CORNWALL IN THE AGE OF THE INDUSTRIAL REVOLUTION

CORNWALL

IN THE AGE OF THE

INDUSTRIAL
REVOLUTION

by

JOHN ROWE

FORMERLY READER IN HISTORY
IN THE UNIVERSITY OF LIVERPOOL

with introductions

by

A. L. ROWSE

&

E. V. THOMPSON

SECOND (ENLARGED) EDITION
Cornish Hillside Publications

1993

First Published 1953

Second (Enlarged) Edition Published 1993
Paperback Edition Published in 2006

This edition published by
Cornish Hillside Publications
12 Hillside Road.
St Austell

© John Rowe 1993

ISBN   1 900147 467

Printed in Great Britain by Short Run Press Ltd, Exeter.

FOREWORD

By A. L. ROWSE

CORNWALL has impinged on English history at three very significant moments. During the Middle Ages the Cornish people remained wrapped up in the womb of their own inner-regarding Celtic experience, cut off by language and remoteness from the main stream of the nation's life. They were swept into it in the course of the sixteenth century, reluctant and making their protest in the rebellions of 1497 and 1549. That story is the subject of my *Tudor Cornwall*. In the next century their devotion to the Royalist cause made the Cornish army the King's best fighting instrument in the West ; under its valiant leaders, its brave progress from victory to victory, from Bradock Down and Stratton to Lansdowne and Roundway Down, until it was decimated in the siege of Bristol, makes splendid and poignant reading in the pages of Clarendon. The whole story is told in Miss Mary Coate's admirable *Cornwall in the Civil War*.

But Cornwall's most important contribution to the life of the nation came with the Industrial Revolution, with her tin-mines and then her brief dominance in the world-production of copper, and the technical concomitants in the development of steam-engines, the steam-locomotive, the scientific and inventive genius of Sir Humphry Davy and Richard Trevithick. This is the theme that Dr. J. Rowe courageously tackles here in the first of two volumes which together will cover this pullulating, crowded, most creative epoch in our history.

So much energy and industry generated within the small confines of our county upon a stock that is naturally keen, intelligent and idiosyncratic produced an explosion of talent. So many remarkable men, men of gifts and character, appear on the scene : there has been nothing to compare with it since. One sees them all : Parson Borlase, stern disciplinarian, hater of Methodists, with his antiquarian interests and devotion to duty ; the close, gnarled, astringent characteristics of all the Williams clan—capitalists on an impressive scale ; the Rev. Cornelius Cardew, sagacious and prudent, eye on the main chance, schoolmaster to them all. There is Davies Gilbert, fussy and philanthropic, with his good-natured encouragement of everything to the fore, from steam-engines to parochial history ; or Francis Basset, Lord de Dunstanville, with his haughty, patrician air, who was no less encouraging of all that was going on. Or we think of John Opie, the painter, " the Cornish Wonder," who accomplished such an achievement after a poignant struggle from what beginnings ; or that genial giant, Richard Trevithick, with his natural flow of inventiveness and lack of any business talent to profit himself by it ; or Humphry Davy, that scintillating, brilliant, mercurial mind, early extinguished : these three, in their different ways, men of genius. What a time it was !

I welcome this book as an excellent introduction to all this period on the side of its economic activity : a work of sound scholarship, wide research and of reliable judgment. Among the many good things in it, I like that about Redgate, where Dr. Rowe tells us that the central one of three parallel ' long ' fields seems to have been an Iron Age fort, the ramparts of which have been denuded into hedges. He has an eye for such things : as a lad he was a practising smallholder himself. For those readers who are not hardy enough for the sterner delights of mining statistics, I suggest that they turn first to the land Dr. Rowe knows so well, which he understands so intimately that he can interpret the very wrinkles on the landscape for us.

The book may well be begun with this chapter—after all the land with its cultivation comes before anything else. But Dr. Rowe envisages this volume as economic history in the pure sense, and has only just resisted the temptation to call it, romantically but with a certain exactness (imagination does not preclude exactitude)—" The Rise and Fall of the Copper Kingdom." For what he intends it, the book is a most valuable study—a contribution alike to the astonishing story of the Industrial Revolution in this country in general, and to the endearing history of Cornwall in particular.

Endearing, for as one reads these pages the image of those ruined engine-houses on the moor, in the valleys, along the cliffs, is always just round the corner of one's eye ; one thinks of those crowded bee-hives of miners, the fairs and feasts in little Cornish market-towns ; the early chapels, the hymn-singing, hard-drinking fellows they were, spending so much of their lives underground (their blood is in our veins) ; and then the day that came when the mines closed down, and thousands of Cornish miners went overseas taking their skill, their industry, their distinguishing characteristics all over the world. I hope that Dr. Rowe will give us a volume on all the social and political life of the period of economic expansion recorded in this ; and that he will then pursue his miners overseas, to give us a history of the most significant of all movements in the life of the Cornish people, that of the Emigration in which their story mingles with that of the modern mining world.

FOREWORD TO SECOND (ENLARGED) EDITION

By E. V. Thompson

During the 18th century a process of industrialisation began in Britain that would accelerate as the century matured and continue until well into the reign of Queen Victoria. It was destined to change not only the country in which our ancestors lived but also re-align the paths along which future generations would walk.

It was a process that would ultimately reach far beyond the shores of these small islands, bridging oceans and continents, gathering itself for an advance into the still undiscovered places of the earth —and beyond.

This most important phenomenon has been written into history as the 'Industrial Revolution'.

As with more conventional revolutions (if such evolutionary spasms can ever be termed 'conventional'), it would be achieved only with painful readjustment, social upheaval, much human suffering and a vicious assault on the dignity of English men, women and even children.

Such changes as were wrought did not occur overnight, nor were they geographically or socially uniform. However, the impact of change hit hardest at those least able to withstand its implacable drive, especially those in agrarian communities. In a bewildering, changing world, they found themselves under attack from all sides.

'Enclosure', that immoral parliamentary peculation whereby land was stolen from the poor and given to the rich, was not as significant in Cornwall as in the counties to the east. Nevertheless smallholdings, of anything from an acre or so up to twenty-five or more, were being merged into larger farms from the late eighteenth century onwards, a process almost certainly facilitated by the widely prevalent three life lease system, causing the shift of population away from the land which continued well into the twentieth century.

Mechanisation and industrialisation accelerated this process, reaching into the most remote regions of the land.

Few regions were more remote than Cornwall in the years before the railway bridged the Tamar. Yet the ancient Duchy spearheaded many of the changes that were to come. Its brilliant, but often controversial engineers revolutionised mining within the Duchy.

Paradoxically, as a result of the expertise it gave to the world the Cornish mining industry suffered a lingering death, forcing exile upon many of its sons and daughters.

Mining had always been an important element in shaping Cornwall's economy and the character of its people. It was in the very soul of the Cornishman. With the advent of new technology the mining industry was given a new, but short-lived, impetus. The steam- engine; improved methods of ore separation; iron and steel to take the place of the wooden beams of its great engines. As the innovations were introduced, engine-houses sprung up like overnight mushrooms. The rattle and reverberation of ore stamps echoed across the hills and valleys and broke the ancient silence of the remotest moorland wastes.

For a while mining, fishing and the infant china clay industry advanced together in Cornwall, absorbing the advancing techniques that left traditional methods behind. However, towards the end of the industrial revolution mining had been left far behind and the fishing industry was fighting for its life in an increasingly competitive world.

The problems posed for Cornwall and its people by the Industrial Revolution are well illustrated in John Rowe's meticulously researched book, with particular emphasis being placed on Cornish mining. This is a period of Cornwall's history with which he has had an abiding love affair. There can be few men in the country with a wider knowledge of the subject.

Also dear to Dr. Rowe's heart is Methodism, another subject of which he possesses expert knowledge. In this edition of *Cornwall in the Age of the Industrial Revolution* he has added two hitherto unpublished chapters dealing with the impact of Wesley and his followers on Cornwall. By so doing he has also presented us with a valuable insight into the influence of Cornwall upon this vigorous, forthright, forceful and, at times rowdy young religion.

John Rowe's research is impressive and the completed book a scholarly, yet eminently readable work of reference. It is a must for every serious student of Cornwall's unique and colourful history.

March, 1993.   E. V. Thompson

PREFACE

Like many another book this study originated in a suggestion made in the hospitable atmosphere of All Souls College, Oxford, and I am happy that the scholar who made that suggestion, Mr. A. L. Rowse, has now written the first and, in my opinion, most felicitous paragraphs in a volume of whose shortcomings I am only too conscious. The fulfilment of the idea has been delayed for many reasons, but I trust that the passing of the years since the fall of 1938 has enabled a more mature and restrained judgment to be made on the nature of the Industrial Revolution in Cornwall. Many a time the magnitude of the task has appalled me as more and more material came—and still is coming—to light on this period of history. There was a problem of beginning and ending—never an easy one in connection with the phrase "Industrial Revolution" in any place; still in Cornwall an era surely opened when copper first, at the very end of the seventeenth century, began to be mined on a commercial scale, and just as surely ended by 1870 when more Cornish miners were to be found, earning a livelihood at their arduous calling, outside than within the boundaries of the south-western county. Considerations of space have forced me to leave a great part of the tale untold, but copper, fish, tin, the fruits of the earth and the animals that fed thereon, were the basis of the social and cultural life of Cornwall during this era, which I hope, someday, will be the subject of a second volume. To my many Methodist friends who may feel that I have done their faith and their founder less than justice, I trust I then will make amends, albeit maintaining the claim that John Wesley would never have visited Cornwall one and thirty times had it not been a land of granite and killas veined with lodes of tin, of copper, and of lead.

It is not possible to enumerate all those who have helped by suggestion and criticism in the creation of this book, but my gratitude to these is none the less sincere. There have been many, however, who by their continuing interest and the nature of their help must have specific mention. Professors G. D. H. Cole and H. J. Habakkuk of Oxford, Professor T. S. Ashton of London University, and Mr. F. L. Harris of Redruth read the whole of the original manuscript and made detailed and valuable suggestions. Professors M. A. Thomson and F. E. Hyde of Liverpool University read a great part of the manuscript and gave me every help and encouragement to complete the work. Professors James Small of Glasgow, R. M. Gordon of Liverpool, and J. B. Brebner of Columbia Universities contributed valuable suggestions when my researches led me into the realms of engineering, medicine, and American mining history.

I owe a special debt of gratitude to Mr. Claude Berry and the management and staff of the *West Briton;* to Mr. T. R. Harris of Camborne; to the late Mr. H. E. Boaden of Falmouth; to Mr. E. M. Cunnack of Helston; to Mr. C. E. Leese of Camelford; to Mr. E. Spurway of Liskeard; to Mr. C. W. B. Parker of Penzance; to Mr. C. C. James of Penzance; to Miss G. Malbon of Liskeard; to the Rev. A. Lane Davies of St. Cleer; and to Mr. A. C. Todd of Penzance. I wish also to express my sincere thanks to the many library and archive staffs who have given aid—the Bodleian Library, the British Museum, the Public Record Office, the Royal Institution of Cornwall, the Royal Cornwall Polytechnic Society, the Royal Geological Society of Cornwall, the Morrab and Penlee House Libraries in Penzance, and the Harold Cohen and Picton Libraries in Liverpool.

I wish to express my sincere gratitude to the Principal and Fellows of Brasenose College, Oxford, for the Senior Hulme Scholarship which enabled me to pursue my historical researches, and my lasting regret that untimely death snatched Dr. W. T. S. Stallybras ('Sonners' to us all) ere this work was completed. To my colleagues at Liverpool University I owe a special debt of gratitude for the interest and encouragement they have given to me and my work. To the Joint Committee on Research of Liverpool University I wish here to express my sincerest thanks for a grant to assist the publication of this work, and to Mr. R. A. Downie, the Secretary of the University Press of Liverpool for his invaluable work in the publication of this book.

Two final acknowledgments must be made; to Miss F. Christopher, who painstakingly but with, I fear, indifferent success, tried to amend the gaucheries of my literary style; and to the bygone host of men of Phoenix, Gonamena, Crinnis, Consols, Botallack, Balleswidden and some twenty score other mines but for whom this book would certainly never have been written.   JOHN ROWE.

Liverpool, November 12, 1952.

PREFACE FOR SECOND EDITION

Re-appearance, forty years on, suggests that a re-introduction would not be inappropriate, especially since two additional chapters have been inserted on religious and social developments to, hopefully, provide a fuller picture of Cornwall during 'the Age of the Industrial Revolution.' This is the only alteration; what happened in history cannot be changed; what changes over the years are the views and reactions, aye, and crochets of individual historians; furthermore there have been many alterations in intellectual fashions and foibles in the writing of history although hardly to the extent as they have been in studies of literature and philosophy.

A second preface provides the opportunity for a few words on bibliography. Since 1953 many works on Cornish history have appeared, and a most helpful and up-to-date bibliography has been provided by Dr. Philip Payton's *The Making of Modern Cornwall*, published last year. Much of my own research was done before the Cornwall Record Office had its first home at Gwendroc and several years before the inauguration of the Institute of Cornish Studies—developments for which Cornish historians are immensely indebted. In Gwendroc my friend, the late Rev. John Pearce compiled his *The Wesleys in Cornwall*, published in 1964, which would have eased researches through multi-volumned collections of Wesley diaries and correspondence. Another friend, P. A. S. Pool has written a masterly biography of William Borlase, although the Methodist *bête noir* was the antiquarian's elder brother, Walter. Possibly some day another pluralist clergyman, antiquarian, and Methodist scourge, Richard Polwhele will attract the attentions of a biographer, while on the other side William O'Bryan deserves more modern research as a pioneering trans- Atlantic travelling evangelist, even though he made his first journey—westward— nearly a century after John Wesley himself had journeyed that way.

Acknowledgements in the 1953 preface can be thankfully and sincerely reaffirmed, although many listed there are sadly no longer with us. Since then other debts should be mentioned, including many friends who have urged re-publication. That this has now come about is, above all, due to the zeal of Charles Thurlow of Cornish Hillside Publications who suggested that 1993, being Industrial Heritage Year was an appropriate time for republishing a work on the Industrial Revolution which, for many years had been out of print. This year, too, was that of the quarter-millenial of the coming of the Wesleys to Cornwall to usher in another 'revolution' in Cornish religious and social life; two lengthy chapters on this had been omitted for reasons of space in the first edition of 1953. So a grafting- publication device was conceived to publish a second edition in a single volume, retaining a feasible chrono-logical sequence, and with no other change save the addition of a supplementary bibliography and index, besides this second preface and, for this extended edition, an up to date second forward, for which I am most grateful to E. V. Thompson, whose deservedly best-selling novel, *Chase the Wind*, has provided by far and away the most enthralling and, even if romantic, outstandingly true picture of life in the Caradon mining district near which my earlier days were spent a century after the Retallicks, their kith, kindred, friends, acquaintances and foes lived, loved, suffered and endured.

To Dr. A. L. Rowse, author of the first forward I remain indebted, although I fear some of the hopes he expressed have ganged somewhat agley. Pursuing West Cornwall miners over to what they termed 'the next parish' diverted my course somewhat from migratory Cousin Jack 'hard rock men' to a more geo-graphical emphasis on the mining frontier hinted at by Frederick Jackson Turner a century ago.

Finally, on the additional chapters; rewritten modifications probably could have been made resulting from researches and work in more recent years by the Rev. Tom Shaw and various members of the Cornish Methodist Historical Association. I can claim to have attempted historical objectivity, although various ortho-dox denominationalists might suspect traces of unreconstructured Bryanism. Possibly, in extenuation, I can plead that the aim was the occupation of ecumenical middle ground between Billy Bray and Parson Hawker.

John Rowe   Rock Mill, Par.
10 March 1993.

CONTENTS

		page(s)
I	The Eve of Change, 1688–1740	1
II	The Years of Transformation	40
II (i)	The Beginning of Religious Change	67.1- 67.40
III	The Years of Conflict, 1775–1800	68
IV	The Age of Power, 1800–1850	114
V	The Fortunes of the Tin Mining Interest, 1775–1845	165
VI	Agriculture in Cornwall	208
VI(i)	Religion and the People after Wesley	261.1-261.48
VII	Men and the Sea	262

Epilogue: The End of the Copper Kingdom — 305

Appendix I Cornish Statistical Material — 327

„ II The Construction and Lease of a Tin Stamping Mill in 1728 — 329

„ III Statistics of Cornish Production of Copper Ore, Value, and Relationship with Smelter's Prices of Fine Copper, 1801–1829 — 331

„ IV The Copper Speculation Mines of 1823–26 in Cornwall — 332

„ V Statistics of the Cornish Pilchard Fishery, 1820–1878 — 334

Bibliography — 337

Supplementary Bibliography — 347

Index — 349

Supplementary Index — 371

TABLES

I	The Average Amount of Tin Coined in Cornwall over Five Year Periods, 1720–1834	58
II	Decennial Production of Fine Copper in Tons, 1801–1880	128
II	Burials in the Parish of St. Cleer, 1813–1859	152
IV	Cornish May Market Prices, 1843–47	163

ABBREVIATIONS

Carew	Carew, R., *Survey of Cornwall* (edition of 1811).
C.R.B.	*Tin Coinage Resolution Book* (MS. in the Museum of the Royal Geological Society of Cornwall at Penzance).
C.S.P.Dom.	*Calendars of State Papers, Domestic.*
C.T.B.	*Calendars of Treasury Books and Papers.*
Drew	Drew, S., *History of Cornwall.*
Hamilton	Hamilton, H., *The English Brass and Copper Industries to 1800.*
Harrison	Harrison, Sir George, *Substance of a Report on the Laws and Jurisdiction of the Stannaries in Cornwall.*
Hunt	Hunt, R., *British Mining.*
J.B.W.	*Journal of the Bath and West of England Society.*
J.R.A.S.	*Journal of the Royal Agricultural Society of England.*
J.R.I.C.	*Journal of the Royal Institution of Cornwall.*
Lean	Lean, Joel, *Historical Statement of the Improvements Made in the Duty Performed by the Steam Engines in Cornwall.*
Maton	Maton, W. G., *Observations of the Western Counties of England, 1794–96.*
Muirhead	Muirhead, J. P., *The Origins and Progress of the Mechanical Inventions of James Watt.*
Observations, 1772	Anonymous, *An Address to the Gentlemen of the County of Cornwall on the Present State of Mining in that County; with some Observations on the Tin and Copper Trade.*
P.R.O.	Public Record Office.
Pryce	Pryce, Dr. W., *Mineralogia Cornubiensis.*
R.C.P.S.	*Reports of the Royal Cornwall Polytechnic Society.*
Report, 1799	Report from the Committee of the House of Commons appointed to Enquire into the State of the Copper Mines and Copper Trade, 1799.
T.N.S.	*Transactions of the Newcomen Society.*
F. Trevithick	Trevithick, F., *Life of Richard Trevithick.*
Unwin	Unwin, G., *Letters, Remarks, etc., with a View to open an Extensive Trade in the Article of Tin from the County of Cornwall to India, Persia and China.*
V.C.H.	*Victoria County Histories.*
Warner	Warner, R., *A Tour through Cornwall in the Autumn of 1808.*
W.B.	*West Briton.*
Welch	Welch, C., *History of the Worshipful Company of Pewterers of the City of London.*
Worgan	Worgan, G. B., *A General View of the Agriculture of Cornwall.*

NOTE : The word *Wheal* prefixed to so many Cornish mines, sometimes spelt *Huel,* means a work or working; the Cornish word for mine is *Bal,* as in Balleswidden, literally "White Mine".

CHAPTER I

THE EVE OF CHANGE

1688-1740

THE Revolution in the late autumn of 1688 left the people of Cornwall almost indifferent, but the triumph of an aggressive and materialistic Parliamentary Protestantism was to affect their lives and those of their descendants to an extent of which few could even have dreamed at that time. Cornwall had had more than enough of strife in the great Civil Wars, which had lasted longer in Cornwall and Scilly than in any other part of England. In those conflicts Cornishmen had participated on both sides, the older landed gentry on the side of Charles Stuart and Laud, the commercial magnates and newer gentry like the Robartes and Eliots on that of Parliament. Many had lost heavily in the prolonged struggle, others had gained, but the main economic result had been the passing of the ownership of land from one to another, the creation of a sense that land itself was by no means a permanent asset but should be used to its fullest extent by its owners while it remained in their possession. Few Cornishmen were ready, when Monmouth made his forlorn bid, to risk life and lands; fewer still were stirred, despite the tradition created by the one Cornish poet of the nineteenth century Romantic Revival—Robert Stephen Hawker—to rise to avenge the wrongs of Jonathan Trelawney and the other Bishops in the Tower. The age of the traditional Vicar of Bray had dawned; at the Restoration all but thirty-seven of the Cornish parish clergy had conformed sufficiently to retain their benefices although in the past twenty years the Puritans had ejected or suspended at least ninety-two.[1] Cornish clergy and laity alike had come to weigh religious idealism in the balance against material well-being and comfort and had found it wanting.

Yet Puritanism had left a deep impression on Cornwall as on

---

[1]Edmund Calamy: *The Nonconformists' Memorial* (1802 edition of Samuel Palmer), pp. 347-376. Mary Coate: *Cornwall in the Great Civil War and Interregnum*, App. 15 pp.382-386. A. G. Matthews: *Calamy Revised*, p. xii.

the rest of England. The older ecclesiastical organization which had been taken over from Rome and modified by the Tudor ecclesiastical compromises, was one based upon and catering for the needs of a predominantly agrarian society. Puritanism, from Tyndale to Lilburne, stressing and almost certainly overstressing not only predestinarian dogma but also the parable of the rightful use of talents, had been the spiritual assertion of a rising class of merchants and lawyers, a class formerly widely condemned as parasitic usurers and extortioners, although they were still associated with agrarianism. The Civil Wars had resulted in a compromise imposing a more rigid sabbatarianism and predestinarian doctrine on the framework of the older Anglican Church. This ecclesiastical compromise, however, had made no provision for the increasing number of people who depended mainly on the sale of their labour for a livelihood, a social phenomenon that early appeared in mining districts among which Cornwall had long been prominent. Hitherto Cornish mining had been on a small scale, and working had been on what might well be termed a simple agrarian basis by agreement between the owners of the soil and the working miners. The infiltration of lawyers and merchants into the landowning caste, a process which was accentuated by the complexities of mining laws and customs and still more by the penalties imposed on landowning royalists by the victorious parliamentarians after 1646, meant that mineral wealth would be exploited to the full and not, as in the past, as a subsidiary addition to rents of land, a system which had sometimes meant the conservation rather than the exploitation of mineral resources.

The existence of copper in Cornwall had been proved in Elizabethan times if not earlier, but its exploitation was negligible until the closing years of the seventeenth century. There are tales that the Cornish miners threw out copper ores as worthless *mundic* waste; there are equally credible allegations that copper merchants concealed the value of Cornish ores in order to maintain high prices by limiting supplies. The main reason for the late start of Cornish copper-mining, however, was the lack of accessible markets, whilst it was also difficult to work the relatively deep copper lodes without mechanical power. Most copper discoveries resulted from the extension of tin-workings to deeper levels; as long as alluvial stream tin had been found in fairly considerable quantity, especially since it usually fetched higher prices than "mine" tin, Cornish copper remained hidden.[1] Underground mining had probably started in Cornwall before 1500, but the maximum amount of tin raised in the county in any one year between the accession of the Tudors and the Restoration of 1660 was an output of rather less than 760 tons in 1547.[2] Throughout Elizabeth's reign the average annual output of Cornish tin was rather below 1,225,000 lb., and this dropped to less than 1,210,000 lb. during the first eleven years of the reign of James I, whilst in the last five normal years before civil war reached the land to number Cornish mining among its first casualties, from 1638 to 1642, the annual output had fallen below 1,172,000 lb. No records survive of output during the years of the Republic and early Restoration, but during the decade 1670-79 the average was 2,222,385 lb., whilst in 1677 an output of over three million pounds was first attained.[3] In the following decade the average yearly coinage rose to 3,052,496 lb., but from 1690 to 1699 it was only 2,755,778 lb. per annum although it increased to 3,137,879 lb. a year from 1700 to 1709. In only four years from

[1]The Elizabethan discoveries of copper in certain localities in Cornwall which cannot positively be identified were due to the imperfect geological knowledge of the time rather than to any deliberate search for copper. Stirred by the mineral wealth of Spanish America, many thought that Cornwall might produce gold as well as tin and silver-lead. Occasionally small veins of gold have been found, and some of these may have stirred vain hopes. A superficial resemblance of the Helston district to the Witwatersrand stirred somewhat similar ideas among some "practical" Cornish miners in the 1890s. (Cunnack MSS.).

[2]Actually 1,695,328 lb.; in 1400 an output of 1,758,328 lb. was coined. These figures are based on Lewis: *The Stannaries*, App. J., pp. 252 ff.; they should not be regarded as an absolutely accurate estimate of the production in any single year; until 1749 the year was that ending at Michaelmas, whilst the figures are those of tin which actually paid coinage duties to the Duchy of Cornwall (or to the Crown in abeyance of the Duchy); by law all tin raised in Cornwall had to be taken in blocks to a coinage town, weighed there and taxed prior to sale; some tin must have been smuggled untaxed out of the county, whilst tin was not always taken to the coinage immediately on being mined; there were fixed coinage days, at first half-yearly, later quarterly. Coinage accounts are complete from 1563 to 1614 save for the year 1583; from 1563 to 1582 the annual amount of tin coined averaged 1,172,419 lb.; from 1584 to 1603 it averaged 1,275,993 lb.; in the first period the coinage was only 10 per cent above the average in five and 10 per cent below it in six years; in the second, three years were 10 per cent above and four below average, so suggesting controlled production, or at least a limitation of the amounts coined which itself regulated the amount of tin coming on to the market. The greatest variation from the mean of the entire forty recorded years of Elizabeth's reign was 24.3 per cent below in both 1571 and 1572, and 22.5 per cent above in 1602; 21 years fluctuated less than 10 per cent either way from the average, and only nine years recorded a coinage 10 per cent above that level.

[3]This figure may be unduly low, as 2 per cent has been deducted from the figures of the three years 1670-72 which may have included a small quantity of tin from Devon.

1710 to 1749 were less than 3,000,000 lb. of tin coined, but the
coinage of nearly 2,143 tons in 1710 was not surpassed for forty
years although in the 1740s the average yearly coinage was
almost 1,743 tons. These figures indicate a significant and
steady increase in Cornish tin production after 1660 that may
be contrasted with earlier conditions; output had risen from a
yearly figure of about 1,000 tons in the early years of the
Restoration to 1,400 tons in the reign of Anne and had reached
levels but little short of 1,750 tons between 1740 and 1749; in
the reign of Charles I, however, output seems to have been less
than the 550 tons it had averaged in Elizabeth's time, and that
figure had been exceeded as far back as 1337 and 1338 and may
not have been much in excess of the levels of tin-production
reached in the reign of John.

This increase in Cornish tin mining, contrasted with the
virtually static conditions prevailing throughout the four centuries before the outbreak of the Civil War, mark the beginning
of the Industrial Revolution in Cornwall. When certain deposits
of alluvial stream tin were exhausted the miners sought, found,
and exploited the underground lodes; going ever deeper they
at length came to the copper lodes just as, more than a century
and a half later, the lower zone of tin-veins were found beneath
the by-then exhausted copper-bearing strata of Dolcoath and
other deeper mines. This vastly increased exploitation of deep
tin itself explains why copper production began in Cornwall in
the closing years of the seventeenth century and not earlier.
The increasing depth and drainage problems of the mines led
to the improvement of pumping machinery and to the application of mechanical power to work these pumps. Methods of
raising the ores from the depths of the mines to the surface were
devised and improved. Explosives, which had already been
used for several years in Midland mines, were introduced.

Nowhere is the truth of the old adage that necessity is the
mother of invention more apparent than in the history of
Cornish mine drainage. Obsessed by the achievements of steam
power and dominated by the individualist spirit of their own
day, writers, in the past, magnified the achievements of more
famous inventors and lost sight of the smaller but no less essential improvements made by a number of unknown men. The
Scotsman Watt, the Cornishman Trevithick, and even their
forerunners the Devonians Savery and Newcomen, were not

inventors but radical improvers; their achievement was the application of a new power agency more and more effectively to pumping machinery which had been introduced and improved since the problem of drainage had first been faced by Cornish mines adventurers. Some radical improvements in pumps may have been made by the German workmen brought by Ulrick Frosse to St. Agnes in 1582,[1] but for at least another century the majority of mine-pumps were worked by hand. Perhaps the most effective and most exclusively Cornish hand-pump was the rag-and-chain pump, described by Dr. William Pryce whose connection with mining as both adventurer and mine surgeon went back to 1750, as consisting of an iron chain:

"with knobs of cloth stiffened and fenced with leather, seldom more than nine feet asunder; the chain is turned round by a wheel of two or three feet diameter, furnished with iron spikes, to inclose and keep steady the chain, so that it may rise through a wooden pump of 3, 4 or 5 inches bore, and from 12 to 22 feet long, and by means of the leather bands bring up with it a stream of water answerable to the diameter of the pump, and in quantity according to the circumvolutions of the pump in any given time. Several of these pumps may be placed parallel upon different Stalls, Sollers, or stages of the mine. . . . The men worked at it naked excepting their loose trousers, and suffer much . . . from the violence of the labour which is so great that I have been witness to the loss of many lives by it. . . . A rag-and-chain pump of four inches diameter requires five or six men, every six hours, to drive twenty feet deep; and to keep it constantly going, 20 or 24 men must be employed monthly at 40 or 50 shillings each man. The monthly charge of one of the engines cannot be less than £50 or £60; and they are now pretty generally laid aside on account of the great expense and destruction of the men."[2]

Using hand-pumps miners could not go very deep, although water was not met so near the surface in some mines as it was in others; this, too, made for the lateral extension of mines rather than for working in depth, save where deposits of ores were found in waterlogged levels rich enough to warrant the employment of sixty or eighty men at the pumps while, at most, ten or a dozen men worked away at digging the valuable minerals. This lateral extension of tin mines away from the granitic rocks would also lead to the copper lodes.

[1] C.S.P.Dom., 1581-1590, pp. 134, 172-73, 179, 185, 191, 194, 196-97, etc. On August 21, 1584 Frosse wrote that the men were working at the water day and night (*ibid:* pp. 196-97).
[2] Pryce, pp. 150-151. (published in 1778).

The late seventeenth century saw the extension if not the initiation of the practice of using water to fight water. In very early times water had been employed to work ore-crushing mills or stamps, whilst long after the days of Watt and Trevithick water power was used wherever it was available and cheaper than steam power. The simple overshot water-wheel was the main source of power, and many such wheels were being used to drain mines in the St. Austell district before 1700.[1] Water power, however, was rather limited in Cornwall, but it was turned to the utmost account in some places by the most fantastic devices and expedients; in more than one place water drained from a mine was conveyed along a leat to work stamping mills and then run along to turn an overshot wheel operating the pumps of another mine. Rentals from water-rights added considerably to the incomes of their owners, but they were also a fruitful cause of litigation, increasing the fees of lawyers who, by one method or another, possibly made more out of the mines than any other section of the Cornish community.[2] Wherever the terrain made it possible mines were drained by the simple method of driving adits to bring the water out of the hills to the valleys below, where, again, it could be used to drive stamping-mills and water-wheels.

Before the end of the seventeenth century it was obvious that if the mines of Cornwall—and elsewhere—were to be wrought deeper something more than hand-pumps would have to be devised. From Hero of Alexandria down to the Frenchman Denys Papin many men, the majority of them forgotten, experimented with steam power, but none of them turned their

---

[1]C. Morris (Ed.): *The Journeys of Celia Fiennes*, p. 258. Celia Fiennes also mentioned the use of horses to work pumping and other machinery in the tin mines of the St. Austell district, and men working night and day, seven days a week, to deal with the waterlogged mines.

[2]The dispute between Viscount Falmouth and the Earl of Radnor over Cornish water rights came before the House of Lords in 1728. Many harsh attacks were made by Cornish writers and others against the predatory lawyers, notably by William Hals whose history was too libellous to be published in full even posthumously. Great fortunes were made by the lawyers who acted as agents for landowners and mines adventurers; the Hawkins family acted in such a role for the Godolphins in the early eighteenth century whilst a century later the Daveys of Redruth were agents of the Gwennap Consolidated Mines to give but two examples. Others augmented their practices and wealth by acting as agents and officials of the stannary organization, notably the Boscawens and Gregors as well as the less well-known families of the Sprys, Coles, and Collinses who by the early nineteenth century were intermarrying with the older gentry, holding lucrative church livings, and even sitting in Parliament.

experiments to any practical use until Thomas Savery, a military engineer, patented a "fire engine" in 1698; four years later, having set up an engine manufactory in London, he described this machine in a pamphlet significantly entitled *The Miner's Friend*. It was not a success, and Savery only made a few engines. Whilst the underlying principles of the machine and the utilization of the power of high-pressure expansive steam were sound the materials Savery had to build it were not; a series of breakdowns and explosions, however, apparently led another practical Devon man, Thomas Newcomen a Dartmouth chemist and ironmonger, to use steam simply to create a vacuum on which the pressure of the atmosphere would act and move a beam connected with pumping rods.[1] The engine erected at Wheal Vor before 1716 may have been constructed on Savery's design, but the three engines which were working in Cornwall in 1741[2] were all Newcomen "atmospheric" engines. Despite many faults and defects in these engines, they did, where employed, drain mines effectively. The great disadvantage was the amount and cost of the coal they consumed. It was only after the monopolistic patent rights of Savery and Newcomen came to an end in 1733, followed eight years later by the remission of the duties on coal brought by sea to work "fire engines" in Cornwall, that Newcomen's atmospheric engine came into general use in the county and, in the hands of Hornblowers, Trevithicks, and other Cornish mining engineers was to be transformed out of all semblance to its original design.

Whilst the drainage of the progressively deepening mines was the greatest difficulty Cornish miners had to face in this period, there were other obstacles to be overcome. The deeper the mine the more difficult and costly it became to raise the ores to the surface. There is no record that the Cornish employed their women-folk to carry tin and copper ores on their backs up ladders as was done in the coal mines of Scotland and Cumberland;[3] in fact there is little evidence of any extensive employment of female labour even on surface jobs until the end of the

[1]This description has been perhaps oversimplified; the fullest account of the work of Savery and Newcomen from a technical standpoint is that of Rhys Jenkins: "Savery, Newcomen, and the Early History of the Steam Engine", *T.N.S.*, Vol. III, pp.96ff., and Vol. IV, pp.113ff.

[2]*T.N.S.*, Vol. X, p.17.

[3]T. S. Ashton and J. Sykes: *The Coal Industry of the Eighteenth Century* pp. 23-24, 171.

eighteenth century.[1] The *whim*, used for drawing up ore and water, was devised by the Bristol man John Coster when in Cornwall about 1720, and consisted of:

"a perpendicular axis, wherein a longer hollow cylinder of timber turns, called the Cage, round which the rope winds horizontally, being directed down the mine by two pullies fixed in what are termed Puppet Heads over the mouth of the Shaft: this axis has a transverse beam, called the Arm, infixed; at the end of which are fixed two horses that go round upon a platform named the Whym-round, and draw more or less according to the number of their circumvolutions in any given time, the largeness of the barrels (60 or 120 gallons) and the depth the Whym is to draw."[2]

In many of these devices for pumping and hauling leather buckets were used, as in the collieries, and the expenditure of mines on rope and on leather was considerable ; in the 1750s North Downs mine was using some fifteen hundredweights of hempen ropes a month and about four and a half hundredweights of leather.[3] As the mines went deeper these quantities of rope and leather also increased.

[1]Lack of evidence does not necessarily prove that female labour was not employed. Only three or four women were recorded as being paid for work at Dolcoath and Cook's Kitchen in the late 1780s. George Skerry of Chiverton wrote in 1799 that female surface workers were only employed in summer. (*Annals of Agriculture*, Vol. XXXV, p. 273). Many now living, however, remember *bal maidens* at work winter and summer alike. It is likely that female labour was increasingly used as mines became larger, and whenever and wherever more and more families became entirely dependent on mining as their source of livelihood. In February, 1818, Wheal Unity in Gwennap was employing 38 females in a total labour force of 107 whereas in 1795 it had only employed two or three. (MS. Abstract of Wheal Unity Accounts per C. C. James, Esq.). An estimate of 1787 stated that out of 7,196 hands employed in copper mines, 2,648 were "women, boys, and girls," whilst John Vivian told a Parliamentary Committee in April, 1799, that the copper mines employed five to six thousand men and between four and five thousand women and boys. (Hamilton, pp. 323-324). At most two-thirds of these may have been females, i.e. about 1,800 in 1787 and 3,000 in 1799, but it is possible that the respective figures should be 1,200 and 2,200. Vivian, too, for his own interests, was most unlikely to have underestimated the numbers employed in mining. Women almost certainly made up a larger proportion of the total labour force on mines where more hands were engaged in preparing the ores for the markets than in actually mining it; this would account for the few women employed at Dolcoath, which, by the 1780s had already gone so deep that much of its labour force was engaged in underground mining and mine-maintenance and in bringing the ores to the surface. One of the earliest references to female mine labourers is to be found in a letter of the Rev. William Borlase of Ludgvan, dated March 1, 1736, wherein he complained that his household was "under the greatest necessity for a servant, no woman to be hired here in this parish for friendship or money being employed about copper." (Borlase MSS).

[2]Pryce, p. 150. Coster had gone to Cornwall to manage some mines in the Chacewater district which had been leased to a group of Bristol copper manufacturers by Lord Falmouth. (Hamilton, pp. 165-166).

[3]Borlase MSS: letter of William Lemon to William Borlase, May 8, 1756; Lemon also gave figures for Polgooth which, however, whilst using up a ton of rope in a month, only bought half a hundredweight of leather in the same period.

The other innovation at this time was the introduction of gunpowder. For at least two centuries Cornish underground miners and surface quarry-workers had used the crude direct application of fire to crack rocks; a few faggots of furze would be taken to the end of a level, placed against the rock face, and burnt, the heat being generally sufficient to crack the rocks particularly along metallic veins and also along the natural joints of granite. Nevertheless the fissures thus caused were shallow and the process might have to be repeated a dozen times or more to penetrate a fathom or even a yard of "hard country". Gunpowder had first been made in England in 1413 and exactly two centuries later Martin Weigal, a mining superintendent at Freyberg, had suggested drilling and blasting in mines, yet there is but little evidence that it was at all widely used even in the Staffordshire collieries before 1670. The first man to use explosives in Cornwall was Thomas Epsley in 1689; within a year his name was recorded in the Breage burial register, nor is it impossible that he was the first of many Cornish miners to lose their lives in blasting accidents, too many of which were simply due to sheer carelessness. Nearly five generations passed before another Cornishman, Bickford, patented a safety-fuse which reduced the number of mining accidents and fatalities considerably.

New methods were also being applied at this time in refining and smelting metal. The essential principles of tin-smelting had been known in Cornwall for at least a thousand years; the principal innovations at the end of the seventeenth century were the use of coal in smelting and the improved reverberatory furnace. The increased output of Cornish tin by itself might have completed the deforestation of the county, even had forests been exploited for smelting only; deeper mines meant an additional demand for timber for pit-props and for pump shafts even without reckoning the demand for oak-bark used in tanning to meet the increasing demand for leather. True, wood-smelted tin was some ten per cent more pure and valuable, but before 1700 it had come to be, in many places, either coal-smelted tin or no tin at all. One sign of the times was the provision, in 1710, for a drawback of the duty on all coal used in smelting tin or copper in Cornwall, one of the last of many favours Godolphin was to win for the Cornish mining interests during his tenure of the Treasury.[1] Another sign was the

[1] 9 Anne, cap. 6, clause 54.

concentration of the tin-smelting houses at or near tide-water.

At the end of the seventeenth century there were twenty-six smelting-houses in Cornwall. Their location roughly indicates the main tin-mining districts of the time. There were still two smelting-houses in Devon, but in Blackmoor and Foymoor, two of the four ancient Stannary divisions of Cornwall with their coinage centres at Liskeard and Lostwithiel in medieval times, the only smelting-houses were at Calstock, Linkinhorne, and St. Neot. In 1689 these three houses, the two in Devon, and another "newly built" in St. Agnes, were under the supervision of Nathaniel Lugger; his successor to the post, which carried a salary of £80 a year in 1702, had also to supervise another house in St. Blazey. The other smelting-houses were under three more supervisors. An older smelting-house in St. Agnes, with others in Redruth, Gwennap, St. Allen, and two near Penryn, one of which was the "newly built" Trecoos house, was allotted in 1689 to George Collins, but this area overlapped that of William Upcott who supervised three houses in Kenwyn, one each in the parishes of St. Stephens, St. Austell, and St. Ewe and the "lately built" house at Bissoe in Kea. The fourth supervisor, Francis Cole, superintended Chyandour and another house in Gulval, Godolphin House in Breage, three in Wendron, and the new Reskymer House at Mawgan in Meneage.[1] The four new houses at St. Agnes, Bissoe, Penryn, and Reskymer were all within easy reach of the sea over which coal was brought to Cornwall, and the same applies to the St. Blazey smelting-house which had either been overlooked or temporarily closed in 1684. Of the older houses, the three in Kenwyn were on the Fal estuary or near it, and those at Chyandour, St. Agnes, and Penryn were all near tide-water. The amount of work done by the various smelting-houses further emphasized the predominance of those near the sea. Greatest of them was Kelynack in Kenwyn, on a reach of the Fal that has in all probability suffered greatly by silting from mining detritus and an accelerated denudation of the surrounding hills through deforestation in the last two centuries. Chyandour, the second, was near Penzance, though its fuel may have come overland from the port of Hayle.[2]   Godol-

---

[1] *C.T.B., 1689-92*, pp. 243-244, 322, and *C.T.B. 1702*, p. 264.

[2] Small barges may have come up to Chyandour itself; comparatively recent road and railway construction has led to the pushing out of the coastline between Marazion and the Penzance railroad terminus.

phin House probably lost third place to the Polgooth House in
St. Ewe[1] after the closing of Wheal Vor about 1715, and the
fifth in importance were the St. Agnes Houses, though the
great days of the Polberro mine only came in the middle of the
eighteenth century.

Dependence on imported fuel meant that tin-smelting came
under the control of merchants and shipowners with a fair
amount of capital. In the hands of these tin-smelters commercial banking developed in eighteenth century Cornwall;
they were in a position to advance credit to the mixed group
of miners who brought their tin to the smelting-houses—to the
men with three or four partners who might have scratched
together a few hundredweights of alluvial stream tin or to men
like John Borlase of Pendeen or Nicholas Donnithorne of Polberro whose mines employed some scores of hands. Godolphin
and Polgooth smelting-houses may have been the last associated
with a single large mine; Chyandour served at least twenty
mines centering on Ding Dong and running in an arc from
St. Just in Penwith to St. Ives; the three houses in Wendron
smelted the ores of a number of mines whose names are well-
nigh forgotten. To the smelting industry they brought in-
increased efficiency; the days were passing when the old blowing houses would be burnt down every five or six years to recover the particles of tin lodged in their thatched roofs. The
cost of coal accelerated the introduction of reverberatory furnaces in which greater heat was obtained and conserved by a
dome-shaped fireplace that threw back the heat and flame on to
the ores. First used for gun-founding in Germany in the sixteenth century, reverberatory furnaces, using coke and not coal
at first, were used in copper-smelting at Neath by 1600; later
George, Viscount Grandison, obtained a patent "to melt and
refine lead ores in close or reverberated furnaces with pit coal",
and set up smelting-works in the Bristol area, whence it is
likely that Bristol copper merchants took the knowledge of their
utility to Cornwall by the close of the seventeenth century.

In spite of all these new techniques and methods the hand of
the past lay heavily upon the Cornish mining industry. The

<hr>

[1]Polgooth House was using reverberatory furnaces before 1700, according to
Celia Fiennes (C. Morris: *The Journeys of Celia Fiennes*, p. 257), but Pryce (p. 282)
put its introduction rather later, instancing the patent of Liddicott and Moult
for "Smelting Black Tin with fossil coal in Iron Furnaces" of 1703. Polgooth,
however, may have still been using wood at the time of Celia Fiennes' visit.

1688 Revolution swept aside one obstacle that helped in no small measure to delay the exploitation of the copper deposits of Cornwall; an obsolete Act of 1405 prohibiting "the multiplying gold and silver" was repealed by a statute which contained a declaration that "no mine of Copper, Tin, Iron, or Lead, shall hereafter be judged to be a Royal Mine, although Gold or Silver may be extracted out of the same."[1]   Five years later this was slightly modified by an explanatory Act laying down that mine-owners should "enjoy" them without let or hindrance, but a certain right of pre-emption of their produce was reserved to the Crown.[2]   This ended the monopolistic rights granted to the Mines Royal Company in 1568, but the Act of 1694 made it plain that the even older rights and obligations of Cornish and Devon "tinners," going back at least to Plantagenet times, were not affected. These privileges had been amended and changed during the course of centuries. What had not changed was the fundamental principle of the Stannary organization that the "tinners" in return for taxes on their product enjoyed wide rights of legislation for and jurisdiction over the management of their industry; these taxes had been granted to the Duchy of Cornwall in the reign of Edward III, a Duchy appertaining to the eldest son and heir of the reigning monarch or, in default of such son and heir, to the Crown itself.[3]   Although the institution had some resemblances to

---

[1] 1 Gul. & Mary, Sess. 1, Cap. 30.
[2] 5 & 6, Gul. & Mary, Cap. 6.
[3] G. R. Lewis in his study, *The Stannaries* (1907), does not deal with the period after 1750 when the last Cornish Stannary Parliament met; stannary law and stannary courts survived until 1894. Lewis stressed the point that the essential difference between the guilds and the stannary system was that the principle of the former was restriction, that of the latter freedom of production which promoted the early development of capitalist enterprise in Cornwall; he failed to emphasise sufficiently that the term "tinner" included a variety of trades and all sorts and conditions of men. The stannary system should be regarded as one superimposed by the Crown on pre-existing local liberties that may have had wider applications than the mere regulation of tin-working; strong local sentiment, a distinct Cornish Celtic language, and isolation from the rest of England were powerful factors making for the survival of local laws. It is even possible that, before the expansion of the powers of Justices of the Peace by the Tudors, the majority of Cornish people had little direct contact with any law outside local manor courts save that of the Stannaries, for the Assize town was Launceston situated within a mile of the Devon boundary; Bodmin only became an Assize town in 1736, despite the protests of the Judges on circuit who were credited with the remark "Out of the world into Bodmin." It is possible that the earliest Plantagenet charters to the tinners were not grants of privileges and immunities so much as limitations of older and wider jurisdictions, jurisdictions which had embraced every type of case, criminal as well as civil, and may have been based on Celtic rather than on English "customary" law.

medieval craft guilds, the Stannaries of Cornwall and Devon possessed far wider jurisdictional rights than any guild; moreover, besides a local court in each of the four stannaries into which both counties were divided, there was also a higher court of the Lord Warden of the Stannaries. The custom of periodical meetings of the tinners of both counties in the so-called *stannary parliaments*, to review and, if necessary change and add to the body of stannary law, conferred what might almost be termed territorial semi-independence, although this had been reduced and put under strict control by Henry VII in the case of Cornwall, whilst, in Devon, the exhaustion of the tin deposits had led to the decay of the stannary system there to comparative impotence even before Tudor times. The stannary courts, however, continued in Cornwall, but many old customs fell into abeyance and were forgotten, first through subservience to the Tudor and early Stuart despotisms, and secondly through the destruction of the Stannary Records at Lostwithiel during the Civil War.

Whatever the privileges of the tinners had been their obligations had never been left in any doubt by the Duchy authorities. Before sale every block of tin produced in Cornwall had to be brought to one or other of the coinage towns to be coined or marked as having paid the coinage duties, the mark consisting of removing a corner off each block. There may have been some intention behind this originally of insuring that good tin was produced, but numerous complaints by London pewterers suggest that often tin adulterated with lead, or even baser material, was passed and coined by the Duchy officials. In medieval times the coinages took place at Liskeard, Lostwithiel, Truro, and Helston,[1] but the increasing importance of far western deposits led to Penzance becoming a coinage town in 1663. The system promoted the concentration of marketing in the coinage towns, and the fact that coinages were held at first only twice a year and later quarterly improved the economic position of merchant-smelters who had capital from which to advance loans to working miners. Even more important was the existence of the monopolistic royal right of pre-emption of tin, which had quite frequently been used by the impecunious Tudor and Stuart monarchs to raise money. The farm of the

---

[1]Bodmin had been designated a coinage town by its charter of 1305, but had ceased to be such before Tudor times. (Lewis, p. 240).

pre-emption had been leased to groups of merchants, but, until the rise in tin prices during the Commonwealth, the Crown had usually fixed rates which had benefited the working tinner by guaranteeing a price for his product. Pre-emption was resorted to for the last time in 1703, when temporary overproduction and the renewal of war with France had caused a slump, the measure being arranged by a Stannary Parliament. In 1710, through another Stannary Parliament, the period of pre-emption was extended for a further seven years, until 1717 when it ended. It is doubtful whether the pre-emption would have been extended in 1710 had not a mob of miners marched into Truro, where the Stannary Parliament was holding its sessions, and demanded that it and tin-prices be maintained.[1] There was some clamour for a revival of pre-emption in 1740, but then the Norfolk squire, Walpole, was in charge of the English Treasury and not Sidney, Earl Godolphin, whose family's fortunes had been maintained, and even created, during two centuries by Wheal Vor.

Only Godolphin's influence can explain the favourable terms of the pre-emption gained by the Cornish tinners in 1703. The price was fixed at 70/- per hundredweight, the highest price since 1688 and an advance of a third over the general level of tin prices in 1702.[2] The actual purchase of the tin was entrusted to John, Lord Granville, the Lord Warden of the Stannaries, to whom by December, 1703, £40,000 had been granted from the Treasury to purchase tin, which was followed by numerous further grants in the next few years. Moreover, these "State" purchases of tin were to amount to 1,600 tons per annum, although the total output of tin in Cornwall and Devon had only averaged about 1,250 tons a year from 1690 to 1699. These extremely favourable terms to the tinners were possibly detrimental to the London pewterers, who had virtually controlled the market and exportation of tin since 1660, and who, even when a farm of tin had been made by the Crown, had been closely associated with the merchants to whom the

---

[1]Hunt (quoting Tonkin), pp. 76-77. The Stannary Parliament of 1710 had split into factions, and there is some ground for believing that the minority he aded by Hugh Boscawen, the Lord Warden and Godolphin's nephew, had stirred up the miners to make their demonstration. Fear of the recurrence of such troubles and the long Whig hegemony explain why no further Stannary Parliament was convened until 1750 and then, not at Truro, but first at Lostwithiel and then at Helston, where there were fewer turbulent miners in the near neighbourhood.

[2]*C.T.B., 1703*, p. 346; Lewis, p. 277.

farm had been leased and had usually been allowed the privilege of buying not less than fifty tons at prices from 15 to 20 per cent below the London rates. While Cornish tinners had been suffering the grips of depression, there were complaints that the pewterers completely controlled the export of tin, and even now the adoption of the farm still meant that all tin was sent to London in the form of blocks where "pewterers" still monopolised its reduction into small bars and ingots for exportation. Whereas it was the intent of Cornwall and of the Crown to produce and sell as much tin as possible, the pewterers wished to restrict exports of bar-tin in order to keep foreign markets of manufactured pewter, although their exports of finished goods in Anne's reign only averaged 200 tons weight per annum, or about an eighth of the total output of Cornish tin. Some pewterers at times wished to prohibit the export of tin altogether, but most of them preferred to enjoy the moderate profits of manufacturing tin-ware for export, despite the already-existing risk that the Dutch might bring enough tin from the East Indies to supply part if not all the demands of their continental competitors.

The Crown's interest in promoting Cornish tin-mining contributed in no small degree to its expansion in the latter part of the seventeenth century. Whilst London manufacturers forced prices and production down in the 1690s, they were torn by their own conflicting interests as manufacturers of finished goods and as exporters of semi-manufactured tin. For this reason they acquiesced in Godolphin's policy, confining their complaints in the next few years to allegations that the quality of Cornish tin had deteriorated. It is probable that the four surveyors of the smelting houses took their duties lightly ; one of them did seize eleven blocks of tin from the smelter William Rawlins in 1702, thereby gaining £60 over his yearly salary of £80 as a reward and compensation for his trouble, but he seized the tin not because it was inferior in quality but because Rawlins had tried to evade coining it.[1] Coinage officials and the Crown cared little about the complaints on the part of the pewterers that the smelters were providing them with inferior tin;[2] all they worried about was the collection of

[1]*C.T.B., 1689-92*, pp. 1582, 1635, and *C.T.B., 1693-96*, pp. 5, 48.
[2]Both Penryn smelting-houses were sending inferior tin to London in 1697. (Welch, Vol. II, p. 169).

the various coinage duties on every block of tin which came to
the market. By 1707 there were complaints that, instead of
keeping the produce of various mines separate as had been done
in days when practically every mine had its own blowing-house,
a few smelters were buying up the entire produce of several
mines and smelting the whole altogether, so making it:

"unfit for abundance of uses wherein tin is wholly consumed (its
quality and lustre being changed) as (by) scarlet dyers, tin foil
workers, potters for all white ware, pin makers, painters, plumbers
and glaziers . . . nor is the said tin of itself so fit to be sent to Turkey,
and other places in bars, or for making fine pewter."

The pewterers, however, were confident that, when the farm
came to an end and a free market was restored :
"there will be a difference made in price between tin blown as
formerly and this now complained of."[1]
The complaint may have had some justification, but any
deterioration in quality could also be ascribed to the growing
proportion of mine to stream tin and to the increasing use of
coal, not wood, in smelting. Nor should it be forgotten that
the larger smelting houses could force the London merchants
to pay higher prices than the multitude of smaller concerns in
the past. Growing dependence on coal fuel and the increased
use of the new and more costly reverberatory furnaces had
helped to concentrate smelting into comparatively few hands;
from the Duchy viewpoint this was a desirable development
since it reduced the number of smelting-houses to be supervised,
thereby helping to ensure that all tin raised paid coinage dues.
At any rate, by 1700, the smelters had gained a dominating
position in the tin-mining industry, although controlled to some
degree by Duchy officials who were a legacy of the Middle Ages.

Another, perhaps even stranger, legacy of the past was the
right of tinners to claim bounds, a right which divorced the
proprietorship of mineral rights from ownership of the soil. On
waste, unenclosed land, by customary stannary law, any
tinner was free to stake a claim, usually about an acre in extent,
which he wished to reserve either to work himself or to claim
dues of one-fifteenth part of the mineral raised from those whom
he licensed to work it. Before demarking and claiming such
bounds, the bounder was required to give three months' notice
to a stannary court and to the lord of the soil.   Where land

[1]Welch, Vol. II, pp. 175-176.

was not in common or wastrel, however, the landowner enjoyed full mineral rights. Bounds had to be renewed yearly and
were a fruitful source of litigation in the stannary courts. By
inheritance extensive mineral rights might come to belong to a
man who did not own a yard of ground. Where bounds were
worked by lessees of the bounder, dues had to be paid to both
bounder and to the lord of the soil; if, within such bounds, 150
tons of tin-stuff were raised, 10 tons would go to the landowner
and another 14 or 15 tons to the bounder, leaving the actual
working mine adventurer only about five-sixths of the ores he
had been at the whole risk and expense of raising. Litigation
arose from the conflicting claims of landowner and bounder,
especially since the majority of bounds were only marked by
upturned turves or by little piles of stones, and not by natural
landmarks.[1] Even more disputes must have arisen from claims
that bounds had or had not been regularly renewed every year.
True, bound-owners could be bought out, and there tended
to be some consolidation of adjoining sets with the passing of
time, but often inheritance led to fantastic sub-division of sets,
particularly when the original bounds had been claimed by a
group of partners. Thus, in 1751, the Rev. Walter Borlase had
the extremely complicated share of a twelfth of $3\frac{1}{2}$ in 9 of the
sets known as Great Wheal Malkin and Little Wheal Malkin
in Bussuliack and Buskednan Commons in Gulval and Madron
parishes; he had one-fourteenth of one-ninth of the bounds
known as Nine Maids or Myne Andrennze and a quarter of a
nineteenth part of both Ventonegue Well and Ding Dong
bounds in the same moorland district. In all Walter Borlase
had some share in no less than ninety-two sets of bounds; many
of them were probably worthless, but Ding Dong, Botallack, and
Boscaswell occur in the list and must have swelled the income
of the man who probably neglected his duties as vicar of Madron
to act as Vice-Warden of the Stannaries, in which capacity he
must have presided over many a case of disputed tin bounds[2].

The past and its customs, however, affected the copper-
mining industry but little. With the Acts of 1689 and 1694 all
restriction on the exploitation of copper by the owner of the
soil or by those to whom he leased his rights was swept away;
the only limitation was the amount of capital available to start

[1]Pryce, pp. 137-141; Henderson MSS., Vol 18, pp. 39ff.
[2]MS. Bounds Book of the Rev. Walter Borlase.

mining operations. Even in the period of the Mines Royal Company's monopoly, copper-smelting came to be concentrated near the coalfields of the Bristol area and South Wales, and smelting companies located in these districts, with their knowledge of markets and with their available capital, began the free exploitation of Cornish copper-ore deposits. The first area to be worked was that west of Truro, extending down to Ludgvan, where tin-workings had, doubtless, already revealed the existence of copper.[1] In the first quarter of the eighteenth century it is likely that tin and copper were worked together, with copper still widely regarded as a by-product of the tin lodes. No other explanation can account for the contradictory evidence on the state of Cornish mining in the 1720s. When the brass and copper manufacturers petitioned for protection against foreign competition in 1721 they alleged that no less than 12,350 families were employed in raising copper ore in Cornwall and Devon and in taking it to the coast;[2] yet the first records of Cornish copper production reveal that in the years 1726 to 1730 the average yearly output of copper ores was but 6,500 tons, worth less than £50,000 per annum. To raise this quantity of ore a labour force of 1,500 should have been more than adequate.[3] The brass and copper interests to

[1]Early records of specific mines are lacking. Both Celia Fiennes (C. Morris: *The Journeys of Celia Fiennes*, p. 260) and Defoe (*A Tour Thro' the Whole Island of Great Britain*, 1927 edition, Vol. I, p. 238) vaguely refer to extensive copper workings between Truro and St. Michael's Mount, and stress the fact that the ores were sent to Bristol and to South Wales for smelting. The contemporary Cornish historian, William Hals, mentioned the existence of copper lodes in St. Enoder, probably at Castle-an-Dinas, now worked for wolfram, but the only Gwennap mine he named was Poldice which he referred to as a tin mine. (*Parochial History of Cornwall*, pp. 116, 155). Poldice was probably one of the mines started soon after the Restoration of Charles II. (Drew, Vol. II, p. 205). In all probability Pednandrea, near Redruth, was an early copper mine for the lower lodes of tin in it had been reached by 1765. (G. Jars: *Voyages Metallurgiques*, Vol. III, p. 142). Pryce, who may have had access to old ticketing records, listed Wheal Fortune in Ludgvan, Roskear, and Pool Adit as the chief copper mines in 1725 (p. 287). William Borlase was the first writer to mention North Downs, but it was in full production before 1740. (*Natural History of Cornwall*, p. 156).
[2]Hamilton, p. 120.
[3]The estimate that 7,517 persons of both sexes and of all ages were engaged in mining, transporting, and shipping copper ore from Cornwall in 1787 (Hamilton, p. 323) related to the output of 38,047 tons of copper ore in that year, gives a product of five tons of ore per unit of labour; the same product per hand can be obtained by relating the mean of the estimate of the labour force given by John Vivian to the Parliamentary Committee of 1799 with the output of 51,273 tons in that year. If each labourer raised five tons, between 1,000 and 1,400 persons must have been engaged on Cornish copper mining in the 1720s; whilst the average output per hand may have increased during the eighteenth century with improved methods of working and increased manual skill, the improvement was offset by the increasing depths and difficulties of working the mines.

make a good case for themselves had, apparently, not only listed all the tin as well as the copper miners, but had added the casual hands who now and again did work about the mines but who were also employed about the farms and fisheries. Until 1740 copper, although rapidly gaining in importance, was less valuable than tin to Cornwall; in the ten years 1730-39 it brought nearly £600,000 to the county as against about £900,000 realized by Cornish tin in the same decade.[1]

Between 1689 and 1740 the Cornish copper-mining industry assumed many of the features which characterized its entire existence. From the first it depended to a large extent on outside capital of which a fair proportion was supplied by the copper smelting interests of Bristol and South Wales. The Glorious Revolution was followed by an age of financial speculation which, starting with or before the establishment of the Bank of England, reached its peak in the boom days of the South Sea Bubble. In that period several must have invested in Cornish mining, some to gain, others to lose, thereby. It was not long before the wealth of the "foreign" smelters, who carried Cornish ores off to Bristol and South Wales, aroused acute and enduring suspicions among Cornish people that they were being deprived of gains that rightfully should be theirs,[2] and a series of rather luckless attempts to smelt copper ores in Cornwall began. Rather strangely, since there is no evidence of any copper being mined in that district at the time, one of the earliest ventures was at Polrudden near St. Austell, by a member of the Scobell family in partnership with a certain Vincent and Sir Talbot Clark.[3] Despite the distance from the copper deposits then being worked, this venture only failed through bad management and dishonest workmen, and its failure did not convince Cornishmen that it was impracticable to bring fuel to Cornwall for smelting copper.[4] The rather

---

[1]Copper figures based on Pryce, p. xv. The tin figures are a rough approximation based on Lewis's records of tin coined (pp. 252 ff.) and the assumption that the average price of tin during this decade was 50/- per hundredweight, which is probably rather low.
[2]Carew (p. 21) had been the first to make this suggestion as far back as 1603.
[3]Hamilton (p. 110) identifies him with Sir Gilbert Clark later associated with the Welsh copper works of Elton and Wayne, who may have been one of the promoters of the Cornish Copper Company of 1694 which foundered in the financial crisis three years later.
[4]Drew, Vol. II, p. 38.

earlier failure of the venture of John Pollard and Thomas Worth at St. Ives was attributed to similar causes.[1]   The attempt begun at Penpol in Phillack by Gideon Collier, and carried on later by Sir William Pendarves and Robert Coster, was rather more successful, and Coster, who was connected with smelting works at Swansea, believed that copper-smelting could be carried on as economically in Cornwall as elsewhere.[2] Yet another attempt was made at St. Agnes, probably by the proprietors of one of the tin blowing-houses there. The cost of fuel and the competition of the Bristol and Welsh smelters, with more capital to hand, drove these ventures out of existence, but the Cornishmen were not convinced that their venture had been fairly defeated. Godolphin was probably responsible for the measure of 1710 which gave a complete drawback of duties on all coal brought to Cornwall for smelting tin and copper. Four years later the sudden death of Queen Anne frustrated a Cornish demand for extending the coinage system to copper. The scheme proposed extending the stannary laws to copper mining in:

"all things (except being under bounds) and have the copper coined at the neighbouring coinage towns, as the tin is, under a duty of one shilling per hundredweight of fine copper to be paid to the Duke of Cornwall; which, as it would be an addition to the ducal revenue, and managed without any surcharge by the same coinage officers, so would it effectively secure the smelting and refining of all the Copper Ores within the county, by degrees let us into the true value of our commodity and the management of it, as easy as that of tin; and furthermore confine the labour and profits in the manufacturing thereof, among ourselves. . . ."[3]

With Godolphin and Anne both dead the Cornish mining interests abandoned hopes of "State intervention" and braced themselves to withstand the shocks of free capitalist enterprise. Landowners, notably Lord Falmouth,[4] began leasing mineral rights on their lands to "outside" speculators, whilst others, even more venturesome, started more or less active capitalization of mining enterprise on their own estates.

The copper industry, however, was dominated by the small group of smelting companies, who, by agreement among them-

[1]Carew, pp. 21-22 note *q* (by Tonkin).
[2]Pryce, p. 278.
[3]Pryce, p. 279. (Quoting Tonkin's MS papers).
[4]Hamilton, pp. 145-146.

selves, monopolized the markets for Cornish ores, and who gave
the mine adventurer as much or as little as they pleased for his
produce.[1] At least two of these companies and their associates,
the English Copper Company and Wayne and Company,
actually embarked on mining in Cornwall. The latter company
sent John Coster, the inventor of the whim, to superintend
mines in the Chacewater district,[2] but its interest had possibly
terminated before 1730. These and other smelting concerns
made contracts with mines adventurers to buy up all the ores
the latter raised over long terms of years at prices ranging from
£2 10s. to £5 a ton,[3] but prices were forced up when a new
smelting company appeared in the market about 1720. Hitherto the Bristol men had apparently been undisturbed in Cornwall, but now a Welsh Company appeared and bought at
£6 5s. per ton some 1,400 tons of ores which had been lying
unsold for some time, the older smelters having refused to pay
more than £4 5s. per ton for it.[4] The newcomer then bought
a further 900 tons from the Roskear adventurers and other
ores to bring his total purchases up to 3,000 tons, or about half
the annual Cornish output at that time. The fact that this
Welsh Company cleared a profit of 30 or 40 per cent on its
transactions[5] increased Cornish resentment against the older
smelters, who, they thought, were working in close association.

Nevertheless, the number of smelters was still small, and
it was likely that before long they would act as a united body
again to the detriment of the copper mining interest. While
the unity of the smelters was temporarily broken, however, the
mining concerns, probably late in 1725, instituted the *ticketing*
system of marketing copper ores, a system that, with one short
break,[6] was to last as long as there was any considerable
quantity of copper ore to be sold in West Cornwall.[7] Hence-

---

[1]Pryce listed four companies—the Brass Wire Company, the English Copper
Company, Wayne and Company, and Chambers and Company—as active
about 1720, but the second and last of these were amalgamated in 1720. (Hamilton,
pp. 244-245).

[2]Hamilton, pp. 145-146.

[3]Pryce, p. 286.

[4]Hamilton (pp. 146-147) suggests that this was Lockwood, Morris, and
Company who acquired the Landore Copper Works, near Swansea when their
original owner was bankrupted by the South Sea Bubble.

[5]Pryce, p. 287.

[6]The period of the Cornish Metal Company, 1785-92. (See below, pp. 82 ff).

[7]The year 1725 is suggested as that in which the ticketing system was introduced
because the statistics for copper production given by Dr. Pryce (p. xv.) begin with
the year 1726, and were probably derived from ticketing records that were at his

forth all ores ready for sale were brought to a convenient marketing centre at least a fortnight before the sale was to take place; there the agents of the various smelters took samples of the different parcels of ore, and, a fortnight later, on instructions from their principals, all attended the ticketing where, after a sumptuous dinner, every agent produced on separate tickets, or slips of paper, the prices his company were ready to pay for each separate lot of ore. The system did not preclude combination and collusion between the agents of the various companies in Cornwall or between their principals in Bristol or South Wales, especially when communications between Cornwall and the smelting areas were vastly improved with the increasing magnitude of the copper traffic itself. The chief disadvantage of ticketing, detrimental to both smelters and mines adventurers, was that bids had to be made for every lot of ore; it might happen that at a particular sale no smelting firm really wanted certain lots and so all had sent tickets with very low bids; one of these bids had to be accepted, and the firm which made it would find itself encumbered with ores which it did not want; at the same time the mine adventurer who had brought those ores to the sale would have to accept a much lower price than he might have secured had he been able to withhold them until a later ticketing. From the miner's viewpoint, prompt sales were generally necessary to meet current running costs, particularly since the cost-book system of dividing profits as and when made left no reserves of capital which might have enabled stocks of ore to be withheld until copper prices rose.

disposal. Later writers have tended to take too literally and uncritically Pryce's references to "about eighty" or "about fifty years ago"; although his *Mineralogia Cornubiensis* was published in 1778, it may have taken many years to write. Thus Hamilton (pp. 146-147) has been misled by Pryce's "about fifty years back" to attribute the copper glut ended by the appearance of the Welsh interloper to the year 1730; and the amount at Roskear and Wheal Kitty then unsold was not 14,000 but 1,400 tons of ore. (Pryce, p. 287). Even if it is not certain that the records beginning in 1726 were ticketing statistics, Hamilton's dates should be set back about ten years; it was in 1720 that Lockwood and Morris set up as copper smelters at Landore, and it is unlikely that they lost much time before making their approaches to the Cornish mines adventurers. Moreover a glut of copper was more likely to have occurred about 1720 than ten years later; there is little reason to doubt that Cornish mining schemes were a feature of the speculative craze of the South Sea Bubble period just as they were in the South American boom a century later. W. R. Scott, it is true, only listed two schemes which were possibly connected with Cornwall during the South Sea Bubble days (*Joint Stock Companies*, Vol. III, pp. 445-458), but it is more than probable that a number of local cost-book schemes were then launched in Cornwall entirely independently of the operations of London speculators and company promoters.

The cost-book system, another legacy of the older tin-mining adventures, originated from the simple partnership of a group of labouring tinners working a tin-stream. With deep mining no group of ordinary working men had the capital reserves on which to live while spending months sinking shafts or driving levels fathoms below the surface of the earth, nor even to provide the equipment necessary to work and maintain deep levels once they reached productive lodes. The capitalist mine-promoters came on the scene, but few of them were ready to risk all their available capital in a single mine, preferring to spread it over a group of, perhaps, widely scattered mines, holding small shares in each and running the risk of no great loss if one or two adventures failed completely. All sorts and conditions of men were willing to venture in such concerns—landowners who had hopes of exploiting the underground wealth of their own estates but who lacked adequate fluid capital to start operations, professional men, especially lawyers who often held landlords in the palms of their hands, not a few clergymen who hoped to gain the money to buy better livings for themselves or for their sons or even to pay a curate's wage, some doctors, blacksmiths and carpenters who could do with the extra work mining operations afforded them, and, above all, merchants who traded in many commodities for which there would be a greater demand if more mines were put to work. Such "adventurers" had long been engaged in tin mining, and, in the early eighteenth century the sight of "foreign" adventurers coming down to work "their" copper deposits from regions far to the east of the Tamar stirred them to emulation. But whether the capital was provided by Cornish or by "foreign" adventurers, the system was the same. The adventurers met, decided to start a mine, and agreed among themselves what share of the costs each was prepared to contribute. Usually a skilled, practical miner had made an estimate beforehand of the capital necessary to work the proposed set and the potential profits to be gained by working it for a certain time. The individual adventurers, knowing how much capital they were willing to risk, had their names put in the *cost-book* for a share, usually an eighth part or a fraction thereof, in the venture. A purser was appointed to take charge of this cost-book of expenses and to manage all financial transactions, whilst a mine captain or manager was put in charge of actual mining operations.[1] The purser was authorized to make all necessary purchases up to the total credit of the mine which the adventurers had agreed to contribute for immediate working. At the end of a month, but more often after two or three, and, in some cases, even four, months had passed,[2] the adventurers or their agents met again, and the purser submitted his accounts. If the mine had already come into production and sold ores exceeding the value of the capital subscribed either in money or materials, a dividend of the whole amount of the profit was declared and shared among the adventurers in proportion to their individual shares at the time; if, however, no profits had been made, and further expenditure was necessary, a *call* would be made on each adventurer in proportion to his share to raise the amount deemed necessary to carry on mining operations until the next meeting of the adventurers. Failure to meet calls meant forfeiture of shares, whilst shares could be transferred with little more formality than notification to the purser.

The cost-book system was a reasonably effective and efficient method of financing mines in Cornwall. It had the merit of "spreading the risk", and enabled the richer capitalists to speculate in several undertakings instead of committing themselves absolutely to the fortunes of a single mine. The system of working from month to month might be criticized, and even more the immediate division of profits as dividends which fostered the notion that a working mine should always be paying for itself. Had there been a capital reserve, ores could have been held back from poor markets and reserved until prices rose. Frequent stocktakings meant a complexity of numerous small accounts; at one meeting a profit of £500 might have to be divided among sixteen adventurers, at the next perhaps £800, but the following meeting might have to make calls amounting to £400 and the next of £600, to be followed by a dividend of perhaps £100, instead of a single dividend of £400

---

[1]As mining concerns became larger the mine captains and managers became separate groups, the former declining to the status of overseers or foremen supervising the daily working of the mines, the latter becoming a managerial class some of whom, like the Williamses and Daveys, had by Victoria's reign risen to the highest ranks in "county" society. At the same time the pursers tended to decline to being mere accountant-clerks.

[2]The period seems generally to have lessened as the mining concerns grew in size; a four months' interval between account-meetings was common in the eighteenth century; later two-monthly accounts became general.

for a year or eighteen months' working. Moreover, of the sixteen shares one man might hold six, or three-eighths of the entire mine, whilst another adventurer might only hold a sixty-fourth and a third some such holding as three five-hundred-and-twelfths, even if there were no forfeited or dead shares to involve such fractions as fifteenths or sixty-thirds. The purser's task was certainly no sinecure, but he was often one of the principal adventurers in a mine and an active promoter of mining adventures; in other cases he and the mine captains were given small shares by the mines adventurers over and above their salaries.

The purser and, still more, the mine captains or managers were the link between the various capitalists interested in the mines and the labouring miners. Other men also occupied intermediate places in the socio-economical order of the mining world, especially as the increasing depth of the mines meant specialization of function. By 1740, besides the "practical miner" who could look at a rock and say with convincing finality whether or not it contained copper or tin in proportio . enough to be worth the working, engineers had appeared whose sole business was making and maintaining pumps and whims, and also skilled carpenters who, among other tasks, could be relied upon to see to the adequate propping of an underground level or the even more difficult shoring up or *collaring* of the sides of a shaft through loose rock and rubble. Another group of foremen supervised the preparation of the ores, once they had been brought to the surface, for sale. Both copper and tin ores had to be crushed and refined before being taken to ticketings or blowing-houses, and so there arose another group of middlemen who owned or leased stamping or crushing mills. Their activities seem to have employed the greatest amount of female and juvenile labour in the mining industries.[1] Stamping-mills were sometimes worked as part of a mine, particularly where the mine was large, but, until the latter nineteenth century, their location depended on the availability of water-power. Many stamping-mills were the property of landowners who leased them to contractors; these contractors must normally have made a reasonably comfortable living, enjoying as they did a more reliable and regular income than the adventurers and mine labourers. Stamping was a trade which gave

[1]Pryce, p. 230; Borlase: *Natural History of Cornwall* (1758) pp. 180-181.

much scope to the inventive mind; there was much experimentation to secure the most economical use of power, whilst
it was discovered very early in the eighteenth century that the
lighter and more flakey copper ores required different treatment
from tin-stuff. Most types of copper ore, indeed, were not
crushed by stamps but were broken into small lumps by hand;
then the whole was *jigged*, or washed in a sieve, so that the
heavy ores sank to the bottom. Only the poorer copper-ores
were crushed at stamping-mills, and the same process of separation by water used to remove the waste rock. By 1750 much
juvenile labour, paid at fourpence a day, was employed in these
processes.[1]

The wealth of smelters, merchants, landowners, stamping-
mill proprietors, and part of the revenue of the Duchy of
Cornwall, all depended on the working miner. Although this
class outnumbered all others connected with the tin and copper
mining industries of Cornwall comparatively little is known of
the actual conditions in which they lived. Unlike smelters and
landlords they left no written records. Sometimes they
appeared before the magistrates, called to prove that they had
a legal settlement in the parish where they resided when, perhaps worn out by years of toil or disabled, they seemed likely
to ask for parish relief. Occasionally cryptic entries in a burial
register recorded accidents that caused their deaths in their
dangerous calling. They ranged from the free miner working
a tin-stream or small mine on his own account to casual
labourers working for a weekly or even a daily wage. From
medieval times, however, the number of free miners had been
declining, that of wage-earners increasing, but in between were
a variety of *tributers* and *tut-workers* labouring under contracts
made with the adventurers. It is impossible to give an estimate
of the proportion of each type of labourer employed in the
Cornish mines at any time; if towards the end of the nineteenth century simple wage-earners outnumbered all the other
groups, yet the free miner still survived.

Nor was there ever any clearly-cut division between the

[1]W. Borlase: *Natural History of Cornwall*, p. 203. When copper-ores were
crushed at stamping-mills, dry and not wet stamps (as used in tin-stamping) were
employed; this must have increased the incidence of silicosis and ensured that
many women and girls died of "consumptions" and "declines" as well as men.
Women tended to live considerably longer than men in the mining districts, but
before 1813 hardly any parish registers of burials recorded ages of death.

different categories of labour in the Cornish mines. Tributers came near to free miners; they contracted to work a mining pitch[1] paying to the owners or lessees of that pitch a proportion of the ores raised by them from it during the period for which they contracted to work it. Contracts were made by open auction, and the competition for pitches which were regarded as rich sometimes meant that the tributer who made the final bid had bound himself to allow the adventurers as much as nineteen shillingsworth of every pound's worth of ores he raised. The tributer also provided his own hand tools. Pitches were usually taken for a period of two months, but sometimes for three. It was to the interest of both adventurers and tributers that the maximum produce be obtained. If a pitch suddenly deteriorated the tributer had the right to abandon it at the end of a month's working, paying compensation to the adventurers for the broken contract in proportion to the number of men he had working with him on it. Agreements were almost invariably verbal. The position of men working as partners of the contracting tributer who took the pitch is not at all clear; some of them, perhaps many, by the eighteenth century were wage-earners paid by the tributer; although the risks of loss through the sudden deterioration of a pitch may have tended to a system of equal partners sharing alike, the chance of a rich strike led many sub-contractors to pay wages to the partners or *pare* working with him, especially when the numbers engaged on a single pitch were fairly large. It is impossible to ascribe the introduction of the tribute system to any particular date or even century, but its extension coincided with the increasing depth of mines which demanded the investment of more and more capital to maintain workings in production; four or six working miners could carry on tin-streaming or even a small shallow mine on their own, but they could not maintain the shafts and levels, adits and pumps, of a concern going fifty or sixty fathoms below the level of the ground.

The tutworker contracted to do a certain amount of work for a specified sum of money, generally within a certain time. He was usually employed to sink shafts and drive levels, but towards the end of the eighteenth century there was a tendency in many mines to employ more and more tutworkers in the actual excavation of mineral ores. This feature, however, seems

[1]A section of a lode believed to be productive of ore in any part of the mine.

to have been rather more marked in the case of copper than in that of tin-mining, owing to the greater distance and rather more complicated transactions involved in the marketing of copper ores. Towards the end of 1786, for example, Dolcoath was only employing tributers irregularly, though in October that year it paid nearly £600 to twenty-three groups of tutwork partners and £492 to casual hands, whilst Cook's Kitchen at the same time was employing seventeen groups of tutworkers and but eleven sets of tributers.[1]

Estimates of the number of persons employed by the Cornish mining industries at this time vary. In a period of depression in 1677 Andrew Yarranton, perhaps over-obsessed with his schemes to start tin-plate manufacturing in England, stated that 60,000 persons depended on Cornish tin mining; some forty years later it was alleged that western copper mines maintained 12,000 families. Both estimates were exaggerated, yet it is likely that the livings of a third of the inhabitants of Cornwall were affected in a less or greater degree, directly or indirectly, by the fortunes of the mines, ranging from landowner to *buddle boys* working on the tin stamps, from merchants' wives to *bal maidens* breaking up lumps of copper ore, from adventuring lawyers and parsons to free miners and muleteers who took the ores from mines to ticketing sales. In all they may have numbered more than 30,000 in the first half of the eighteenth century, although the number wholly dependent on the mines for their livelihood probably did not exceed half that number. Many spent only part of their working life about the mines; at other times they were cultivating small-holdings or taking part in the seasonal pilchard fishery. Yet the fortunes of the mines meant to most of the thirty thousand the difference between tolerable comfort and dire distress.

What they regarded as tolerable comfort would be described as privation today. Few ventured far outside the limits of their own parishes, fewer still, except sea-farers, ever left their native county. If they travelled it was by sea rather than by land, but both were perilous—the sea from storm, shipwreck, and priv-

---

[1] Cook's Kitchen and Dolcoath Accounts, October 19 and 20, 1786. (MSS., in possession of T. R. Harris, Esq.). The Dolcoath Accounts on this occasion did not specify whether the 23 sets of partners paid were tribute or tutworkers, but other Dolcoath accounts specify when tributers were paid. Three of the eleven groups of partners receiving money as tributers at Cook's Kitchen were also paid for tutwork at the same time.

ateers in the long wars that raged periodically between 1689 and 1815, the land from highway robbers and roads so-called only from courtesy. In fact, Cornish roads were a by-word in the eighteenth century; Celia Fiennes nearly broke her horse's neck and her own in a pot-hole when she journeyed from Looe to Fowey;[1] the Cornish historian Tonkin seems to have lost the sight of one eye struck by a bramble overhanging a narrow sunken lane along which he rode.[2] Nor were potholes and unpared hedgerows the only perils and inconveniences the traveller faced. Over the unenclosed moorlands of the mining districts there was danger after nightfall, or on frequent foggy days, of losing the trackway altogether and stumbling headlong into an unfenced mine-shaft. Some of the few bridges which existed were unsafe, and even much later there were some casualties on the road from Marazion to Penzance which ran alongside a tidal marsh; John Wesley attempting a short cut across the sands and tidal marshes near Hayle, was once almost cut off by the quickly rising tide and several others had or did not have similar narrow escapes near Par and St. Blazey.

In the course of the eighteenth century many fine mansions were built by the gentry of Cornwall, but before that time such houses—and many of those who lived in them—left much to be desired. Celia Fiennes was sensitive to the fumes of the tobacco smoked by Cornish folk of both sexes round the inn-fires where she lodged, but her younger contemporary, Mary Granville, had more to complain of when she came to Roscrow, near Penryn, as the bride of Alexander Pendarves, a man old enough to be her grandfather. She found Roscrow with rotten floors, broken-down ceilings, and badly provided with windows.[3] She made no complaints about her husband, but his relative Sir William Pendarves, the copper-smelter was an offensive, boastful, hard-drinking man who had had

"a coffin made of copper (which one of his mines that year had produced) and placed in the midst of his great hall, and instead of his making use of it as a monitor that might have made him ashamed and terrified at his past life, and induce him to make amends in the future, it was filled with punch, and he and his comrades soon made themselves incapable of any sort of reflection; this was *often* re-

[1] C. Morris: *The Journeys of Celia Fiennes*, pp. 255-256.
[2] Carew, p. 143, note q.
[3] Mrs. Delany: *Autobiography*, Vol. 1, pp. 35-36.

peated, and lured him on to that awful moment he had so much reason to dread."[1]

Nevertheless the future Mrs. Delany seems to have accommodated herself to the life of the Cornish squirearchy, and years later when she visited Ireland she remarked that the heartiness and sociability of the people there were more like those of the Cornish people than she had encountered in any other place.[2]

True it was only the eccentrics among the Cornish gentry who left memories and traditions of their characters and actions behind them, whilst the majority were prosaic and even conventional enough. In a hard-drinking age only gargantuan dissipation attracted much attention, or the antics of a man like Sir William Pendarves, whose contempt of his latter end in a credulous age might well have led to rumours of ungodly covenant with the powers of darkness. Another striking figure of the time was John Borlase, squire of Pendeen, landowner and mine adventurer, a Justice of the Peace and for a time Member of Parliament; in 1709 he shocked his more conventional neighbours by horsewhipping a man in Madron church; later he bought the incumbency of that church for his oldest surviving son, Walter. John Borlase seems to have grown more headstrong as he grew old; when he was eighty-five Walter Borlase wrote him a peremptory advice immediately to turn to doors a female servant, who had lately given birth to an illegitimate child, and thereby "put a stop to that scandal and offence which the contrary conduct casts upon your character".[3] Far different was Sir John St. Aubyn, who gained a reputation as the one Member of Parliament Walpole could not bribe; he spent his short lifetime between parliamentary duties and the improvement of his estate at Clowance. Many other gentry also lived honest and temperate lives, but the example they set to the "lower orders" may have been offset by the conduct of the rakes and adventurers whose conduct was far more sensational.

The clergy were closely allied and inter-related with the

[1]Mrs. Delany: *Autobiography*, Vol. 1, p. 66.
[2]Mrs. Delany: *Autobiography*, Vol. 1, p. 291.
[3]Walter Borlase MSS: Walter Borlase to John Borlase, July, 1751. It is not unlikely that Walter Borlase was stirred to write this admonition by rumours that John Borlase was the father of the child, rumours not a little disturbing to the dignity of the Vicar of Madron and Kenwyn and Prebendary of Exeter.

squirearchy. Four of the great mining parishes by 1740 were in the rather indifferent hands of two of the sons of John Borlase; Walter held Madron and Kenwyn, William Ludgvan and St. Just in Penwith. The Pendarves and Bassets were using livings in the Redruth and Camborne district to provide for younger sons or other family connections; St. Aubyns and Godolphins along with the Duchy interests held most of the remaining livings in the western mining region. Temporal and spiritual affairs had come into the hands of a narrow caste whose rather meagre fortunes in landed estates had been increased greatly by the exploitation of the tin and copper deposits on those estates. Yet these clergy were not so notorious for lack of zeal as some of their detractors have alleged. Some clergy may have taken their duties lightly, but even absentee rectors and vicars held religious views every whit as sincere as those of the itinerant Wesleyans. There was Walter Borlase who held the livings of both Madron and Kenwyn besides a prebendal stall in Exeter cathedral; his activities as a magistrate, mining adventurer, and Vice-Warden of the Stannaries can hardly have left him much time for his three-fold clerical duties; in his private correspondence with his many sons and daughters he was almost invariably advising great care in money matters. Pluralist and man of the world, Walter Borlase gained notoriety by persecuting the early Methodists in Cornwall; his faith was not their faith, yet it was one acceptable to many thinking men of his day, for it was he who wrote :

"the plan of providence with regard to man not being limited to his station here, which is but a grain of his duration, this ought to satisfy us, that whatever particular Evils fall to our lot, tend in the whole system of things to universal Good and that whatever is, is Right, with regard to the Disposition of God and to its ultimate tendency. . . . Without this persuasion, how think you I could sleep under the oppressions of anxiety and solicitude for so many children depending for their subsistence and provision upon the breath of one frail infirm man?"[1]

It is strange to find this quietist resignation in a man whose family, despite good claims to Norman blood, had only attained affluence by the rapid progress of mining in West Penwith. True, it was a faith that would keep the lower orders in what

[1]Walter Borlase MSS: Walter to John Borlase, December 12, 1747.

was regarded as their rightful station, but it was not a religion that could move mountains nor one which appealed to the enterprising spirit of the age. It was the best that the majority of learned clergymen had to offer Cornwall at that time, but it was as much out of tune with the spirit of an age of industrial expansion as the semi-pagan superstitions of the illiterate masses.

Clergy and people had drifted apart, and religion no longer held society together. The individualist assertion of self-made men who gained fortunes by mining enterprise set the tempo of a new age. It was not the Sir Roger de Coverleys who seized the imaginations of the Cornish masses as leaders of men, but dynamic characters like Sir William Pendarves and John Borlase who seemed to hold nothing sacrosanct that lay in the way of the gratifications of their lusts or their hates, and a host of smaller men who pushed themselves forward by fortunate and often sharp speculations. With such examples before them it is little wonder that the Cornish people gained a reputation for drunkenness, violence, and lawlessness. It was not an up-surge of primitive barbarity, but the reverse side of the victory of predatory and anarchic capitalist enterprise; the Methodists who denounced it have failed to give due recognition to the fact that John Wesley's victories in Cornwall were gained largely because the Cornish folk regarded him as a courageous insurgent against inert traditional institutions whose magnitude might have been expected to crush him.

Roistersome traditional sports, like hurling and wrestling, survived from an earlier age and were not confined to the "lower orders." They, too, came under the ban of Methodist excommunication. True they were violent recreations in which serious and even fatal injuries sometimes occurred; hurling matches between adjoining villages provided opportunities to pay off old scores and to gratify long-rankling feuds and hatreds; cock-fighting and bull-baiting have been condemned by a more enlightened and perhaps more sensitive age, although they were the only means in those days of gratifying the ineradicable craving of men for exciting diversion and gambling in their leisure hours. Cornish wrestling matches, however, were exhibitions of physical skill and grace in which sheer brute force rarely gained the victory. Hurling was a game which called forth communal activity; in some inter-parochial matches

every fit male was a participant, and glory in a communal
victory of hamlet or village in which each had taken part was
to be commended rather than despised. Maypole dances and
village feasts, celebrations like the Helston floral dance and
that of the Padstow Hobby Horse, even if rooted in pagan
antiquity, all fostered and kept alive that sense of community
which a later age was to lose and mourn. Even a more repre-
hensible practice like the Skimmington Ride was, in the last
resort, the communal vindication of the sanctity of marriage
vows imposed by a Church that had proved powerless to enforce
them. Not infrequently a clergyman rebuked a sinner in the
face of the congregation, but his audience regarded him as
expressing only his personal views or, at most, those of his
ministry; the censure of the entire community, crudely and
blatantly expressed, was a virtual decree of outlawry on
offenders and a deterrent, more potent than any ecclesiastical
warning, to those who might have been tempted to err against
the mores of the community in the same way.

But there were grimmer occasions on which the Cornish
assembled in violent groups. In April, 1710, the tinners had
invaded Truro in their thousands to compel the Stannary
Parliament to fall in with their wishes.[1] Twenty years earlier
another body of tinners had invaded Falmouth, boarded a
ship, and seized a cargo of salt, with some loss of life.[2] Food
riots in 1729 led to the execution of three or four ringleaders,
whilst six Cornish Justices of the Peace who took an active
part in their apprehension, shared a Treasury reward or Compensation of £120 for their trouble.[3] In 1737 there were to be
further similar troubles at Falmouth which led the alarmed
Treasury to consult the Secretary at War. The tinners had
assembled either to prevent the exportation of corn by the
merchants, or to seize it from ships which had arrived in Falmouth harbour; demonstrations of this type had hitherto been
rare if not unknown, but were to be fairly common between
1770 and 1850.[4] Incidents such as these, coupled with the
Jacobite sympathies of some of the Cornish Tory squires, were
doubly alarming to Walpole's Ministry, but the threat was one
to property rather than one to life.

[1]Hunt, pp. 76-77.
[2]*C.S.P.Dom.*, *1690-91*, pp. 26, 29, 34.
[3]*C.T.B.*, *1729-30*, pp. 113, 559: Carew, p. 66, subnote by Tonkin.
[4]*C.T.B.*, *1735-38*, p.341.

Property was also menaced by the far more frequent "riotous" assemblies that went *wrecking*. Later romancers have created the idea that wrecking consisted of the practice of luring ships on to the rocks and reefs of the Cornish coasts by displaying lanterns, sometimes lashed to the necks or tails of donkeys or cattle. Assize rolls do not record any such practice, although there were some convictions, sometimes accompanied by sentences of death, for the offence of "wrecking" which was simply plundering vessels which had been cast on to the rocks of the Cornish coast. Wrecks "by the hand of God" were so frequent as to render unnecessary the trouble of going abroad with a lantern on the cliffs on dark, stormy nights in the hope of deluding the helmsman of a tempest-tossed vessel into a fatal alteration of his course; not only were such lights more likely to lead friendly neighbouring fishermen to doom, but no man in his senses would venture on to the cliffs by night, hazarding limb and neck, on such a slender off-chance of gain. But if news came of a wreck on the shore there was a stampede to the scene, all hoping to salvage something from the doomed vessel— part of a cargo of goods that might help to feed and clothe them in an unwonted luxury, timbers from the shattered ship to repair a house or even merely for firewood, and, perhaps not always last but first, the lives of some of the luckless crew and passengers. Life-savers and salvagers might have got into each other's way, and doubtless many rushed to secure some valuable-looking chest or keg from the waves when they might have helped to try and save a fellow-mortal from destruction. Scenes of violence occurred when men and women bickered and fought for the possession of spoils thrown up by the seas; a seamen might struggle ashore and see a wrecker making off with property he recognized as his own only to be threatened with violence if he attempted to retrieve it.[1] Customs officials might attempt to assert the Crown's right to wreckage but that was a law unrecognized by the common folk, who believed that if any man ran the hazard of saving something from the sea and succeeded, to him it belonged. To the poorer classes a wreck

---

[1]Defoe: *A Tour Thro' the Whole Island of Great Britain,* (1927 ed.) Vol. I, p. 245 The exact date of Defoe's visit to Cornwall and Scilly is unknown; whilst it may have taken place in James II's reign, the description of a sea-fight with a French privateer off the Lizard suggests that it occurred during his electioneering tour of 1705; had it occurred later than 1707 it is hardly likely that he would have omitted to mention the wreck of Sir Cloudesley Shovell off Scilly.

was a gift of God; sometimes it meant a taste of luxuries otherwise hopelessly beyond their reach; more often it meant
nothing more than a few fragments of broken timber, fit only
to make a fire—but a good fire was a luxury in many poor
homes by the treeless coasts of western Cornwall.

Wrecking was almost a major occupation of the inhabitants
of Scilly in the early eighteenth century. For days after heavy
gales they would be found wandering about the shores looking
for any chance wreckage that might have been cast up, neglecting their farms and fishing nets—a fact not to be wondered at
when it is remembered that in times of distress and dearth the
staple, and almost the only, food of many of them was limpets.
Defoe, however, also found some ambitious Scillonians whom
he described as "engineers" attempting to salvage the cargoes
of sunken wrecks by elaborate devices, resembling more modern
diving-bells, in the hope of finding pieces of gold and other
treasure.[1] Almost a century later the Anglican incumbent of
Scilly, Troutbeck, is reputed to have uttered the prayer—
"Dear God, we pray not that wrecks should happen, but if it
be Thy will that they do, we pray Thee let them be to the
benefit of Thy poor people of Scilly." The tale may not be
true, but that it was possible for it to be told and noised abroad
is testimony enough of the importance of the "wrecking industry" of the islands. The Scillonians may be acquitted of
the charge of having murdered the luckless Admiral Sir
Cloudsley Shovell for an emerald ring he was wearing when
cast up alive from the wreck of his fleet in 1707; the tale of a
death-bed confession by his murderess has a ring of romance
rather than of truth, besides being about the only tale of a
wrecker overtaken by qualms of conscience at his or her latter
end; nor is it likely that the Admiral alone of all those on his
ship was swept ashore alive by the waves.

It was the men of Breage and Germoe, however, who gained
the reputation of being the most barbarous of all Cornish
wreckers. The coastline of these adjoining parishes was a
graveyard of ships. Vessels which failed to get into the harbours
to the west of St. Michael's Mount were driven on to the reefs
and sands further east, for it required the greatest skill in
navigation and intimate knowledge of the coast to bring sailing
vessels into the tiny harbours of Prussia Cove, Porthleven, and

[1]Defoe: *A Tour Thro' the Whole Island of Great Britain* (1927 ed.) Vol. I, p. 245.

Gunwalloe. The inhabitants of the region wrested a hard and
scanty living from poor soils, from fishing, and from tin-mining,
none of which normally maintained them in any real or steady
degree of comfort. It is possible that they more than other
miners felt a grievance against the merchants who alone seemed
to batten on the arduous and dangerous labours of the tinners,
and when a merchantman went aground they rejoiced and
looted the possessions of a class whom they regarded as their
enemies; that sailors suffered as well went unheeded. Native
and foreign wrecks were plundered indiscriminately; indeed,
the plunder of foreign vessels sometimes attracted more attention in the governmental circles of the day, for it might easily
provoke or aggravate critical international relations. That
Breage and Germoe men paid no heed to the Crown's claim
to wreckage went without saying, but they were also rather
lax in their definition of wreck, plundering vessels that limped
into haven which would have been able to sail away again after
slight repairs had been effected. Thus, in 1730, Thomas Richards,
alias Luggervan, was apprehended looting the *Battle of Hastings*
while it lay at anchor by the pier at St. Michael's Mount,[1] whilst
early in 1750 troops were called upon to arrest the Breage and
Germoe men who had plundered a vessel lying safely at
anchor, though somewhat storm-damaged, near the Mount.[2]

---

[1]*C.T.B., 1729-30*, pp. 392, 576.

[2]Walter Borlase MSS: Letters of Walter Borlase to Hawkins, December 15,
1749; to Gregor, January 3 and 25, 1749/50; to Harris, January 6, 1749/50;
and to Lord Edgcumbe, January 29, 1749/50. The attitude of this clerical Justice
is revealed in his letter to Harris—"The rifling of a little frigate in the way of
contraband trade is a petty larceny not worth mentioning 'tis so common. The
late public plunder of a vessel near the Mount after she was safely anchored surpassed all former acts of that kind in barbarity and violence. Breage and Germoe
led the way and were followed by too many out of the adjoining town and
parishes." The first letter of the series, that to Hawkins, suggests that Borlase was
worried by hints that the very Justices themselves had connived at wrecking, and
he also feared lest the continuance of such practices adversely affect the trade of
Mount's Bay :—"I doubt not but you have heard of the plunder and robbery
committed near the Mount last Wednesday on the vessel in Distress by the Barbarians of Breage, Germoe, etc., which act of inhumanity and rapine if laid before
our superiors in all its flagrant circumstances will, I fear, produce this natural
inquiry—Are there in that county no Justices? Where were they when the laws
were violated in so daring a manner? Or if they could not prevent such violences
what did they do in order to punish them? It is therefore my opinion, but which I
submit to yours, that we who are thus concerned, should for our own vindication
forthwith meet somewhere to take informations, such as we can get, of the fact.
And not only this but best consider further drawing up some proposal for general
subscription of all Gentlemen in the neighbourhood for the prosecution of these
offences, which, the longer they are suffered to pass off with impunity will grow
the more ambitious and desperate to the infinite reproach of our county and the
loss of trade to this Bay in particular."

Wrecking and riots were not confined to Cornwall, but the Skewis incident in 1734 excited alarm even beyond the borders of the West Country in the "pacific" days of Sir Robert Walpole. In the law courts Henry Rogers had failed to make good a claim to the tenement of Skewis in Crowan, near the seat of Sir John St. Aubyn at Clowance, against his brother's widow, arguing erroneously that freehold property could only devolve on male next of kin. In the widow's absence, Rogers seized the house, fortified it, and on June 18th and 19th, 1734, beat off two attempts of the sheriff's men assisted by some troops to drive him out, three men being killed. In August Sir John St. Aubyn called the Justices together to discuss the matter, but nothing was done until March 16th, 1735, when two more men lost their lives; cannon were then brought up from Pendennis castle, whereupon Rogers fled but was arrested at Salisbury, tried at Launceston Assizes in August, 1735, condemned and hanged for murder. Yet the long delay in bringing Rogers to justice fostered an impression that the gentry and lower classes alike in Cornwall were indifferent to the maintenance of law and order, and that the land beyond the Tamar was a foreign country to which the name "West Barbary" might well be applied.[1]

Yet, before 1740, times were changing. The old Celtic language of Cornwall, to all intents and purposes, was dead; Dolly Pentreath, the last person to speak the ancient tongue died in 1745, in Paul, sixty years after the last service in Cornish

[1] The fullest account of the Skewis affair is that of Davies Gilbert, *Parochial History*, Vol. I, pp. 207 ff. The MS letters of William Borlase, however, shed more light on the affair. Among them is a copy of the note Rogers sent to Sir John St. Aubyn, dated March 9, 1734/5, which suggests that it was not Rogers but the forces of law and order who "started the shooting", Rogers writing—"I was this day shot at three times by Bennetts, Pengwidna, and Arthur Toby, and they say it was by your order, and if it's not your order I desire you may write per the bearer or any of your servants, but if it is, forbear writing to your Honour's honourable servant." The Arthur Toby named in this note may be a relative of if not the "Andrew Willis alias Tubby" killed on March 16, 1735, whose head, according to one of the witnesses at the Assizes, Rogers threatened to cut off "and stick it on the chimney" at Skewis (Gilbert, Vol. I, p. 217). On April 14, 1735, soon after Rogers had been arrested, William Borlase wrote to an unnamed correspondent, probably John Harris of Kennegy—"you seem to be under a mistake and imagine that the resistance of Rogers was abetted almost by the whole county", and went on to deny that any criminals let alone any man with the name or character of a gentleman gave Rogers any aid, but that he was abetted by "the wickedness of the common people who out of their false compassion scruple not to secrete and conceal this man though they might have £500 for taking him at the same time they would not hesitate to knock a poor shipwrecked sailor on the head for a sorry piece of timber, perhaps not worth sixpence."

had been held at Landewednack church in the Lizard. Crom-
wellian Puritanism had put an end to the old religious plays,
the only vestige to survive being the mummers' short interlude
dealing with the exploits of St. George in English. Even before
1700 Bishop Trelawney had thought it necessary to get the
Marazion scholar Keigwin to translate Jordan's *Creation* which
had been written in Cornish about the same time as Shake-
speare was writing *The Tempest.* Contacts with England were
multiplying through the increased exploitation of tin and the
rapid rise of copper mining; more and more merchants and
speculative investors were developing interests in Cornwall
and sending agents there to look after those interests. Whereas
Savery and Newcomen had gone from neighbouring Devonshire to start their engineering business in London, the latter
had, before 1740, sent three of his machines and the first of the
Hornblowers as an engineering expert and technician down to
Cornwall. The colonial wars of William and Anne in America
and the West Indies attracted some attention to the natural
advantages of Falmouth harbour. By 1737 trading contacts,
legal or illegal, between Cornwall and the Mediterranean were
so extensive that William Elliott, the Receiver-General of the
County, was petitioning the Treasury that he had incurred
great losses in complying with the order of the Board of Taxes
that all the moneys he collected should be sent up to London
in specie; he had found it both difficult and costly to change
the taxes he received from the Cornish people who paid him
in Portuguese gold and "moydores, a specie not current at the
Exchequer or Bank."[1]   In the age of Walpole, too, the
notoriety of the Cornish "rotten" parliamentary boroughs
began; in 1688 the greater number of the Cornish contingent
of forty-four members had been natives of the county; in the
Parliament of 1741 there were still to be found Carews and
St. Aubyns, Boscawens and Rashleighs, Bullers and Godolphins, but a Clive was representing Mitchell and Horace
Walpole Callington. Trade and politics were linking Cornwall
more closely to the rest of England and to England's mercantile
empire; English traders and politicians were taking growing
interest and concern in the county that offered both classes of
men golden opportunities for "adventuring." In the county
itself population was increasing; in 1588 it had been about

[1] *C.T.B., 1735-38,* pp. 314-315.

70,000, in 1688 it had perhaps reached 100,000, by 1756 it
must have almost attained 135,000.[1] Something like a quarter
of this total population, a proportion which too was steadily
increasing, was dependent to greater or less extent on Cornish
mining industries. Those industries were changing the very
distribution of population within the county. In the mining
parishes of both Redruth and Camborne the working classes
had settled to the east of the old medieval parish churches. The
same feature could be seen in Kenwyn where a mining settlement developed at Chacewater more than three miles from the
old parish church, and in St. Just in Penwith with the rise of
mining hamlets as large as the older village that gave the
parish its name between Trewellard and Pendeen, whilst in
Gulval a sizeable hamlet sprang up in the valley below Ding
Dong. Such hamlets were beyond the reach of the older
villages and their parish churches, villages and churches for
the most part associated with an agrarian social order and
community. Landowners and large tenant farmers were no
longer the leaders of social life, save where they possessed
mineral rights and interests as well. These changes had all
begun and progressed far before 1740, and more rapid and
greater changes were yet to come.

[1]Sir C. Lemon: "Notes on the Agricultural Produce of Cornwall", *Statistical
Society Journal*, Vol. IV, p. 202.

CHAPTER II

THE YEARS OF TRANSFORMATION

CHANGE had been in the air long before, but in the fifth decade of the eighteenth century there began a period of revolutionary transformation in the economic and social life of Cornwall. Already, in 1740, exports of copper ore were more valuable than those of pilchards and, moreover, were rapidly overhauling in value the exports of tin. The increasing exploitation of copper meant that more and more of the Cornish mining population had become dependent on deep mining enterprises which differed fundamentally from the older tin workings. The era of large-scale organization and of division of labour within the mining industry itself had begun. Formerly a small group of men and boys could work a tin stream with no implements save a spade, a pick, and a sieve to wash out the dross from the valuable grains of tinstuff in the nearest running stream, whilst a single packhorse, the property of one or other of the working tinners who resorted to streaming as a means of adding to the income of a smallholding, was all the transport necessary to take the ore to the smelting house. Copper mining, however, meant going deep underground, for little orestuff containing this metal was found within forty fathoms of the surface; it meant, therefore, a division of labour between men expert in sinking shafts and in driving underground levels, men whose practical knowledge of the varying richnesses of orestuff meant their exclusive employment in actual excavation of the lodes, men and boys who brought the ores to the surface, and the considerable number of workers of all ages and both sexes who, at the surface, 'dressed' the ores and prepared them for marketing. More and more capital was required to work mines as they increased in depth and to maintain the shafts and levels that were absolutely necessary to enable mining to be carried on at all; capitalist control replaced the casual groups of working miners that, in earlier times, had joined together to exploit a surface tin-work, a development that had first, in all probability, appeared in the deep tin mines like Ding Dong, Wheal Vor, and Drakewalls; in brief, capitalistic partnership, characterized by legal deeds and agreements, formalities, and conventions, replaced the co-operation of actual labouring 'free' miners[1]. As more and more mines were worked by the costbook system a managerial group, distinct from landowners, working miners, and capitalist adventurers alike, grew in importance; the actual operations on the larger and deeper mines demanded supervision by an increasing number of mine 'captains' both above and below ground. Industrial mining society was becoming stratified, and this tendency was intensified by the appearance of a group of engineers. Moreover, even from the beginnings of Cornish copper mining, the proportion of capital provided by 'foreign' adventurers, like the Bristol and Welsh smelters, had been considerable and had increased rather than diminished as time went on, and this thrust increasing responsibility and social prestige on local mine pursers, captains, and managers.

In the late 1730s the value of the copper ores raised in Cornwall had averaged about £57,000 a year, but in 1740 only 5,000 tons were sold, and it was not until 1751 that the 11,000 tons sold in 1739 was exceeded; thereafter output steadily rose to 29,000 tons a year by 1770. The decline in production and rather lower prices meant the reduction of the value of copper ores sold in Cornwall in the 1740s to less than £46,000 per annum.[2] Average yearly output in the decade 1730-39 had been nearly 7,750 tons, but in the next ten years it was only 6,262 tons, and this decline can be reasonably attributed to the exhaustion of the shallower copper workings and the difficulty of working deeper deposits. To work deep mines either better or more cheaply operated pumping machinery was essential. The outbreak of war with Spain in 1739, followed the next year by the outbreak of a general European war, led many to anticipate an increased demand for copper. Mining interests started exerting political pressure for assistance and relief ; the tottering administration of Walpole, too well aware of the phalanx of Cornish members in Parliament, gave way, and agreed to grant a complete drawback of duties on all coals brought by sea to Cornwall for working 'Fire engines' from and

[1]A similar development occurred with the exhaustion of the alluvial gold deposits of California and Victoria in the 1850s; *vide* W. P. Morrell, *The Gold Rushes*, pp. 98-103, 112, 249-256.
[2]Pryce: p.xv,

after Midsummer Day, 1741.[1] The remedy, however, only took effect slowly for there were, at that time, only three Newcomen engines in Cornwall, those at Wheal Rose, Wheal Busy, and Polgooth. Nor were there any skilled engineers in Cornwall who knew much about the Newcomen machines until the arrival of the elder Jonathan Hornblower and his brother, Josiah, in 1745.[2] Even after that, continued dependence on outside manufacturers of various machine parts meant that it took at least two or three years to design an engine, erect it, and set it to work. When recovery did come, a decade later, it was not due to the remission of duties on fuel so much as to improvements in engines, often trivial in nature, by the actual mine engineers, like John Nancarrow[3] and the elder Richard Trevithick,[4] who took charge of the machines once the Hornblowers had designed and erected them. During the war years, too, any abnormal demands for copper were more than offset by the activities of French privateers, although tin going up the Channel to London was affected far more than copper ores crossing the Bristol Channel to South Wales.

Although there is no suggestion that overproduction of copper had occasioned any significant decline in prices at this time, the case of tin was different. When the farm ended in 1717 the domination of the tin market passed to the London merchants, many of them pewterers themselves, who could virtually fix their own price—usually one that was not very remunerative to the 'tinners' of Cornwall. In no year between 1717 and 1740 did the price of tin exceed the £3 10s. or £3 5s. per hundredweight of the seven-year contracts in Anne's reign, whilst in some years the price was barely £2 15s. Fruitless

[1] 14 Geo. 2 cap. XLI cl. 3.
[2] The fullest accounts of the Hornblower engineering dynasty are those of L. F. Lorre, "The First Steam Engine in America", *T.N.S.*, Vol. X, pp. 15-26. and of Rhys Jenkins, "Jonathan Hornblower and the Compound Engine," *ibid.*, Vol. XI, pp. 128-154.
[3] Little is known of Nancarrow; he supplied Dr. William Borlase with the details of 'fire engines' that the latter used in his *Natural History* (pp. 172-5). Letters preserved in the Borlase MSS. suggest that William Lemon put Borlase in touch with Nancarrow, although Lemon himself had been instrumental in bringing the Hornblowers to Cornwall. The surviving letters of Nancarrow to Borlase were written in 1757; although it is likely that Borlase might have entertained sectarian prejudices against Hornblower, this may indicate that by this time Nancarrow was the most well-known engineer in Cornwall. It is possible that he, like Josiah Hornblower, ended his days in America.
[4] Details of the elder Trevithick are given in the biographies of his son; *vide* also A. Titley: "Account Books of Richard Trevithick, Senior." *T.N.S.* Vol. XI, pp. 26-39.

proposals were made in 1742 to convene a Stannary Parliament in order to establish another farm of tin, which would ensure prices of £3 5s. for common tin and £3 9s. for the superior charcoal-smelted grain tin, which was mostly derived from streamworks; apparently a group of merchants had expressed their readiness to buy up 2,400 tons a year, or 300 tons more than the average annual production of recent years, at these rates.

The war and the activities of French privateers made matters worse. It is possible, too, that the tinners lost rather than gained by their association with the Duchy of Cornwall at a time when the family relationships of the monarch and his heir apparent were at their worst. Whether Frederick, Prince of Wales, took any great interest in the Duchy is doubtful, although it was one of the main sources of his revenues. Petitions to him in April, 1744, and again in the following year, asking for the convocation of a Stannary Parliament met with no response, although the obstruction may have been the Pelham ministry rather than the Prince himself.[1]

Peace came in 1748, but it was a year in which the harvests of both land and sea had been bad.[2] The threats of the western miners against corn-merchants who thought that they could secure higher prices elsewhere, led the authorities to intervene and ban the exportation of grain from Cornwall.[3] Copper prices fell and tin was almost unsaleable.[4] A meeting of the adventurers in tin mines met in Truro in August, 1749, discussed the post-war depression, and again recommended the convocation of a Stannary Parliament. It was, however, not until June, 1750, that the Lord Warden of the Stannaries, Thomas Pitt, was instructed to call this Parliament, and when it met to:

"assent to all such good Laws, Orders, and Constitutions as shall be agreed upon, and presented to you by the said Convocation, or Parliament, in such Manner, as hath been accustomed, so as the same be for the Advancement, Welfare, and good Government of our Stannaries, and of our Revenues, and be not repugnant to the Laws of the Land."[5]

[1]The words of the 1745 petition indicate that Frederick had encouraged the idea of reviving the farm of tin. *A Statement of the Proceedings of the Convocation or Parliament for the Stannaries of the County of Cornwall . . . "* (1751), Appendix pp. 53-56.
[2]Walter Borlase MSS: letters of Walter Borlase to Peggy Borlase, August 18, 1748 and to J. Harris, October 20, 1748.
[3]*Ibid:* W. Borlase to F. Gregor, October 21, 1748.
[4]*Ibid:* W. Borlase to Harris, February 23 and April 29, 1749.
[5]*A Statement of the Proceedings of the . . . Stannaries* (1751), pp. 67-70.

The Stannators, as had been customary since early Tudor times, were elected by the corporations of the four ancient Stannary towns of Liskeard, Lostwithiel, Truro and Helston,[1] and were summoned to meet at Lostwithiel on August 28, 1750.

It seems probable that the tinners had agreed at the Truro meeting to force the Prince to summon the Stannary Parliament by withholding their tin from the coinages. In 1749 only 1,154 tons of tin were coined as compared with an average of over 1,800 tons during the preceding decade and of 2,658 during the following ten years. Tin could be mined, but only if the 'miners' chose to bring it to the coinages and then sell it would it bring any revenue to the Duchy of Cornwall. Furthermore, it was late in 1748 or early in 1749 that the phenomenally rich Polberro lode was struck in St. Agnes. This mine for some time after this discovery, produced over 500 tons a year, whilst in the same period Polgooth was producing over 350 tons a year.[2] Neither of these mines was situated in the chief tin-mining district of the time, but their small number of share-holding adventurers were in a stronger position to dictate terms to the Duchy than the numerous small adventurers in the Helston and West Penwith regions. It may, therefore, be concluded that the last meeting of the Stannary Parliament was occasioned not by distress but by the pressure of flourishing capitalistic interest;[3] moreover, this convocation was to spend much of its time passing legislation detrimental to the smelters and to the small independent stream-tinners.

London mercantile circles expected that the convocation of the Stannary Parliament would lead to a renewal of the farm of tin which offered vast financial possibilities. The amalgamated companies of the Mines Royal and the Mineral and Battery Works[4] planned to secure a monopoly of Cornish tin

[1] At this time these boroughs were controlled by the families of Eliot, Pitt himself, Boscawen, and Godolphin.

[2] William Borlase MSS: letter of Walter Rosewarne to Wm. Borlase, February 11, 1756. Also Walter Borlase MSS : letter of Walter Borlase to J. Harris, November 2, 1749.

[3] In the midst of 'depression', on June 3, 1749, Dr. Walter Borlase wrote to the famous Dr. Oliver of Bath—"I have a share in a very flourishing tin-mine. I receive it from the hand of providence with a most humble and thankful heart, and . . . with more satisfaction than I should any worldly preferment. This does not render me dependent on any men. I am not to dissemble or cringe or do any dirty work for it. I have none to thank but Him whose excellencies I cannot flatter, whose favours and protection I can safely and joyfully acknowledge, whose service is perfect freedom.

[4] For the earlier history of these Companies *vide* W. R. Scott: *The Constitution and Finance of the English, Scottish, and Irish Joint Stock Companies to 1720*, Vol. II, pp. 383-405, 413-429.

for twenty-one years; it proposed to buy up to 2,200 tons of tin per year, at the price of £3 10s. per hundredweight[1] for common and £3 14s. for grain tin—but it would not undertake the purchase of more than 190 tons of grain tin in a single year.[2] To raise the necessary capital, estimated at £150,000, the promoters proposed a division into 15,500 shares, 4,000 of which were to be 'transferred' to:

"Gentlemen in Cornwall and Devonshire, who at their Will and Pleasure may, or may not accept thereof. Now from this generous equitable Distribution of Things, the Purchasers of the said 4,000 Shares, in becoming Proprietors . . . will, if they should close with that Offer, stand Intitled to an adequate Share of all the Profits . . . from this Undertaking; and by virtue of such Admission, they will be qualified to form a proper Judgment concerning the Conduct and Management of the Tin Trade in the hands of these Societies.

"From the whole scope and Tenor of this Proposal it appears evident that all imaginable regard hath been paid to the interest of the Cornish Gentlemen, who upon being thus fairly and candidly Dealt with, will not only forward an Agreement, but also cheerfully contribute towards raising the said Joint Trading Stock of £150,000, or at least such part thereof as a General Court shall direct and appoint."

The suspicious Cornish, however, seem to have thought little of this offer; they saw that they were only to have rather more than a quarter of the shares in a London dominated Company, and they may have doubted if a fund just enough to purchase the total yearly production of tin at the suggested rates was really adequate; some of the "miners", too, wanted higher prices, although tin was, at that time, only realizing £2 15s. per hundredweight in Cornwall.

The last of the Stannary Parliaments did little to alleviate economic depression, but it adjusted some of the ancient laws and customs of the Stannaries to new conditions. This, however, was only done after prolonged disputes which had nothing to do with the welfare of the mining community, but which were closely connected with the more obscure political undercurrents of the day. The Stannators selected by the corporations of Liskeard and Truro were nominees of the Eliot and Boscawen families who were staunch supporters of the Pelham ministry; the Helston group represented a Godolphin interest

---

[1]The Cornish Stannary hundredweight of 120 pounds.
[2]*A Proposal for Raising a Fund of 150,000£ to Encourage the Tinners in Cornwall and Devonshire, and for the better carrying on and Improving the Tin Trade in General*, (August 9, 1750); there is a copy of this rare prospectus in the Bodleian Library.

that was rather more friendly to the Prince of Wales; only the Stannators chosen by the corporation of Lostwithiel out of deference to Thomas Pitt of Boconnoc could be regarded as real supporters of the Duchy interest; moreover, Pitt's influence at the last town was challenged by the Edgcumbe family which was Pelhamite in its political affiliations.

With the time and place of meeting left to his own discretion, Thomas Pitt, rather unwisely, decided to hold the Stannary Parliament at Lostwithiel. True, that town had been the ancient meeting place, but the Parliaments of 1703 and 1710 had been held in Truro, whilst in the mid-eighteenth century the most important tin-mining district lay west of Truro, scarcely any tin at all being produced east of Lostwithiel. After quarrelling with Pitt over the choice of a Speaker of their convention, the Stannators demanded that the Parliament be adjourned to Truro. Pitt denounced this as an infringement of the prerogatives of the Duke of Cornwall, alleging, furthermore, that even the Parliament of the Realm had no constitutional right to adjourn itself. Finally the Prince himself intervened and adjourned the Stannary Parliament to Helston, possibly with the design of winning the support of the Godolphins rather than from reflection that Helston was then the most convenient centre for the Cornish tin mining regions. The Parliament met in Helston on October 20, and a fortnight later adjourned until the following July, continuing its intermittent sessions thereafter until 1752. The political dissensions and intrigues ended after the death of the Prince in March, 1751. Had the Stannators made good their claim to a right of adjournment, they might have proceeded to a demand for regular future sessions; but they failed, and this failure meant the end of the Stannary Parliament. Moreover, the legislative pretensions of the Stannators were contrary to the contemporary tendency towards the assertion of the sovereign legislative omnipotence of the Parliament of the Realm. There is every reason to believe that the claims brought forward by the Stannators in 1750 were only advanced by supporters of the Pelham administration in order to embarrass, weaken, and discredit the clique of politicians that had grouped themselves around the heir to the throne.

The work actually accomplished by the last Stannary Parliament can hardly have appealed much to the speculative interests supporting, or likely to support, the projects of the Mines Royal Company. Laws were passed to bring the new larger smelting house concerns as completely under the ancient laws and customs of the Stannaries as the old 'Blowing Houses' had been; this can be regarded as evidence that the 'miners' were convinced that their economic misfortunes were partly and perhaps mainly due to the activities of these smelters. The smelters, too, were ordered to produce regular accounts at the Stannary Court of all the blocks of tin they had smelted and to keep records of every sale they made. The London Pewterers, who had long been complaining of adulterated tin, were gratified by a law imposing penalties of £50 fines or six months imprisonment on smelters who 'falsified' tin by inserting into it metal of less value. The ancient claim of stream-tinners to divert watercourses, which had proved detrimental to farmers, and still more to certain stamping-mill proprietors, was virtually abolished; this may have been regarded by land-lord interests as a preparatory step towards the abolition of ancient bounding rights, although the further provision of penalties against streamers whose works silted up rivers and harbours indicate general concern for a more public welfare. Finally a sop was thrown to the increasing number of absentee 'foreign' adventurers in cost-book concerns by laws imposing penalties up to £50 for frauds on 'associates.'[1] In short, the legislation of the last Stannary Parliament was designed to promote the interests of the 'adventurer' class of landlords, small capitalists, local merchants and so forth; it cared little for the interests of the labouring miner, but, on the other side, it attacked the large smelting concerns whose malpractices were blamed for the low prices that tin in the form of large blocks, weighing between three and four hundred pounds, fetched in Cornwall in comparison with the price small bars or ingots made by melting down, recasting, and, where necessary, purifying the blocks realized in London.

Legislation either by Parliament, in the case of the copper mines, or by the Stannary Convocation, in the case of tin, did comparatively little to alleviate depression, and the Cornish mines were left to survive or fail by their own devices. Price levels indicate that the plight of the mines was certainly not due to any over-production of copper, and it is doubtful if there

[1] G. Jars: *Voyages Metallurgiques*, Vol. III, pp. 529-535.

was a vast amount of unsold tin-stuff at the end of 1750. Any
decline in the English demand for pewter was offset by the
demands of the new tin-plate industries in South Wales,
whilst the expansion of the various British textile industries
meant the utilization of more tin in the preparation of scarlet
and purple dyes. 'By-products' of mining activities were turned
to some account. About 1745 a certain Dr. Rouby, described
by Pryce who in all probability knew him personally as a
"curious foreigner," began making Roman or blue vitriol at
Treleigh, near Redruth, from the waste slimes of the tin-
stamping mills. Apparently the venture was short-lived, owing
to disagreements between the partners concerned in it; in any
case, the cheaper methods of making vitriol at Birmingham,
developed a few years later, would have driven the Cornish
product from the market.[1]

Little effort was made to utilize the cobalt found in association with the copper lodes of Cornwall, or the arsenic associated
with both tin and copper. This period, however, saw the small
beginnings of the china or porcelain clay industry, which was
destined to survive copper mining and to become the most
important industry in Cornwall. Although credit for the discovery of the properties and value of Cornish china clays has
been given to the Plymouth chemist, William Cookworthy, it
is possible that the tinners of both the St. Austell and Breage
districts had encountered the white clays and china stone long
before he first began to take an active interest in the mineral
wealth of Cornwall about the year 1745.[2] Before Cookworthy
established his Plymouth porcelain works, Cornish clays were
being used by the porcelain manufacturers of Worcester and
Staffordshire. Before 1755 a small porcelain manufactory
which had been established at Calstock had failed; whilst a
Staffordshire man, Horn, came into Cornwall in 1755 with
plans of establishing porcelain works at Penryn.[3] There is
evidence suggesting that these plans to establish porcelain
works in Cornwall resulted from the suspicion that 'foreigners'
were taking the clays of Cornwall and making fortunes thereby.

---

[1]Pryce: p. 33.   William Borlase MSS: letters of John Nance to Borlase,
March 15, 1747, and of W. Churchill to Borlase, April 9, 1748; also Borlase to
da Costa, April 12, 1747.
[2]L. Jewitt: *The Wedgwoods*, pp. 223 ff.
[3]William Borlase MSS: Borlase to Lord Edgcumbe, March 31, 1755; John
Trehawke to Borlase, May 23 and December 23, 1755.

The many plans, most of them abortive and forgotten, to enable Cornwall to derive the full benefit of her mineral resources at this time—to smelt her own copper,[1] establish porecelain works, and make pewter-ware[2] indicate not only outside interest in and exploitation of Cornish natural resources but the existence of what might be termed an active and progressive industrial spirit in Cornwall itself before 1760.

If porcelain was slowly but surely replacing pewter-ware in popular esteem, any decline in the demand for tin for the manu-facture of the older ware was partly compensated by the increasing demand for the china clays of Cornwall. A new market for tin was provided by the expansion of tin-plate works in South Wales.

Tin-plate manufacture had been slow in establishing itself in Britain. The first British works had been set up at Pontypool in 1675, using processes that had been kept a close secret by the Saxons and Bohemians until the 'industrial spy', Andrew Yarranton, had visited Germany. Progress was slow until the 1720s, when the energetic Major John Hanbury established a second tin-plate works at Kidwelly. Two more manufactories of tin-plate were started in the four years 1747-1750 at Ponthir, in Monmouth, and at Carmarthen, and the new industry and new market for tin could then be regarded as firmly estab-lished, although in the next fifty years but five further tin-plate concerns were established, four in South Wales and the other in Herefordshire. Before Hanbury and John Payne invented a process of rolling sheet iron in 1728, iron had to be hammered out in sheets by heavy hammers driven by water-power, but the really vital discoveries affecting the demand for tin in this industry were improvements in methods of preparing the sheet-iron for coating with molten tin which were made between 1745 and 1760.[3]

With the demand for copper growing and that for tin cer-tainly not declining, the Cornish mining interests sought relief from local depression by expanding their output. Cheaper coal made deeper mining possible through the employment of New-comen pumping engines, although dependence on sea-borne supplies retarded recovery during the war years when enemy

---

[1]See below, pp. 63 ff.
[2]William Borlase MSS: letter of John Trehawke of December 23, 1755 referring to the plans of the Lostwithiel tin-smelter Drake to establish a local pewter manu-actory.
[3]P. W. Flower: *A History of the Trade in Tin*, pp. 44-49, 93-94, and 209-210.

privateers were active in the narrow seas. However, before
these machines were used, places where they could be used
most productively had to be discovered. In earlier times it had
been easy for miners to trace detrital tinstuff up the sides of
valleys to outcropping lode-bearing rocks; copper, however,
lay deeper underground, and the early discoveries of this
mineral had been made when the upper tin veins had been
worked far down into the earth. Thenceforward all mining
depended on skill and judgment in driving deep levels underground, either along the direction of mineral veins or, in
certain cases, across the prevalent run of the lodes in the hopes
of cutting into rich metallic deposits. Geological knowledge
was scanty, but through practical experience working miners
learnt a great deal about the formation of the rocks in which
they worked and became quite adept at recognizing signs of
mineral-bearing veins. To ensure that working miners carried
on prospecting along with exploitation many mineral leases
granted by the landowners of the time required the adventurers
leasing the mineral sets to drive exploratory levels a certain
distance, either yearly or within a stipulated time, on pain of
forfeiture. Thus, in July, 1761, John Vivian undertook to
drive a level of two hundred fathoms, or nearly a quarter of a
mile, in two years, when he leased the Wheal Ram set from
Francis Basset, whilst, in April, 1762, the same landlord
granted a mining set on Treswithian Downs to William Johns,
and required him to:

"drive with due and true levels from the Western end of the Downs
on the course of the level 60 fathoms within two years and 60
fathoms more within three years from thence, and sink 10 fathoms
under the adit in seven years."[1]

Other leases stipulated the minimum number of workmen a
lessee adventurer must employ, nor was it unusual to demand
that for two, three or four months during the year mining
'below adit' be carried on. Landlords, in short, took care that
mines be developed and kept in production; their usual share
of a sixth part of the value of the minerals raised was often a
considerable part of their income; they preferred a regular

[1]Tehidy MSS: Tehidy and Nancekuke Setts, Tehidy Setts Nos. 26 and 33.
The number of grants of mining setts for 21 year periods recorded in this book of
abstracts of leases of mining setts on the manor of Tehidy was 35 in the 16 years
from March, 1748 to July, 1764; ten more were granted on the smaller manor of
Nancekuke.

income to spasmodic gains from rash exploitation. In addition, provisions for adit-driving not only improved mine drainage and kept the sett in workable condition during and after the term of the lease, but also assisted the discovery of new lodes.

Exploration of this nature was the only sure method of finding mineral ores, but it is significant that it was during this period that the divining or dowsing rod was first used in Cornwall. The first Cornish author to describe it was Dr. Pryce, in 1778. It was apparently not known to Carew in late Elizabethan times, but it is rather strange that Dr. William Borlase was apparently unacquainted with it twenty years before Pryce, unless he forbore mentioning it either through scepticism or a belief that it was meddling with dark occult powers. Pryce attributed its introduction to Cookworthy, who had been instructed in its use by the Spanish commander of the Plymouth garrison, Ribiera, and who used it to trace lodes in the St. Austell district in 1754 or 1755.[1] Scientists, unable to explain the properties of the rod, contented themselves with expressing doubts of its efficacy or with simply ignoring it. In one respect, however, its significance is unquestionable; the fact that many miners believed in it promoted the continuing quest for mineral wealth. The divining rod, too, was generally used only in places where the presence of mineral was already suspected. If the rod did not locate metal, at least it encouraged prospectors to make the efforts necessary to sink deeper shafts and extend levels in promising country.

Once the richer lodes had been discovered, the difficulties of exploitation began. In the deeper levels the greatest problem was drainage, and more and more of the greater mines installed steam engines to counter this difficulty. The elder Jonathan Hornblower and his associates and, possibly, rivals erected more than forty engines in Cornwall between 1745 and 1775;[2] even if, at the latter date, less than half of them were working owing to the high price of fuel, yet it was apparent that steam-power was absolutely indispensible in Cornish mining. Few details of these early engines survive, but it is likely that some of them incorporated several devices that could not have been found in the original types designed by Savery and Newcomen.

[1]Pryce, pp. 115-124.
[2]Letter of Boulton to Watt of September, 1775, quoted by Erich Roll: *An Early Experiment in Industrial Organization*, p. 67.

In 1757, for example, John Nancarrow described machines at Great Work in Breage and at Herland in Gwinear, which he supervised and probably had designed; these had devices for lengthening and shortening the stroke of the engines, for reducing the pressure of the steam, and for using some of the water raised to feed the boilers. Indeed, Nancarrow's references to 'strong steam' suggest that he was inclined to use high-pressure steam rather than the low-pressure atmospheric principles of the Newcomen engine which Watt over-cautiously retained.[1]

Another Cornish engineer of this time was Sampson Swayne who, in 1754, had established copper smelting works at Entral near Camborne.[2] Swayne might well be regarded as the precursor of the compound engine, for he conceived the notion of using more than one furnace or boiler, an idea less likely to achieve fuel economy than to attain greater power. In 1762 Swayne and an associate, John Weston, were granted one of the Nancekuke mining setts by Francis Basset, on condition that they erected:

"their new invented Engine with as many furnaces as may be wanted to work same and all such other erections as they may want . . . within eighteen months. To work the deepest bottoms 20 fathoms under the Adit two months in every year. To make reasonable satisfaction to the tenants for extra drainage. To be void in case of failure to perform any part after twenty days notice."[3]

The readiness of the landlord Basset to allow engines to be erected on his property is also an indication of the progressive spirit of the age.

The most radical innovator, however, was the elder Richard Trevithick; his fame has been overshadowed and his achieve-

---

[1]William Borlase MSS: John Nancarrow to Borlase, October, 1757. In this letter Nancarrow referred to other engines at Ludgvan Leas and at the 'Mannour'.
[2]See below, p. 63.
[3]Tehidy MSS: Tehidy and Nancekuke Setts; Nancekuke Sett, No. 10, December 14, 1762. Swayne's engine, however, may have been designed with the dual purpose of working pumping machinery and also calcining copper ores, in view of his known interest in the Entral and (later) Hayle Copper Smelting Works. It is possible that it was Swayne's engine that was alluded to in the anonymous pamphlet *An Address to the Gentlemen of the County of Cornwall on the Present State of Mining in that County* (1772); primarily concerned with projects of establishing copper smelting works in Cornwall, the author stated (p. 41) "Though nothing would have prospered in the hands of those who broached the doctrine of boiling and roasting at the same fire, yet the double purposes of calcination and fusion were actually effected in the one instance, and this application of the fire by no means delayed the working of the engine itself." John Weston may have been one of the capitalists associated with Swayne in the Entral Copper Smelting Works.

ments obscured by those of his more famous son. He became chief engineer at Dolcoath mine, near Camborne, sometime before 1765; there he began his battle against water by constructing a deep adit. Under his supervision the Dolcoath workings were deepened and extended, and before 1770 he had introduced some type of artificial ventilation, probably an air pump.[1] Trevithick is also said to have introduced the method whereby miners excavated up from a level; hitherto they had dug away below their feet, a method which greatly impeded the carriage of excavated material from the ends of the levels to the surface.

The elder Trevithick's greatest achievement, however, was the radical transformations he made in the old Carloose engine, bought by the Dolcoath adventurers from a nearby mine in 1775. Surviving accounts reveal that the adventurers bought the engine for £414 12s. 3d., but Trevithick's alterations added £2,040 to the bill. In all likelihood the engine had been originally designed and built by the older Jonathan Hornblower between 1745 and 1750.[2] Trevithick's transformed engine worked nearly twenty years, and then his son made further alterations in it. The elder Trevithick improved the gear and the valves, which he made self-acting, but his great improvement was his:

"new semi-circular boiler-top, which . . . took the place of the original flat-top weighted down by slabs of granite. The cylindrical sides, and indented or curved bottom, of the Newcomen boilers gave strength to these parts, but its flat top prevented the use of steam at a higher pressure. Newcomen's steam boilers were simply the ordinary household boiler used in cooking on an enlarged scale, with the lid on top weighted down, to enable them to retain steam of one or from that to two pounds on the square inch."[3]

These alterations made it possible for 'stronger steam' to be used,

---

[1] Artificial ventilation had been used at Goon-lez in St. Agnes as far back as 1696. (Pryce, p. 202).

[2] Francis Trevithick says that the engine was fifty years old (*Life of Richard Trevithick*, Vol. I. p. 21), but this would imply that it had not been erected by Hornblower. There is a possibility that it had been brought to Carloose from North Downs or even from Wheal Vor. The other possibility is that, before 1730 there had been other engines in Cornwall besides the three or four Savery, Newcomen and their agents had erected, the Carloose engine being one of them especially as it is not certain from surviving details that it was of the Newcomen type. Moreover, if the tradition that the turf-burning Balwath machine, near Porkellis, was the first steam engine in Cornwall (Hunt, p. 411) has any foundation, there is a possibility that it was working before the days of either Savery or Newcomen.

[3] F. Trevithick, Vol. I, pp. 22. The younger Trevithick added a Watt condenser to this engine in 1799, and replaced the old boiler with a globular one; he altered it again in 1811 (*T.N.S.*, Vol. XI, pp. 33-34).

but Watt's all-inclusive patent delayed the development of the use of high-pressure steam for a quarter of a century. It was long practical experience not academic theoretical research which led the elder Trevithick to move the cylinder :

"from its objectionable seat on the granite boiler-top, and placed on cross beams from wall to wall of the engine house; thus avoiding the jar of the steam cylinder resting on the rock boiler and masonry, which had been the source of trouble in the early Newcomen."[1]

With the coming of Watt the history of the steam-engine in Cornish mining becomes clear, but it is certain that considerable improvements had been made between 1740 and 1775 when forty or more engines had been erected in the western county. Cornish engineers, as mines went deeper and drainage difficulties increased, simply made the cylinders and other parts of their engines larger;[2] the 70 in. cylinder Herland engine,[3] erected before 1757, was probably far larger than any Newcomen himself ever saw or even projected. Unfortunately these engines were costly to erect, maintain, and work; there must have been numerous suggestions put forward to reduce expenses; some suggested reducing the size of the boilers, others "increasing the elasticity of the steam."[4]   The last idea led Nancarrow, the elder Trevithick, and possibly Swayne, towards the use of high-pressure steam. Then came Watt's separate condenser and the patent which checked this tendency; the condenser did achieve economy of fuel, but the principle underlying it was the conservation not the increase of power.

The cost of erecting and working steam-engines led to the construction of many adits to drain mines. More ambitious even than the deep adit of the elder Trevithick at Dolcoath was the Great Adit, started by John Williams, the manager of William Lemon's Poldice Mine in 1748.[5] It took Williams nearly twenty years to drive this adit from an outlet near Bissoe Bridge to the western limits of Poldice; branch adits driven to other mines then and later gained this undertaking the name of the County Adit, for, in all, it extended over thirty miles and drained at least forty mines. Adit construction not only solved drainage difficulties, but also frequently led to rich

[1]F. Trevithick, Vol. I, pp. 23-24.
[2]Borlase: *Natural History of Cornwall*, pp. 172-3.
[3]Wm. Borlase MSS: Nancarrow to Borlase, 1757.
[4]Borlase: *Natural History of Cornwall*, p. 173.
[5]C. C. James: *History of Gwennap*, pp. 176-178.

lodes that otherwise might never have been found. Construction, however, was difficult. Even the 'killas' rocks were not easy to penetrate, and granites and elvans were far worse; there were no effective rock-drilling machines until the middle of the nineteenth century; the only explosive known was gunpowder, which was costly on account of the East India Company's monopoly of saltpetre; the wonder is not that Williams took so long to drive the adit to Poldice but that he ever reached it at all or even embarked on so ambitious an undertaking. Nevertheless, the time taken suggests that the average rate of driving the adit was only about 200 fathoms a year.[1] The past and continuing riches of Poldice, however, justified the work, and its extensions were an incalculable boon to the Gwennap mining district.

The elder Hornblower, the elder Trevithick, and John Williams played a role in Cornish economic development that is fairly clear, but equally important, perhaps, were improvements effected by unknown men in every branch of the mining industry from prospecting lodes to the final stages of preparing tin and copper for the market. Some experience gained in producing block tin through the centuries helped the comparatively new copper industry; outside knowledge helped even more, but even if 'foreigners' taught the Cornish 'new-fangled' ways, yet their knowledge would have benefited them but little had there been no mineral resources in Cornwall to which to apply it. If some outside capitalist shareholders in Cornish cost-book mines suggested improvements derived from collieries and metallic mines elsewhere, Cornish capitalists and adventurers on the spot, especially those involved in a mine that was working between a profit and a loss, might use all their ingenuity to transform it into a profitable concern, especially when they were convinced that the ores were there and that the only thing to do was, somehow or other, to work them at a profit. Only in Cornwall on the site of the mine was it possible to determine if it would be more economical to employ manual labour or stamps similar to those used by the tinners to break

[1]*Cf.* the grant of Francis Basset of Wheal Ram to John Vivian in July, 1761 (p. 50 above). The greater part of the County Adit ran through killas which made for easier working. As late as 1876, mechanical boring machines, operated by a gang of ten men and two boys, took twenty-four hours to cut a level 8½ feet square a mere four feet, in harder granite and tinstone, and these machines were reckoned to be four times more effective than hand labour. (Hunt, pp. 555-558).

up copper ores preparatory to calcination, and if the stamps were used to determine whether to work them wet or dry, and at what rate they should work to achieve the best results. Only experience could prove the most effective type of furnace and the nature of fires to be employed in calcination, whilst even more experience was needed to gauge the best ways of treating different types of copper ore. It was the local ingenuity of men on the spot that was required to turn water-power to the best advantage; outside men are hardly likely to have dreamt of using subterranean water wheels to work stamps and pumps, as was done by a 54-foot diameter overshot wheel in Cook's Kitchen in 1797.[1]

All these developments increased production. The number of mines producing copper more than trebled between 1740 and 1775, whilst the average yearly production taken over five year periods increased from about 11,000 to over 29,000 tons in the same time.[2] By 1770, however, a fall in price suggested that copper supplies were in excess of demand. Till 1765 the price of copper ore had averaged well over £7 per ton, in 1772 this had fallen to £6 14s. 9d., and in the next two years was down below £5 7s. 6d., although over the following five years the average price was to be about £6 3s.[3] The check in the progress of copper-mining is even more apparent from the statistics of the total output in value and amount; the value of ores raised in 1772, about £190,000, was only slightly exceeded in one year before 1783, eleven years later, when the total value was rather less than £220,000; moreover, whilst the increase in value was about 16%, to achieve it actual output had been stepped up by over 28%.[4] Quite apart from the higher costs of working as mines deepened, profits were falling off, and by 1772 the Cornish copper mining interest was talking of depression.

The fortunes of the tin-mining interests were even worse. Production had fluctuated since 1750, although the general tendency was upward. It was an industry that was extremely sensitive to prevailing conditions of peace and war. In peace-time between half and two-thirds of the total output of tin was ultimately exported. If war, in those times, did not mean complete cessation of trade even with enemy states, it meant that

[1]Maton: Vol. 1. p. 238.
[2]Pryce, p. xv.
[3]Figures based on Hunt, p. 842.
[4]From 27,965 to 35,799 tons: Hunt, p. 892.

cargoes of tin might be captured by privateers at sea, these risks were increased by the sending of nearly all the tin of Cornwall by sea to London, whose merchants still maintained their hold of the trade, whether destined for a foreign market or not; the higher insurance costs during war years often made all the difference between profit and loss to the mining interest. In no year between 1750 and 1760 did the Cornish price exceed £3 9s. per hundredweight; the Cornish mines could just pay their way if the price was £3 4s., and the price hovered between these two levels between 1762 and 1769; prices began falling in 1770 and three years later were down to £2 14s.; the outbreak of the American war limited rather than delayed recovery, prices averaging about £3 for the six years 1775-80, and after that there was a fairly rapid rise to £3 10s. by 1782. By this latter date, however, other factors had come into operation.

The depression of 1772 was not confined to the mining industries. It had been caused by a wave of speculation in the late 1760s which, together with improved mining techniques, sent the Cornish output of tin up to above 3,000 tons per annum. In 1772 over 3,150 tons were coined, a figure not attained again until 1786, and one followed by a recession of over twenty per cent in the next two years. The 'peak' of 1772 was partly the delayed result of mining speculation three or four years earlier, and partly the consequence of a rush to sell off available stocks of tin before the prices fell even lower. The foreign markets in these years were adversely affected by the protracted war between Russia and Turkey, which restricted trade with the Ottoman Empire, and by the confused political situation that culminated in the first Partition of Poland, which by no means helped trade in the Baltic.[1] At home the pewter

---

[1] Statistics of eighteenth century foreign trade are extremely fragmentary and show violent fluctuations in the value of trade from year to year. In the years immediately before the outbreak of war with Revolutionary France about 20% of the exports of tin went to the Baltic and about 7% to the 'Near East'. (Hunt, p. 891); but these were estimates of value which differed from records of bulk consignments. It is likely that a considerable amount of tin represented as sold to Italian markets was re-exported to the Levant. It is likely that a considerable amount of tin was smuggled out to Mediterranean markets by those engaged in the pilchard trade—tin which never appeared in any records since it had never paid coinage duties. In Northern Europe the advanced metallurgical industries of Sweden and Germany were better customers than the Dutch, who could force prices down by bringing in East Indian tin. No real estimate of the value of the trade can be made without taking into account the value of the commodities brought back in exchange; for this reason the tin exports to the Levant were more important than the actual statistics of exports would suggest.

industry was really beginning to feel the growing popularity of 'porcelain'. True, new markets were found, but neither the development of the tin-plate industry in Britain nor the increased use of pewter and tin ware in African slave trading and in the fur trade with the Indians of North America, compensated for the falling away of older markets. It should be remembered, too, that the total output of tin only increased by ten tons per year during the whole period from 1750 to 1775, a fact which suggests that overproduction may not have been a contributory cause of the 1772 slump, although there had recently been one or two abnormally productive years.

TABLE I

THE AVERAGE AMOUNT OF TIN COINED IN CORNWALL OVER FIVE
YEAR PERIODS 1720-1834[1]

Period	Average Yearly Coinage (Tons)	Period	Average Yearly Coinage (Tons)
1720-24	1398	1780-84	2667 (W.P.)
1725-29	1560	1785-89	3237
1730-34	1652 (approx.)	1790-94	3405
1735-39	1627	1795-99	3085 (W.P.)
1740-44	1757 (W.P.)	1800-04	2677 (W.P.)
1745-49	1729 (W.P.)	1805-09	2572 (W.P.)
1750-54	2588	1810-14	2340 (W.P.)
1755-59	2728 (W.P.)	1815-19	3598
1760-64	2610 (W.P.)	1820-24	3772
1765-69	2842	1825-29	4776
1770-74	2854	1830-34	4224
1775-79	2647 (W.P.)		

In earlier times such a depression would, doubtless, have roused a demand for the convocation of a Stannary Parliament, but the failure of the last to achieve more than limited legislative reforms, the minority of the then Duke of Cornwall, the development of *laissez faire* economics (long before Adam Smith reduced them to a philosophical theory), and, perhaps, the progress of the doctrines of Parliamentary sovereignty

[1]W.P. indicates war period. The figure for 1730-34 is an approximation on account of the loss of half the records for 1731, arrived at by doubling the figure of the half-year coinage which survives; the average of the other four years of this period would give the rather high figure of 1718 tons. The five-year periods eliminate minor fluctuations, and reveal recessions, or rather delayed expansion, associated with periods of war. (Based on Lewis, pp. 257-58). It should be stressed that these are figures of the amounts of tin which paid coinage duty and not records of actual production.

recently popularized by Blackstone, all predisposed the tin mining interests to seek salvation by their own efforts. The coinage system and more recent technical improvements in smelting had thrown the Cornish side of the industry into the hands of the larger smelting houses; periodically their principals and agents met at the coinages at Truro, Helston, and Penzance, and discussed business conditions. For a long time past bills of credit they gave, based on tin, had been used almost as circulating currency in the West, for even longer had they been advancing credit to mining adventurers; in fact they had built up a system of banking based on the tin industry, and it was one of their number, James Vivian of Pencalenick, then Sheriff of Cornwall, who, after the Midsummer coinage of 1772, convened 'a general meeting of the Tinners of Cornwall' to meet at Truro on July 18th.

This meeting agreed to meet the crisis by forming an 'exclusive company' to control the sale of tin. A committee of twenty-three was elected to draft details of organization, which were to be laid before another general meeting on August 3rd. At this meeting it was agreed to raise a sum of £66,000 to buy up all the tin remaining on hand at £3 5s. per hundredweight.[1] Sir John Molesworth, one of the two county members of Parliament, was chosen to be President of this 'Cornish Tin Company'; he had agreed to contribute £5,000 of the £66,000, whilst he also had a share in a further £12,000 offered by the attorney, Francis Bennelleck, who acted for Molesworth and for the commercial house of Quick, Dagges, and Company. Sums of £10,000 were in the names of Henry Rosewarne and Company, and in that of Thomas Daniell, then head of the great Truro merchant dynasty. Humphrey Mackworth Praed, who had joined with Molesworth and Edward Eliot in founding a bank in June, 1771, put his name down for £5,000, as did also the Penzance and Gweek merchants, James Blewitt and William Cornish. Philip Richards of Penryn, a partner in the London banking house of Lubbock and a shareholder in Tincroft, Dolcoath, and other mines in the Camborne district, offered £3,000. The other county member, Sir John St. Aubyn, put down £2,000. Sheriff Vivian was prepared to invest a thousand, as were also Thomas Devonshire, a Truro copper assayer, and the Gwennap mine-owner, William Paul.

[1] *i.e.* indicating an unsold stock accumulation of 1,015 tons.

The Church was represented by the Rev. Trevanion, who had considerable mining interests in the Helston district, and who offered £2,000, whilst a further £4,000 was advanced by William Tremayne, the rest being made up in smaller amounts.[1]

This group of capitalists, bankers, merchants, smelters, miners, landowners, and clergy, failed to check the fall of tin prices; indeed, the fall accelerated in the later months of 1772. To dispose of the unsold stock of tin new markets and consumers would have to be found either at home or abroad. Lower prices could restrict production to some extent by compelling the less profitable mines to stop, but a group of men who did not represent the entire tin-mining, or even all the tin-smelting, interests of the county could not hope to gain anything like control of production. The Truro area was rather better represented than Helston and Penzance districts; the adventurers of the great mines of Polgooth, Poldice, Polberro, and Ding Dong did not participate, nor did the great Chyandour smelting house and the rising firms of the Bolithos, Oxnams, and Daubuzes; the now established Gwennap mining dynasty of the Williamses and the extremely influential Lemon family had no part in the concern. The relatively insignificant tin concerns in the Lostwithiel and Liskeard districts were not represented, nor were the quite considerable interests of St. Just in Penwith. For the project to succeed, every tin mine and every smelting house would have to co-operate; otherwise the Cornish Tin Company would merely squander its capital by buying up surplus tin, and all the while 'outside' miners and smelters would go on producing on the same scale as before thereby aggravating rather than amending the situation.

Economic recession brought its inevitable attempts to find scapegoats, but in 1772, for the first time, along with the usual outcry against the London pewterers and merchants, was summoned up the bogy of East Indian Competition.[2] True, some

---

[1]MS. Minutes of the Meeting of July 18, 1772, preserved with the Tin Coinage Resolution Book of 1780-1818 in the Royal Geological Society of Cornwall, Penzance; details of the shareholders are found in G. C. Boase: *Collectanea Cornubiensia*, under their individual names.

[2]Anonymous: *An Address to the Gentlemen of the County of Cornwall on the Present State of mining in that County: with some Observations on the Tin and Copper Trades.* This pamphlet is henceforth cited as *Observations on the Tin and Copper Trades*, 1772. The London Pewterers first became aware of Dutch imports of eastern tin nearly a century before, in 1675. (Welch, Vol. 11, pp. 150-151).)

tin was being brought from Banca to Holland, but it is difficult to assess the extent to which it enabled the Dutch to undersell Cornish tin in European markets. It must, however, be remembered that the international trade in tin at this time was extremely small; it was unusual for England to export more than 1,500 tons of tin in a single year, usually as part of mixed cargoes of merchandise to various ports in Europe, and in much smaller quantities to Africa and America, so that the arrival of a few Dutch East Indiamen with anything like appreciable quantities of tin would inevitably flood a local European market with a commodity which was still a luxury rather than an article of necessity, thereby forcing prices down. Through the intermittent risks of war in the West and the perennial menace of piracy in the East, too, the Indiamen almost invariably sailed in convoys, thus making still further likely the flooding of markets. It may be concluded that the Cornish mining interests had some grounds for complaining about foreign competition, even if they failed to produce statistics to prove their case. The solution that they suggested in 1772, probably at the August meeting which set up the Cornish Tin Company, was to petition Parliament to abolish the export duty on tin.[1]

Whilst the depression in Cornish mining was associated with the collapse of the speculative boom of 1768-70, the situation in the South Western county was aggravated by certain local features. The copper mines, in particular, were facing a complex crisis. Exploitation had almost overtaken demand just at the time when the copper resources of Anglesey began to influence prices. Mechanical efficiency and economy in working machines had improved, but had failed to keep pace with the

[1] The actual output of tin from the East Indies in these years was small by modern standards. The deposits of Banca (off northeast Sumatra) had long been known to Chinese merchants, but the first recorded considerable cargo to Europe was in 1734 when the Dutch brought about 160 tons to Europe (W. Torrens McCullagh: *Industrial History of the Free Nations*, Vol. 11, p. 347 quoting J. Macgregor : *Commercial Tariffs*, Pt. VI, Introd. p. 23), but the output of the Cornish mines in that year was nearly 1840 tons—practically twelve times as much. In only one year between 1760 and 1789 did the amount of Banca tin brought to Europe exceed 500 tons. From 1760 to 1769, 2723 tons of tin came to Holland from Banca, whereas Cornish production averaged 2725 tons per year in the same decade; if only half the Cornish product was exported, the Dutch had gained only a fifth of the European market of tin. A tribute to the high quality of Cornish tin was made by the Dutch; they cast Banca tin in blocks and marked them with forged Duchy of Cornwall stamps to make them appear to be of Cornish origin. (Maton, Vol. I. pp. 171-2).

increasing difficulties of working the deepening mines. The
very expansion of mining had weakened the unity of the adventurers in their relations to the markets and marketing agencies
of the day. The margin of profits between costs of production
and selling prices had grown narrower. Again complaints were
voiced about a 'conspiracy' of 'outside' smelting interests designed to keep down and even to reduce the price of copper;
as always, smelters and middlemen were blamed for the declining fortunes of the mines adventurers. It could not be
denied that copper ores calculated to produce a ton of pure
copper realized only £70 in Cornwall, whereas smelters sold
the finished product to the East India Company at £100 or
more per ton;[1] it was widely believed that if the smelters
reduced their prices, the East India Company could gain wider
markets and thus prevent the accumulation of unsold stocks.
There were also complaints about the growing costs of materials
and of labour, but the tribute and tut-work systems tended to
limit the reduction of labour costs.

In many ways the cost-book system of financial organization
hampered the Cornish adventurer. Monthly or bi-monthly
accounting, the deriving of costs from produce, and the short-
sighted division of profits as and when made, prevented the
creation of reserves of capital, besides making it impossible to
hold back produce from market to wait for a rise in price. The
system even aggravated the glutting of markets by tempting
losing concerns to make up deficiencies in costs one month by
producing even more the next. It might even be said that the
cost-book system left the adventurers in productive mines in
times of economic crisis but two alternatives—the meeting of
costs by still greater production or, alternatively, the partial
or total suspension of their operations.[2]

The ticketing system, too, had played into the hands of the
merchants who, once again, had become a closely united group.
There were only about ten copper-smelting concerns in 1770,
and their agents in Cornwall frequently acted together. There
were even reasons to suspect collusion between the assayers or
'samplers' employed by the 'rival' smelting houses to estimate

---

[1] *Observations on the Tin and Copper Trade*, 1772, pp. 33-34.
[2] The mines which continued working at a loss and making continued 'calls'
on their shareholders were generally concerns in which there were hopes of making
rich discoveries, although often it was merely throwing good money after bad or
sheer human reluctance to admit defeat and to acknowledge loss.

the value of the various lots of ores for sale prior to the ticketings. The highest price offered for a particular 'parcel' of ore,
no matter how absurdly low it might be, had to be accepted
without quibble or demur. In theory the adventurer was not
bound to bring his ores to a sale, but, if he did not do so, he had
not only to pay tut-workers, engineers, and other casual
labourers, but he also had to meet the demands of the tributers
for their share of the value of the ores raised during the last
working period besides the proportionate dues, usually amounting to a sixth of the entire output, to the lord of the soil for that
same period.

In these circumstances it was not surprising that proposals to
smelt copper in Cornwall were again made, although apparently not by the mining adventurers themselves, probably because the mines had exhausted their available capital. Those
who supported the idea could point to the success of the copper
works at Hayle, but the Cornish capitalists who realized the
extremely moderate success of that enterprise were unwilling
to risk their money in embarking on similar undertakings.[1]
The Hayle works had been originally started by the engineer
Sampson Swayne and some local mines adventurers at Entral
near Camborne in 1754. After a few years the establishment
had been moved to Hayle in order to eliminate the heavy costs
of the land carriage of coal to a site at least four or five miles
from tidewater.[2] The older smelting firms had combined to
do all in their power to ruin this new competitor; prices of
copper ores had been forced up and those of refined copper
down, but the Cornish company had managed to survive.[3]
Once its existence was assured, however, the Cornish adventurers realized that, although they could pay their way, the
cost of fuel was far greater than they had anticipated. No
second venture, therefore, was likely, especially since the consumption of coal in mining operations had increased even more
rapidly than the output of the mines, and copper ore provided

[1]Pryce (p. 280) mentioned in 1778 a 'recent' establishment of copper smelting
works at Redruth associated with North Downs mine; it was later moved to
Falmouth, and may have been a subsidiary enterprise of the Fenton Copper
Company which had acquired a considerable interest in the Chacewater mines.
[2]The harbour of Portreath, itself four miles away, had not been constructed
by the Bassets of Tehidy when the Entral works were set up; Hayle, the nearest
port, was over five miles distant; the route was practically that of the present
railway from Camborne to Hayle.
[3]Pryce, p. 274.

a return cargo to South Wales which helped to reduce freight charges. It can be doubted, moreover, whether the Cornish labouring classes regarded the proposals to smelt copper in Cornwall with much favour, especially since accounts of the ill-health and mortality of the employees in the Hayle works circulated, and possibly, were magnified by rumour. Superficially, tut-work and tribute agreements suggested that the labourer was on equal terms with the adventurer with whom he contracted to do a certain amount of work; labouring in copper-smelting works was a species of 'wage slavery' to which the mining population of Cornwall had not been accustomed.[1]

The price of fuel was the main deterrent to establishing a copper-smelting industry in Cornwall, but it was closely connected with the economics of transportation. It was costly to send coal-ships back in ballast to Wales, and it was necessary, too, to use land transport to the best advantage. The cost of bringing coal by pack-horse and mule to Entral from St. Ives, Hayle, and the tidal creeks on the Fal estuary, had led to the removal of the works to Hayle. It was more economical to use land transport in both directions to full capacity than to bring up sufficient coal to reduce the bulk of the produce of the mines to a mere tenth that had to be taken down to the ports for exportation. The copper had, in any event, to be exported to find a market,[2] and, other things considered, it was every whit as economical to send it in the form of ore as to go to all the trouble of smelting it in Cornwall. The cost of starting smelt-

[1] Maton made some reference to the ill-health of the Hayle copper workers (Vol. 1, p. 233). He indicated (Vol. 1. pp. 231-232) that the total output of fine copper at Hayle in 1794 was only about 30 tons a year, and that 150 men were regularly employed. The works smelted about 360 tons of ore a year, or less than 1% of the total Cornish output, costing about £1,250; the value of the copper sold was hardly more than £2,500, yet the annual wage bill can hardly have been less than £4,000. Possibly the works reduced a larger quantity of ores to regulus for export, and only produced this small quantity of finished copper to prove that refined copper could be produced in Cornwall. Maton's data, however, cannot be regarded as very reliable, and particularly his estimate of the number of men employed to tend sixteen furnaces in four different operations.

[2] This factor also accounts for the failure to establish successful pewter manufactures in Cornwall, quite apart from the opposition of 'vested' London interests. In earlier times London Pewterers had objected to the manufacture of small tin bars in Cornwall, but once tin had been coined into large blocks it was more economical to export them from the coinage towns than to send them back to Cornish smelting houses, melt them down, and recast them into bars, before exporting them. The manufacture into small bars would have facilitated the evasion of coinage duties. The substitution of a simple export duty for the coinage dues would, of course, have been detrimental to political place men and their hangers-on.

ing works was considerable, and it is significant that the Entral works had been set up in the period of economic recovery consequent upon the depression at the close of the War of the Austrian Succession, whilst their hard struggle to survive, even under favourable economic conditions, was a warning against the establishment of similar works in times of economic recession. Moreover, the highly-skilled copper-smelting industry had been so long firmly established in South Wales that new competitors, and especially those in regions lacking both local fuel supplies and local large-scale consumers of the finished product, would be placed at an almost insurmountable disadvantage. The power of the smelters could be curbed by control and restriction of the production of copper ores, but such a course demanded a degree of co-operation between the mines adventurers which it was difficult, if not impossible, to achieve.

The cost-book system was one obstacle to co-operation, since it multiplied the number of individual adventurers. Whilst, by 1775, the greater part of the copper ores sold in Cornwall was raised by less than twenty mining concerns, double that number or more were responsible for the rest;[1] any one of these mines might, by the accidental discovery of rich lodes, be liable to flood a particular ticketing sale, with detrimental results on prices.[2] A few mining concerns had already been amalgamated, whilst quite a number might employ the same managerial personnel—managers, pursers, engineers, and so forth—but the majority must be regarded as independent units. One capitalist might have shares in a number of mines, but the number of shareholders in the various copper mines of Cornwall about 1770 can hardly have been less than five hundred, and it was possibly nearly twice that number, since many mines had been in operation long enough for subdivisions of the original shares to have come into the hands of heirs, creditors, and business associates of the original shareholder. Moreover, the number of 'foreign' adventurers had

[1] A note book of the elder Richard Trevithick listed 86 mines selling copper-ores in 1777 (*T.N.S.*, Vol. XI, p. 39); his grandson, Francis Trevithick, (Vol. 1, pp. 35-36) only listed 64 mines, but these were those making sales at a single ticketing; a list of all mines selling ores over a period of at least three years would indicate more accurately the number of selling concerns.

[2] The chance availability of transport facilities, too, often led certain mining concerns to send abnormally large quantities of ores to a single ticketing sale, but this was the case with the smaller rather than the larger concerns.

increased; although many of them had fully accredited and
instructed agents in Cornwall, others had not, and their consent
was necessary for the mines in which they were interested to
adopt new policies necessitated by emergency conditions; if
they were not consulted, resulting troubles, quarrels, and mis-
understandings might easily bring final disaster to a concern
already in the throes of crisis; on the other hand, time lost in
achieving unanimity between the scattered shareholders of a
single mine might be equally fatal to its destiny.

One factor favouring the development of increasing co-
operation was the concentration of copper mining in a comparatively small area; the mines of the single parish of Gwennap were in time to come to produce about a third of the total
output of Cornish copper, and even at this earlier period were
probably raising over a fifth of the copper ores sold in Cornwall;
very little copper-ore, indeed, was then mined outside the
seven parishes of Gwennap, Kenwyn, Redruth, Illogan, Camborne, Crowan, and Gwinear; practically the entire copper-
mining region was within eight miles of the summit of Carn
Brea—itself only four miles from the Northern Channel. Even
with the poor communications of those times a hard riding man
could have gone round the entire perimeter of the copper-
mining area, and brought in many of the tin mines as well, in
a day. Had they wished, the local Cornish mines adventurers
could have met together with comparative ease.

The limited geographical bounds of the copper-mining
region, however, brought other problems, whatever opportunities they may have afforded for the concentration of enterprise and for close co-operation among mines adventurers. In
that area between 1670 and 1770 population had vastly increased, doubling in some parishes, possibly increasing five-
fold in others;[1] in it were concentrated by 1770 between
twelve and fifteen thousand people who were mainly dependent
on the mines for their livelihood. Any check in the progress of
the mines threw on the parochial rates not the infirm young,
the impotent aged, and the hapless sick envisaged and pro-

[1]Estimates of population suggest that the total for Cornwall was about 100,000
in 1670, and that by 1770 it had nearly reached 150,000; the 1801 census gave a
return of 188,269. There is little doubt that the greatest increase occurred in the
mining parishes, whilst in some agricultural parishes, and especially the moorland
parishes of East Cornwall, there may have been a decline. (N. J. G. Pounds:
"Population Movements in Cornwall and the Rise of Mining in the Eighteenth
Century" *Geography*, Vol. XXVIII (1943), pp. 37-46).

vided for by the framers of the Elizabethan Poor Law, but many able-bodied persons destitute from sheer inability to find employment. This problem only became acute, however, towards the end of the eighteenth century, whereas long before the inability of the old ecclesiastical organization to provide for the spiritual needs of the increased population had brought the Wesleys to Cornwall with momentous results upon the social life of the people.

THE BEGINNINGS OF RELIGIOUS CHANGE

1740-1791

The failure of the Anglican Church to adapt itself to economic change meant that it no longer adequately fulfilled the role in society that was demanded of a religious organization. Harsh judgments have been passed on it and on its members for that failure, especially by later Methodist writers; these condemnations, however, have been prejudged to greater or less extent by the religious fanaticism of succeeding generations, and, still more, by changed and changing conceptions of conventional morality. The detractors of the eighteenth century Anglican Church, moreover, both at the time and subsequently, through indiscriminate confusion of the terms 'religion' and 'church', failed to realize that the duties of a church included the reconciliation of the individual soul with other individual souls in society in this world. The real and tragic failure of the Anglican Church was its failure to comprehend that economic changes had revolutionized the structure of society. That Church had fulfilled its functions in the agrarian order, but did not realize or refused to realize that in the new industrial order it must seek out a new reconciliation of the individual and society in order to survive as an established church. The very fact that, theologically, it represented a compromise between Roman Catholicism and puritanical Presbyterianism meant that it lost dynamic living force when the struggles of the two extreme factions, that had lasted nearly a century and a half, ended in the virtual elimination of both in Cornwall by the beginning of the eighteenth century. A mild predestinarian sentiment, modified by survivals of the Catholic faith which stressed the beneficence of the Deity, suited well an agrarian society dependent on co-operation with the inevitable processes of Nature with seed-time never failing and harvest but rarely. Such a belief, however, was out of place in a society that was becoming increasingly dependent on tearing from Nature riches hidden in the earth, riches that once removed could never be replaced even though, at the time, the vast mineral reserves remaining to be exploited encouraged a quite widely prevalent idea that mineral deposits grew in the depths of the earth just like trees on its surface.[1] The difficult and hazardous nature of mining predisposed men to believe that by their own efforts alone they could win or conquer the bounties of God or Nature. Increasing practical knowledge lessened the belief of the fortunate ones in luck, fate, or predestination. They no longer believed that their own good fortunes were testimonies of their individual favour in the eyes of the Deity although, for some time yet, there was still a tendency to attribute the misfortunes of others to their individual unregenerate spiritual condition. The successful miners, in brief, for purely mundane reasons, were ready to accept the Wesleyan re-assertion of the ancient, but rather obscure, doctrine of Justification by Faith.

There was general agreement that man was by nature a religious being, but, whereas the progress of mining enterprise called for the assertion of an active faith, the majority of the clergy frowned on any tendency to zeal or "enthusiasm." They remembered only too well the trials, tribulations, crimes, persecutions, and disturbances that aggressive sectarianism had brought in its train since the middle of the sixteenth century. Many clergy realized that conflicting theological dogmas were irreconcilable, and the greater number of them, like Charles II after the Restoration, had no desire to travel again—unless it was to a more lucrative living. The outcome of all the storm and stress had been the triumph not of any of the fanatical sectaries but of such men as the Vicar of Bray, men who believed that a show of outward conformity was all that could be obtained in this world—nay even that that was all that it was desirable to obtain; above all, controversial theology which had proved so disastrous to church and to state, to laity and to clergy alike, was

---

[1]Pryce in 1778 wrote—"The most common opinion among the miners in Cornwall is, that certain immature Minerals do nourish and feed the Ores with which they are inter-mixed in the mines, and that the Minerals themselves will, in process of time be converted into Ores productive of those metals to which they have the closest affinity, and with which they have the greatest intercourse . . . Those of most experience seem to have a contrary notion of the matter, and yet differ among themselves . . . It is reasonable to conclude, that Metals were made and implanted in veins at or very soon after the creation of the world. Tin Ore will particularly evince the justness of this conclusion; for it is frequently found in its richest and purest state, in large spots and bunches in blocks of stone of the most hardened consistence, such as Granite, Elvan, and the like which have been above the surface ever since the first induction of solids, have experienced no revolution, nor have been water-charged with metallic particles, unless from the clouds of heaven." (*Mineralogia Cornubiensis*, p. 4.)

to be avoided and shunned. The Church came to be identified with an ecclesiastical order wholly of this world, and, although thinking men might have honestly believed that this was the best solution attainable, the irrational emotions of the masses of the people were left unsatisfied.

The gap between the Anglican Church and the people was still further widened by the identification of the former with a social order and by the transformation of its clergy into a caste of worldly society. Formerly the Church had unified society; all members were equal, at least theoretically, in the presence of the Divinity, but by the early eighteenth century this was no longer true. In time past clergymen had been drawn to a greater or less extent from all classes of society but by 1700 the majority of beneficed clergymen were the younger sons or relatives of the landowning classes with only rarely a member of the lower social classes appearing; whereas in the early Tudor period it had been possible for the son of a butcher to become Archbishop of York and a Cardinal, it is extremely doubtful if Wolsey in Hanoverian times would have been more than a Vicar's churchwarden. The few adventurers who without landed forbears did come slightly to the fore had, almost invariably, some other source of wealth to further their advance in the ecclesiastical order.

As time went by, too, there appeared clerical families like the Collins, Borlases, and Trists, and the caste stratification was still further developed by intermarriages. Walter Borlase, eldest son of the squire of Pendeen who had recouped his family fortunes by lucky adventures in the tin-mines of westernmost Cornwall, held the livings of Madron and Kenwyn; he had married a daughter of the Reverend Henry Pendarves a scion of that formerly great landowning family; on his death, in 1776, the Madron living was 'inherited' by his son, William, who, for the past eight years, had been Vicar of Zennor, bordering on Madron to the north, and who had also held the smaller parish of Gulval, adjoining Madron on the east; Kenwyn passed to the Rev. John Trist, who was also enjoying the livings of Veryan and of Kea. Walter Borlase's younger brother, William, the antiquarian and historian, held the livings of Ludgvan and of St. Just in Penwith for close on half a century; he had married the daughter of the Rev. William Smith, another

[2]Ecclesiastical Returns of 1779 (*Henderson MSS*). Letter of William Borlase to Huddesford, May 13, 1772. (*Borlase MSS*)

pluralist holding both Camborne and Illogan parishes, in 1724. When William Borlase died in 1772 St. Just passed to the Rev. G. P. Scobell of Sancreed, who carried on Borlase's system of employing curates to attend to the spiritual needs of the far western mining parish. Ludgvan, that for fifty years had had a resident vicar, now came under the care of a curate, John Penneck, the son of the then Vicar of Gulval, since the Rector, Herbert Praed, resided at his other benefice, Cheriton Fitzpane in Devon. Pluralism, absenteeism, and the extensive employment of curates meant that the "independent" parish priests had declined greatly in numbers. The Anglican clergy had become imbued with narrow class loyalties, and were using religion to serve the interests of that class of society from which they were drawn to an increasing extent; they were no longer intent on reconciling all classes in the communion and community of the all-embracing Church.

The class to which the clergy belonged was the landowning one whose importance was declining with economic change, although its decline was retarded by the long-lasting social prestige conferred by the possession of land. The established church, however, offered extremely limited opportunities for the host of 'self-made men' who rose to positions of relative affluence and importance in ordinary society with the expansion of mining industry; opportunities were actually being lessened by the development of pluralism and by the rise of local clerical "dynasties". The new industrious middle class men were shut out from positions that they thought should be theirs in religious life by the caste monopoly of squires and parsons; a churchwardenship might occasionally be available, but the lesser positions of parish clerks and constables had no attraction to men who had gained some position in the world by their own ambitions and exertions.

In a still lower position in worldly society were the masses of working people. Democratic meanings implied in the scriptures and by the Magnificat may not have stirred them, especially since the clergy only stressed texts enjoining that each man be content in his own station. The unlettered and untaught poor, however, must have drawn a lesson of democracy from life itself or rather from death. Squires and parsons, blacksmiths and paupers, all came to the same end and resolved into dust, even though the dead squire might have been pompously laid away in a family vault, that might, perhaps, still be inside the church, and the pauper huddled away in a corner of the churchyard where grass and nettles soon obliterated all trace of a newly made grave. Against that stark reality the arid formalism to which many clergy had reduced the services of the Anglican Church seemed to matter but little, and it was the fault of these clerics that so many people had come to regard the parish church as merely the place to which they were brought to be baptised, married, and buried. Fees exacted for these services were resented, as were the lesser tithes that fell on the smaller occupiers of land and 'commoners', tithes that were apportioned to the incumbent, whether Rector, Vicar, or mere hireling curate, like those on pigs, geese, and honey allotted by the pluralist Marshall[3] to the curate who looked after Cury and Gunwalloe for him in 1779.

The employment of curates in some cases may have lessened the gap between the church and the people; in many places, however,

---

[3]Marshall held the livings of Breage and Germoe which he served himself, residing in Breage and officiating at Germoe every third Sunday: Cury and Gunwalloe were served by the Curate John Passmore for only £30 a year, the tithes mentioned, fees, and Easter offerings which probably did not amount to much since there were less than thirty communicants out of a total population in both parishes of about 350. Marshall also held the living of St. Erth where he paid a "locum tenens" 1/6d a week to conduct services till he could find a regular curate. Breage and its "three daughter churches" were still held by one man in 1821—the Rev. R. Garvey Grylls who then paid a resident curate just £110 and a non-resident curate merely £60 a year to look after them while he himself lived in his other living at Luxulyan. Poverty may gave dictated the amalgamation of livings, but any gain to the worldly station of the incumbent and any gain thereby to the prestige of the Church was offset by the poverty of the hireling curates. The system had been defended by William Borlase in a letter to Sir John St. Aubyn dated December 31, 1736:-

"conferring two livings on one person is neither contrary to scripture nor reason . . . for that livings have been pannelled out and divided one from the other long since the canon of scripture was settled, that it is no more than enlarging the trust, and consequently no more contrary to reason than conferring many civil or military offices upon one and the same person, a privilege which no government in the world would suffer itself to be deprived . . . Abolishing pluralities will be a dangerous amputation and such as the wound (i.e. abuse) does by no means require. All degrees of Clergy must suffer—but the parochial most of all as being deprived of the only method of advancing themselves into leisure and a capacity of studying without falling into any inferior occupation to maintain themselves or educate their families . . . As for that other wild scheme of making Pluralists share their income with their Curates, I say nothing of it but the more I think upon it the more I think it impracticable." (*Borlase M.S.S.*)

Pluralism was, however, only a method of enabling a few clergy to live in greater state and worldly comfort; William Borlase holding the livings of Ludgvan and St. Just-in-Penwith, his father holding Madron and Kenwyn his nephew later holding Madron, Morvah, and Zennor, his successor Scobell at St. Just holding Sancreed, Marshall and Grylls holding five livings apiece ranked with the gentry; the curates they employed unless they had family means belonged to a lower order and their poverty may have been truly apostolic but hopelessly at variance with 18th. century notions of social prestige and seemliness.

a petty curate over-conscious of his puny shreds of dignity widened the gulf. Just as the servants and minions of many jovial and affable squires exaggerated the shadowy prestige distinguishing them from the common rut of humanity, so did many curates, aping the features of their employers, superiors, and masters. In this way the curates exaggerated the features that distinguished the clergy as a caste, instead of minimizing those traits and establishing any real communion between the various social groups that made up, or should have made up, the congregation. The identification of the established religion with a narrow social caste accounted, in no small degree, for the smallness of many congregations; religion itself, like the church establishment, came to be regarded by many as a perquisite of the upper classes. Nevertheless an affable rector or vicar, or a curate who forgot that he was on the fringe of an ecclesiastical hierarchy, could still draw and hold large congregations.

Some of the clergy kept a close watch on the curates they employed, and even on the congregations they committed to their charge, but when they did their main purpose was the maintenance of outward conformity and seemliness. William Borlase seems to have regarded the Church and its officials as little more than a type of spiritual police when he wrote to Tregarthen, the Curate of St. Just in May, 1734, instructing him to send the churchwardens and Parish Constables round the ale-houses during the hours of divine service to apprehend all they found therein when he, Borlase, would present for breakers of the Sabbath. He had adopted this policy himself in Ludgvan "with some success" as he regarded "intemperance and profaning the Sabbath" as "the two great inlets of all vice". At the same time he ordered Tregarthen to hold services regularly, and insisted on the catechizing of all children[4]. Tregarthen, however, paid little attention and four years later Borlase wrote him a lengthy letter upbraiding him for neglecting services in St. Just in order to officiate for other clergymen; for holding services at times inconvenient to the folk living in the outlying hamlets of the parish; for absenting himself from a populous parish in which burials were frequent and not even putting in appearances at times he had arranged with bereaved parishioners to bury their dead; for failing to insist that godparents

----

[4]*Borlase M.S.S.* Wm. Borlase to Tregarthen: May 18, 1734.

at baptisms were confirmed communicants; for failing to keep the registers of baptisms, marriages, and burials regularly; for undertaking to perform fortnightly afternoon services at Paul to the neglect of the people of St. Just, without first asking Borlase's permission. The Vicar concluded with the threat that, if Tregarthen did not, within a week, promise to mend his ways, the matter would be brought to the attention of the Archdeacon or even to that of the Bishop[5]. Tregarthen may have mended his ways, but by the end of the year he was dead and Borlase was asking the Bishop of Exeter to appoint "Mr. G. Hawkins, son to the late Vicar of Sithney" in his place[6]. This new curate, however, did not prove entirely satisfactory, for, in a letter sending an excommunication against a "Mr. Polkinhorne", Borlase wrote:-

"I am concerned to know that your health did not permit you to officiate in the forenoon of the Sunday after Christmas Day . . . I must desire you also to bury the dead according to your appointment let the weather be what it will and not let the Parishioners wait with the corpse at the style of which they will complain and I am obliged to take notice of their complaints. I suppose you had very good reasons for neither bidding nor officiating on the 30th. of January (two years following) though a day that no Clergyman in England ought to leave his Church without service, considering the guilt that day brought upon this unhappy nation; I suppose therefore I can say that you had the most weighty reasons for leaving your Church of which I beg you would write me as also whether your health will permit you to change with me once a month during the long days which it will be my duty to desire of you. Of this please to send me your resolutions for if the duties of the Church are too frequent for and inconsistent with your health you are a Gentleman of too good a fortune to be long deliberating whether you will continue or resign the Cure."[7]

A poor curate, apparently would sell his services to the neglect of his charge; a rich one might not go to any personal inconveniences to hold services and conduct burials in stormy weather.

William Borlase probably took more interest in his second parish, which he acquired in 1732, than many other pluralists in theirs, for it was the parish in which he had been born and spent his early

[5]*Borlase MSS.* William Borlase to Tregarthen, May 15, 1738.

[6]*Borlase MSS.* William Borlase to the Bishop of Exeter, December 7, 1738.

[7]*Borlase MSS.* William Borlase to the Curate of St. Just, February 11, 1739/40.

days. There is little in his correspondence with his curates, however, to suggest that he did more than intervene when some scandalous or unseemly conduct was brought to his notice. It was to his credit that he took occasional services in his second living but the journey was not formidable on horseback along the trackway by which tin had been taken from St. Just to Helston before Penzance had been made a coinage town in 1663. Borlase was ready to use the law to force people to attend Church; he was ready, perhaps, to preach sermons against Sabbath-breaking; nowhere did he suggest that the Church should draw people by providing them with those things of the spirit they needed or felt they needed. Outward conformity and unquestioning obedience to the existing social order was the supreme necessity and it is striking how a good Whig of the mid-eighteenth century regarded the execution of Charles I—not as the triumph of his own class interests but as productive of anarchy in Church and State.

The best of the vicars and curates may have been a little better than William Borlase, Tregarthen, and Hawkins; the worst of them were far more negligent. The system of pluralism and absenteeism had not only reduced preferment in the church to a stock-jobbing business but had also left vicars and curates evading and shuffling the responsibilities of the care of souls. There is nothing to suggest that Hawkins and even less that Tregarthen were fitted to take charge of the extensive tin mining parish with a population of about two thousand. Borlase's own interest in the place was only spasmodically roused by appeals and complaints which probably came from the tenantry or household servants of Pendeen manor where he had been born; and whatever, his undoubted abilities as an antiquarian or as a historian, there is little to suggest that he looked on the Church other than as a comfortable source of income for himself and his family while he pursued his reading and his researches. So Methodism was able to establish one of its earliest footholds in St. Just in Penwith, just as its development in the "eastern" copper mining district was promoted by the absenteeism of Borlase's elder brother, Walter, from Kenwyn.

The state of the Anglican Church in St. Just in Penwith was comparable to its condition in the more easterly copper-mining region. In that entire area, roughly bounded by the villages and towns of St. Agnes, Penryn, Helston, Marazion, and Hayle, there were some eighteen parish churches and about the same number of incumbents, usually eight at least being curates, to look after a population which, by 1740, exceeded 20,000;[8] about a century later the single parish of Gwennap had no less than eleven chapels belonging to various Methodist denominations, a Baptist church in St. Day, besides the parish church and the newly built Anglican churches in St. Day and Lanner to cater for the population of the parish which, by 1841 had risen to 10,794.[9] East of Gwennap the Chacewater mining district lay in the parish of Kenwyn; if Walter Borlase's curates were as unreliable as those of his brother, they were not likely to bestir themselves on Sundays or on weekdays for a weary eight mile journey from Kenwyn and back. Towns like Redruth and Camborne grew up at some distance from the parish church, and in many other parishes the mines were at a considerable distance from the ancient "church- towns." The answer to this, provided by John Wesley and his followers, was the open air services at Gwennap Pit and elsewhere, and the numerous tiny meeting-houses and chapels that sprang up later throughout the mining districts.

It does not seem, however, that the Wesleys were drawn to Cornwall originally by any apprehension that the mining districts were suffering from the neglect of religious duties by the clergy, or through any realization that the increase in population, incidental to the expansion of the mining industries, had outgrown religious facilities provided nearly four centuries before when the greater number of the Cornish churches had been rebuilt or enlarged. John Wesley's desire as an ordained Anglican clergyman was to supplement and reinvigorate the life of the Church, and to do so with the greatest effect he naturally concentrated on the most populous districts. He gloried in numerous congregations; the salvation of individual sinners he tended to leave to his followers, men whom he encouraged to teach small classes, that gathered

[8]An estimate of the population, based on the returns to Bishop Ross, gives this mining district a population of 29,650 in 1779, viz: Kenwyn (including part of Truro) 2,300; Redruth 1,400; Illogan 540; Camborne 2,450; Gwennap 3,000; Stithians and Perranarworthal 1,125; Wendron (including Helston) 9,000; Sithney 900; Breage and Germoe 2,800; St Hilary (including Marazion) 2,250; Ludgvan 1,000; St. Erth 560; Phillack and Gwithian 675; Gwinear 900; Crowan 1,250; no return was made from St. Agnes. Figures derived from a rough estimate of 4.5 persons per "family" (*Henderson MSS.*)

[9]William Francis: *Gwennap—a Descriptive Poem* (1845), pp. 129, 136-140. Francis estimated that only 2,000 parishioners attended thirteen places of worship; the Methodist New Connexion Chapel had been forced to close for lack of support. In 1779 the curate, Robert Hoblyn, admitted that there were only 40 communicants out of a population of nearly 3,000, although, as in 1845, it is likely that only a fourth of the congregation participated in the sacraments, even if they were only administered four times a year.

here and there, as, in earlier days, the Oxford Holy Club had met in his rooms in Lincoln College. These clubs or classes were the foundation of his evangelical work, and it was the news of the existence of some such body in St. Ives, brought by a certain Captain Turner to Bristol, rather than accounts of the depths of spiritual darkness prevalent in the western county, that determined him to make his first journey to Cornwall. It was a later age that created the legend of pre-Wesley heathendom and barbarity in Cornwall, maximizing over-lusty wrestling and hurling matches into sins but one whit removed from cannibalism, over-stressing drunkenness, exaggerating tales of smugglers and wreckers and so forth, just as converted hysterics, at the penitential bench, magnified their glorified individual salvation by the confession of lurid past sins, many of which, in an atmosphere of rational reflection, would seem very trifling indeed, and not a few of which might well be dismissed as a figment of the great emotional strain they were undergoing at the time these confessions were made.[10] If hurling and wrestling declined it was doubtless due to the springing up of meeting houses that provided another outlet for communal emotionalism; revival meetings were more interesting than

[10]Thus the Cornish miners in the St. Just district were described a century later as being, in the 1730s "ferocious in manners, obtuse in intellect, alternatively servile and riotous, their more serious employment, when disengaged from the mines were smuggling and wrecking, while their amusements partook of the same savage and brutal character . . . The facilities for concealment supplied by a range of mines along the coast, gave every encouragement to smuggling, and with it came a train of other ills—drunkenness especially in its more debasing forms. Nor was wrecking uncommon, though there is no evidence that it was ordinarily accompanied by the atrocities for which other places were infamous." Richard Treffry, Junior: "*Memoirs of Mr. John Edwards Trezize*" (1837), pp. 10-17. A similar vague account had been given by the Rev. Richard Warner a generation earlier in his "*Tour Through Cornwall in the Autumn of 1808*", pp. 300-302. Yet William Borlase accused his western parishioners of nothing worse than neglect of the Sabbath and drunkenness; true it is possible that his father John Borlase, squire of Pendeen had little respect for inconvenient laws and decorum and the fogou at the back of Pendeen Manor might well have been used as a private cellar. Smuggling and even wrecking went on long after the day not only of Wesley but after that of Treffry for in the Burial Register of St. Just in Penwith against the date January 9th, 1878, recording the burial of George Hall of Bosorn, aged 24, the officiating clergyman added the comment "drowned on Epiphany (Sunday) wrecking the Anne of Bilbao." The entry John Wesley himself made in his journal for April 7, 1744 "it is remarkable that those of St. Just were the chief of the whole country for hurling, fighting, drinking, and all manner of wickedness; but many of the lions are become lambs, are continually praising God, and calling their old companions in sin to come and magnify the Lord together" (J. Weslsy: *Journal*, Curnock edition, Col. III, p. 129) seems to have been rather premature. Wendron Parish Registers record that in 1795 "James Hall, aged 24, a man of good repute, was shot by a volunteer of Helston at the wreck of a vessel stranded in Poljew sanding cove" (Canon G. Doble: "*Sithney and Wendron*", p. 41.)

cock-fights if only for the greater scope they provided for the occurrence of the unexpected; it was easier and far more comfortable to crowd into a chapel than to brave the rain and winds in a hard hurling match across the moors. If some came away from these religious meetings sadder and wiser men so much the better; nor were the more youthful elements of the community neglectful of opportunities offered by religious meetings to strike up acquaintances with members of the opposite sex. Drunkenness may have declined but that in part was due to changing fashion and the introduction of tea—particularly, perhaps, the cheaper smuggled variety. As for more serious crime and immorality Methodism can claim much but prove little; possibly the numbers transported in the 1840s were rather less in proportion to the total population than in 1740 but most evidence surviving seems to link "crime waves" with periods of economic distress irrespective of religion; antagonists of Methodism and of evangelical preachers generally have alleged that their watchnight services and later camp meetings promoted sexual immorality, but even were full statistics of illegitimate births available their testimony would be rather less that the flimsiest circumstantial evidence to support or to refute the contentions of the Methodists or those of their opponents.[11]

The Wesleys first visited Cornwall in 1743, Charles arriving in mid-July and John at the end of August. Both made St. Ives their centre, most likely at the invitation of the trading associates of Captain Joseph Turner, himself a Bristolian convert who seems to have been employed in the coastal trade between Cornwall and Bristol in copper-ores, coal and the general merchandise that went by the name of Bristol ware. Their trials, tribulations, and triumphs in their early visits to Cornwall have become well-high legendary. Charles Wesley clashed with the pluralist Rector of St. Ives and his curate, Hoblyn, but was loyally supported by the Presbyterian

[11] At the Spring Assizes of 1743 in Cornwall, three men were sentenced to transportation to America for terms of seven years each; at the Spring Assizes in 1841 two men were sentenced to ten year periods for stealing a sheep, and a third for the same term for stealing a pony, whilst a man charged with "wrecking" was found not guilty after judge and counsel had expressed doubts if the charge were a mere larceny or a capital felony. (P.R.O. Ass. 24/25, and *West Briton*, April 2 and 9, 1841.) The Spring Assizes of 1843 had an even stranger variety of cases, including the trial of the fortune-teller Statton for witchcraft, of which he was found not guilty—he had apparently offered to find a lost or stolen heifer for 3/- by white magic; there were four sentences of transportation—two for life on convicted burglars, one for fourteen years on a forger of assay marks, the other for ten years on a highway robber; two Boscastle "wreckers" were sentenced to twelve months hard labour each. (*West Briton*, March 31, 1843.)

mayor of the borough, John Stephens. Violence was not the monopoly of the enemies of Methodism, for at Pool a drunken miner who threatened to assault Charles Wesley was nearly lynched by the congregation, whilst the Redruth miners threatened to stone any who dared speak against the Methodists. Not all churchmen were antagonistic. George Thompson of St. Gennys, who may have met John Wesley in Georgia, John Bennet of Tresmere, and John Torney of Week St. Mary gave them very active support in the early days.[12] Nevertheless the most formidable antagonist the Wesleys had to face was Walter Borlase, who used his position as a magistrate to harry them at every turn; using or mis-using his powers as a Justice of the Peace in the late summer of 1744 he committed the preacher Thomas Westall to the House of Correction.[13] In June 1745, along with his father and another local Justice, Usticke of St. Buryan, he tried to draft another regular Methodist itinerent preacher Maxfield into the army as a vagrant; the Borlases on this occasion issued a general warrant to the constables and overseers of several parishes ordering them to "apprehend all such able-bodied men as had no lawful callings or sufficient maintenance"; Maxfield had been apprehended at Crowan and was described in the warrant as "A person, his name unknown, who disturbs the peace of the parish." Crowan had no great reputation for law-abidingness and the memory of Henry Rogers and the sieges of Skewis was still green; nor was all the violence on one side, for the Constables moved him out of the parish "having received timely notice that a body of five hundred

---

[12]Three of the 1745 returns to Bishop Cleggett's letter asking for information about the population, numbers of Dissenters, etc., from the clergy of Cornwall show that Thompson and Bennet were regarded as the real leaders of Methodism in Cornwall. John Cory of Marhamchurch wrote that there were no Dissenters in his parish "but only one Family whom I am informed frequent Mr. Thompson's irregular meetings and accompany him on his circumferaneous vociferations. There is no licensed meeting house in the parish nor any who take it upon them to teach unless in the said family where (I have been told) some of those deluded people who style themselves methodists, Thompson's and Bennet's followers, who meet together in private." Thomas Serle of Treneglos and Warbstone returned that there were no Dissenters in his parishes—"unless they may be called dissenters who go by the name of Methodist—a set of people who are chiefly encouraged and abetted by a neighbouring clergyman." William Leaver, Vicar of Kilkhampton, where he employed a curate whilst he himself acted as domestic chaplain to the Earl of Cardigan in London, wrote that in Kilkhampton sixteen persons dissent—" who call themselves Methodists. They have no licensed meeting house, but assemble at the house of William Simons, Officer of Excise, and their leader is Mr. George Thompson, Vicar of St. Gennys." (*Henderson MSS.*) John Bennet held the poor livings of Laneast and North Tamerton besides that of Laneast.

[13]J. Wesley, *Journal* (Curnock Edition) Vol. III, pp. 150-152.

Methodists were coming to take him away by force." Other magistrates were reluctant to follow the lead of Borlase, and after the refusal of a naval captain to take Maxfield on his ship unless Borlase was prepared to pay him wages as a regular chaplain, he was released about a fortnight after his arrest.[14] Nothing daunted, or, perhaps, rather infuriated by this set-back, Borlase, Usticke and Francis Beauchamp then resorted to warrants to arrest Wesley himself and his companion Shepherd, an expedient whereby they were checked from preaching. When the preachers were brought first to Castle Horneck and then to Pengreep in Gwennap, however, the magistrates who had ordered their arrest refused to see them; and servants told them that they were free to go.[15]

Mobbing, arrests, and on occasion the reading of the riot act were features of the third visit of John Wesley to Cornwall which lasted from June 16th to July 16th, 1745. The opposition of the Justices was largely on account of fear of disturbance, and they made the most of baseless rumours that Wesley was the ally of the Pretender—even that he was the Pretender himself—and that he was a secret emissary of Rome. The episode of Maxfield's arrest at Crowan had shown that the mob was a two-edged weapon. None of the magistracy seems to have lifted a finger to apprehend those who had destroyed a meeting-house at St. Ives to celebrate a naval victory over the Spaniards early in 1744,[16] but in the troublous political situation aggravated, furthermore, by depression and distress in the mining industries, they were alarmed at that time lest emotional evangelical preaching should incite mobs to riot and to the destruction of property that did not belong to Methodists. Borlase always believed the Methodists were "mad, crazy-headed fellows".[17] He was now convinced that they were dangerous to the security of the realm, and was ready to strain his magisterial powers to suppress the menace, albeit not going so far as the hot-headed curate of St. Ives, Hoblyn, who, in April 1744, had stirred up mob emotions by denouncing Wesley and his adherents as enemies of the Church, as Jacobites, and as Papists.[18] There were some who would not have hesitated to rouse the mob against the Methodists to distract it from other mischief in those

[14]*ibid.* Vol. III, p.182 ff. vide also C. Wesley *Journal* for July 3, 1745.
[15]J. Wesley: *Journal,* Vol. III, pp. 186 ff.
[16]J. Wesley: *Journal,* Vol. 111, pp. 127-8.
[17]*Ibid,* Vol. III, p. 130.
[18]*Ibid,* Vol. III, pp. 130-131.

dangerous times. Others preserved the peace by threatening their
tenantry against attending Wesley's services,[19] whilst it is even
possible that the clergyman Thomas saved Wesley's life at Falmouth
from the infuriated mob on July 4, 1745. Whatever may be said
of the rational basis of Wesleyan evangelicanism, its opponents were
fighting it not with reasoned arguments but by even more irrational
appeals to mob prejudices, and the most violent opposition that
manifested itself in 1745 derived from one of the deepest and often
one of the most irrational of all human emotions, fear—the fear
of an established order that the turbulent and evil days of the
seventeenth century were returning.[20] It is significant that violent
manifestations against the Methodists in Cornwall practically ceased
after the collapse of the invasion of Charles Edward Stuart when
the Whig gentry and their clerical relatives and dependants were
able to breathe freely again.

Rationalism, if such it can be called, only entered into the lists
against Methodism in 1747[21] when George Lavington who had
succeeded Claggett as Bishop of Exeter issued the first part of his
lengthy "Enthusiasm of Methodists and Papists compared." It was
an attack from the secluded study by a man of considerable
learning, but whose whole career had divorced him from the harsh
realities of the world: His own connections with and knowledge of
the West Country, although he had been born in Devon, were
slight before the great Whig peers, Hardwick and Newcastle,
promoted him from the prebendal stall at Worcester, which he had
acquired after being domestic chaplain to George I, to the see of
Exeter two months after Claggett's death in December, 1746. His
knowledge of Methodism was almost entirely confined to the
writings of some of its protagonists, which revealed ignorance,

[19]Thus Sir Francis Vyvyan, squire of Trelowarren had "solemnly declared, nay, and that
in the face of the whole congregation, as they were coming out of the church, 'If any man
does hear the fellows he shall not come to my Christmas feast.'" (*Ibid.* Vol. III, p. 142). The
threat seems to have been effective, but it might not have been had the parishioners of
Mawgan in Meneage foreseen that Sir Francis's next Yuletide feast was to be with
Polonius—"Not where he eats but where he is eaten: a certain convocation of politic worms
are e'en at him. Your worm is your only emperor for diet: we fat all else to fat us, and we
fat ourselves for maggots: your fat king and your lean beggar is but variable service—two
dishes but to one table; that's the end." (*Hamlet*, IV, 3.)

[20]Typical of the clergymen of the Established Church was the man who told the Methodist
Jonathan Reeves that "he wished the Bible was in Latin only, that none of the vulgar might
be able to read it. Yet there are the men that rail at us as Papists". Charles Wesley *Journal*,
July 30th, 1744 (quoted Thomas Jackson "*Life of Charles Wesley*', Vol.I, p. 396.).

[21]This work originally appeared in three parts; the first appearing in 1747, and the
complete work being published in 1754.

inability and even superstition besides their zealous and emotional faith and to the stories that lost no descriptive detail in the telling by rumour's multitudinous twisted tongues of the scenes of emotional frenzy and madness attending revivalist meetings. His was an attack on Methodism in general and not merely or particularly on their conduct in the western part of his new diocese.[22] Moreover, the Journals of both the Wesleys suggest that as yet there had been relatively few of these scenes of wildest religious frenzy, although they became common later, and perhaps most frequent of all in the revivalist meetings that were held in the half century following the death of John Wesley:[23] It is possible, however, that some of the non-ordained itinerant preachers, lacking the academic training and discipline the Wesleys had undergone at Oxford, allowed feeling and sentiment to carry them away, whilst all Methodists alike, in the early days, directed their appeals to the emotions rather than to the reasoning faculties of their congregations. It was only the second and third generations of Methodists that penetrated far into the arid deserts of theological speculation and reasoning, and when they did many of their congregation drifted away to the schismatic sects of Kilhamites, Primitive Methodists, and Bible Christians and others who still had sublime faith in religious sentiment unencumbered by academic theology.

Only the appeal to their emotions could have any affect on the largely illiterate working miners of Cornwall; the theological reasoning of the academic oligarchy of the eighteenth century to which men like Lavington belonged left them uncomprehending, perhaps bewildered, certainly unmoved. Whilst the proportion of those who could just read and write was, perhaps, larger than may

---

[22] The last of the great clerical opponents of Methodism in Cornwall, the Rev. Richard Polwhele, as late as 1833 saw fit to re-issue Lavington's work with a lengthy preface and an appendix that, also not erring on the side of brevity—more than doubled the size of the work.

[23] The accounts given by John Wesley himself in his *Journal* of his early visits to Cornwall mention some instances of violent conversions, but give little hint of his moving his congregations to mass hysteria; the nearest approach to such was that when Charles Wesley concluded his second mission to Cornwall in 1744 at Tresmere when it seems that the preachers rather than their congregation were carried away by emotion; Charles Wesley declared that he had been dead to God, asleep in the arms of the devil, and secure in a state of damnation for eighteen years; his itinerant colleague Meriton went even further and said he had been in that state for twenty-five years; Vicar George Thompson claimed thirty-five years in unregeneracy, whilst the aged clergyman John Bennet eclipsed them all by claiming "far above seventy".

be supposed, yet comparatively few had any wider knowledge than rudiments taught them by old women, by men fit for no other employment, or by catechizing curates and vicars and wisdom which they gained by harsh experience in the hard school of life itself. Life itself, however, was changing; the agrarian love of nature of olden times was derived from a far different mode and experience of living than that developing from the pursuit of mining. Older Anglican Protestantism had coincided with the decline of the mediaeval agrarian community; Methodism, perhaps without the realization of its founders and earlier preachers and teachers, had coincided with the appearance and development of a new industrial community. In this lies the main reason for the progress and eventual triumph of Methodist dissent in Cornwall without any recourse to vague notions of peculiar Celtic racial traits. The intermingling economic and social conditions that promoted the early progress of Wesleyan evangelicanism in Tyneside, in the colliery and manufacturing districts near Bristol, and in London, were closely related to the economic and social development of Cornwall in this period—a development that did more to destroy Celtic provincialism than to promote it and one that had led to the disappearance of Cornish as a living language just before Wesley arrived in Cornwall. Celticism, however, was perhaps as important as the lyrical genius of Charles Wesley in imposing hymn-singing on Methodists a living communal spirit in their congregations far different from that uninspired reference in the Anglican Prayer Book to "quires and places where they sing"; all could and would join in the Methodist hymns but in the Established Church not only were squire and parson monopolising control, but choiristers and musicians and bell-ringers had well-nigh become minor castes in the ecclesiastical congregation.[24] However conservative his political and social views, Wesley regarded the Church

[24]It may be postulated too that the Eucharist had become monopolized by the higher classes in the community, judging by the limited numbers participating; the class conscious clergy may be blamed for this, not because they debarred communicants—William Borlase indeed made a violent appeal to insist on all Godparents at baptisms being communicants but because their attitude led the people to regard the Church and all that belonged to it as the perquisite of their "social betters". Not the least heinous offence of the humbler Methodists in the eyes of the clergy of the day was their assurance of their own personal salvation; thus when John Wesley questioned a "little gentleman" of St. Just about the arrest of Edward Greenfield in June 1745, he received the reply, "Why, the man is well enough in other things; but his impudence the gentlemen cannot bear. Why, sir, he says he knows his sins are forgiven." (J. Wesley, *Journal*, Vol. III, p. 186.).

as a democratic communion; others, more worldly and more realistic than he, foresaw and dreaded the consequence of such views that were menacing the established social order. Wesley's Arminian theology and the new emphasis he put on the doctrine of justification by faith were irreconcilable with predestinarian ideas of the blessed lot of the few elect both in a future existence and in this.

Walter Borlase and his fellow justices, squires and parsons, especially the less learned ones, were inclined to believe that conversion to the doctrine, now by many of them denounced as "Popish", of justification by faith alone, meant that the half or wholly illiterate and unthinking might confound it with a faith in their own righteousness or salvation and lead them to challenge the hardly won and delicate compromises on which the security, tranquility, and very existence of the social order of the day depended. More especially had they come to dread the "hydra-headed multitude" which had already shown its disregard of property rights not in mere spasmodic plundering of wrecks but in the riots in the St. Austell district in 1728 and in the raid on Falmouth in 1737. It was to men of this class that Wesley was appealing when he attracted crowded congregations at Gwennap and St. Just; in a fury of patriotism mobs could be turned against Wesley, but there had been incidents when they had supported him and his followers. There was no evading the fact that the evangelical preaching of the Wesleyan itinerant preachers appealed to the working miners and fishermen already nursing a grievance against landlords, who claimed anything up to a sixth of the ores they raised, and against clergymen, who claimed tithes—and in some cases double tithes[25]—of the fish they caught not merely by hard labour but ofttime to the very imperilling of their lives. Only as time went by was it seen that Wesleyanism, by offering the common folk the hope of a better life hereafter, diverted their attention from concerted action in remedying their grievances in this world at the expense of those classes representing, property, education and a narrow modicum of uninspired reasonableness that was limited to their own immediate welfare. The lower classes,

---

[25]Double tithes might be claimed when the fishermen belonged to one parish but landed their catch in or operated from another. Over claims of this nature the Borlase's came into conflict with neighbouring clergymen, Walter with the Rev. A. A. Sykes, Dean of Buryan (Penlee MSS.—see) below and William with the vicar of St. Hilary (Borlase MSS. U.D. c. 1730-32. William Borlase to Sir John St. Aubyn.).

starved in mind and far from well fed in body, were rich only in emotions, and it was to the emotions that the evangelical preachers appealed.[26] By so doing they may have provoked several cases of hysteria but in a far greater number of cases they provoked sober thought about the mysteries of the human spirit and the universe it inhabited. Their demagogic theatrical methods offended the intellectual ecclesiastics and the upper caste fashions of rigid decorum and strict seemliness. Their faith in miracles was mocked, derided, scorned, and, in some cases, feared by the rationalist churchmen of the day, who did not realize that "rational theology" was incomprehensible to an unlettered congregation. But where the Methodists differed above all, despite the intense individualism of the doctrine of justification by faith, was in reviving the belief in the congregation as a communion and as a community: Whereas in the majority of Anglican churches communion services only took place about four times a year, the Methodists turned every service into a communion whether or not the Eucharist was celebrated; their frequent class meetings made religious services communal acts and not the mere gathering of many or few individuals to watch the parson perform a service in which they really hardly participated at all, comprehended little of what was said or done, and went away with no real satisfaction of their needs of communion with their fellows through only too often with vague realization of the different worlds in which they and the parson lived.

It is not surprising, therefore, that Wesley and the Methodists so

---

[26]Lavington recognized this when he wrote that the "lamentable disorders, horrid convulsions" associated with religious revivals were "natural distemper" occasioned by "stifling air in close rooms, bad diet, indigestion, conditions, and flatulencies (not realizing standards of living); to being exposed to wet, cold, and violent heats; to long watchings and fastings; to suppressions, to sudden frights, wounds, and blows giving a concussion to the brain; to divers affections, passions and perturbations of the mind—love, jealousy, fear, shame, sorrow, anger, envy, malice, great disappointments, or great expectancy; to ambition and pride, swelling till they are ready to burst; to deep cogitations, especially intent upon one object, etc. Those operating in various kinds and degrees, according to men's different humours and constellations; working strongly in enthusiastic heads, when the animal spirits and brains are not disturbed . . .' (Lavington—*Enthusiasm of Methodists and Papists Considered* (1833 edition), p. 255). The appeal of Wesleyanism to the lower classes is also stressed by Walter Borlase (vide his letter to Dr. Oliver of Bath of June, 1749, quoted Note 39 below) who wrote in a letter to his friend Gregor in the summer of 1749—"The Bishop has been pleased to send me the second part of the 'Enthusiasm of Papists, etc. and (I) am going to sit down to it as to an exquisite regale . . .' (*Walter Borlase MSS.*: letter of Walter Borlase to Gregor, August 24, 1749.

speedily gained a hold in the populous mining districts of Cornwall where clergymen were few, some of those few not over-active in their performance of their spiritual duties, and those most active apparently more concerned with the observance of outward conformity that, to their congregations, seemed more inconvenient than necessary. Besides the two Wesleys, several other itinerant preachers visited Cornwall in those years, and a number of native class leaders did not hesitate to "expound" religion to smaller or larger gatherings with growing frequency. The promise of salvation, welcome at all times, was doubly welcome in the trying times of economic depression that prevailed throughout most of the 1740s, and the numbers of professed Methodists grew. As early as 1746 Cornwall was one of the seven Methodist circuits of England, but there is no record of membership for the next twenty years; indeed such records of membership by the Methodist Conference were a sign of that secession from the Church of England which Wesley himself sought, to the very end, to avoid. Nevertheless, professed Methodists must have been considerable in numbers, whilst those attending Methodist revival meetings and services if only out of curiosity were vastly greater. In the uneventful visit in September, 1746, John Wesley held services in several crowded houses and to an "immense multitude" at Gwennap;[27] when he preached in the last parish the following July he was afraid that his "voice would not suffice for such an immense multitude; but my fear was groundless, as the evening was quite calm, and the people all attention."[28] During this visit in 1747, Wesley met the stewards of all the local Methodist societies and found that schisms in Cornish Methodism had already begun because, out of the eighteen "exhorters" in the county, four had no gifts and a fifth, though talented, "had evidently made shipwreck of the grace of God. These therefore I determined immediately to set aside, and advise our societies not to hear them."[29] During this visit, the fifth of John Wesley's thirty-one missions in Cornwall, there were minor incidents, hardly worth the name, at Newlyn and at Port Isaac, the latter the place where earlier Edward Greenfield had nearly been lynched; but, by 1748, all violent resistance to the preachers had

---

[27]Not at Gwennap Pit which was first used for services by Wesley in 1762 (J. Wesley: *Journal*, Vol. IV, p. 528. C. C. James: "*A History of Gwennap*", p. 20.).
[28]J. Wesley: *Journal*, III p. 306.
[29]*Ibid*, III p. 307

disappeared, and John Wesley rejoiced that out of the hundred and fifty persons in the St. Just society more than a hundred had experienced "true conversion"; most of the societies were smaller, but there were perhaps a thousand Methodists in Cornwall.[29a]

If the Methodists were comparatively few in proportion to the total population they were enough to reinvigorate and enliven Cornish religious life. Besides Thompson and the elderly Bennet, other clergymen became active in evangelical work, notably the Rev. Samuel Walker of Truro, no convert of Wesley's but of the Truro Grammar School Master, Conon. The numbers of Methodist preachers and exhorters active in Cornwall was increasing steadily, whilst in self-defence or self-justification some few of the Anglican clergy must have bestirred themselves into greater activity. Yet it may be questioned how far the evangelical preachers extended their influence. Far from all "conversions" were permanent, and some of the preachers themselves lapsed from grace;[30] even in the early days of the Methodist movement there were some who professed conversion and remorse at one of Wesley's revivalist meetings, lapsed again in face of the convival temptations of the world, but, in some cases, returned to the fold again later.[31] The human psychological craving for novelty and change attracted, not merely to revivalist services but even into the societies, some who were only to drift away later and it seems that the numbers of Methodists declined somewhat after revivalism, whilst the sheer persistance of Wesley and his followers became a normal religious routine by the middle of the century. The return of a modicum of prosperity even to the labouring classes of the mining population inevitably meant a recession of religious zeal, but the set-back to the progress of Methodism was only

[29a] *Ibid*, pp. 377-379.

[30] The case of John Trembath may be mentioned; an itinerant in the mid-'forties he had fallen from grace by first getting married, then adopting the pursuit of agriculture becoming one of the fraternity who kept no company but those whose "talk is of bullocks", lapsing further by becoming a frequenter of the hunting field and worse places and by 1755 was alleged to be abetting if not aiding smugglers. (John Wesley—*Letters* ed. John Telford, Vol. III, pp. 141-143).

[31] One of the most striking examples of this was the "tinner" James Roberts of St. Ives; he was one of the first Methodists in that town, but failing to resist the temptations of the bottle, was the leader of the mob that destroyed the meeting-house early in 1744, but, after a short time, was again convinced of his sinful ways and rejoined the Society. (J. Wesley: *Journal*, Vol. III, pp. 127-8 & Vol. IV, p. 413.).

temporary,[32] and after 1750 numbers gradually increased with minor recessions now and again. Yet even by the time of Wesley's last visit to Cornwall, in 1789, the total membership of the various scattered and usually small societies did not exceed four thousand, a figure, however, that compared favourably with the number of communicants of the Anglican church about that time even although it was less than three per cent of the total population.

It was these democratic religious groups or societies that were the significant contribution of Methodism to Cornwall in Wesley's own life-time. The long reluctance of Wesley to ordain preachers left them to their own resources and to their own searchings of heart, to the word of the Bible and to the rapidly increasing number of tracts couched in simple terms that relatively uneducated laymen could understand. The mysteries of religion induced many to the effort to educate themselves not in solitary studies remote and secluded from the bustle of every day life, but in the homes of ordinary folk where the Methodist classes met; theological speculation only came later when a regular Methodist priesthood appeared and theology after all is more often than not a sign of religious decline; it was not accidental but almost inevitable that, with the first really theological Methodist works, schisms appeared.

Whilst it may be granted that the influence of Methodism extended further than the relatively few society members would at first sight suggest, the resounding claims of contemporary, and still more those of later, propagandists and apologists that it effected a moral revolution in Cornwall must be discountenanced. What finally almost entirely suppressed smuggling in Cornwall was the employment of naval cutters after the end of the Napoleonic wars,

[32]Walter Borlase in a letter to Dr. Oliver of Bath, suggested that the decline in Methodism was even earlier writing in June 1749—"The sect you speak of is well known in these parts, having been chiefly propagated by the personal labours of the Wesleys. They have worked upon many of the most vile and ignorant and such as were of a complexion disposed to catch their Enthusiasm, so as to produce some very bad effects, such as violation of order and subjection, remissness of industry, and of course indigence and almost ruin to the circumstances of those poor deluded folk, but such consequences being severely and quickly felt, and their itching was pretty well scratched; this together with the moderation and patience of their lawful partners seems to have reduced them to their senses, and so that the party is by degrees dwindling away. (*Walter Borlase M.S.S.* letter to Dr. Oliver, June 3, 1749). Walter Borlase, for the most part was a level-headed man and sound in judgment, but it is possible that he was here carried away by prejudice and by wishful thinking especially as he had been just telling Oliver of the success of a tin mine in which he had a share.

and one of the smuggled commodities, tea, probably had more to do with the alleged reduction in drunkenness—that cannot be either proved or disproved—than all the sermons preached in Methodism's first century of life. It is equally impossible to prove that wrestling matches and hurling games became less frequent as the eighteenth century went by; they probably did and doubtless it was because frequent Methodist "preachings" provided a counter-attraction. Nor must it be forgotten that the increasing production of copper and tin was achieved by the development of a capitalistic system of enterprise that left labourers with less time for holidays, even although this tendency was slowed down by the survival of tut-work and tribute; the competition of tut-workers and tributers among themselves left them with longer working days and shorter leisure hours; few, if any, would be inclined, even if the days were long enough, after their hard toils in the mines to indulge in hurling but they might slip along to the neighbouring cottage where the week-night Methodist class meeting assembled. The decline of popular festivals, pastimes, and sports coincided with and was occasioned by the triumph of the doctrine of utility, which included the Methodist belief that a thing of real worth could only be such if it contributed to religious salvation as well as the sombre materialism of utilitarian economics.

Wrecking was not entirely suppressed, but it certainly seems to have declined somewhat in the period of Wesley's mission to Cornwall, although not on account of his denunciations of the practice but through the control of the coercive powers of the state by men who had far different notions of the sanctity of private property than the wreckers. Indeed Wesley's preaching seems to have had little real effect in amending the ideas of the men of Breage and Germoe about the impropriety of plundering vessels cast on the rocks on the eastern side of Mount's Bay. The opposition

[33]J. Wesley, *Journal*, Vol. III, pp. 262-3. The entry for September 13, 1746 states that between one and two o'clock he preached "before Mr. Probis's house at Brea . . . Many were there who had been vehement opposers, but from this time they opposed no more." Curnock identifies Brea with Carn Brea, and it may have been the hamlet on the north-western side of that granite massif, but this is unlikely as Wesley had been at Camborne, little more than a mile from Brea on September 11; there is no entry in the journal for September 12th, but before going to Brea he had "taken leave of the brotherhood of St. Ives', and at six that evening he was preaching at Sithney. Had he gone to Carn Brea from St. Ives and then back to Sithney, it was an extremely round-about route, whereas Breage would have been practically on a direct track from St. Ives to Sithney.

of the local gentry and parsons had kept him out of the Wheal Vor tin mining region in his tumultous 1745 visit, but in September, 1746, he was preaching in this district,[33] and in 1747 visited "Breag" where "neither the house nor the yard would contain the congregations; and all were serious and the scoffers are vanished away."[34] In 1748 he preached at Sithney again before proceeding to Crowan and then to Penryn, starting off in the morning from St. Ives. But before John Wesley visited the Wheal Vor mining region again in August, 1750, the men of Breage and Germoe had surpassed all their former exploits as wreckers by plundering a vessel, somewhat storm damaged, which had safely anchored near St. Michael's Mount in December, 1749. Warrants for the arrest of the ringleaders were issued by Walter Borlase and one or two of his fellow justices, but when it became apparent that the parish constables to whom these warrants were given were either in collusion with the wreckers or afraid to take action against them, an extraordinary meeting of the justices of the western hundred of Penwith and Kerrier was held, in consequence of which the Lord Lieutenant of Cornwall approached the Government and obtained troops to execute the warrants.[35]

Only drastic action could curb the plundering of wrecked vessels, and the drastic measures taken on this occasion, and on that later

---

[34] J. Wesley, *Journal*, Vol. III, p. 306.—entry for July 6, 1747.

[35] *Walter Borlase MSS.* Letters of Walter Borlase to Hawkins, December 15, 1749; to Gregor January 3 and 25th, 1749 (O.S) to Harris January 6, 1749 and to Lord Edgcombe, January 29, 1749. The attitude of this clerical justice of the peace is revealed in the letter to Harris—"The rifling of a little frigate in the way of contraband trade is a petty larceny not worth mentioning 'tis so common. The late public plunder of a vessel near the Mount after she was safely anchored surpassed all former acts of that kind in barbarity and violence. Breage and Germoe led the way and were followed by too many out of the adjoining town and parishes." The first letter of the series, that to Hawkins, suggests that Borlase was concerned by hints that the very justices themselves had connived at wrecking, and he was also concerned by the prospect that the continuance of such practices would badly affect the trade of Mount's Bay: "I doubt not but you have heard of the plunder and robbery committed near the Mount last Wednesday on the vessel in Distress by the Barbarians of Breage, Germoe, etc., which act of inhumanity and rapine if laid before our superiors in all its flagrant circumstances will, I fear, produce this natural inquiry—Are there in that county no Justices? Where were they when the laws were violated in so daring a manner? Or if they could not prevent such violences what did they do in order to punish them? It is therefore my opinion, but which I submit to yours, that we who are thus concerned, should for our own vindication forthwith meet somewhere to take informations, such as we can get, of the fact. And not only this but best consider further drawing up some proposal for general subscription of all Gentlemen in the neighbourhood for the prosecution of these offences, which, the longer they are suffered to pass off with impunity will grow the more ambitious and desperate to the infinite reproach of our county and the loss of trade to this Bay in particular."

one in 1767 when the aged reprobate William Pearse,[36] convicted at the Assizes for stealing a piece of rope from a wreck, despite appeals made by many that he be reprieved, was hanged, obviously as a warning to others. It was the enforcement of the law that brought about any decline in wrecking in the eighteenth century, rather than Methodism's rise and progress; it is noteworthy too, how the Breage and Germoe incident that shocked Walter Borlase and his brother justices into appealing for military aid came in that year of depression in tin mining, 1749.

In the following decade the work of the Methodists went on, John Wesley himself visiting Cornwall in 1750, 1751, 1753, 1754, 1755 and 1757. There were still a few cases of resistance, but the persecutions of the 1740s. were a thing of the past; but in the course of the 1750 visit Wesley complained that "through all Cornwall I find that societies have suffered great loss from want of discipline" and the seriousness of the set-backs is revealed by the fact that the St. Just society, still the largest in Cornwall, only had forty-five members in that year, which also saw the first watch-night service in Cornwall.[37] By the summer of 1753, however, the Society had recovered with some fifty or sixty recent converts joining it, but it is of some significance that this recovery was made during a two-year absence of the founder of Methodism, who, moreover, in his previous visit in 1751 had concentrated his attentions on East Cornwall. In 1755 Wesley found the "lions of Breage" turned into lambs, but he did not attribute this, rather uncharitably, to the activities of Borlase and his fellow magistrates but to the suicide of the minister who had enlarged from his pulpit on the alleged sexual immoralities of Wesley and his followers;[38] at St. Just membership had increased and Wesley preached at the laying of the foundation stone of a new Meeting House. In 1757 Wesley drew consolation for the complete disappearance of the

[36] *Cal. Home Office Papers, 1766-1769*. Nos. 548, 549, 557 & 564. Pearse is referred to being "above fourscore years" and despite the appeal of Humphrey Morice to Lord Shelburne that if he were not reprieved his borough interests in Launceston and Newport would be imperilled he was hanged. It is possible that Pearse is one of those that plundered a French vessel (ibid. No. 13) and went to the gallows as a proof of English goodwill to France after the conclusion of the Seven Years' War.

[37] J. Wesley: *Journal*, Vol. III, p. 491. Another reason for the decline may have been that Wesley himself had not visited Cornwall in 1749, and this is the decline that was mentioned by Walter Borlase in his letter to Dr. Oliver in June, 1749. (See above, Note 32. pp. 174).

[38] J. Wesley: *Journal*, Vol. IV, pp. 132-133. The "minister" was the Rev. Edward Collins, Vicar of Breage from 1722 to 1755, and also Vicar of St. Erth where he was buried.

Society in Gulval by the existence of a flourishing one in the adjoining parish of Ludgvan, a development typical of this decade of early Methodist history. Most of the old persecutors now held their peace or had died; the opposition of the clergyman who also held the office of Mayor of the already notorious parliamentary borough of Grampound in 1757 was more than compensated by the assistance given to Wesley by Walker of Truro, by Vowler, the curate of St. Agnes, and by the wealthy Donnithornes in the latter parish; in St. Just and Gwennap fortune had ebbed to flow more strongly than before; Port Isaac and Mevagissey which had been more than a little boisterous at his first appearance now furnished attentive and sober congregations of fisherfolk; in East Cornwall there had been a little trouble in the earlier visits at Launceston but now there were sufficient societies scattered in that area to warrant the establishment of a separate "steward's" meeting from that of Western Cornwall; zeal, however, seems to have flagged somewhat in Thompson's parish at St. Gennys and Bennet was now growing very old, and it was a young Sancreed miner, Richard Rodda, who by the end of the decade was Wesley's "right-hand man" in Cornwall.[39]

This very progress of Methodism was, however, widening the gulf between it and the Established church; on nearly every mission Wesley found his way to some new centre of population; from the mining villages of the west he had gone to the trading and fishing ports, and from there to the St. Austell mining district,[40] and later still to certain villages and towns in the east of the county. His widening mission field in Cornwall and elsewhere lessened the attention and care he could give to any particular place, and as yet there were insufficient regular itinerant preachers to assume the burdens of regular care; more and more spiritual responsibility was perforce thrust on lay stewards and exhorters drawn from the miners, fishermen, small tradesmen and a few farmers. Walker of Truro suggested that the Methodist Society be merged into the Established Church, and, in 1755, had warned Wesley that the course he had pursued was leading to separation from that Church. Both Walker and Wesley agreed at the time that separation from

---

[39]J. Wesley: *Journal*, p. 274.: "*Methodist Biography*"—edited Thomas Jackson (1865), Vol. III, pp. 295 ff.
[40]The many references to St. Mewan in the Journal can be associated with the extensive Polgooth mine.

the Church was inexpedient, but they differed over the doctrine of
Predestination; whilst Wesley refused to bind himself to certain
forms of the Prayer Book which he deemed contrary to Scripture,
referred to many of the laws of the Church as "the dregs of Popery"
in especial the anti-Christian penalty of excommunication, and
believed that the more emphasis the Church placed on order and
laws and not on worship and doctrines, the stronger would be the
case for secession.[41] Both men were sincere, but whereas Walker
could contentedly confine himself to the care of souls in Truro and
with regular meetings of a "holy club" together with monthly
meetings of like-thinking clergymen, Wesley could not; travelling
had been second nature to him; itinerism was a fever in his very
soul; maybe, too, he was not altogether lacking in personal vanity,
and desired to continue to rule the organisation he and his helpers
had built up in face of the opposition of the Church. Above all,
he was reluctant to entrust the brands he had plucked from the
burning to the all too numerous ministers who had no real calling
from God. Walker and Vowler, Bennet and Thompson were rare
exceptions, and even Thompson had by now slipped into Moravian
quietism.[42] Wesley did not forgive the slanders of the Vicar of
Breage, and though later he was somewhat reconciled to Lavington
he still, at the time of these proposals by Walker, remembered the
slander-mongering visitation that prelate had made of the western
part of his diocese a short time before.[43] A little later Wesley wrote
to Walker expressing the belief that if he withdrew the itinerant
preachers the Methodist Societies would secede from the Church
before long.[44]

Wesley agreed with Walker that separation was inexpedient at

[41] J. Wesley, *Letters* (ed. Telford) Vol. III, pp. 145-155, 192-196, and 221-225. Edwin
Sidney: "The Life . . . of the Rev. Samuel Walker (1855) pp. 195-197, 281 ff. etc. J. C.
Ryle. *"The Christian Leaders of the Last Century"* (1869) pp. 318 ff. *Arminian Magazine*—1779,
pp. 368, 641-644
[42] *Evangelical Magazine:* Vol. VIII(1800), pp. 318-319.
[43] J. Wesley: *Journal:* Vol. III, p. 492 (August 25, 1750). The particular story Lavington
propogated seems to have been that Wesley had defrauded Mrs. Morgan with whom he
had lodged at Mitchell; in the telling doubtless swindling was metamorphosed into seduction
by rumour. Wesley himself believed that the woman herself had started the tales from sheer
malice or sensation- seeking.
[44] J. Wesley: *Letters*: Vol. III, p. 222. This letter dated September 19, 1757 refers to a
schism in the Falmouth society that is not mentioned in the Journal; Wesley himself hinted
that this was proof of what would occur if the itinerant preachers were withdrawn; he himself
was still an ordained clergyman and in the light of what later transpired after his death, the
implied claim that he and his itinerant preachers were alone keeping the Societies within the
Church is justified.

the time and still claimed to be an ordained minister of the Church of England, yet Walker had put considerable stress on the points on which Wesley differed from that Church; not all the Prayer Book was acceptable to him; he did not believe in excommunication though he and his followers later excluded many errant members; he wanted to shift the whole emphasis of the Church from orders and laws to worship and doctrines. To an unknown correspondent in a letter from Truro written in September 1757 he stressed still further differences between the Methodists and the Anglicans. For the past three weeks he had been labouring in Cornwall and it was with the practices of Cornish Methodism fresh and clear in his mind that he wrote:-

"The longer I am absent from London, and the more I attend the service of the Church in other places, the more I am convinced of the unspeakable advantage which the people called Methodists enjoy: I mean even with regard to public worship, particularly on the Lord's Day. The church when they assemble is not gay or splendid, which might be a hindrance on the one hand; nor sordid or dirty, which might give distaste on the other; but plain as well as clean. The persons who assemble there are not a gay, giddy crowd, who come chiefly to see and be seen; nor a company of goodly, formal outside Christians, whose religion lies in a dull round of duties; but a people most of whom do, and the rest correctly seek to, worship God in spirit and in truth. Accordingly they do not spend their time there in bowing and curtsying, or in staring about them, but in looking upward and looking inward, in harkening to the voice of God, and pouring out their hearts before him.

"It is also no small advantage that the person who reads prayers, though not always the same, yet is always one who may be supposed to speak from his heart, one whose life is no reproach to his profession, and one who performs that solemn part of divine service, not in a careless, hurrying, slovenly manner, but seriously and slowly, as becomes him who is transacting so high an affair between God and man.

"Nor are their solemn addresses to God interrupted by the formal drawl of a parish clerk, the screaming of boys who howl out what they neither feel nor understand, or the unseasonable and unmeaning impertinence of a voluntary on the organ. When it is seasonable to sing praise to God, they do it with the spirit and with the understanding also, not in the miserable, scandalous doggerel of Hopkins and Sternhold, but in psalms and hymns which are both sense and poetry, such as would sooner provoke a critic to turn Christian than a Christian to turn critic . . . (sung) not by a handful of wild, unawakened striplings, but by a whole serious congregation, and those not lolling at ease, or in the indecent position of sitting, drawling out one word after another, but all standing before God and praising Him and with a good courage."[45]

Wesley concluded this letter defending Methodist worship by asserting the genuineness of the Methodist preachers and the religious graces of those Methodists who were admitted to the celebration of the Lord's Supper, stressing that they were real Christians and not mere outward conformists to formalities they did not either understand or appreciate. There was no attempt to deny their religious enthusiasm; that it offended against worldly canons of seemliness was ignored.

This letter might be regarded as Wesley's most happy answer to the allegations of Lavington and other detractors. Perhaps he had ignored the specific charges critics of Methodism had levied against individuals, but his implied and implicit denunciation of the dead formalism that so many of the clergy of the day regarded as the practice of religion was now more effective than a retaliatory catalogue of miscreant Anglican clergymen would have been. Above all he stressed the communal aspect of Methodist worship; the preacher led the congregation, set an example to them, but yet was one of them; if he was more swayed by emotions than by reason so were the majority of men—In that is the key to the ultimate triumph of deviating forms of Methodism at the expense not only of the older Anglican Church, before it was changed first by Evangelicism and later by Tractarianism, but also at the expense of the hierarchy of Conference that attempted to impose its will on Methodism.

These developments, the final secession from the Church of England, and the long-enduring schisms in Methodism itself, lay, however, far in the future. While Wesley lived he was able not only by sheer force of personality to preserve a considerable degree of unity among his followers and adherents, but also to stave off the final break with the Established Church, aided, perhaps, in this last, by the fears of the Anglicans that the religious disorders of the previous century might recur if they drove the "Enthusiasts" to secession. For the next quarter of a century, therefore, the work of Wesley and his followers went on partly within, partly without the framework of the Anglican Church. The tendency towards separation, however, was accelerated through the gradual superimposition of more and more elaborate doctrine and dogma upon Methodist

[45]J. Wesley: *Letters*, Vol. III, p. 226-228.

preaching, and still more by the split among the Evangelists themselves between Arminians and Predestinarians although both these parties agreed that the first consideration was the conversion of the masses to a more active religious way of life.

In the 1760's and 1770's John Wesley conducted twelve more revivalist missions in Cornwall; sometimes there was a three year gap between his visits; sometimes he came two years in succession; the general picture left by his Journal is one of progress, perhaps slow, but uninterrupted. In 1767 when the minutes of Conference first began recording the numbers of Society members there were 558 in East Cornwall, served by three ministers and 1608 in West Cornwall served by four; the total numbers in the British Isles were 25,911 so that Cornwall contained approximately 8.3% of all Wesley's British followers; Cornish membership then rose to a temporary peak of 2,497 in 1771 only to fall by a fifth to 1994 in 1773, rallying to a level of about 2,150 which was maintained until 1781, a figure which towards the close of the period represented barely a twentieth of the total numbers of British Methodists. In some places zeal flagged; in others members quarrelled among themselves.[46] No considerable part of the real decline in Methodism in these years can be attributed to the anomalous position caused by Wesley's continued adherence to the Church of England.[47] There were still a few scoffers and one or two ready to create a disturbance, and even as late as 1765 the parson of Redruth appeared at one of Wesley's open-air meetings in his parish and proceeded to read the Riot Act to which no heed was paid except that Wesley hurried his discourse to a close to enable the congregation to disperse within the hour;[48] incidents of this nature, however, were becoming very rare, and quite a number of wealthy gentry were now attending Wesley's services in Cornwall through sincerely religious motives, though some, doubtless, came out of sheer idle curiosity.

An impetus towards secession from the Established Church, however, came from an unexpected quarter. After the death of Samuel Walker in 1762, the religious society he had formed in Truro broke away from St. Mary's Church and within a few years

[46]J. Wesley: *Journal*, Vol. IV, p. 406—entries of September 3 and September 5, 1760 referring to the Launceston and Camelford Societies.

[47]Out of the 98 members of the St. Agnes Society in 1760 all but 4 or 5 had given up attendance at the Eucharist. (*ibid.* iv, p. 407).

[48]*ibid.* Vol. V, p. 147.

set up a Congregational Church in Truro—an ironic commentary on the work of the man who had tried to get Wesley to merge his followers into the Anglican Church and a foreboding of what would come when Wesley's own labours ceased.[49] Moreover the followers of Walker were now denouncing the Methodists as heretics on account of their Arminian views, and there was a real danger that if the evangelicanism of Anglican clergy persisted along the Presbyterian lines to which it had hitherto been confined the Methodists would be driven out despite themselves. In addition to this, the older dissenting creeds had made some progress in this period at the expense of the Anglicans and, to some extent, at the expense of the Methodists.

The Baptist movement in Cornwall, indeed, is even more clearly linked with the economic transformation than the Methodist, for it was the engineer Jonathan Hornblower the Elder who took a prominent part in fostering the establishment of the first Society at Chacewater where he had settled in 1761. With the assistance of William Pollard, a member of the Anglican Calvinistic society formed by the succession of curates at St. Agnes that had been more or less intimately connected with Walker, this engineer started weekly "Conversation Meetings" where they opened proceedings with prayer, sang a hymn, then discussed religious subjects, before concluding with another hymn and a final prayer. It was only a small group of about six members at first, but in 1767 (a year when John Wesley did not visit Cornwall) the Plymouth Baptist minister Heath preached at one of their meetings. It seems that this meeting attracted a considerable congregation for sometime later Heath:-

"made them a second visit; but having no convenient Place for any considerable number to attend, Mr. Wesley's People were asked on that occasion for the use of their House; which with difficulty was granted, though not without first stipulating that nothing should be delivered contrary to Mr. Wesley's Principles, and though Mr. Heath endeavoured carefully to avoid everything of that nature yet he was given to understand that such another Request would not be granted. It was then proposed to erect a House convenient to hold such who were disposed to attend, when such occasional opportunities afford."[50].

[49]*ibid.* Vol. V, p. 185.
[50]*M. S. S. Materials for the Second Part of the State of the Dissenting Interest in England and Wales."*—c. 1772-3. (M. S. S. in possession of Dr. A. L. Rowse).

The first Baptist meeting house was then built at St. Day in 1768, but in 1770 there was some disagreement with the two or three surviving members of an older dissenting society at Penryn over the appointment of a regular minister which led to the secession of the Penryn and Falmouth members from the original Chacewater group in 1772.

If these Baptists were comparatively few in numbers yet they were zealous to make converts and it is clear that almost from the beginning they were antagonistic to the Methodists; adult baptism, particularly by total immersion was something new and strange, and these people made no pretence of being members of the Established Church. Yet in the years that followed they made little progress; the main challenge to Wesleyan Methodism came from the revival of Congregationalism, patronized by the Countess of Huntingdon who paid a visit to Cornwall in 1775, probably at the invitation of Thomas Wills, the curate of St. Agnes who had married her niece and who, a few years later, became one of her itinerant chaplains. Meeting places financed by the Countess and her associates were erected in several places in Cornwall and, though she, like Wesley, regarded herself as a member of the Established Church, the tendency towards separation was accelerated especially as these meeting places were licensed like those of the Methodists as houses for dissenting worship to comply with the letter of the law as laid down in the Act of Uniformity. Conformity was not strengthened by the careers of several of the Evangelical preachers; when Wills left his curacy at St. Agnes in 1778 to become a chaplain to Lady Huntingdon he sold his family plate to provide the funds to erect a meeting place in that parish since he had little faith that his successor there would carry on his zealous labours; nine years before that Walker's Truro society, after his death, had built their own meeting house on the site of the former cock-pit; and, a little later, that strange character Sir Henry Trelawney had built a meeting house at West Looe, where he conducted services for his own tenantry and the fisherfolk before religious speculation led him to declare himself a "rational dissenter" with pronounced anti-Trinitarian views, for he closed this chapel and rented it to a maltster with a clause in the lease forever prohibiting its future use as a religious meeting house.[51]

Sir Henry's religious vagaries, that were eventually to bring him

[51] *Life and Times of the Countess of Huntingdon*, Vol. II, pp. 419-421.

to the Church of Rome, may have discredited the Evangelical movement and certainly incurred the unforgiving and uncharitable anger of the sects he successively patronized and abandoned, but his career in many ways was typical of the confusion into which religion had fallen in the last quarter of the eighteenth century with the failure of Wesley and Walker alike to achieve the renaissance of the Anglican Church, a failure that is best shown by the "religious census" of 1779. In that year Bishop Ross of Exeter sent out a questionnaire to the incumbents in his diocese, and the returns from Cornwall suggest that, at the very most, only one in twenty ever participated in the sacraments—and probably a considerable proportion of these were Methodists—and that in all likelihood more than three-quarters of the population never entered within the portals of their parish church, save for the purposes of being baptized, married, or buried.[52] Nor do the activities of the itinerant preachers, whether supported or opposed by the beneficed clergy, seem to have done anything to check a decline in church-going, for in a group of fifteen parishes in Eastern Cornwall, several of which Wesley and his followers must have visited now and again, the proportion of the population taking part in Communion services in 1779 was little more than half what it had been in 1745.[53] It was little wonder, indeed, even after John Wesley and his followers had been labouring in Cornwall for a full generation, that Lady Huntingdon could write of "thousands and tens of thousands of poor perishing creatures whom all seem to neglect"; her efforts stirred the Methodist preachers to even greater activity and by the end of Wesley's long life the numbers of society members

---

[52]In 113 parishes in which a return was made of the estimated number of communicants that number was only from 4354 to 4802 communicants and the population of those parishes was between 92,328 and 92,558 souls, giving the maximum percentage as less than 5.2. This represents rather more than 62 per cent of the total population of Cornwall and may be taken as a reasonably fair indication of the whole; it may be assumed, therefore, that the total number of communicating members of the Anglican Church cannot have exceeded 7750 or at most 8000. The number of Methodist society members in that year was 2130. In the parishes of the great mining district (See Note 8 above) the total number of communicants, excluding Camborne for which no return of communicants were made and the parish of Wendron for which the return of "2000" families made by the resident vicar, the Rev. Jacob Bullock, seems abnormally high, the total number of communicants was 708 to 805 out of a total estimated population of 18,700 or at most 4.3 per cent. In the tin-mining and fishing area along the northern shore of West Penwith which might well be termed the birth place of Cornish Methodism the five parishes of St. Ives, Towednack, Zennor, Morva, and St. Just in Penwith had 350 communicants out of a population of 6,400 or rather less than 5.5 per cent. (Return of 1779—*Henderson M. S. S.*).

[53]Ref. Appx. p. 67.40 below.

in Cornwall rose to over four thousand, or nearly double what they had been about ten years before.

The last decade of Wesley's life is characterized by concerted efforts of religious reformers, irrespective of theological disagreements, that, within a short time, were to lead to bitter sectarian quarrels and schisms. Wesley's last six visits to Cornwall were characterized by attentive and large congregations; if, for the time, the Methodists had been driven out of Launceston, further to the west there was no effort made to check them or their leader, although in August, 1789, Wesley could not reach the Truro meeting-house since the street was thronged by miners who had invaded the town not to listen to Wesley but to "beg or demand an increase of their wages, without which they could not live."[54] Thousands were congregating to the Gwennap Pit meetings and in most places, when Wesley came, meeting-houses were so packed that open-air preaching had to be resorted to no matter what the weather. New and larger meeting-houses were being erected in several places and it was in these that Wesley now preached and no longer in parish churches, though some clergymen were friendly enough, notably Richard Miles of Kenwyn who entertained Wesley during his visit in September 1787.[55] It was only a question of time before Methodism finally seceded from the Anglican Church, and this increasing number of meeting places brought problems of finance, administration, and organization that were to be the cause of great trouble once Wesley's hand was removed. The people felt that the houses, built largely by their money, and, in some cases, by their own hands, belonged to them; Wesley they respected, revered, loved and obeyed, but in time to come they would not submit to the claims of a conference of preachers whose members were seldom in one district longer than two years to control their communal proprietary claim to the place where they met to worship. They were willing to follow the founder of Methodism; but their individualism had been fired by the preaching of justification and salvation by faith; but it was sooner or later to come to the realization of the equality of the saved in the sight of God and man; the ministers from wisdom and experience might claim to supervise and advise, but if they claimed ruling control resentment might easily and did lead to schism.

[54]J. Wesley: *Journal.* Vol. VII, p. 328 (August 18, 1789)
[55]*ibid.* Vol. VII, p. 326.

Passion and emotion had been the driving power behind early
Methodism and behind the antagonism to it. Long before the
end of Wesley's life, however, the controversy had been shifted
to theological grounds with Arminianism and Predestinarianism
grappling in a conflict complicated by a host of deviationist
"heresies" that by the majority of people were regarded as hard
names. To the labouring miners, fisherfolk, and farmers, many of
whom could barely read or write, controversies about the Trinity,
about baptism, about the Sonship of Christ meant little even if they
were the breath of life to college-trained preachers; the only popular
power behind the religious revival was the psychological craving
for assurance of a blissful immortality; any preacher with a message
of salvation was welcome, but they had not the knowledge to
appreciate the subtle distinctions that harassed men like Sir Harry
Trelawney, drove George Thompson and Thomas Wills from the
Anglican Church, the former to Moravianism the latter to that new
form of Calvinistic Congregationalism that resulted from the zeal
and wealth of the Countess of Huntingdon. Unable to discredit
"enthusiasm" the Church of England fell back to theological
weapons in its efforts to discredit Wesley; the Methodists resorted
to similar means; but it may be doubted if the common people
tortured their minds or souls overmuch with arid academic
arguments that might well be in keeping with the rationalist spirit
of the age but seemed to have little connection with the basic
common-sense apprehension that to each man the ultimate concern
is his personal destiny.

Thus it was that when the former curate of St. Agnes, Thomas
Wills, returned to Cornwall as one of the itinerant preachers of the
Countess of Huntingdon he received but an indifferent welcome
from beneficed clergymen in Bodmin, St. Columb, Falmouth and
Buryan, but the whole-hearted support of the Methodists, although
Wills himself was convinced that the doctrines he taught "of the
total apostasy and helplessness of men by nature, and the only way
of justification by the righteousness of God our Saviour"[56] differed
fundamentally from those of the Wesleyans and could only ascribe
his welcome to the fact that he was a Cornishman and that the
Methodists were probably "glad to see an ordained clergyman on
the itinerant plan".[57] Nor did Wills realize that when he came

---

[56]"*Memoirs of the Life of the Rev. Thomas Wills* (1804). p. 52.
[57]*ibid.*, p. 53.

back at special request to preach to Sir Harry Trelawney's deserted congregation at Looe and enlarged on the "awful apostasy of ministers" that religious societies could and did survive without the supervising care of ordained clergymen. After a five week mission Wills left Cornwall at the beginning of August 1781; Wesley came down for eight days at the end of the month and visited some of the same places, receiving much the same warm welcome and preaching to similarly thronged congregations; in one place only did their experience differ; Wills summarily dismissed Camborne as "a very careless and drunken parish" but Wesley after preaching there believed that "the hearts of all the people were bowed down before the Lord" and at nearby Redruth stressed the Arminian doctrine of the text "Ye are saved through faith" that was probably more welcome than the Calvinistic texts of Wills.[58] Wesley drew vaster audiences than did the Cornishman who was looked upon by his congregations as one of many who felt themselves called to conduct revivalistic missions, some of the latter were Cornish born, but Wills differed from them, as he himself realized, by being an ordained clergyman.

Yet it may be this connection with the Established Church, this effort of aristocracy and wealth to stir the dry bones of that Calvinistic theology that had never, even in its literally militant phase, seized much control of the religious life of Cornwall, accounts for the failure of the alliance of the still declining Anglican Church and Lady Huntingdon to check the people of the South Western county on the course towards dissent and separation into which the Wesleys had been driven. The quarrel of Wills with the rather imperious Countess in 1788 did not help the latter's Connexion in Cornwall. In his lifetime Wills stood alone but, whilst the people of Mithian and St. Agnes had a ready welcome to give their former curate, elsewhere in the county he was regarded as another itinerant, and his gloomy convictions of human depravity, wrongheadedness, and sin found little response in an era of social and economic advance save, possibly, in bad years and even in those the consciousness of the riches of the county made its people

---

[58] *ibid*, p. 53. J. Wesley: *Journal*, Vol. VI, p. 334. It might be noted too that whereas Wills estimated the congregation he had at Gwennap Pit on Sunday, July 1st at 10,000, Wesley on Sunday, September 2, reckoned his audience then to number between 22,000 and 33,000; both men preached at 5 o'clock in the afternoon, a time that would not clash with Church services.

look rather to a faith in a future that they could achieve, partly at least, by their own efforts.

It is in economic forces rapidly advancing towards domination, not only in the tin but also in the copper mining industries, and not in any alleged mystical appeals to a Celtic temperament, that the reason for the eventual triumph of Cornish Methodist dissent is to be found. All that can with any justice be ascribed to Celticism is the reassertion by some of the later Bible Christians and Wesleyan Reformers of clan egalitarianism in the chapels that ignored the Established Church and Methodist Conference alike, and the singing of hymns composed by Charles Wesley and others. Behind that freedom and independence of the Cornish "Methody" chapels stands the worldly living tradition of the free mining partnership— indeed not a few chapels were created on a cost-book system of financial management.

All this, however, was not to be revealed until the age following Wesley. In his long life-time he had become a myth, yet, even though he paid no fewer than thirty-one visits to Cornwall in the last forty-eight years of his life, intermittent revivalism would hardly have succeeded in keeping the movement alive but for numbers of unknown people who quietly and regularly attended society meetings, but for exhorters and lay preachers who attended to the congregation when no regular minister was available, and but for the zeal of lesser ministers. Among the last may be named Peter Jaco of Newlyn, like another Peter a fisherman, who was converted by the "plain, honest tinner" Stephen Nichols at the age of seventeen and became a regular itinerant preacher seven years later in 1754;[59] the Sancreed miner Richard Rodda (1743–1815); John Murlin (1722–99) who came of farming stock in the parish of St. Stephen in Brannell.[60] Jaco, Rodda, and Murlin were among those who lived at the same time as Wesley, whilst later Cornish Methodist ministers were to include Richard Treffry Senior, and Theophilus Lessey who became Presidents of the Methodist Conference. They form no unimpressive group in the annals of Methodism but just as the earlier men were overshadowed by Wesley himself, the later were to be dwarfed by the Luxulyan man, William O'Bryan, who was to be driven out by the ministers and

[59]Jaco died at the age of 52 in 1781—*Methodist Biography*—ed. Thomas Jackson (1865), Vol. I, pp. 260-267.
[60]*ibid*, Vol. II, pp. 295 ff and Vol. III, pp. 293, ff.

to start the new sect of Bible Christians, all the while loudly accusing the Orthodox Methodists of the same formal deadness which in their early days had been the main feature of their own denunciations of the Church of England.

Even in the closing years of Wesley's life some of the Cornish Methodist societies had been more than a little insubordinate. The tendency of the Cornish to welcome any itinerant preachers, so evident during the visit of Thomas Wills, in 1785 led Wesley to take the trouble to send a letter from Lisburn in Ireland to Francis Wrigley who was then stationed in St. Austell, telling him that "you cannot suffer anyone to preach either in St. Austell or elsewhere that is tainted with Calvinism or Antinomianism. 'Tis far easier to prevent the plague than to cure it."[61] All he had said or written in sermon or tract failed to check the activities of the smugglers and he told Pitt that he believed that half a million of revenue was lost every year through it in Cornwall alone.[62] He did not scruple to use his influence in Cornwall to try to secure votes for the Government in the 1790 election, but whether his advice was heeded or not it is impossible to say, for a little later he wrote to John Mason, a minister at St. Austell:-

"As long as I live people shall have no share in choosing either stewards or leaders among the Methodists. We have not and never had any such custom. We are no republicans and never intend to be. It would be better for those who are so minded to go quietly away. I have been uniform both in doctrine and in discipline for above these fifty years; and it is a little too late for me to turn into a new path now I am grey-headed . . .'[64].

Only affection for their aged founder kept the Cornish Methodists—or the majority of them—in line and under control; in his last years a new generation of itinerant preachers, many trained in the Kingswood seminary, had risen to prominence, men who were rather too eager to assume the responsibilities of ecclesiastical organization at the expense of evangelical preaching. Mason had apparently run into trouble in the St. Austell district which included Gunwen, home of William O'Bryan, who was then

[61]J. Wesley: *Letters*, Vol. VII, p. 273.

[62]*ibid.* Vol, VII, p. 235.

[63]J. Wesley: *Letters*, Vol. VIII, p. 173—Letter to John Mason of St. Austell of October 1, 1789—"If, as I am informed, Mr. Gregor is a lover of King George and the present Administration, I wish you would advise all our breathren who have votes to assist him in the ensuing election."

[64]*ibid.* Vol. VIII, p. 196. Wesley to John Mason: January 13, 1790.

a twelve-year old boy, and hardly likely yet to have caused any serious heart-burnings among the sober fathers of Methodism. A little later John Valtan ran into trouble in St. Ives—the Mecca of Cornish Methodism, and Wesley rather sadly wrote to him: "You do not know the Cornish yet. Many of them have little sense and a great inclination to criticize."

In the past Wesley had restored unity to many of the Cornish societies that had been shattered by personal bickerings and quarrels. Perhaps it was in the hope of doing so again that, early in 1791, he was planning another tour of the Western County. But it was not to be; long before summer came Wesley was in his grave; his work was done. The ministers in conference thought that his mantle had fallen on them; the congregations of Western Cornwall had rather different ideas. For the past years he had been checking progress, shrinking back from separation, reluctant to loosen his grip on the spiritual kingdom he had raised up in this world. Instead of a triumphal religious progress of John Wesley the summer of 1791 saw the Methodist laity of Redruth demanding that they chose their own class leaders and stewards by election, and that they and not the ministers should decide who was to be admitted to their societies, besides claiming power to bring about the removal and even the dismissal of preachers. It might almost be said that the first Jacobins in Cornwall were the Methodists of Redruth; but they had already clashed with the minister Benjamin Rhodes in 1788 who, backed by Wesley, dismissed certain of the stewards and restored the "good old Methodist discipline."[65] It can be said that with the death of Wesley the era of religious change gave way to the era of religious revolution; even the sober, conservative Minutes of Conference record the fact that in the years when Wesley's own physical powers were failing, Cornish Methodists had doubled their numbers; in the following ten years they were to more than double again.[66] It cannot be denied, however, that these "revolutionary years" like the 1740's which had seen the turbulent beginnings of Methodism in Cornwall were years of economic depression that drove the poor and needy labouring classes to look for leaders with messages of consolation

---

[65] J. Wesley: Letter, Vol. III, pp. 102, 109 and 133.

[66] In 1780 there were 2071 Society members in Cornwall; in 1791 there were 4192; the revival of 1799 sent numbers up to 10,729, although there was to be a recession to 6148 in 1804 after which there was a gradual recovery to the 1799 level by 1813.

and salvation; it was fortunate for the tranquility of the realm that they found those leaders associated with the Methodist movement and not in "radical" political societies; had they not done so it is just possible that at the cost of riot and bloodshed they might have effected an improvement in the general standards of material welfare. The immaterial consolation so many of them drew from Methodism was something very real to them, however, in their little meeting-houses and chapels, these common men gained self-assurance and qualities of character that enabled them the better to seize and turn to account any opportunity that the material day-to-day world in which they lived offered them. Methodism, marred here and there by hypocrisy and superstition, was nursing and rearing a more democratic society that, once it became conscious of its own strength and worth, was able to challenge Wesley himself and the ministerial oligarchy of Conference that succeeded him.

Appendix

The Decline in the Number of Communicants of the Anglican Church in Proportion to Population as revealed by the returns of the Clergy to Bishop Clagett in 1745 and to Bishop Ross in 1779 from Sixteen Parishes in Eastern Cornwall.

	1745		1779	
Parish	*Estimated Population*	*Number of Comms.*	*Estimated Population*	*Number of Comms.*
Anthony	290	40 to 60	610	50
St. Austell	1,350	100	3,150	80
St. Blazey	135	30	360	30
Botusfleming	105	20 to 30	165	12
St. Cleer	765	50 to 80	735	24
St. Dominic	225	60	270	40
Duloe	485	20	585	30–40
Egloshayle	675	80	585	90
Forrabury	50	7 to 15	110	20
Fowey	520	30 to 80	900	70–80
Lawhitton	225	30 to 50	243	20–40
Menheniot	730	50 to 80	745	35
St. Neot	585	30 to 100	700	20–30
St. Pinnock	180	25	200	20
Sheviock	240	24 to 38	210	20
St. Stephens by Saltash	1,350	120 to 200	1,375	40
	7,910	716 to 1048	10,943	591–641

(Based on *Henderson MSS.*)

CHAPTER III

THE YEARS OF CONFLICT:

1775-1800

CHAPTER III

THE YEARS OF CONFLICT:

1775-1800

THE LAST quarter of the eighteenth century was, for the
Cornish copper mining interests, a period of conflict and of
stress. The old antipathy towards the 'foreign' adventurer
suspected, often wrongly, of exorbitantly profiting at the
expense of Cornish people, persisted; their own local rivalries
intensified. In bad times the smelting interests of South Wales,
Bristol, and Birmingham, themselves often bitter competitors,
were denounced as profiteers by mines adventurers who, bearing all the risks of financing the mining of copper, thought they
saw ruin staring them in the face. Cornish engineers came
into collision with James Watt and Matthew Boulton of Soho,
over the monopolistic patent rights which, originally secured
in 1769, were prolonged by a subsequent Act of Parliament
from seven to thirty-one years. Cornish mines adventurers had
to face the cut-throat competition of Thomas Williams of
Anglesey, nor could they agree amongst themselves whether
to restrict production in the hope of maintaining prices or to
flood the markets with copper ores in the hope of driving the
Welsh mines to ruin first. The situation was aggravated by the
rivalry of certain individual Cornish adventurers and landowners who derived profits and dues from copper mining, and,
in especial, the feud of Francis Basset of Tehidy and the Boscawen family. At times further complications were caused by
the unemployment of labouring miners when certain mines
closed down, either from an effort to restrict production, or
from financial necessity, or even, in some cases, from the
natural exhaustion of the deposits of ores. If the working of
mines on the tribute system tended to preclude industrial combination on account of unemployment, increasingly frequent
periods of grain shortage could, and on occasions did, unite
hungry and riotous mobs.

The depression which affected the Cornish copper mines in
1772 can be attributed chiefly to over-production of copper

ores, itself partly the result of a recent speculative boom. During the Seven Years War production had been comparatively steady, averaging 16,220 tons of copper ore annually from 1756 to 1762; it had never exceeded that figure by more than five per cent and had only in one year, 1758, fallen more than seven and a half per cent below it.[1] In the next seven years, however, the average yearly output was 20,890 tons, or nearly thirty per cent above the level of the war years, despite the greatly diminished demand for military and naval purposes. In 1770 the sales of copper ores in Cornwall reached 30,776 tons, whilst annual sales from 1770 to 1776 averaged 29,100 tons, or an increase of nearly forty per cent above the level of the preceding seven year period and one of nearly eighty per cent above the level of the war years.[2] The result of this over-production and of the general economic recession was indicated by the fall in the price of copper ores sold in Cornwall. In 1772 the price had been £6 15s. 6d.; in 1774 it was only £5 7s. per ton, a drop of more than twenty per cent, and one of nearly thirty per cent from the price that had varied but a little from £7 7s., and which had come to be regarded as almost customary during the twenty years from 1746 to 1765.[3]

Speculation had even graver consequences than a temporary economic recession; it had led to the reckless exploitation and sometimes to the exhaustion of the more accessible and richer deposits of ores. The fall in prices after 1772 in part reflected the pouring into the market of progressively deteriorating qualities of ores; greater and greater quantities of ores had to be raised to maintain the ultimate produce of fine copper. The system by which the dues of leasing landowners were paid by a proportion of the produce had a similar tendency and result. Had the costs of labour and of materials used in mining

[1]Pryce, p. xv; Hunt, p. 891. The year 1758, of course, was the year in which Britain's political fortunes reached their lowest ebb.

[2]Pryce, p. xv; Hunt, p. 892. Hunt's statistics are taken from Pryce until 1771; they then vary slightly for the next four years, but the total discrepancy amounts only to the addition of 347 tons by Hunt, *i.e.* less than ·3%.

[3] Regular records of copper prices only survive from 1772 and are given by Hunt (p. 892); Pryce had consolidated his statistics of prices into decennial periods from 1726 to 1775 (p. xv). The later statistics are further complicated by the adoption of a *Standard* which was related to the final production of fine copper, not to the actual production of ores whose *produce* varied considerably—not only from mine to mine but for different *parcels* of ores obtained from the same mines. The highest average produce recorded of the Cornish copper mines was 10% in 1808; it may have been higher in earlier times; by the 1860s it rarely exceeded 7½%, and in some years only 6½%.

remained the same—and there is reason to believe that they also rose during the speculative period—no mine adventurer could ignore the fact that it cost as much to raise ten tons of ores yielding but fifteen hundredweights of copper as to raise ten tons which yielded a full ton or more of fine copper. The mines adventurers, therefore, began to look around for opportunities of economies.

Since it was the largest single item in all accounts of mining costs, there is little doubt that they first considered the possibilities of reducing the labour bills, but found little scope for economy in that direction. Unskilled day-labour, mainly that of women and juveniles, would have suffered had it not been that the demand for such labour grew in proportion to the progressively declining produce of the ores; where ten persons previously would have, in a given time, broken up the quantity of ores to produce a ton of copper, it now required the labour of twelve or fifteen. It is possible, however, that female and juvenile labour replaced adult male labour wherever practicable. The skilled underground tribute workers were in a strong position for they made their monthly, bi-monthly, or quarterly contracts on the basis of a proportionate share of the ores they raised; although they lost when prices fell rapidly, yet when they came to make new contracts with the adventurers they demanded more in proportion to their pre-judged opinion of the qualities of the lodes they undertook to work. Moreover, with the necessity of raising greater quantities of ores, tribute-labour was scarce rather than abundant; it was not a question of unemployed labourers competing against each other for work so much as one of rival groups of mines adventurers competing for their services. Only when the poorer mines closed down and when adventurers combined to restrict production, did unemployment appear and wages fall. Meanwhile labour costs could only be reduced by adopting mechanical labour-saving devices wherever and whenever practicable; already many mines had installed 'fire-engines' in place of 'rag and chain' hand-pumps, whilst many adventurers had experimented with stamping mills, long used in preparing tin-ore, in order to reduce the amount of labour employed on the surface breaking up rocks containing copper ore.

The increasing depth of mines also directed the attention of adventurers to mechanically-operated pumps. Nearly all the copper ore raised in Cornwall before 1770 had been mined in the region between Truro and Hayle, and the deposits nearer the surface had been well-nigh exhausted.[1] There were numerous indications of vast deeper reserves, but the 'fire engines', pumping to depths of sixty or seventy fathoms were extremely expensive. Cornish engineers had developed the Newcomen engine and made it powerful enough to drain even the deepest mines of the time tolerably well, but some of the older engines were no longer adequate, and the proportionate coal bill had become even greater than it had been in 1740. Other charges of working and maintaining the mines had also risen, but it was both dangerous and difficult to attempt to reduce expenditure on timbering, explosives, ropes, candles, and other such items. Nor, at the time, did there appear to be any real hope of reducing the coal bills. It was little wonder that many mines adventurers saw no prospect of making some profits themselves save by reducing the alleged exorbitant gains of the smelters, and that they again began to talk about setting up Cornish smelting houses to deal with Cornish copper ores.[2] It seems, however, that several Cornish mines adventurers and their merchant associates were better acquainted with the balance sheets of the Hayle Copper Works than the theorists who publicised such notions, and they shrank from embarking on further ventures of this kind. Moreover, the number of mining concerns in Cornwall, along with the system of selling copper ores at ticketings without price reserves in order to meet the claims of tributers and landlords, made a combination of the 'Miners' against the smelters to get a higher price for ores sold to the latter almost impossible.

The Cornish mines might have recovered fairly quickly from the commercial slump and temporary glut of copper but for the Anglesey mines which, at that very time, made the first challenge to the Cornish domination of British copper mining. The 'open-cast' copper deposits of Parys Mountain had been discovered in 1768; the produce was inferior to that of Cornish ores, but this was over-compensated by cheapness of working,

[1]The list of 86 mines selling copper ores given in the account books of the elder Trevithick (*T.N.S.* Vol. XI, p. 39) only mentions one mine, Gunnislake, in East Cornwall; the copper mines of the St. Austell district only became prominent after 1812, and those of Caradon were not opened until 1835.
[2]*Observations on the Tin and Copper Trade*, 1772, pp. 39-40 ; Pryce pp. 242-243, 270-280.

by ready access to the sea for transport, and by proximity to the rapidly developing new industrial regions of north-western England. When Thomas Williams gained a virtually absolute managerial control over the Anglesey Mines, the Cornish mining interests were threatened with ruin, unless they could meet the challenge by finding more economical methods and by achieving greater unity among themselves than ever before. The immediate consequence of the appearance of Anglesey ores in the markets, in and after 1770, was the strengthening of the control of the 'ring' of smelters over the industry; the rivalry of Cornwall and Anglesey prevented any recovery to the higher prices for copper ores which had prevailed a few years earlier; but, in the long run, the smelters nearly brought disaster upon themselves by forcing the combination of the miners of Cornwall and Anglesey with the Birmingham manufacturing trades which had become one of the main consumers of fine copper.

The rapidly growing competition of the new Welsh mines, and the increasing depths of their own mines, together with diminishing profits and rising costs caused grave alarm among the Cornish mines adventurers before 1775. Aware of the developments in mechanical technology in other British industries, they turned their attention to the further development of steam power along lines indicated by the Hornblowers, Nancarrow, and other Cornish engineers; in 1771 they called in the aid of John Smeaton who, in a year, effected improvements which almost doubled the power of the Newcomen atmospheric engine,[1] but the costs of fuel were still so heavy that, in 1775, only eighteen of the forty engines in Cornwall were being worked.[2] A year later the Cornish miners made their first approaches to James Watt, who, in association with the manufacturer Matthew Boulton, was to dominate the mechanical side of copper mining for the next quarter of a century.

[1] Lean, pp. 5 and 7. The exact extent of Smeaton's improvements cannot be estimated since the early methods of calculating the *duty* of steam engines (*i.e.* how many pounds weight could be raised one foot by the consumption of a bushel of coal) left wide margins for error, especially since the bushel was an extremely variable measure in Cornwall ; nor was any allowance made for different qualities of coal. These conditions applied until Joel Lean's calculations of duty began in 1811, eleven years after the end of Watt's connection with Cornwall. The Leans estimated the duty performed by the Newcomen engine as 5,000,000 and that of Smeaton's most effective engine in 1772 as 9,450,000, whilst Watt's engines averaged about 20,000,000.
[2] Erich Roll: *An Early Experiment in Industrial Organization*, p. 67.

Watt had become mathematical instrument maker to Glasgow University in 1757, and six or seven years later had been asked to repair a model of a Newcomen engine there. Experimenting with this model, he was struck by the fact that:

"by far the greatest waste of heat proceeded from the waste of steam in filling the cylinder with steam. In filling the cylinder with steam, for every stroke of the common engine a great part of the steam is chilled and condensed by the coldness of the cylinder, before this last is heated enough to qualify it for being filled with elastic vapour or perfect steam; he perceived, therefore, that by preventing this waste of steam, an incomparably greater saving of heat and fuel would be obtained, than by any other contrivance. It was thus in the beginning of the year 1765, that the fortunate thought occurred to him of condensing the steam by cold in a separate vessel or apparatus, between which and the cylinder a communication was to be opened for that purpose every time the steam was to be condensed, while the cylinder itself might be preserved perfectly hot, no cold water or air being ever admitted into this cavity."[1]

Thus, by experimenting with a model engine, in the academic seclusion of a laboratory workshop in a Scottish University, Watt had discovered a way whereby it might be possible to double the efficiency, or the economy of operating, of a steam engine that was similar to or the prototype of those then being employed in Cornish mines; it was the discovery of a scientist, not one of a practical engineer.

Scientific discoveries, however, might have extremely practical uses, and Watt's friend, Dr. Joseph Black, University Lecturer in Chemistry and Medicine, put him in touch with the industrialist and colliery owner, Dr. Roebuck,[2] who had encountered similar drainage problems to those of the Cornish copper miners, and who wanted to reduce the costs of working certain unprofitable coal-mines which were eventually to lead him into bankruptcy. Roebuck was willing to support Watt's further experiments and introduced him to both Smeaton and, in 1768, to Boulton who was already interested in the possibilities of applying mechanical power to manufacturing processes, having just established the famous works at Soho for

[1] J. P. Muirhead: *The Origin and Progress of the Mechanical Inventions of James Watt,* Vol. 1. pp. xxxvi-xxxvii, quoting from the account by Dr. Joseph Black, written thirty years after the invention for evidence in the lawsuit between Watt and Hornblower in 1796-97.

[2] Roebuck had abandoned the practice of medicine to establish a manufacture of sulphuric acid, and then founded the Carron Iron Works in Stirlingshire before becoming entangled in colliery activities.

the production of metal wares. Almost at once Boulton wished
to set up a business for manufacturing engine parts, but Watt
was financially dependent on and bound to Roebuck who,
along with his friends Dr. Black and John Robinson at the
University, had helped to draw up the patent specification of
1769. Roebuck would only allow Boulton a licence to make
engines with Watt's separate condenser within the limited area
of the English Midlands thereby delaying the progress of the
practical application of the device. Watt's own activities as a
surveyor, on which he depended for his livelihood, also delayed
matters. The slump of 1772, however, numbered Roebuck
among its victims, and Watt was then able to enter into
partnership with Boulton and to devote himself entirely to the
development of steam engines.[1]

Through Boulton an Act of Parliament was secured in 1775
to extend the period of Watt's patent rights to 1800.[2] Had
the period not been extended it is likely that the Cornish mines
adventurers would have waited until the original patent
expired in 1783 before acting; some of them might have risked
copying the separate condenser with minor variations in the
structure of the machine described in the patent specification in
which the condenser was incorporated; it is rather unlikely
that they would have come to terms with Watt himself. Nevertheless in the Black Country engineering technique had
developed further and on more scientific lines than it had done
in the West.[3] In time past satisfactory and still more amazing
results had been secured by Cornish engineers who had used
sledge-hammers to refashion machine parts, or who had used
split links made by local blacksmiths for a variety of purposes.
It can, however, be doubted if, in 1775, there was a single forge
in Cornwall capable of casting the more minutely designed

[1]For Watt's early partnerships with Roebuck and with Boulton *vide* H. W.
Dickinson: *Matthew Boulton*, pp. 74-88.
[2]The Act of 1775 was piloted through the House of Commons by Heneage
Finch (Lord Guernsey), Member for Maidstone, Adam Ferguson, Member for
Ayrshire, and Lord Frederick Campbell who sat for the group of burghs which
included Glasgow. (*J.H.C.*, Vol. XXV, pp. 142, 168-9, 207, 313). The period of
the original Newcomen patent had also been extended by Act of Parliament.
[3]Before Watt's connection with Cornwall began, the Darby firm at Coalbrookdale had supplied machinery and engine parts to Poldory, Dolcoath, Wheal
Virgin, Chacewater, Rosewarne, and other Cornish mines. (*V.C.H. Shropshire*,
Vol. 1. p. 464). The same firm had cast a 74 in. cylinder as far back as 1762; it
weighed 6½ tons, the whole engine weighing over eleven tons, (*Annual Register*,
1763, p. 66) whilst as early as 1724 the Darbys had supplied an engine weighing
74 hundredweights. (*V.C.H. Shropshire*, Vol. 1, p. 462).

cylinders and other engine parts that Watt regarded as essential to the successful working of a steam engine. True, in time, the Cornish foundry workers would acquire that greater skill and precision, but, as yet, the Midland foundries enjoyed a considerable lead. But it was only a question of time before the increasing use of machinery in western copper mines would stimulate Cornish engineers and engineering to supply more and more intricate machine parts in order to eliminate the loss of time occasioned by dependence on the Midlands for spare parts whenever an engine broke down. The slow means of communication in those days, together with the difficulties of transporting heavy machines and parts of machines,[1] led to the transformation of some of the blacksmith's shops in the Cornish mining region into foundries, and before long Boulton and Watt realized that it would pay them best to get the Cornish smiths to provide all but the more intricate machine parts.

Watt's attention was first directed to the potentialities of Cornwall as a market for his machine in February, 1771, by Boulton's physician Dr. William Small, who informed him that four or five Cornish copper mines were on the point of closing down simply on account of the heavy costs of fuel necessary to keep them working. Thereby a legend was born— the legend that Watt's engines saved the Cornish copper mines from extinction. Small had got his information late in 1770, the year in which speculative overproduction had raised the

---

[1] Some indication of the transport problems of the time is given in the correspondence of Thomas Wilson, the agent of Boulton and Watt in Cornwall. On February 19, 1784, Watt wrote Wilson: "The noyles for Poldory have been delayed there six weeks by the frost on the canal and river, both which are still fast and likely to be so. . . . If the frost does not go before I get your answer, shall I send them by land? They are about 30 cwts. besides the steam case which is either at Bristol or froze up by the way." In 1785 the delivery of engine parts to North Downs Mine was delayed by the abnormally dry summer impeding navigation on the Severn. (Wilson MSS: Boulton and Watt to North Downs Adventurers, January 23, 1786). Such difficulties inevitably led the Cornish mines to seek local machine parts wherever and whenever possible. One bulky article sent by Boulton and Watt to Cornwall was a wooden beam for an engine in 1793, an indication of the deforestation of Cornwall. The bill sent to R. W. Fox and Co. (*Ibid:* J. Pearson to Wilson, January 7, 1794) read:
"To an Oak Tree for a working Beam . . . sent 10 Sept.
Last £62 4s. 8d. £62 4 8
"To Cash paid a Carpenter for time and Expenses in going to Middleton Wood, Bar Wood, Stowport, etc. to look out a tree fit for a beam £1 11 6
£63 16 2

amount of ores sold in Cornwall to 30,776 tons, and a year, too, in which rash speculation had doubtless caused attempts to work mines which, in saner days, no adventurer would touch. Not for another seven years was a machine designed by Watt to work in Cornwall, and in the intervening period the average sales of ores only fell by seven per cent from those of 1770. The legend becomes well nigh impossible to sustain when it is remembered that eighty-six mines sold copper ores as against but thirty-seven mines making sales twenty years later, although in 1797 forty-two other mines incurred costs though making no sales.[1]   All that can be justly attributed to Watt is that the saving of fuel by his separate condenser enabled Cornwall to fight back in the bitter price war with Anglesey which forced the price of copper ores down from £5 16s. per ton in 1779 to £3 13s. in 1784.[2]   The four or five mines that closed down—if they did—in 1770 or 1771 should be regarded

[1] *T.N.S.* Vol. XI, p. 39.   *Report 1799*, App. 23.
[2] A. H. Dodd: *Industrial Revolution in North Wales*, p. 158. Hunt's statistics (p. 892) are rather different; their inclusion of the amount of copper derived from the ores suggest that Hunt obtained them from smelters rather than from miners; he could not find accounts for the years 1790–93, nor did he estimate the average value of a ton of ore.

	Ores sold in Cornwall: tons.	Copper tons.	Value.	Standard.	Value of a ton of ore.		
1779	31,115	3,724	£180,906	£73	£5	16	3
1780	24,433	2,932	£171,231	£83	£7	0	1
1781	28,749	3,450	£178,789	£77	£6	4	5
1782	28,122	3,375	£152,434	£70	£5	8	5
1783	35,779	4,296	£219,937	£76	£6	3	0
1784	36,601	4,392	£209,132	£72	£5	14	4
1785	36,959	4,434	£205,451	£71	£5	10	2
1786	39,895	4,787	£237,237	£75	£5	18	1
1787	38,047		£190,738	£67	£5	0	3
1788	31,541		£150,503	£57	£4	15	5
1789	32,281		£184,308	£63	£5	10	9

This table shows that 1788 was the worst year. There is a great discrepancy between the *Standard* of 1789 compared to that of 1785. The records of finished copper cease with the great fall in price, and also with the entry of the Metal Company on the scene (see below, pp. 82 ff.). The low standard of 1788 may indicate a desperate attempt by some smelters to get rid of accumulated stocks. If Professor Dodd's figure for 1784 is correlated with the low level of 1788 it seems that the miners only obtained about 75% of the prices calculated above as average values of a ton of ore. Another discrepancy between smelters' and miners' statistics is shown by the difference between Hunt's records of the total value of copper ores sold in Cornwall from 1794 to 1798 and those produced by the miners at the Parliamentary Committee of 1799 (*Report*, 1799, Apps. 20–24).

	Hunt's Statistics.	Miners' Statistics.	Percentage discrepancy.
1794	£320,875	£293,654	8.5
1795	£326,186	£305,820	8.4
1796	£356,654	£348,837	2.2
1797	£377,838	£320,607	15.2
1798	£422,633	£405,489	4

as the victims of rash speculation during the boom, as transient concerns hastily organized and nearly as hastily abandoned when the bills began pouring in even more rapidly than their projectors' visions of rich lodes faded.

Watt probably did not forget Small's suggestion, but for the next few years he was still experimenting with his engine, carrying on his work as a surveyor, worrying about Roebuck's bankruptcy, and then entering into partnership with Boulton when Roebuck gave up his share of the patent of 1769. There followed the preparations to persuade Parliament to extend the period of the patent; in Committee the proposed bill led to a violent attack by Burke on monopolies, and the claims of William Blakey to prior invention had to be disproved.[1] Although the Bill was finally passed without a division, it had been considerably amended, whilst a proposal to insert a clause permitting any person to use and erect the engine after Watt's patent expired only after paying compensation to him was rejected. Burke's opposition may have had some connection with the Bristol copper smelters among his constituents; there is no record of opposition or support from the host of Cornish borough members. The most active part in the preparation of the Bill was taken by certain Scottish and Midland members; Sir Adam Ferguson, Lord Frederick Campbell, one of the Dundas family[2] the Staffordshire member, Sir William Bagott, and the Lichfield representative, Thomas Gillert all took part in the committee proceedings.[3] Whilst the Bill was under consideration, Boulton was approached by a certain Mr. Glover[4] on behalf of some Cornish mining interests, but it was not until November, 1776, that he could write of obtaining a positive order from Ting Tang Mine.[5] That order, however, had not come until some months after a deputation of Cornish mines adventurers had visited Soho,[6] and after Boulton and Watt had offered to erect an engine in Cornwall

[1]*J.H.C.* Vol. XXV, p. 206.
[2]Probably Henry Dundas who had just begun his political career as member for Edinburghshire, although there were four other members of the Dundas family in this Parliament, three of them sitting for Scottish constituencies and the fourth for Richmond.
[3]Muirhead, Vol. 11, letter No. 146, Boulton to Watt, April 24, 1775.
[4]Possibly Richard Glover, Member for Penryn along with Sir Francis Basset in 1790.
[5]Muirhead : Vol. 11, letter No. 161, Boulton to Watt, November 31 (*sic*), 1776.
[6]"Less for the purpose of negotiating the purchase of a Watt engine than for that of gleaning some information about the new invention." (Erich Roll: *An Early Experiment in Industrial Organization*, p. 68).

at their own expense as an advertisement. The order actually came from the elder Jonathan Hornblower, but the Ting Tang engine, despite the efforts of the Soho firm to speed construction, and thereby all the more quickly convince the Cornish miners that Watt's engine was superior to all then existing, was not working until the summer of 1778, by which time a small 30-inch cylinder engine had already been erected and set to work at Wheal Busy near Chacewater.

To supervise the erection of these machines Watt came down into Cornwall himself in the summer of 1777, and almost immediately quarrelled with the Cornish engineers and mines adventurers. The younger Jonathan Hornblower, who perhaps thought that his father might have waited on the success of his own experiements before ordering the Ting Tang engine, declared that Watt's machine was not worth twopence-half-penny.[1] Watt's biographer wrote that he was confronted:

"not only with such obstacles as nature presented, in the dark abysses of desperately flooded mines, but also with the deeply-rooted prejudices of a rude and obstinate class of men, generally as incredulous of the power of the new machine, as they were ignorant of the causes of the imperfections of the old ones."[2]

Doubtless there was much professional jealousy, and a sour-visaged, diabetic Scot met but a poor welcome from the tough, hardy engineers of West Cornwall. For the past twenty years he had consorted with scholarly men like Black and Robinson in Glasgow, and with philosophers like Small, Priestley, and other members of the famous Lunar Society in Birmingham; he now found himself among a society which, in its moments of deepest thought, attained no higher levels than the wild emotionalism of a Methodist revival meeting. It was little wonder that Watt came to believe that his engine only appealed to a race of uncouth barbarians on account of the noise it made.[3] Even less to his liking were the wild moors of Cornwall; its sea-coast had no charms for him; the wet climate and gloomy lowering skies depressed him; the conditions of extreme poverty prevalent among many of the mining folk sickened him; it turned his stomach when he saw a Cornish engine attendant scrape the grease off a machine and eat it.

[1] S. Smiles: *Lives of the Engineers, Boulton and Watt*, p. 177.
[2] Muirhead, Vol. I, p. clxviii.
[3] Muirhead, Vol. II, letter No. 170—Watt to Boulton, from Truro, undated, probably 1777.

Despite Cornish scepticism the engine trials were successful. The engine worked, and effected a phenomenal reduction in the quantity of coal consumed. Watt transformed an old engine at Chacewater in 1778 so that it easily drained away waters that two of the largest of the old engines together had failed to cope with, and, moreover, only used a quarter of the fuel. By the end of 1778 five engines, equipped with the separate con-condenser, were working in Cornwall, and eight more were ordered.[1] The Chacewater adventurers agreed to pay Boulton and Watt £700 a year for the saving of fuel, but, with other mines, difficulties soon arose as to the means of payment to the inventor and his business associates, since they were only designing and erecting machines for which the mines adventurers bore all the costs of materials used in construction. Finally, Boulton and Watt arrived at the by no means satisfactory expedient of making agreements with the individual mining concerns, which had installed their machines, to the effect that the users of the engines should pay premiums amounting to a third of the value of the coal saved. Watt prepared elaborate tables to calculate these savings, but it was extremely difficult to arrive at a just figure or formula which would allow for the variety of conditions under which different machines worked at different times and places. These premiums were to be paid as long as the machines were working during the time of the extended patent. At first, desperately concerned to make their mines pay, adventurers were ready to agree to these premiums, but, as time went by and Watt and Boulton continued to claim their dues, grumbling increased at paying a continued levy on engines erected and maintained at the adventurers' own cost.

The sums actually paid were great. By the end of 1791 Boulton and Watt had received over £76,000 in premiums from Cornwall from forty-two engines, or about £150 per annum from each machine, besides the money received for supplying machine parts which they made themselves or sold to the mines as agents of other manufacturers. These figures, too, bore no relation to the actual working times of the various engines; not one of them worked for the full period of twelve years; one machine, indeed, that at Wheal Butson had only

[1]Muirhead, Vol. 11, letter No. 70—Watt to Dr. Black, from Redruth, December 12, 1778.

started in October, 1791, whilst the old Chacewater engine,
which Watt had fitted with a separate condenser, had been
worn out and scrapped late in 1785. Indeed, the average engine
in this period was only working six months out of ten and the
average premium for full time working was therefore £250 a
year. This may not seem excessive, but a few large engines
with 58 and 64 inch cylinders were paying far more than the
small ones like the 18 inch installed at Wheal Maid in May,
1785. Moreover, one mining concern, the Consolidated Mines,
ran seven engines, and Poldice another four; with North
Downs and the United Mines, these mines acounted for more
than half of the working time of all the Watt engines in use in
Cornwall during this period; in other words, four groups of
mines adventurers were liable for over half the premiums
claimed by the Soho firm in Cornwall.[1] With profits diminishing through the competition of Anglesey, these and other
groups of adventurers, seeking possibilities of economy, quite
naturally began to question the continued payments, especially
when more and more machine parts were being provided by
local foundries and forges, and the Soho firm, although
actually making more machine parts itself than it originally
had done, appeared to them to be not manufacturers of engines
but mere middlemen dealers in machine parts which, the
Cornishmen suspected, were not bought from the cheapest
makers.

Watt once said that he had been willing to sell the patent
rights of his invention to the Cornish miners for seven or ten
thousand pounds, and the history of the copper mining industry in this period would have been happier had he done so.
Yet the separate condenser did enable the Cornish mines to
carry on against Anglesey. Watt's engines, during the term of
the patent, saved the Cornish mines adventurers about £40,000
a year, or roughly £1 on every ton of copper ore raised.[2]
Eliminating the third payable as premiums to Boulton and
Watt, and allowing for the costs of installing and maintaining
the engines, this should have enabled the adventurers to reduce

[1]Estimated from "Account of B. & W's. engines built in Cornwall" and
"Sums actually Rcvd. by B. and W for premiums of their Engines in Cornwall",
drawn up by Thomas Wilson in connection with the lawsuits against Bull and
Hornblower. (Wilson MSS.).
[2]Estimated from Wilson's account, February 2, 1799 (Wilson MSS.): H. W.
Dickinson, *Matthew Boulton*, p. 176.

the selling price of ores by about 10s. per ton without lessening profits or increasing losses. In the first five years in which the new engines were in general use in Cornwall, before the formation of the Cornish Metal Company in 1785, the average price of ores in Cornwall was £6 1s. 3d. as compared to £6 14s. 6d. during the ten-year period, 1766-1775,[1] a price which probably meant a profit of at least five per cent, and which indicated that in the years immediately preceding the arrival of Watt and his machines in Cornwall, copper ore could be produced at £6 8s. per ton. Watt's invention meant that a profit of 3s. 3d. could still be made on every ton, or 2¾%, which, with the prospect of further economies, and the use of the additional power now available to work the rich deposits of ore suspected to lie at deeper levels, was enough to encourage the adventurers to pursue their speculations, other conditions remaining unchanged.

Through the appearance of Anglesey ores on the market, however, they were not unchanged. The alternative source of ores enabled the smelters to force down the prices they paid the adventurers. The situation was aggravated by an accentuation of the old policy of trying to maintain gross profits in a falling market by increasing production, a policy encouraged by the very existence of the more powerful new machines. The premium system, too, meant that agents of Boulton and Watt pushed the full time and full power working of their machines. The results of this policy were fully shown in 1783, when, with some twenty Watt engines working in Cornwall, the output of copper ore in the county was 35,799 tons as against 28,122 tons the previous year.

Even before 1783 there had been complaints about the premiums; these increased when hitherto profitable mines began incurring losses. Several mines had already paid as premiums sums exceeding the value of the engines designed and erected by Boulton and Watt. Cornish mines adventurers, too, tended to value the technical advice provided by Watt and his subordinate engineers, like William Murdoch, at the low rates which they had been accustomed to pay their native engineers and mine captains. Already the younger Jonathan Hornblower and his brothers had been making suggestions that they could erect better and cheaper machines than Watt,

[1]Hunt, p. 892. See note 15.

without infringing the Scotsman's patent rights, and thereby save the payments of such heavy premiums. To safeguard their premiums, Boulton and Watt became shareholders in some Cornish mines, so gaining representation at the adventurers' meetings, but it was impossible for them and their friends to secure a controlling interest in at least a score of different mines.[1] Nevertheless this closer participation in Cornish mining enterprise, together with his own experience as a manufacturer consuming refined copper, made Boulton realize that Cornish complaints that smelters made exorbitant profits were not without foundation; he turned his attention to devising a new method of marketing copper which would help to reduce the gap between miner and manufacturer. At the same time, his direct and indirect interests in Cornish mines led him to oppose the demands of other Birmingham manufacturers for heavy duties on the export of copper which would have reduced the market demand to a quantity little more than the current Anglesey output.[2]

After lengthy negotiations in London, in which Boulton and the Cornish mine adventurer John Vivian took the leading part, the Cornish Metal Company was formed in September, 1785. The Governorship of this Company was given to the youthful and ambitious landowner, Sir Francis Basset of Tehidy; Vivian was Deputy Governor, and there was a board of thirty-six directors, two-thirds of whom were to be nominated by the mines adventurers.[3] Working in uneasy conjunction with Thomas Williams of Anglesey, this was an attempt to create a monopolistic cartel controlling the marketing of copper. The Company was to buy all copper ores raised in Cornwall for the next seven years; sales were to be shared between Cornwall and Anglesey in the ratio of three to two, but there was no agreement to restrict production. The smelters were to be relegated to the position of agents of the Company, the influential connections of John Vivian being

[1]The chief mines in which Boulton and Watt became shareholders were the Consolidated Mines, North Downs, and Wheal Jewell. They were not always successful in their efforts to induce their business associates to take further shares. (Wilson MSS.: Boulton to Wilson, July 24, 1784; August 20, 1785).
[2]Wilson MSS: Boulton to Wilson, January 26, 1784; Watt to Wilson, January 27, 1784.
[3]G. C. Allen: "An Eighteenth Century Combination in the Copper Mining Industry," in *Economic Journal,* 1923: H. Hamilton: *English Brass and Copper Industries,* pp. 162 ff.

sufficient to induce the English Copper Company, Lockwood, Morris and Company, the Gnoll Copper Works (the successors of the Mines Royal Company), and Freeman and Company, four of the smelting concerns, to agree to buy and smelt the stocks besides advancing credits. The entire risks of sales were undertaken by the Company, and the ticketing system was suspended.[1]

The success of the Cornish Metal Company depended on a degree of co-operation not only between Cornwall and Anglesey but also between the various Cornish mines which was not easy to attain. For a time the ring of smelters had been broken, but those outside the agreement naturally began offering favourable terms to the mines in order to starve their rivals of supplies and ruin the venture. Thomas Williams did not co-operate wholeheartedly, and increased the difficulties of the new Company by increasing production in Anglesey and by starting his own smelting works—an example John Vivian did not forget. Nor had Williams any intention of allowing Boulton and his Midlands associates to gain control of the copper market. In Cornwall divisions were accentuated by the personal and political rivalries of three great landlords, adventurers, and borough-mongers—Basset, who dominated Cook's Kitchen, Dolcoath, and other mines in the Camborne district, Lord Falmouth the principal landowner in the Chacewater and Gwennap district, and Sir Christopher Hawkins landlord of the great Hallamannin Mine and of the silver-lead mines of the Chiverton Valley. The majority of "miners" on the board of directors of the new Company, and the association of John Vivian with some of the Welsh smelters whose monopoly Boulton had challenged, suggested that the Soho manufacturer had not secured control of the copper trade but had, instead, achieved a union of mines adventurers and smelters at the expense of the consumers of copper. The slight recovery in the price of copper following the establishment of the Company only led to further overproduction, especially by the smaller mines, in Cornwall. The Company, too, was committed to buy all ores that came on the market. Moreover, a fair amount of copper was imported from Hungary, Spain,

[1]The ticketing sales were revived when the Metal Company came to an end in February, 1792, as a result of the decision of a meeting of "Miners" at Truro. (Wilson MSS: Watt to Wilson, June 30, 1785, and Boulton to Wilson, February 2, 1792).

Sweden and Holland, and there was an abortive attempt to induce the Swedish copper producers to enter the association early in 1786.

Much depended on the relations between Boulton and Sir Francis Basset, who soon convinced Boulton and Vivian that he was no figurehead Governor. Possibly Boulton knew little of the character and ambitions of the squire of Tehidy, although in 1781 one of Watt's largest engines had started working on Basset property in Dolcoath. That in itself did not necessarily make for amicable relations between Boulton and Basset, for it is not unlikely that the elder Trevithick, as manager of Dolcoath, was before long hinting to Basset that he could, if given a free hand, improve the performance of Watt's engine just as, a few years earlier, he had transformed the Carloose engine. Boulton's refusal to advance credit to Pool Mine in 1782[1] may have incurred Basset's displeasure, whilst the Tehidy steward, Thomas Kevill, was associated with the Tincroft adventurers who later were to be allied with Hornblower in his assault on Watt's patent. Nevertheless, it seems that in 1784 Boulton and Basset were on good terms, and Boulton had sought the aid of the Cornish squire and his protégés in the House of Commons to thwart the effort of the Birmingham Commercial Committee to secure Parliamentary legislation imposing heavy export duties on copper and tin. Basset's part in the actual creation of the Metal Company had been less active than John Vivian's, but without the credit of his wealth to back it the Company might never have been formed.

Boulton's other manufacturing interests, however, made him, like many others of the time, an ardent suitor for the favours of whatever administration happened to be in power, whereas Basset had followed Fox and North into the political wilderness in 1784. The principal and most influential supporter of the younger Pitt in West Cornwall was Basset's rival, Lord Falmouth, who, moreover, proved more generous than the squire of Tehidy in remitting the dues he claimed on copper mined on his lands.[2]   In addition, the Soho firm had heavier

---

[1]Wilson MSS: Boulton to Captain John Vivian, December 8, 1782; this Vivian, one of Basset's mine managers, and a member of the Camborne engineering family was not related to the future deputy-governor of the Cornish Metal Company.

[2]Wilson MSS : Boulton to Wilson, May 6, 1787. This was Edward Boscawen, third Viscount Falmouth.

stakes in the mines on Boscawen property than in those on Basset lands.

The crisis between Basset and Boulton came in the autumn of 1787. The finances of the Metal Company were then in a very precarious state for, at the very beginning, shareholders who had subscribed £130,000 of its capital of £500,000 had been promised eight per cent interest on their advances,[1] whilst the unchecked exploitation of the Anglesey mines by Williams had made it apparent that the Company would never clear the estimated £15,000 per annum over and above the interest promised to the shareholders. The intensified "price war" had forced North Downs and other Cornish mines to suspend working, and a formidable demonstration of unemployed workmen had marched into Truro.[2] The situation was so ominous that Vivian and Boulton rushed down to Truro and called a committee meeting of the Metal Company on October 11th. It was a stormy meeting which was graphically described by Boulton himself:

"Our business on Thursday was conducted entirely by the little great man (*i.e.* Basset), who on a former occasion made a motion to deprive another great man of his 50 votes and hath now made other motions which will, I have no doubt, deprive him of his 50 (five hundred £) shares. The little man hath just found out that he is engaged in a Trading Company under the form of the Cornish Metal Company and that his great property is liable to the payment of all deficiencies and therefore let what will be the consequences he seems determined to annihilate the Company.

"He hath also discovered that the interest, etc, of the Metal Company capital and debts is so great as to lay a heavy burden upon the mines and therefore it is thought wise, just, honourable and reasonable that the Cornish Metal Company shall lose all their money and shall not sell more of their 7,000 ton of copper than 1,300 ton per year.

"It is also thought right to break the last and all other bargains made with Williams, and in future to sell the Cornish ores to the Ex-Companies (*i.e.* the Welsh Smelters) either by the old mode of ticketing or by any other that can be agreed upon. It is also thought right that all responsibility for the Cornish Miners to the Metal Company shall be done away with and thus by selling the ores to Companies who are not loaded with copper or debts but on the contrary have large sums unemployed there is no doubt that they

[1] E. Roll: *An Early Experiment in Industrial Organization*, pp. 91-92. The Metal Company was a joint stock organization with unlimited liability; the initial subscription of £130,000 had probably led some of the Cornish shareholders to believe it similar to the Cornish cost-book mining companies.

[2] Wilson MSS: Boulton to Wilson, October 11, 1787.

can give a better standard than the Metal Company can do, and thereby Dolcoath and other poor mines can work.

"In order to accomplish these salutary points a conference was held between the Metal Company Committee and the Miners' Committee and it was proposed that the Miners should pay to the Metal Company (if the Miners find they can afford it and are in the humour to pay it) fifteen thousand per year although the Metal Company now are saddled with interest, salaries, etc, to the amount of more than twice that sum and that the Metal Company shall not sell more than 1,300 tons a year and consequently are deprived of (the means of) lessening their debt. A Committee was appointed to go to London to lay themselves at the feet of the old Ex-Companies and prevail upon them to support the Miners against Anglesey.[1]

"As to myself I declared at the General Meeting that I did not regard the loss of my capital but as to my absent friends who are large subscribers I must in justice to them protest against the proceedings but Sir Francis Basset thought all absent members were bound by the acts of the two Committees although they tended to take away their property . . . "[2]

Obviously the interest of the Cornish "Miners" had clashed with those of a group of speculators who had sought to set up a monopolistic organization for the sale of copper. Refusing to restrict production, the mining interests were trying to compel the "outside" speculators to buy all the ores they raised but at the same time to restrict their sales in order to maintain prices. The Metal Company tried to insist upon a reduction of price, but finally had to give way and come to terms with the Welsh smelters. There is little doubt that Basset wanted to end the Cornish Metal Company forthwith; had that been done he and others would have lost heavily; as it was, by 1792, the Company had just cleared off its debts when it came to an end. Boulton thought that Basset was too cautious to risk his own property and was yet only too ready to sacrifice the capital of others. It is apparent, however, that Basset had thought that the Company was similar to Cornish cost-book concerns, from which it was possible to withdraw at any time; he was only reluctant to incur the risks of further losses which seemed inevitable, but there is no suggestion that he was trying to evade liability for losses he and the other shareholders had already

[1]The names of the Committee to go to London were written on the margin of this letter; headed by Basset and John Vivian, it also included Boulton himself, Richard Fox, and R. A. Daniell, the later ally of the Hornblowers. The merchant John Edwards also went with the Committee to London. It was, therefore, a Committee of merchant adventurers in the mines.

[2]Wilson MSS: Boulton to Wilson, April 17, 1788.

incurred. Basset, too, could criticise not only the high rates of interest promised subscribers of the Company but could also point out that the concern had created an excessive number of "jobs" for connections of the non-mining shareholders. Moreover, the miners were a majority on the Committee, and they were incensed against Williams of Anglesey who was bent on achieving a domination over the copper industry which would be far more injurious to their interests than the old Welsh smelting ring had ever been. Even Boulton at times doubted his own ability to check the Anglesey man. Yet, at the time, this Cornish "declaration of war" against Anglesey seemed more likely to lead to the ruin of the deep mines of Cornwall than to check the progress of Williams towards control of the entire copper industry.

The Cornish Metal Company had been set up as a marketing organization; not only had it failed to arrest the fall in copper prices but it had proved extremely expensive to those who had been induced to participate in it. The suspicion that it had been designed to provide lucrative posts for persons connected with the Midland manufacturers rankled; it was generally realized that those manufacturers were interested in keeping the price of finished copper low; the very failure of the Company to achieve its object increased suspicions of mismanagement. These suspicions may have been illfounded and unjust but the fact of their existence was all that mattered at the meeting of the mining interest in October, 1787.

Nevertheless, united action of some sort was necessary to avert greater disasters in the Cornish mining industry. The real trouble was the immense stock of copper in hand; the only solution lay in restricting production. The march of the miners into Truro, however, made it evident that the closing down of any great mine or mines would lead to unrest and rioting; indeed, that demonstration of the unemployed forced the North Downs adventurers to resume operations. Sir Francis Basset did not see any reason why he should allow the Dolcoath adventurers to suspend working in order to allow North Downs to continue production, even if Lord Falmouth had waived his lord's dues, particularly since there was less than no guarantee that Anglesey would also limit production. He may have suspected also that Boulton and his associates would try to keep those mines going in which they were personally interested and those in which more of their machinery was installed than there had been in Dolcoath.

After lengthy negotiations Williams was brought into a scheme to limit production, but at the price of making him the sole agent for all the Metal Company's sales and with a two per cent commission on those sales. There then followed a long dispute over the settlement of rates of compensation to be given by the associated mines to those mines which had closed down, Basset standing firm for higher rates than those proposed by John Vivian. At last agreement was reached, and Dolcoath was among the mines which closed down. Yet if mine owners, landlords, and adventurers were satisfied the working miners were not, and further demonstrations by the unemployed in the spring of 1788 led James Watt to express his conviction that troops ought to be stationed at Truro and Redruth.[1]   Boulton, perhaps more humanely and certainly with more business-like acumen, suggested the permanent removal of the surplus copper mining population to western lead mines and to the more distant coalfields of the Midlands.[2]

In the light of the subsequent history of the mine it seems strange to find Dolcoath a "knacked bal". Destined to become the deepest and most famous mine in Cornwall, its different levels varied greatly in riches and poverty of metallic lodes and veins. Under the skilful management of the elder Trevithick and his subordinate engineers, the richer upper levels of copper had been very thoroughly exploited before a 63 inch Watt engine was installed in 1781. For the next five or six years production was maintained at a high level, and in the year ending at Michaelmas, 1786, rather more than 5,400 tons of Dolcoath ores fetched about £30,700. The output and quality of the ores then declined rapidly, and in the year ending at Michaelmas, 1790, only 890 tons, or a sixth of the former amount, were sold for barely £1,250, or less than a fourteenth part of the sums realized but five years before.

This fall cannot be wholly explained by lower copper prices, but indicates that very inferior ores were being sold,

[1]Wilson MSS: Watt to Wilson, April 17, 1788.
[2]Wilson MSS: Boulton and Watt to Wilson, April 18, 1788 (in Boulton's handwriting).

and possibly some that had been cast aside as *halvans* in more prosperous days.[1] Dolcoath started again in 1798, but it was not until November, 1804, that a profit of £1,600 was divided among its shareholders; in the second half of 1805 its profits reached some £37,500 and it went on paying dividends for many years; late in the 1830s there was a temporary suspension of its lower levels, partly owing to the financial crisis of 1837, but the discovery of the lower zone of tin strata soon afterwards gave Dolcoath a new lease of life which lasted over eighty years.[2]

It was easy for a Birmingham industrialist to advocate the suspension of several Cornish mines, but Boulton had little if any idea of the difficulties and costs of setting a closed-down mine to work again; it would take three or four years to drain off the waters accumulated in the deeper levels during the period of abandonment, without allowing at all for the rapid deterioration of surface and underground structures of mines in the corrosive Cornish atmosphere. Basset may have had some knowledge of this, but his main concern, apart from his personal income, was the riotous disposition of unemployed miners. Whilst it is true that disorderly conduct was the only mode of protest open to the lower classes in eighteenth century England, there had been rather too many "incidents" in Cornwall since 1773. Many of the disturbances which occurred could be associated with periods of food-shortage, but that problem, too, had been accentuated by the increase of population in the mining regions.

The succession of crises in the mining industries found Cornwall facing problems of local over-population and unemployment with the antiquated administrative machinery of the Elizabethan Poor Law. Emigration, suggested by Boulton, was only possible to a few mining areas of the United Kingdom, areas

---

[1]The Watt engine ceased working at Dolcoath on April 30, 1788, but although the number of tribute groups working at the mine fell almost immediately to three or four *partners*, the last payment to tributers for this period of working was not made until March 19, 1790 (Cook's Kitchen and Dolcoath Account Book, MS; in possession of T. R. Harris, Esq.).

[2]Accounts of the sales made by Dolcoath in the years 1785-90 are given by Wilson in an undated paper drawn up in connection with the patent lawsuits; the dividends of 1804-05 are calculated from the shares paid to Lord de Dunstanville as adventurer (Tehidy Estate Accounts, MSS. in possession of F. L. Harris, Esq.). The exhaustion of copper in Dolcoath became apparent at the end of 1836 (*W. B.* January 6, 1837).

in which wages were rather lower than in Cornwall.[1] The Laws of Settlement, too, deterred miners from migrating rather more than other men; they were aware that theirs was a dangerous avocation, and many would not run the risk of going elsewhere and of being sent back to their home parishes when and if accidents befell them; moreover it was the partially disabled miners who suffered most in times of unemployment, and they would find it particularly difficult to obtain work and gain a settlement elsewhere. Over and above this, it should be remembered that the tradition of the "free miner" was strong in Cornwall, and only the direst destitution and absolute despair could have driven many of them to migrate to the coalfields; they knew something of conditions in the South Wales collieries from the men who brought coal in to Cornwall even if they knew nothing of the conditions of peonage still prevalent in the Scottish coal mines. A few of them may have drifted away to the new clay works in St. Stephens in Brannel,[2] but the copper and tin miners regarded clay-working as an inferior occupation and as one positively derogatory to their skill as miners. Basset and one or two other land-owners did something to promote subsidiary small-holdings and waste-land reclamation which provided some employ-ment and helped to alleviate the problem of the scarcity of food,[3] but the industrialization of the textile man-ufactures in northern England left it too late in the day to promote spinning, knitting, and lace-making as domestic industries in Cornwall.

Despite the closing down of certain mines and the reduction of the scale on which others were worked, the situation in Cornwall was not hopeless. A few despairing souls talked of utter ruin and of the imminent end of Cornish copper mining, but the very conflict with Anglesey had aroused a fighting determination to curb Thomas Williams. Camborne men had been prospecting in Anglesey some time before the dis-

---

[1]In the closing decade of the eighteenth century the average level of weekly wages in Cornwall was estimated at from nine to fifteen shillings; in Anglesey it ranged between six and ten shillings; nowhere in the South Wales Coalfield did it exceed twelve shillings, whilst on Tyneside it was about nine shillings. (A. H. Dodd: "Parys Mountain during the Industrial Revolution"; *Anglesey Anti-quarian Society and Field Club Transactions*, 1926 pp. 97-98: T. S. Ashton and J. Sykes: *The Coal Industry of the Eighteenth Century*, pp. 136 ff).

[2]The population of St. Stephen's rose only from 1575 in 1744 to 1738 in 1801.

[3]See p. 225 below.

covery of the copper deposits at Parys,[1] and they had formed a very true estimate of the limited nature and extent of those deposits; besides there had already been similar discoveries in Cornwall itself of lodes which, for a time, dominated ticketing sales and then petered away—Dolcoath might well be quoted as an example. From direct knowledge and from the analogy of their mining history Cornish miners foresaw the ultimate exhaustion of the Anglesey mines. By 1790 the quality of the Anglesey ores, never very rich, had deteriorated considerably, whilst Williams was hastily exploiting the better lodes. There was little prospect of finding further deposits in Anglesey that could be worked by opencast methods. By 1790, too, the copper market had revived and the accumulation of unsold stocks in the hands of the Metal Company was rapidly being reduced; a year later Boulton was seeking desperately for copper to execute manufacturing and coinage contracts he had undertaken.[2] The price of copper late in 1793 was a third above the average level of 1789, while, by 1799 it was nearly double that of ten years before.

Costs of production, however, more than kept pace with the revival in the copper market, and, with the expiration of the Metal Company in 1792, the main conflict was transformed from a struggle for markets between Cornwall and Anglesey to one between certain Cornish adventurers and engineers, on the one side, and Boulton and Watt, on the other, over questions of patent rights. Two factors embittered this conflict—the tendency of the very use of steam power to concentrate production to a limited number of mines, and the attempt to restrict production that had exhausted the more accessible resources of those mines which had continued working. It was no longer the mines which raised and sold the greatest quantities of copper ores which made the greatest profits; indeed a few of them incurred considerable losses in some years. Thus, in

[1]"One James Thomas, a Cornishman, an ore washer in Drws-y-Coed, took a lease from Owen Thomas within the two years and gave Owen money for it. But after examination, the ore, if ore it be, was not worth anything. . . . James Thomas is (now) working here and there. . . . Sir George (Young) sent the steward for £60 pans from Cornwall; and Sion had to go to superintend the lead mine at Llanrhychwin." (*Morris Letters*, ed. J. H. Davies, Vol. 11, p. 358, William to Lewis Morris, July 2, 1761; I am indebted to G. Melville Richards, Esq., for drawing my attention to this passage and for the translation).

[2]Wilson MSS: Boulton to Wilson, January 13, 1791; Boulton and Watt to Wilson, September 12, 1791; Watt to Wilson, October 28, 1791.

1792, five mining concerns[1] sold ores worth in all £179,000, two others a further £40,000 worth, whilst the remaining sales valued at £60,000 were made by fifteen other mines, and there were thirty-eight other working mines which made no sales although incurring costs. The greatest sales were those made by Consolidated Mines, amounting to £47,000 but only gaining a profit of £4,100 (to be submerged by losses of £7,800 the next year), whereas Wheal Unity selling less than half the value of Consols' ores cleared a profit of nearly £15,650 in 1792.[2] By 1797 the greatest sales were made by North Downs which accounted for £56,650 in the total sales of Cornish copper ores valued at £320,600, but which thereby only cleared a profit of just over £850 contrasted with Tincroft's profits of £27,750 on sales of ores worth £39,500 and with Wheal Unity's profits of £16,250 from sales amounting to £37,750.[3] The five-year period from 1792 to 1797 reveals an even more startling contrast between North Downs and Tincroft, the former actually losing £10,545 on sales totalling £245,875 and the latter clearing profits of £37,207 from selling less than £91,050 worth of ores,[4] whilst its actual sales had increased eightfold in the period. Mining, undoubtedly, was a very speculative enterprise, and the strange differences between the profits and losses of different mines might be accounted for by the variable nature of mineral reserves and the ease or difficulty of exploiting them. But the difference that struck contemporaries was that North Downs was using engines designed by Watt and paying heavy premiums for them whereas Tincroft was employing other machines, designed by engineers who claimed that they were not covered by Watt's patent specifications and who refused to pay the premiums. The fortunes of Tincroft threatened not merely the income Boulton and Watt derived from the Cornish mines but the very reputation of their engine, and a prolonged and bitter contest in the law courts resulted.

The challenge to Watt's patent came from the younger Jonathan Hornblower. After condemning the Watt engine his father had ordered for Ting Tang, he had carried on his

---

[1]Consolidated Mines, United Mines, Poldice (all in Gwennap), North Downs, and Cook's Kitchen.
[2]*Report, 1799*, Appendix 18.
[3]*Report, 1799*, Appendix 23.
[4]*Report, 1799*, Appendices 18 to 23.

own experiments, showing the utmost determination to better the engine he had disparaged so scathingly. Watt's engine, however, could not be surpassed by any machine which did not incorporate the separate condenser and thereby infringe Watt's patent. The invention of this comparatively small, and not very costly, device had given Watt and his partner monopolistic control over the use of steam power in Britain.[1] Hornblower, after prolonged experiments, patented an engine in 1781 which sought to evade the patent by using not one cylinder but two. It has been claimed that this was the first compound engine,[2] yet all Hornblower had devised after years of experimenting was an alteration, or rather an extension, of existing machine component parts in order to use the same steam twice over. Twenty years before Sampson Swayne had had somewhat similar notions,[3] but it is more likely that Hornblower got the idea from the common sight of water running through streams or leats to work a series of machines and mills in its course, for he was only, like all the engineers of the day, attempting to use steam in place of water power. His actual patent specification was vague, merely stressing the utilization of two cylinders, whereas Watt, assisted by academic and businessmen friends, had, in 1769, drawn up a patent specification which had, by its elaborate and painstaking description of the entire engine, the engine created by Newcomen and others, almost obscured his own cardinal contribution of the separate condenser. Jonathan Hornblower's vagueness led Watt to declare that if the Soho firm made an engine on the lines indicated by the 1781 patent specification the law could not touch them; Watt also thought that any gain from using two cylinders would be more than lost through the greater amount of heat lost by radiation from a greater area of exposed surface.[4] This belief in the inferiority of Hornblower's engine, and Watt's own unsuccessful experiments with double-cylinder machines, partly account for the fact that Boulton & Watt did not bring actions for infringement of patent

[1]Some collieries, in which coal cost little, could and did continue to use the older types of Newcomen engines, but in the Cornish mining districts economy of fuel was of paramount importance.

[2]Rhys Jenkins: "Jonathan Hornblower and the Compound Engine", *T.N.S.*, Vol. XI, pp. 128 ff.

[3]See above, p. 52.

[4]Wilson MSS: Watt to Wilson, October 31, 1786, and Boulton to Wilson, November 2, 1786.

rights for more than ten years after Hornblower took out his patent.

Other factors also delayed the contest. By 1781 the merits of Watt's engine were obvious to the majority of Cornish mines adventurers, and, for the time being, that engine served their purposes and their pockets quite well. Even apart from their innate conservatism, they were not prosperous enough to embark on further experiments. Rivalry with Anglesey and the fall in copper prices made them even less disposed to subsidise costly experiments on an engine that certainly took no little time to prove its merits and one, moreover, that was being constantly maligned by Watt and his associates to whom the adventurers were bound by close business ties. It was far cheaper to adapt older engines to the Watt type by the addition of the separate condenser than it was to add extra cylinders as Hornblower suggested. Nor were they willing at the time to allow themselves to become involved in costly litigation, for it was evident that Boulton and Watt would not hesitate to defend their patent monopolistic rights which had created, as yet, no great feeling of real hardship in Cornwall. As time went by, however, and the amount of premiums claimed by, if not paid to, Boulton and Watt increased, as profits diminished, as the progress—if such it could be called—of the Cornish Metal Company suggested that Boulton, besides monopolizing their steam power, had released them from thraldom to the Welsh smelters only to lure them into the control of Midland and London manufacturers and speculators, the mines adventurers turned against the Soho men and became more and more ready to listen to the claims Hornblower made.

Soon after he had taken out his patent, Hornblower approached some Cornish adventurers, but these seem to have been smaller men, embarked on newer mines, with little resources to employ him and even less to risk on the litigation that Soho threatened.[1] In the background of the struggle of the rival engineers in Cornwall can be seen the fortunes and misfortunes of the shaky patent of Richard Arkwright. The Lancashire man's patent had not been upheld in his action against Morduant in 1781—the very year in which Hornblower took out his patent. The Court of Common Pleas

[1] Wilson MSS: Watt to Wilson, August 16, 1783; Watt to James Tooker, November 21, 1783.

reversed this decision in February, 1785, and until then it was unlikely that the Soho firm would resort to the courts to defend a patent that, like the Lancastrian's, incorporated so many features which could unquestionably be attributed to earlier inventors. In June, 1785, however, Arkwright lost his action against Nightingale in the Court of King's Bench, and that decision made the challenge to Watt's patent inevitable.[1]

Moreover the Soho firm had achieved a monopoly of the engines employed in Cornwall. Finding it impossible to get anyone in Cornwall to take a costly machine that had yet to prove its worth, Hornblower went to Bristol, entered into partnership with the iron-founder John Winwood, and installed a double-cylinder engine at Radstock colliery where there was no need to use the Watt condenser since fuel was cheap and abundant. For the time his rival inventor was content to utter very calumnious reflections on the performances of this engine,[2] but Hornblower gradually improved it whilst dissatisfaction over the continued payment of premiums grew in Cornwall. The recovery in copper prices then encouraged the more extensive working of old and speculation in new mining ventures, and this hastened the conflict of the rival engineers.

Lying behind the conflict were the well-nigh ineradicable prejudiced suspicions of the Cornish that "foreigners" were attempting to deceive and best them in business transactions. The dour and diabetic Watt had alienated them from the very start, whilst the more convivial Boulton had been forced by the conditions of fierce competition prevalent in the world of industry and business to adopt methods that were not above criticism. Yet Boulton was no worse, and, perhaps, a great deal better than most business men in a self-seeking generation; it can be said to his credit that in pursuance of his business he made lasting friends and not mere acquaintances; but he made enemies as well. The unfortunate affairs of the Cornish Metal Company had alienated him from the influential Sir Francis Basset, nor does it seem to have improved his relations with the scarcely less influential John Vivian; the engine disputes were to alienate Sir Christopher Hawkins and incurred the bitter

---

[1]Wilson MSS: Boulton and Watt to Wilson, February 26, 1785; Watt to Wilson, June 18, 1785. P. Mantoux: *The Industrial Revolution in the Eighteenth Century*, pp. 225–239.

[2]Thus Watt said of the Radstock engine—"it was obliged to stand still once every ten minutes to snore and snort." (*V.C.H. Somerset*, Vol. 11, p. 384).

hostility of the Daniell's of Truro who had stood by the Metal Company to the very last. Prejudices and pecuniary considerations weighed heavily with a host of lesser merchants and mines adventurers, and the first challenge to the monopoly of steam power in Cornwall came when they encouraged the former Soho employee Edward Bull to erect an engine which, although it inverted the cylinder and did away with the cumbersome and rather costly beam, differed in no essential way from Watt's engines.[1] The revolt was encouraged by knowledge of Arkwright's discomfiture, and by the publication of a certain amount of evidence purporting to show that Watt's separate condenser, let alone the other parts of his engine, had not been a new invention.[2]

Edward Bull apparently broke away from Boulton and Watt when, after employing him to erect an engine on the Wheal Virgin set of Consolidated mines, they had put William Murdoch in charge of all their engines in Cornwall. Already some of the Consols adventurers had become embittered by the premiums,[3] and they induced Bull in August, 1789, to effect certain alterations in the Wheal Virgin engine which he and they alleged transformed it so much that it was no longer covered by Watt's patent and therefore exempt from further liability to premiums. Hornblower was consulted and agreed with this opinion. Litigation seemed imminent, but Watt believed that the Hornblower-Bull alliance would be fatal to the claims of Jonathan Hornblower to have invented a radically different type of engine.[4] The initial failures of Bull's engine delayed recourse to the law courts, whilst forcing Bull to adopt devices which may have further lessened the superficial differences between his machine and the orthodox Watt type;

[1]H. W. Dickinson and A. Titley: *Richard Trevithick*, p. 21.

[2]This line was taken by Jonathan Hornblower in 1788 in his *Address to the Lords, Adventurers, and others concerned in the Mines of Cornwall.* Since the House of Commons had rejected the claims of William Blakey to prior invention in 1775, Hornblower resorted to allegations of even earlier descriptions of machines, notably the *Machinarium Hydrauliconum* of the German Leopold (*c.* 1724). His attention may have been drawn to this by Rudolf Erich Raspe, the creator of Baron Munchausen, who had found it expedient to settle in Cornwall at this time. Raspe seems to have been connected with Boulton and Watt men in Cornwall, but even Boulton, a man far less distrustful of his fellows than his Scottish partner, did not trust this German adventurer. (Wilson MSS: Boulton to Wilson, October 15 and November 11, 1792).

[3]Wilson MSS: Watt to Wilson, November 20, 1788. The Consols adventurers in 1799 included Jethro Hornblower, and John Winwood, Jonathan Hornblower's partner, besides Boulton and Watt. (*Report, 1799*, Appendix 30).

[4]Wilson MSS: Watt to Wilson, September 2, 1789.

they also encouraged Hornblower to advance the claims of his
invention which had by now proved itself at Radstock. For the
next two years Boulton and Watt were more concerned with
the activities of the Hornblowers, and suffered Bull to go on erecting engines in the belief that they would not work and that, if
they did, they could easily be proved infringements on Watt's
patent and liable to the payment of premiums during the
whole period they worked until Watt's patent expired.
Bull had erected ten engines before the lawsuit was decided
against him, after ten months in the courts, late in 1793. Even
then the Court merely decided that an engine which Bull had
erected at Dolcoath infringed the patent, but refused to give a
definite decision that the patent itself was valid. Bull returned
to Cornwall, engaged to erect more engines, but was stopped
from executing these contracts by a court injunction in March,
1794.[1] The Soho men would not allow him to finish the engines
he had started erecting at Hallamannin and Ding Dong, and
were determined to drive rival engineers out of Cornwall.[2]
If they stopped Bull with injunctions, however, the younger
Richard Trevithick, who had given evidence for him in the
trial, was ready to carry out the contracts to build engines he
had made. Incensed by Bull's actions and allegations against
him in Cornwall, Watt furiously talked of bringing an action
of perjury against him.[3] In fact, the Soho men were desperate.
The validity of their patent could only be proved by further
litigation, and the Arkwright precedent caused them grave
alarm. All the while the number of mining concerns refusing
to pay further premiums increased.

The contest between Hornblower and Soho developed on
rather different lines. Hornblower's early setbacks with his
machine had led Boulton and Watt to disparage his abilities
an engineer, but his bitter criticisms of their machines and his
own boastful claims at times made them consider bringing
actions against him for libel and slander, since they damaged
their credit and reputation in Cornwall. Preoccupation with
the Metal Company and other matters, however, engrossed
their attention at the very time when Hornblower solved his
technical problems at Radstock; the challenge he made in

[1]Wilson MSS: A. and T. Weston to Wilson, March 22, 1794.
[2]Wilson MSS: A. and T. Weston to Wilson, March 29, 1794.
[3]Wilson MSS: Watt to Wilson, March 22, 1794.

D

1788 came as a shock ; they had never thought that he could
even copy their own engines let alone perfect a compound
engine which Watt, from his own over hastily abandoned
experiments, had regarded as impracticable. They now
admitted their rivals' ability by instructing Thomas Wilson in
Cornwall to try to buy the Hornblower patent from Jethro
Hornblower. Jethro would have been willing to sell the patent,
which still had six years to run and might, like Watt's own, be
extended by Parliament, but at the time he was hardly on
speaking terms with his brother and the negotiations came to
nought. Winwood was then approached, but he would do
nothing without consulting Jonathan who flatly refused to sell
on the terms offered, although the possibility that he was merely
holding out for a higher price may have delayed the appeal of
the Soho men to the courts against him.[1]

By themselves these transactions reveal that Boulton and
Watt were genuinely alarmed by the new engine Hornblower
had designed, and that alarm grew when the Tincroft adventurers started using one of his compound engines in March,
1790.[2] Before that time Wilson had been instructed by Soho
to become a shareholder in Tincroft in order to gain admission
to the adventurers' meetings and discover their plans and
dealings with Hornblower,[3] whilst in May, 1790 Boulton and
Watt considered bringing an action against the Radstock
colliery rather than against Tincroft for infringing their
patent.[4]

For the time, however, the Arkwright decision had made
Boulton and Watt reluctant to risk a legal action which might
invalidate their patent or end in a Court decision that Hornblower's engine was different from that described in the patent
of 1769; instead they resorted to Hornblower's own methods
of newspaper advertisements to persuade people that Watt's
engine was superior. With their approval, Wilson started
publishing accounts of the performances of their engines,
and tried to arrange competitive trials to ascertain the
efficiency of the rival machines. Litigation was also
delayed because each of the three groups concerned in the

[1]Wilson MSS : Wilson to Boulton and Watt, October 2, 1789 and February 26,
1790; Watt to Wilson, February 19, 1790.
[2]Wilson MSS: Wilson to Boulton and Watt, April 13, 1790.
[3]Wilson MSS: Watt to Wilson, January 30 and March 11, 1790.
[4]Wilson MSS: Watt to Wilson, May 19, 1790.

Tincroft engine[1] denied that they could allow Watt's agents to inspect that machine without the consent of the others, an evasiveness which naturally strengthened the suspicions of the Watt party that Hornblower had infringed the patent. The trials to prove the superiority of Watt's engine were not so convincing as the Soho men had anticipated. Calculating the *duty* of an engine by the weight of water in pounds raised one foot by the use of a bushel of coal was extremely unsatisfactory because, even if the bushel of coal had been a uniform measure in Cornwall, there could be endless disagreement about the uniformity of the quality of coal used in working different engines.[2] With the failure of the Soho firm to make good their petition against the extension of Hornblower's own patent early in 1792,[3] actual proof of the superiority of Watt's engines was essential if the Soho men wished to retain their engine market in Cornwall. Allegations that Hornblower's engines were inferior had to be backed by positive proof. Wilson claimed in September, 1792, that the Wheal Butson engine which had only been working a year and which was the only Watt engine erected in Cornwall since 1786, could perform a duty of thirty-three millions,[4] but at the trials held a month later, despite all attempts to reduce friction to a minimum, its best performance only registered 28,466,782.[5] The secrecy of the Tincroft men, however, encouraged Wilson to make and publish calculations showing that Hornblower's engine was only a third as efficient as the Wheal Butson machine,[6] but his figures must have been incomprehensible to the laymen of the time, whilst his painstaking calculations of the actual surface areas of the cylinders in the different engines[7] did not convert the Tincroft adventurers, who promptly

[1] *i.e.* Winwood, the Tincroft adventurers and Hornblower. Wilson MSS: Watt Wilson, March 18, May 2 and 17, 1791.

[2] Wilson MSS: Boulton to Wilson, August 23, 1790.

[3] *J.H.C.*, Vol. XLVII, pp. 416-17, 478, 514, 546, 756 and 762. Basset was a teller in one division against Boulton and Watt.

[4] Wilson MSS: Draft of Advertisement in Answer to Hornblower's Advertisement, September 25, 1792.

[5] Wilson MSS: John Vivian to Wilson, November 27, 1792. The duty at these tests was calculated by one of the Moyles (probably the Marazion physician, see below, p. 228), who do not seem to have been friendly to the Soho firm. Boulton, however, blamed the poor result on to the inferior coal used (*Ibid:* Boulton to Wilson, October 31, 1792; Boulton and Watt to Wilson, November 15, 1792).

[6] Wilson MSS: Boulton to Wilson, December 27, 1792.

[7] Wilson MSS: "Table comparing B. & W. Engines with Tin Croft Engine," December 29-30, 1792.

commissioned Hornblower to build them another compound engine, double the size of the first, which was working by January, 1794. Other mines followed suit, notably Tresavean and Wheal Unity. The defection of Wheal Unity to the Hornblower camp was a bitter blow to the Soho firm, for it was the most profitable copper mine in Cornwall, clearing profits of over £85,000 on sales of £156,200 worth of ores in the six years from 1792 to 1798. Indeed, in these six years, Tincroft and Wheal Unity, selling less than fourteen per cent of the value of the copper ores raised in Cornwall,[1] cleared over forty per cent of the total profits of all mines that made profits in the period;[2] moreover, whilst the absolute profits of all Cornish mining concerns in this period only amounted to £44,927 13s. 8d., the combined profits of these two mines were £124,008 13s. 6d.[3]

The part played by Hornblower's engine in contributing to the fortunes of Wheal Unity and Tincroft may actually have been very small, but his association with these two mines and their evidently growing prosperity in these years, contrasting so sharply as it did with the ill fortunes of concerns associated with Boulton and Watt, attracted notice—and highly unfavourable and unfriendly notice insofar as the Soho men were concerned. Other factors aggravated the feud of the rival engineers. Most of the Watt engines in Cornwall had been working since 1783; some of them had been assembled from parts taken from older machines; they were showing signs of wear and tear and, in some cases, careless and neglectful supervision. When these engines had been new it had been easy for Watt to mock Hornblower's set-backs; it was a different story when, in December, 1791, the Herland engine became a worthless wreck.[4] After the Wheal Reeth engine had been completed early in 1786, no new Watt machine was erected in Cornwall until the Wheal Butson engine was completed in October, 1791, whilst in the next few years, during which Bull and Hornblower each erected ten engines in Cornwall,[5] all the Soho men did was to put a 64 inch cylinder to an old Poldice

[1] Approximately £254,000 out of £1,832,000.
[2] Approximately £124,000 out of £303,000.
[3] *Report, 1799*, Appendices 18-23.
[4] Wilson MSS: Watt to Wilson, December 17, 1791.
[5] Rhys Jenkins: "Jonathan Hornblower and the Compound Engine", *T.N.S.*, Vol. XI, pp. 141-2, 155.

engine at Herland and to make a new engine at Hewas in the St. Austell district, which was far from the main copper mining region of the time. By 1794, instead of monopolising the use of steam power in Cornwall as they had done ten years earlier, Boulton and Watt had control and claims upon barely half the machines working in the county and their connections were with the less flourishing and losing mines.

The decline of the monopoly can be attributed partly to Boulton's association with the restrictive policy adopted by the Cornish Metal Company and partly to his failure to grasp, late in 1789, that the state of the copper market demanded the reversal of that policy. Many mines using Watt's engines had continued full-scale working during the period of restriction and of low prices, and they had, thereby, worked at a loss which had to be made up; moreover, to cut labour costs, they had exhausted their more accessible and richer deposits, and now would have to clear away masses of "deads" and barren "country" before they had any hope of tapping new rich deposits; such mines experienced a lag of profits behind a rising market until the rise accelerated late in 1795. The claims of Boulton and Watt to have saved the mines using their engines from ruin, too, made it obvious that those mines would, sooner or later, be facing similar crises when Watt's atmospheric machine could no longer drain the deeper levels that would have to be worked if the mines were to continue in production.

Contemporaries, however, were probably more influenced by the fact that Wheal Unity and Tincroft had never used Watt engines, nor is it without significance that the mines which commissioned Hornblower were those in which there were comparatively few "foreign" adventurers. The only outside adventurer in Tincroft was the Cheshire man, Roger Wilbraham, who had probably only taken a sixteenth share in it as a means of securing a Cornish seat in Parliament. A quarter of the shares of Wheal Unity were held by Sir William Lemon, the county member, and he may have been partly responsible not only for the choice of General William McCormick's election as a Truro member in 1784 but also for the acquisition of three of the 128 Wheal Unity shares by the future governor of Cape Breton

Island.[1] Peter Tippetts, an adventurer in Baldhu, was a resident of Bath who had in all probability been associated with Hornblower at Radstock. Known "enemies" of Boulton and Watt like the Reeds were adventurers in Baldhu, Tresavean, Wheal Pool and Wheal Tregothnan, whilst the firm of Daubuz, with whom Boulton had had difficulties in dealings in tin, had interests in Wheal Margaret and the Lostwithiel Mine. On the other hand, friends of the Soho men, had shares in mines connected with Hornblower, notably the Foxes of Falmouth who held eleven of the sixty-four Tresavean shares and had interests in Wheal Pool: Thomas Wilson's share in Wheal Pool, however, had probably only been acquired to enable him to attend its meetings and to watch over the interests of Boulton and Watt.[2]

The situation early in 1794 was not promising to Boulton and Watt. They had stopped Bull from erecting engines by injunction, but they had not stopped Hornblower nor the even more dangerous younger Trevithick. The Courts had not declared their patent valid, and this encouraged the mines using their engines to refuse further premiums or, at least, to demand reduced premiums. Considerable sums were involved since the patent had still six years to run, whilst the very reputation of Watt's engine was at stake. Their lawyers started the lengthy preparations necessary to bring Hornblower before a Westminster law court. Had the case been tried in Cornwall the verdict would have gone against Boulton and Watt, but already, in the early stages of their action against Bull, they had defeated the effort of their opponents to make Cornwall the venue of cases involving their patent rights despite contentions about the costs entailed in bringing witnesses from Cornwall to London.

After securing the injunction against Bull, Boulton and Watt immediately took legal steps to recover premiums from the engines Bull had erected and worked and to get control of his unfinished machines at Ding Dong and Hallamannin.[3] The

---

[1]Wilbraham, supported by Basset, failed to get elected at Mitchell in 1784, but came in for Helston on a vacancy in 1786, and sat for Bodmin from 1790 to 1796. McCormick resigned his Truro seat on acquiring his colonial governorship in 1787.

[2]Wilson MSS: List of Adventurers concerned in Hornblower's Engines. (Undated—drawn up between 1796 and 1799).

[3]Wilson MSS: Weston to Wilson, April 5, 7, and 8, 1794.

threatened mines then came out in open combination[1] to challenge the validity of the patent, urged on by Bull who alleged that Wilson had told him during the course of the action against him that the Soho men had not prosecuted the Horn-blowers because they were afraid that their patent was not good in law.[2] The Soho men, perhaps not altogether wisely, rejected the request of the mines to stay costly legal proceedings pending a general meeting of the mines adventurers to suggest terms, and further alienated the miners by expressing confident hopes that the Lord Chancellor would commit Bull to jail for contemptuous evasion of the injunction.[3] The law cases dragged on, the judges being more concerned with the Hastings impeachment and with "treason trials", and hesitating to pronounce on the validity of Watt's patent on account of the reversal of the decision in the Common Pleas in Arkwright's case by the King's Bench.[4] The Soho men, however, were free to carry on actions to recover arrears of premiums from mines using either their own or Bull's engines, but when Hornblower advertised new technical improvements in his engine in the summer of 1794 Watt admitted that they could do nothing for the time.[5] The only new engine order came from the declining mine of Poldice, and even then the majority of its adventurers had wished to employ Bull. R. A. Daniell had flatly refused to pay premiums and induced the Consols adventurers, weary of the long-continued drain of premiums, to follow his lead. By the end of 1794 the Soho firm was in an even worse position than it had been at the beginning, and the Cornish "rebels" were trying to win over William Murdoch to whom Boulton and Watt had denied the opportunity of using certain technical improvements he had devised simply because they would benefit men who had shown "ingratitude" for their own past boons.[6]

While the rival engineers and adventurers were at logger-heads and enabling the lawyers to reap a goodly harvest, an

[1]Wilson MSS: Watt to Wilson, April 17, 1794.
[2]Wilson MSS: Watt to Wilson, March 22, 1794.
[3]Wilson MSS: Watt to Wilson, April 18, 1794.
[4]Wilson MSS: Weston to Wilson, June 29, 1794; Watt to Wilson, July 4, 1794.
[5]"If Jonathan's new schemes are like his old ones they will not gain him much credit; our backs being at the wall at present we must be very quiet and let them contrive a way." (Wilson MSS: Watt to Wilson, October 30 ,1794).
[6]Wilson MSS: James Watt, Jr. to Wilson, November 23, 1794; Boulton to Wilson, January 13, 1795.

undercurrent of social unrest swept to the surface. Capitalists and technicians were quarrelling over the division of profits, but the working miner, badly paid and badly fed, was showing a disposition to disturbance and riot; over-aware of events in France the richer classes feared the worst. There were complaints that some dissenting ministers were not praying for the welfare of the monarch and of the royal family as often as more orthodox ministers deemed either seemly or necessary.[1] Early in 1793, when local armed "Associations" were being set up to resist possible French invasion, some of the gentry doubted the wisdom of arming the working classes.[2] When it was proposed to form an Association in Ruan Lanihorne the Vicar, the learned antiquarian John Whittaker, told his congregation that they would be armed by the Government and thereby "be always prepared to give a warm reception to the tinners, who had so lately been visiting us." Yet before the meeting dispersed, talk among the labourers that the price of corn ought to be reduced and among the tenant farmers that rents should be lowered, roused the fears of Whittaker and of Jeremiah Trist, the Vicar of Veryan, that the:

"volunteers may turn their arms more against the farmers and the gentry, than against any invading French."[3]

In the mining districts there was far more discontent than in rural Roseland whose parsons were so alarmed by the temper of the "common men". Years later Sir Francis Basset told the artist Joseph Farington that the miners had terrorized the corndealers into accepting "Laws of the Maximum", and that the local justices were afraid to intervene. He had rushed down from London, called some of the magistrates together to swear in fifty special constables, whom Basset led by night to the houses of the ring-leaders, fifty of whom were arrested and taken to Bodmin jail to await trial at the next Assizes. Three of them were sentenced to death and others to transportation. Despite pleas for mercy, Basset insisted that one must be hung as an example, which he believed had a most salutary effect on the mining people since

[1] Rev. R. Polwhele: *Reminiscences*, Vol. 1, p. 85 (copy of a letter of Rev. J. Whittaker to Sir C. Hawkins dated January 6, 1793).
[2] Polwhele: *Reminiscences*, Vol. 1, p. 89; Whittaker to Hawkins, February 16, 1793.
[3] Polwhele: *Reminiscences*, Vol. 1, pp. 92-93; Whittaker to Hawkins, February 28, 1793.

"the manners of the people were suddenly changed from rudeness and disrespect to proper obedience."[1]

The actual Assize records suggest that Basset's story had been somewhat improved with the passing of the years. At the Assizes held in Bodmin in July, 1796, seven men only were tried for:

"Stealing fifteen bushels of wheat value £5 of Samuel Phillips in his Dwellinghouse on 5th of April last at the Parish of Redruth, the said Samuel Phillips then being therein and put in feare."

and on seven other counts. Four of the men were acquitted; the verdict against another is not recorded, but capital sentences were passed against William Sampson alias William Rose and John Hosken; Hosken was hanged and the other respited and transported for seven years.[2] At Bodmin Assizes, three years earlier, two other men had been acquitted of a charge of stealing 540 bushels of corn from a Padstow store, and the only other cases of riot before the Assizes in these years were nothing more than drunken brawls. Yet the Court records of that time do not give any conclusive idea of the social unrest prevalent in Cornwall; the fear that judicial prosecutions and punishments might only provoke worse incidents was a powerful deterrent to the gentry; at the same time the inefficiency of parochial constables was notorious.[3]

These inarticulate protests of the underpaid and underfed were alarming to the Cornish richer classes. The French Revolution had frightened the upper orders of English society; the concentration of poorer people in the mining villages and towns of Cornwall, together with an awareness of the illicit French contacts of the smuggling fraternity whose activities had been not only suffered but condoned by the gentry in less troublous times, redoubled alarm in the south-western county. In such circumstances, Cornish landlords and merchants were

---

[1] J. Farington: *Diary*, Vol. VI, p. 134 (entry of September 12, 1810); A. K. Hamilton Jenkin: *The Cornish Miner* (1948 ed.) pp. 163-4, follows Farington's account, and ascribes these events to 1795 not 1796 as the Assize records suggest was the correct date.

[2] P.R.O. Assizes 23/8. On April 13, 1796, alluding to these troubles, James Watt wrote to Thomas Wilson—"I hope the military will settle your rebellion and rejoice they (the rebels) have been kept from Truro." (Wilson MSS.).

[3] The formidable riots in Cornwall in 1847 only led to one case at the Assizes, when the maximum sentence imposed was two years imprisonment (*W.B.* August 6, 1847: see below p. 162); earlier, however, at the Midsummer Quarter Sessions two men had been transported for seven years each for looting a Redruth corn store (*W.B.* July 2 and 10, 1847).

not averse to diverting the violent passions of the working classes against Boulton and Watt[1]—against the men and not against their machines, for the most uneducated miner realized that destruction of engines meant the annihilation of the deeper mines and of the employment they provided. Formidable riots occurred at Poldice in July, 1795. The Poldice adventurers had rejected the liberal terms for a new engine offered by Boulton, a new engine that might have restored the fortunes of the mines, and asked Bull to erect an engine; when the agents of Boulton and Watt obtained a legal injunction to stop this, rioting occurred and the terrified Soho agent Lander asked his employer for permission to leave Cornwall.[2] Simon Vivian, who had given evidence in one of the actions against Bull, had already fled to Birmingham;[3] other Soho employees had been intimidated or bribed into leaving the service of Boulton and Watt. A group of mines adventurers had, in short, determined to drive the Soho men from Cornwall, and added to their troubles by haling their agents before the Stannary Courts when they refused to meet "calls" on some tin mines in which they held shares—a refusal provoked by those very mines refusing to allow them their due shares of the tinstuff which had been raised.[4] At Ding Dong the younger Trevithick went on constructing the engine Bull had begun; when, at last, the legal advisers of Boulton and Watt found out his Christian name and secured an injunction against him, they could not find a man bold enough to serve it on the young "Cornish Giant", who had threatened to throw a man down the engine-shaft and who was strong enough and quick-tempered enough to carry out such a threat.[5]

Bull's appeal in Chancery for setting aside the injunctions against him was turned down in July, 1795; his bearing in the Court, and his expressed contempt of it in Cornwall turned the judges against him and against his efforts to bring a counter-action seeking to invalidate Watt's patent.[6] Yet 1795 passed

---

[1] Just as Whig gentry half a century earlier had turned the mobs against Wesley and his followers to divert them from possible Jacobitism.

[2] Wilson MSS: Watt to Wilson, January 21, 1795; J. Watt, Jr. to William Wilson, August 3, 1795; J. Watt, Jr. to Wilson, August 4, 1795.

[3] Wilson MSS: J. Watt, Jr. to Wilson, July 21, 1795.

[4] Wilson MSS: Watt to Wilson, January 20 and 21, 1795.

[5] Wilson MSS: Weston to Wilson, June 11 and November 17, 1795; J. Watt, Jr. to Wilson, December 15, 1795.

[6] Wilson MSS: Weston to Wilson, July 20, 1795.

by with no legal pronouncement that that patent was valid. A business quarrel with John Wilkinson,[1] who had for so long been supplying them with cylinders and other engine parts, led the Soho men to decide to become engine manufacturers themselves instead of acting merely as consulting engineers assembling machines from parts supplied by other manufacturers.[2] This decision, which led to the establishment of the Soho Foundry at Smethwick in the closing months of the year, made it more necessary than ever to vindicate the reputation of their engines. A hint was circulated that had the Cornish adventurers been more grateful Boulton and Watt would long before have provided them with vastly improved engines,[3] whilst Wilson was asked to draw up an account listing all the benefits which their engines had provided the Cornish mining industry.[4] This extension of the activities of the Soho firm was necessary, too, if they wished to retain their connection with the steam engine business, for in a few years the patent would expire—if it were not invalidated earlier by the Courts. Meanwhile litigation must continue to vindicate the reputations and prestige of Boulton and Watt and to recover the withheld premiums. There was some chance that they might secure the services of Trevithick and other engineers associated with Bull, and the very scarcity of skilled engineers was an immense advantage to the Soho men in their new venture, which was the first attempt of free capitalist enterprise to capture the markets for steam engines. All that vindication of the patent meant to them for the future was the retention of business and technological prestige.

The litigation in 1796 was chiefly directed against the Hornblowers, Bull having practically given up the fight when, in January, the Attorney-General refused to grant him a writ of *scire facias* like that which had defeated Arkwright.[5] Other "pirates" in the North of England were coming to terms with Boulton and Watt, but in Cornwall there was a formidable alliance of the Hornblowers with the Truro merchant and mine

[1]Wilson MSS: J. Watt, Jr. to Wilson, March 24, 1795.
[2]Boulton and Watt, however, had been progressively increasing the number and proportion of the machine parts made in their own factory at Soho. (H. W. Dickinson: *Matthew Boulton*, p. 164).
[3]Wilson MSS: Watt to Wilson, April 22, 1795.
[4]Wilson MSS: Weston to Wilson, June 22, 1795.
[5]Wilson MSS: J. Watt, Jr. to Wilson, January 16, 1796.

adventurer, Daniell, backed to some degree by John Wilkinson.[1]   Jonathan and Jethro Hornblower had forgotten their earlier quarrel, perhaps only because the Soho men had opened hostilities by seeking an injunction against a third brother, Jabez,[2] to which the family countered by filing nine affidavits in Chancery asserting that Watt's invention had not been new, and that his patent specifications were not adequate in point of law.[3]   The legal actions were then delayed by the general election of 1796[4] and by the overtures of Hornblower's partner, D. A. Maberley, for a settlement which lasted until October.[5]   Finally, despite the "croaking" despondency of Thomas Wilson, harassed by his other business worries, racked with gout, and forced to live among the enemies of Soho,[6] a decision was obtained against Maberley and Hornblower for "piracy" in December, 1796.[7]   Even yet, however, the patent had not been declared valid, but the attempt of the Hornblowers to secure a new trial was rejected by the judges.[8] The overtures made earlier by Maberley and, long before, by Hornblower's first partner, Winwood, demonstrated, however, that the challenge to their machines was made by working engineers and not by merchant manufacturers who might establish engineering works to compete against the new Soho foundry.

The most startling events of 1796, however, arose from the strange conduct of the younger Trevithick. No one in Cornwall would serve an injunction on him, but Boulton and Watt could get injunctions against the mines working the machines he made. In July he offered his services to the Soho firm, either in Cornwall or, preferably at Soho, through the mine adventurer Thomas Gundry. After considerable hesitation, perhaps

[1]Wilson MSS: Watt to Wilson, March 4 and 20 and May 9, 1796; Boulton and Watt to Wilson, March 18 and 28, 1796.
[2]Wilson MSS: J. Watt, Jr. to Wilson, January 5, 1796.
[3]Wilson MSS: J. Watt, Jr. to Wilson, May 13 and 18, 1796; Watt to Wilson, May 17, 1796. The affidavits were those of the four Hornblowers, Jonathan, Jethro, Jesse and Jabez, of their employees Strode and Arthur Woolf and of Bramah, David Watson and Rowntree whom the younger Watt denounced as pirates themselves.
[4]Wilson MSS: J. Watt, Jr. to Wilson, May 24, 1796.
[5]Wilson MSS: Boulton and Watt to Wilson, September 20, 1796; J. Watt, Jr to Wilson, October 27, 1796.
[6]Wilson MSS: J. Watt, Jr. to Wilson, November 26, 1796.
[7]Wilson MSS: Boulton to Wilson, December 26, 1796.
[8]Wilson MSS: Watt to Wilson, February 8, 1797; M. R. Boulton to Wilson, February 13 and 19, 1797.

because they suspected that the offer was not genuine and that he only wanted to come to Soho to spy out their most recent devices, Boulton and Watt offered to employ him in Cornwall; Murdoch opposed this, but Trevithick, scorning a wage of a guinea a week which was much less than Stray Park had been paying him as a retaining fee years earlier, made no answer to this offer. Then, in December, he appeared at Soho along with Bull and Andrew Vivian. It is possible that he came as a "spy" at the behest of the "rebel" Cornish adventurers with whom he was connected, although natural professional interest in the progress of his trade could justify and explain his visit. His appearance at Soho gave the agents of Boulton and Watt their long awaited opportunity to serve on him the injunction debarring him from erecting and working any more engines which incorporated Watt's patented devices, whether they were designed by Bull or by himself.[1] Yet it was but a hollow victory for the Soho men; they had stopped Edward Bull; the expenses of litigation were to bring Jonathan Hornblower into a debtor's jail; Richard Trevithick, however, after visiting Wilkinson at Coalbrookdale, was to return to Cornwall all the more determined to evade the patent if possible. In the next year, 1797, he was working the Ding Dong engine with an open-topped cylinder and devised his first plunger-pole engine, the type which, improved as the years went by, was to supersede many of the earlier Watt machines; moreover, no less than nineteen Cornish mines were employing him or men connected with him as consultant and as working engineers.[2]

Whilst Trevithick improved and transformed the steam engine, Watt and Boulton began to realize that they had dissipated their energies and abilities on litigation instead of furthering the progress of mechanical invention and power. Rather too late they became aware of the fact that they had lost the good will of many of the most influential Cornish mines adventurers; there was a very real risk that they would lose the Cornish engine market unless they were more accommodating in the future. The slowness of lawyers and Courts, it is true, gave time to settle feuds amicably, but they failed to make use

[1]Wilson MSS: Thomas Gundry to Boulton and Watt, July 5, 1796; M. R. Boulton to Wilson, July 12, 1796; J. Watt, Jr. to Wilson, July 19 and August 9, 1796; Boulton to Wilson, December 26, 1796. F. Trevithick, Vol. 1, p. 56.
[2]Wilson MSS: Boulton to Wilson, December 26, 1796; J. Watt, Jr. to Wilson, December 30, 1796. F. Trevithick, Vol. 1, pp. 60-70.

of this opportunity. When Trevithick again approached Boulton and Watt, in the summer of 1797, and asked for terms allowing him to erect machines of their type at the United Mines, they were in a quandary. If they refused, their Foundry would lose work, probably to Wilkinson at Coalbrookdale; if they accepted, they would have to accept reduced premiums for the remaining three years of their patent and sacrifice some past arrears, thereby jeopardising their chances of recovering arrears from other defaulting mines; above all, they distrusted Trevithick, on whose employment all the Western mines were insisting. Underlying all was fear—fear that the improvements Trevithick claimed could be substantiated and fear that the Courts might even yet disallow their patent. Nevertheless, whatever lawyers and judges might decide, the real conflict now was one between a manufacturing establishment, engaged in constructing machines, and an engineer who was all-powerful in the richer western mining districts of Cornwall, an engineer of a different calibre from Jonathan Hornblower, Edward Bull, and even from James Watt himself. Trevithick was ready to go further than Hornblower and Bull in changing the designs and principles of the steam engine; whereas the older engineers and Watt had reached their final conclusions by patient experiment and research, the Camborne man had an entirely different approach; most of his results were achieved not by the processes of slow cogitation but by flashes of intuition which left reason far behind. Whilst the mental processes of Watt and Hornblower had been those of painstaking thought fostered by the theological and religious background of the older dissenting sects, those of Trevithick had been developed in that Methodist background wherein sudden intuitive conversions were regarded as the greatest if not the only manifestations of divine grace. Few of his friends thought Richard Trevithick paid much heed to religion, yet his widespread wanderings to install different types of steam engines to increase the wealth of mankind can be likened to the travels of itinerant Methodist missionaries and their call to go into places of spiritual darkness with their messages of salvation through divine power.

Eventually Trevithick came to terms with Boulton and Watt about the engines he erected at Ding Dong and in St. Agnes.[1]

[1]Wilson MSS: J. Watt, Jr. to Wilson, March 22, 1798.

Hornblower and Bull carried on their struggle against Soho, with but indifferent success.[1]   Not until January, 1799, did the Court of King's Bench finally decide that Watt's patent was valid; next year the patent expired, and the age of conflict came to an end, perhaps to the relief of both engineers and adventurers although lawyers may have felt some regret.

Whilst the services of James Watt to Cornwall were great, the methods employed by him and his partner, Boulton, to secure recompense for those services can be criticised. Their initial mistake lay in the failure to establish the engine manufactory which Watt had originally suggested; had they done so the Cornish mines adventurers would have paid a fair price for their engines instead of being compelled to buy the component parts from a number of firms, to pay all the costs of erection and of maintenance, and, above all, to continue to pay premiums on the savings of fuel for so long as the patent lasted. Watt's patent specification had been drafted in such a form that hardly any type of steam engine could be designed without infringing it. The efforts of Bull, Hornblower, and others to evade this patent had diverted mechanical inventiveness from other lines of practical development which might have been far more useful. Even when men did discover better methods and devices they could not use them without licence from Boulton and Watt. On occasion, too, Watt displayed a petty jealousy of younger and more daring inventors, even dissuading the loyal William Murdoch from effecting improvements which would have been both practicable and valuable. Nevertheless, no one could have foreseen in 1775 that the extension of monopolistic patent rights for a quarter of a century would, before that time had passed, come to be a brake on the progress of industrial expansion which had accelerated to a rate hitherto unprecedented.

Watt's engines were efficient in their own day, and even later, after 1800, Jonathan Hornblower himself erected machines of the Watt type,[2] but Boulton, the business man of the partnership, had failed to make adequate provision for the expanding demand for steam power. The continued exaction of premiums was a tax on progress, aggravated at times by the failing

[1]Wilson MSS: Boulton and Watt to Wilson, December 9, 1797; J. Watt, Jr. to Wilson, December 20, 1797; Boulton and Watt to Messrs. Foxes, June 25, 1798.
[2]Rhys Jenkins: "Jonathan Hornblower and the Compound Engine": *T.N.S.*, Vol. XI, p. 151.

fortunes of certain mining concerns and by more general economic recessions. Monopolistic rights, linked with the restriction of production, failed to meet the increasing demand for copper which came in the closing years of the Cornish Metal Company ; while, after 1793, the war needs of Britain, coinciding with the declining produce of Anglesey, despite an embargo on the export of copper, created a demand on Cornish mines which offered unprecedented opportunities to adventurers and engine-makers alike. Unfortunately, by that time, the feud of the rival parties had been so embittered by costly litigation that some of the mines adventurers had virtually declared that they would be independent of the Soho men at all costs; they would get their engines elsewhere and employ their own men to build and maintain them. The new Soho Foundry was set up too late for Boulton and Watt to regain control of the Cornish engine market.

The feud had also stimulated Cornish inventiveness. The much maligned Bull machine proved rather more efficient and economical than Wattite propaganda admitted; Hornblower's double-cylinder was developed into effective compound engines. If no reliance can be placed on the early competitive tests of the rival engines and on contemporary claims as to the the magnitude of the duty they attained, there can be no doubt that Hornblower's engines worked to the general satisfaction of the Tincroft and Wheal Unity adventurers; furthermore, the demands of some of the Consols and United Mines adventurers that Hornblower and Trevithick be employed furnishes proof of their belief that these men's engines were not only cheaper but more efficient than those of Watt, for, if the machines of the "pirates" were identical with those of the patentees, there was no point in embarking on costly litigation to save premium charges that would have to be partly devoted to paying for the services of the rival engineers.

What the Cornish engineers and adventurers wanted was freedom to use new machines and to adapt them to changing conditions. Personal enmities embittered and confounded the issue which was fundamentally a clash between monopolistic control and free enterprise. The separate condenser was of the greatest utility and value to Cornish mining, whilst the greater precision on which Watt insisted in the making of machine parts was a great step forward. The example of Boulton and

Watt led some Cornish adventurers to adopt more businesslike methods in their enterprises. Yet, after 1788, Boulton and Watt impeded the progress of Cornish engineering and mining; they could or would not supply enough machines on reasonable terms; they checked some considerable improvements in engine designs; and they stirred up rancours and hatreds which festered long after their patent rights expired.

CHAPTER IV

THE AGE OF POWER

1800-1850

THE END of Watt's patent rights did not immediately lead to radical changes in the engines used in Cornish mines. For several years Watt engines continued to drain those mines. Indeed, the withdrawal of the Soho men from Cornwall seems to have led to an immediate deterioration of the performances of the pumping engines after 1800. The early engine tests were of little value, but even if Watt engines, using the best fuel and with friction artificially reduced to an absolute minimum, had exceeded twenty-seven millions, their average duty under normal working conditions can hardly have exceeded two-thirds of that duty. But when the Soho party left Cornwall they took the majority of the skilled engineers with them, and, deprived of their painstaking supervisory care, the Cornish engines showed a marked decline in efficiency that was not to be redeemed for some years. In 1800, too, the greater number of Watt's engines in Cornwall had been in operation for at least fifteen and in most cases for over twenty years; some of them had been moved more than once from one mine to another and must have been impaired in dismantling, removal, and re-erection despite the care taken by some of the engineers in charge. Now and again an engineer like Joel Lean would improve the performances of the engines in his care, but it can be doubted if many of the engines in Cornwall averaged a duty of more than twelve millions in the first decade of the nineteenth century.[1]

Apart from the men taken away by the Soho firm, other engineers were no longer working on Cornish mines. Jonathan Hornblower's reputation had been blasted and his financial resources annihilated by the litigation of the 1790s. Arthur Woolf had gone to London, where he remained until 1811.[2]

[1]Lean, pp. 6-9.
[2]Rhys Jenkins: "A Cornish Engineer: Arthur Woolf" : *T.N.S.*, Vol. XIII, pp. 55-56.

Richard Trevithick, after successfully adapting the principle of the plunger-pole to pumping engines, had turned his attention to wider engineering fields. Trevithick had demonstrated to his own satisfaction that the efficiency of pumping engines could be vastly increased by using expansive steam and that the pump itself could be improved by replacing buckets with plungers;[1] if conservative and over-cautious mines adventurers did not choose to adopt these ideas that was their affair, not Trevithick's. Instead of working away at these devices and perfecting them to improve mine drainage, Trevithick left that painstaking, humdrum, and tedious task to lesser engineers, devoting his own energies to locomotives, shipping, and other problems—his genius would not suffer itself to be confined to a single narrow field of the engineering realm.[2] Time and time again in his career Trevithick was a pioneer, but he never settled down to develop any of the fertile fields of invention into which he stumbled more often by flights of intuition than by painstaking *a priori* reasoning. He was a restless, inspired genius, a type of man not uncommonly encountered in other spheres of human creative life and endeavour but one rarely associated with practical engineering. It has at times been suggested that had he found a Boulton to back him, Trevithick would not have ended his days a virtual pauper; but he was too much an individualist to co-operate for long with any other man, and it might be questioned whether any shrewd business man would have risked entering into partnership with a volatile adventurer who would, almost without warning, throw everything aside to go to revolutionary Spanish America on a renewed rumour of the riches of El Dorado.

The locomotive venture was typical. After four or five years casual experimenting, the "Dragon" was tested on the road between Camborne and Redruth at Christmastide, 1801. Accounts of the trial differ; it may well have been prematurely initiated in a spirit of drunken bravado. Whether the engine was badly steered and upset in a ditch, or whether it was merely

[1]F. Trevithick, Vol. 1, pp. 67-69. The plunger pump had been first invented and patented by Sir Samuel Morland in 1675; William Murdoch had used one as a temporary makeshift in Ale and Cakes Mine in 1796, but Trevithick had asserted in 1797 that it should be used in preference to bucket-pumps on all occasions, since it required less elaborate and less costly "pit-work" besides reducing friction in all pumping operations.
[2]H. W. Dickinson and A. Titley: *Richard Trevithick, the Engineer and the Man*, Appendix 11, pp. 278 ff.

left outside a public-house by its "crew" who forgot to shut off
steam with disastrous consequences, is not clear from second-
hand accounts and recollections of the venture or escapade.[1]
Trevithick, however, did not lose faith in this locomotive, and
patented it in March, 1802.[2] Then, instead of doing anything
to perfect this "road carriage", Trevithick experimented,
rather spasmodically in the intervals of other engineering works,
with locomotives designed to run on specially-constructed railway tracks or tram-roads. One of these later locomotives had
relatively successful trials at Penydaren in South Wales early
in 1804, but the ill-success of trials on a circular track in London
in 1808 were wholly due to defects not in the engine but in the
permanent way. Had Trevithick then attempted to improve
the construction of permanent ways his claim to be considered
the real pioneer of railway locomotive transport would have
been unassailable, but he seems to have been constitutionally
incapable of such unspectacular but vital work.

Trevithick's interest in locomotives sprang from the problems
of commercial transport in Cornwall in his own time. The
growing output of ores from the mines and the increased
demands for fuel to raise and to prepare those ores for sale
required more and better transportation facilities than
the old pack-horse and mule transport that had served in
earlier times. The increasing mining population, too, meant
more extensive arable farming for grain and potatoes, which
not only increased the calls on animal labour but also reduced
the area of pasture-lands whereon these animals had lived. The
situation was partly met by the development of wheeled transport, but the greater number of Cornish roads were unfit for
carts and waggons, whilst for years to come there were complaints, not limited to Cornwall, that narrow-wheeled vehicles
were damaging the roads to an incredible extent by cutting
deep ruts.[3]

To solve this problem, the first Cornish "railway" or tramroad, running from the mines of the Redruth district down to
Portreath haven, was projected at the time when Trevithick was
engaged in making locomotives and steam dredgers in New-
castle-on-Tyne and London. The moving spirit was Sir

[1]Dickinson and Titley: *Richard Trevithick*, pp. 46 ff.
[2]Dickinson and Titley: *Richard Trevithick*, Appendix 1, pp. 269 ff.
[3]*W.B.*: February 5, 1819. P. Mantoux: *The Industrial Revolution in the Eighteenth
Century*, pp. 120-121.

Francis Basset, now Lord de Dunstanville, who had taken an active interest in Trevithick's locomotive experiments, and who may have been told of the tramroads already used by the South Wales and Tyneside collieries by the vagabond Camborne engineer. By 1806 a group of speculative adventurers had agreed to construct a line from Portreath to Dolcoath, de Dunstanville taking a controlling interest of thirty-one out of sixty shares.[1] The total cost of the undertaking came to some £16,000, but early in 1814 it started paying dividends which soon reached $4\frac{1}{2}$% on the investment. In 1824 the "Eastern" mining interest, aware of the financial success and of the value of the Portreath railway to the "Western" mines, secured an Act of Parliament to enable them to construct a line from the Chacewater mines to Restronguet Creek on the Fal estuary, and this was opened for public use early in 1826.[2] The third "railway" in Cornwall was that projected between St. Austell and Pentewan in August, 1826, to serve the needs of the already quite considerable and progressive local china clay trade; four years later this line was running a regular passenger as well as "goods" service.[3]

The mining industries served by these engines and transportation facilities experienced rather variable fortunes in the early years of the nineteenth century. With the virtual exhaustion of the Anglesey copper deposits by 1800, Cornwall became the premier copper producing region of the world. The high prices of copper during the years of the French Wars, however, do not accurately reflect the state of the Cornish mines in that

[1] De Dunstanville contributed £1,194 2s. 5d. to the first call of £2,300 to acquire iron plates and other materials on May 23, 1826; later, however, he only held a sixth of the shares (Tehidy MSS Accounts, 1798-1842.).

[2] *W.B.*: February 3, 1826. *Old Cornwall* : October, 1926, pp. 9-12. Trucks running on these tram-roads went on down gradients by the force of gravity; on the up-gradients they were drawn by horses, and rather later in certain cases (notably at Portreath, at Angarrack near Hayle, and at Pont's Mill near St. Blazey) by stationary engines installed at the summit of steep inclines.

[3] *W.B.*: September 1, 1826, and June 11, 1830. Passengers were taken the whole distance of the railway, about four miles, for 3d. At this time Pentewan was one of the principal china clay exporting ports; it also exported some granite; it declined after J. T. Austen provided Par with superior harbour facilities. The actual output of china clay and china stone in Western England had risen from below 4,000 tons in 1816 to nearly 13,000 tons in 1826; the greater part of this came from the district between St. Austell and St. Stephens in Brannel, but the number employed in the clay works of that area can hardly have exceeded 400 in 1826, although a greater number may have been casually employed. In the clay works scattered in other parishes of Cornwall and Devon the number of persons engaged thereon can hardly have exceeded the number of carpenters and blacksmiths working in those parishes. (D. Cock: *A Treatise on China Clay*, p. 123).

period. The fluctuations in the "standard" of the smelters were extreme, rising from £121 in 1799 to nearly £170 in 1805, and falling to below £101 in 1808. Over the whole period of seventeen years from 1799 to 1815, however, the standard only fell below £110 in one year and exceeded £140 in two, whilst in six years it ranged between £130 and £140 and in seven between £120 and £130.[1] Although the prices obtained by the miners for their ores bore some relation to the standards, the declining produce of 'fine' copper from those ores meant smaller profits; produce, too, varied inversely with the standard because higher prices made it profitable to sell lower grade ores, although the profit per ton was less. The high standard of 1805 coincided with the low average produce of $7\frac{7}{8}$, whilst the low standard of 1808 occurred in the only year of the nineteenth century in which the average produce of Cornish ores was 10. It is not likely that the miners ever secured more than three quarters or less than two thirds of the standard price—the rates that were general in the closing years of the previous century; in 1808 they probably obtained between £70 and £75 per ton, but it is unlikely that the low grade ores of the boom year three years before realized more than £140 per ton and may not have been much above £120.[2] Profits were reduced by the general rise in prices of necessary materials for working in the war years, whilst it must be remembered that a general price of copper which assured a handsome profit to one mine would leave another working at a loss. On the average, Cornish copper mining paid during the war years, but there were mines which incurred heavy losses.

The actual production of copper ore in Cornwall was increasing, but the high prices of 1805 led to overproduction in 1806, the output of 79,269 tons in that year not being surpassed until 1818, whilst the low prices of 1808 reduced production to little above 66,000 tons in 1810. Whereas the quantity of copper ore mined in Cornwall rose by nearly forty per cent between 1800 and 1815, the amount of fine copper from those ores only

---

[1] Hunt, p. 892.

[2] See p. 76 n. 2 above. Adequate data to obtain an accurate estimate of the prices obtained by the miners is lacking; it would entail complete details of all sales made by all the working mines in Cornwall. The relationship of the standard to miners' prices, too, cannot be accurately gauged in the absence of full details of the comparative costs of smelting and refining low and high grade ores, and in the absence of complete details of the expenses incurred by every working Cornish mine in raising these ores.

increased by about twenty-five per cent.[1] Remembering the recent fate of Anglesey mining, some thought that this declining produce betokened the imminent exhaustion of the Cornish copper mines, especially since a larger proportion of the ticketing sales were made after 1810 by newer mines, particularly by Crinnis and other mines in the Par district. Optimists might aver that improved methods made it possible to work and sell inferior ores at a profit, but no one could deny that the older mines had to be worked deeper and at increasing costs and that every experience showed that the richness of copper lodes did not increase with depth.

The fluctuations in copper prices during the war years can be attributed to many causes. Renewed hostilities with France in 1803 increased naval and military demands for copper; the economic warfare initiated by the Berlin and Milan Decrees and the retaliatory British Orders in Council were partly responsible for the low prices in 1808 and in one or two later years. The activities of enemy privateers were the main cause for the reduction of copper sales to the East India Company from about £370,000 in 1803 to little more than £45,000 in 1806, although the average annual sale for the ensuing five years rallied to above £260,000.[2] The East Indian market had become important in the days of Thomas Williams and the Parys Mines as a means of disposing of the surplus production of British copper,[3] and with Continental markets closed by Napoleon's Decrees it had become more important, especially since the British Government took every care to prevent the sale of war materials to neutrals who might resell to the enemy. Like the 'tinners', the Cornish copper mining interest adopted the policy of combining to set aside part of their ores to supply the East India Company; thus, in 1810, they agreed, at Redruth, to set aside a sixth of the next year's output for the Company, but, a week later, they reduced the period to six months only.[4]

A drastic fall in copper prices in the late summer of 1810 led to a further meeting of the copper mining interest on November

[1]In 1800 55,981 tons of copper ore produced 5,187 tons of copper; in 1815, 78,483 produced 6,526 tons. (Hunt, p. 892).
[2]J. Macgregor: *Commercial Statistics*, Vol. IV, p. 410.
[3]Wilson MSS: Boulton to Wilson, May 5 and July 30, 1787, and June 29, 1789; Watt to Wilson, August 11 and 21, 1787.
[4]*W.B.*: August 17 and 24, 1810.

1st, with Lord de Dunstanville in the chair.[1] The slump was attributed to abnormal foreign imports, and the prohibition of foreign copper was demanded, although no one stated where these imports were coming from.[2] The meeting, perhaps rightly, asserted that the French were getting all the copper they required for military and naval purposes, and that, therefore, the continued ban on exports of British copper only injured British mining and manufacturing interests without inconveniencing Bonaparte to the slightest degree. A few oɪ the men present at the meeting, aware of the currency difficulties of the day, wished to press the Government to institute a new pure copper coinage.

The situation, however, was ameliorated by reduced output and by a new agreement with the East India Company, concluded by agents of the copper miners in London, whereby the Company undertook to buy 300 tons of copper at "reasonable terms". In consequence of this, and aware that the Company's "reasonable terms" was considerably below the normal market price, the 'miners' met at Redruth again on December 17th. to discuss the best way of sharing among themselves the cost of this agreement, a cost that to most of them entailed no actual pecuniary loss but a diminution of prospective profits. All they attained agreement on was a resolution that:

"to facilitate the said sale we will contribute and pay to the sellers £10 per ton on 300 tons £3,000 . . . to be raised by adequate and equal percentages, on the amounts of all Ores that have or may be sold or stocked in the last four months of 1810.

"It being distinctly understood that we engage each other for himself only, and not the one for the other, not however, in the least doubting that all persons will co-operate with us, and accede to a measure so obviously for the interest of the Cornish Miners."[3]

Eight months later, in August, 1811, the East India Company offered to take 1,500 tons of copper at £115 per ton; the offer was accepted, though many thought the price rather low;[4] most "miners", however, felt small profits preferable to running the

[1]*W.B.*: November 2, 1810.

[2]The Peninsular War may have occasioned the unloading of an accumulation of several years from Spanish American copper mines, particularly those of Cuba, on the British market. World production of fine copper outside Great Britain only averaged 2,600 tons in the decade 1801-10. (N. Brown and C. C. Turnbull: *A Century of Copper*, p.2).

[3]W.B.: December 21, 1810.

[4]*W.B.*: August 16, 1811.

risk of a glutted market which would eliminate all profits. A similar agreement was made in July, 1812,[1] and in return the copper mining interest was prominent among the groups petitioning Parliament for the renewal of the East India Company's charter in February, 1813.[2]

The gap of never less than £25 and often more than £30 between the prices the "miners" obtained for their ores and the smelters' standard[3] caused some grumbling against the extortions and exorbitant profits of the smelters. This, however, was not so pronounced as it had been in earlier times, mainly because influential groups of mines adventurers were now associates in smelting concerns. In 1810 Richard Hussey Vivian and John Henry Vivian, the sons of Boulton's old associate in the Cornish Metal Company, started the Hafod Copper Works at Swansea; twenty-one years later the Williams family of Gwennap acquired the site of the adjoining Morfa Works. Even before this, in 1803, Pasco Grenfell, who had considerable interests as a merchant and mine adventurer in western Cornwall, had entered into partnership with Owen Williams, son of Thomas Williams of Parys, in the Copper Bank Smelting Works near Swansea, and by 1826 the Grenfells had secured the whole interest in these works.[4] The copper industry was becoming closely integrated; what adventurers lost as miners they more than recovered as smelters, but as time went by the miner-smelter was faced with a dilemma arising from the increased production of foreign copper ores; when that crisis came the Grenfells were inclined to sacrifice the protection of Cornish copper mining to extend their smelting of foreign copper ores, whereas the Williamses were inclined to fight for the retention of prohibitive duties against imports.[5]

During the war years it had been the policy of the Government to admit foreign copper ores, and, at the same time, to restrict and at times prohibit the exportation of copper from

---

[1] *W.B.*: July 24, 1812.
[2] *W.B.*: February 26, 1813.
[3] *Vide* Appendix No. III, p. 331 below.
[4] G. Grant-Francis: *The Smelting of Copper in the Swansea District*, pp. 121-2, 126, 136, 141, etc.
[5] Both families had acquired interests in foreign mines before Peel's Budgets drastically cut the duties on imported copper ores. The Grenfells were among the main shareholders in the Cuban Cobre mines; the Williams family were rather less directly interested, through the holdings of their co-adventurers and managers of the Consolidated Mines, in the Real del Monte Mexican Silver Mining Company of 1823.

Britain, a policy first adopted during the American Revolutionary War. In 1814 the duties on imported copper were only 9½d. per ton, the average price of Cornish ores in that year being £8 15s. 6d. per ton. The smelting interests were further protected by duties of 9/11¼d. per hundredweight on unwrought bricks and pigs of copper and of £1 10s. 5¾d. per hundredweight on 'partly wrought' copper plates and bars, besides a further duty of £1 per hundredweight on these categories of copper which, imposed in 1812 as a revenue duty for the duration of the war was extended for a further five years in 1815. Manufacturers of copper goods were protected by an *ad valorem* duty of 59⅜% on foreign copper manufactures. Soon after the end of the war these duties were changed to the detriment of the manufacturers, to the doubtful benefit of the smelters, but unquestionably to the benefit of the miners; by 1819 the duty on foreign manufactured copper goods had been lowered to 50%, that on unwrought copper raised to £2 14s. 2d. and on partly wrought to £3 15s. 6d. per hundredweight, but the duty on foreign copper ores had been raised to £21 per ton.

These import duties had been imposed to raise revenue rather than to protect the mining interest. It is doubtful if they really stimulated Cornish mining enterprise. Only in one year—1819—between Waterloo and the final abolition of import duties on foreign copper ores, in 1848, did the price obtained by Cornish miners for their ores represent more than £100 per ton of fine copper, and when the speculative boom began in 1823 the price was hovering around the low £75 level.[1] At these low prices many mines, especially the smaller concerns, were working at a loss, but with some three or four score mines normally raising and selling ores every year during this period it is impossible to arrive at any real estimate of the fortunes of the entire mining interest; in the best years hardly a third of the working mines paid dividends, whilst, through the different sizes of the various mines, a relatively small proportion of the capital sunk in the industry might gain a very disproportionate share of the total dividends paid out by copper mines in one year, although in another year there might be a more equitable division of perhaps smaller total profits.

The great profits made by a few mines inevitably attracted the greatest attention and stimulated new speculations. Crinnis

[1] *Vide* Appendix No. III, p. 331 below.

sprang into prominence in this way early in 1814, and before long the older western mining interests were fearing that a second Parys had been discovered in Cornwall itself.[1] There were to be further discoveries in the Crinnis district but, for another generation, the Camborne-Redruth copper mining region maintained its predominance, with Dolcoath, a better-managed Consolidated Mines in the control of the Williamses, and, for a short period, Tresavean making great profits. Other mines struggled on, but the managers of even the most profitable mines realized that copper deposits once mined were gone for ever, and devoted their attention more and more to the problems of reducing costs by greater and more efficient use of mechanical power. The deeper the miners pursued the richer lodes the more expensive and more dependent on steam power mining became.

The problems of economical deep-mining explain the phenomenal developments in Cornish engineering after 1810 when Trevithick returned to his native county to be followed by Arthur Woolf a year later. At the same time Joel Lean started inducing mine managers to register and publish monthly accounts of the engines working in the mines they supervised; the comparative performances, he felt, would stimulate friendly rivalry and benefit all by revealing the most efficient types of machines in use. The average duty of a dozen engines reporting in 1811 was only seventeen millions. Lean was then appointed Register and Reporter of the Duty of Engines, and persuaded an increasing number of mine captains to send in monthly engine reports; by 1814 32 engines were reported, the average duty having risen to 20,600,000; in 1820 the average duty of 45 engines was 28,700,000, whilst by 1829 the average duty of 53 engines was no less than 41,700,000.[2]

The first new engine presaging this vast increase in efficiency was that erected by Trevithick at Wheal Prosper in Gwithian. In it he employed a plunger-pole and used steam at a pressure of a hundred pounds to the square inch. Hitherto 'strong' steam had only been used in a few small whim-engines in Cornwall, simply because the mines adventurers had been afraid of using high-pressure steam on any extensive scale—not that they can be condemned outright for excessive prudence for the

[1]*W.B.*: April 14, 1815 and March 22, 1816.
[2]Lean: pp. 10-11, 32, 97.

disastrous explosion of one of Trevithick's own boilers at Greenwich in September, 1803, when four persons were killed, revealed the dangers of high-pressure steam, although, as a consequence of this disaster, which he attributed to leaving the engine in charge of a boy who played truant to go eel-fishing, Trevithick had promptly devised "fool-proof" safety devices.[1] The great advantage of this new engine, apart from the vast increase in power it effected, was that it cost less than £500,[2] whilst its small size compared to that of the older low-pressure atmospheric pumping engines made it easier and cheaper to move from one mine to another or to move to different places on the same mine. Trevithick only regarded this engine as a small model designed to demonstrate what high-pressure steam could do. He claimed no patent rights for it; others were free to copy it if they would. Trevithick then experimented successfully with steam-threshing engines, and early in 1812 told Sir John Sinclair, the President of the Board of Agriculture, that all agricultural operations could be performed by steam power; then, receiving little encouragement in England, he induced some West Indians to install his machines on their sugar plantations.[3] His assertions that steam power could accomplish everything were far in advance of his time, and met little response from the more prudent and conservative mines adventurers and still less from the contemporary farmers.

Arthur Woolf's claims were less revolutionary. In London he had patented a tubular boiler in 1803, and had then experimented with high pressure steam in compound engines of the Hornblower type but with little success. His employers, the Meux brewery, tired of his prolonged experiments and installed a Watt engine whereupon Woolf, a brusque and jealous man who did not get on well with his fellows, left out of pique and entered into partnership with Humphrey Edwards.[4] Not until 1811 did Woolf complete an engine which, working in a flour mill, performed nearly three times the duty of the Watt machine hitherto employed there, but it should be added that this Watt engine was old and practically worn out. Returning to Corn-

[1]H. W. Dickinson and A. Titley: *Richard Trevithick, the Engineer and the Man*, pp. 59 ff.
[2]F. Trevithick, Vol. II, pp. 69 ff.
[3]F. Trevithick, Vol. 11, pp. 43 ff.
[4]Rhys Jenkins: "A Cornish Engineer—Arthur Woolf", *T.N.S.* Vol. XIII, pp. 55 ff.

wall, Woolf was soon put in charge of the engines at Wheal Crenver, Oatfield, and Wheal Abraham in Crowan. In 1814 he erected a double-cylinder engine at Wheal Abraham which maintained an average duty of over 32,000,000 for four months; he improved it and in 1816 it recorded a duty of nearly 57,000,000.[1] He erected a second engine of the compound type at Wheal Vor which attained a duty of about 50,000,000 in 1816.

Woolf had many critics, and as late as 1824 some of them were alleging that he had attained no higher duties than Watt had done a generation earlier.[2] His claim to have invented the tubular boiler has not gone unquestioned, nor can it be denied that in his great pumping engines the fundamental principles were those of Hornblower and Trevithick. Had they worked together Trevithick and Woolf might have done much, but both were poor collaborators, Trevithick from the natural impatience of an intuitive genius that leapt to conclusions that others could not see or grasp and from a rather quick temper, Woolf from sheer misanthropy and from a consistently bad temper. The dislike Woolf aroused among his fellows injured his reputation irreparably; the adventurous career of Trevithick created a sensational haze about his life and work which has obscured the judgment of later ages on Woolf and many other engineers of the early nineteenth century. Woolf had one great quality which Trevithick lacked—a dogged patience that enabled him to plod away and thereby achieve final success; he took consummate pains to gain results; the tortoise to Trevithick's hare, Woolf was the first to prove convincingly that high pressure steam could be safely and economically used, and it was he, not Trevithick, who first doubled the duty reached by Watt's best engines. Woolf was not a man who would reach conclusions, right or wrong, by flashes of sheer intuitive genius, nor one to quickly assemble a machine from any material that lay to hand, achieve an initial success with it, and then, when a breakdown occurred through defective materials, stand back asserting to the world that the engine was a success and that the world must make the best shift it might to put it together again, preferably with better materials, while he devoted his attention to something entirely different.

[1] Lean, p. 31.
[2] *W.B.*: July 2 and August 14, 1824.

Trevithick lacked more than a Boulton—he lacked contact with teachers like those of Glasgow University who had given Watt some inkling of the way to communicate knowledge to others of lesser abilities with patience and a fair modicum of success.

Yet it was not entirely a coincidence that during the years Trevithick was in Latin America little further progress was made in developing the pumping engine in Cornwall. Just before he sailed, Trevithick patented a plunger-pole pumping engine, which, however, does not seem to have eclipsed the performances of Woolf's compound engines.[1] Just before Trevithick returned in October, 1827, another engineer, Samuel Grose, erected an immense 80 in. cylinder engine at Wheal Towan which, through the most careful precautions to limit wastage of steam, averaged a duty of over 60,000,000 over a period of six months.[2] Not to be outdone, Woolf erected a 90 in. single engine at the Wheal Fortune set of the Consolidated Mines, but in the earlier trials could not reach a duty of 63,700,000,[3] whereas Grose at special trials in May, 1828, stepped up the performance of his engine to 87,209,662.[4] It was then a race to reach the hundred millions duty. Captain Richards of Wheal Vor reached 91,353,246 with an 80 in. engine in 1832,[5] but in October, 1835, William West, a former assistant to Grose, smashed the record with an 80 in. engine at Fowey Consols which exceeded 125,000,000.[6] West's rival and Trevithick's former partner, James Sims, however, quickly pointed out that over a period of six months the Fowey Consols engine had only been able to maintain an average duty of about ninety millions.[7] Still, in 1838, the average duty of no less than 61 engines in Cornwall was 48,700,000[8]—a fourfold increase in efficiency in the space of a generation, achieved by the Cornish engineers themselves, using materials made for the

---

[1]The best recorded performance of one of the earlier plunger-pole engines was 45,000,000 at Wheal Chance in 1814, nearly 12,000,000 less than the performance of the Wheal Abraham engine in the same year. Some years later Trevithick's partner, James Sims, attained 54,000,000 at Polgooth with an engine of this type. (Lean, p. 32).

[2]Lean, pp. 57 ff.

[3]*W.B.*: December 28, 1827.

[4]*W.B.*: May 9, 1828.

[5]Otherwise known as Borlase's Engine; *W.B.*: November 6, 1835.

[6]Lean, pp. 95-97; *W.B.*: October 30, 1835; otherwise known as Austen's engine after J. T. Austen, owner of Fowey Consols.

[7]*W.B.*: November 6, 1835.

[8]Lean, p. 139.

most part at the Cornish foundries at Hayle, Perranarworthal, and elsewhere.

By 1840 Cornish engines and Cornish engineers had attained a pre-eminent position. Trevithick's wanderings had helped to propagate the gospel of steam power; in Cornwall his relatives, the Harveys of Hayle, transformed what had once been a blacksmith's shop into one of the greatest foundries in the kingdom, catering for the needs of mine engineers. They were almost wholly engaged in constructing pumping engines, and, perhaps, their greatest triumph occurred in 1840 when a group of Dutchmen visited Fowey Consols to inspect the engine they had built for William West. As a result of this visit the Harveys received an order for the greatest engine ever made to drain Haarlem Lake. An immense 144 in. cylinder was cast in July, 1843; the area of the piston was 16,286 square inches; the achievement of the Harveys in melting over 25 tons of iron for this work in less than six minutes amazed the county at the time. Less than a year later this great engine, then by far the largest in the world, was delivered at Amsterdam, and by October, 1845, part of the lake had been successfully drained.[1] Many other Cornish engines found foreign markets; Trevithick's engines arrived in South America before he did himself; others were taken to Mexico to work in the Real del Monte mines in 1825.[2] In time to come a phrase was to gain currency that wherever there was a pit in the world a Cornishman would inevitably be found at the bottom of it digging for metals; it might have been added, and with more truth, that wherever miners used pumping machinery, rock drills, or safety fuses in the later years of the nineteenth century those devices were more likely than not to have been of Cornish manufacture.

These engineering developments enabled the mines to be worked profitably to greater depths; thereby the output of Cornish copper ore increased, relatively steadily, thoughout the first half of the nineteenth century. In the years following Waterloo a moderate prosperity was enjoyed by the copper mining industry, although in 1816 the standard fell to £98 13s. It recovered rapidly, however, to £134 5s. in 1818, but this

[1] *W.B.*: September 4, 1840; August 11, 1843; July 5, 1844, and October 3, 1845. A second 144 in. engine for Haarlem was made by the Harveys in 1846. (*W.B.*: January 29, 1847).
[2] *W.B.*: March 11 and August 26, 1825.

level was not exceeded until 1853; in the long intervening
period of generally declining prices between these peak years
only four years recorded an average standard of £100 or less,[1]
although in only three years did it exceed £120.[2] Such figures
indicate a progressive and healthy industry, relatively unaffected by drastic fluctuations in either output or price. But
there were some ominous features; the declining produce of the
ores obtained, especially from the older mines, was no portent
of long-enduring fortune. Even more ominous was the decline
in the relative importance of the Cornish copper mines. In
the decade from 1801 to 1810 Cornwall had been responsible
for more than two-thirds of the world production of copper,
and continued to be responsible for that proportion until the
1830s when it dropped to $53\frac{1}{2}$%; the next ten years from 1841
to 1850 saw it down to less than 40%, whilst in the 'fifties when
Cornish output reached its peak it only provided about a

Table II: Decennial Production of Fine Copper in Tons,
1801-1880.[3]

Decade	Cornwall	United Kingdom	World
1801-10	60,597	65,000	91,000
1811-20	67,030	73,000	96,000
1821-30	91,295	106,000	135,000
1831-40	116,161	143,000	218,000
1841-50	115,499	138,000	291,000
1851-60	121,548	142,000	505,999
1861-70	90,614	116,000	900,000
1871-80	36,224	47,000	1,189,400

quarter of the world's copper, and in the next disastrous
decade less than a tenth. Until the middle 'forties Cornwall
dominated the copper production of the world, but the decline
had begun some ten years earlier, and the Cornish copper
mining interest had then begun raising a sustained outcry
against foreign competition.

In the early nineteenth century the two greatest non-ferrous
mining regions of the world were Cornwall and Latin America.
True, minerals were known to exist elsewhere, notably the

[1]*Viz*: 1831 and 1832 £100; 1848 £97 10s.; 1849 £92 11s.
[2]*Viz*: 1819 £127 10s.; 1826 £123 3s.; 1842 £120.
[3]Based on Hunt, p. 892 for Cornwall, and on N. Brown and C. C. Turnbull:
A Century of Copper, pp. 1-22, for decennial production of the United Kingdom and
for estimated world production.

alluvial tin deposits of the East Indies, but exploitation had been on a minute scale. All the explorations of three centuries since the days of Cortez and Pizarro had not revealed much more in the way of mineral wealth than had been known in the Middle Ages save in Spanish America. Some prospectors had found their way to the copper deposits of the Lake Superior region a few years before the secession of the American Colonies, but these deposits were not to be commercially accessible for nearly another century.[1] The fabled riches of Cathay and of the Orient had turned out to be little more than gemstones. Africa and Australia from the mineralogical viewpoint were *terrae incognitae*. South and Central America, however, had long been producing silver and copper, besides some gold and other minerals, but, until the Wars of Independence, they had been the exclusive economic preserve of Spain.

From Elizabethan times the British had unceasingly coveted the riches of Spanish America. Late in the eighteenth century the younger Pitt had seriously considered supporting colonial revolutionary movements to gain markets and sources of raw materials for Britain, whilst throughout the long French wars British industrial and commercial interests kept their eyes on Spanish America, which they regarded as a fruitful vineyard for speculation that was hopelessly neglected and mismanaged by its incompetent Spanish owners. Whilst the new race of Anglo-Saxon industrial magnates wanted markets and sources of raw materials, their most urgent need was a greater quantity of the gold and silver regarded, then and for long to come, as essential to cosmopolitan commercial transactions and even, though to rather a less extent, to "domestic" trade and commerce. England's supplies of gold and silver had been drained down to what was thought a dangerously low level by Eastern trade; Spain still possessed the greatest known or suspected reserves of both minerals. The British commercial interests were impelled to accept any opportunity to gain access to the Spanish colonial mines; if the Spaniards, through the international political crises of those stormy times, could be pressed to make concessions, well and good; if not, revolutionary governments in the Spanish Colonies might be more amenable; the political but not the economic independence of the New

[1]Pryce, p. 61. The mining region round the Lakes was only ceded to the U.S. by the Chippeway Indians in 1843.

E

World was finally recognized by Britain to redress adverse trade balances in the Old.

The long struggle against Napoleon had made the Spaniards more ready to develop their imperial resources, and to come to terms with the English mercantile classes, although, by 1815, many of the latter had reached the conclusion that the political independence of the Spanish Colonies would benefit them more. It had been an employee of the Spanish colonial authorities, Francisco Uville, who had induced Richard Trevithick to send some of his machines to Peru to work the Cerro de Pasco mines. In the course of his own travels and adventures in South America,[1] Trevithick discovered or re-discovered the copper deposits of northern Chili and encouraged their exploitation. Mexico, however, rather than Peru, was the greatest magnet to British enterprise ; within two or three years of the revolt against Spain that country attracted a host of British speculators; in 1824, the Camborne mine captain, John Rule, arrived at Real del Monte to install modern machinery,[2] and other miners and engineers quickly followed. Then, bereft of her mainland possessions, Spain began to rework the copper deposits of Cuba on modern lines, and those deposits along with those of Chili revealed by Trevithick were to deprive Cornwall of its world pre-eminence. Before long new competition came, first from South Australia and then from Michigan.

Spanish governments, constitutional or revolutionary, in the Old World or the New, lacked the financial resources to develop mines, but British investors had capital to spare and the outcome was the tidal wave of speculation in 1823 and 1824. Some of the speculative projects were quite genuine; others were devised by scheming sharks to trap a host of gullible persons only too eager to be led to perdition by the prospect of easy riches. Soon after the first Latin American mining company flotations there appeared persons with the persuasive and patriotic argument that speculators would be better advised to invest their capital nearer home—in Cornish mines. The fate of these speculations rendered proposed investments in Cornish mines suspect for ever after. Yet, had the luckless speculators of 1823 and 1824 only exercised a little common

[1]F. Trevithick, Vol. 11, pp. 196 ff.
[2]*W.B.*: August 6, 1824.

sense, and had they only taken a little trouble to acquire a little knowledge of Cornish mining conditions, they would never have thrown their money away on wild-cat schemes. The very nature of the cost-book system of financing Cornish mines meant that shares in the best dividend-paying mines could only be obtained rarely and then at a high price; the only cheap shares were those in losing mines or those in new unproved projects—and the less likely of success the latter, the cheaper shares in them would be.

A few of the projectors were honest men who had been decoyed by "salted mines" or by the specious tales of some rascally mine captains and adventurers. For a considerable time there had already been much adverse "outside" criticism of Cornish mining agents who "worked-up" concerns in which they took a few shares for themselves and for their local trading connections, induced outside adventurers to take the rest of the shares, and then, at subsequent account meetings where only Cornish adventurers could attend, pass accounts without let, hindrance, or question, for goods they themselves had sold to the concern.[1] But in the dawn of speculative hope all this was forgotten. A *bonanza* find at Pembroke mine near St. Blazey in August, 1822, sent the value of a forty-eighth share in it to £640.[2] Early in 1823 the mine projector Stanley of Rosemunday arranged the amalgamation of Great and East Towan mines in St. Agnes; the recent successes of the Consolidated Mines in Gwennap was well known,[3] so the new venture was promptly given the name of the Great Towan Consolidated Mines; the prospectus issued to intending shareholders vaguely stated that some years ago the Great Towan mine set alone, worked only at shallow levels, had yielded profits of £146,000 to the well-known and reputable Truro merchant, Ralph Allen Daniell, and his associates. Stanley now proposed dividing the mine into 150 shares, and asked for a deposit of £20 on each share.[4] In point of fact, this venture was genuine and honest,[5] but Stanley knew "all the tricks in the trade", and made no allusions in his prospectus to difficulties en-

---

[1]*W.B.*: November 2, 1821; G. Abbott, Jr.: *An Essay on the Mines of England,* (1833) pp. 28-30.
[2]*W.B.*: August 30, 1822.
[3]*W.B.*: September 26, 1823.
[4]*W.B.*: February 28, 1823.
[5]G. Abbott, Jr.: *An Essay on the Mines of England,* p. 82.

countered in the earlier working nor reveal that the earlier
works had been suspended through inadequate mechanization.

Other genuine revived adventures which gained much outside investment were those to rework Polgooth in St. Mewan,
Herland in Gwinear, Wheal Alfred in Phillack, Wheal Busy in
Kenwyn, and Wheal Sparnon and Penandrea in Redruth.[1]
Herland alone, however, recouped its shareholders in this
period, whilst the unfortunate adventurers in Wheal Alfred
lost nearly £60,000 and those in Wheal Sparnon and Pednandrea about £40,000.[2] But apart from these there were a
number of mining ventures that can only be described as bubble
speculations. Such swindles may have been inevitable in a
period of financial boom, but their failure brought lasting discredit upon Cornish mining ventures among the British
investing public.

The most notorious of these mining companies was the
Devonshire and Cornwall Mining Association, projected by the
attorney John Wilks, junior, Member of Parliament for Sud-
bury until his shady financial transactions made it expedient
for him to apply for the Chiltern Hundreds. Wilks made a
deal with a group of Cornish mine agents for rights to work
thirteen mines for £78,500. He then organized a company to
work these mines, transferring his rights to the company for
£121,000. Among the mines were Crenver and Oatfield which
had been fairly productive if not sensationally profitable in the
past, and which adjoined the still profitable Wheal Abraham;
Wheal Dream, however, had gained a poor name when
Boulton and Watt were associated with Cornwall, and had not
gained a better reputation since; West Wheal Vor was a name
likely to attract those who had heard of the recent great finds
of tin at Wheal Vor; Great Wheal Fortune, too, was an
attractive name, although an earlier working had ended in the
bankruptcy of the chief adventurer. Wilks in the prospectus of
the Company mentioned that Wheal Barnard had hardly ever
been worked in the past simply through lack of capital: any
cautious investor might have asked the pertinent question
whether any moderately promising mine had failed for such a
reason in a district where copper had been mined for nearly a
century. The same prospectus stressed that in a single year

[1] *W.B.*: September 26, 1823.
[2] G. Abbott, Jr.: *An Essay on the Mines of England*, pp. 82, 84-85.

Crinnis had cleared £84,000 in profits; it did not mention that not one of the mines Wilks had bought and sold to the Company was situated in the Crinnis district. Wilks also appealed to patriotic investors to buy Cornish mine shares rather than risk their money on grandiose South American schemes, writing that there was abundant knowledge available on Cornish mines whilst very little was known of the mines in the New World.

The best that can be said of the mines now owned by the Devonshire and Cornwall Mining Association was that they actually existed and contained mineral. Under good management that mineral might have been worked fairly successfully, but it was managed not by practical miners but by a group of questionable financiers, some of whom were rogues and the others deluded fools. Wilks had made a good profit when he sold his mining rights to the Association for £42,500 more than he had given for them, and his attempt to convince the House of Commons that this profit only existed on paper and that he had actually risked and lost more of his own money was unconvincing. This, however, was mere sharp business practice. More suspect was the way in which "dummy" directors of high public standing had been inveigled into patronising the concern, thereby luring the small and not very intelligent investors to speculate in it; Wilks induced the easy-going Lord Palmerston to become a director without being asked any difficult questions, but the more astute George Canning refused a similar offer accompanied by a bribe.[1]

Although Wilks and a few associates had formed the Association for their own financial advantage, yet they may have thought that the venture would pay dividends not only to themselves but also, though perhaps in less amount and degree, to the small investors. With the modicum of luck that is essential to all mining enterprise, and good management, the Association might have gained a moderate success. By acquiring thirteen mines the risk of loss was spread and the chance of gain increased. The system of joint-stock financing tapped a vaster reserve of capital for investment than the old cost-book system could have done, and that at the very time when the cost-book system was proving less and less able to cope with

[1]Hansard: *Parliamentary Debates*, Second Series, Vol. 17, 299-343, 845-853
W.B.: July 24, August 4, 11, and 25, September 8 and 15, October 6 and 27, 1826; April 13, May 11 and 25, and November 9, 1827.

the increasing expense of mechanizing deeper mines. The small "foreign" investor could not and would not normally venture to assume the responsibility of even a sixty-fourth share in a Cornish cost-book mining concern; that, or even a more infinitesimal share, was all that a "small man" could afford. The small investor, however, was willing to subscribe to £50 shares, like those of the Devonshire and Cornwall Mining Association, paying a deposit on each share and agreeing to pay the rest in instalments, especially when by so doing he acquired a share not in a single mine but in thirteen—one mine might fail and lose him all his money but it would be ill-fortune indeed if as many as thirteen mines incurred nothing but loss.

Some of the other speculative ventures of this time, quite apart from considerations of financial and technical management, were less sound than the Devonshire and Cornwall Mining Association. The British Mining or Royal Stannary Association made very dubious investments indeed when, in the Truro district, it bought Wheal Malkin for £4,700 and Wheal Charles for £5,000 although it spread the risk by buying up some silver-lead mines in North Devon at the same time.[1] Many of the mines acquired by the British United Mines Company and by the Cornwall United Hills Copper Mines were alleged, in alluring prospectuses, to have been worked by machinery; all that was needed to gain great profits was the judicious application of steam power; the latter concern did spend much on machinery in 1825.[2]   The projectors of Copper Hill Mine, near Camborne, informed prospective investors that the mining property they had bought had last been worked by "scavengers" about 1775, but that fully a century had elapsed since the last working of the bottom levels, and then, of course, not with steam power.[3]   These and other company projectors and mining adventurers gave an impetus to engineering; many new engines were installed in new and old mines; elsewhere second-hand engines were moved from mines that had proved unsatisfactory to ones that promised better gains. An

[1]H. English: *A Compendium of Useful Information relating to the Companies formed for working British Mines*, (1826)—Prospectus of the British Mining Association, pp. 57, 112-114.
[2]H. English: *A Compendium of Useful Information relating to the Companies formed for working British Mines*—Prospectuses of the British United and of Cornwall United Hills Mining Companies, pp. 6, 10, 87, 92; *W.B.*: September 23, 1825.
[3]H. English: *A Compendium of Useful Information relating to the Companies formed for working British Mines*—Prospectus of the Copper Hill Mine Company, pp. 13, 94.

indication of this development is given by the engine reports
of the Leans; in 1817 only 30 engines reported giving an
average duty of 26,500,000, in 1825 the average duty of 50 was
over 32,000,000.[1] Over the same period, too, the output of
Cornish copper ore increased nearly fifty per cent—from less
than seventy-seven to a hundred and seven thousand tons.

While speculation stimulated and expanded copper mining
in Cornwall, the collapse of the financial boom in 1825 had a
more detrimental effect on "outside" adventurers than it had
on the industry itself. In the entire period from 1815 to the
peak of Cornish copper production in 1856—a period in which
the output of copper ore trebled—there were only eight minor
recessions from temporary peak levels of production;[2] the
greatest set-backs were those from an output of 104,500 tons
in 1822 to 95,750 tons in 1823, or a drop of $8\frac{1}{2}$% in a single
year, and a decline of rather less than 11% over four years
from 162,500 tons in 1845 to 145,000 in 1849. The "outsiders"
had speculated in a host of less well-known mines, whereas
more than half the Cornish output of copper ores came from
eleven mines[3] not one of which figured in the mining pro-
motions of 1823 and 1824.

The continuing fortunes of Consols and Dolcoath, of
Lanescot and East Crinnis, and of Penstruthal were no consolation to the persons induced by Wilks and other promoters to
invest in western mines. With the collapse of the speculative
boom and the bursting of bubble South American schemes,
the new investors in Cornish mines thought, and in many cases
only too rightly, that they had been swindled as well. There
is ample proof that some Cornish mine owners or agents had
sold some extremely unprofitable concerns to outside company
promoters, selling mines which had already been worked out
or mines whose prospects only seemed promising in the eyes
of those who did not know the first thing about copper
mining.[4] Even the more honest outside company promoters

[1]Lean, p. 32.

[2]The peak years were 1815, 1822, 1828, 1831, 1835, 1839, 1842 and 1845.

[3]*i.e.* Consolidated Mines, Penstruthal, Dolcoath, East Crinnis, Lanescot,
Poldice and Unity, Fowey Consols, Wheal Buller and Beauchamp, Pembroke,
Wheal Montague and Harmony, and Binner Downs. The ores of most of these
mines was low grade, and they only accounted for a third of the value of the ores
sold. (John Taylor: *Records of Mining*, p. 170).

[4]*W.B.*: August 18, 1826 (Goonhavern Mine), and June 15, 1827 (Cornish
Equitable Mining Association); also May 12, 1826 (West of England Cobalt and
Copper Company).

must be censured for a general failure to get expert opinions on mining properties before purchasing them. One or two may have been deceived by "salted" mines, but only a credulous idiot would have thought that he could get for two or three thousand pounds mining property alleged to be worth twenty or thirty times as much. Nor is there any indication that the "spec" promoters tried to acquire any interest in the great copper-producing adventures like Consols, Dolcoath, or Lanescot; had they done so they would have quickly discovered that Cornish mines adventurers like the Williamses, Lord de Dunstanville, and Joseph Thomas Austen, or any other Cornish business man were not inclined to part lightly from productive and profitable mining concerns.

It was not the company projectors but the small outside investors that suffered. On the whole, Wilks and men like him, now and again engaged in bulling and bearing the shares of the companies they directed,[1] now and again selling to those companies at no small profits to themselves "mining property" they had acquired, and all the time drawing directors' salaries for mere attendance at an inordinately excessive number of company meetings which they called themselves, profited by these transactions. When the financial collapse came the small investor began to ask questions, began to quibble about making further payments on the shares he had acquired, and started criticizing the directors' methods of conducting affairs. The storm broke in November, 1825, when the Gwennap Tin and Copper Mining Company was exposed; the shareholders found that instead of owning a valuable mining property they had made themselves liable to subscriptions of £90,000 to the promoter, a certain Mr. Cooke, who had, for about £500, secured a dozen of the 127 shares in the Cathedral Mine and had forthwith set up his Company; some shareholders were deluded into subscribing by an allegation that Lord Nugent was a director of the Company; with picturesque justice a contemporary newspaper dismissed the "spec" as one that could only be surpassed by promoting "a Company to work the mines of the moon".[2]   Still Cathedral Mine and shares in it

---

[1] Wilks was also a director of the Welsh Iron and Coal, the Patent Wood, the British Annuity, the Medway Lime and Coal, the Welsh Slate, the Kentish Railroad, and the Norfolk and Suffolk Railroad Companies. (*W.B.*: September 8 and October 7, 1826, and December 12, 1828).

[2] *W.B.*: November 11, 1825. (*Vide* also issues of Nov. 2, 1825 and May 12, 1826).

did exist unlike the "Consols Mine" whose promoters were trying to sell £50 shares to unwary speculators in November, 1824.[1] Then the shareholders in the Devonshire and Cornwall Mining Association grew restive; Wilks was evasive; a series of meetings of shareholders and the more honest directors failed to come to terms for winding up the concern; a petition of a shareholder who had lost heavily was presented in the house of Commons in April, 1827; Wilks made a long speech defending himself and free enterprise; Lord Palmerston, more briefly but equally unconvincingly, explained his "sleeping directorate." Later Palmerston retrieved his reputation by making good some losses the Association had incurred, but Wilks contented himself by applying for the Chiltern Hundreds. After lengthy and costly litigation by directors seeking to force shareholders to pay up their subscriptions and by creditors to recover the value of goods they had supplied the Association, the adventure came to an end.[2]

These transactions brought Cornish mine speculations into lasting discredit. The closing law actions were rather farcical. Wilks brought an action against Palmerston and certain other directors for refusing to abide by the bargain to buy the mining rights for £121,000 alleging that they had only paid him £54,000; if indeed he had lost £24,500 he truly and justly had been hoist by his own petard, for he lost this action. The successful defendants, however, were told by the Vice-Chancellor that, had the mines turned out prosperous, they would have found difficulty in proving their right to share the profits; it was also pointed out that as a director of the company Wilks ought to sue himself.[3] Behind these and the other law cases resulting from the activities of this Association can be seen little more than greedy speculation and swindling dishonesty. It is doubtful whether Wilks lost much for he had left a loophole in the agreement he had made with the Cornish agents for buying the mining rights for £78,500 by a stipulation that the mines were to be worked. Nor is it likely that the Cornish agents, William Carne and Thomas Teague, who sold him the mining rights, incurred any losses; they may even

[1]*W.B.*: November 26, 1824. This affair was an attempt to delude speculators into the belief that they were acquiring shares in the Consolidated Mines which had recently taken over the United Mines and were then very prosperous.
[2]References as in note 1, p. 133 above.
[3]*W.B.*: July 27, 1827.

have been party to his proposed methods of "working" the mines. The association of Wilks with so many other dubious financial schemes, however, proves that he was mainly if not wholly responsible for the Association; the other directors were either passive accomplices or dupes.

The Court of Chancery also put an end to the Royal Stannary or British Mining Association in May, 1826, when it dismissed the case of the directors who sought unpaid subscriptions of £5 per share on 1690 shares, the defence successfully pleading that the Company prospectus had been fraudulent.[1] The total number of shares in this concern had been 8,000; if the other 6,310 shares had been subscribed the directors would have cleared a threefold profit on their outlay on Wheal Malkin and Wheal Charles.

Along with the swindling promoters, the Cornish adventurers and agents who had sold them mining property were discredited. The directors of the Cornish Equitable Mining Association, however, merit little sympathy. When that concern failed its directors alleged that they had been "gulled" into buying three mines by Cornish agents, one of them complaining that :

"It really appears to me that they looked upon us as foreigners, and considered us fair game to be plucked at their pleasure, when they had once gotten us into this net."[2]

This director could well have been asked what sort of mines he thought he could buy at the rate of three for £300—less than twenty tons of normal grade copper ores from each of the mines would repay such a small outlay. Yet many small investors had lost heavily in Cornish speculations. The far greater number that had lost even more heavily in South American mines were rather quickly forgotten, but thereafter Cornish mining promoters were suspected, often unjustly, on the stock market, thanks to the sharp practices of the agents who had sold dream mines and to the even sharper methods of company promoters who erected grandiose edifices of commercial speculation on the unsubstantial foundation of those dreams. Nor should those who expected vast fortunes by investing next to nothing have escaped uncensured.

It may have been rather fortunate for Cornish mining that

[1] *W.B.*: May 23, 1828.
[2] *W.B.*: June 15, 1827.

the South American ventures had attracted the speculators and company promoters, honest and dishonest alike, even more than Cornish mines. The sounder concerns were able to carry on undisturbed by the vagaries of wildly fluctuating shares on the stock market, and the purely financial crisis had comparatively insignificant repercussions on actual Cornish mining operations. From the beginning of the speculative boom in 1823 to its collapse late in 1825, however, about forty new copper mines started in Cornwall; only a dozen of these mines were still active in 1830. The most productive of these mines was South Wheal Basset which, opening in 1825, in the next thirty years sold about 95,000 tons of copper ore for over £600,000; second was Wheal Unity Wood which, starting in 1823, sold 33,000 tons of ore during the same period for some £190,000; the resumed working of Wheal Busy was to sell 33,500 tons of lower grade ores for £125,000 and another revived mine, Wheal Trenwith, raised 13,000 tons of high grade ores worth £115,000 during the same time. No other mine, opened or re-started during the boom, however, cleared more than £50,000 over extended periods of working. Among the short-lived concerns, Wheal Raven was the best, getting nearly £10,000 for 1,450 tons of copper ore raised between 1825 and 1828. The most luckless mine was Great Towan Consols, which worked only a few months and marketed but twenty tons of ore for less than £100, whilst neither West Wheal Prudence nor George the Fourth made sales of more than £500 in value, and the Friendly Mines dragged on for nearly three years to scrape up 160 tons of ores sold for less than £1,200.[1]

Some local unemployment resulted from the failure of the boom mines,[2] but most of their employees soon found work elsewhere. On the eve of the boom the great enterprises of Fowey Consols and Levant had started in the St. Austell and St. Just areas, whilst in 1826 the Cardrew and United Hills mines began a fairly extended working life near Redruth; older mines like Dolcoath in Camborne and Penstruthel in Gwennap were at their zenith as copper mines in this period. In fact, until the 1850s, as one Cornish mine declined another rose to take its place, or more than its place. Speculation, too, helped to reveal the prospective wealth or poverty of mining

[1] J. A. Phillips and John Darlington: *Records of Mining and Metallurgy*, pp. 256-265.   [2] *W.B.*: June 9, 1826.

sets hitherto either untouched or very imperfectly worked. There was no indication yet that the copper reserves of the Camborne-Redruth area were near exhaustion; great resources were being revealed in the St. Austell region; the deposits in East Cornwall were virtually inknown, although finds of relatively high grade ores at St. Cleer[1] and at Gunnislake augured well for the future.

Whatever the ill-fortune of certain over-hopeful mining projects and the losses of individual speculators, Cornish copper mining was in a reasonably flourishing and progressive state throughout the 1820s. The collapse of many South American mining schemes may even have emphasized the economic stability of copper mining in Cornwall. Already, however, a challenge to the world pre-eminence of the "Cornish Copper Kingdom" had been made, and after the financial crisis of 1825 the Cornish adventurers were fighting a losing battle to retain their supremacy. The first threat came early in 1822 when, possibly pressed by merchant interests, the Government proposed to anact a Warehousing Bill permitting the importation, warehousing, and re-exportation free of duty of foreign copper and tin; it was too late for this measure to be passed Session, but it was passed next year and came into force in July, 1823.[2]   There was some agitation in Cornwall against this Act, which undoubtedly stimulated trade and still further encouraged investment in foreign copper mines; it may have reduced exports of British copper, but this was more than compensated by the increasing domestic demands, and it had very little effect on price levels. Then, in March, 1825, Huskisson proposed halving the duties on foreign tin and copper ores, with further progressive reductions to follow;[3]   the Cornish mining interest alleged that a return to the pre-1808 duties would ruin them. The slump in copper prices in July, 1826, however, was generally attributed to rash speculation.[4] A further threat came in June, 1827 when the Government proposed the free admission of foreign copper ores for smelting in Britain, the produce being returned into bond for re-exportation, Huskisson maintaining that this would not affect home copper markets.[5]

[1]At Cutcare Wood on the fringe of the Caradon copper zone. (*W.B.*: September 10, 1824).
[2]*W.B.*: July 21 and 28, 1822; April 4 and 25, June 27 and July 5, 1823.
[3]*W.B.*: March 18 and April 1, 1825.
[4]*W.B.*: August 18, 1826.   [5]*W.B.*: July 6, 1827.

The actual imports of foreign copper into Britain at this time were small; some fifty years before a fairly large proportion of the copper used in British industries had been imported from Spain, Sweden, Russia and elsewhere, but these imports had almost ceased during the French wars. During and after the war years British consumption of copper had increased, the Cornish output had increased, but the output of other copper mines in Europe had remained stationary or had fallen. The real challenge came from Latin America—from the Cobre mines of Cuba, in which the Grenfell smelting house had invested, and from the Chilean mines Trevithick had stimulated into production. During the boom British investments in foreign mines had increased amazingly, and the ores of the Chilean Mining Company first reached Swansea late in 1829.[1] The battle of free trade and protection then began in earnest. Smelting firms at Liverpool and in the North West looked to Latin America to offset the end of the Anglesey mines; George Canning, member for Liverpool and representative of its commercial interests, had called in the New World to redress the balance of the Old in a commercial and industrial sense, to offset the copper hegemony of Cornwall as well as the political threat of the Holy Alliance. Cornish approaches to the Board of Trade early in 1830 met no favourable reception, and a meeting of the mining interest was held at Truro on March 3rd. At this meeting the Earl of Falmouth asserted that the measures passed in 1827 and 1828 to allow the free importation of foreign copper ores for smelting were absolutely unnecessary; Cornwall was raising more than twice the copper ore used by those British manufacturers who were urging Parliament to adopt free trade; he alleged, not entirely convincingly, that during the past generation the price of copper had fallen by thirty per cent and the Cornish output had increased a hundred and sixty per cent, the produce, however, having only doubled. To the moderate but now-threatened prosperity of the Cornish mines he attributed the relatively fortunate position of Cornish agriculture at the time, whereas in the Home Counties, landlords and farmers were living in terror of "Captain Swing".[2]

In 1830, however, although interested in securing cheap

[1]*W.B.*: November 27, 1828 and January 22, 1830.
[2]*W.B.*: February 19 and 26, and March 5, 1830.

copper, the British manufacturing interests were not in the van
of the free trade movement; the main free traders were the
British investors in foreign mines, merchant shipping interests,
and some of the copper smelters. Together they were powerful
and influential, and it gradually became apparent that the
domination of the smelters in the copper trade meant the
inevitable triumph of free trade. The smelters feared that, if
the British Government refused to admit foreign ores or imposed
any but low duties on those ores, foreign smelters would be
encouraged to the ultimate deteriment not only of the British
smelters but of the entire copper industry of Britain in all its
branches from mining to the production of the finest metal-
ware. At the time the fettering impositions on trade were being
swept away one by one; free trade was in the air; even the
Cornish mining interest itself benefitted by the abolition of the
duties on coal transported coastwise early in 1831.[1]

One of the strongest arguments for the retention of heavy
protective duties against foreign copper and ores was the high
protection given to agriculture by the Corn Laws; the protectionists argued that it was unfair that one industry should be
favoured and others neglected or even harmed. Arguments
that the Cornish labouring classes were relatively well-off and
contented through the protection of agriculture and mining
were, however, rudely contradicted by certain incidents in the
winter of 1830-31. Discontent, distress, and unrest among the
farm labourers of North Cornwall led the magistrates of
Stratton hundred, in December, 1830, to order that wages be
increased from 1/- to 1/4 a day; the farmers quickly retorted
that they could not afford higher wages unless rents and tithes
were reduced; the landowning gentry on the Bench then
thought it wise to swear in extra constables to maintain order.[2]
"Swing" attacks on corn-ricks and machinery were threatened
at Morval and St. Winnow a little later,[3] whilst early in
February, 1831, the miners of mid-Cornwall "paid visits" to
Wadebridge and to Padstow to prevent the "exportation" of
corn to other parts of England.[4]

Incidents of this nature had occurred in the past in times of
scarcity and distress, but late in February, 1831, the first open

[1] *W.B.*: March 4, 1831.
[2] *W.B.*: December 17, 1830.
[3] *W.B.*: December 24, 1830 and January 7, 1831.
[4] *W.B.*: February 18, 1831.

collision between capital and labour in Cornish industrial history took place in the St. Blazey district. In an attempt to change the regulations under which Lanescot Mine was being worked, the miners organized a combination against the mine agents; the men of the adjoining Fowey Consols Mine joined them. It was an effort to end the system whereby the mine-owning adventurers had profited by the competition among the labourers themselves at the setting days for taking tribute pitches. The men, however, were not unanimous, and one or two refused to join the combination, preferring the freedom to make their own terms with the mine agents even at the cost of retaining the system whereby labourers, bidding against each other for pitches in the mine, only lowered their own "wages" to the gain of the adventurers. Two of these "blacklegs", threatened by their fellow-labourers, took refuge in Lanescot counting house, where they were besieged. Magistrates, including Austen the mine-owner, were summoned to the scene; the Riot Act was read; the men refused to disperse; seven of the ringleaders were arrested by the constables; their colleagues attempted to rescue them, but failed after a struggle lasting an hour, and the prisoners were taken to Bodmin jail. There was then another demonstration by the miners outside the jail, but the presence of additional special constables and militia there made them ready to listen to the pleas of the High Sheriff, John Hearle Tremayne, for the maintenance of law and order, and they were induced to depart after each had been given "a pint of beer and a penny loaf". The coming of troops to St. Blazey convinced the Lanescot men that it was best to return to work, and the first strike of Cornish copper miners ended. At the Assizes a month later the seven leaders were tried; the Judge laid down that an attempt to coerce others into combining with them was a capital offence, but they were discharged since the prosecution wisely chose not to press the charge.[1] Had the charge been pressed there might have been further disorders, and possibly destruction of costly mine machinery which might end a profitable mine. On their side, the men were aware that they were getting wages higher for the most part than those obtained by copper miners elsewhere in Cornwall.[2]

[1] *W.B.*: February 25, March 4, and April 1, 1831.
[2] The higher wages in the St. Austell and St. Blazey area were only those paid to tut-workers and day-labourers; the tributers of the Redruth district tended to

The example of the Lanescot men was not followed by any other group of Cornish miners until a much later time. The tribute and tut-work systems were generally satisfactory to men and adventurers alike. Occasionally, but very rarely until after the slump of 1866, there was ill-feeling when a man consistently underbid his fellows at tribute-settings. If a man made a bad "bargain" he generally stuck by it, but took good care not to repeat the mistake; both adventurers and men wanted so make as much as they could from the mines. Moreover this strike took place at Lanescot. In most other great Cornish mines the cost-book system meant division of ownership among several adventurers who, perforce, were obliged to leave the actual management of the mines to captains whose sympathies were often with the labourers from whose ranks many had risen themselves. At Lanescot practically all the shares were held by Austen, and this incident was the direct collision of an individual industrial magnate with the men he employed.

Labour troubles, however, concerned the Cornish mining interests very little during this period but the threat of foreign competition worried them greatly. By 1832 the competition of South America was becoming formidable, and the policy of all governments, Whig and Tory alike, to lower tariff barriers and to promote the smelting interests, always suspected of making exorbitant gains at the miners' expense, alarmed the men concerned in a mining industry more than half of whose raw product had, hitherto, eventually been marketed abroad. The mines adventurers, closely allied and connected as many of them were with the smelting interests, were, however, inclined to compromise. Whilst foreign mines were worked by cheaper labour and were usually richer in produce than those of Cornwall, the costs of transporting foreign

get the highest tribute wages. This was partly due to the competing demand for less-skilled tut-work and day labour by the clay works in mid-Cornwall. In 1837 it was calculated that the comparative monthly rates of wages were :

	West of Penzance	Redruth District	St. Austell District	Average
Tributers	47/6	68/-	59/-	58/2
Tutworkers	45/-	57/2	59/-	53/8
Day Labourers	42/-	41/-	45/-	42/8
Average	44/10	55/5	57/8	51/6

(Sir Charles Lemon: "The Copper Mines of Cornwall": *Journal Statistical Society,* Vol. 1, p. 73. Lemon, however, was a mineowning adventurer himself, and was hardly likely to have minimized the wages paid; he did not take any account of the tools, candles, etc., provided by the men at their own cost, or of such items as doctor's pence; these wages, too, were wages per calendar month).

ores to Britain offset these advantages for a considerable time; there seemed to be no real reason to deprive British smelters of an opportunity to expand their business, especially as it was likely that if the foreign ores were not smelted in Britain they would be elsewhere to the ultimate detriment of the British copper industry. It was felt that it was far better to retain control of the world copper trade than to persist in a narrow and short-sighted policy of prohibition and protection which only benefitted a comparatively small number of mines adventurers. As time went by, without any great decline in copper prices, and as it became apparent that the demands of home and foreign markets kept place with the increasing output of both Cornish and Latin American mines, advocacy of protection lessened although, at every reduction of import duties on foreign copper ores, there was a noisy outcry from a few that Cornish mining would be utterly and irretrievably ruined.

The challenge of Chile to Cornish copper supremacy resulted from the speculative boom of 1823. By the end of 1823 the agents of three English mining companies—the Anglo-Chilian, the Chilean, and the Chilean-Peruvian Mining Association—had been sent to Coquimbo.[1] Among the directors of the Chilean Mining Association were George C. Fox and Alfred Fox of Falmouth, and John and William Williams of Truro,[2] whilst Pasco Grenfell, besides his interest in the Cuban Cobre mines was a director of the Columbian Mining Association founded in December, 1824. The collapse of the boom had brought hardships and losses to these Companies, but they had led the way for the large-scale exploitation of Latin American copper resources. Other miners and engineers had followed Trevithick from Cornwall to South America and helped to develop its mines. Rich ores and cheap Indian labour offset difficulties arising from the political troubles of the infant republics. In three centuries the Spaniards had barely scratched the surface of these deposits. The new high-pressure Cornish steam engines proved their efficiency in the rarified atmosphere of the high Andes. In the 1830s Chile provided nearly a fifth of the world output of copper as against more than half provided by Cornwall, but by the end of another

[1]R. A. Humphreys: *British Consular Reports on the Trade and Politics of Latin America, 1824-26*, p. 95 note 2.
[2]H. English: *An Inquiry into the Plans, Progress and Policy of the American Mining* Third Edition (1825) pp. 52 ff.

decade Chile had overtaken the western county, and in the
'fifties when Cornwall produced barely a quarter of the world's
copper supply, Chilean mines provided over forty per cent.[1]

The alarm of Cornish mining interests at the appearance of
foreign competition may have been premature but it was not
ill-founded. Mines adventurers fought grimly for the retention
of protective duties, but they were fighting not only against
mercantile and manufacturing interests but against the very
spirit of the age. The smelters dominated the copper industry,
and one by one they became convinced that their true
interests lay in free trade; they hoped that free trade would
enable them to gain world markets through their advantages of
cheap fuel, long experience and technical skill—all that they
thought that they required to achieve international economic
supremacy in their industry was cheap high-grade copper ore,
and that the free trade economists and politicians promised
them.

The potential exhaustion of the Cornish mines might have
been used as a convincing argument for free trade. Every ton
of ore raised in Cornwall reduced the reserves of mines, many
of which had been worked for two or three generations. Now
and again rich lodes were found, but the increasing poverty of
lodes in depth, revealed in Dolcoath and other deep mines,
was a warning. Many Cornish adventurers might have recalled
the fate of Parys, worked almost to apparent exhaustion in less
than forty years; nearer home there was North Downs which,
hardly paying costs when it sold ores valued at over £52,000 in
1798, only made £6,200 for 970 tons of ores sold in the year
ending June 30, 1828.[2] The very scale of past and present
copper-mining in the Camborne-Redruth area made further
great discoveries in that region more and more unlikely with the
passage of every year, although the opening of new mines in
other districts might prolong the existence of Cornish copper
mining for many years. Gwennap was still the greatest mining
parish in the late 1820s, but in 1828 the fourth, sixth, and
seventh places in the list of productive mines were taken by

[1]N. Brown and C. C. Turnbull : *A Century of Copper*, pp. 2-20.
[2]In the forty years from 1815 to 1855 North Downs sold ores worth £127,951;
in the four years 1795-8 it had sold ores worth £178,581; Cook's Kitchen sold
only £185,000 worth of ores between 1815 and 1856, whereas in the seven years
1792-8 its sales had been worth £172,300. (*Report, 1799*, pp. 709-713; J. A.
Phillips and J. Darlington: *Records of Mining and Metallurgy*, p. 259; John Taylor:
Records of Mining, p. 170).

Crinnis, Lanescot, and Fowey Consols, all in the region east of
St. Austell, whilst a new "far eastern" mine, Wheal Mary in
St. Neot, sold over £1,800 worth of ores in its first year of
working, and in the next thirty-three years was to sell about
12,000 tons for £56,400.[1]

Cornish copper mining was expanding by lateral extension
to new districts rather than by the deeper and more efficient
operation of older mines. For many years prospectors had been
active in the Caradon area in St. Cleer as they had been in
Anglesey for years before the discovery at Parys in 1768. The
rock formations and topographical features were similar to
those of Carmenellis where so much copper had been mined in
the West; in Caradon, too, there had been extensive workings
of the "old men" for tin. A small group of adventurers, some
of them experienced in copper mining in St. Austell and Camborne, started working on South Caradon in 1836; in 1837,
after initial disappointments, they found a rich main lode; in
1838 the sale of 130 tons of ores for £1,198 cleared all the past
costs of these persistent adventurers, and the era of the Caradon
mines had begun. Other adventurers quickly came to the
district. West Caradon opened in 1840 whilst another new
company took over the old tin-mining set of Marke Valley to
the north-west of Caradon Hill. In 1842 the more sanguine, or
obstinate, adventurers of the luckless Cornwall Great United
Company which, since 1835, had spent £50,000 with no success, secured from the Duchy of Cornwall a new lease of the
more westerly Phoenix sets, and, after further heavy expenditure, was able to pay dividends ten years later. More and more
capital and miners were attracted to the district; some adventurers made fortunes, others were less fortunate, but by 1850
the Caradon district was recognized as one of the richest
mineral areas in Cornwall, whilst ten years later over twenty
mines were working there, six of them paying reasonably good
dividends.[2]

The exploitation of Caradon was somewhat hampered by
lack of transportation facilities, and by the conservative
prejudice of many mines adventurers against new districts.[3]

[1] J. Phillips and J. Darlington: *Records of Mining and Metallurgy*, p. 261.
[2] Webb and Geach: *History and Progress of Mining in the Caradon and Liskeard Districts*, (1863), *passim;* John Allen: *History of Liskeard*, pp. 395-399; J. H. Collins: *Observations on the West of England Mining Region*, p. 253.
[3] *A Concise Description of the Marke Valley Consolidated Mines*, (1839) pp. 3-4.

It had been working miners rather than capitalist adventurers who had made the first great finds at South Caradon, notably the Clymo and Kittow brothers; once they struck rich lodes, however, they found support from local investors, like John Allen of Liskeard, who soon gained great profits from the Caradon mines. In 1843, to solve the transport problem, an Act of Parliament was secured to construct a railway from Liskeard to the new mines;[1] unexpectedly heavy costs made it necessary to get a second Act in 1847 to raise additional capital; by that time, however, the railway had reached Cheesewring from Moorswater whence ores were taken by barge down the Liskeard and Looe Canal to Looe.[2]

The construction of the Caradon Railway coincided with the mania of railway speculation which collapsed early in 1846. Since the Pentewan Railway had been completed numerous railway schemes had been mooted in Cornwall. Plans in 1830 to link Perranporth with Truro and the Upper Fal came to nothing through the rivalry of two groups of railway promoters,[3] but the Bodmin and Wadebridge railway, projected in 1831, was officially opened on September 30, 1834.[4] In 1833 and 1834 plans for a railroad to link the clay and granite-working parish of St. Stephens in Brannel to tidewater on the Fal were widely publicised,[5] but nothing came of a scheme that earlier, in pre-Reform Bill days, might have gained formidable support from the notorious boroughs of Tregony and Grampound. Projects to construct lines from Padstow, via Delabole and Camelford, to Launceston and Plymouth, failed to gain adequate support, but in 1834 the Hayle Railway Company secured an Act of Parliament for a line from Hayle to Tresavean, with branches to Redruth and the great Roskear and Crofty mines, which would also link up with the older Portreath tram-road; it was planned to run a locomotive from a point a little to the west of the present station of Gwinear Road to Tresavean, but on the Angarrack incline down to Hayle a stationary engine was to be used to draw up trucks just as was done on the steep gradient at the harbour end of the

[1]6 & 7 Vic. cap. 63.
[2]J. Allen: *History of Liskeard*, pp. 399-402. *W.B.*: May 26, 1843.
[3]*W.B.*: November 5 and 19, and December 10, 1830.
[4]C. F. D. Marshall: *A History of the Southern Railway*, pp. 22 ff.
[5]*W.B.*: January 11, 18, and 25, 1833, and November 7, 1834.

Portreath line.[1] This railroad was completed by 1837, and in October, 1838, the first locomotive built in Cornwall—the *Cornishman*, built at Hayle by Messrs. Sandys, Carne and Vivian—had completed its successful trials along this line.[2] Before the Hayle line was operating plans had been made for a line from Truro to Penzance, but the West Cornwall Railway only obtained its Act of Parliament and took over the Hayle Railway in 1846.[3] The collapse of the railway boom made investors reluctant, and the line was not completed until August, 1852.[4] Plans for a railway linking Cornwall to London were held up even longer, the great obstacle being the Tamar river which occasioned the formation of two rival groups of railway promoters. One party thought that a line to Plymouth over the river was possible; the other planned a route along the height of land from Redruth eastward, via Bodmin and Temple to Okehampton and Exeter—a route which by-passed the considerable towns of Truro, St. Austell, and Liskeard to cut across the most extensive and desolate moorland wastes of Cornwall. As early as 1839 there had been eloquent Cornish railway projectors like John Paynter boasting that they would make Falmouth the Atlantic port of London,[5] but only twenty years later did Brunel conquer the Tamar for these visionaries. Until 1859 the quickest way for a West Cornishman to reach London was to get a steamer at Hayle for Bristol, and there get on a train to London. The greatest obstacle to railway communication in Cornwall was that which Trevithick had failed to meet; the engines were powerful enough but it was difficult to build a permanent way on which they could run. By the time the "iron way" had been laid down for the whole distance between London and Penzance, the output of the western mines had dropped ominously, and even the riches of the Caradon and Tamarside regions were not enough to check the declining amount of ores raised from Cornish copper mines.

The immediate challenge of Caradon to the supremacy of the Carmenellis area in Cornish copper mining, however, should not be overestimated. Until 1856 South Caradon had

[1]E. T. MacDermott: *History of the Great Western Railway*, Vol. 1, pp. 298-301.
[2]*W.B.*: November 2, 1838.
[3]E. T. MacDermott: *History of the Great Western Railway*, Vol. 1, pp. 301 ff.
[4]E. T. MacDermott: *History of the Great Western Railway*, Vol. 1, pp. 305-306.
[5]*W.B.*: November 1, 1839.

only sold ores worth about £450,000, West Caradon £462,000, and Marke Valley only £67,000, but by June 30, 1868, South Caradon sales of copper ores over thirty-two years had exceeded £1,650,000, and the total "calls" had been but £637; at nearly every bi-monthly account there had been smaller or greater dividends to be shared between its fortunate adventurers.[1] Although the other mines in the district did not make such phenomenal profits, it was not surprising that outside investors were attracted to the new Eastern district rather than to the older mining areas where even the most profitable mines were forced on occasion to make heavy calls; the actual proportion of the total Cornish output of copper ores provided by the Caradon mines was, of course, a matter of secondary importance to share-brokers and stock-speculators. Another challenge to the western mines came with the opening of Devon Great Consols, just over the river county boundary in Tavistock parish, in 1844; in the first twelve years of its existence this concern sold ores worth over £1,400,000 or £35,000 more than Dolcoath's total copper output in the forty years after Waterloo and half the value of the ores marketed by the great Consolidated Mines of Gwennap in the same forty years.[2] By 1845 the sun was going down over the older western mines, but the day of the eastern copper district had just dawned and promised to be exceedingly fair.

The successful beginnings of South Caradon coincided with another period of speculation which began in the summer of 1835. Many small investors were now attracted by "scrip-holding" speculations,[3] although the Caradon adventures were organized on traditional cost-book lines. Some hopeful speculators with what must have been an entire lack of geological knowledge even started mining operations in Veryan,[4]

---

[1] J. H. Collins: *Observations on the West of England Mining Region*, p. 253; J. A. Phillips and J. Darlington: *Records of Mining and Metallurgy*, pp. 257-261.

[2] J. A. Phillips and J. Darlington: *Records of Mining and Metallurgy*, pp. 256-265.

[3] Under the scrip system the investor first paid a deposit to be registered as a shareholder; on payment of the first instalment or "call", a scrip was issued to him, on which he was to have subsequently entered receipts for his further subscriptions up to the total value of the share. Most shares were for £50, but they varied from £10 to £100 or even £200. This system left the management entirely in the hands of two or three organizing directors. Abuses crept in through the defective laws of the time, for although shareholders were only liable to the scrip company to the value of the shares they had undertaken to buy, their liability to outsiders was unlimited unless the company was legally incorporated, which few if any of them were. (*W.B.*: November 13 and 20, 1835; *Cornwall Gazette*: December 25, 1835).

[4] *W.B.*: April 8, 1836.

whilst rather more cautious investors took shares in the West Cornwall Mines Investment Association, a Company which spread risks by acquiring shares in a number of mines including the once extremely profitable Tresavean which latterly, however, had fallen on difficult times.[1] Inevitably the lucky-charm name "Consolidated" appeared on attractively baited prospectuses again; the St. Cleer and St. Neot Consolidated Mining Association was formed to work Goonzion Down, Wheal Bank, Tin Hatches, and Trengale, which might have been good tin-mining "specs" in the Middle Ages, and which the promoters of this venture still deemed promising.[2] Several other scrip concerns attracted investors, particularly those which spread the risk of loss over several mining adventures, but by November, 1836, the boom had collapsed; during the next year most of the scrip companies were wound up or, like Wheal Triumph in Camborne, reverted to the cost-book system.[3] Some investors lost heavily, but practically all the mine-promotions of this speculative period, unlike those of a dozen years before, were genuine enough, although the clash of absentee Leeds shareholders with the Cornish directors of the Redruth Consolidated Mining Company, culminating in the law courts, brought afresh to the memory of investors the excursions of John Wilks and Palmerston in Cornish mining.[4]

There is, however, another side of the picture, very different from the comfortable bank-balances of lucky speculators and from the statistics proudly showing the increasing output of Cornish mines. The increasing population of mining parishes has rightly been regarded as a sign of material prosperity. Before the Caradon discoveries, St. Cleer was an agricultural parish whose population only rose from 774 in 1801 to 982 in 1830; then copper was found and by 1861 the population reached 3931. In that generation mining boomed, and St. Cleer was a little California to some mining adventurers. But a heavy price was paid for this prosperity, a price revealed by the parish burial registers, which show a smaller proportion of the parishioners living out the Psalmist's span of three score years and ten, an alarming increase in the proportion of infants dying under five years, and the virtual halving of the average

[1] *W.B.*: June 16, 1836.
[2] *W.B.*: April 8 and 22, 1836.
[3] *W.B.*: September 8, 1837.
[4] *W.B.*: January 4, 1839.

expectancy of life from over forty to less than twenty-two years. Much the same tragedy is revealed in the burial registers of

TABLE III: BURIALS IN THE PARISH OF ST. CLEER, 1813-1859.

	Males				Females			
Period	Total Burials	Under 5 years of age	Over 70 years	Average Age	Total Burials	Under 5 Years of age	Over 70 years	Average age
1813-19	31	6	12	51, 6m.	37	2	12	45, 3m.
1820-29	69	13	22	46, 4m.	65	14	23	44, 6m.
1830-39	82	18	31	42, 6m.	88	27	32	42, 8m.
1840-49	135	49	30	35, 2m.	118	41	33	35 yrs.
1850-59	259	130	26	21, 10m.	214	103	24	21, 3m.

other mining parishes. At St. Just in Penwith in the decade 1840-49, 600 males were buried; their average age was 25 years and 8 months; only 56, or nine per cent were over seventy, whilst 261 were infant boys of less than five years. The 477 females buried in St. Just in the same period averaged 27 years of age; 82 had passed seventy, but 220 girls never reached five years. The explanation of these tragic figures lay in the overcrowded and insanitary cottages in which the miners and their families lived—and died. Many of them were hovels of cob and thatch, sometimes raised overnight by the communal effort of the miner and his workmates after their shift at the mine was over; all that was deemed essential was a roof and the walls to support it; water supply was a secondary consideration; sanitation came last of all. Measles, smallpox, diptheira, typhoid fever took a heavy toll; silicosis and phthisis carried off many of the males who had survived the hazards of childhood; maternal mortality was high; accidental deaths were little more numerous in proportion to population than in agricultural parishes, rarely averaging in St. Cleer, for example, more than two or three a year. Poverty, dirt, and malnutrition killed more than did occupational diseases.

The poverty of the miners in the second quarter of the nineteenth century is revealed by the fact that the majority of them earned an average weekly wage of less than 13/-; a few fortunate ones might get 15/-. In normal times it was a bare living wage but nothing more; it left but little to be set aside for the proverbial rainy day, even when sons and daughters made some contribution to family budgets—and rainy days often came to the miners. Till the 1870s, when there were strikes against the practice, it was the custom of mine managers to hold back a month's wages, and, through the tribute, tutwork, and ticketing systems, wages were paid monthly not weekly. The system of "subsist" advance allowances was general, but on many mines it was associated with truck shops. The poorer and less fortunate miners were nearly always in debt to local tradesmen and shop-keepers. With wheat prices usually over 60/- and not infrequently 80/- or 100/- the quarter, more than half the wages of the poorer miners with large dependent families went on grain alone, although for years to come many used barley and not wheaten bread. Only a small proportion of the total mining population of Cornwall possessed smallholdings or gardens of any size.

Before 1840 there was some investigation of the ill-health and mortality among miners. Pulmonary and cardiac complaints were found to be especially fatal and prevalent. Investigations into occupational diseases began and made considerable headway. Yet phthisis and silicosis alone were not accountable for the low average expectancy of life in mining districts; they only affected the male underground workers and perhaps a few surface hands employed in breaking up orestuff. Poverty, malnutrition, and insanitary conditions were the underlying causes of the high rates of infant and maternal mortality. Not infrequently a bad tribute bargain reduced a fully-employed and hard-working miner to the direst straits; other men and their families experienced the depths of destitution at the end of the monthly working period with wages, savings, and credit all exhausted. Many mines had their own friendly societies to help the widows and families of those killed in their dangerous calling, and to relieve injured and certain sick miners, but these did nothing for the far greater number of men—and their dependents—who were just physically worn out by hard labour, past work but often living on for years. A broken limb caused by falling from a ladder in the depths of a mine might mean months of privation for the injured man and his family. In nearly every mining parish were one or two miners who had been blinded in mining accidents.

Facilities for the treatment of injuries were extremely bad. The surgeons and doctors paid by the subscription of a penny or two a week deducted from the pay of the miners were usually conscientious, but were extremely hampered by the lack of hospitals until much later. In 1844 the mining adventurers and their friends at Redruth set up a "Practical Miners' Society" which sought to remedy this. At their second meeting in May, 1844, they were told by the surgeon Tobias Mitchell that:

"In many cases requiring surgical treatment the surgeons often had the greatest difficulty to encounter through the want of accommodation in the miners' cottages. These buildings often consisted of only two or three rooms, and it often happened that when a miner was brought home wounded, the first thing that had to be done was to get poles to prop up the bedroom so as to admit the additional weight of a surgeon and the other persons that might be necessary at such a time. Then the staircases were so narrow that a wounded man could hardly be got up many of them without the greatest difficulty and danger. Often there was only one bed in the house in which a man and his wife and children usually slept, and the children, in times of accident, had to be quartered on their neighbours. Even the beds were of such a character that . . . a miner's fractured leg frequently had to be reset in consequence of the sacking of the bed giving away."[1]

Schemes for starting a miners' hospital came to nothing. It was only the landlords, mine-owners, surgeons, and a few philanthropists that favoured such plans. The miners themselves were indifferent, and even hostile; when an outbreak of cholera had alarmed the mining district some years before the mine-owning Member of Parliament, E. W. W. Pendarves, had offered to turn a mine counting house into an emergency hospital, but the miners had threatened to pull it down if a single patient was taken to it.[2]

The work of mine doctors, backed by adventurers and ratepayers who realized that something must be done to reduce the poverty caused by accident and disease and the consequent heavy burdens on the rates, effected some amelioration in working conditions in the mines. Many injuries sustained by miners were due to falls from ladders, and by 1840 some doctors were attributing the high incidence of cardiac disease among labouring miners to the strain of climbing ladders, and warning the younger men against racing against each other up the ladders to see who could get to the surface quickest at the end of their

[1] *W.B.*: May 24, 1844.
[2] *W.B.*: August 23, 1844. The first proposal for a miners' hospital was made by Dr. William Pryce of Redruth in his *Mineralogia Cornubiensis*, pp. 176-178. This work was published in 1778, but it is more than probable that Pryce had talked over such a project with his fellow mine doctors and adventurers long before that time. The Miners' Hospital at Redruth, however, was not opened until January, 1866.

shifts. In 1836 the use of lifts in mines was advocated[1]; the offer of a prize by the Royal Cornwall Polytechnic Society was later secured by the Liskeard engineer, Michael Loam, for a "man engine" which was working in Tresavean by October, 1842.[2] Before that time warm baths had been instituted for miners at Roskear, whilst at the suggestion of Dr. Carlyon, Lady Basset provided for the issue of hot soup to the men when they came to the surface on leaving work.[3] Proposals to consolidate all the payments to doctor's pence and to the many small friendly societies into a single fund were made in 1821 and again in 1846, but without result.[4] These small friendly societies did good work with their limited funds, but they only lasted as long as the mine they were associated with worked, and made no provision for the "worn-out" miner whose only refuge was parochial relief or the dreaded Union Workhouse.

Few miners were able to save much for their old age in a comparatively short working life. A miner of fifty was old. In youth they had to help support their parents and younger brothers and sisters; then, usually marrying young, they quickly found themselves with a growing family of their own, the youngest member of which would hardly be old enough to maintain himself or herself by the time the miner—if he lived so long—was fifty; if and when he reached that age, a miner was usually suffering from diseased heart or lungs, or from the after-effects of accidents, and was hardly able to earn a mere living wage.[5] Thereafter life was little more than a struggle

[1] *W.B.*: May 27, 1836.　　　　[2] *W.B.*: November 4, 1842.

[3] *W.B.*: December 10, 1841. By this time the difference in temperature between the hot bottom levels of a mine and those at the surface had attracted much attention, and it was realized that it contributed to the ill-health of miners. Thus, in 1842, Cyrus Redding wrote: "A Cornish miner can work in a level 60 feet from a shaft without inconvenience, owing to the good ventilation but they have been known, notwithstanding, to lose 5 lb. or 6 lb. at a single spell of labour from perspiration at the bottom of a deep mine, where the temperature is often nearer 90 than 80." (*Illustrated Itinerary of the County of Cornwall*, footnote p. 204). The temperature at the 184 fathom level in Poldice was 100°F.; in Wheal Clifford a hot spring sent the temperature up to 125°F.: the copper mines in killas were generally hotter than the tin mines in granite. (C. C. James: *History of Gwennap*, p. 235).

[4] *W.B.*: July 6, 1821; May 1 and June 5, 1846.

[5] It is impossible to arrive at any age-grouping of the miners who worked underground; some indication is given by the recorded ages of the men who perished in the East Wheal Rose disaster in Newlyn East on July 9, 1846; 7 were under 20, 13 aged between 20 and 29 years, 8 in their thirties, 2 between 40 and 50, and the eldest 58; the youngest victim was 15, and the average age of the 31 but 26 years. (*W.B.*: July 17 and 23, 1846; the disaster was caused by a cloudburst flooding the mine). About 1840 Dr. Richard Lanyon found the average age of 1101 working miners to be 31 years; only 15 of them were over 60, and he estimated the average working life of a miner to be only 16 years and 2 months. (C. Redding: *Illustrated Itinerary of the County of Cornwall*, p. 201 footnote).

to keep out of the Union Workhouse, whilst economies on the necessities of life shortened their days. How hard they lived may be gauged from a recipe for making a gallon of soup for fourpence recommended by a philanthropic lady early in 1847 when famine threatened many mining districts; an ounce of dripping and three ounces of beef "cut small" cost three-halfpence, a quarter pound of barley a penny and the same amount of "seconds flour" another halfpenny; a few shreds of unrinded turnip, with a flavouring of leeks and other greenstuff, with a dash of salt and the cost of fuel made up the other penny.[1] In reasonably good times the mining population had rather better food than this, but "short commons" were all too prevalent; too many meals consisted of sour barley bread washed down with boiled water slightly discoloured with tea, occasionally varied with a few turnips, sometimes stolen from a field, fried in grease that had been purloined from the mine engines.

It would not have been surprising had widespread riot, crime and unrest resulted from such conditions. Yet Chartism made but a slight impression in the county that had been the birthplace of its first great leader, William Lovett, who had, however, only engaged in political and social agitation after he had left Newlyn to live in London.[2] Until the Truro church rate troubles early in 1838 there does not seem to have been a single active Chartist agitator in Cornwall, but then, after a riotous distraint sale, the carpenter Richard Spurr gained the reputation of being the leading Chartist in the county, although he also left for London by 1840.[3] Early in 1839 the Chartists adopted Wesley's former methods of sending itinerant proselytisers to the western county, but their "missionaries", Duncan and Lowry, arrived at the very time when firebrand temperance advocates were conducting extremely active missions in the mining districts. Opponents of Chartism spread tales of drunken men signing the Charter under the impression that they were taking the pledge.[4] Faced with the rivalry of Methodist and Temperance revival meetings, Chartism made little progress, although on one occasion it

[1] *W.B.*: March 5, 1847.
[2] William Lovett: *Life and Struggles*, (1876 ed.) pp. 1-24.
[3] *W.B.*: February 22, March 15, April 5 and 19, May 3 and 17, 1839, and January 24, 1840.
[4] *W.B.*: March 22, 1839.

invaded the "temple" of Wesleyanism and held a meeting at Gwennap Pit on April 1, 1839.[1] Chartist activities, however, did arouse alarm, and in June, 1839, over sixty professional men and shopkeepers in Camborne, headed by the vicar, Hugh Rogers, and the doctors, Richard Lanyon and Philip Vincent, saw fit to issue to the world their adherence to what amounted to a solemn league and covenant against Chartism, declaring that they:

"the Undersigned, Inhabitants of the Town and neighbourhood of Camborne, being anxious to preserve the peace and good order which have so peculiarly characterized this place for so many years past, and to prevent it from being the arena of political discussion by certain persons calling themselves Chartists, and who are propagating statements false in fact, and political doctrines destructive alike of the peace, prosperity, and security of the country—do hereby express our abhorrence of such attempts, and our determination individually and collectively to suppress them by all the means placed at our disposal, being fully assured that should they succeed the labouring classes in particular will be the deluded victims of such efforts to disturb the good order now so happily subsisting."[2]

Chartism then fell on evil days, particularly after John Frost's attempted march on Newport; at a Redruth meeting held on Good Friday, a collection to help pay for the legal defence of Frost and his associates was alleged not to have raised a single penny; in the same week Methodist Anniversary Services in St. Ives took collections exceeding £200.[3] During the next two years, however, the non-militant Complete Suffrage Movement made some progress in Cornwall, although it gained most support not in the mining areas but in the Launceston district where, despite the 1832 Reform Bill and the annihilation of the borough of Newport, the Duke of Northumberland still controlled elections to the solitary seat left to Launceston borough.[4]

Chartism had practically vanished from Cornwall when the hard winter of 1846-47 began. In December, 1846, bread tickets and blankets were distributed among the poor at Truro, Callington, Helston, Grampound and elsewhere, whilst benevo-

[1] *W.B.*: April 5, 1839.
[2] *W.B.*: June 14, 1839. The good order subsisting in Camborne seems to have been imaginary; "disturbances and depredations" led to a public subscription to get one of Peel's London policemen in the hope of improving "peace and good order" in 1841. (*W.B.*: March 12, 1841).
[3] *W.B.*: April 16, 1841.
[4] *W.B.*: June 16 and August 18, 1843.

lent landlords like Philip Rashleigh of Menabilly, John
Paynter of Boskenna, and Sir Richard Vyvyan of Trelowarren
made munificent gifts.[1]   But these were mere palliatives, and
on January 16, 1847, the Par Consols miners were threatening
to march on Pentewan to stop the "export" of corn; they were
dissuaded from violence by the personal intervention of the
aged Joseph Thomas Treffry,[2] who subsequently induced his
fellow mines adventurers to subsidise the sale of flour and grain
to their employees, besides advancing loans to the more needy,
unfortunate, and distressed tributers.[3]   Elsewhere soup
kitchens and blanket clubs helped ameliorate the worst conditions of poverty, whilst even in these times of dearth considerable collections were made at Falmouth, Truro, Penzance,
and elsewhere in Cornwall for the relief of the starving
peasantry of Ireland and of the Western Highlands of Scotland.[4]   But charity was not enough to span the gulf between
the general wage levels of the day and wheat at 120s. the
quarter.

Rumours, often only too well-founded, that dealers and corn
factors were profiting by scarcity were prevalent, and increased
as dearth intensified. The old idea of Cornish labourers that
they were being starved to fill the pockets of profiteering
merchants again appeared. The trouble came to a head at
Wadebridge on May 12th., when two or three hundred miners
and clay workers from St. Austell, Roche, and Luxulyan invaded that town to prevent the "export" of corn, and, moreover, demanded that they should be supplied with the grain
stored in the warehouses at their own prices. The magistrate,
Edward Stephens, tried to dissuade them, but for the first time
for years the working men of Cornwall were indisposed to
listen to the reasoning of their "superiors and betters". Stephens
was shouted down and struck by one of the mob, but not injured; with another magistrate he then swore in about a
hundred special constables. Night fell, and the rioters went to
their homes after failing to get Stephens' promise that the corn
in the warehouses should not be taken from Wadebridge. Next
morning the corn merchants hastily loaded the grain on board
a ship, hoping to catch the first tide and send it beyond the

[1] *W.B.*: December 18 and 25, 1846; January 1 and 8, 1847.
[2] J. T. Austen had taken the name of Treffry in 1838.
[3] *W.B.*: January 22 and 29, and May 21, 1847.
[4] *W.B.*: February 5 and 12, 1847.

reach of labourers whose idea of a just price did not agree with their own idea of sound business or economic principles. Before the ship had been loaded a band of Delabole quarry workers invaded the town, but were persuaded to leave after they had been given a half loaf of bread apiece. They had hardly crossed back over the bridge when the miners of the St. Austell district arrived on the scene again. The two "armies" joined forces. The half-laden ship hoisted anchor and put off down-river, the captain preferring to risk running aground on sand-banks to being boarded by hungry miners and quarrymen. The mob leaders grew threatening, and the magistrates thought it wise to admit them to the warehouses so that they could see for themselves how little corn was left. Even then they did not disperse, but paraded up and down the streets behind leaders, one of whom carried a red flag. As night approached fears of violence and of fiery destruction grew, but soon after sunset the demonstrators dispersed, although the tradespeople of Wade-bridge were living in terror until a detachment of troops arrived next day.

The Wadebridge "riots" were nothing more than an attempt to prevent the exportation of corn, with some hint that dealers should be forced to accept "fair" prices. Similar attempts had frequently occurred in times past, and with the same result—failure. No property had been damaged or destroyed. The injuries suffered by Stephens had been trivial, but it was significant that violent hands had been laid on a justice of the peace. Many threats had been uttered, but there was no dis-position on the part of the labouring miners and quarrymen generally to do more than threaten.

Elsewhere Cornish working men adopted rather more revolutionary tactics. On the first day of the Wadebridge troubles, a band of Caradon miners visited Callington market and forced the sale of corn and butter at what they deemed fair prices. Their proceedings were orderly and restrained. Every farthing made by the wheat sold at 8os. and the barley at 40s. the quarter, and the butter at 11d. the pound, was handed to the farmers who had brought those commodites to the market—though in the hope of getting much higher prices. After all the stock in the market had been sold the miners seized the stores of grain in the public houses and sold them at the same rates, again giving the entire proceeds to the erstwhile owners. It was feared, however, that such measures would deter the farmers from bringing their produce to the next weekly market, and two days later the local justices met in Callington and promised the farmers "protection" of their property. The next evening, Saturday, May 15th, some three hundred miners attended a mass meeting in the Town Hall; there they pledged themselves not to drink any liquor in the public houses of the town for the next six months—a pledge occasioned not by teetotal fanaticism but simply for conserving grain and for saving their wages for the necessities of life; anyone breaking this pledge was to be "horsed round the town on a pole". Magistrates, publicans, and farmers chose to see in this a threat to property; it was rather a threat to the prevalent economic notions of unrestrained *laissez faire* and to capitalistic notions of the sanctity not of property but of profits; the labouring classes were fighting, perhaps unconsciously, for the stabilization of real wages.

The example of the Caradon miners was followed by others elsewhere. On May 15th working men imposed maximum prices in Launceston market; in other districts bands of miners and quarrymen were visiting farms and ordering the occupiers to thresh supplies of corn, take the grain to market, and sell it at "fair" prices. In West Cornwall trouble began at Helston when a group of women mobbed a dealer who was suspected of attempting to corner limited grain supplies, but the presence of troops prevented any violent demonstration at the next Helston market on May 22nd. It was reported that agitators were going from mine to mine trying to organize mass support to enforce fair prices in the western markets. Similar unrest in Devonshire, where shops had been looted in Exeter and and actually burnt in Torquay, increased the alarm of the Cornish magistrates. On May 27th, the miners of West Penwith entered Penzance in force, but came to an agreement with the justices that the maximum price of barley, until the harvest was reaped, should not exceed 42s. 8d. per quarter for men earning less than 55s. a month; the previous week the price had been 60s.

All this passed by without real violence. In many mines the owners took steps to provide grain at reduced prices to their workers, either standing the loss themselves or making agreement with the labourers that the latter should pay the cost when times improved. But actual violence broke out in the Camborne-Redruth area on June 4th. A corn store was looted at Pool; later, the same day, special constables were driven out of a Redruth corn store, but troops arrived in time to prevent worse befalling. Some arrests were made, and at the subsequent Midsummer Sessions two men were transported for seven years each for their part in this riot, whilst three of the women who had played no small part in inciting the mob to violence and looting were, perhaps, fortunate to get sentences of only three months hard labour. On this occasion only the restraint of the troops had averted bloodshed. The actual amount of property stolen was small. The Redruth mob had got out of hand mainly, if not wholly, because it lacked leadership of the calibre which had enabled the West Penwith miners to make terms with the justices about the price of barley and the Caradon men to impose maximum prices in the Callington market.

Worse rioting occurred on June 11th, when a mob of casual mine-labourers and clay-workers invaded St. Austell and started looting some shops. The conduct of the High Sheriff, Nicholas Kendall, who arrived rather belatedly on the scene, was rather ill-advised; having induced the mob to appoint a delegation to state their grievances, he then only railed at the spokesman of that delegation as a disgrace to the community, berating him that he ought to be content with and thriving on a wage of 10s. a week, and telling him that if that was not enough he could work harder and get another fourpence a day, although Kendall did not think that needful since the earnings of the man's son brought the family weekly income up to 16s. Thus browbeaten, the deputation promised to get the mob out of town; they failed to do so, perhaps not attempting very much to carry out the behests of the unsympathetic representative of law and order they had encountered. The Riot Act was read, amid the jeers of men who swore they would pull down the Town Hall; a few departed to get picks to carry out their threat, and had started hacking away at the building when troops arrived. Several arrests were made, but the authorities fearing that their prisoners would be rescued by their fellows if they were taken to Bodmin jail by the direct road over the moors sent them thither by way of Lostwithiel. A few other prominent rioters were arrested later, including

F

the firebrand William Tellam who had struck the magistrate
Edward Stephens at Wadebridge. At the Assizes Tellam was
sentenced to eighteen months for his part in the Wadebridge
riots and a further nine months for his activities at St. Austell.
The heaviest sentences on the St. Austell rioters were the two-
year terms inflicted on Richard Kestall and Charles Faull, the
law coming down upon them severely since they were not
content with a wage of about 16s. weekly: seven others were
sentenced to terms of from six to eighteen months imprisonment, but six of the men tried were acquitted.[1]

With the St. Austell riot the disturbances came to an end in
Cornwall. The authorities had been gravely alarmed, but very
few men had been ready to resort to violence. The majority of
the people apparently knew that scarcity of food was general
throughout Britain, and that the authorities had little power to
remedy matters. The readiness of many magistrates and mines
adventurers to alleviate the crisis by supplying grain at less
than cost price was enough to reconcile the majority of the
labouring classes. No one suggested that wages ought to be
raised; agitation was directed against a few farmers and
profiteers who tried to gain exorbitant prices through the
emergency. Part of the trouble resulted from the inadequacy
of the old system of local weekly markets to supply the needs
of a population that, in most of the mining districts, had more
than doubled within a generation. In those markets prices
reflected a relationship of local supply and demand, and
fluctuations were considerable from season to season and even
from week to week. Miners, clay-workers, and quarrymen
alike seem to have considered that the tribute, tut-work, or
day-work contracts represented a fair bargain that they had
made with their employers; what they fought against were
what they thought unfair prices demanded for the necessities of
life. The new economic creeds might declare that scarcity and
high prices went together, but the Cornish labouring classes
still clung to the old order in which the prices of both labour
and of the necessities of life were fixed by custom and agreement and, in the last resort, by the fiat of local magistrates.
Only when it became obvious that the price of living had been

---

[1]Full accounts of the riots were given in *W.B.*: May 14, 21, and 28, June 4,
11 and 18, July 2 and 9, and August 6, 1847 for East and mid-Cornwall, and by
the *Penzance Gazette and West Cornwall Advertizer*: June 2, 9 and 16, 1847, for the
Penzance and Helston episodes.

TABLE IV: CORNISH MAY MARKET PRICES, 1843-1847[1]

	1843	1844	1845	1846	1847
Penzance					
Wheat	6s. 4d.	7s. 3d.	6s. 1d.	7s. 7d.	13s. 0d.
Barley	2s. 10d.	4s. 4d.	4s. 2d.	4s. 2d.	7s. 6d.
Beef	6¼d.	6d.	7½d.	6d.	7½d.
Butter	8½d.	7½d.	9d.	8¾d.	10¾d.
Potatoes	5s. 0d.	6s. 0d.	9s. 6d.	10s. 0d.	—
Eggs	5d.	—	5d.	5½d.	—
St. Austell					
Wheat	6s. 2½d.	7s. 6½d.	5s. 8d.	8s. 1½d.	13s. 0d.
Barley	2s. 8d.	3s. 8d.	3s. 8d.	3s. 8¼d.	7s. 6d.
Beef	6d.	6d.	6d.	6¼d.	—
Butter	8½d.	9d.	1s. 1d.	11d.	1s. 2d.
Liskeard					
Wheat	4s. 10d.	7s. 0d.	6s. 0d.	7s. 0d.	13s. 6d.
Barley	2s. 6d.	3s. 9d.	4s. 3d.	4s. 3d.	7s. 6d.
Butter	11d.	10d.	1s. 1d.	1s. 1d.	1s. 2d.

left unsheltered to face the storms of free competition did anything like a general agitation for higher wages begin. In the crisis of 1847 some local authorities and a greater number of mines adventurers fell back on the expedient of subsidizing wages, occasionally in money but more generally in kind—a policy virtually identical with the Speenhamland system which had been swept away by the Poor Law Amendment Act of 1834.

The famine months before the harvest of 1847 were a temporary crisis. There had been much distress and privation, some unrest, and a few riots. But there was no general uprising; there was no cohesion and unity between the labourers of the various mining, clay-working, and quarrying districts. Since the working classes lacked general leadership, and since a better harvest was confidently predicted, no lasting result could be expected. All that had been revealed was the powerlessness of the labourers to improve their own lot and the impotence of local authorities to effect more than mere palliative relief measures. Where mines had closed down, as in St. Agnes, unemployed men were given work repairing old roads and making new, whilst a few landowners, like the mines adventurers Stephen and Richard Davey of Tywarnhayle,

[1]Wheat, barley and potato prices per imperial bushel; beef and butter per pound; eggs per dozen. Based on *Penzance Gazette and West Cornwall Advertiser*: May 24, 1843; May 22, 1844; May 21, 1845; May 27, 1846; and May 26, 1847.

started land reclamation schemes to provide work and reduce local food shortages in time to come.[1] Unemployment, however, was not general, although a warning had been given that high prices, low wages, and unemployment might lead to intense distress. On this occasion the Cornish mining industry did not have to experience depression in all its ugly entity. Twenty years later a greater crisis was to come when the failing resources of the Cornish copper mines were no longer able to withstand foreign competition. In 1847 the fortune of copper mining still seemed bright, and with better harvests followed by the higher copper prices of the early 1850s all seemed to be well, although it was to be but the brief and illusory Indian Summer of the Cornish copper mining industry.

[1]*W.B.*:   June 11, 1847.   The Daveys employed some sixty miners on their "model" Tywarnhayle farm.

CHAPTER V

THE FORTUNES OF THE TIN
MINING INTEREST

1775-1845

THE DEVELOPMENTS in steam power and in *laissez faire*
capitalism profoundly influenced the Cornish tin mining
industry in the closing decades of the eighteenth and the
opening years of the nineteenth centuries, but the main interest
of this period arises from the expedients suggested and adopted
to meet the problems of a saturated market. The Cornish Tin
Company, established in July, 1772, failed to give the tin
mining interest lasting prosperity; there was a slow rise in
prices from the disasterously low levels of 1772, but this must
be associated primarily with a reduction in the amount of tin
mined and sold in Cornwall. In the crisis of 1772 the cry of
East Indian competition had first been raised, yet in only one
year before 1789 did the amount of "Banca Tin" brought to
Europe exceed 500 tons; for years to come Holland was to
import nearly as much tin from Cornwall as it did from the
East Indies. The outbreak of war in 1778 and again in 1793
reduced exports of Cornish tin for a time, creating more stocks
of unsold mineral.

To deal with the glut of tin on the markets, in 1772 and later,
a variety of expedients were suggested—the making of pewter
and tinplate in Cornwall itself, transferring the marketing of tin
abroad from the control of the ring of London pewterers whose
interests lay in keeping prices low, and the abolition of the
export duty on tin. In 1772, however, the London merchants
were able to prevent a Parliamentary inquiry into the conduct
of and the conditions prevailing in the tin trade.[1] About
1770, the invention of Britannia metal, an alloy in which tin
was the main constituent provided a new market.[2] The
London pewterers looked around for new overseas markets,

[1]*Observations, 1772*, pp. 17-24.
[2]The constituents were 90% tin, 7% antimony, 1.5% copper, and 1.5% brass.
(Lardner's Cabinet Cyclopedia: *Manufactures of Metal*, Vol. III, 'Tin, Lead and
Copper' (1834) pp. 103 ff.).

and developed a profitable connection with the Liverpool African slave traders whilst some of their produce found its way to distant Kamchatka.[1]

When France became the ally of the American Revolutionaries in 1778, the tin industry suffered a check. The British navy, neglected since 1763, could not adequately protect merchantmen plying between Cornish ports and London from the ravages of privateers; the long siege of Gibraltar cut off Mediterranean tin and pilchard markets. There was, however, a temporary removal of East Indian competition when Britain declared war on the Dutch in 1780. In this crisis the tin mining interest again combined and, dominated by the Truro merchant and mine adventurer Henry Rosewarne, set up a Committee of Correspondence at Helston on February 29, 1780. This Committee met at Truro on April 8, 1780, and agreed to fix the price of tin at the Coinage at £3 per hundredweight. "Agents" in London and Bristol were required to furnish accounts of the amounts of tin they had received from the Cornish tin proprietors, and to give details of tin sales they made. The Committee arranged to meet again at the next Coinage at Penzance, and also moved a vote of thanks to Sir Francis Basset for his help and trouble in furthering the objects and endeavours of the Tinners' Association. The minutes of this meeting were signed by Rosewarne as Vice-Warden of the Stannaries, and by John James, Benjamin Nankivell, Thomas Reed, William Edwards, William Cornish, Ralph Allen Daniell for Thomas Daniell, Thomas Warren, Collan Bowden, John Messer and James James—most of whom were connected with the mines west of Truro.[2] From this time until 1818 the Association of the Proprietors of Tin dominated the tin trade. It was a group of merchants, smelters, and a few owners of mineral rights; the ordinary working miners were unrepresented, but the tribute system of working mines meant that their interests and those of "capitalists" were, for the most part, identical.

At successive Coinages the price of tin was raised, reaching 70s. in April, 1782. At the meeting of the Committee held at Truro on October 21, 1780, it was agreed to limit credit for tin

---

[1]Lardner's Cabinet Cyclopedia: *Manufactures of Metal*, Vol III, 'Tin, Lead and Copper', pp. 92-3.
[2]*C.R.B.*: April 8, 1780 Minutes.

to no longer period than three months; a general meeting of the "Tinner" unanimously agreed on July 14, 1781, to meet increasing insurance costs in transporting tin to market the price in London should be 8s. above that in Cornwall (per hundredweight) and that in Bristol 7s. 6d. above as against 7s. and 6s. 6d. previously, but the general annual meeting, held at Helston on September 6, 1781, made the Bristol rate the same as that at London. The minutes of this September meeting of 1781 also passed a resolution never to have further dealings with agents in London or Bristol who banded together to "counteract the Resolutions of the meetings of the Associated Tinners in Cornwall"; possibly pewterers and other purchasers of tin had "corrupted" the agents the Association had previously appointed. A month later it was resolved that no member of the Association should sell tin at prices below that fixed by the associates at the Quarterly Coinage Meetings.[1] The system of coining tin, originally designed merely to secure the dues claimed by the Duchy of Cornwall, provided the tin mining interests with excellent opportunities for meeting and concerting a common policy of which, at this time, they availed themselves to the utmost extent. A little later, meeting at Penzance, the "Associated Tinners" resolved unanimously:

"Whereas a Report has prevailed that the Tinners in this Neighbourhood were no longer bound to abide by the Association entered into at Helstone.

"That it is the Opinion of this Meeting that the Association of the Tinners has been attended with the most beneficial Consequences to the Tin Trade of this County and that we will support it by every means in our Power in its utmost Extent being fully convinced that by so doing we shall render the greatest service to the Mining Interest and the Tin Trade."[2]

Whilst the increased demand and a slight fall in output contributed to the rise in price, some rather disgruntled pewterers, no longer enjoying control of the tin trade, began complaining against the "monopoly" achieved by the Cornish Association. To meet these complaints, when the Association agreed to raise the price to 70s. per hundredweight at the Truro Coinage Meeting held on April 13, 1782, it expressly laid down that this price was not to be changed for six months in order "to prevent any groundless jealousies, that we mean to push the price of tin

[1] *C.R.B.*: October, 1781.
[2] *C.R.B.*: November 3, 1781.

to an exorbitant height"; at the same time provision was made to alter the price if the imminent end of the American War justified any such alteration. These changes were only reductions made in the Bristol and London tin prices.[1] The Cornish price remained at 70s. until January, 1785, when it was raised to 72s, a level maintained until a 2s. reduction in July, 1788, indicated the onset of another catastrophic slump. By January, 1789, the Cornish price of tin was down to 58s. Until this new crisis, however, the Association had succeeded in stabilizing prices, and had controlled the tin trade; it had not hesitated to dismiss agents who sold tin at lower prices than it dictated;[2] the power of the London pewterers had been broken.

In October, 1787,[3] the Associated Tinners resolved to codify the resolutions made at their earlier meetings, and, on January 19, 1788, a general meeting accepted a series of seven articles. The first of these laid down:

'that the price of tin shall be fixed at the last day of each Coinage at Truro as has always been the Custom at the Meeting then to be held, and that no person sell any tin at a less price till the same is altered at a like Meeting; that no Tin shall be sent for sale to London, Bristol, or Birmingham but to Agents appointed by the Associated Tinners."

Six London and two Bristol Agents were named, but the choice of a Birmingham Agent was deferred until the next meeting, and the first article concluded with a declaration:

"that no further Agents be appointed unless nominated by a Person who shall have coined Fifty Blocks of Tin per quarter for three years preceding in his own name or name of the House of trade in which he is a partner, or shall engage to consign 100 Blocks per quarter at London or 50 Blocks per quarter at Bristol or Birmingham at least to said Agents, and that such person proposed as Agent is first approved of by a Majority of Tinners at one of the usual meetings . . . at Truro. That said Agents are to sell all the Tin consigned to them by different persons without any partiality and rateably as far as can be, except only when prevented by necessity of supplying their Customers with particularly required marks.[4]   That the Commission in each place be 1/- per hundredweight and no more."

[1]The Bristol price was reduced 6d. per hundredweight below that of London in April, 1783, since "there is full that difference in the freight to the two markets"; in October, 1783, London price levels were lowered to 7/6d. and those of Bristol to 7s. above the Cornish levels. (*C.R.B.*: April 12 and October 25, 1783).
[2]John King of Bristol was dismissed from his agency in April, 1783, for selling tin at a shilling below the fixed price (*C.R.B.*: April 12, 1783).
[3]*C.R.B.*: October 20, 1787.
[4]*I.e.* the smelting-house marks by which blocks of tin coming from particular smelting-houses were distinguished.

This shows beyond question that the Association was dominated by the larger tin smelters; a quantity of four hundred blocks a year would represent at least fifty tons worth £3,500 at the then price; the total output of Cornish tin in 1788 had been just over 3,350 tons.

The second article stipulated that prices in London and Bristol were to be "invariably governed by the price in Cornwall, *viz*: 7/6 per hundredweight at London and 7/- per hundredweight at Bristol above it, for all Tin sold for Home Consumption, and 3/6 per hundredweight further if Exported by the Agents for Duties and all Charges if shipped in Blocks, and further 1/6 per hundredweight if shipped in Barrels." The purchaser from the Agents was to be allowed the customary one pound weight in every block that had been granted to London, Bristol and Birmingham buyers for "breakage". The third resolution, besides limiting credit to a mere two months, stipulated that no person was to be retained as an Agent "if he shall sell tin consigned to him by any person not a party hereto at a less price than that fixed by the Associated Tinners." The fourth article still further emphasized the monopolistic nature of the cartel that had been set up by the Associates when it decreed:

"we will not carry our Tin to any Smelting House now working or to be put on, unless the owners and proprietors thereof become parties to this agreement and the Owners of Smelting Houses hereby engage not to smelt or deliver any Tin to persons who refuse or have not consented to become parties hereto. Nor to any persons who have supplied the Buyers of Tin at London, Bristol, or Birmingham with Tin which has or shall be sold at a price less than stipulated herein."

Only a small concession to "private trading" was made by the fifth article which stated that:

"If any Pewterer or other person give orders for Tin to be shipped for London or elsewhere in Great Britain on his own account, any member of this Association shall be permitted to fulfil such order at the Coinage price, charging other duties . . . with 6d. per hundredweight for Commission and 1/- per Block for the Charges of Shipping and at three months credit, but if such Pewterer or other person employ such Tin to undersell the Agents of this Association . . . (they) shall not be supplied hereafter with Tin by any member of this Association, unless by buying it at one of our Agents at the Stipulated price."

The sixth article provided that complaints should be heard at subsequent meetings, whilst the last article declared that since:

"there is every reason to believe that some shippers of Tin have recently been offering it at a Price under what has been fixed for Exportation by the principal Shippers, and which conduct must injure the Trade very considerably by sending forth an Opinion that the price is falling in the County which will keep back many orders. We as Tinners and Smelters declare our strongest dis-approbation of such Measures and that we will discountenance it as much as possible, and if proof of such Conduct is brought forward at the next or any future Coinage meeting, we will take effectual means to prevent any Continuance of it."

These articles were approved unanimously at the Truro meeting, and, five weeks later, on February 26, 1788, were submitted to the Western Tinners at Helston. Whilst Benjamin Nankivell presided at both the Truro and Helston meetings, at the latter meeting four parties dissented from the seventh article, including the Falmouth houses of Fox, Phillips & Fox and of George C. Fox & Son, which had assented to it at Truro; the other dissentients were John Batten of Penzance and the Heam & Trieve partnership. The Penzance merchants Oxnam and Bolitho secured the appointment of John Harris as an additional London agent. At Helston it was also agreed to pay William Skues, the secretary of the Association, to take the book of resolutions around to all "Tinners and Associates" who had not attended the meeting, and to print five hundred copies of the articles for circulation amongst "the proper Rank of this County". Even more significant was the passage written in the Resolution Book by Thomas Glynn, and later struck through, that he, Glynn, approved the articles but only:

"provided that the tin-smelters will swear, when required, that they will give the tinners a just price for their tin."

Comment on this is almost superfluous; it only emphasized that the merchants and smelters had seized a monopolistic control of tin-marketing and were running the tin industry in their own interests, not in those of the working miner with whom they were not always identical.

After prices had been falling for nearly a year, the Truro Coinage Meeting held on July 18, 1789, elected Nicholas Donnithorne to the permanent chairmanship of the Association in place of Nankivell, and appointed a special Committee from the "coiners" of tin to meet at Redruth on July 29th, to investigate the causes of the low tin prices and to suggest methods whereby "a fair price" might be regained. This Committee attributed the slump to over-production, and recommended withholding supplies from the markets by a stocking system, each "coiner" or producer of tin keeping back a proportionate part of his tin so that "no more than the annual consumption should come into the markets", but no suggestion of any specific quantity to be sold each year was made.[1]

The Redruth meeting concluded its session with a vote of thanks to persons who had put forward plans for improving the Cornish tin trade, and particularly George Unwin "for the useful discoveries and communications he has given to this Committee respecting the Tin Trade in India." Unwin, a former employee of the East India Company, had returned to England with the idea that the "war" with Banca could be carried to the very heart of the rival tin-producing district. During his years in the Orient Unwin had been impressed by the considerable Dutch tin trade with China. Henceforth, mainly through Unwin and Donnithorne, the affairs of the Associated Tinners became closely connected with those of the East India Company. As far back as 1749 the East India Company had taken some Cornish tin to China, and there had been some shipments of that metal thither in the 1760s.[2] In all, however, less than 250 tons of Cornish tin had reached China before 1789, and more than three-quarters of that total amount had been sent out by the East India Company in the two years 1762 and 1763, losing some 23% on the transaction since the price of tin in Canton was only about £3 above the current London price of £65. By 1789 the price of tin in Canton had reached £96 per ton, and with Cornish prices standing at £60 or below, the Directors of the East India Company were persuaded to make another trial of the Chinese tin market.

The Chinese market offered another attraction to the tin

[1] The average output of Cornish tin in the decade 1780-89 had been slightly more than 2,950 tons, and it seems that the Association regarded this quantity sufficient to meet the demand; output, however, had increased from only 2,550 tons in 1782 to 3,350 tons in 1788; it was not to fall below 3,000 tons until 1798, but thereafter was not to exceed that amount until 1815. In 1816, the Cornish output first exceeded 4,000 tons. (G. R. Lewis: *The Stannaries*, App. J., pp. 255-56).
[2] Unwin, p. 27.

speculators; metal sent thither was not manufactured into durable products but was destroyed by being beaten into tin-leaf that was burnt at the countless shrines of family idols venerated by the hosts of heathen yellow men. Unwin was confident that the Chinese market could consume more tin than was raised at Banca and the other East Indian Islands,[1] whilst David Scott, a director of the East India Company believed that £100,000 worth of tin[2] could be sent to China every year without having "any visible impression on that market".[3] Unwin believed that the Dutch could be deprived of the China trade, and reckoned that this would benefit British revenue, since the principal commodity the Dutch took from the Chinese in exchange for tin was tea which, first brought to Holland, was subsequently smuggled into northern England and Scotland. Cornish tin, too, would probably redress in part the extremely adverse balance of Anglo-Chinese trade.[4]

Influenced by Unwin's arguments and by the recommendations of the Committee meeting at Redruth, the general meeting of the Association on September 29, 1789, appointed a Committee of Correspondence to negotiate with the East India Company; arrangements were made for each smelting house to supply its due proportion of the tin allocated to the East India Company, thereby revealing the fact that the smelters had now assumed direct control of all tin sales from Cornwall.[5] A month later the price of tin in Cornwall was raised to £65 per ton.[6] In July, 1790, Donnithorne informed his associates

[1]Unwin, p. 39; this may be contrasted with the "bogy" raised in 1772, in *Observations, 1772*, pp. 17-18.

[2]*I.e.* over 1,000 tons at the Canton price, and over 1,400 at the Cornish price, or at least double the surplus production of the Cornish mines at that time.

[3]Quoted Unwin, p. 39.

[4]Estimated at £1,300,000 against £150,000. (Unwin, p. 2).

[5]No minutes of this meeting survive; the minutes of the Truro meeting of September 15, 1789, made no reference to any Committee of Correspondence, but that of October 24th, asked the Committee of Correspondence to meet on the next Thursday in terms indicating that it had already come into existence; it is possible, although not certain, that the Committee appointed on July 18th, and which met on July 29th, called itself a Committee of Correspondence.

[6]*C.R.B.*: Minutes October 24, 1789. At this meeting and at most of the following meetings the chair was taken by the Truro merchant R. A. Daniell; since he had been elected as chairman in Nankivell's place, Donnithorne had not attended a single meeting, being absent in London negotiating with the East India Company and, moreover, being almost exclusively concerned with the marketing rather than the actual production of tin. John Thomas, the future Vice-Warden of the Stannaries had taken the chair at the July and September meetings. At the meeting of October 24th, no less than 38 Associates signed the resolutions besides Daniell, either in person or through agents including Thomas Wilson "for Boulton & Watt etc. and self."

that he had agreed to supply the East India Company with 1,200 tons of tin—three-eighths of the total amount coined in Cornwall that year—and the Penzance Coinage Meeting, on July 31st, not only resolved to give Unwin a commission of 6/8 on every ton of Cornish tin sold east of the Cape, but furthermore declared that they would not smelt any tin for anyone who refused to participate in the contract with the East India Company. To meet this East Indian contract the entire produce of the Truro Michaelmas contract was set aside, and by January, 1791, the Cornish price had risen to £76. Every effort was made to ensure that each Associate contributed his fair and proportionate share to the stock of tin reserved for the East India Company. The surplus of unsold tin vanished, and on May 2, 1792, an extraordinary meeting had to be called to make provision for borrowing from the East Indian stock to meet the demands of the home market, the price in Cornwall having now reached £90.

If the price in England had risen over fifty per cent since the beginning of 1789, the East India contract remained at the same rates, and this led to quite considerable feeling in Cornwall that the Company should pay more for Cornish tin. Late in 1793, with the time drawing near for the East India Company to seek the renewal of its charter from Parliament, Francis Gregor suggested to the Associated Tinners that, if the Company refused to take any tin they offered, at higher prices than those of the contracts, the Associates should themselves seek permission and licence to use the Company's ships, paying freightage dues, and themselves export tin to any place within the limits of the Company's charter; the Company was to be debarred from levying any duties on such tin, whilst the Tinners were to appoint their own agents to the Orient to conduct the trade.[1] The Company promised some concessions, since the value of the trade was considerable; in the five years 1791-5 it had exported nearly £400,000 worth of unwrought tin to China, whilst for the whole decade 1791-1800 the average yearly export was £79,320 8s. This, however, declined by nearly half during the next decade to an average yearly export

[1] *C.R.B.*: Minutes December 8, 1792. These proposals were referred to a special Committee by a "General Meeting of the Lords, Adventurers, and others concerned in the Tin and Copper Trade of the County of Cornwall" at which Lord Falmouth presided.

valued at £48,920 12s., whilst by 1821 tin was being transported in the opposite direction.[1]

The outbreak of war with France in 1793 did not have the disastrous repercussions on the fortunes of Cornish tin mining that many may have expected. The surplus of Cornwall was absorbed by the East India Company, even though in 1788 "France and French Flanders" had taken over a quarter of the total exports of British tin.[2] The activities of French privateers impeded the trade somewhat, especially in 1796,[3] but by 1797 the Associated Tinners were less concerned with war troubles and impediments to trade than with the discrepancy between the Cornish tin price of £88 and the £72 stipulated in the contracts with the East India Company. Furthermore the declining output of the Cornish tin mines made it difficult to fulfil the contracts with the Company; early in 1797 it had been necessary to borrow 158 tons of tin from individual mercantile concerns to meet the contracts,[4] whilst in October, 1798, the Associated Tinners reduced the proportion of tin stocked for the East India Company,[5] and, with output still declining, this was further reduced in July, 1799, and the Company informed that the Associates could only guarantee a delivery of 600 tons instead of 800.[6]

In brief, a new crisis had developed and, for the first time within memory, the demand for tin had exceeded the output of the Cornish mines. The amount of tin coined in 1798 had fallen to 2,820 tons, whilst by 1801 it was down to 2,328 tons, the lowest level since 1751; in the next five years the average yearly coinage was about 2,800 tons, but there followed a further decline until it was down to hardly more than 2,000 tons in 1810; after that until the end of the Napoleonic Wars the average was around 2,400 tons a year, but in 1816 the amount coined was just short of 3,350 tons, and the following year saw it leap to 4,120 tons.

The decline in Cornish tin production in the closing years of the eighteenth century coincided with an expanding home market, principally for the manufacture of tin-plate. Despite

---

[1] John Macgregor: *Commercial Statistics*, Vol. IV, p. 432.
[2] 666 tons out of 2,321. (Unwin, p. 32).
[3] *C.R.B.*: Minutes, April 9 and July 16, 1796.
[4] *C.R.B.*: Minutes January 21, 1797.
[5] *C.R.B.*: Minutes October 20, 1798.
[6] *C.R.B.*: Minutes July 20, 1799.

this greater home demand, the Cornish smelters persisted in their efforts to supply the East India Company and China. In August, 1800, the price of tin at Penzance had reached £94,[1] whilst at Truro the position was described as alarming at the meeting held on December 23, 1800, since an extremely difficult and complicated situation had arisen from repeated borrowings of tin in advance from certain merchants and from the stock reserved for the East India Company to meet the demands of home consumers. Nevertheless, with many European markets closed by the "convulsed state of that Continent", the Associated Tinners agreed on January 24, 1801, to increase their sales to the East India Company to 700 tons. Three months later, however, with Northern European markets re-opened, the Associates resolved to ask Unwin and the two county Members of Parliament, Lemon and Gregor, to approach the East India Company "to endeavour to obtain some relief by an increase in price in consequence of the distressed State of the Mines and declining condition of this valuable branch of commerce."[2] When they met on August 7, 1801, the Associated Tinners agreed to reduce the contract offered to the East India Company to 300 tons at £75 per ton, but during the next six months the Cornish price of tin rose a further £6 to £100. Perhaps anticipating that further contracts with the East India Company would not be possible, the Coinage Meeting held on July 17, 1802, agreed to grant George Unwin an annuity of £300 for the rest of his life, raised by a levy of 4½d. on every block of tin coined, "in consideration of the services rendered to the Tin Trade of the County of Cornwall".

Unwin's scheme of the China market and the increasing home demand for tin had helped to eliminate the reserves of mined mineral that had for so many years been encumbering the markets. Contributing even more to this result had been the temporary decline in Cornish output caused by the exhaustion of the more shallow deposits of stream and mine tin. The output of tin in Cornwall was not to increase again until the high-pressure steam engines of Trevithick and other Cornish engineers came into general use. In addition, concentration on copper-mining, which increased the output of copper ores

---

[1] *C.R.B.*: Minutes August 2, 1800. The London price was now fixed at £103 and that at Bristol £102.
[2] *C.R.B.*: Minutes April 25, 1801.

in Cornwall from less than 43,000 tons in 1794 to about 76,250 tons in 1809, made demands on limited resources of capital and labour to the detriment of the older mining industry. In these years of scarcity, however, some of the most incredible expedients were resorted to by Cornish miners in their efforts to arrest the declining output of tin. Visitors to Cornwall were amazed by the risks run to gain the precious ores from veins lying below the sea as well as in the depths of inland hills. "Foreigners" were particularly impressed by the Wherry Mine, near Penzance, which closed down in 1798 after a relatively short life, where the adventurers had sunk a shaft below high tide level by employing huge iron vertical tubular pipes, a method later employed in the Carnon Valley.[1] In St. Just in Penwith levels were already being run out below the sea from the shafts of Botallack and Wheal Cock, although these submarine workings were by no means as extensive as they later became.

The closing of the Wherry Mine in 1798, in consequence of increasing costs and damage done to its insecure superstructure by storms, marked the beginning of depression; if the price of tin had increased by more than fifty per cent since the slump of 1772, the costs of production had risen in even greater proportion. Within the next ten years the Carnon Stream works and the great Polgooth mine in St. Mewan had also suspended operations, the latter closing down in 1807 after returning more than £100,000 in profits to its adventurers.[2] In 1800 the Porth stream workings were overwhelmed by the sea, and were not resumed until some years later, when the Wherry method of sinking iron cylinders to form a shaft was adopted; this venture was nearly wrecked by another storm in 1815, but later another shaft was sunk even nearer low-tide level.[3] The great tin and copper mine of Pednandrea near Redruth was also suspended in this period, and was only to be restarted in 1852, although an unsuccessful attempt to resume it was made in 1822.[4] With these older workings falling on evil days a greater proportion of the tin raised in Cornwall came from "mixed" mines which produced both copper and tin, for the fluctuating prices of the two metals had made

[1] Maton, Vol. i, p. 209; Warner, pp. 148-150; Drew, Vol. ii, p. 441.
[2] Drew, Vol. i, pp. 619-620.
[3] Drew, Vol. ii, pp. 66-69.
[4] Cunnack MSS.

adventurers more ready to risk their capital in concerns in which losses on tin might be made up by profits on copper, and mines like Cook's Kitchen in Illogan and Wheal Unity in Gwennap became the most important tin-producing adventures in Cornwall. In addition to the declining fortunes of the mines of western and mid-Cornwall, the eastern tin concerns had almost entirely ceased production.[1] Yet it might be doubted if actual Cornish tin production had fallen off to such an extent as the coinage statistics suggest; the brief recovery after the Peace of Amiens and the startling increase after Waterloo were rather too sudden and marked to be entirely explained by post-war speculation and enterprise. It will never be known how much crude tin-stuff, which never reached a smelting-house controlled by the Associated Tinners let alone the Coinage Halls of Truro, Helston and Penzance, went over in the war years as ballast in the smuggling ships which ran back cargoes of brandy, lace, gin, tea, salt, and other heavily-dutied commodities; a mere ten tons of such ballast was worth well over £600.

Nevertheless, even had the Peace of Amiens endured, it is likely that the European consumers of tin would have been forced to seek East Indian supplies, for the proportion of Cornish tin exported was declining considerably. The bitter memory of unsold and unsaleable stocks of metal, however, died hard, and the Associated Tinners still persisted in the policy of reserving a considerable part of their produce for the East Indian market, especially when the renewal of hostilities with Napoleon again cut off many Continental markets from regular and legal trade. On July 16, 1803, they agreed to supply five or six hundred tons of tin to the East India Company at £75 per ton, although the Cornish price was then £100 a ton. At the same meeting they passed a vote of thanks to the smelter Richard Oxnam and to Unwin who had prevailed upon the Government to forego the three per cent export duty. on tin sent to China and the twelve and half per cent duty on timber imported for use in Cornish mines. Until 1808 this quantity of tin was regularly set aside for the East India Company, but after that date it was progressively reduced, a natural development in view of the continued decline in

[1] No "Eastern" mine was mentioned by Dr. Berger as producing tin in 1800. (Drew, Vol. 1, p. 619).

Cornish output and the high prices which reached £112 in 1806 although receding to £104 in 1808.

The first challenge to the Associated Tinners came in April, 1808, when the Trevenen adventurers refused to stock any tin to sell at the £75 rate to the East India Company, and the Associates approached the Vice-Warden of the Stannaries to call a "General Meeting of Lords, Bounders, Adventurers and Tinners" to consider this matter. The root of the trouble was a growing suspicion that the smelters were "borrowing" excessive quantities from the reserves stocked for the East India Company, for which the mines adventurers were only receiving £75 less deductions of various charges per ton, and selling it to home consumers at £104 plus charges.[1] These suspicions increased when the Truro men agreed to stock five-ninths of the Midsummer and Michaelmas Coinages of 1808, whilst those of Penzance only agreed to reserve four ninths,[2] but the western smelters later agreed to stock a third of the Ladyday Coinage of 1809 as against a fifth stocked by the eastern smelters for that and the next two Coinages.[3] The continued opposition and refusal of some tinners to agree to the stocking system led to the calling of a general meeting of the mining interest which, on August 11, 1809, apparently convinced the defaulters that stocking tin for the East India Company was of great benefit and to the interest of all; moreover, on February 4th, the Associates had already taken steps to ensure that the various smelting houses were keeping accounts of the quantities of tin they smelted and coined and sold, and submitting such records to the Association. The decline in Cornish output, however, despite the closing of European markets by Napoleon's Continental System, made it well-nigh hopeless to continue the policy of reserving tin for China at prices much below those obtainable in the home markets. The Penzance Ladyday Coinage Meeting of 1810 agreed that:

"in Consideration of the present reduced State of the Tin Mines, the consequent Diminution of nearly half the quantity of Tin, occasioned by the increased prices of Labour and mining materials, it becomes necessary for the preservation of the mines to advance the price of coined Tin to 147/- per cwt., exclusive of duties and charges, 160/- in London and 159/- in Bristol."

[1] *W.B.*: January 18, 1811.
[2] *C.R.B.*: Minutes July 16 and 30, 1808.
[3] *C.R.B.*: Minutes February 4 and April 8, 1809.

A quarter of the next three Coinages, however, was still reserved for the East India Company, but the Associates agreed to ask:

"the County Members to request that when notice is given in Parliament for the renewal of the East India Company's Charter that they apply for a clause to permit the Tinners to export Tin to the Countries within the Limits of their Charter if the Directors do not incline to purchase it. . . ."

Sir William Lemon and John Hearle Tremayne, the County Members, seem to have exerted their influence on behalf of the Associates, and for this, along with Davies Giddy the Bodmin Member, were accorded a vote of thanks at the next Penzance meeting on July 28, 1810. "Increased demand", however, led to a resolution at that same meeting to reduce the proportion stocked to a fifth, and that only with a proviso that all participated in their fair proportion; the opinion was voiced that only the exportation of tin had saved the Cornish mining industry when the Associates offered a service of Block Tin to Sir George Wesley, the British Ambassador to Persia, as a token of appreciation of his efforts to promote trade with Eastern merchants. Finally, the Tinners concluded the business of that day by raising the price of tin to £154 per ton. The price remained at that level until March, 1811, when it fell to £142, and a further £6 drop four months later led the Associates, meeting at Truro, to ask the East India Company to pay more than £75 a ton, although agreeing to stock four-ninths of the current and five-ninths of the next three Coinages for the Company.

The mining interest, however, was becoming increasingly dissatisfied with the smelters and their dealings with the East India Company. The Porth Towan Smelting House refused to stock tin but was induced by its landlord, Lord de Dunstanville, to express its willingness to join the Associates in the summer of 1811. The Associates then summoned a "Special Meeting of Lords and Adventurers in the Tin Mines, and Tin Smelters" to discuss "the deplorable State of the Tin Mines and Tin Trade". This meeting at Redruth on August 26, 1811, resolved that:

"application be made to the Lords and Bound Owners of Mines earnestly entreating that they will grant no setts nor renew old ones without inserting a condition that the respective Takers shall be subject to the Resolutions of the Associated Tinners, nor grant any

Plots (of land) for erecting Smelting Houses, or of Water Courses for this purpose without being subject to such Resolutions."

This resolution, however, apparently did not gain the desired results, for, at a special meeting held at Redruth on November 21, 1811, the refusal of the Porth Towan and Ludgvan Smelting Houses to co-operate in the stocking system was blamed for the "present most deplorable states of the Tin Mines and Tin Trade". Indeed, the industry had fallen into a state of depression again, for since July, 1811, the Cornish price of tin had fallen from £136 to £100 a ton. The mining interests refused to believe the declaration of the Smelters that the stocking system had enabled them to dispose "of the excess of our produce at a reduced price beyond the demands of the European market." They suspected that smelters and speculators had made exorbitant gains from price fluctuations, and even that speculation with the tin stocks had caused the slump in price. The Ludgvan Smelting House came into line, but the Porth Towan concern was only forced into compliance when the Associates induced the miners to boycott it by taking their ores elsewhere for smelting.[1]

The days of the system of stocking tin, however, were numbered. A general economic recession had brought the old feud of miner and smelter to life again. Resentment grew when tin was taken from the reserved stocks to meet European demands by the London agents of the Association. The smelters were believed to be hand in glove with "foreign" London speculators, whilst in Cornwall the mining areas were suffering extreme distress through the scarcity and high prices of grain and provisions. In the early spring of 1812 the plight of the mining districts was so bad that the landed gentry and mining magnates combined to call a special meeting at Redruth on April 3rd to discuss the distress caused by high prices. Gaunt, ill-fed, half-starving and ragged miners might have cynically remarked the way these meetings of the Cornish landed and mining interests invariably assembled at the best hostelries just before the time of the midday repast. At this meeting the Rev. Hugh Rogers of Redruth took the chair, and it was agreed that the western mining parishes should each, in vestry meetings, elect two representatives to a Committee, which was to meet at Truro on April 29th, to discuss and make plans for

[1]*W.B.*: February 13 and 27, 1812.

relieving the labouring classes. This Committee was particularly enjoined to make suggestions designed to reduce the consumption of corn, whilst the meeting at Redruth itself recommended the planting of early potatoes, the raising of subscriptions for general relief, and purchases of barley by
parochial authorities. The parish vestries proceeded to elect
a Committee consisting of men belonging to the Associated
Tinners with the addition of a few clergymen. Kenwyn sent
John Moyle and Thomas Trestrail, Perranzabuloe George Fox
and Benjamin Sampson, Illogan William Reynolds, Kea
Robert Mitchell, and Gwennap Michael Williams along with
the clergyman Booth, whilst Camborne elected the landowner
Edward Stackhouse and the engineer Andrew Vivian, Redruth its Vicar, Rogers, a member of a family of landowners and
mines adventurers, along with the mine manager William
Teague, Stithians the smelter Michael Bath and its Vicar,
Nankivell, and Crowan Thomas Grylls, a member of the
Helston family of lawyers and clergyman. Not a single parish
thought it fitting, but may well have thought it dangerous, to
send a representative of the class most affected—the working
miners.[1]

Before the Committee met the situation had grown ominous,
and when the Quarter Sessions assembled at Truro on April
7th, a Redruth brewer, Magor, appeared to complain that the
miners had occupied his premises and seized his stock of barley
although he had already sold considerable quantities of that
grain to the poor at less than cost price. Elsewhere in the
mining region between Truro and Redruth groups of miners
had been visiting the farmers and compelling them to sign an
agreement to sell wheat at ten and barley at five shillings the
bushel; some of the miners begged for bread, avowing that
they had not seen or tasted any food for several days; although
some threats had been uttered, no instances of physical violence
had occurred. Faced by this crisis the answer of a group of
landowning, clerical, and mine-adventuring justices[2] to half-
starved labourers was a declaration that the low stocks of grain

---

[1]*W.B.*: April 10 and May 1, 1812.
[2]The Justices present at this Sessions were the landowners Francis Gregor
(in the chair) Edward Stackhouse and E. T. Glynn, the "Tory" parsons John
Trist of Veryan and Richard Polwhele of Manaccan, the "Whig" parson Robert
Walker of St. Winnow, the mines adventurers John Thomas and John Vivian, and
the Padstow merchant Thomas Rawlings. (*W.B.*: April 10, 1812).

throughout the country made frugality in consumption absolutely essential, that they hoped to get outside supplies, and
that:

"although the high price of corn is a grievance, yet it is the best
check upon consumption and guard against waste.

"We observe, with much concern, the deluded Miners leaving
their work, to the great disadvantage of those who employ and
maintain them, going to the Farmers' houses, and by their threats
endeavouring to lower the price of corn, whereby, in addition to the
CRIME of riotously assembling, they produce at length a contrary effect, and increase the evil of which they complain, by
intimidating the Farmers in general, from carrying their Corn to
Mill and Market, lest they should be plundered on the road."

Furthermore, the Justices declared that the ranks of the disorderly included very few respectable men with family cares
and responsibilities, but were mostly irresponsible youths led
by "some men of the worse characters in their Parishes". The
miners were told that corn had been ordered from other
counties, and that every class must observe the most stringent
economy in the use of corn; men with families were advised to
apply to their Parish Overseers for relief, but, on no account
would riotous assemblies be tolerated.[1]

Although they were ready to await the arrival of imports of
corn, the Justices took extremely prompt action to prevent the
risk of riot. The High Sheriff, John Vivian, signed an order to
call the Brecon and Monmouth Militia, then stationed in Pendennis Castle, to Redruth. Edward Stackhouse and the Rev.
Hugh Rogers were sent to Redruth to take charge when the
troops arrived in that disturbed town; the promptitude of
these proceedings can be gauged from the fact that the Welsh
militia men left Pendennis before eight in the evening the
day the justices had met. Their stay in Redruth was very short,
partly because Rogers and Stackhouse had persuaded the
groups of miners thronging the streets to return to their homes,
but mainly because the Militia themselves found it impossible
to procure bread in the town. Leaving a hundred men behind,
they went back to Pendennis the next day, but they took the
precaution of carrying back with them the ammunition and
bayonets of the Stannary Local Militia Royal Artillery which
had been stored at Redruth—had the miners seized these

[1] *W.B.*: April 10, 1812.

military stores and not Magor's Brewery a different and more tragic tale might have been told.

After a few more "visits" by hungry miners to isolated farms the situation grew quiet. Although many realized that the miners' wages were inadequate with grain at the exorbitant level of 120s. per quarter,[1] it was also obvious that in many parts of Cornwall no grain could be found. Proposals were made to eke out flour with rice, whilst the "Associated Attorneys of Cornwall", a group that probably never had cause to complain of inadequate earnings, met at Truro to pass a resolution that:

"during the present Scarcity of Corn, we will not permit Pastry or Puddings of any kind of which Flour shall form an Ingredient, to be made use of in our respective Families, and that we will in every other respect, as far as we possibly can, contribute to lessen the Consumption of Flour."[2]

Nor was the dearth confined to the mining regions, for in the farming and slate-quarrying parish of Lanteglos-by-Camelford a special committee was set up by the parish authorities to assess and distribute the quantities of grain in the parish in May, 1812.[3] The situation was alleviated in the western mining district by the arrival, at Falmouth, of two American ships with cargoes of flour, consigned for London, which the principal persons at Camborne and Redruth promptly bought up; other ships arrived with Norfolk barley and helped to dispel the spectre of famine in Cornwall. The riots and unrest in the western county were not so formidable as those caused by dearth in Northern England at this time, nor was there any sign of the epidemic of machine-breaking which had swept through parts of industrial Yorkshire. Within a few days most of the Cornish miners had returned to work, apparently satisfied that the local farmers were not hoarding grain.[4] The condition of the labouring poor in the mining parishes, however, is revealed by the immense sums paid out as parochial relief in these "starving times": for the year ending at Ladyday, 1812, St. Agnes had paid out £2,700, Redruth £2,900, and Gwennap no less than £3,300—or nearly £10 a day. Indeed, in Gwennap, a further £200 was paid out in ten days after the

[1] *W.B.*: April 10, 1812.
[2] *W.B.*: April 17, 1812.
[3] Lanteglos-by-Camelford Churchwardens' Accounts.
[4] *W.B.*: April 17, 1812.

appointment of new overseers on the March quarter day.[1]

While the working miners were existing on the verge of famine there was no evidence to suggest that the profits of the smelters or speculators or their agents were declining. The "borrowings" from stocked tin went on, and, on April 25, 1812, the Penzance Coinage meeting passed a resolution that this practice had made the stocking system less efficient, and that :

"to remedy this evil and to induce the Coiners of Tin to deliver Quarterly the full proportion of Tin agreed to be Stocked: It is agreed that the Tinners' Committee be desired to produce at the end of every Coinage an Account of the Quantities coined by any individual Coiner, and also of the Quantities respectively Melted into Ingots and shipped from London for the supply of the East India Company . . ."

It was agreed to impose penalties of 10s. per hundredweight on the defaulting Coiners, but it was expressly stated that this penalty:

"is by no means to be considered as exonerating the Coiners from the delivery of the full Quantity of Tin agreed to be stocked."

The same meeting, since the Government had just revoked the Orders in Council banning all trade with Napoleonic Europe, asked that its representatives in London approach the Board of Trade "to procure the insertion of the Article of Tin in all future Licences granted by the French Government."

The end of the Orders in Council and relaxations in the Napoleonic Continental System made it seem likely that more normal trade relations with Europe would soon be resumed whatever the fate of the French expedition now being prepared against Russia. European markets, deprived of tin for so many years, were likely to offer better prices than the East India Company. It was not surprising that the Associated Tinners, perhaps partly to distract attention from their own profits, now started to demand that the East India Company pay £85 per ton for its tin since:

"considering the present very distressed State of the Tinners and Tin Mines in Cornwall, and the excessive price of every article consumed in the Mines it appears to this meeting that the Tinners cannot furnish the East India Company with Tin at a less price."[2]

[1] *W.B.*: April 24, 1812. The population of St. Agnes at the 1811 census was 5,024, that of Redruth 5,903, and that of Gwennap 5,303.
[2] *C.R.B.*: Minutes November 17, 1812.

The Company offered to buy 800 tons at £80 per ton—£46 below the Cornish price at the time;[1] this was rejected but a further offer by the Company to buy a quantity "not exceeding 1,200 tons" at £80 was accepted.[2] The defeat of Napoleon at Leipzig, six months later, however, led a special meeting of Tinners and Smelters on November 24, 1813, to reduce the quantity of tin stocked for the Company from a third to a fifth of the total output for the next year. This quantity could be changed if a further general meeting saw fit, and with the first abdication of Napoleon and the increase of the price of tin in Cornwall to £160 per ton in April, 1814, the proportion stocked was reduced to an eighth. Three months later it was agreed to raise this to a quarter since tin prices had again fallen, but the continuance of the stocking system was made contingent upon general agreement[3] and it was obvious that it would only survive if the ring of smelters remained unbroken.

The actual outlook was obscure. Domestic demand had increased considerably during the war years, and there were now about a dozen tin-plate works in Wales and England[4] which, by 1815, were using well over 500 tons of tin annually. It was significant, however, that the tin-plate manufacturers preferred alluvial "grain" tin, which was free from iron and sulphur, to the metal obtained from the deep mines,[5] and they were soon to be demanding the free importation of Banca tin. The output of Cornish tin was no longer declining but increasing, and it was left to the future to show if there would soon be a glut of tin on the markets. A drastic slump in prices might again lead to a race to unload stocks to cut losses, whilst Cornish miners and smelters alike distrusted "foreign" speculators and adventurers who had been largely responsible for the opposition of the Porth Towan smelters to the stocking system. Only one thing was certain—that the man to gain least and suffer most would still be the working miner; he alone had shown no ability to combine and organize in order to protect his material welfare; the most he had done was to disturb the peace a little when the pangs of hunger were most acute,

---

[1] The actual miners were getting £100. (*C.R.B.*: Minutes July 18, 1812).
[2] *C.R.B.*: Minutes January 23 and April 9, 1813.
[3] *C.R.B.*: Minutes April 22 and July 18, 1814.
[4] P. W. Flower: *A History of the Trade in Tin*, pp. 209-210.
[5] P. W. Flower : *A History of the Trade in Tin*, pp. 85-86, 93-94, and 152.

although working men, like armies, could never put up any real fight on empty stomachs.

Apparently, however, there was no really prolonged or acute unemployment problem in the tin-mining districts in these years; the population of St. Just in Penwith was only 2,779 in 1801 and that of Breage but 2,534, whilst that of St. Austell had reached 3,788. In the last parish and district alone is there any evidence of a marked decline in tin-production in the early years of the nineteenth century, and, if some of the miners regarded employment in clay-works as professionally degrading, the opening of the Crinnis copper mines in this period offset the decline of the tin workings. The fortunes of Breage were revived by the re-opening of Wheal Vor by the Gundrys. Wheal Vor was mainly responsible for the great increase in Cornish tin output in the post-war years. One of the oldest mines in Cornwall, it had ceased working in 1715, after an apparently unsuccessful attempt to use an early Savery or Newcomen engine,[1] and was not worked on any considerable scale—if at all—until Captain John Gundry of Goldsithney came on the scene in 1814. The long suspension of Wheal Vor can be attributed to the failure of the early engine, to alternative and more accessible reserves of tin elsewhere in Cornwall, and to the concentration of speculative interests on copper rather than on tin throughout the eighteenth century since copper mining was not subject to the restraints of any antique Stannary system. Gundry, doubtless, had heard tales of Wheal Vor from the "old men", who, then as now, had an unshaken faith that there were abundant mineral riches deep down if men would only bestir themselves to get at it. The time had now come for workings to go deeper if Cornish tin-mining was to survive, and Wheal Vor, by all accounts, had only been worked to merely sixty fathoms. The start was unpromising, for Wheal Vor at the time consisted of two long, deep "coffins" or open-cast excavations, overgrown with brambles and nettles, but an old shaft was located, and an engine erected thereon by Gundry's engineer Bratt. Some forty years later, reminiscing on those day, the "self-instructed ingenious man, Joseph Bawden of Poldour" told R. J. Cunnock:

"When the engine was first started she only made a few strikes and the people were disappointed; on asking Mr. Bratt the reason,

[1]Cunnack MSS.

he replied "She wean't go wethout some beer." However (perhaps after the beer was furnished), the engine went to work and after the water was forked[1] down a little way a sollar or platform was met with, and in the sollar were six holes corresponding to six rods which were traditionally reported to have been hung first to the end of the beam of the original engine to work the six drawing lifts into which the 60 fathom level was divided. When the water was pumped out, a good branch,[2] but not very large, was found in the shaft and this was followed down in the hard ground. . . ."[3]

Under Gundry and Bratt, Wheal Vor made steady if not spectacular progress; the difficulties in locating and draining ancient workings which had been abandoned for a century were immense, whilst the Gundrys were financially embarrassed by certain other rather rash adventures. Nevertheless, Wheal Vor was promising enough for Arthur Woolf to be called in to work a double-cylinder compression engine in 1816.[4] Lawyers, bankers and creditors of the Gundrys then induced them to buy the mine outright, which led to their bankruptcy and thereby caused a sensation in Cornish mining circles.

The personal financial difficulties of the Gundry family, however, had little bearing on the fortunes of Wheal Vor. Mild excitement was caused by the discovery of some gold 150 fathoms down, but soon after the first tin lode petered out. The mine captain, Beaglehole, then drove a level in the opposite direction to find the richest lode of tin ever found in Cornwall. Following this discovery the Wheal Vor adventurers employed Thomas Richards to install an 80 in. cylinder, the greatest ever yet in Cornwall which, in December, 1832, reported a duty of 91,353,244.[5] By employing Woolf and Richards, Wheal Vor contributed much to the progress of Cornish engineering; about the time Richards' engine was started Wheal Vor, in a single month, produced 220 tons of tin and, for a year or so, despite the financial plights of its owners and adventurers, was producing between a quarter and a third of all the tin raised in Cornwall.[6]

[1]Cornish mining term meaning unwatered or completely drained.
[2]Western Cornish term for mineral vein or lode.
[3]Cunnack MSS.
[4]Rhys Jenkins: "A Cornish Engineer—Arthur Woolf", *T.N.S.*, Vol. XIII, p. 59, gives the date as 1818, but the contemporary, Lean (p. 31) states that the engine, the second Woolf erected in Cornwall, attained a duty of fifty millions in 1816.
[5]Lean, p. 95.
[6]Cunnack MSS.

From 1790 to 1814 inclusive the average yearly production of Cornish tin had been 2,816 tons; for the next twenty-three years it averaged 4,127 tons, or an increase of 46½%.[1] Possibly a third, perhaps even a half, of this increase can be attributed to the resumed working of Wheal Vor, and much of the remainder came from the lower zone of tin strata reached in the deeper copper mines. Other mines were more extensively worked, whilst numerous small concerns would account for the remainder. Yet, until 1837, output only exceeded 5,000 tons in the two years 1824 and 1827 and this can be related to the speculative wave lasting from 1822 to 1825. Probably fewer "foreigners" invested in Cornish tin mines than in copper, but even before the Gundrys revived Wheal Vor a new set of adventurers had resumed operations at Polgooth which had been idle for four years, whilst there had been another attempt to restart the Carnon Stream works in 1814.[2] Some tin was again being worked in East Cornwall, but there is no record that the London adventurers who took over the "ancient" mines of Stowes and Wheal Jenkin in Linkinhorne, in 1824, met with much success, although they probably lost less than unwary and ill-advised speculators in South American schemes.[3]

The resumption of Wheal Vor marked the beginning of an era of mechanization and speculation in Cornish tin mining. Before 1812 hardly any of the tin workings outside the Wherry Mine and Ding Dong had used much machinery; practically every one of the Cornish engines of Boulton and Watt had been installed in mines whose main concern was raising copper rather than tin, hereafter machinery and capital was applied on a large and increasing scale to tin mining, and almost at once capitalistic enterprise felt the cramping effects of the old stannary organization and the impediments of the coinage system. Increasing production sent prices down from £156 10s. per ton in 1814 to £93 10s. three years later, and in the next twenty years the price in Cornwall hovered between £75 and £95, only exceeding £100 in 1836—the year which recorded the lowest coinage since 1822. These figures indicate that, although output had vastly increased, the industry was not

[1]G. R. Lewis: *The Stannaries*, pp. 255-256.
[2]*W.B.*: February 22, 1814.
[3]*W.B.*: June 18, 1824.

making great profits, and in the three years from 1819 to 1821 and in the nine years from 1826 to 1834, when prices in Cornwall were below £80, it is hardly likely that many mines were doing more than barely paying their way. The speculative boom of 1823-24 may have led to a temporary glut of tin in the markets, whilst the end of the wars had freed the eastern trade routes; every year an increasing amount of "Banca" tin was arriving in European and English markets, offsetting the gain of lowered insurance costs on sea-borne tin that came with the cessation of privateering activities.

Late in 1818 an attack was made on the mineral dues claimed by the Duchy of Cornwall. It was not the coinage dues that were assailed but the claims of the Duchy to mineral royalties on estates, some of which had been sold, and sold in many cases some considerable time ago. In 1817 these dues had been leased to Edward Smith for twenty-four years; his exactions in St. Agnes led to the suspension of several mines in that parish, and to a more general cessation of mining operations at depths below which adit drainage was impracticable.[1] Ill-feeling was aroused and rankled; the position was not improved by the obscure legal position created by the death of George III; though there was now no Duke of Cornwall, until the birth of a male heir to the Crown in 1841, in law the Duchy had not merged into the Crown. The personal unpopularity of George IV aggravated matters still more; it was not wholly a coincidence that Queen Caroline's staunch supporter, Alderman Wood, was interested in Crinnis Mine, disputes over which lasted for years, culminating in the seven-days action of *Rowe v. Brenton* in the King's Bench in November and December, 1828; in this case a hundred and thirty witnesses were called and one set of documents brought in as evidence weighed three-quarters of a ton.[2] This particular trial merely ended in a decision that conventionary tenants of the Duchy had no rights to mine, quarry, or cut timber on lands to the surface of which they possessed a right of perpetual renewal. The tenant, Brenton, "won" his action against the executors of Josiah Rowe, who had died bankrupt long before the case reached the King's Bench, to recover the value of some copper Rowe had removed from Crinnis Mine, in the manor of Tewington which the

[1] *W.B.*: January 1, 1819.
[2] *W.B.*: November 21 and December 5, 1828.

Duchy had sold with express reservation of mineral rights in 1798. It was followed by attempts, both in and out of court, to eject the tenant Brenton, whilst a further action, *Rex v. Rowe and Brenton*, was instituted by the Duchy to recover the mine. All told it was a lawyer's holiday; Brenton was claiming £10,000 in costs, whilst the total costs exceeded £40,000; the costs of bringing witnesses to London from Cornwall was considerable, particularly as many of them seem to have thought it a golden opportunity to live on the best food and liquor in the land at the expense of the litigants, one group of witnesses being alleged to have consumed 370 grogs and 50 bottles of wine one single evening on their way to attend the Court.[1]

Whilst the production of evidence going back to Domesday and beyond in this intricate case may be fascinating to the student of law, the Crinnis case is significant mainly because it represented the clash of restrictive antique custom and obsolete ideas of property rights with the new spirit of free enterprise. The medieval conception of property was entirely different from the new capitalistic one, and holders of the newer ideas had little patience with rights reserved to absentee owners and still less with the entanglement of property with such an abstraction as the Duchy of Cornwall which could exist without there being a Duke of Cornwall. The Crinnis case revealed the costliness of litigation, and there was the chance that the working of any mine on land which had at any time, no matter how remote, belonged to the Duchy of Cornwall would lead to similar litigation. Men like Edward Smith, to whom these rights were leased, were as intent and as able to make the most of their "property" as the most level-headed business men of the new age of industrial capitalism. The possible exaction of anything up to a tenth of all the minerals raised on these undefined estates was a threat against the further expansion of mining enterprise, whilst in the places where they were actually being exacted they reduced if they did not entirely eliminate the profits of the mines adventurers. Yet the real trouble lay in the fact that, in an age of competitive enterprise, the men who leased Duchy rights, like any other owner of "property", meant to get all they could from such rights. Henry Creese, who had succeeded Smith as lessee of the Duchy mineral claims precipitated a crisis in 1834, by making it clear

[1] *W.B.*: September 11, 1831.

that, if unchecked, he intended to claim rights to dues on
no less than 238 Cornish manors which had formerly belonged
to the Duchy. The more learned landowners and mines
adventurers, who knew how vague Domesday descriptions of
manors were, faced a menace that was very real; the law, as it
stood, was on the side of antiquity, for in the case *Creese v.
Barrett* Lord Lyndhurst ruled that what belonged to the Duchy
when granted to it by the Black Prince still belonged to it unless
limited by Act of Parliament.

This decision, a threat to nearly every landowner in Cornwall,
led to the convention of a general meeting of the mining
interest, with the Earl of Falmouth in the chair, on December
12, 1834. A resolution was passed declaring that Lord Lyndhurst's decision:

"would bring into jeopardy, not only the mineral rights which
thousands of His Majesty's loyal subjects have enjoyed by grant,
purchase or inheritance during many past centuries; but would
threaten to unsettle property in land to a vast though unknown
extent, for their enjoyment of which may have no other security
than that of undisputed usage prior to, or supported by deeds of
transfer, bequests or other documents of very ancient date; and
that such a principle is proved to have been thought intolerable by
the fact of an Act of Limitations having been passed on the 21st.
James I (210 years ago)[1] and confirmed more positively by the
Act of 1768, called the Nullum Tempus Act,[2] whereby the Crown
itself is barred from all claim after adverse possession of sixty years."

It was decided to petition the King to instruct his Ministers to
introduce a Bill in Parliament extending the Act of 1768 to the
Duchy of Cornwall. The Earl of Falmouth promised to
approach the King himself, but it was not until another general
meeting of the Cornish mining interest was held on December
29, 1835, that he was able to state that William IV was inclined
to agree, although Lord Chancellor Lyndhurst had expressed
himself strongly in favour of retaining the Duchy rights.[3] The
"new order" had gained a moderate triumph, but delays
followed; nothing had been done when William IV died, and it
was not until 1844 that the Nullum Tempus Act was extended
to the Duchy of Cornwall in an extremely prolix act of ninety-
four clauses.[4]

[1] 21 Jaq. 1, cap. 2.
[2] 9 Geo. III, cap. 16.
[3] *Cornwall Gazette*: January 1, 1836.
[4] 7 & 8 Vict. cap. 105.

In another matter, however, economic free enterprise met a reverse. The judicial powers of the Cornish Stannary Courts had never been liked by "outside" mines adventurers, and the sharp practices associated with every financial boom and its attendant collapse had led to much litigation. Since the sessions of the last Stannary Parliament in 1750-51 the Stannary organization in Cornwall had changed; all judicial functions had been taken over by the Court of the Vice-Warden of the Stannaries and the four Steward's Courts—one in each of the four Stannary divisions of the county—had disappeared. There is little evidence that the Vice-Warden's Court was being conducted badly, but neither is there any suggesting that it was efficient. Since Blackstone's time legalistic philosophy and thought had developed on lines inimical to the survival of peculiar local jurisdictions and, with more and more outside capital being invested either directly or indirectly in Cornish mining, the Stannary jurisdiction came in for much adverse criticism. The peculiar privileges conferred on the ill-defined group of men known as "tinners" ran counter to the now generally accepted notion of equality before the law. The rare use of juries to decide cases in the Vice-Warden's court in recent years increased "outside" criticism.[1] Impatience with antique privilege had been aggravated by the necessity of securing Parliamentary legislation to employ military forces recruited from tinners outside Cornwall in Ireland and elsewhere during the Napoleonic Wars.

Matters reached a crisis in 1823 when the Vice-Warden, John Vivian, made a decree against Frederick Hall in a suit for recovery of debts incurred for work done in and materials supplied to Baldhu Mine in Kea by tradesmen who had no interest in the mine as adventurers. Hall lost an appeal he lodged in Chancery, but the case then went to the King's Bench as an action for trespass, and that Court decided that the Vice-Warden's Court was a court of original jurisdiction in matters of equity only, and that the Steward's Court was the Stannary court in which actions at law should originate.[2] All records prior to 1750 had been lost, and the decision of the King's Bench meant the virtual suspension of the Stannary

---

[1] The case of *Moyle v. Tyacke* early in 1823 was the first tried by a jury of tinners for twenty years. (*W.B.*: March 7, 1823).

[2] Harrison, pp. 15-16.

jurisdiction for four years,[1] but, in September, 1828, the new Vice-Warden, John Wallis, and the Steward John Borlase resumed their courts, Borlase even reviving the court of Foymoor, which had hardly met within living memory.[2] The dubious validity of the Stannary Courts, the general hatred of irresistible capitalistic utilitarianism towards the fettering traditions of the past, the question whether John, in 1202, or Edward I, in 1305, had not exceeded their constitutional powers when they had conferred such extensive privileges,[3] the difficulty of defining a "tinner" or what constituted a tin mine in law, and the undefined local limits of Stannary jurisdiction, made recourse to Parliament for decision inevitable.

Most of the "new men" and "foreign" adventurers would have welcomed the abolition of the Stannary Jurisdiction by Act of Parliament. The spirit of the age was on their side. It seemed anomalous that this particular jurisdiction appertaining to the Duchy of Cornwall should survive when "royal courts", as an attribute of sovereignty, had been subordinated to an omnicompetent Parliament in 1688. The case for the resuscitation of Stannary Jurisdiction, but in an expressly defined form, was taken up by three men; by Davies Gilbert,[4] a moderate Tory who sat for Bodmin in Parliament as the protegé of Duchy interests, by Sir Richard Vyvyan, the ultra-Tory county member, and by the other county representative, E. W. W. Pendarves, a Whig Reformer and Cornish mineowner who believed that the suspension of the Stannary Courts was to the:

"manifest inconvenience and serious injury of all owners of mineral property throughout the county, in regard to these most important local and peculiar interests."[5]

Many Cornishmen, too, favoured the revival of the Stannary Courts, one mining agent writing that it was to the:

"great benefit to the Mining Interests of Cornwall to have their disputes settled in the Stannary in which they arise, instead of being dragged into the Courts of Westminster, where the counsel address

[1]Harrison, pp. 12, 110-111, 124-125.
[2]*W.B.*: March 13, 1835.
[3]In point of fact these Plantagenet kings had merely confirmed pre-existing rights and privileges.
[4]Davies Giddy, the patron of Trevithick and Humphrey Davy, and a Fellow of the Royal Society, took the name of Gilbert on his marriage in 1817.
[5]Harrison, p. 12.

the Jury as if a mine was a spinning-jenny; whilst the latter take it for granted and give their verdict accordingly. With every respect for these gentlemen, a London jury cannot know anything about mining matters."[1]

It was long before Parliament took action, being pre-occupied by the Reform Bill crisis which also divided the Cornish landowning and mining interests into opposing camps. The mining interests who wished to define and retain the Stannary Courts were at the same time objecting to the payment of the Duchy Coinage dues, the great part of which had been devoted to the maintenance of that very Stannary jurisdiction. The Duchy, while willing to maintain the Stannary Courts, had alienated Cornish landowners through the exorbitant claims of the lessees of its mineral royalties. Radical Reformers, triumphant in 1832 and obsessed against anything that smacked of traditionalism, were eager to sweep away another vestige of "antique privilege", and made the most of the connections of certain Stannary officials with the Cornish boroughs that had become notorious in the annals of political corruption; truly the cause of Stannary Jurisdiction gained nothing from owning the Marquis of Hertford, Thackeray's notorious Marquis of Steyne, influential in the boroughs of Camelford and Bodmin, as its Lord Warden, and even less from granting the post of a Supervisor of Blowing Houses to Nicholas Middlecoate whose political activities at Tregony had almost occasioned the disenfranchisement of that borough long before 1832.[2] Duchy officials were extremely dilatory in conducting the inquiries preparatory to drafting a Parliamentary Bill, whilst the Bill presented by Davies Gilbert in 1827 was dropped since it was unacceptable to some Cornish mines adventurers. The death of George IV was followed by an attack of the mining interest on the coinage duties which caused further delay, and only in the spring of 1834 was Sir Richard Vyvyan able to make a move in Parliament towards the restoration of the Stannary Courts. In the reformed House of Commons the appearance of an uncompromising ultra Tory like Vyvyan supporting a measure to restore a medieval or pre-medieval jurisdiction was hardly a harbinger of success. Vyvyan, however, did little, preferring to leave matters to the

[1] *W.B.*: March 13, 1835.
[2] *W.B.*: February 8, 1833.

Duchy's legal advisers; the Cornish Whigs then grew impatient and, after first even seriously considering the practicability of of summoning a Stannary Parliament,[1] induced the Earl of Falmouth to convene a general meeting of the mining interest at Truro on November 4, 1835.

This meeting was dominated by Sir Charles Lemon who said that there was no need to set up a new Court or new Stannary Code; all that was necessary was to secure the prompt and equitable administration of justice and that the most expedient means of doing so was:

"to re-establish the Vice-Warden's Court, and amend and define its Jurisdiction, giving it such additional powers as may appear to be essential to the Mining Interest, and assimilating it in principle and practice to the Courts of Westminster Hall, so far as that can be done with due regard to the peculiarities of Mining Concerns."[2]

For that purpose a committee, headed by the Earl of Falmouth, was set up to draft a bill. The Committee, consisting of the most prominent mines adventurers and landowners in the county, appointed three lawyers to investigate the existing Stannary laws with the aid of Joseph Thomas Austen, then the greatest mine adventurer in Cornwall, Stephen Davey, the agent of Consolidated Mines, and four or five other "practical miners". Falmouth submitted their proposals to a further general meeting in January, 1836; it was accepted and transmitted to the Duchy officials. Some opposition to the proposals came from the "foreign" adventurer, George Concanen, who alleged that it was useless appealing to the Duchy to reform its own Courts, the proposed court of equity would be a curse to the mining interest, and that powers of equity should not be entrusted to mere placemen dependent on other placemen. To this one of the Committee retorted that:

"It may suit Mr. Concanen and the 'Foreign Capitalists', whom he represents to carry their mining disputes to Westminster Hall, but I trust that no Cornishman can be found who would not prefer a domestic tribunal, where the subject under dispute is sure to be much better understood, the judgment of the Court more speedily obtained, and the expense of the suit comparatively insignificant."[3]

objected to the proposed new Stannary Bill, and petitioned

---

[1] *W.B.*: November 6, 1835.
[2] *W.B.*: November 6, 1835.
[3] *W.B.*: February 19, 1836.

Henry Creese, the lessee of the Duchy mineral dues also
Parliament that it should not become law, as did also some
London shareholders in Cornish mines and some Cornish
adventurers living in St. Agnes, Truro, Falmouth, Penryn and
Linkinhorne.[1]

The main objections to the proposed Bill were the continued
association of the Stannary Courts with the Duchy and the
inconvenience of attending a court held in Cornwall to outside
adventurers. The conduct of Stannary jurisdiction in the past
had aroused suspicions that it was neither impartial nor equitable. Until the appointment of John Wallis as Vice-Warden
in 1827 that post had been held by some of the greatest mine-
owners, speculators, and adventurers of their day, Wallis's
four immediate successors being the Rev. Walter Borlase,
Henry Rosewarne who, indeed, had disposed of most of his
mining shares in 1779 soon after his appointment, John Thomas
and John Vivian, the last two being not only adventurers
themselves but also related to many other adventurers. Nevertheless, a Bill, based on the recommendations of the Cornish
committee, was drafted by the Ministry and introduced in the
House of Commons by Alexander Baring, then President of the
Board of Trade, on June 27, 1836; amended somewhat it was
passed and became law at the end of September. The only
concession to the "foreign capitalists" was the appointment of
lawyers to conduct the new Stannary Court, but they resented
the extension of Stannary jurisdiction to copper and other
metallic minerals, and, perhaps even more, provisos for summoning witnesses from and serving the original processes of
the Court in any part of England and Wales. The new Vice-
Warden, John Lucius Dumfee, held his first Court at Truro
on November 3, 1836; there was little business on that occasion,
but the session held in July, 1838, lasted a full week.[2] The
judicial organization of the Stannaries had been given a further
sixty years of life, and in that period there were few complaints
that it failed to provide an impartial and necessary administration of justice in mining concerns.

The new Stannary Court had hardly been instituted when
there was a renewed demand for the abolition of the Coinage
duties, this time associated with the first real threat of foreign

[1] *J.H.C.*: Vol. 91, pp. 638, 652, 673, 681, 685, 715.
[2] *W.B.*: July 13 and 27, 1838.

competition. Despite Cornish opposition a Warehousing Bill, permitting the importation, warehousing, and re-exportation of foreign tin and copper free of duty had been passed in 1823. Faced by foreign competition, the Cornish tin-mining interests felt themselves doubly injured by the coinage system; Cornish tin had to be brought to the coinage towns to be coined only four times a year, whilst the actual coinage duty was a tax on Cornish tin from which the re-exported foreign tin was exempt. The Duchy officials were, however, willing to arrange additional coinage days and towns; in February, 1821, an additional coinage was held in Truro to meet an East India Company contract,[1] but it was not until March, 1833, that provisions were made to hold coinages every six weeks and to add Hayle to the list of coinage towns; a few weeks later St. Austell also became a coinage town.[2] This meant that there were now about 150 coinage days throughout the year,[3] but there was still normally in the main tin-mining region, served by Hayle and Penzance, an interval of twenty-five days between one coinage and the next, whilst transportation difficulties still restricted many mines to one coinage town, so creating an interval of at least five weeks between coinages. On the question of the coinage dues the Duchy was adamant, and when the Cornish mining interest approached the Reform Government of Lord Grey, it was told that the Ministry could not interfere with the coinage duties as they belonged to the King as Duke of Cornwall.[4] The Duchy, however, consented to abolish a few minor incidental fees.

Talk in Cornwall about the menace of foreign competition was exaggerated. Although the direction of the trade in tin between England and the Far East had been reversed, yet England only imported 2,456 tons of tin from 1815 to 1829, or an average of less than 164 tons a year, whilst in the same period the average annual Cornish output had been nearly 4,050 tons a year.[5] Agitation against foreign competition coincided with

---

[1] *W.B.*: February 9, 1821.
[2] *W.B.*: March 29, April 5 and 19, and May 24, 1833.
[3] Six day coinages were held at Truro and Penzance, a three day coinage at Hayle, and a two-day coinage at Helston eight times a year; the other coinage towns, Tavistock, Liskeard, and St. Austell held quarterly coinages lasting generally but a single day.
[4] *W.B.*: April 5, 1833.
[5] Figures based on Hunt, p. 887, and on P. W. Flower: *A History of the Trade in Tin*, p. 203.

low prices; it had quickly died down after the 1823 Warehousing Act when the Cornish price was £94 15s. per ton, but in December, 1826, when the price had fallen to £77 a meeting of tin-mining adventurers was held in Redruth to consider petitioning for the removal of the coinage duties, whilst in April, 1828, with the price down to £73 5s. the consistent and prolonged outcry against foreign competition began. This recession was really the aftermath of the boom of 1823-24 and the over-production it had occasioned. The mines adventurers who were alarmed by the diminished value of British tin exports seem to have ignored entirely the vast increase in the demand at home by British tin-plate and other industries. The smelters, as always, came in for censure, and one of them, the Cornish-born Grenfell, did not improve the relations of miners and smelters by asserting that if he was not allowed to smelt foreign tin in Wales he would set up as a tin-smelter in France. Grenfell later denied that he had made any such declaration,[1] but it is likely that smelters, eager to expand their works, were ready to force the Government to agree to free trade in foreign tin by such threats. Some of the more reasonable "miners" were willing to meet the smelters half-way by agreeing to a duty on foreign tin-ore that would represent rather less than the difference in cost between smelting tin in Britain than on the Continent, but it was realized that East Indian alluvial tin was cheaper to produce and perhaps of better quality than Cornish mine tin, and fears were already entertained that ultimately foreign tin would force the abandonment of the Cornish mines.[2]

After 1830 imports of foreign tin rapidly increased, but it was practically all re-exported after smelting, having paid a duty of £2 10s. per ton, since the heavy 60% *ad valorem* duty on the domestic consumption of foreign tin was still retained; thereby a difficult situation was averted, for whilst the British consumer had to use British tin, his foreign competitor was supplied by the British smelters with a rather cheaper foreign product; the cheapness of that foreign tin excluded British tin from the foreign market so tending to reduce the price of British tin on the home market to which it was thus confined. Whilst the smelters had little reason to complain, both the

[1] *W.B.*: April 18 and 25, 1828.
[2] *W.B.*: May 9, 1828.

miners and the domestic consumers of tin felt that they were penalized by the Duchy coinage duties, which, with sundry additional fees, amounted to five guineas a ton and represented a levy of between eight and ten per cent on British tin, most of which went to pay the salaries of the officials who administered the coinage system and contributed but little to the support of the heir apparent to the throne.[1] Early in 1833 the Cornish "miners" denounced the duties as "wholly inconsistent with the spirit and character of British commerce",[2] but only secured the concession of the extra coinage towns and the abolition of a few trivial additional fees. Thereupon Michael Williams, one of the most prominent "miners" of the time, at a meeting held in Truro on April 12, 1833, suggested asking Parliament to redress a pernicious system "which considered a raw material produced in this country as a fit object of taxation", but he opposed the suggestion of a non-landowning "miner" that landlords remit their dues to enable the Cornish mines to defeat the competition of Banca tin in British markets.[3]

In 1834 the price of tin rose to £78 per ton in Cornwall, an increase of five guineas above the level of the preceding year. This only precipitated another crisis, for, on June 5, 1834, the tin plate manufacturers met at Newport and decided to ask the Government to abolish or, at least, reduce the prohibitory duty on foreign tin, alleging that the Cornish smelters charged them exorbitant prices and that the cheaper Banca tin used on the Continent lost them foreign markets. Twelve days later, summoned by the Penzance smelter L. C. Daubuz, the Cornish "mining" interest met; resolutions were passed alleging that although the rise in Cornish tin prices only increased the cost of tin plates by 10d. per box, the Welsh manufacturers had advanced their prices by six or seven shillings the box. The tin-plate makers were told that if the smelters asked too high prices they were free to buy ore in Cornwall and smelt it themselves. The Cornishmen then passed resolutions to the effect:

"That any measure which would introduce Foreign Tin into England for home consumption, would at once stop many of the Tin Mines, and by preventing new Mines from being set at work, would gradually render England dependent on a Foreign and very

[1] *W.B.*: September 7, 1832, February 8 and March 15, 1833.
[2] *W.B.*: April 19, 1833.
[3] *W.B.*: April 19 and June 7, 1833.

distant country, for all her Manufactures, of which Tin forms a part, as it is perfectly impossible for the Cornish Tin Mines, subject as they are to a heavy duty on their produce (payable to His Majesty) as well as to other direct and indirect imposts, to compete with those of a Country, where labour is so much cheaper, and where there are no duties, either on the articles consumed, or on the produce.

"That the present application of the Tin Plate Manufacturers is most unreasonable, as it is well known, that, at the present price of plate, this trade is highly prosperous; they, however, called upon the Government, to risk the destruction of the Cornish Tin Mines, not to preserve from loss, but to increase the profit of a trade, which in point of importance, as a national object, bears no comparison to this."[1]

By 1835 tin had risen to £91 10s., and the tin plate makers sent a deputation to the Board of Trade to ask for the reduction of the duty on foreign tin. Hard on their heels came a Cornish deputation headed by the Tory Earl of Falmouth and the two West Cornwall Whig Members of Parliament, Sir Charles Lemon and E. W. W. Pendarves, to protest against any such concession. They were told that it was too late in the present parliamentary session for anything to be done, but that the matter was likely to come up the next session and that then the Cornish interests would have to put up a strong case if they hoped to carry the day.[2] By the end of the year, 1835, many in Cornwall realized that:

"A system that sends the tin smelter to Belgium to refine his foreign tin, to be brought back to this country in a marketable shape, for the supply of the export demand, at £7 or £8 below the price of British tin, places the British consumer in such an unfavourable position, and with such anomaly, that with all the energy of the Mining interest, we doubt its being perpetuated, even if it were desirable, which we do not think it is, for the interest of the tinners. We believe that a well regulated duty on tin and tin-stuff, would immediately, or at least within a short period, advance the price of tin throughout the world, and maintain this country in its position in the tin trade."[3]

Yet it was another vicissitude of speculation, boom, and depression rather than the reasoned arguments of economists that brought about the abolition of the coinage duties. In 1836 the price of tin reached £109 10s; some older mines had re-

[1]*W.B.*: June 13 and 20, 1834.
[2]*W.B.*: August 19 1835.
[3]*W.B.*: November 20, 1835.

opened, but many new ventures were the product of hope rather than that of reason, and some of those who bought £3 shares of Larkholes Mine in St. Cleer, on a report of rich finds beneath the "old men's working" lived to regret it.[1] New finds in Wheal Vor and in St. Just in Penwith were rather more promising, but by November, 1836, the boom had collapsed. Once more "monopolistic smelters" were made the scapegoats. It was alleged that a close ring of four smelting concerns in the last five years had shared profits averaging £70,000 a year, or something like a fifth of the value of all the tin mined in Cornwall. The Wheal Vor adventurers made another attempt to set up their own smelting works, but were forced to abandon them by 1840, since the smelting firms combined in the London markets to buy up the Wheal Vor tin at very low prices. Proposals that the mines adventurers combine to set up co-operative smelting houses and to maintain their own marketing organization came to nought.[2] The smelters too complained of bad times, and by May, 1837, were considering making another application for the abolition of the coinage duties. The death of William IV provided an opportunity, and a meeting of the mining interest was held in Truro on October 27 "to consider the propriety of petitioning Parliament and the Duchy that a remission of the Duchy duty on Tin may form part of the arrangement for Her Majesty's future revenue." The smelting firms of Daubuz, Bolitho, and Williams were mainly responsible for convening this meeting, which was told by E. W. W. Pendarves that this was the proper time to petition both the Queen and Parliament for the abolition of the coinage duties since the Civil List had not yet been granted;[3] had the "miners" acted more quickly after the death of George IV, in Pendarves' opinion, the duties would have been abolished seven years before.

The outcry against the profiteering smelters may have induced them to attack the coinage duties as a diversion. The matter had hardly reached the attention of Parliament when rumours were circulating in the Cornish mining districts that the abolition of the coinage duties would be accompanied by the reduction or entire abolition of the duties on imported tin.

[1] *W.B.*: April 1, 1836.
[2] *W.B.*: November 4 and 11, 1836. Cunnack MSS.
[3] *W.B.*: October 20, 1837.

The question was raised in the House of Commons on December 15, 1837, but was postponed. Shortly afterwards it became known in Cornwall that the tin plate manufacturers were again to ask Parliament to reduce the import duty on foreign tin, and that they were alleging that they could not get enough tin for their needs and blaming the scarcity of tin and not the general economic depression for the reduction of their exports from a value of £297,000 in 1836 to £250,000 in 1837.[1] News of this led to the convention of another meeting of the mining interest at Truro on January 17, 1838. At this meeting the division of opinion among the various groups connected with the tin mines was evident. The October meeting which had sought the abolition of the coinage duties had been called by L. C. Daubuz as chairman of a combination of Cornish smelters, the survivors of the Association of 1780 who had continued to meet irregularly and without publicity since the East India contracts and the stocking system had come to an end; the January meeting, convened by the Earl of Falmouth was a general meeting of the "Mining Interest", similar to those Falmouth had presided over when the questions of the Duchy claims and of the Stannary jurisdiction had been raised. The former question had not been settled, and Falmouth himself seemed inclined to advocate the retention of the Duchy coinage duties, perhaps because, as a landowner, he thought that in return the Nullum Tempus Act of 1768 might be extended to the Duchy, but he made no reference to the Duchy mineral claims at this meeting. Instead he argued that the retention of the coinage duties alone justified the continuance of protective duties against foreign tin. Michael Williams, however, declared that an eight per cent levy was too much to pay for a "friend at court", that it looked as if the duties on foreign tin were doomed, and that they should seek whatever relief they could, although he believed that the prospects of Cornish mining if free trade came were extremely grim and would prefer a prohibitory duty against imported tin. Robert Taylor stated that they could only reasonably ask for a protective duty since prohibition merely meant that foreign tin would be smelted elsewhere. Falmouth then vacated the chair to assert that the abandonment of prohibition for mere protection would give an impetus to Banca tin that would ruin Cornwall,

[1] *W.B.*: January 19, 1838.

and that protection would mean that foreign tin would be smelted in Britain and re-exported to monopolize overseas markets. Sir Charles Lemon and E. W. W. Pendarves were inclined to agree with Taylor. Lemon said little except that they did not wish to abolish the coinage duties without compensation, whilst Pendarves questioned whether any "interest" had the right to expect benefits to the exclusion of all other trades in the country without making it clear if he was referring to the tin-plate, the smelting, or the mining interest. Despite their differences of opinion, however, the meeting agreed to appoint a deputation to approach the Government.[1]

This deputation met the Chancellor of the Exchequer on April 30th. Davies Gilbert and John Basset may be regarded as representing the landowning interests; Michael Williams, Thomas Teague, and Joseph Thomas Austen the mines adventurers, and Thomas Bolitho and Joseph Carne the smelters.[2] They were told by Spring Rice that the question of the coinage duties was connected with the import duties, and that the existence of the former had been one of the strongest arguments for a prohibitory duty on foreign tin; the Government had determined to abolish the coinage duties, but asked the Cornish deputation to suggest a protective revenue duty since they had offered to compensate the Duchy. On May 4th the Cornishmen told the Chancellor that a duty of £15 per ton was indispensable. The Government agreed, and in August the coinage dues were abolished as from October, 1838;[3] provision was made to compensate the holder of the Duchy from the consolidated fund of the United Kingdom, whilst minor officials affected by the abolition of the coinage system were also to be compensated. The only impost left on Cornish tin was a levy of one farthing in the pound which had already, by the Stannary Act of August, 1836, been imposed on all other metals and metallic minerals raised in any Cornish mine to maintain the Stannary Court. For the time it was a satisfactory compromise to all interests—to tin-plate manufacturers, to

---

[1] *W.B.*: January 19, 1838.
[2] No hard and fast line of division can really be drawn between the three interests; Basset was a mine adventurer as well as a landowner, as was also Austen; Michael Williams was a copper-smelter as well as a "miner", and Carne a banker and merchant as well as a smelter.
[3] 1 & 2 Vict. cap. 120.

smelters, and to the Cornish "miners," although a few of the last were still fearful of the future.

When the Cornish price of tin slumped to £70 a ton early in 1840, however, the old cry against the smelters was raised anew; the reduced duties on imported tin were not blamed since Banca tin still cost £77 on importation without reckoning the duties and smelting charges which raised it to £93. At the "Tinner's Meeting" held on June 3, 1840, when ninety-five per cent of all the tinners in Cornwall weresaid to be present or represented, a resolution was passed that:

"in order to protect the Adventurers in tin mines, and obtain for that important article of consumption, tin, a fair and reasonable price, it is necessary to adopt some measures to destroy the ruinous system at present and for many years pursued by certain parties engaged in smelting."[1]

Talk of the miners smelting their own ores was again general, and a scheme of a general Mining and Smelting Company, similar to the old (copper) Cornwall Metal Company of 1785, was mooted early in 1841. The "hungry 'forties" had dawned, and a Camborne miner, blaming the smelters for the hard times, but also critical of the mine proprietors whose complaining meetings almost invariably ended in electing committees, passing votes of thanks, and then finally settling down to substantial dinners, wrote that higher wages alone, which mine-owners could well afford, would alleviate the lot of the working miners; no man could maintain a family in food and clothing, and pay house-rents and poor rates on fifty shillings or so a month; philanthropists might stress the dangers and diseases of the miner's calling, and draw up tables of his rates of mortality, but all he needed was enough food to fill his belly.[2]

The discontent of working miners and the complaints of adventurers against the smelters were overshadowed by Peel's reduction of the tin import duties in 1842. The duties on foreign tin ores were reduced to £2 10s. per ton, but only 10s. was charged on ores coming from British possessions; tin in blocks,

---

[1] *W.B.*: June 5, 1840.
[2] *W.B.*: January 29, 1841—letter of "A Miner" dated Camborne, December 29, 1840.

ingots, bars, and slabs, was subjected to somewhat higher
duties of £6 per ton foreign and £3 per ton colonial, whilst all
imported manufactures of tin were to pay an *ad valorem* duty of
15%.[1] At one time it looked as if protection had been abolished for, through an oversight on the part of the Treasury, tin
had been omitted from the draft of the tariff submitted to the
House of Commons, but this was remedied when Sir Charles
Lemon questioned Gladstone on the matter.[2] Threatened
also by drastic and rather complicated reductions of the duties
on copper ores by the same tariff, the mining interest met at
Redruth on March 28, 1842, and passed several resolutions,
including one stating that:

"the proposed duty on tin ore appears to have been fixed without
due enquiry into the metallic produce of foreign ores, and will be
ruinous to the most ancient mining interest in the kingdom, being
that of Cornish tin; and more particularly this meeting is of opinion
that a differential duty between tin or tin ore brought from a
foreign country, and that brought from a British settlement, will
prove very prejudicial, and lead to fraud and evasion."[3]

A deputation was sent to the Government, but failed to convince Peel and Gladstone that free trade would be detrimental
to Cornish mining; Gladstone, indeed, openly stated that the
Ministry hoped these lower duties would increase British
smelting.[4] The concern of the "Tory" Ministry for manufacturing interests was shown by the relatively heavy *ad valorem*
duties still imposed on manufactured articles. Scathing
Cornish denunciations of Peel as the "Joseph Surface of the
Imperial Parliament", and suggestions that a deputation of
working miners should have been sent instead of one of
capitalist mine-owners, were mere echoes of impotent frustra-
tion, nor was Peel disturbed greatly when the ultra-Tory Sir
Richard Vyvyan "revolted" against the Government a few
weeks later.

The final blow came early in 1843 when Peel abolished the
import duties on foreign tin-ores altogether, although he retained duties on refined and manufactured tin. At the time tin

[1] 5 & 6 Vict. cap. 47.
[2] Hansard (Third Series), Vol. LXI, 594. (March 15, 1842).
[3] *W.B.*: April 1, 1842.
[4] *W.B.*: May 27, 1842.

prices were rising, mainly on account of a fairly considerable
decline in Cornish output during the past few years. It does
not seem that the tin plate manufacturers had pressed Peel to
abolish the duties, although their industry had expanded considerably recently. The Cornish adventurers again raised the
cry that this would encourage foreigners to over-produce and
flood the markets, although not one of them had stated or could
state that the reduction of import duties in 1842 had had this
result, and that reduction was far greater than the total abolition now decreed.   Until 1845, Cornish tin output was greater
than that exported from Java, but the latter had increased from
825 tons in 1826 to 4,516 tons in 1845.[1] Only about a third of
this tin came to Britain,[2] either directly or through Holland,
but by 1845 the alluvial deposits of Malaya were being exploited by British adventurers on a considerable and growing
scale with Chinese coolie labour.[3]   It was these virgin deposits
of the Malay Peninsula, not the long-worked deposits of Banca,
that were the real menace to the Cornish mines. Yet, for years
to come, skill acquired through centuries in mining and in
preparing tin for market enabled Cornwall to withstand
Malayan competition, especially since the advantage of cheap
coolie labour was offset by brigandage and by transportation
difficulties in the East. Peel's free trade policy did not bring
immediate disaster to Cornish mining. The progress of industry
in Britain and the "West" could use all the tin raised by
Cornishman and Oriental alike. By the end of 1852 tin was
again fetching more than £100 per ton; in the following twenty
years it only fell once below that level, and then only in the
depression year 1866 when it fell to £88 12s. 6d., but it was
to recover and soar to above £150 in 1872.[4]

The complaining Cornishmen of 1845 had failed to gauge the
rate at which the industrial demand for tin was to increase in
the near future. British exports of unmanufactured tin, it is
true, were falling, but those of manufactures of tin were rising

[1] J. Macgregor: *Commercial Statistics*, Vol. V, p. 29. Javanese tin exports
averaged 2,633 tons from 1836 to 1840, and about 3,720 tons annually during the
next five years.

[2] British imports of tin from places "East of the Cape" averaged 830 tons a
year from 1836 to 1840, only 91 tons of which came yearly from Java or Holland;
this explains the outcry against imperial preference in 1842. (Figures based on
Macgregor: *Commercial Statistics*, Vol. I, pp. 917, 991, and Vol. V, pp. 425 ff.).

[3] J. Macgregor: *Commercial Statistics*, Vol. IV, p. 1008.

[4] Hunt, p. 889.

more rapidly,[1] and the domestic consumption was increasing on a comparable scale. Whether or not the free traders had a clearer vision of the future is beside the point, but a Cornish editor may later have wished that he had not hastily written when the tin import duties were ended:

"Sir Robert Peel says we must no longer confide in protective duties. A new era is begun; and free trade principles must be boldly carried out. So he sweeps away the duty of 50s. a ton on tin ore from foreign mines! He is mute as a ghost before the agriculturalists or the West Indians, but applies his theory in full force to the Cornish tin-miner. The Premier is a reasonably bold man. He is resolute against all personal opposition when the men he opposes are to be feared. He adheres with unswerving fidelity to his principles when there is no risk in enforcing them."[2]

The Corn Laws, however, had but little longer to run. It was soon to be the turn of another hitherto protected interest to protest against a "death sentence" passed against them. The Cornish farmers were not the least vocal in that protest, but, like the Cornish mines adventurers, they, too, survived.

[1]Statistics for five year periods show the following yearly average for the years 1830-1844:

Period	Unwrought Tin Quantity	Exported Value	Value of Exports of Pewter, Tin Ware and Tin Plates
1830-34	1,184 tons	£82,992	£268,458
1835-39	906 tons	£76,807	£394,415
1840-44	1,806 tons	£122,939	£409,961

(Macgregor: *Commercial Statistics*, Vol. V, p. 101). For the three years 1845-47 the average annual value of exports of unwrought tin was £72,243 and of manufactures £593,556. (*Ibid*, Vol. V, p. 108).

[2]*W.B.*: March 7, 1845.

CHAPTER VI

AGRICULTURE IN CORNWALL

FARMING, till recent times, was the Cinderella of the Cornish economic order. Even in late Elizabethan times, Richard Carew, a landowning squire, could write that, until the mines began to fail, the Cornish people had neglected husbandry, preferring the chances of quickly gained wealth from the rich minerals scattered below the surface of the earth to the unceasingly monotonous toil and moil of ploughing and reaping;[1] only when the tin streams of East Cornwall became poor and promised little further riches to be gained by the then-known methods of mining, did the Cornish people remember the Biblical promise that seed-time and harvest would not fail—provided, of course, that the right seeds were sown in the right places by the best methods known.

Agriculture, to be productive and beneficial to man, can be defined as human co-operation with climatic and soil conditions to bring forth the best that the earth can produce in animal and vegetable life. Climate is, perhaps, the first consideration, but it is modified by the hill and valley, mountain and plain, structure of the land. In Cornwall the prevalent winds come from the Atlantic; there is no land barrier to lessen the surge of salt-laden vapour clouds swept in by gales from the wide ocean. Rainfall, therefore, is comparatively heavy; it would be heavier had not the Cornish hills been denuded down to a relatively insignificant height. For the same reason, the Cornish peninsula does not experience the extremes of temperature of continental land masses, extremes between winter and summer or between day and night of heat and cold. The average rainfall of the whole county is about sixty inches a year; the average range of temperature between winter and summer is from 44° to 60°F.; and the range of temperature between day and night rarely more than a few degrees. The prevalence of southwesterly oceanic winds means that rain may occur at any time of the year, although November and February are generally the wettest and May and June the driest months; if a drought

[1]Carew, p. 61.

occurs and lands scorch, the reason lies in the porous nature of the soils in certain localities and not in any real deficiency in rainfall, for, even in a dry year, rain falls in greater or less quantity on two hundred days of the year. Frost is more devastating than drought in Cornwall; it can occur in seven or even eight months of the year, and does most harm when a damp and warm winter, after encouraging the precocious development of vegetation, changes, sometimes very suddenly into frost and "black" east wind; too often a warm March may be followed by blighting frosts in May. Rather low summer temperatures prolong the growing season and delay the wheat harvest especially until late in August—a factor of great account in the times when all harvest labour was performed by hand and little could be done either to reap or harvest crops saturated with dew.

These general climatic conditions are modified by the relief of the land, which is, in simplified geological terms, the result of the upthrust of granite through older Cambrian rocks. The four main granitic areas of the Cornish mainland[1] are in West Penwith, popularly known as the Land's End district although it is in fact an irregular plateau, with its greatest heights within a mile and a half of the coast between Morvah and Zennor, sloping gently down to Mount's Bay on the southeast; the Carmenellis massif south of Camborne and Redruth; the Hensbarrow area in "Mid" Cornwall; and, most extensive of all, the Bodmin Moors dominated by Brown Willy and Roughtor. These granite uplands run roughly parallel to the north Cornish coast; on them the clouds condense to rain, clouds driven in by south-westerly winds for the most part, so that the district between Bodmin and Alternun gets nearly twice as much rain in the year as Newquay, and considerably more even than the Scilly Isles though on the latter there are, on an average, some thirty more "rainy" days throughout the year. The different directions of hill slopes create a great variety of climatic conditions; a two-hundred foot difference in altitude may mean a difference of three or even five weeks in the time of harvest, perhaps on lands belonging to a single small farm. In Charles II's reign Daniel Coxe wrote with truth that, in Cornwall, it was possible to travel from Spanish

[1]The Scilly Isles are a fifth granitic upthrust.

to Orcadian conditions in a single afternoon.[1] Even in the absence of heavy rains, sea fogs, more prevalent on certain parts of the Cornish coastlands than on others, have a deleterious influence on growing and ripening crops unknown in more favoured inland districts. In addition, whilst the highest hill in Cornwall, Brown Willy, is only 1,375 feet in altittude, a considerable area of the county lies above the six hundred foot contour level which is widely regarded as the upward limit of cultivation in the British Isles.

The upthrust granite masses dominate soil conditions even more directly than they affect climate, weathering down as they do to infertile *black growan* soils which support little vegetation other than heath, furze, and poor grasses that decompose into peats more useful as fuel than for raising other types of vegetation. Only pockets of deeper soil support even bracken, let alone thistles and docks which only grow on better soils. The sedimentary Cambrian rocks around the granite afford rather more kindly soils; Carew, in 1602, classed all these as *slatty* or shelvy soils, and it was not until the mid-nineteenth century that his general classification of growan and slate soils was amplified and several distinct sub-regions distinguished.[2] Both granite and slate soils were deficient in lime, and by early medieval times Cornish farmers were remedying this, wherever and whenever possible, by liberal applications of sea-sand.[3] The use of sea-weed and of the waste products of the pilchard fishery as fertilizers, which attracted considerable interest among the agricultural innovators of the late eighteenth century, was probably of more recent origin and was confined to a few localities whereas sea sand was used practically throughout the county.

Cornish agriculture had a bad start for, in the days when wool was truly the golden fleece of English trade and industry,

[1] Daniel Coxe: "The Improvement of Cornwall by Sea-sand": *Philosophical Transactions*, Vol. X, pp. 293-296.
[2] By W. F. Karkeek, "On the Farming of Cornwall", *J.R.A.S.*, Vol VI (1845-46), pp. 404 ff. Karkeek distinguished thirteen regions of Grauwacke or slate soils, but some of these were loam soils which one or two earlier writers had regarded as a third type of Cornish soil. Karkeek also classified the Meneage as a third "main" region, subdividing it into four sub-areas of which the barren "serpentine" plateau of Goonhilly was the most extensive.
[3] Richard, Duke of Cornwall and King of the Romans, in the mid-thirteenth century granted to the Cornish the right "to take sand freely out of the sea and carry it through the whole county. to manure their ground withal." (Carew, p. 89, note *o* [by Tonkin writing *circa* 1720]).

Cornish farmers were still raising a type of sheep whose wool was so coarse that it went under the name of "Cornish hair", and was allowed to be freely exported when, to foster the manufacture of woollen goods in England and to reduce competition in finished cloth in European markets, the export of raw wool from England was prohibited. Nevertheless, this was being remedied in Tudor times by selective breeding, a method of increasing English wool production that was perhaps preferable to the enclosure of open arable fields and laying them down to pasture which was going on at that time in parts of the south-eastern Midlands. In the same period enclosing was going on in Cornwall, but it was mainly the reclamation of open waste lands, and was designed to increase the production of grain crops; this continued throughout the Stuart period, keeping pace with the demands of a population which increased from about 70,000 in 1588 to nearly 100,000 in 1700.[1] It was this steady increase in the population, not any calamitous decline in tin-mining, which accounts for the progress of Cornish agriculture in Tudor and Stuart times.

Improvement, however, was slow; for a long time there was land enough and to spare in Cornwall. Until the last years of the eighteenth century no one criticised a practice that was more like contemporary colonial than English agrarian usage of the time—the practice of clearing a large croft, burning the waste vegetation that had been rooted up, giving it a dressing of sand, taking one or two cereal crops from it, and then allowing it to revert to furze again for thirty or forty years.[2] Permanent cultivation only became necessary about 1750, whilst a generation later every third or fourth year saw a scarcity of grain in Cornwall, sometimes marked by distress and riots among the labouring classes. Yet if Cornwall had felt the pressure of population upon agricultural production earlier than other parts of England, its farmers seem to have done little to relieve the situation until 1780 or 1790.

[1] Sir C. Lemon: "Notes on the Agricultural Produce of Cornwall": *Statistical Society Journal*, Vol. IV (1841), p. 202.

[2] Tonkin (Carew, p. 63, note *i*), writing about 1720, stated that six crops were taken off such crofts; this was possibly the case in some populous areas like the flourishing mining parish of St. Agnes where Tonkin lived; it is possible, too, that this particular number of crops were harvested to evade the payment of tithes for, by a statute of Edward III, no claim could be made for tithes of hay and corn on "barren" land until it had been in cultivation for seven years: this statute was successfully appealed to in the case of *Paynter and others v. Permewan* in 1823. (*W.B.*: April 4, 1823).

Whilst enclosure was extensively practised by the improving landlords and tenant farmers of Cornwall, the situation was rather different from that in eastern counties. The open-field agrarian system probably existed in parts of Cornwall but had practically vanished by Tudor times. That system was ill-adapted to the irregular valleys in which were found the most fertile Cornish soils; there were but few comparatively level tracts of five or seven hundred acres like those which made open-field farming practicable in the plains of eastern England; on the very extensive tracts of rocky granite it was particularly impracticable. Nevertheless, although long, regular strips of land could not be shared out among the members of Cornish hamlet and village communites, the periodic re-allocation of irregularly shaped pieces of ground in order to achieve an equitable sharing of soil-fertility among all the folk of those communities was possible and was frequently done, especially in West Cornwall where the fantastic shapes of many small fields today are partly the result of such practices. It was this system, a modification of the "run-rig" husbandry of Celtic peoples, which Richard Carew had alluded to when he wrote that, in his own lifetime:

"they fell everywhere from commons to inclosure, and partake not of some eastern tenants' envious dispositions, who will sooner prejudice their own present thrift, by continuing this mingle-mangle, than advance the lord's expectant benefit after their term expired."[1]

For a full century after Carew's time, however, this system persisted in many parts of western Cornwall, whatever may have taken place in the south-east where the Carew estates lay. References to *stitches* of land are found in many leases of late Stuart and early Hanoverian times, and there are also many designations of small *closes* of lands appertaining to the holdings of particular tenants. As late as 1799 in the 28½ acre holding of Penheske, part of Trewoone Manor in St. Mewan, the Down Closes were 15 acres in extent, the Great Meadow but 3 acres, and a piece simply described as "Stitch" was half an acre.[2]

The term *stitch* only means a small piece of ground, not

---

[1]Carew, p. 119. Carew was born in 1555 and died in 1620, eighteen years after the publication of his *Survey of Cornwall.*
[2]Hoblyn MSS.

necessarily a long strip. There are several narrow, elongated
fields to be found in Cornwall today, but many of them are only
survivals of the wide trackways which were in use before
narrow "metalled" roads were laid down in the closing years
the eighteenth century and later; when one part of these trackways had become rutted down, hardly passable and even
dangerous, another track was simply made alongside it; when
that too became bad, parochial waywardens might, perhaps
after repeated behests of the local magistrates, arrange for the
worst ruts to be filled with rubble or stones, or start another
track alongside. There are some fields, as, for example, near
Mitchell where there is a comparatively wide extent of moderately level ground, whose length suggests that they may have
been formed by the consolidation of two or three adjacent
strips, but most Cornish fields are roughly square or quadri-
lateral in shape, usually only about four acres in area, whilst
extremely irregular field patterns occur on the many rounded
hills.[1] There was an open-field system near Penryn in late
Tudor times, which had possibly been introduced there by the
ecclesiastics associated with Glasney College,[2] and its relics
caused considerable trouble and disputes in the eighteenth
century over the bounds and tenure of certain lands at Car-
vennick. The issue had become hopelessly complicated through
the loss of records of small tracts of land on the borders of three
or four different estates. Alexander Pendarves of Roscrow had
leased "3 Stitches in Boyers new Closes and the Rack Park" to
Thomas Worth in 1708, and this was followed in 1717 by a
deed of:

"Lease and Release from Edward Johns and Richard Ludgey to
Thomas Worth the younger, By which is Conveyed from them to
the said Thomas Worth in fee One Stitch or piece of land in the
new Close in Belwathland fields in Gluvias by estimation half an

---

[1]The lack of references to open-field cultivation in surviving records suggests
that the practice was rare in Cornwall. Archaeological research, and particularly
air photography may bring more cases to light, but it may be added that at
Redgate, near Camelford, the central one of three parallel "long" fields seems to
have been an Iron Age fortification whose denuded ramparts form the present
hedges.

[2]An Elizabethan map (reproduced in T. C. Peter's *Glasney Collegiate Church*)
shows open-field strip cultivation to the west of the College site, and also on the
other side of the creek below Gluvias Church; the latter strips, however, adjoined
the enclosed fields of Treviscon, so suggesting that the map was made at a time
when the transition from open fields to enclosed was practically complete in that
locality.

acre of land—formerly the lands of Lukey—Bounded with the Bishop of Exeter's on the north, the lands of Pendarves on the South, and a field called Carvinick Meadow on the East in posession of the said Johns. And all that Stitch of Land in Gluvias aforesaid, One Acre of Land lying in a field called Carvinick Meadow. Between the lands appertaining to the Bishop of Exeter on the South and the lands of Bickford to the North."[1]

This deed went on to convey two more stitches which had been granted by Alexander Pendarves to Edward Johns, and a third let to Johns by Lord Godolphin as "farmer", not owner, of the Manor of Penrhyn Foreign. In March, 1724, Lord Godolphin leased this last stitch to Worth for ninety-nine years determinable on the expiration of three lives. In June, 1733, these stitches were leased by further deeds from William Bickford to Edward Hodge. Other deeds of leases were lost, and when, in November, 1756, Edward Hodge asked Francis Basset to renew the lease with three new-named lives it took over seven months to conclude the business.

This may have been a legal labyrinth but from a purely agrarian standpoint certain facts stand out. Firstly, these stitches are described as being in certain meadows and closes. Secondly, in 1756, the bounds were ill-defined in the extant deeds in the hands of Francis Basset, the owner of the manorial rights. Thirdly, it seems apparent that the tenantry were, now and again, making agreements among themselves and transferring lands to each other without consulting the lord of the manor who was only concerned when the expiration of lives named in the current lease meant that a heriot was due to him or that the lands reverted into his possession. This particular case may have been rather exceptional since the lands of more than one lord of the manor were involved, although those lands were less than five acres in extent, and there must have been many similar cases in which comparatively insignificant holdings kept stewards and lawyers busy searching out records to prove or disprove manorial ownership rights.

The holding of Edward Hodge seems to have consisted of four or five scattered stitches of land, probably unenclosed and ill-marked, and, moreover, situated in meadow or pasture land. It is a clear example of a survival of the old Celtic run-rig

---

[1] Tehidy MSS. Belwathland or Behelland Fields lay near to Gluvias Church; the name means "the dwelling by the water near the church". Carvinnick, a name meaning "stony town", lies on the boundary of Gluvias and Mylor parishes.

system; on all the original inconveniences of that system had been superimposed manorial rights and the claims of manorial owners to "enter into their own again" when leases expired on the death of the last of the three lives named in the lease.[1] In this particular case, moreover, it does not seem that a single lease covered all the stitches occupied by Hodge; lives on one lease might expire long before those on another, thereby forcing the tenant to seek a new lease to retain all the lands which he had been working as a single agrarian unit or, otherwise, adjust his economy to a smaller holding.

Such inconveniences probably played no small part in the decline of the life-leasehold system during the eighteenth century in Cornwall. Although for long afterwards cottages continued to be leased for three lives, the larger farms were increasingly let out at "rack" on leases for fixed periods—usually for fourteen years, although sometimes for only seven years and still more rarely for twenty-one. By this system the tenant took a farm on payment of a fine which often amounted to ten or twelve years value of the land, undertook to pay a certain conventionary or quit rent, and named the three lives—usually his own and those of two of his children or grand-children. In many leases it was provided that the lessee could add another life when one of the original three died on pay-ment of a fine; heriots were charged on the deaths of each and all of the lives. By 1700 the older obligations of performing harvest "journeys" on the lands of the lessor, the only labour service which had survived in Carew's time, could be com-pounded by the payment of about sixpence. The payment of capons at certain times of the year was also generally com-pounded for a similar sum by this time.[2] Thus, at Midsummer, 1722, Wearne Nicholas of Tregithio, in Manaccan, leased part of Trenant in St. Keverne to Anthony Tonkin, on the lives of three of the latter's grandsons, reserving mineral and timber

---

[1] A good picture of the consequences of the three-life system is given by Thomas Hardy in *The Woodlanders*.

[2] The lease of Chynalls in St. Levan of 1702 provided for the payment of both harvest journeys and capons. Harvest journeys were also mentioned in the leases of Treago in St. Columb Major in 1709 and of Mellioneck in Colan in 1731; the the rate of composition in both these cases was only 4d. whereas in the case of Chynalls it had been 6d.; possibly at St. Levan harvest labour was scarcer, a fair number being engaged in the pilchard fishery there at harvest time. The demands of the mines for labour might account for the harvest journey at Kayles in Phillack being rated at 6d. in 1731, whereas at Boskidden in nearby St. Erth the rate was 4d. in 1734. (Hoblyn and Penlee MSS.).

rights. For this Tonkin paid £255 10s., a yearly rent of 23s. 8d. payable quarterly, a yearly capon of 6d. and heriots of 30s. on the deaths of the named lives. Tonkin was responsible for all repairs and would forfeit the farm if he failed to pay the quit rent within forty days of the quarter days. It was a hard bargain, for the tenement was small, consisting of:

"all that field or close of land formerly in one field and now in two fields called by the name of the great Gow . . . of six acres . . . the new close . . . two acres; all that part of the furz-croft adjoining with the new close, one and a quarter acres; . . . (and) all that croft called Calavounder the lower part of the orchard as now divided by the Mowhay with use of the Town place next the orchard . . ."[1]

An even harder bargain was made by John Boddy of St. Keverne in 1764 when he secured from Wearne Nicholas the thirteen-acre holding of Tregaminion with certain common rights for £180, a yearly rent of 47s. 4d. payable quarterly, a capon or one shilling at Christmas, and a heriot of 40s. for a "best beast"; the term was 99 years determinable on the two lives of Richard Boddy, aged 35, and Barbara Roskelly, aged 25, probably the son and daughter of the lessee.[2]

This ancient system had withstood the first shock to its existence in the sixteenth century caused by the price inflation consequent upon the influx of Spanish-American silver and gold into Europe, although, in 1602, the landowner Carew had compained that the parson was getting more from his tithes than the squire from his rents.[3] In Stuart times prices became stabilized and there was little further inflation until the era of the Revolutionary and Napoleonic Wars; inflation then dealt the death-blow to life-leases of farms in Cornwall. Long before 1800, however, many landlords had preferred setting leases for terms of years at rack rents, thereby securing a considerable yearly income from their lands instead of irregular windfalls when third lives lapsed. The older system gave the tenant reasonable security for himself, his own being usually one of the named lives, but his heir might have to pay crippling fines for renewal of a lease at an unforeseen and unexpected time. The fine on entry was heavy, and the lessee often was forced to resort to a mortgage which he could sometimes only raise by insuring the three lives at the behest of the

[1]Boaden MSS.
[2]Boaden MSS.
[3]Carew, pp. 118-119.

mortgagor at a cost of something like ten per cent of the annual value of the holding.[1] On the other side landlords suffered when a holding, hanging on the thread of a single aged life, was mercilessly racked by the tenant—a process that might go on for a dozen years or more. Leases for terms of years appealed particularly to the generation of improving landlords that came into their own with the accession of "Farmer George" to the English throne in 1760. Such leases made it easier to exert pressure on the tenantry and compel them to adopt better systems of husbandry and modern crop rotations. A short-term tenant who hoped for a renewal of his lease was more likely to keep the land in good heart and farm buildings in reasonable repair.

The small size of many Cornish estates and the very fact that a considerable number of landowners enjoyed other sources of income led many to regard land primarily if not solely as a source of monetary revenues; men like the Vyvyans and Bassets who derived such great riches from the copper deposits of Carmenellis during the eighteenth century easily came to look upon their lands as a source of regular income; from the tin deposits of West Penwith the Borlases of Pendeen were able to acquire Castle Horneck and the church livings of Madron and Ludgvan; Eliots and Molesworths resorted to banking to supplement the incomes of their landed estates. Others were less fortunate, and some of the old landed gentry disappeared to be replaced by new "county" families. The practice, not always scrupulous, of law by the Hawkins family enabled them to acquire the extensive Trewithen estate in Probus;[2] the copper mines of Kenwyn and Gwennap enabled the Lemon family to purchase Carclew and to rise to the rank of knighthood. A century later saw the end of the Trevanions and the purchase of Carhayes by the Williams family of Scorrier and of the Consolidated Mines.

The agrarian revolution of the sixteenth century was little more than a desperate attempt to make landowning and farming profitable in a period of rapidly rising prices; that of the eighteenth century arose from the sheer and stark necessity of making the land more productive in order to support a rapidly increasing population. "Turnip" Townshend showed the way

[1]Worgan, p. 20.
[2]W. Hals: *The Parochial History of Cornwall*, p. 76.

on his Norfolk estates to eliminate the wasteful practice of frequent fallowing. The cultivation of turnips not only helped to maintain and increase live-stock breeding for meat, but it also enabled heavier crops of wheat and barley to be raised; the rapidly growing London market had to be supplied, and if the East Anglian farmers had not revolutionised their methods England would have become dependent on foreign grain supplies decades before she did, and at a time, too, when paying foreigners gold for grain would have sorely vexed the mercantilist conscience of the age. Many before Townshend had devoted attention to the problems of maintaining and enhancing the fertility of the land, especially among the members of the Royal Society. Chemists had begun analysing rocks and soils, and in 1675 Daniel Coxe, a doctor of medicine, had contributed a paper to the Society on the use of sea-sand as manure in Cornwall.[1]

Coxe had written up his paper from data supplied to him by the nonconformist minister Charles Morton, who had been ejected from the living of Blisland in 1662.[2] Classifying sands by colour, Morton reckoned the reddish-yellow sands of the Camel estuary most valuable, the grey-blue sands of the Southern coasts second, and the white sands of the Land's End district inferior in quality; he mentioned the coralline sands found near St. Mawes which, a century later, William Borlase regarded as the best obtainable as fertilizer.[3] These last sands, according to Borlase, were dredged up by canvas bags from below low-tide level, and were taken by barges up the Cornish rivers as far as possible, a barge load costing rather less than ten shillings about 1750 and being ample to dress an acre of ground. It is possible that in the period of the Commonwealth and Restoration these sands were more extensively used than Morton's passing reference suggested. The schemes of Charles Trevanion to make the Fal navigable once more up as far as Grampound, on which he lost a considerable fortune in the reign of Charles II, may well have been designed to transport Falmouth harbour sands further inland.[4] By the end of the

---

[1] D. Coxe: "The Improvement of Cornwall by Sea-sand": *Philosophical Transactions*, Vol. X, pp. 293-296, 305-306.
[2] Calamy: *Nonconformists' Memorial*, (1802 ed.) Vol. I, pp. 347-348.
[3] W. Borlase: *The Natural History of Cornwall*, pp. 83-84.
[4] W. Hals: *The Parochial History of Cornwall*, pp. 80-81. Charles Trevanion was a member of Parliament for Grampound from 1661 to 1679, and then for Tregony until 1685.

eighteenth century sand barges on the Fal could only reach Tresillian, and in 1787 Charles Burrows was paid about 12s. 6d. per barge load for the land carriage of twenty-two loads from Tresillian up to Trewithen.[1]

Morton and Coxe suggested that sands should be chemically analysed, but were inclined to think that empirical experimentation would provide the best proof of those most valuable as fertilizers. They and Borlase were inclined to lay vague stress on the organic properties of the various sands, and it was not until the middle of the nineteenth century that detailed chemical analyses were made of sands and of the soils to which they were applied.[2] Morton, Coxe, and Borlase regarded the blown sands of the *towans* or dunes on the coast from Hayle to Perranporth as of little value, Morton and Coxe flatly dismissing them as "of no use" and Borlase remarking that they were deficient in lime and salt.

Blown sand was certainly a problem on the north coast until reeds were planted to stay its advance; not only had churches and houses been buried at Gwithian and Perranzabuloe, but there was even the legend of a lost city beneath the sands. All the towans provided, according to Borlase, was a species of snail on which the sheep of Gwithian fed and thereby provided mutton of a superior quality.[3] In the late summer of 1833 violent sand storms led to fears that the entire cultivated area of the valley running down from Bolingey to Perranporth would be overwhelmed.[4] Nevertheless, the Spring Assizes of 1834 revealed that farmers had been using towan sands for manure, and had been doing so from "times beyond the memory of man". Some time before the landowners Enys and Sir Richard Vyvyan had stopped men from taking sand off their properties, and in 1833 the Dean and Chapter of Exeter Cathedral instructed their tenant, Blewett, to fence off certain towans, not for the purpose of stopping the "Sanders" so much

[1]Trewithen Farm Accounts MSS. Coxe and Morton reckoned that the cost of the land carriage of sea sand in Cornwall amounted to £32,000 per annum in the 1670s. It is likely that the value of the Fal sands as fertilizers declined in the eighteenth century; the best sands had been dredged away by centuries-long exploitation, whilst now the waste material from the Carnon Stream Works and the even more deleterious mundic brought down after 1755 by the Great Adit from the Gwennap copper mines were pouring into the estuary.
[2]Dr. A. Voelcher: "Use of Lime, Marl, and Shell Sand in Agriculture", *J.B.W.*, Vol VI, pp. 242-44.
[3]W. Borlase: *The Natural History of Cornwall*, p. 286.
[4]*W.B.*: September 13, 1833.

as for that of exacting a toll from them. There had, apparently, been no protest when Enys and Vyvyan had stopped the removal of sand from the towans on their property, but the ecclesiastical authorities had already alienated the farming community by tithe exactions, and on May 29, 1833, a formidable concourse of four or five hundred farmers and their labourers, headed by "some gentlemen", came with carts, broke down the new fences, and carried off sand. Blewett, as tenant of the Dean and Chapter, subsequently brought an action against Tregonning one of the farmers who had not only taken sand away but had destroyed pasture ground. After a nine-hour hearing at the Assizes during which aged persons from Perranzabuloe, from which parish the sand had been taken, and from St. Erme where Tregonning farmed, testified to the existence of an immemorial right of taking sand to farms as far distant as the parishes of Merther and Probus, the Judge instructed the Jury to give a verdict:

"negativing any particular Presumptive right to the Defendant's Estate, or any particular Grant, but affirming the existence of the custom in all the parishes mentioned, and the point was reserved for the opinion of the Court of King's Bench, how far such a custom for the whole neighbourhood without limits to go on a particular estate for such purpose was valid in law."[1]

The final decision denied the validity of the custom, but in September, 1835, landowners and tenants:

"in the several parishes of Perranzabuloe, Crantock, Cubert, St. Allen, Newlyn (East), Kenwyn, Kea, St. Clement, St. Erme, St. Enoder, Ladock, and all others who have derived or might derive benefit from the privilege hitherto enjoyed by and now wrested from the public of taking the valuable Shell sand from the Perranzabuloe Sand Pits for manure."

were invited to attend a meeting at Truro at which a subscription was to be raised to defray the costs of the lawsuits and to discuss the expediency of bringing another test case before a jury.[2] Nothing was done; *laissez faire* individualism and the protagonists of the rights of private property had won another triumph over older customary communal rights. Another group of individualists, however, appeared on the scene and

[1] *W.B.*: April 11, 1834.
[2] *W.B.*: September 4, 1835.

proposed the construction of a railway from Perranporth to Truro, with a branch line to Zelah and Newquay, which would make the sea sands of Perranporth available to the farmers who had been denied access to the towans.[1] The promoters of a Padstow Railway scheme and of the Cornwall Central Railroad from St. Just Pool up the Fal Valley to Tregony, Grampound, and St. Stephens also stressed the value of such undertakings to farmers by enabling sand to be transported cheaply just as, half a century earlier, similar arguments had been advanced by the promoters of canals to link Bude and the Tamar and the Camel and Fowey rivers.[2]

Sea-weed, generally referred to as ore-weed in Cornwall, had long been used as manure there. Carew briefly mentioned it,[3] whilst William Borlase described it at some length though stressing the fact that it fostered weeds as well as more desired crops.[4] Borlase, however, and later writers reckoned the waste products of the pilchard fishery—bruised, damaged, and small fish, and waste salt—to be the richest manure used in Cornwall, but although a mere forty-eight bushels of this waste material were reckoned ample dressing for an acre of ground, it was more costly than sand or sea-weed, and during the Revolutionary and Napoleonic Wars the cost rose from £2 to over £4 an acre.[5] The closing of the foreign pilchard markets by the Napoleonic Continental System, however, benefitted the farmers living near the fishing ports; thus at Penzance in August, 1808, over 10,000 hogsheads of pilchards were sold at 10d. the cartload for manure.[6] From the point of view of the fishing trade matters were even worse in May, 1872, when pilchards which had been brought back from the glutted markets of Italy were offered for sale as manure at 7s. per hogshead.[7] Another valuable fertilizer was the waste oil drained off from the pilchards in the curing process.

In the application of fertilizers to their lands Cornish farmers did not lag behind those of Eastern England. They made the most of their local resources. For centuries they had been using

[1] *W.B.*: July 3, 1835.
[2] *W.B.*: March 15 and November 8, 1833, and July 22, 1836.
[3] Carew, p. 89.
[4] Borlase: *The Natural History of Cornwall*, p. 87.
[5] Worgan, p. 123.
[6] Warner, p. 190; also see below, p. 283.
[7] *J.R.I.C.*, Vol. IV (1872), p. xiii.

sand to remedy the lime deficiencies of their granitic and silurian soils, although sometimes they may have used it to excess in places where it was most easily accessible. They were, however, backward in adopting more scientific and less wasteful rotations of crops, although the practice of sowing grass seeds with the fourth or sixth successive grain crop after which the land was allowed to remain as pasture for four to eight years was probably more economic than the old English customary rotation of two years grain followed by a year of fallow.[1] This Cornish rotation might seem to be unduly exhaustive of the soil, but practical experiments with grass and clover seeds before 1700[2] suggest that the old Cornish farmers could advance a claim to be considered among the pioneers of modern ley-farming.

Cornish farmers, however, had no propagandists to state their merits in Stuart and early Hanoverian times, and by the time of George III agricultural "improvers" had become obsessed with two crops—wheat and turnips. Cornish farmers might have taken more readily to turnips had they not already started growing potatoes on a fairly considerable scale, although, in 1758, Borlase wrote that several Cornish "gentlemen" had "of late" begun tilling turnips.[3] It does not seem, however, that turnips and mangolds were at all extensively grown in Cornwall until after the collapse of grain prices in 1815; this may be ascribed to a variety of reasons, not the least being that, whatever qualities of fertility turnips restored to the soil, they took from it three times as much lime as potatoes and more than nine times that taken by wheat. Seed-drills were only introduced in Cornwall about 1800 or even later, whilst the demands of the mines for labour meant that men, women and children were not available as in Eastern England for

[1]Carew (p. 62), stated in 1602 that the Cornish farmers usually took two crops of wheat and then two of barley from their fields and then allowed them to remain fallow for seven or eight years. Grass seeds however may have been sown with the second barley crop. A century later, Tonkin, whose knowledge of farming may, it is true, have been limited to West Cornwall, stated that six grain crops were possible, the rotation being wheat, oats, oats, wheat, oats, oats with grass and clover seeds, then pasture for three or four years—"but if the land be but ordinary and not worth the keeping up for inclosure, they let it run amain, and such will not answer the tilling anew under forty years or more, except it be furzy, which may bear a good crop again in twenty or thirty years." (*Ibid.* p. 63, note *i.*). This suggests that in 1700 enclosure for tillage was the rule in West Cornwall but that pasture lands were held in common.

[2]Carew, p. 18, note *k* by Tonkin.

[3]Borlase: *The Natural History of Cornwall*, p. 89.

hoeing crops.[1] The best results from turnip husbandry, moreover, were only obtained in conjunction with stock-raising, but for generations the general Cornish practice had been to rear stock on the moorland pastures and despatch them "on the hoof" to fatten on richer eastern pastures. It is also probable that the concentration of the woollen textile industries in northern England led to a decline in Cornish sheep-breeding in the eighteenth century. One or two "gentlemen farmers" might grow turnips of a quality to earn the praise of "foreigners", but there seems to be no foundation whatever for the Rev. Richard Polwhele's assertion that Cornish farmers had been winter-feeding their stock with turnips in pre-Roman times.[2]

Cereal production in Cornwall, till about 1780, was probably in most seasons more than adequate to satisfy local demands; the earliest riot against the exportation of corn took place in the St. Austell district in 1729,[3] and such riots only became frequent after 1770. Although the cool Cornish summers delayed the maturing of wheat crops, barley ripened quickly, whilst extensive crops of the now extinct pillas or

[1] This labour problem explains the criticism made by some of the writers whom Arthur Young induced to study Cornish farming. In 1794 Robert Fraser wrote that in Cornwall turnips were neither drilled nor hoed, but were so smothered in couch grass and weeds that "it would not be supposed at a distance that there was a single turnip in the field." Fraser also criticised Cornish farmers for never practising fallowing, which would have checked weeds, writing that it was "difficult to persuade them that the land will grow more corn in proportion to the destruction of the weeds. (*Survey of the Agriculture of Cornwall*, p. 43). A few years later G. B. Worgan scathingly wrote (p. 71)—"A more general and perfect use of the hoe in turnip husbandry over the county, is of the most essential consequence, as is evidenced by the very superior state of cultivation of the lands about Menheniot and St. Germans, where it has been longest in practice," and where incidentally, Worgan himself had farmed and gone bankrupt.

[2] Polwhele: *History of Cornwall*, Vol. I, p. 161. The term "winter-feeding" deserves emphasis. The mild Cornish winters enabled the hardy native breeds of cattle and sheep to be kept out of doors all the year round with little more fodder than that on which they grazed. Cornish farms were generally very poorly supplied with buildings to house cattle, and too many beasts had to take their chance of survival by finding a "loo hedge" against the storms and gales. Most of them may have survived, but comparatively few cattle were kept. Dairying was in its infancy in the eighteenth century, although Celia Fiennes enjoyed the treat of Cornish clotted cream when she visited the county in the 1690s. (C. Morris: *The Journeys of Celia Fiennes*, pp. 256-257). In 1793 Sir Francis Basset was only keeping 35 head of cattle on the 750 acre Tehidy "Home Farm"; 15 of these were draught oxen, and only one a milch cow. (*Annals of Agriculture:* Vol. XXII, p. 146). By the time that Robert Bakewell was experimenting with sheep and cattle breeding, a pig and potato husbandry, supplemented by fish and a chance rabbit, had become the mainstay of the Cornish labouring classes, and when small-holders kept milch cattle it was often primarily to obtain skim milk to raise more pork.

[3] Carew, p. 66, subnote by Tonkin.

avena nuda were grown, especially in western districts. During Stuart times the area of wheat production in the county was extended through the supersession of the unbearded knot wheat, which produced a coarse and dry flour, by the bearded dredge wheat which could thrive on poorer soils and which yielded a finer flour.[1] These cereals, together with the extension of potato culture, made Cornwall virtually self-sufficient in necessary foodstuffs save for a few years of dearth until the last quarter of the eighteenth century. Even then it was a question in Cornwall not of making two blades of wheat grow where but one had grown before, but of bringing into cultivation tracts which, hitherto, had grown no wheat or barley at all. So began the encroachments on the waste common lands of Cornwall, especially in the western mining districts where the increase in population was greatest and proceeding most quickly.

Long before this time many farmers had been taking occasional crops from enclosed furze crofts on their holdings, cutting down the gorse, burning the scrub, ploughing and tilling the ground, and taking one or two grain crops therefrom every ten, twenty, or even only every forty years. In the mid-eighteenth century it cost from thirty to forty shillings to bring an acre of furze croft into cultivation,[2] and it can be surmised that these crofts were only cultivated when the farmer had an excess of labour at his disposal and when he, too, had a good furze rick to fall back upon for fuel. In fact, the land was required for raising both food and fuel, and even as late as 1839 the sowing of furze seeds appears to have been quite a common practice.[3] It should be remembered, too, that with corn prices rising high, the farmer could afford to buy Welsh coal, a fuel by this time extensively employed by mining operations and in those processes of smelting tin which activities had, moreover, long since stripped many Cornish woodlands and left more land ready for the plough.

It is impossible to reach any but a vague estimate of the area

---

[1] Carew, p. 63, note *m* by Tonkin.

[2] Borlase MSS: Letter of the Rev. R. Buckland of St. Allen to William Borlase, May 15, 1753.

[3] *W.B.*: April 19, 1839. As late as 1861 there were no less than 30,000 acres in Cornwall classified as "furze brakes and plantations", and double that acreage of "large enclosed crofts", but only 20,000 acres of "timber and oak coppice" out of a total area of 860,000 acres. (N. Whitley: "The Development of the Agricultural Resources of Cornwall", *J.B.W.*: Vol. IX (1861), p. 196).

of waste land brought under cultivation in Cornwall during the eighteenth and early nineteenth century. Enclosure in Cornwall was a process of irregular and intermittent attrition of wastelands by individual landlords and tenants, rarely, if ever, with parliamentary sanction. Most of the more fertile lands had been enclosed generations before, and the eighteenth century enclosure movement in Cornwall was essentially different from the processes of enclosing open arable fields which went on in the country east of a line drawn from Hull to Exeter. Instead of a process which eliminated the small yeoman farmer the Cornish changes tended to increase the number of small-holders, especially in the mining districts, although there were some cases of the amalgamation of small holdings into larger farms. It is probable that 25,000 to 30,000 acres of wastelands were reclaimed between 1700 and 1860, but there is no accurate estimate of the total area of wastelands until the latter year when it amounted to 191,500 acres out of a total area of 860,000 acres.[1]

The most extensive reclamation of wasteland in the later eighteenth century probably went on in the Camborne-Redruth mining district, and especially on the Basset manors of Tehidy and Nancekuke. When Sir Francis Basset began corresponding with Arthur Young in December, 1793, he stated that he had encouraged poor labourers, who were chiefly employed in mining, to build cottages and enclose a few acres of waste lands. During the past "few" years he reckoned that about fifty cottages had been built on his estates. The cottagers were granted their tenements on leases of three lives with quit rents of 2/6 a year; he was inclined to think that this rent was rather high, although his father had reduced it from 3/4 in 1762.[2] On the manor of Nancekuke between fifty and sixty-five acres had been enclosed to form such cottage holdings in the thirty years from 1756 to 1786, whilst on the manor of Tehidy a number of cottagers and small farmers had enclosed tracts of Reskajeage and Treswithian Downs and from Carn Entral in the same period.[3] Some proposals by the

---

[1]N. Whitley: "The Development of the Agricultural Resources of Cornwall", *J.B.W.*, Vol. IX, p. 196. In 1808 Worgan (p. 106) had been content to state that there were "at least from 150,000 to 200,000 acres of unenclosed waste lands" in Cornwall.

[2]*Annals of Agriculture*, Vol. XXII, p. 154.

[3]Tehidy MSS: Proposal Book, 1756-86. Francis Basset, father of Sir Francis, succeeded to the Tehidy estates in 1756.

tenants to enclose lands had been turned down for various reasons. Thus, at Michaelmas, 1757, Humphrey Langdon asked to be allowed to enclose eight or nine acres of Nancekuke Downs, but only offered a quit rent of 6d. per acre, but the elder Francis Basset asked for 3/4; Langdon then enclosed a small plot of ground at Porth Towan, part of which did not belong to the Basset estate. The request of John Willoughby for leave to enclose four acres adjoining Portreath Cove was rejected in September, 1760, because the land was already leased to another tenant. Arthur Benny's request for three acres which he wished to enclose and build upon was first granted but subsequently withdrawn, because, "on enquiry Benny is not a parishioner of Illogan, and (is) a man of bad character". Whatever may have been Arthur Benny's moral deficiencies and delinquencies, it is certain that Basset selected his tenantry, taking good care that his wastelands were not occupied by any thriftless race of ne'er-do-well squatters likely to become a burden on the parish rates. No answer was given to the application of John Hockin, who had already built a cottage on Nancekuke Downs without a permissory lease, when he asked for three acres in 1767, he was described as "a parishioner, but very poor, would obstruct no roads, nor prejudice the tenement." Nor is there any record that Basset granted Thomas Hawke's request to be allowed to enclose two acres near Forge, although Hawke was a man of means who "keeps 20 or 30 mules, and if (the land is) granted could keep 20 or 30 more." On the other Basset manor, Tehidy, there were two requests for a tract of land with the ill-boding name of Labour in Vain near Illogan Churchtown; no answer was given to the application of Henry Magor in October, 1757, but in June, 1773, it was granted to Andrew Uren. Nicholas Hockin's request for Pengigan Moor on Carn Entral was acceded to in July, 1760, but on reconsideration permission was withdrawn, because "this proposal would be improper; it is the watering place of the tenants' cattle, and where they lie in summer."[1]

The Bassets and other landlords seem to have rigidly controlled the growth of cottage tenements on the waste lands belonging to their estates. There is no indication of any scruple about reducing the furze crofts and turf pits of poor cottagers, but the withdrawal of permission to enclose Pengigan Moor

[1] Tehidy MSS: Proposal Book, 1756-86.

from Nicholas Hockin shows that care was taken not to inconvenience the tenants of larger holdings. Precautions were also taken to prevent overstocking common lands; when Joshua Eva was allowed to enclose eight acres of Reskajeage Downs in 1768, he was restricted to keeping not more than eight horses or oxen and not more than twenty sheep. As a condition to the grants of three or four acres the tenants were required to build a house within a year. The tenant named the three lives on which the tenement was to be held before it fell back into the hand of the landlord again. When the quit rent was reduced from 3/4 to 2/6 a year in 1762, however, it became the practice on the Basset lands to demand that the house to be built within the year should be worth £20 and not £10 as in the earlier grants. Similar leases and grants were probably being made at the same time on the adjoining estates of the Vyvyans, St. Aubyns, and Boscawens.

Nevertheless, extensive common lands remained, and on them Cornish pastoral husbandry became almost a ranching economy; selective breeding was impossible, nor was "rustling" of cattle and sheep unknown.[1] The extension of corn tillage led to a more extensive use of summer moorland pastures during the Napoleonic period. The vast Bodmin moors were widely used, herdsmen collecting the cattle from various places, even as far down the county as St. Allen, early in May and returning them to their owners at Michaelmas. The cattle of different owners were distinguished by ear-marks, notches of particular shapes cut in the ears of the beasts. The charges made by the owners of moorland grazing rights varied between 2/- and 21/- a season per head of cattle, and about a penny per head for sheep; on the Hawk's Tor and Butter's Tor "ranges" in 1836 the charge for cattle was 5/-; elsewhere 8/- was sometimes charged; horses cost double the rate of cattle.[2] Few sheep were taken to the moorland pastures; not only were they more susceptible to summer diseases and the ravages of fly and maggot, but they had also to be taken away for shearing in the midst of the season, and offered greater temptation to thieves than did cattle. The types of rough grass on the moors did not suit sheep which, usually after a month or six weeks, would

[1]*W.B.*: July 17, 1829.
[2]Worgan, p. 106; *W.B.*: May 6, 1836. The charge of 21/- per season was one in all probability for horses only.

become "moor-sick", and have to be taken back to "inland" pastures to recuperate. Sheep, too, are liable to a greater number of infectious diseases than cattle, and early in the nineteenth century a new "scab" disease had appeared; about 1825 the sheep-farmers in the hundred of Lesnewth formed an association to prosecute persons who depastured scab-infested sheep on the commons of the hundred, and in the next few years half a dozen persons were prosecuted successfully at petty sessions for offending in the parish of St. Juliot; in other parishes in the hundred the precautions taken were successful and the disease was stamped out.[1]

Outside the granite and "serpentine" moorlands there was little land in Cornwall which could be "reclaimed" except a few acres of low-lying marshlands. In 1793 Dr. Richard Moyle successfully drained about seventy acres of tidal marsh near Marazion, using a pipe with a valve outlet which was automatically closed by the rising tide, an idea which he may have conceived by seeing a tidal mill in operation.[2] Crops raised on the reclaimed land were not good for the first three or four years, but after that it produced good harvests of corn and potatoes, and materially extended the area that later came to be known as the winter garden of England. In 1839 Trevanson Marshes below Wadebridge were reclaimed,[3] whilst rather earlier, the completion of the Liskeard and Looe Canal must have improved the drainage of the narrow valley below Liskeard, besides facilitating the transport of lime up to the Liskeard district.

Enclosure and reclamation in Cornwall were designed to a single end—the extension of the area of grain, potato, and good pasture lands. Cornish arable practices attracted considerable attention from agricultural writers of the "Agrarian Renaissance"—from Arthur Young and his associates Robert Fraser and William Marshall; some of these methods, however, had been mentioned by Borlase and even Carew in earlier times. A practice that somewhat increased the fertility of the soil and which was, apparently, confined to south-west England was that known as sod-burning, burning beat, or Denshiring, the last term originating from a supposition that the practice had

[1]*W.B.*: June 29, 1836, and February 9, 1827.
[2]Drew, Vol. 11, p. 330.
[3]*W.B.*: November 29, 1839.

its beginnings in Devonshire.[1] Stubbles, roots, weeds, and grass were all dug up, allowed to dry, raked into small heaps and then burnt slowly with a "smothered heat".[2] Although this was criticised as wasteful of the fertilizing constituents as far back as 1708,[3] it persisted until, faced with foreign competition after the repeal of the Corn Laws, the farmers of the south-west began to abandon it simply to reduce labour costs for, on some farms, burning beat lasted a full month or even longer.[4]

The "arrish mow" attracted even more interest from "up-country" visitors. The practice of putting up small round mows in the fields, each containing up to two hundred sheaves, has not yet entirely disappeared from West Cornwall, although, by 1800, it seems to have vanished from the south-eastern districts. Tonkin, the first to describe arrish-mowing, said that it had been adopted to protect the corn from damage by rain and winds;[5] this explanation was accepted by later writers, especially as it seemed to account for the disuse of arrish-mowing in the drier south-eastern districts. It is, however, probable, that the practice originated from and survived the older Celtic common field, one arrish mow being the entire crop of an individual holding within that field. It is certain that it was more convenient from the point of view of transportation and threshing in the eighteenth century. It was only at the very end of that century that the first four-wheeled waggon appeared in the eastern Liskeard district;[6] in other districts the two-wheeled Cornish wain had appeared a little earlier, and incidentally with a carrying capacity of about two hundred sheaves; elsewhere transport was by the sledge or sliding butt or by pack-saddle. It is little wonder, indeed, that the Cornish farmers preferred to make these "hand" mows out in the fields in which all the work was performed by human labour. Threshing, too, was done by hand, and a single hand

[1]W. Marshall: *Rural Economy of the West of England*, pp. 8, 227 ff.; Worgan, pp. 67, 118.
[2]Worgan, p. 67; Borlase MSS: R. Buckland to William Borlase, May 15, 1753.
[3]Dr. A. Barry in *Philosophical Transactions*: Vol. XXVI, pp. 142-143. In 1845, nearly a century and a half later, the Cornish veterinary and agriculturalist, W. F. Karkeek, called the practice "pernicious" since it destroyed or wasted carbon and humus. (*J.R.A.S.*, IV, p. 433).
[4]Marshall: *Review and Complete Abstracts of the Reports to the Board of Agriculture from the Southern and Peninsular Departments of England*, p. 543.
[5]Carew, p. 66, note *n*.
[6]J. Allen: *History of Liskeard*, p. 337.

mow represented a full day's work of two men with flails. After threshing by flail, the straw could be left on the ground where it lay for cattle to feed upon, and the grain easily carried by pack-horse or, not infrequently, on the shoulders of the farm labourers themselves to the farmstead and there be immediately sold.[1] The arrish mow, therefore, survived until the introduction of mechanical threshing appliances; these came into wider use after the repeal of the Corn Laws; left unprotected to face foreign competition the farmer could profit best by speedy threshing and the immediate despatch of his grain to market before supplies reached England from Odessa; quick harvesting and threshing also produced a cleaner grain since there was greater risk of fermentation in the arrish mows.[2]

The actual yields of grain varied from year to year and from farm to farm, but differed little from those secured elsewhere in England. In the eighteenth century a wheat crop of from 20 to 25 bushels to the acre was reasonably good, although in 1808 Worgan found some fields yielding 40 or even 45 bushels per acre. In 1753 the Rev. R. Buckland of St. Allen reckoned that the furze crofts of that parish, when tilled with wheat yielded from 15 to 25 bushels to the acre.[3] Worgan's figures, published in 1808, were deemed excessive by William Olver of St. Pinnock, and he informed his landlord Thomas Bond that, in a reasonably fertile district, he rarely raised more than 16 bushels of wheat to the acre, that 30 bushels of barley per acre was a "very good crop" although Worgan had said the average was between 30 and 40 bushels, and that 30 bushels of oats was "a decent crop" from a single acre whereas Worgan had mentioned crops of between 40 and 60 bushels.[4] In 1845 Karkeek gave the production of cereal crops in the Perranzabuloe—St. Enoder—Mawgan area (which he regarded as the best wheat and barley growing district in Cornwall) as averaging from 20 to 32 bushels of wheat and 24 to 36 of barley per

[1] Reporting on the harvest of 1794, John Thomas of Chiverton stated in February, 1795, that all the corn threshed in Cornwall to that date had already been sold, "our farmers having no granaries." (*Annals of Agriculture:* XXVI, p. 226).

[2] *W.B.*: September 7, 1849.

[3] Borlase MSS: R. Buckland to William Borlase, May 15, 1753. The figure stated above is an estimate based on Buckland's own statement that 48 Cornish acres were equivalent to 57 statutory acres; the yield per Cornish acre was from 18 to 30 bushels.

[4] Worgan, pp. 63 (wheat), 65 (barley), and 66 (oats); the information of Olver to Thomas Bond is handwritten as marginal notes in the copy of Worgan's book formerly owned by Bond.

acre; he also described oat yields of 40 to 55 bushels per acre as "very heavy."[1]

The corn riots of 1774 mark the end of the period when Cornwall could rely on harvesting enough grain to meet the needs of its own population every year. Not even the supplies of the less thickly-peopled farming districts of eastern Cornwall and the Meneage were enough to supply all the needs of the western mining districts, and by 1795 it was estimated that half the bread consumed by the Cornish mining population was made from flour imported from the Isle of Wight.[2] The failure of the harvest of 1794 caused much distress and some disturbances in the mining districts, but the worst crisis came in the spring of 1812 when there was a dearth of grain not only in the mining area but in the agricultural districts as well, and when food shortage was further aggravated by the general economic depression which affected every aspect of Cornish economic life. At Lanteglos-by-Camelford, a predominantly agricultural district, the parochial authorities set up a special committee in May, 1812, to assess the quantities of grain in the parish and to decide how much of it could be distributed among the labouring poor. The farmers were to be paid the market price for the corn they supplied (which was not surprising since six of the committee of eleven members were farmers themselves, and a seventh was described as a small-holder), but the poor were to get it at a reduced price, the already over-harassed rate-payers bearing the loss. If there was not enough grain in the parish the committee was empowered to purchase corn or flour from outside on the best terms it could make.[3]

It was the "starving times" of the wars with Revolutionary and Napoleonic France which brought the potato into general prominence as a field-crop to supplement, and, in some cases, to take the place of cereal crops. The early associations of the south-west with the New World might have led to the early cultivation of potatoes in Cornwall, but it seems that it was its utility in Ireland as a preparatory crop for barley on heath and bog soils that led to its wide cultivation in the south-west after 1700. By 1758 Borlase was writing that the potato was "a more useful root" than the turnip, and that it was

[1] *J.R.A.S.*: Vol. VI, pp. 406, 412.
[2] Letter of John Thomas of Chiverton in *Annals of Agriculture*, XXVI: p. 226.
[3] Lanteglos-by-Camelford Churchwardens' Accounts: MSS.

grown all over Cornwall, thriving best on shallow, poor lands.[1]

When Borlase wrote there were two main types of potatoes being grown in Cornwall. The flat or kidney potato was planted in November or December, dug about midsummer, and would keep until about Christmas; it can be regarded as the fore-runner of the early potato industry of the Mount's Bay district where Borlase lived. The second type, a round potato, was planted in the late spring and not harvested until December, and could keep until the following autumn. By the 1790s two potato crops a year were being raised by some growers in the Marazion district, the total yield being from eight to nine hundred bushels to the acre, at least two hundred bushels more than the best "up-country" potato crops of the time.[2] About a third of the total was "earlies", dug in May—the month in which grain supplies approached exhaustion and the month in which most of the formidable food riots in Cornwall occurred. Robert Fraser, who first publicised this to the world, however, suspected that such double crops would rapidly exhaust the fertility of the soil. He also criticised the Cornish for only raising potatoes for local markets and for human consumption, and took some pains to point out to the Cornish farmers that, if they raised more, thereby eliminating the menace of dearth, any surplus could always be fed to cattle and pigs, such being the practice of the most progressive farmers of the day in Somerset and Wiltshire. He mentioned the attempt of the Cornish Judge, Buller, to grow potatoes on Dartmoor in the hope of stirring the Judge's compatriots to emulation on the more westerly wastelands. Fraser, too, stressed the excellence of sea-weed as potato fertilizer, which seems to have been rather gratuitous advice unless, as was only too likely, some Cornish farmers were planting potatoes without any manure at all. They seem, however, to have taken the advice of Fraser and others to use potatoes as cattle-feed for, by 1808, out of seven different types of potato raised in Cornwall, two were grown specifically for animal food.[3]

Today the Cornish potato-grower, mainly concerned with supplying the early market, dreads the late frost, but, in the winter of 1794-95, it was an early frost that wrought havoc,

[1] Borlase: *The Natural History of Cornwall*, p. 89.
[2] *Annals of Agriculture*, XXIII: pp. 61-68.
[3] Worgan, pp. 75-83.

trebling prices where the crop was not utterly destroyed, and causing immense hardship to the labouring classes which had become largely dependent on a staple diet of potatoes and fish.[1] It might seem recklessly and culpably wrong to allow the potatoes to remain in the ground until December, but such a practice was not confined to Cornwall at that time. The labour problem was the main cause of the late potato harvest; cleaning stubbles, burning beat, and ploughing kept the available supply of farm labour in Cornwall fully employed till December, and any or all of these operations might be long delayed by heavy autumn rains. Even when potatoes were dug and gathered, storage in earthed-over clamps, already practised in 1794, was far from ideal for preservation against frost.

The extension of cereal production, the reclamation of waste-lands, and the improvement in potato cultivation in Cornwall after 1790, were the outcome of the conditions of siege imposed on Britain by the long French wars; the pressure of population on the means of subsistence had been increased by war and by blockade, counter-blockade, and privateering. All that mattered at the time was to increase food-production; considerations of economy were relegated to the background; prices and wages rose. In Cornwall the competition of the mines for labour aggravated the situation, but the very example of the mines fostered the introduction of mechanical methods to agriculture. In 1812 Richard Trevithick constructed his first steam threshing engine for Sir Christopher Hawkins of Trewithian, a man notorious for his parsimonious economies; he then constructed a second machine for Lord de Dunstanville, a third for a Padstow farmer, and a fourth was bought by a Bridgenorth farmer.[2] Elsewhere flails were being superseded by threshing machines worked by horses and, in a few instances, by water power. The great improvement during these years, however, was in farm transport. Fraser had written in 1794 that everything in Cornwall and Devon was carried by pack-horse or mule, but Worgan, fourteen years later, stressed the number of wheeled vehicles used by western farmers, ranging from four-wheeled waggons to wheelbarrows. The two-wheeled Cornish wain, in particular, was a great advance on the old sliding butts or sledges and on the far more costly pack-horse

[1] *Annals of Agriculture:* XXIV, p. 232.
[2] F. Trevithick, Vol. II, pp. 36 ff.

and mule transport. There was also some experimenting with
ploughs, mainly with heavier types of "sub-soil" plough which
could break into the marl clays lying beneath growan top-
soils; till the end of the the French Wars, however, the old
Cornish types of plough remained in general use, although
"up-country" ploughs were entered into a few Cornish ploughing
matches.[1] Trevithick's schemes for 500 horse-power steam
engines which could perform every possible agricultural operation and make horse and ox unnecessary were, however, more
than a century in advance of the time.[2]

Great improvements were effected in the breeds of livestock,
though even greater were to be achieved after 1815. By the
middle of the eighteenth century Cornish wool was sufficiently
good for the Williams family to set up a factory in Perranarworthal employing five or six hundred hands;[3] a generation
later the customs officials and wool merchants were alarmed by
the amount of wool smuggled out of Cornwall to France. The
old four-horned sheep had disappeared, but the majority of
Cornish sheep, according to Sir Francis Basset, were still as
wild as cats. Basset, himself, in 1793 had a small flock of
Dorset sheep; Sir William Molesworth had given him a pair
of ewes from Robert Bakewell's flock, and he was considering
obtaining a Leicestershire ram if he could "get a tolerable one
at a price not immoderate".[4] The largest flock of Dorset sheep
in Cornwall was that kept by Lord Camelford on his Boconnoc
estate; apparently these did not prove very profitable owing to
the low prices fetched by early lambs in Cornwall, and their
wool clip only averaged four pounds to the fleece.[5]

Many types of cattle were introduced by the landlords. The
small black native Cornish variety had not disappeared by
1815, but was being widely superseded by superior Devon
breeds. Sir Francis Basset experimented with Scottish cattle
at Tehidy, whilst the Eliots brought some Gloucestershire
cattle to St. Germans. The first to introduce any of Robert
Bakewell's cattle to Cornwall was Sir Harry Trelawney of
Pelynt; he did not induce any of his neighbours to follow his

[1]Worgan, p. 42.
[2]F. Trevithick, Vol. II, pp. 40-47.
[3]Borlase MSS: Letter of Richard Williams to William Borlase, August 27,
1757; Borlase: *The Natural History of Cornwall*, p. 318.
[4]Letter of Basset to Arthur Young, December 16, 1793, published in *Annals of
Agriculture*, XXII.
[5]R. Fraser: *Survey of the Agriculture of Cornwall*, pp. 46-47.

example, and, apparently, these cattle did not answer well in Cornwall for later, on Bakewell's own advice, Sir Harry replaced them by North Devons.[1] By Worgan's time many Cornish dairy farmers had some Jersey and Guernsey cattle.

If, in 1815, there were some strange crosses among the sheep and cattle, the Cornish pigs were mongrels indeed. The aboriginal type had been a large long white, razor-backed, long-eared beast that was frequently kept for three years before slaughtering. Crosses with Devon, Suffolk, Leicester, and Chinese White varieties were made and a vast improvement effected by many farmers, and especially by the Rev. Robert Walker of St. Winnow and by R. L. Gwatkin of Killiow in Kea. Worgan's main criticism of Cornish pig-breeders was not the quality of their stock but their practice of allowing them to wander in fields, orchards and lanes, often trespassing upon and damaging the fields and gardens of neighbouring farmers and cottagers; if they were kept in sheds or yards, in his opinion, they could be fattened more quickly and the farmer would also gain their valuable manure.[2]

The system of renting cows in West Penwith was one of the strangest features in Cornish pastoral farming. When Worgan was making his survey in 1808 he was told that the farmers of that district, who usually had tenements of between twenty and sixty acres, used the crofts of waste, upland moors as pasture for cows from November to near their time of calving; after they calved the cows were leased out:

"to labourers and poor people, at £6 or £8 per cow, for seven or eight months; four, six, eight, or ten cows to each person. The hirer pays his cow-rent by milk or butter, for which he finds a ready market and sale in this populous (mining) district. When a cow approaches her time of calving, the farmer is obliged to take her, and provide the person with another, flush in milk. These cow-renters generally have a piece of ground allotted them by the farmer, on which they grow potatoes; with these, and with the scalded milk which has yielded cream for the butter, they fatten a great many young porkers."[3]

This practice can hardly yet be called a thing of the past, but in the first part of the nineteenth century it was a regular feature of the husbandry of West Cornwall. It declined when a general

[1] R. Fraser: *Survey of the Agriculture of Cornwall*, pp. 45-46. *Annals of Agriculture:* XXXIII, pp. 636-637, and XXXV, p. 106.
[2] Worgan, pp. 155-157.
[3] Worgan, p. 140.

transition to pastoral husbandry occurred after the great slump
in corn prices in the 1870s; it had, even before, become less
prevalent as oxen became less important for draught purposes
on the larger farms; it was doomed when modern transportation facilities made large-scale milk production the main-stay
of Cornish farming. The system in all probability originated in
comparatively modern times for mutual convenience—the
farmer wanting only draught and beef animals, the cottager
milk for his family and his pigs. Known locally as "dairying",
this system has analogies to the still prevalent setting of sheep
to "half crease" whereby the person providing the pasture for
the flocks during the breeding season is paid by being allowed
half the number of lambs born and reared. It might be added
that the setting of pigs and even of geese to half crease has not
been unknown in West Cornwall.[1]

With the ending of the French Wars hard times came to
British farming, and they were bitterly felt in Cornwall where
so much marginal land, which could only yield profitable grain
crops in seasons of high prices, had been brought into cultivation. Moreover, to meet the exigencies of the Napoleonic siege,
the more fertile lands had been racked nigh unto exhaustion
by taking grain crops from them year after year. Although
prices slumped there was no great reduction in the area under
grain. The adage that the corn mow paid the rent had become
traditional, and Cornish farmers were already notorious for
their reluctance to depart from the ways of their fathers.

[1]In 1845 W. F. Karkeek described the dairying system at some length.
(*J.R.A.S.*, Vol. VI, p. 407). By this time, however, things had changed considerably. The "dairyman", as the lessee was called kept the calves, although in many
cases the farmer had a right of pre-emption. The rent per cow was now £8 per
year, but the dairyman, besides a quarter acre of potato ground, was now allotted
1¼ acres for the upkeep of each cow, two cart loads of turnips, about half a ton of
straw, and some fuel, whilst a dairyman renting five or more cows was provided
with a cottage and houses for pigs and for storing potatoes. Hardy's reference to a
similar system in the Dorset part of his "Wessex" country ("The Withered Arm",
Wessex Tales) lends some support to the suggestion that the system was due to
mutual convenience to farmer and to cottager rather than to mere survival of an
older Celtic communal farming practice. William Borlase, a native of West
Cornwall, made no reference whatever to the system in 1758, and this supports
the view of its comparatively recent origin. On the other hand it was going on in
Borlase's time: on June 11, 1763, William Eddy was examined by the Gulval
magistrates, when he claimed to be legally settled in that parish, he revealed that
he had kept "dairies" in both Gulval and in Zennor twenty years before. (Gulval
Parish Documents, preserved at Penlee House, Penzance). In 1850, at the annual
dinner of the Kerrier Agricultural Association, Samuel Harvey of Sennen stated
that he was then renting out about fifty cows to various dairymen. (*W.B.*: June 21,
1850).

Tenants, too, were often bound by the conditions of their leases to cultivate a stated proportion of their holdings and to follow prescribed crop rotations. Under the shelter of the Corn Laws grain production continued to dominate Cornish arable farming, whilst, despite the slump in prices, wheat was still the most profitable—or least unprofitable—crop to raise.

Wool prices fell even more disastrously than those of grain after 1815. The ban on exports of raw wool was retained for a few years longer, but the woollen textile industries of Western England were in a perilous state at this time. Insofar as the home market was concerned, the ruling consideration was that, in hard times, people are likely to cut down expenditure more on their wardrobes than on their larders. The limited class that believed in being decked in costly garments at any price and inconvenience were, in those days, less likely to want British broadcloths and homespun than the new cotton fabrics of Lancashire and the silk-stuffs that could now be easily obtained from France with the end of the wars. The Western woollen industry, like the tin and copper interests, had become dependent to a fairly large extent on bulk contracts with the East India Company, which, it was alleged, frequently drove a hard bargain detrimental to farmers and weavers alike.[1] In the case of wool a fall in price might be remedied to some extent by increasing production, although there was always the risk that this policy would flood the markets and precipitate more disastrous price reductions. Through the replacement of short-woolled breeds by the long-wool Leicester sheep Cornish wool production rose nearly 75% between 1800 and 1828, largely through the efforts and example of John Penhallow Peters who had started a flock of Leicesters at Philleigh in 1790, and who held regular ram sales until 1840. Peters was also fairly successful in crosses of Leicesters and Cotswold sheep.[2] Robert Walker, Vicar of St. Winnow, and Colonel Francis Hearle Rodd, squire of Trebartha, also played a prominent part in introducing Bakewell's Leicester sheep into Cornwall after 1815.

Cattle rearing offered an alternative to corn production, but

---

[1] *W.B.*: February 10, 1826.
[2] W. F. Karkeek: "On the Farming of Cornwall," *J.R.A.S.*, Vol. VI, pp. 448-449.

there were only local markets for dairy produce until Brunel built the railway bridge over the Tamar at Saltash in 1859. In beef-production progress was made by the almost complete elimination of the smaller native cattle in favour of Devon breeds, by speedier fattening, and by slaughtering a greater proportion of beef animals in Cornwall rather than sending them off on the hoof to eastern dealers and markets. Feeding methods were improved, and more housing for livestock was provided on the farmsteads. Besides the Devons, shorthorns were introduced into Cornwall, again principally by J. P. Peters; another man to experiment with this breed was Colonel John Scobell who, having given up an active army career at the end of the wars, devoted much of his attention to improving the agriculture of West Penwith by precept and example. Transport problems limited the chances of gain by raising early vegetables, although potato cultivation for "up country" markets increased considerably between 1815 and 1825, but this increase was mainly effected on the smaller holdings.

Cornish farmers attempted to withstand the post-war slump by reducing the prices of production. Few reductions in wages were possible, some farmers were paying their men about 9s. a week in 1815, but in the Stratton district, where no mining or fishing industries competed for labour, wages remained as low as 7s. until the middle of the century showing no increase for two generations.[1] Around Truro in the 1840s the average wage of agricultural labourers did not exceed 10s. a week, but with perquisites of cheap grain, housing in some cases, and so forth, this was reckoned to be worth 14s.[2] As elsewhere, the farmers of Cornwall had relied on the poor rates to make up the pay of their employees to a living wage in some parishes. After 1815 labour costs were reduced by employing less regular and more casual labour on contract jobs, and by an increased use of machinery. The former, however, tended to increase the number of able-bodied men who were forced to seek parish relief when unemployed, whilst the latter was not at all widely resorted to until after the repeal of the Corn Laws. In one or two parishes something was done to alleviate the lot of

[1] *W.B.*: January 8, 1847. Wages might have fallen in this district but for the considerable emigration of labourers from it to the mining districts and to Canada between 1815 and 1850.
[2] *W.B.*: June 4, 1847.

labourers by the institution of allotments whereon they could grow potatoes and a few vegetables for their own use, notably in Crowan in 1833 through the instrumentality of the squire, Sir John St. Aubyn, and the Vicar, the Rev. William Grylls, and in Breage in 1839 where the moving spirit was the improving farmer Hendy of Penbria.[1] The practice of binding pauper children as apprentices to husbandry meant that many farm houses were overcrowded with youthful apprentices,[2] and this, too, lessened the demand for adult able-bodied labour. In some places gangs of paupers were hired out by parish overseers to farmers for casual extensive jobs, but the demand was not great, and in the harvest season of 1822 some Ludgvan farmers were able to secure virtual slave labour at 2d., 3d., or 4d. per man per day.[3] The final desperate resort was emigration, and from Padstow there was almost a regular service of emigrant ships to Canada in this period; many emigrants were assisted by parochial funds to leave their native country, and many more might have gone had they been able to raise enough capital.[4]

The amount of labour employed in arable farming, however, could only be considerably reduced by mechanisation, and comparatively little was done in this direction until the repeal of the Corn Laws increased the threat of foreign competition. In addition, the greater number of Cornish holdings were small enough to be worked by the farmer and his own immediate family. In the spring of 1822 out of 444 farmers who signed a requisition for the High Sheriff to convene a county meeting on the subject of agricultural distress, 371 had holdings of less than two hundred acres, and the total number of men employed by the 250 who farmed less than a hundred acres cannot have been very large. Several of the larger farms, moreover, consisted mainly of moorland tracts on which hardly any labour was employed.[5] The supersession of the flail by threshing machines reduced the labour required for threshing grain to a quarter of what it had been before, whilst successive improvements in these machines meant a tenfold reduction of the

---

[1] *W.B.*: April 5, 1833 and May 31, 1839.
[2] *W.B.*: March 15, 1822.
[3] *W.B.*: August 16, 1822.
[4] *W.B.*: April 2, 1830 and April 6, 1832.
[5] *W.B.*: March 22, 1822. In all these 444 farmers occupied about 60,000 acres or less than a tenth of the land of Cornwall, but they were probably representative of all the farmers and farms in the county.

labour employed in threshing by 1850.[1] The superiority of
these machines over the flail also reduced the amount of grain
lost in threshing, and the quantity of grain thus conserved
might well mean the difference between an average and a poor
harvest.[2]   Despite Trevithick, Cornish farmers made sur-
prisingly little use of steam-power in the first part of the nineteenth century, although they did follow the example of mining
adventurers in making the utmost possible use of water power,
often constructing leats to take water one, two, or even three
miles to serve two or three farms.[3]

The replacement of pack-animals and sleds by wheeled
waggons and wains also reduced the amount of labour employed on farms to some extent besides reducing the number of
draught animals kept. Gradually, too, horses replaced oxen,
but whereas the draught power of a horse was about twice as
efficient as that of the ox it cost nearly twice as much to maintain in fodder, although it perhaps required and almost
certainly got far less care and attention. Horses, in fact, were
one of the black features of Cornish husbandry; they had been
improved somewhat from the small beasts in Carew's day that
had been ruined by being over-burdened with pack-loads on
their backs, but as late as the Bath and West Show at Truro in
in 1861 were condemned as "rather inferior".[4] The deficiency
of Cornish horse-breeding was partly due to the extensive use
of mules, especially by the mines, for transport; it was far easier
to rear a mule than to go to the trouble of breeding and raising

[1]The Daveys of Redruth, agents of Consolidated Mines, used a machine made
by the St. Agnes miner Michael Harris on their "experimental" farm at Tywarnhayle in 1844. Portable and worked by a single pony, this machine threshed a
thousand sheaves in eight hours; it would have taken two men five days to thresh
this quantity with flails. The modern threshing machine can deal with a similar
quantity in about an hour. (*W.B.*: August 16, 1844, and information supplied by
W. P. Batten, Esq., Penhale, St. Keyne).

[2]*W.B.*: January 7, 1831 (Report of speech by E. W. W. Pendarves, M.P.).

[3]The Liskeard engineer William Morshead, junior, specialized in the provision
of water-power installations on Cornish farms in the middle of the nineteenth
century. (*J.B.W.*: Vol. IV, 1856, pp. 24-52.).

[4]Carew, pp. 79-80; *J.B.W.*, X, p. 30. In 1845 Karkeek had flatly denounced
Cornish brood mares as inferior, whilst the "majority of the stallions that have been
introduced have been unfortunately either broken down by premature labour,
or having exercised their vocations, and been condemned as breeding stallions
in other places, have been sent into Cornwall by way of a finish." (*J.R.A.S.:*
Vol. VI, p. 453). Worgan rather discreetly hinted that Cornish farmers would be
well advised to feed their horses better, and wrote that Cornish "farm horses are
as rude and cheap as they can be." (p. 153) Tonkin, however, reckoned that the
rough and not "over handsome" Cornish horses were well-adapted to the needs
of a hilly country in which more shapely Eastern horses rapidly foundered.
(Carew, note p. 79).

a pedigree colt, and there was always a ready market for a mule. The inferior Cornish horse was also an inevitable result of depasturing animals on the lime-deficient moorlands which caused stunted if not mal-formed bone development.

After 1815 Cornish ploughs were improved and horse-drills came into more general use, although these developments were slow and retarded by conservative prejudice. Previously an old type wooden plough, supplemented by the so-called "tormentor" which has some claim to be considered as the forerunner of the disc harrow, had been in general use, and it was only replaced slowly by more modern and improved types. The old Cornish plough was little more than a simple blade fixed to a wooden beam with handles attached, the whole arrangement being more like a modern hay-sweep than any plough now used; the actual blade was small but it was designed to cut fairly deeply; its most commendable feature was that it could be easily turned on the steep hillsides and in the irregularly shaped fields. New eastern types of ploughs were brought in by some landlords, and one of them was tried with marked success at Tehidy in April, 1819, where it saved about a third of the animal labour and dealt successfully with wastelands on which older Cornish ploughs had broken to bits.[1] Further west, in the Penzance district, Colonel John Scobell (1779-1866) did all in his power to promote better methods of cultivation, bringing in eastern harrows, which greatly excelled the tormentors, and making extensive use of drills. He had a stiff fight against conservative prejudice, not only from the smaller tenant farmers but from men like John Boase (1771-1836) who was farming the Castle Horneck estate and who would hardly suffer strange-looking labour-saving devices to be brought into his fields.[2] Scobell introduced a new iron plough and a turnip drill to western Cornwall; by 1850 the new plough had practically superseded the old cumbersome and relatively weak wooden Cornish plough, but it took much longer for the turnip drill to come into general favour with the Penwith farmers.

The drill cannot be regarded as a great labour-saving device, but it effected a great saving of seed compared to the old

---

[1] *W.B.*: April 30, 1819.
[2] *W.B.*: June 15, 1849. (Report of John Scobell's speech to a meeting of the Penwith Agricultural Society of which he was a founder member).

broadcast methods of hand-sowing, and seed corn and turnip seeds were no inconsiderable items in farm accounts in those days. Every small economy helped in the hard years to narrow the margin between loss and gain. Some economies may have been short-sighted, notably the rough treatment of horses, and the leaving of implements in the fields rather than go to the expense of making sheds to house them. Yet if the farmer treated his live and dead stock hard, he was not wallowing in the lap of luxury himself. Only at harvest home might farm tables have groaned beneath loads of food and drink. At other times farm fare was meagre indeed. John Boaden of Skyburriowe (1828-1904) wrote that in his boyhood days in the Helston district:

"Things went on with the greatest regularity and order in the household. We rose at 5 o'clock a.m. in summer and 6 in winter, breakfast was at 7.30 so a tolerable lot of work was done before breakfast, dinner at noon, just before which was the calling of the people from the fields to dinner by the different servant girls, very few people had watches in those days making the calling necessary. They generally knew before they came in what the bill of fare would be, and it was the same almost in all well-regulated Farmhouses in the district. On Saturdays and Mondays it would be fish and potatoes; two days potato pie with a rind or crust around it with a piece of salt pork washed on top; on Sundays there would be a piece of fresh meat instead. Another day it would be broth with apple dumplings in season, and hard dumplings otherwise; this with either salt or dried pork formed another day's dinner. Fridays was a sort of odd day about which there was some uncertainty, sometimes peas at other times fry, when a pig was killed it would be pig's fry. I should say that after the pork and potatoes there would be tea and sometimes a piece of apple pie, or a slice of white bread and butter. For breakfast and supper, as the evening meal was called there was invariably milk and bread with mornel after; the bread for both meals was barley bread, except on Sunday evenings when it would be either white bread or cake."[1]

Such food may have been "substantial", but it lacked much variety, nor is there much doubt that the farmers lived hard and worked hard in their—generally successful—struggle to pay their way.

During these hard times, lasting with but few breaks until the middle of the nineteenth century, farmers and tithe-owners came into collision. A few tithe-owners in bad years remitted

[1] John Boaden: MS. Autobiography.

ten or twenty per cent of their claims, but the majority tried to exact every penny due to them. Although these troubles were not confined to Cornwall but were general throughout the Kingdom and were to lead to the Tithe Commutation Act of 1836, the agitation and law suits that resulted were something new in the West Country. Clergymen were rather more lenient and accommodating than lay impropriators in making compositions for tithes, but in the greater number of Cornish parishes the great or corn tithes were in the hands of laymen, who, where a composition had been arranged, had been exacting sums amounting to more than an eighth, and sometimes nearly a sixth, of the rent of the farm.[1] The great trouble and difficulty arose from the custom of taking tithes in kind or, alternatively, of accepting a composition based on a valuation made in the harvest-field which, if anything, caused more trouble and dispute than taking tithes in kind. After 1815 there were many Cornish complaints that agriculture was unfairly burdened with tithes in addition to taxes and rates, but the real storm broke in 1821 when Anthony Geake of Trecarrel in Lezant successfully sued the Rector, Johnnes, for the non-removal of a tithe of hay in a civil court. Johnnes then brought an action in the ecclesiastical courts as a result of which Geake was imprisoned. The threat that this would establish a precedent leaving the determination of all tithe cases to ecclesiastical courts led to a mass meeting of the Cornish "yeomanry" at Bodmin on December 1, 1821. The meeting raised a subscription for Geake and resolved to take the case to a higher court. Geake was then released by writ of habeas corpus, although only on account of some obscure legal technicality.[2] However, tithe-warfare had begun in Cornwall. A further meeting at Bodmin on May 22, 1822, passed resolutions condemning the ecclesiastical courts and proposing to petition Parliament on the question of tithes.[3] In July, 1822, a prolonged dispute began in Kea parish over the titheability of rakings; this culminated in a legal decision that can only be described as obscure, for it declared that *involuntary* rakings were not titheable and that the rightful way of taking tithe was as corn was reaped and not after the sheaves had been erected

[1]Worgan, pp. 32-33.
[2]*W.B.*: November 23, December 7 and 14, 1821, and January 18, 1822.
[3]*W.B.*: May 24, 1822.

into shocks or mows. Geake at once pointed out in a public letter that this meant that in a wet season corn would be ruined by being left lying on the ground in scattered sheaves until tithe proctors came to estimate the value of the crop and of the tithe from it. He might have added that all rakings were involuntary since no farmer would wish to go over his fields a second time to gather his whole crop, and that the decision left the way open for a farmer to argue that the use of a rake left the entire crop raked exempt from tithe.[1]

Lawyers, if not the law itself, seemed to be on the side of the farmers; it was one aspect of the revolt of the age against traditional privileges for which no rational justification could be adduced. At times tradition was fought with its own ancient weapons. In the case of *Paynter and others v. Permewan*, in 1823, a statute nearly five hundred years old was brought forward to defeat the claim of tithe-owners to take tithes of hay and corn from waste lands in Buryan, the statute having laid down that tithe could not be taken from "barren land" until it had been in cultivation for seven years. In this case reclaimed lands had only been cultivated for four years before they had been allowed to lapse into waste again.[2] In 1824 the case of *Facey v. Harden* arising from a tithe dispute in Egloskerry parish ended in a decision in favour of the plaintiff who had brought an action against the tithe-owner for the non-removal of a tithe in kind thereby further weakening the position of tithe-owners; Facey had stated that in Egloskerry it had not been customary to give notice to tithe-owners to collect the tithes; the decision of Justice Bosanquet that tithe owners must prove a long-established custom of notice being given by the farmers to the proctors to collect the tithes meant that the collection of tithes in kind might become impossible in many parishes.[3]

Tithe agitation then merged into the general demand for Parliamentary Reform, which, for the farming interest, represented an effort to reduce the burdens on agricultural enterprise. Heavy rates to maintain the poor and tithes to maintain speculators rather than clergymen who fulfilled their spiritual functions weighed heavily enough, but to them had been added a crushing burden of taxation imposed by a Parliament con-

[1] *W.B.*: July 26, August 2, 9, and 16, 1822.
[2] *W.B.*: April 4, 1823.
[3] *W.B.*: May 21, 1824.

sisting mainly of members whose main preoccupation was the successful manipulation of a spoils system which ensured to themselves, their relatives, and their friends, the enjoyment of sinecure offices and places. Since 1760 "up-country" moneyed interests like the banking family of Baring, coal-owning magnates like the Dukes of Bedford, and East Indian "nabobs" like the Barwells had gained control of Cornish boroughs that hitherto had returned members acceptable to the local gentry. Mine-owners like the Bassets, Boscawens and Hawkins and bankers like the Eliots and Molesworths, it is true, could hold their own in politics against or in co-operation with these "foreign" moneyed interests, but the small Cornish landowner could not. By 1820 the latter class was beginning to feel the pinch of reduced rental as fourteen-year leases granted during the high price period of the war expired. The failure of Lord Liverpool's Government to effect any considerable reduction of taxes more than offset any advantage given by the Corn Laws. So the Cornish landed interest allied itself with the cause of Reform; it was conservative radicalism, dictated by pure self-interest, a demand for economy and not for revolutionary change. The great County Meeting at Bodmin on April 2, 1822, opened with spirited denunciations of governmental extravagance, went on to demand the reduction of taxes which, in turn, would enable tithes and rents to be reduced, condemned the resumption of cash payments, wanted more protection for agriculture against foreign competition, and finally demanded that Parliament should be reformed in order to bring about the abolition of sinecure offices.[1] Such were the demands of Cornish freeholders. It was no accident, nor was it really inconsistent, that the same men were largely responsible for the return of the "Ultra Tory" Sir Richard Vyvyan as a County Member of Parliament four years later.

There followed a short spell of prosperity, but with the bad harvest of 1829 hard times returned. A series of local meetings demanding protection, economy, and reduced taxes culminated in the County Meeting of March 22, 1830, summoned by eight magistrates after the High Sheriff refused to convene it. The radicals dominated this meeting, the financial policy of the

---

[1]*W.B.*: March 22 and 29, and April 5, 1822. Similar meetings of the "agricultural interest" were held at the same time in many other English counties and were derided by Cobbett in his *Register*.

recent succession of Tory governments was roundly condemned; the improving farmer-parson, the Rev. Robert
Walker of St. Winnow, delivered a lengthy Jeremiad against
borough corruption, to be followed by the forthright declaration of John Rundle that the borough members no more
represented Cornwall than the man in the moon.[1]

A little later in the Home Counties the "Swing" riots drove
the farming interests into hard and fast alliance with conservatism. In Cornwall the only incidents were at Morval and
St. Winnow, the Rev. Robert Walker taking prompt action in
the latter parish to secure the arrest of a drunken bargeman who
had threatened to organize the destruction of every threshing
machine in the district.[2]   A week or two later Walker took a
leading part in convening another radical County Meeting
which assembled at Bodmin on January 19, 1831.[3]   During
that winter of 1830-31 the demand for tithe, tax, and rate
reductions had been raised anew; at South Petherwin the
local justices had considered introducing the notorious Speenhamland system of making up the wages of labourers from the
rates; the parish of Linkinhorne drafted a petition to Parliament asking for an all-round reduction of rates, tithes, and
taxes; in St. Neot tithe troubles nearly culminated in riot.[4]
Matters improved slightly with the coming of spring, and the
great national Reform Bill crisis thenceforth overshadowed all.
After the Reform Bill had been passed Cornish farmers resumed their campaign against the tithe system, alleging that
it was out of date, that it deprived the poor of employment,
and that it was a formidable obstacle to the improvement of
waste land.[5]   Grumblings of discontent died away after the
passing of the Tithe Commutation Act in 1836, although
several farmers of the Truro district and in West Cornwall
declared that Act to be far from satisfactory.[6]   The new Poor
Law met the farmers' demands for the reduction of rates, and
it is noteworthy that the only rioting in Cornwall against the
new workhouses occurred in the agricultural unions of Stratton
and Camelford, where troops had to be called in to protect the

[1] *W.B.*: March 5, 12, 19, and 26, 1830.
[2] *W.B.*: December 24, 1830 and January 7, 1831.
[3] *W.B.*: January 14 and 21, 1831.
[4] *W.B.*: December 17 and 24, 1830. The only real tithe riot at this time was
that at Mousehole against fish tithes. (See below, pp. 296-7).
[5] *W.B.*: April 5 and 19, June 28 and July 12, 1833, and May 21, 1834.
[6] *W.B.*: April 15 and 29, 1836.

Poor Law Commissioner, Gilbert, in 1837. There were, however, minor disturbances at St. Ives and at St. Just in Penwith against the new Union Workhouse system, which might have been worse had the mining and fishing industries not been reasonably prosperous at that time.[1] On the whole Tithe Commutation and the Poor Law Amendment Act alleviated the burdens on agriculture considerably, but they had been the work of Whig Reformers and Radicals. The price had yet to be paid by the termination of protection and the abolition of the Corn Laws.

There was no real unity in the Cornish farming community on the desirability of maintaining protection. A few landlords and farmers declared that if miners were paid better wages they could afford to buy protected breadstuffs, but they were voices crying in the wilderness. Religious Nonconformity became the ally of the Anti-Corn Law League; tithe troubles had led many farmers to abandon the Church of England for Wesleyanism, whilst an even greater number had joined the Bryanite or Bible Christian movement which, initiated by a Luxulyan man, William O'Bryan, had made its greatest appeal to the more rural districts that older Methodism had rather neglected in the West Country. The Bible Christian chapels, too, enabled the larger farmers to take a role that the land-owning squires still monopolised in the Anglican Church. The first great Cornish follower of Cobden and Bright was Sir William Molesworth of Pencarrow, whilst the Earl of St. Germans became the main defender of the old protectionist order. Some landowners, who might have been expected to defend the Corn Laws to the last, were too involved in mining operations and speculations not to realize that cheaper bread would enable wages to be kept low, and many of them may have hoped that free trade in corn would put an end to the unrest which prevailed in the mining districts every time there was a dearth of corn and prices ruled high.

Agitation began early in 1839 with anti-Corn Law meetings at St. Agnes and Penryn and pro-Corn Law meetings at Callington and Launceston.[2] At the Launceston Meeting, however, John Rundle, now Member for Tavistock, declared his

[1] *W.B.*: February 10, 17, and 24, March 3, June 16 and July 21, 1837.
[2] *W.B.*: January 11, 1839 (Launceston meeting), January 25, 1839 (Callington and Penryn meetings), and February 22, 1839 (St. Agnes meeting).

outright opposition to all Corn Laws, whilst other speakers
questioned the statistics quoted by supporters of the Corn Laws,
particularly those showing the relative numbers of agricultural and other labourers, and denied that free trade would
reduce the English labourer to "black bread and chicory";
no one, however, suggested a rise in wages, and although a
resolution was passed to petition Parliament to continue the
Corn Laws, several opposed it and others refused to vote either
way. An even stormier meeting took place at Truro in February, 1839, when a Free Trade resolution was passed despite
the alliance of the Tories with a handful of Chartists who had
become prominent in that borough by assuming the leadership
of an agitation against church rates.[1] Late in May, 1839, the
Devon landlord Acland toured the agricultural district of
North Cornwall making speeches against the Corn Laws;
his meetings at Stratton, Launceston, Callington, and Liskeard
passed off without incident, but at Camelford he was greeted
with a shower of stones.[2]

During the next few years meetings for and against the Corn
Laws were held up and down the county, but even in 1840 two
or three of the most prominent landowners in the great wheat-
growing district around Wadebridge refused to sign a petition
asking Parliament to retain the Corn Laws.[3] In April, 1843,
John Bright addressed a crowded meeting at Liskeard, and at
the end of that year Sir William Molesworth told the Wadebridge Farmers' Club that free trade would benefit both agriculture and industry since they were interdependent; two
years later the members of that club debated the question and
many of them were inclined to believe that free trade would not
bring ruin in its train—but it should be remembered that not
a few of them were Molesworth's own tenants.[4] By the
beginning of 1846 the Corn Laws were under sentence of death,
and William Rashleigh, one of the East Cornwall Members of
Parliament, had the mortification of being voted down at a
Bodmin meeting which rejected his resolution that English
farming needed protection in favour of an amendment demanding the total and immediate repeal of the Corn Laws.[5]

[1] *W.B.*: February 22, 1839.
[2] *W.B.*: May 31, 1839.
[3] *W.B.*: March 20, 1840.
[4] *W.B.*: April 21 and December 29, 1843 and December 26, 1845.
[5] *W.B.*: February 13, 1846.

Indeed, protectionists failed to put up any real fight in Cornwall until the beginning of 1850 when Cornish farming, too long depending on the corn mow to pay the rent, was in the depths of depression. At this time the Cornish wheat producer admitted that he could just pay his way if wheat was 56s. the quarter; in the Cornish markets it had fetched rather less than that price in 1844, had averaged about 50s. in 1845 and 60s. the following year; in the starving times of 1847 it had reached 85s. in some markets, but had generally fallen to 56s. in 1848, the fall continuing throughout 1849 so that by January, 1850, many Cornish farmers were only getting 40s. From this low level recovery was rather slow to 50s. in 1852, although in January, 1854, wheat was fetching 84s. in some Cornish markets. This later high level was not long maintained; during the twenty years from 1855 to 1874 wheat prices only averaged 56s. and upwards in twelve years, but in five years the price was less than 45s., four of these being the years from 1862 to 1866, the last of which saw the collapse of the Cornish copper mining industry. After 1875 lean times began again, and from 1877 onwards a series of bad harvests coincided with the first really considerable importations of grain from the New World, whilst agrarian distress was accentuated by heavy losses of cattle and sheep through epidemic diseases.[1]

With the onset of agricultural depression in 1848 two courses lay open to Cornish farmers—either to sit back and grumble or to push forward and make the best of matters. For those who favoured the former the old traditional scapegoats were there to hand—the weather and the government, and in the confused political situation of the time there seemed every hope of changing the latter. Remote from the centre of the political scene, western farmers were inclined to underestimate the popular backing for free trade, and to look upon Cobden and Bright as the tribunes of the cotton-manufacturing oligarchy of Lancashire whose only concern was that of diverting the resentment of their underpaid workmen against the producers of the food on which they lived. They mocked the henchmen of Cobden and Bright who were still heading parades with big loaves and little loaves stuck at the end of poles, little realizing

[1]The market prices of wheat are based on weekly market reports printed in the *West Briton*, the *Cornwall Gazette*, and the *Penzance Gazette and West Cornwall Advertizer*. Highest prices occur for the July markets; those for January, after the completion of the main threshings, are the lowest.

the effectiveness of such propaganda. In vain protectionists argued that where in Asia the necessities of life were cheapest there the conditions of the poor were the worst in the world; to the ordinary working man Asia was as remote as the dark side of the moon, and he would not be convinced by any such specious argument to a belief that high costs of living and a high standard of living went hand in hand. On the other hand it had been emigration not free trade which had relieved the distressful condition of Ireland, nor had the Free Traders been able to stifle the last, futile demonstration of the Chartists in 1848. Cornish farmers had vague notions of all these but it is unlikely that they had heard that Toryism's white hope, Disraeli, had pronounced protection dead and damned.

Unaware that the country was committed irrevocably to a policy of free trade, a group of East Cornwall landlords and farmers demanded a return to the protectionist system in order to relieve agricultural distress. They were led by a few landlords whose main concern was to avoid wholesale and permanent reductions of rents. The western mining district took no part in this movement which was confined to East Cornwall and began with meetings at Polperro and Callington in the closing weeks of 1849.[1] Other meetings were held in 1850, but at the annual meeting of the Wadebridge Farmers' Club on December 28, 1849, not only did the Molesworth free trade line prevail but an unrepentant protectionist like Olver of Trescow avowed that it was hopeless to demand a revival of the Corn Laws, that it was up to the tenants to adopt better farming methods, and that landlords should introduce a system of rents graduated according to the price of corn; even more scathingly contemptuous of the latter day protectionists was the Chairman of the Club, Edward Stephens of Trewornan, who condemned a race of farmers so lacking in initiative that they would call in Parliament to keep down the rabbits on their farms.[2]

The protectionists, however, secured the convention of a County Meeting at Bodmin on February 12, 1850, by the High Sheriff to whom a requisition of no less than 3,706 signatures had been presented. The only Member of Parliament present, T. J. Agar Robartes, declared that he would never support any proposal to tax bread merely to keep up the splendours of the

[1] *W.B.*: November 23 and December 14, 1849.
[2] *W.B.*: January 4, 1850.

landowning aristocracy, whilst his fellow representative, the Conservative W. A. Pole Carew, sent a letter apologising for absence but stating that recent divisions in both Houses of Parliament made it clear that there was not the remotest chance of a return to protection. Nevertheless, the Meeting proceeded to pass resolutions demanding protection of agriculture against foreign competition, although the only noteworthy speeches on their side were the diatribes of Olver and of Edward Archer, squire of Trelaske in Lewannick, against the cotton lords. Archer, indeed, was the one real leader the die-hards possessed, but his criticism of a Government that had spent millions in "stuffing opium down the throats of Chinese", and the reminder he gave to Cornish freeholders that the big-loaf Mancunian philanthropists had been forced to call in eleven regiments to protect their lives and property whereas in Cornwall "the staff of your old crippled parish constable is quite enough for your protection",[1] was not enough to get him a Parliamentary nomination, even had he desired it. Instead the Protectionists put forward Nicholas Kendall of Pelyn as their candidate in the East Cornwall election of July, 1852, the first contested election since that division had been formed in 1832. Kendall was elected, but only by ousting the Conservative Pole Carew, since Robartes easily headed the poll.

Protectionists made frequent accusations that Cobden, the arch-bogey, was trying to drive a wedge between landlords and tenantry. Rents were high, it is true, but this was mainly the result of the keen competition of the tenants themselves for farms when leases expired. Substantial remissions of rents were made in 1850 and the following years by many landlords, notably by the free traders Robartes of Lanhydrock, Fortescue of Boconnoc, and Gilbert of Trelissick, and by the protectionists Kendall of Pelyn, Archer of Trelaske, and Lord Falmouth of Tregothnan. Yet whenever a lease expired and a farm was advertised to be let by tender, some would-be tenant would offer the same high rent as paid before. The agricultural crisis of 1848-51 brought about no permanent reductions in the general levels of rents; indeed, in the years that followed rents actually rose slightly.

Complaints about excessive taxes and rates brought no amelioration at this time; it was left to the Cornish farmers to

[1] *W.B.*: February 15, 1850.

make the best they could of matters. A few of them and a fair number of the more enterprising labourers emigrated. Vercoe of Pendavey, the Treasurer of the Wadebridge Farmers' Club went off to New Zealand; Nicholas Boaden and several others left the Meneage district to find new homes in South Australia.[1] The population of the hundred of Stratton declined more than ten per cent from 1841 to 1851, falling from 9,436 to 8,496; in the twelve Meneage parishes the population dropped over five per cent in the same decade from 7,876 to 7,458. Although many of the emigrants only moved to other parts of Cornwall or of the United Kingdom, the actual numbers leaving these districts were greater than the decennial census figures suggest,[2] for they took no account of the excess of births over deaths in this period. Migration prevented any fall in agricultural wages save on a few farms in the Launceston and Looe districts; any attempt by the farmers to reduce wages was met by the threat of men to emigrate and in one or two cases by strikes.[3]

The only hope for the farmers was to adopt more economical methods of agriculture. In Cornwall, as in the rest of England, the area under grain crops actually increased after the repeal of the Corn Laws; farmers were still looking to the corn mow to pay the rent. Economy could be effected by improved methods of tilling and of harvesting. Drills now came into general use for tilling, though they saved seed rather than labour. Harvesting was revolutionized in two stages. The scythe replaced the reaping-hook only to be quickly superseded in its turn by the reaping machines that were first introduced in Cornwall in 1852 by the enterprising Farmers' Clubs of Wadebridge and of Probus. These first machines were of the type designed by the inventor Hussey, which, owing to his failure to secure a patent, only cost £18. Almost immediately a local millwright at St. Stephens in Brannel, L. B. Truscott, improved on Hussey's machine and, with some justice, claimed that he had made an implement as effective as any of the much-vaunted American reapers.[4] By 1870

---

[1] *W.B.*: May 23, 1851 and March 26, 1852.
[2] From the single parish of Mawgan in Meneage over fifty persons went to South Australia in 1850 (John Boaden: MS Autobiography).
[3] *W.B.*: March 8 and April 12, 1850.
[4] *W.B.*: January 16, February 6 and 13, May 21, June 25, and August 13, 1852.

reaping machines were in general use in Cornwall.[1] The Hussey reaper was very similar in design and in operation to the hay-mowing machines used today. One of the reasons for its comparatively slow advance in Cornwall was that it was too wide to go through the narrow gateways of Cornish fields. When this matter was discussed by the Probus farmers in the spring of 1852 it was remarkable that no one suggested the obvious expedient of widening the gateways, but there were a number of suggestions that the machine should be made with detachable parts, so that the cutting gear could be taken off and carried by hand through the gateways, whilst the relatively narrow wheeled-chassis could then easily be drawn through by horses.[2] Farmers liable by the conditions of their leases for the upkeep of gates and fences were, perhaps, chary of altering gateways to accommodate the new machines; they were even more unlikely to adopt even more drastic measures of levelling hedges and fences to merge two or more fields into a single large field in which the new reapers could be worked to the greatest advantage. Still it is doubtful if any progressive landlord would have objected to wider gateways and to the amalgamation of fields; numerous hedges were a waste of space besides being weed and vermin breeders, whilst the increasing practice of stall-feeding and winter-housing of cattle had vastly reduced the utility of hedges as shelter for stock.

The reaper, too, demanded a degree of mechanical knowledge hitherto rarely found among ordinary farmers, and this factor also delayed any considerable application of steam-power to agriculture although for many operations its cost was less than half that of horse labour.[2] For some machines a farmer could, in the mining districts, easily get a mine mechanic to effect repair and maintenance tasks for a trifling sum or, perhaps, a bag of corn or a quarter of mutton, but the reaping machines were entirely different from any machines employed in mining. The adoption of the reaper was particularly slow on the farms where oxen were still employed as draught animals;

[1] John Boaden: MS. Autobiography.
[2] *W.B.*: February 13, 1852.
[3] W. Morshead, jr., "Relative Advantage of Steam, Water, and Animal Power", *J.B.W.*: Vol. IV (1856) pp. 24 ff., and "Practical hints as to the Selection and Management of Agricultural Steam Engines": *J.B.W.*, Vol. X (1861), pp. 87 ff.

if scarcity of labour forced a farmer to get a reaper he often had to buy an additional horse or two at the same time, and all this additional expense was incurred when a succession of poor years had reduced the available capital of most tenant farmers. It cannot be wondered, then, that it took more than fifteen years for the reaper to supersede the reaping hook and the scythe, and the latter still had to be used to "open up" the fields around the hedges before the reapers went around, and even to cut fields when storms had so battered the growing crop that machines could not cope with them.

Ploughs and other implements were also improved, but at a St. Germans ploughing match in October, 1850, E. S. Tucker of Tregannick flatly declared that the old six-ox ploughs of their grandfathers were still as cheap as any, and that some of the best farmers were still threshing with flails, although he concluded, rather inconsistently, by demanding the provision of agricultural schools and for a wider knowledge of the applications of chemistry to farming.[1] The great change in ploughing technique at this time was the elimination of the driver who drove or led the draught horses or oxen whilst another man or youth guided the plough. This practice only became general in Cornwall about 1850, although it had been introduced at Trewithian in 1811 by that economical landowner Sir Christopher Hawkins after he had seen it practised by Scottish farmers.[2] It was the cost and scarcity of labour, vaguely attributed to emigration, which brought about this change, just as it had forced many farmers to buy reaping machines and more horses, which, although reducing the labour necessary in the harvest fields by a half or even three-quarters, did not wholly compensate in some districts for the migration of labour to the mines, towns, or overseas.

The proximity of the mines made Cornish farmers far more mechanically-minded than those in the purely agricultural districts of England. They had been too conservative, it is true, to carry out the ideas of Trevithick, but so had been many mines adventurers when the Camborne inventor had advised them to use high-pressure steam. From the miners Cornish farmers learnt the many uses to which water-power could be

---

[1] *W.B.*: November 1, 1850.
[2] *W.B.*: February 13, 1852.

put. After 1850 they made more use of steam-power,[1] but
the progress of its application to agriculture was retarded by
the development of a more mixed husbandry after the repeal
of the Corn Laws and then by the agricultural depression of
the 'seventies which, it might be argued, ensured the survival
of the horse-plough for another two generations. Only richer
men like the Daveys of Redruth, with the wealth of the mines
behind them, could afford to buy and experiment with steam
ploughs.[2] With an increasing area under permanent pasture
or down to long leys, more and more ploughs were left by the
hedges to rust away or to stop a gap against straying cattle and
sheep.

With the recovery of corn prices in 1853, Cornish farmers
went ahead with improved methods of cultivation which
enabled them and their landlords to live with increasing
comfort until the great debacle of the late 'seventies. During
the bad years in the middle of the century some farmers had
survived by racking the land, starving it of manure, but more
and more, then and later, adopted the stall-feeding of cattle
which conserved farmyard manure and reduced the cost of
lime, guano, and superphosphates which they had already been
using fairly lavishly in the 1840s. Along with this had gone a
demand for agricultural education, and one of the greatest
blows dealt to Cornish farming by the depression of 1848-52
was that it put an end to the plans for establishing an agricultural college in Cornwall as a memorial to Francis Hearle
Rodd of Trebartha.[3]

At the onset of that depression Thomas Olver of Trescow
had bluntly stated that the ways of their grandfathers that did
very well when corn was £5 a quarter were no longer good
enough when it was but £2,[4] and many Cornish farmers
agreed with him. Several, it is true, adhered to the old ways,
but, perhaps most significant of all, was the group of farmers
and landlords who tried to combine the best of both worlds.

[1]W. Morshead, jr., "The Relative Advantage of Steam, Water, and Animal
Power": *J.B.W.*, Vol IV, pp. 24 ff.
[2]*W.B.*: September 23, 1869, and February 2, 1871.
[3]This scheme, first proposed in October, 1846, would have cost at least £5,000
a year. The immediate response was good and subscriptions of £1,500 were
promised at once. In the end, however, less than £1,000 was actually subscribed,
and the scheme was finally abandoned in the summer of 1849. (*W.B.*: October 30,
1846, November 17 and December 1, 1848; July 6 and August 10, 1849).
[4]*W.B.*: October 12, 1849.

Rash experimenters had come to grief in the past as had John Penhallow Peters, who, good sheep-man that he was, failed as a cattleman. Others had gone on more or less successfully experimenting in a small way like John Scobell of Madron, who, nearly forty years after he had helped to found the West Penwith Agricultural Society, and more than twenty years after he had introduced "scufflers" and iron ploughs to improve Cornish tillage, experimented successfully with the seed of black African barley in 1849.[1] Thomas Olver, who had been most sceptical about the possibilities of using the new "American" reapers in Cornwall, was himself the inventor of an improved turnip drill.[2] Other Cornish farmers had been among the first users of guano and superphosphates in England. But, one and all, they had been practical in their experimentations; they tried a little first, if it succeeded, well and good, if not, the loss was not great.[3] Hard-headed men, perhaps too conscious of their own limitations, they stood back to mock at wild experimenters like John Joseph Mechi of Tiptree in Essex who was, through his earlier success as a manufacturer of razor-strops, too ready to advertise his methods to the world. Olver publicly jibed at Mechi when he published a balance-sheet showing a loss of £650 in one year on a farm of 150 acres, a loss double or treble that sustained by the least fortunate Cornish farmer.[4] Edward Archer mocked Mechi's attempts to pump and pipe liquid manure all over his Tiptree Hall farm and told East Cornwall farmers that erudite scientists could try and teach a variety of subjects to them but that the ways of their fathers were good ways yet.[5] Archer's own efforts at agricultural improvement at Lewannick, however, were as extensive as those of any single Cornish land-

[1] *W.B.*: June 15, 1849 and June 21, 1850.
[2] *W.B.*: June 14, 1850 and May 21, 1852.
[3] This may explain the short life a of flax-growing venture initiated in 1850. (*W.B.*: July 4, 1851). Boosted by W. H. Pole Carew and others, flax failed to become a feature of Cornish husbandry, although the propaganda drive supporting it was enough to suggest that it would have superseded cotton to the detriment of Cobden and the "Manchester men". But nature was against it in the soils of Cornwall which were far from deep enough, and it would hardly have made much headway even had corn prices not recovered in 1853 and even had the American Civil War and the Lancashire Cotton Famine occurred ten years earlier. As a "novelty", too, it had to face the formidable competition of rape and mangolds. It would also have demanded the employment of a much greater amount of labour on the farms at a time when every farmer was trying to reduce labour in the few cases where sufficient labour was available.
[4] *W.B.*: January 16, 1852.
[5] *W.B.*: June 8, 1849.

owner of his time. Before 1850 he had reclaimed and brought
over 130 acres of moorland into cultivation; whilst Mechi had
spent £3,400 in buying his farm to start with in 1840, Archer
spent little less than that amount in enclosing, draining, sub-
soil ploughing, removing rocks, erecting buildings, and installing a water mill and a threshing machine.[1] Although Archer
realized the potentialities of this waste land he also realized its
limitations; he was the level-headed practical man who saw
that wastelands could be improved, but instead of entertaining
notions of making the desert blossom as the rose, he was content
if he could raise a plot of cabbages.

The repeal of the Corn Laws did not ruin Cornish farmers,
although many incurred considerable privations and some only
survived through considerable remissions of rents by their
landlords. Many of those rents had been excessively high, and
there was much to be said for Thomas Olver's proposal of a
sliding-scale rental based on the price of corn—if corn was to
be regarded as the staple of Cornish agriculture, and that was a
premise that had never been wholly true and was steadily becoming even less true. Until the collapse in the 'seventies,
however, corn-growing was one of the main features of Cornish
husbandry, and the system of grass leys and green crops, used
to rear live stock, were only stages in rotations designed and
adopted to produce more corn and to produce it more economically. Some farmers started stall-feeding of cattle less to
produce beef more quickly than to conserve farmyard manure
which would reduce their bills for lime, guano, and superphosphates. The cry for protection died away to be replaced by
one for free trade and fair trade all around. Cornish farmers
in 1852 could see no reason why agricultural progress should
be checked by maintaining high prices of guano simply to
benefit the speculators in Peruvian Bonds; indeed some, in
view of the doubtful claim of Peru to the Lobos Islands, voiced
the opinion that a Government which had spent millions to
force the Chinese to buy opium and in acquiring Hong Kong
might, with equal injustice, perhaps, but with more reason,
bestir itself to annex guano sources to the Empire.[2]

Better times returned. An early harvest in Britain and a
temporary dearth on the Continent enabled the British to export

[1]*W.B.*: January 11, 1850.
[2]*W.B.*: June 4, 1852.

I

wheat once more for a month or two in the late summer of 1853. Wool prices soared when the sheep-shearers of Australia rushed off to the gold diggings. With Cornish copper production reaching its zenith in 1856, farmers, facing a scarcity of labour, were forced to make use of mechanical devices wherever practicable. In normal years it became apparent that foreign competition in the English grain market was not so formidable as once anticipated, and that the English farmer could get a good market by harvesting and threshing his crop quickly and selling it before Polish and Ukrainian wheat arrived in the British ports. The majority of Cornish farmers, however, realized by this time that the British Isles could not produce all the grain its people consumed, whilst the south-western county could not, even in the best of seasons, raise grain enough to meet the needs of two-thirds of the Cornish people. The mechanical reaper, improved threshing machines, and the supersession of the massive arrish mow by the seven, eight, or ten sheaf shock all lessened the time-gap between reaping and market. The cool Cornish summers, however, delayed harvesting besides meaning an inferior grain that at best only produced a sixty-pound bushel whereas warmer and dryer climes could produce a seventy-pound bushel of wheat. Some improvement was effected by seed-selection, but late in the 1850s the old type of red wheat was still being sold in the Penzance markets at a price usually two shillings a quarter less than that for "white" wheat. The consequence of all these developments was a growing integration of arable and pastoral husbandry, and by 1880 Cornish farms were carrying nearly twice as many cattle on cultivated lands as the general average for England and Wales; there were eight sheep for every seven elsewhere and three pigs to two, whilst, despite mechanization, the proportion of horses to cultivated acreage was in the ratio of 23 to the 18 of England and Wales; if the total area of the county was reckoned, Cornwall had more than three head of cattle to two in England and Wales, the numbers of its sheep were rather less in proportion, but it had 22 horses to 19 and 7 pigs to 5.[1]

The breed of these animals had been vastly improved.[2]

[1]*Parliamentary Papers*, 1881, Vol. XV, W. Little's Report on Cornwall, pp. 1-2.
[2]John Thomas: "Changes in Agriculture in Cornwall": *Statistical Society Journal*, 1869, pp. 441-445.

The old black cattle were now less than a memory, and, besides the Devon breeds, shorthorns and Jerseys had found a firm footing in the county. John Penhallow Peters had not made a great success of his shorthorns, and after he retired his old farm of Crigmurrion was merged into Polsew by Richard Davey, the son of the former agent of the Consolidated Mines.[1] Tenant farmers like Trethewy of Grampound carried on the work of Peters whilst, as early as 1851, another Cornish cattleman, Kendall of Treverbyn in Probus, was selling short-horns to French purchasers.[2] By 1870 a few Herefords had appeared in the western county.[3] Horses, too, had been improved, though they were judged to be among the more inferior exhibits at the Bath and West Show held at Truro in 1861, where the first steam traction engine to be exhibited at any Bath and West was shown besides no less than five types of mowing machines.[4] The main improvement in sheep was the introduction of Southdowns, the pioneer work being that of the Gilberts of Trelissick who had estates in Sussex. As for pigs they were so vastly improved that Richard Davey, in 1858, reckoned them to be the most profitable feature of his farm at Polsew, even though he had cleared a profit of £124 in thirteen weeks by feeding thirty-two store cattle with fermented turnips and chaff straw.

Although they derided "cranky" experimenters, Cornish farmers in the first half of Victoria's reign were progressive and able to hold their own in the competitive world of free enterprise. When disasters befell them in the late 'seventies, they survived; they had already adapted themselves to a condition of things in which grain was not a staple product but only part of a system of balanced husbandry. At the height of this new great depression in 1880 only one Cornish farmer told the Parliamentary Commissioners investigating agricultural distress that they should return to protection, and he was flatly told by a fellow-farmer that such a solution was madness since the corn they had been able to raise of late was unfit for human consumption.[5] There is no doubt that the majority of Cornish

---

[1]W. F. Karkeek: "Richard Davey, M.P.'s Farm at Polsew in Philleigh": *J.B.W.*, Vol. VIII, pp. 338 ff.
[2]*W.B.*: November 14, 1851.
[3]John Thomas: *Statistical Soc. Journal*, 1869, pp. 441-445.
[4]*J.B.W.*, Vol. X, pp. 2, 19.
[5]*Parliamentary Papers*, 1881, Vol. XVI, p. 426.

farmers were realistic and practical men who knew their work and did it to the best of their ability in times of both prosperity and of adversity. Some of them may have been over-cautious and conservative. Some were probably hard taskmasters to all around them like the Helston farmer who told the Parliamentary Commissioners in 1880 that he did not employ children since he had some of his own,[1] and his neighbour who voiced the complaint that women were "above agricultural work". But if the farmers believed that others should work, few of them were sluggards themselves.

Behind the criticisms levelled by squires like Archer and tenants like Olver against scientific professors and business men who sought to revolutionize farming by the methods of the laboratory and the factory was a deeper psychological trait. They were men of the soil, and they felt that they belonged to it just as the land belonged to them; some of them might rack the land mercilessly if their leases were running out, but not one of them commended such a practice. Sheer economic necessity drove them to use machinery to an ever-increasing extent, but they used those machines in co-operation with Nature whilst the high-farming professors and razor-strop manufacturers were only too patently endeavouring to transform Nature into a machine. To the Cornish farmer the machine was not a master, not even a servant, but only a slave. They might grumble and complain. Many were a little over-slow in adopting new ways, but, living, as so many of them did, on a narrow margin between moderate comfort and straitened circumstances, they were wont to cast a balance before embarking capital on a risk, and many a time they would delay further and make up that balance twice over. Their faith in dark times that better days would dawn carried them through many periods of depression, and they had an inborn ability to make the best of things. They learnt from their own failures and successes and from those of their neighbours; if they could get help from outside they did not spurn it, but if they were absolutely thrown on to their own devices few of them went under. Their self-confidence and self-reliance sprang from the land itself; all else perishes, the earth remains; just as the squires were referred to by the names of their estates—Basset of Tehidy, Molesworth of Pencarrow, Vyvyan of Trelowarren—

[1] *Parliamentary Papers*, 1881, Vol. XVI, pp. 136-142.

so were the tenant farmers invariably referred to by the names of their farms, Peters of Crigmurrion, Olver of Trescow, Tucker of Tregannick, and a host of others; the farm and the man were indissolubly knit together, neither amounting to anything without the other.

RELIGION AND THE PEOPLE AFTER WESLEY

During his later years John Wesley had been increasingly occupied by the cares of ecclesiastical organization rather than by the furtherance of missionary proselytyzing enterprise. The hope, once confidently entertained, of breathing fresh life into the dry bones of the Anglican Church had faded away; Methodism had been driven to virtual secession although Wesley himself would not admit that secession was an accomplished fact. Such an admission would have been an admission of failure by the founder of Methodism. Nevertheless it was obvious to him that the work of the Methodists must go on after he himself passed from the scene of his earthly labours, and that only his followers could be relied upon to carry on that work. The most and nearly the only active section of the Anglican Church was that of the Calvinistic Evangelicals whose doctrines were anathema to Wesley's Arminian faith; the other members of the Establishment seemed even more dead to religion than they had been in 1739. Clergyman and preacher himself it was only natural that John Wesley came to the decision that the only solution lay in entrusting the work to the group of preachers who met in yearly conference, and for that reason he made testamentary provision for the entire methodist organization to be bequeathed to that body on his death. Thereby all power was given to a priesthood; the rank and file of the congregations were apparently ignored; a ministerial oligarchy was given supreme control over the fortunes of Methodism at the time when democratic sentiment in Britain had been stirred into activity by the revolutionary movements in America and in France, a democratic sentiment, moreover, that had its theological counterpart in the Wesleyan doctrine of Justification by Faith.

Even before Wesley died the Methodist congregations in the Redruth district had been uneasy and restive under the control imposed by the ministers sent to them and changed every year by the decision of the annual Conference. Within a few months of Wesley's passing a group of fifty-one Methodist laymen met in Redruth on June 14, 1791, and proceeded to pass resolutions that class leaders should be elected by the majority vote of the members of that class, that no persons should be admitted into or expelled from any Methodist Society without the consent of the majority of the members of that Society, and that the Society Stewards assembled in Quarterly Meeting should elect the Circuit Stewards. These resolutions amounted to a demand for lay control of the local classes and societies, but the Redruth laymen went even further. They demanded that the travelling ministers be nominated by the Circuit Stewards, that the conduct of any minister "charged with not walking worthy of his Vocation, or with being deficient in abilities" be investigated by a committee composed of equal numbers of his fellow ministers and lay stewards, and that, if such charges were proved to the satisfaction of a majority at such a meeting, the preacher in question was forthwith to be expelled from the Circuit. The laity furthermore asked that any new minister coming from a distant place bring with him a certificate of good conduct signed by the stewards of his former circuit, and that lay preachers have an equal voice with the ministers of Conference in practically every question that arose and came under discussion.[1] There is little doubt that these resolutions of the Redruth meeting came as a rude shock to the "priesthood of Conference", when that body next met, nor was it surprising that that body, perhaps a little over-conscious of its own importance and dignity no longer dwarfed by the commanding presence of John Wesley, dismissed them. It was the first of many clashes in Methodism of insurgent democratic groups that believed the Church was made for men not men for the Church and a priestly caste that held fast to a diametrically opposite view.

Conference, controlling Methodist publicity, was in a position to suppress a great deal of the evidence of discontent and unrest among local congregations, whilst its own bickerings and quarrels overshadowed what was going on in the lower levels of the Methodist organization. Of the individual Redruth "rebels" but little is known. Chief among them were the local preacher and pampleteer Richard Williams and the surgeon Dr. William Boase.

[1] The full text of the Redruth "Manifesto" was printed by the Camborne historian of Methodism, George Smith, in his *History of Wesleyan Methodism*, Vol. II. p. 702.

The latter was a personal convert of John Wesley, and had been dissuaded by the founder of Methodism from his early ambition of entering the Church and, instead, had taken up the medical profession. Boase, however, seems to have always entertained regrets of abandoning his first-intended career, and that may in part account for his prominence at this meeting and for his later establishing a separatist chapel of his own in Redruth. Four of the other laymen were prominent in the mining industry; John Budge was one of the best-known Cornish engineers of the day; Richard Trevithick, senior, was captain of the great Dolcoath mine; Paul Penrose was captain of Polgooth; John Martyn was the confidential clerk of the merchant and great mine adventurer Thomas Daniell of Truro and was the father of the later famous missionary, Henry Martyn. Six others, John Vivian, James Sems, Stephen Harvey, William Jeffree, James Matthews, and Nicholas Rodda were in all likelihood mine captains or engineers. The two Carvosa brothers were prominent in West Cornwall Methodism; William was at this time farming at Ponsanooth near Penryn where he had built a meeting house, whilst Benedict had remained at Mousehole, where he was probably living by fishing as may have also been the case of Charles Slade of St.Ives.[2] The demand for greater lay control over the affairs of Cornish Methodism came from the lower professional classes who had joined the movement, men with no little responsibility in their daily work in connection with the mines, with farming and fishing, and with trade.

Although Conference rejected the demands of the laity yet, for the next few years, the men it sent as "travelling preachers" into Cornwall walked with circumspection. The Kilhamite secession had no immediate result in the western county, although Theophilus Lessey the elder, father of a man destined to be President of Conference, who had spent some years in Cornish circuits, on one occasion wrote to Alexander Kilham to find out whether or not Kilham was likely to carry the majority of Conference with him, thereby arousing the suspicions of the young rebel that he only wanted to make sure that he would be on the winning side in a dispute that threatened to split the Methodist organization in twain.[3] Methodism continued to make converts,

[2]George Smith: *History of Wesleyan Methodism*, Vol II, p.702. G.C.Boase and W.P.Courtney: *Bibliotheca Cornubiensis*. G.C.Boase: *Collectanea Cornubiensia*. Lawrence Maker: *Cob and Moorstone*, p. 81.
[3]*Life of Mr.Alexander Kilham* (1799) p. 197.

although there were some backsliders; several able Cornishmen became travelling preachers, including Richard Treffry of Tregony, another future President of Conference in 1792, and his neighbour, Francis Truscott a few years earlier. The struggle in Conference between the more "democratic" followers of Alexander Kilham and the other ministers, especially those who had some design of effecting a reconciliation with Anglicanism that might lead to their promotion to episcopal dignity, possibly had some little bearing on the decline of the numbers of Methodist Society members in Cornwall from 4,230 in 1792 to 3,457 in 1793, but two years later the loss had been more than regained, and by 1798 there were 6,227 members joined in Society in the western county.[4] There is little doubt that the miseries of earthly poverty and privation, and the contrasting promise of a blissful after-life, brought no inconsiderable numbers into the Methodist fold during the years of economic distress that coincided with the outbreak of war against Revolutionary France, and had no little to do with the success of the Great Revival of 1799 which sent the numbers of Cornish Methodists to a temporary peak level of well above ten thousand.

By that time the "High Church" party in Conference had been defeated, a defeat which meant that the breach between Methodism and the Established Church was irreparable. The Revival of 1799, therefore, led to renewed controversy between the adherents of Anglicanism and those of Methodism in Cornwall. The Rev. Richard Polwhele of Manaccan, a man of no mean repute as an antiquarian and of little less as a poet, rashly published, under the imprint of the Anti-Jacobin Press, a collection of *Anecdotes of Methodism*, in which he had gathered together all the gossip and slander he could find about the conduct—or rather misconduct —of particular individual Methodists.[5] It was not long before a Methodist reply was forthcoming, an analytical answer from the pen of Samuel Drew shoemaker, local preacher, and amateur metaphysician of St. Austell.[6] Drew reached the conclusion that:-

"out of about thirty-four anecdotes (related by Polwhele), eight are false, of six I can get no account, nine are misrepresented, five are related with

[4]*Minutes of Conference*, Vol.I, pp. 259, 277, 416.
[5]Rev. R. Polwhele: *Anecdotes of Methodism (to which is added a Sermon on Conduct that Becomes a Clergyman)*.
[6]S. Drew: *Observations (in behalf of the Methodists) on a pamplet . . . by Rev. R. Polwhele . . . entitled Anecdotes of Methodism*: July 2, 1800.

the omission of many material circumstances; all the remainder are (here) revised and corrected."[7]

The strongest point made by Samuel Drew was that the cases of a few miscreants did not condemn the whole membership of the Methodist Societies. He made much of the fact that it was extremely difficult to secure a copy of the Vicar of Manaccan's pamplet in Cornwall; he poured scorn on the way in which Polwhele had admitted that the Methodists were seriously religious but at the same time inconsistently had asserted that they were neither truly nor sincerely religious. Polwhele's creed was denounced as a "compound of deism and contradictions, erected in the suburbs of infidelity",[8] and whereas he had nowhere ventured to question the consistency of Methodist doctrines with the word of God, he, the Vicar, was, perhaps, in the gravest danger of falling into the "Popish" error of denying individual responsibility before God.

Polwhele, whose passion for publication almost amounted to a mania, had been more than over-hasty in publishing stories of "levellers, rogues, debauchers, fornicators, adulterers, robbers, seducers, false prophets"[9] without adequate supporting evidence to back his charges. It cannot be denied that he did not scruple to suppress relevant facts; many of the culprits, whose exploits he related with a zest ill-fitting a minister of the Church, had either no connection at all with the Methodists or had already been expelled from the Methodist Societies for past delinquencies. Had Drew or any other Methodist chosen they could have countered with a collection of tales about Anglican clergy and laity that would have thrown the peccadilloes of Polwhele's alleged Methodists into the colourless shade. Apart from salacious gossip, however, Polwhele did advance some general criticism of the Methodists. He was inclined to follow in the steps of Bishop George Lavington with a general condemnation of the followers of Wesley as a "fraternity compounded of hypocrites and enthusiasts";[10] he strongly condemned a tendency to blind spiritual pride and arrogance born of the assurance of salvation through conversion; in doing so, perhaps, he was overmuch concerned lest converts began calling into

[7]Drew: *Observations*, pp. 69-70.
[8]Drew: *Observations*, p. 34.
[9]*Ibid:* p. 12.
[10]Polwhele: *Anecdotes of Methodism*, p. 7.

question their lower social status in this world, rather than with the less pleasing individual traits it engendered. The main charge he brought against the Methodists was the old one of "enthusiasm", reaffirming the old decorous belief of the conventional eighteenth century that religious zeal had something disgustingly unseemly inherent in it. But it was no longer the Methodists who were being denounced for "Popish" leanings; that particular charge was now being levied against the Anglican clergy.

Three of the anecdotes related by Polwhele were rather inadequately refuted by Samuel Drew. Polwhele was wrong when he accused the Penryn Methodists of "loudly acclaiming" the public attack of a Quaker on the sacrament of Baptism; Drew pointed out that the Quaker had not attacked Baptism, but had stressed the "true baptism of the Holy Ghost";[11] neither, however, made any attempt to grapple with a theological point that was in the future to cause serious controversy and divergences in the Anglican Church itself, and was to be the cause of the clash of the Rev. C.G. Gorham of St. Just in Penwith and Bishop Henry Phillpotts of Exeter that had such disastrous consequences. Samuel Drew failed to meet the charge that certain Camborne Methodists had participated in recent food riots in that place; he admitted that they had been forced to join the rioters "through necessity", but he claimed that they had curbed mob- violence and looting.[12] He failed even more significantly to deal with Polwhele's anecdote that certain Methodists had tried to put a stop to the parish feast at Sithney, and that, when they had been driven from the scene by force they had brought actions for assault against the men who had resisted their interference with popular revels.[13] The last two incidents, however, provide evidence that Methodism was exerting a claim to lead and dominate social life and morality. If they had turned hungry miners into orderly demonstrators it revealed that popular leadership had fallen into their hands. The attempt to suppress a parish revel revealed a tendency on the part of the Methodists to change from proselytyzing to persecution, an

---

[11]Polwhele: *Anecdotes*, pp 9-10: Drew; *Observations* p. 42.

[12]Polwhele: *Anecdotes*, pp. 30-32: Drew: *observations* p. 54.

[13]Polwhele: Anecdotes, pp. 28-9: Drew: *Observations*, pp 53-4. The early antagonism of the Methodists to popular revels is revealed by Richard Treffry's *Diary*; in July, 1802, he visited St. Columb Major on "a day of dissipation; thousands of people were got together for the games; wrestling and ringing bells were the chief pursuit; in the evening I got a handful of People together and preached from Luke 12: 32 (*Mss Diary.* July 19, 1802)

intolerance of the sentiments and feelings and pleasures of others that grew more and more pronounced with the passing of the years. Methodism had become strong enough to challenge the spirit of toleration that had become well-nigh a fetish since the days of John Locke, although Samuel Drew could see no inconsistency on his part when he, in reply to Polwhele, stressed the growth of toleration at considerable length.[14]

The scenes of enthusiasm associated with religious revivals and the cruder manifestations of religious emotion, however, repelled many of the more sober and sedate Methodists, who deemed such to be in flagrant contradiction to the original idea of a seemly and ordered life implied in the very name of their connexion. Secular authorities may not have been displeased that the Methodist preachers and leaders had diverted mass emotions into religious channels in 1799, but, within a few years, the Methodists began to wonder if the revival had been the great blessing they had hailed at the time. Converts began to backslide at an alarming rate to the discredit of Methodism; by 1804 the numerical gains had been lost, with but 6,148 members in society as against 6,227 in 1798.[15] From that time onwards the more prudent and thoughtful Methodist preachers began to rely on sober reasoning rather than emotional appeals to gain converts, but ever and anon they were forced by the more zealous spirits to have recourse to revivalism in self-defence. Over this issue the great schisms in Methodism were to develop; in Cornwall William O'Bryan and in Staffordshire Hugh Bourne and William Clowes were to come forward as the protagonists of revivalism; O'Bryan was finally to be driven out to found the Bible Christian Connexion just as, a few years earlier, the Staffordshire "rebels" had established the Primitive Methodists. Sectarianism was the inevitable consequence of the divergent attitudes of mind of the revivalist preacher on the one side and the church organizer on the other; John Wesley had combined the qualities and abilities of both, but he was nearly unique in this, and hardly any succeeding President of Conference had the twofold gifts. The very growth in the numbers of the Methodists accentuated the tendency on the part of Conference and the ministers to devote more and more attention to the problems of ecclesiastical organization than to the promotion and propagation

[14]Drew: Observations p. 26.
[15]*Minutes of Conference*, Vol. I. p. 424, Vol. II. p. 233.

of religious faith. It was a dilemma that every religious group has had to meet in its history—if indeed it has survived long enough to have a history—and it can be truly said that Wesleyan Methodism met it with less ill-success than some others.

It was not surprising that the first schism in Cornish Methodism took place in Redruth; what was really surprising was that it did not occur earlier. At the Conference of 1802 Thomas Kelk was appointed Superintendent Preacher in that circuit and chairman of the Cornwall District, then composed of the five circuits of Redruth, Truro, St. Austell, Penzance, and Helston, with seventeen "travelling preachers" besides Kelk himself. Within four months of Kelk's appointment the numbers of members joined in society at Redruth had dropped from over five hundred to less than two hundred,[16] the secessionists for the most part following Dr. William Boase who, before long had set up a chapel of his own.[17] Boase had long been a discordant element in the circles of Redruth Methodism; he was a man of no uncommon ability, having assisted William Murdoch in early experiments in gas-lighting besides his professional duties, whilst his over-zealous concern in Methodist organization had made him prominent among those who questioned the authority of the ministers appointed by Conference in 1791. Kelk, for his part, was autocratic and tactless, and refused to renew the tickets of membership to society of Boase and his supporters, and, not content with this act of "excommunication", went on to declare that any member of society who met any of the men whom he had thus excluded from membership in any religious class meeting would themselves be expelled. At a meeting of sixteen of the eighteen ministers of the Cornwall district, held on June 7, 1803, Kelk was removed from the chairmanship of the district, his place being taken by William Shelmerdine, the superintendant of the Penzance circuit.[18] This step came too late to prevent schism, but it may have checked any further great increase in the number of secessionists.

[16] R. Treffry: *MSS Diary*, December 28, 1802.
[17] *Arminian Magazine*, 1823, p. 79 footnote. The revolt at Redruth may have been precipitated by the refusal of Richard Treffry and the other ministers to allow the circulation of a tract certain members of the Society had caused to be printed; the tract dealt with the conversion of a Nottingham woman in the condemned cell awaiting execution for the murder of her child; it was the crude type of religious propaganda deplored by those who held dear the ideal of religious respectability, quite apart from any theological controversy it might well occasion. (R. Treffry: *Diary*, April 30, 1802).
[18] R. Treffry: *Diary*, June 7, 1803. Kelk remained in Cornish Circuits until 1809.

The attack of Polwhele on the Methodists was typical of a new antagonism of the Anglican clergy to the Methodists that arose at the turn of the century. Even when Wesley had taken the revolutionary step of ordaining his own followers as priests he had not lost hope of the eventual incorporation of the Methodists into the Established Church; in homely Biblical phrase he regarded his organization as the leaven that would in the end transform the establishment. A few of the more prominent Methodists after his death had looked to a reunion that might well bring them prelatical honours. It was not to be. The more active "reformers" in the Anglican Church were Calvinists who looked on Wesleyan Arminianism as heresy. Then had come the attack of the French revolutionaries not only on an established church but on Christianity itself; the established order in England forthwith closed its ranks against any attempt of change or reform. The persecution of fifty years before was not renewed in such an openly violent form, but in many places in Cornwall Anglican clergymen set their face hard against the Methodists. In Lewannick the vicar, Mangles, brought all possible pressure to bear against any who afforded facilities for Wesleyan preaching; a shoemaker who had offered to allow his cottage to be used as a meeting-place withdrew the offer when the vicar threatened to withdraw his custom—and possibly induce his congregation to do likewise; a widow who then allowed the Methodists to meet in a room in her house was evicted; the offer of a dilapidated farm cottage was withdrawn when the farmer who made it was threatened with tithe prosecutions; finally in 1810 John Nanscawen Dawe gave the Methodists a freehold site at Trevadlock Cross, Mangles dying before he could put a threat of exacting inconvenient tithes in kind from Dawe into execution.[19] Another persecuting parson was Lindivan of Sithney, who, perhaps, thought that he would gain popular support from the people who had forcibly resisted the attempt of the Methodists to put an end to the annual parish feast; in 1802 he haled the local preacher Giles Paul and one of the Gundrys before a meeting of the justices, the former for preaching without a license, the latter for omitting to license his house for preaching services; in consequence Gundry promised the justices that he would not let his house for such a purpose again whilst Paul promised that he would not preach in

[19]Lawrence Maker: *Cob and Moorstone*, pp. 59ff.

that place any more.[20] The attitude of some of the Anglican clergy who refused burial services to "irregularly" baptized children, however, did more to alienate the common people from the Established Church than the disputes over preaching places; when Methodists were no longer buried in the same "God's Acre" as Anglicans the sectarian breach had transcended the boundaries of this world.[21]

Polwhele's slanderous attacks were imitated by others, but the Methodists did all in their power to check, punish, and expel those persons whose conduct unloosed the malicious tongue of gossip and scandal. The Conference of 1802 expelled one preacher for courting two women and promising marriage to both; another, for a similar offence, was suspended for a year; a third was suspended for a year for drunkenness and swearing.[22] Every attempt was made to reconcile disputes and quarrels among the members of the societies,[23] whilst the local superintendants and ministers kept a sharp eye upon the conduct of members of the societies, reproving some for actions that might be prejudicial to the good name of the Methodists, and summarily expelling those guilty of more heinous offences.[24] The Methodists, moreover, did not hesitate to censure and condemn the shortcomings and failings of their Anglican rivals, and intolerance of this nature intensified with the passage of time.

The discipline imposed by the ministers and their insistence on strictly abiding by a rigid conventional code of morality in all probability aggravated the antagonism of the laity against the "priestly pretensions" of the preachers appointed by Conference.

[20]R. Treffry: *Diary*, February 3, 1802. A reference in the same diary, dated March 11, 1802, suggests that it was Captain John ("Jack") Gundry, the man later responsible for the restarting of Wheal Vor Mine, who had allowed the preachers to hold services in his house; if this was the case it provides further evidence of the support Methodism was gaining from the more prominent and richer men associated with the mining industry.

[21]R. Treffry: *Diary*, November 29, 1803—"Buried for the first time in our Chapel Yard (at Camelford) a child belonging to R. Bosanhoe. Mr. Robins baptised one of his children, and the Priest would not bury, in consequence of which our chapel yard was appropriated to the purpose." The particular "Priest" might have been in a position to argue that the child had lived long enough to have been regularly baptized, since Joseph Robbins, the former superintendant of the St. Austell circuit, from which Camelford had been separated by the 1803 Conference, had left the district nearly three months ago.

[22]R. Treffry: *Diary*, July 25, 1802.

[23]*Ibid*. May 3, 1802; May 14, 1802.

[24]The following entries in Richard Treffry's *Diary* illustrate the powers of excommunication assumed by the ministers. "Excluded two from the Society (at Prospidnick) for being fruitfully intimate without a priestly sanction". "had to erase the names of two persons from the Society (at Tintagel) for quarrelling." (R. Treffry: *Diary*, Feb. 24, 1802 and Feb. 2, 1804)

In February, 1802, the chairman of the Cornwall District, William Shelmerdine was:-

"in a Strait not knowing whether to admit delegates from the People to the District Meeting to be present all the time or not; by admitting them to all the business he thinks he shall merit the censure of Conference and by not admitting them the Censure of the People."[25]

A little later, at a stormy District Meeting in Truro, the preachers spent some time discussing the propriety of recommending to Conference the admission of a certain man as a probationary preacher; they then allowed the laity to come in, and there followed a revolt against the decisions the ministers had reached "relative to the adjustment of certain affairs of a temporal nature."[26] Further disputes arose at the same meeting over the rejection of a request by the leaders, stewards, and trustees of St. Agnes for admission to the Redruth Circuit. On the second day of the meeting, however, the laymen and ministers reached a compromise arrangement. The agreement of the laymen that no Steward was to be eligible to participate in a District Meeting for more than two successive years over a period of nine years precluded the formation of a group of laity whose long terms as members of such meetings would, of necessity, place them in a stronger position than the travelling preachers who were moved from circuit to circuit every one or two years.[27] The ministers, in return, promised that:-

"there be no privileged order of men in our Connexion as Clerks of the Conference, Stewards of Conference, etc., who are in from year to year without being chosen legally . . ."

At this meeting there was a further dispute that might well have excited more alarm among the ministers. The Penzance laymen declared that if one of the ministers stationed in their circuit claimed an extra allowance for his wife, and that if two of the other ministers

---

[25]R. Treffry: *Diary*, February 19, 1802.

[26]R. Treffry: *Diary*, May 18 and 19, 1802.

[27]This might seem to be rather more to the advantage of the preachers than at first appears; although they were rarely in one circuit for more than two years, they often stayed in the same district for six years or even longer; Richard Treffry was stationed in the Cornwall District from 1796 to 1803 when he went to Camelford in the Plymouth Dock District; Thomas Kelk remained in Cornwall from 1802 to 1808; nine of the eighteen preachers of 1802 were left in Cornwall in 1803, and all nine were still there in 1804, though two of them were now retired supernumeries, whilst no less than five of the men of 1802 were still in or had returned to the Cornwall District in 1808. (*Minutes of Conference* Vol. II, pp. 125, 170, 223, and Vol. III, p. 7.

claimed allowances for servants, they would not allow any money at all for the wife of another married minister. It was one of the earliest attempts on the part of Methodist laymen to use the power of the purse and to control the funds they contributed to the Connexion; the ministers might well have been warned that in further crises and disputes the laity would not hesitate to withhold the funds on which they depended for their livehihood. Somewhat later another clash occurred when the society members at Caneggy declared that if they were not allowed to have preaching services on Sunday mornings they would have none at all.[28]

Relations between the laymen and the preachers had thus become rather strained; there is no doubt that many of the latter had become somewhat arrogant in their ministerial pretensions, whereas the people were ready to assert that the Methodist ministry had been created to serve them and that they were not in this world simply to benefit a priestly caste. The ministers, moreover, had come to lay as much stress on outward seemliness and decorum as the most conservative Anglican clergy, and were neglecting the "harvest of souls". Laymen craved for the emotional excitement of revival meetings; they had no interest in the bickerings of the preachers in Conference over original sin and other even more obscure and abstract theological doctrines; many of the more learned preachers had less appeal to the common people than the local preachers who lived among them and worked alongside them during the week. There was a genuine fear that the Methodist movement was falling into the moribund condition of the Anglican Church. Some of the ministers were alleged to have entered their profession not from religious zeal but merely to gain a position in this world.[29] Even the most zealous of the preachers failed to bear any comparison with the memory of the greatness of John Wesley and with the legend that men had created around that memory. Years had passed by and many Methodists had grown old in their faith and, like the old of all generations, looked back with nostalgic regret to the "good old days."

[28]R. Treffry: *Diary*, May 21 and June 20, 1802. It is likely that this demand meant that the Caneggy Methodists wanted to hold their services at the same time as those of the Established Church, and not at different times which had been a widespread custom adopted to enable persons to attend both; if so it is further evidence of the growing breach between Anglicanism and Wesleyanism.

[29]Rev. R. Polwhele: Introduction to Bishop Lavington's *Enthusiasm of Methodists and Papists*, (1833 p. ci.)

Wesley the revivalist preacher and the scenes of triumphant religious emotionalism attending his crowded services were remembered. The way in which he had organized the Societies, ruled them, and in no few instances tyrannized over them was forgotten. Conference, his heir, seemed to have sacrificed the great patrimony for organization and for arid theological controversy. Redoubled stress on the old Methodist ideal, that from which it derived its very name, the ideal of moral decorum, conventionality, and restraint, did not find favour in a progressive age that was becoming increasingly impatient or any form of restraint. Just as the impatiently restless Cornish engineers had thrown off the cautious principles of Watt's low- pressure engines so now did the Cornish Methodists press forward to make the utmost of the religious zeal that could be kindled by the fearful and little-understood power of human emotionalism. John Wesley had now and again appealed to popular sentiments and had played on the emotions of his congregations, but he did not venture so far as many of the later Cornish preachers; especially did caution increase with Wesley as he grew old. Richard Treffry was ready to go a little further and William O'Bryan much further, but it might be argued that the farming antecedents of both these men made them more cautious than the dynamically explosive miner, Billy Bray, a personality who remained fast in the memories of common men and women who had forgotten Treffry, but half-remembered O'Bryan, and regarded the longer dead-and- gone Wesley much as they did the ancient Celtic patron saints of the parishes in which they lived.[30]

Richard Treffry, the son of a Cuby farmer, was admitted by the Conference of 1792 as a probationary itinerant preacher, he being then twenty-one years of age. After four years in Glamorgan, Taunton, Canterbury, and Rochester he returned to Cornwall; in the following nine years he served in various Cornish circuits,[31] before going to Haverfordwest in 1806; he came back to Cornwall for a further eight years in 1813 being stationed successively at Penzance, Redruth, Falmouth, and Truro before going back to

---

[30]Hills Chapel, on the upper reaches of the Looe River in the parish of St. Cleer, now a farm outbuilding, is still spoken of as the place where Billy Bray once preached; about two miles away Trenant Chapel, one of the earliest meeting places of the Bible Christians, is rarely if ever now associated with O'Bryan; somewhere between the two the site where John Wesley first preached in St. Cleer, at Redgate, is entirely forgotten.

[31]The last two years were at Camelford then in the Plymouth District.

Rochester in 1822; later he served in the populous circuits of Hull, Southwark, Leeds, and Bristol, and in 1833 was elected President of Conference. Early during his second period in his native county he came into prominence by a forthright defence of revivalism which he published in the early summer of 1814. The controversy was the outcome of the Cornish revival of 1813, and had been provoked by the Penzance curate, the Rev. Charles Val le Grice. A few years before the more orthodox Methodists had been inclined to suspect the efficacy of evangelical revivalism on account of the reaction that had followed the revival of 1799, but they were forced to resort to the more unorthodox methods of emotional appeal that John Wesley had employed by the actual secession of the Primitive Methodists in the Midlands in 1810 and by the unrest among many of the Cornish local preachers and class leaders. Aided by the economic depression and general distress, that were so widespread in Cornwall in 1812 and the closing years of the French Wars, the revival of 1813 sent the numbers of society members in Cornwall up from about 10,000 in 1813 to over 16,000 in 1814.[32]

Le Grice attacked the revival and the Methodist revivalists in a sermon in the church at Penzance in April, 1814, which was almost immediately published.[33] Although he did little more than reiterate some of the former arguments and more of the former allegations of Richard Polwhele and Bishop Lavington, the situation had now changed, since by 1814 hardly a doubt or hope survived that the Methodists would re-unite with the Established Church. Before this time the Methodists had made little positive defence against the allegations of "enthusiasm" levelled against them by their opponents, but within two months of Le Grice's sermon, Richard Treffry boldly acclaimed enthusiasm as a positive religious good.[34] Lavington, Polwhele, and now Le Grice were exponents of the eighteenth century belief—if, indeed, it could be described by so strong and positive a word—in rational religion; Richard Treffry asserted that "reason is not a rule to prove the total of our faith",[35] and struck even harder at the rationalists with an

[32] *Minutes of Conference:* Vol. III. p. 302, Vol. IV. p. 27.

[33] Rev. C. V. le Grice: *Proofs of the Spirit or Considerations on Revivalism.*

[34] R. Treffry: *Letter to the Rev. C. Val le Grice occasioned by his Sermon entitled Proofs of the Spirit or Considerations on Revivalism,* Second Edition, June 18, 1814. (henceforth cited as R. Treffry: *Letter.*)

[35] R. Treffry: *Letter,* p. 20.

out-and-out declaration that the age of miracles had ceased.[36] The late watch-night services of the Methodists were justified by the example of St. Paul;[37] from Scripture Treffry drew the examples of David, of Christ, and of the Apostles to justify—not merely defend—the violent and passionate utterances of Methodists in their prayers;[38] in conclusion he quoted Paley's remark that "the mildest opinion that ever was entertained in matters of religion, is more rational than unconcern about these matters."[39] Richard Treffry failed entirely to meet Le Grice's telling remark that the Methodists tortured the soul with the terrors of hell just as papal inquisitors tortured the body, but he did not hesitate to charge the Penzance curate of holding "Popish doctrines",[40] and asserted that:-

"Clouds of Sermons, Essays, and Pamplets have arisen like noxious vapours, to darken the moral atmosphere of the country, while Methodism, like the sun in the firmament, has held on its course, burst through the gloom, and illuminated the minds of millions."[41]

Even before Richard Treffry published his answer to Le Grice his fellow Methodist minister, John Riles, at Truro had replied to the attack on the Methodist "Enthusiasts" by asking why men should not be fanatical in the holy life, in the cause of truth, and in their faith, asserting that lukewarmness and indifferency were far worse evils than passionate evangelical emotionalism.[42] Treffry, however, in a rather over-strained effort to be absolutely fair to the man he was attacking, trod on perilous ground, writing, in an opening paragraph:-

"That you, Sir, as a man, and a minister, possess an indisputable right to publish to the world your sentiments on Religion, is a truth which none will attempt to controvert; but as Religion is not the exclusive property of any individual; as its doctrines lie open to all; as every individual is accountable to God for his Religion; so every man has an inalienable

[36]R. Treffry: *Letter*, p. 15. Denial that there had ever been an Age of Miracles was to be the work of the so-called "Higher Criticism" of a later generation.
[37]R. Treffry: *Letter*, p. 32.
[38]R. Treffry: *Letter*, pp. 31-32.
[39]R. Treffry: *Letter*, p. 42.
[40]R. Treffry: *Letter*, pp. 12-13.
[41]R. Treffry: *Letter*, p. 6.
[42]John Riles: *Account of the Revival* (published at Truro, May 28, 1814) pp. iii, 17. Le Grice's sermon had been preached on April 24, 1814.

right to controvert the religious sentiments of another; and this is the only plea I offer for obtruding myself on your notice."[43]

Thus unwarily and unwittingly Richard Treffry, a minister of some twenty years standing or more, virtually admitted the doctrine of the priesthood of all believers. He had assailed the Established Church; he had publicly accused one of its most learned and able clergymen in Cornwall of "Popish" leanings; but he had also given ministerial authority to a belief that could lead to schisms within Methodism itself—and that at the very time when William O'Bryan had already collided once with the "Conference men" and seemed like to do again in the very near future.

Like Treffry, William O'Bryan came of a farming family, but his father and grandfather had also engaged in tin-mining speculations as active adventurers besides being owners of various sets of tin bounds.[44] He was born at Gunwen in the parish of Luxulyan in February, 1778. His parents were devout Methodists, particularly his mother, Thomasine Bryan, nee Lowry, the granddaughter of a Quaker, John Grose. It is possible that the influence of Quaker ancestry on the character and beliefs of William O'Bryan has been over-estimated by some of his biographers; it was most significant in that it had created a family tradition of religious dissent; other Methodists had become such out of simple disappointment with the Established Church into which they had been born; the Bryan family in time past had inhabited a different spiritual home. Other alleged Quaker legacies inherited by O'Bryan can be explained away. The Quaker doctrine or belief in the inner light was but a facet of a more intense religious individualism. Methodist pre-occupation with the conversion and salvation of the individual soul inevitably led to some idea of an alternative to the sacrament of baptism as the mark of admission into the community of a church without there having been any direct connection with the Quaker idea of the true baptism of the Holy Spirit. Above all, there is no need to seek Quaker origins for attacks on ritualistic ceremonialism in the early nineteenth century, an attack already pushed by the rationalists of the previous century so far that there were already

[43]R. Treffry: *Letter*, pp. 5-6.
[44]S. L. Thorne: *William O'Bryan—Founder of the Bible Christians*, pp. 9ff. The family name was Bryan, the preacher himself changing his name to O'Bryan, claiming descent from an ancient Irish noble family, a strange foible, perhaps, but one which bears a parallel to the genealogical mania of a later sect, the Latter Day Saints.

appearing signs of reaction against it. William O'Bryan, however, was profoundly influenced by his early upbringing in a strict and puritanical household in which the Sabbath was rigidly observed, and by living in a house that was frequently visited by itinerant ministers and local preachers paying friendly calls on their way to and from the widely scattered chapels in which they were "planned" to hold services. The worldly circumstances of the Bryan family were comfortable, even well-to-do, for William Bryan the elder occupied three or four farms, running one himself and letting the others to tenants or sub-tenants. Receiving a moderately good education locally and at Fowey, O'Bryan was temporarily apprenticed to a St. Austell draper, but returned to the farm, and at the age of twenty-one was churchwarden at Luxulyan, an indication of the prominent status of his family in the parish and of his own abilities.

Until that time the relationships of the Anglicans and the Methodists in the Luxulyan district were good. The clerical family of Cole was rather too preoccupied with hunting and card-playing, with wine and women, to pay much heed to religious controversies. So long as the parishioners paid their tithes they did not see the point of interfering with them overmuch. One of their curates had been struck by the abilities of the young William O'Bryan and suggested to his father that he should study with a view of taking Orders, obviously convinced that the youth had the talents and his family sufficient social standing and wealth to make such a career possible. It is even possible that this particular curate saw the danger of allowing O'Bryan to persist along the individualist lines he had already shown by his rather unorthodox exhortations to Methodist preachers and class-leaders to preach and live the religious life more zealously; if he could be induced to study for the Church the discipline of Holy Orders would eventually check revolutionary tendencies.

As Churchwarden O'Bryan made an effort to amend the lax ways of the easy-going Anglicans by altering the times of the vestry meetings to a day in the week; he set his face against the old custom of holding them after the Sunday service in the convivial atmosphere of the public house across the road from the churchyard gate.[45] For some time, however, he was diffident about becoming

---

[45] This is one of the earliest indications of the temperance movement among the "people called Methodists".

a preacher himself, since he held an exaltedly high ideal of that profession, one which but few preachers, either Anglican or Methodist, attained. It was not until 1801 that he started revivalist preaching in the Luxulyan district, although it is rather uncertain whether he had been regularly admitted to the ranks of the Methodist local preachers at that time. Indeed, it seems that from the first he laboured independently although in close association with his Methodist friends; in 1809 the itinerant preacher Joseph Womersley thought so highly of O'Bryan that he entrusted him with his own preaching engagements while he attended the Methodist Conference in Yorkshire. Such an engagement as locum tenens, however, only lasted a few weeks; there was another Conference minister in the Bodmin Circuit at the time; Womersley, too, may have thought it all to the good to tie O'Bryan down to fixed "planned" preaching engagements. Then, with no warning, at Christmas, 1809, O'Bryan started an independent itinerant mission of his own in North Cornwall where he reckoned that the regular Methodist preachers had failed in their work. His own zeal and his rather too-outspoken criticism of the lack of zeal of others, together with his refusal to confine himself to the engagements allotted to him on the local preachers plan of the Bodmin circuit led to his public expulsion from the Methodists in November, 1810.[46]

He would not be silenced by the "Conference men"; it was galling to his pride to be expelled from the Methodists in the very chapel he had built for their use and made over to them hard by his home at Gunwen. His neighbours and friends were more than critical of the hasty action of the new superintendant, James Evans, and the majority of them thereafter neglected the chapel to attend meetings O'Bryan held in his own house.[47] In the autumn of the

[46]The first expulsion of O'Bryan from the Methodists occurred shortly after that of the Primitive Methodist leaders, Hugh Bourne and William Clowes. Bourne had been expelled in June, 1808 and Clowes in June 1810; neither of them had preached much before 1805. (John Petty: *History of the Primitive Methodist Connexion*, pp. 3-33.)

[47]Accounts of O'Bryan's reaction to his first expulsion from the Methodists differ. S. L. Thorne states that he carried on his itinerant work and that most of his converts followed him (*W. O.Bryan: Founder of the Bible Christians*, pp. 90-91) but it is certain that he did not make any immediate effort to resume his labours among the various groups of converts he had made in the Newquay district. Evans, too, unlike Kelk at Redruth eight years before, apparently did not withdraw tickets of membership from any who continued to "meet" with O'Bryan. Membership of the Methodist Societies in Bodmin Circuit did not drop in consequence of his expulsion, although the increase of members from 562 in 1810 to 637 in 1811 was wiped out by 1813. (*Minutes of Conference*, Vol. III, pp. 152, 214, 312.

following year he made another itinerant revivalist tour, this time to the villages and hamlets on the fringe of Bodmin moor, visiting Cardinham, Warleggan, Draynes in St. Neot, and going as far as Kingsand on the south-east coast. This journey and his earlier work in the Newquay region shows that O'Bryan was devoting his attention to a class of people the older Methodists had rather neglected—to farmers and their labourers in the less thickly populated districts where mining was not carried on at all or only on a small scale and then, principally, by tin- streamers working individually or in small groups. O'Bryan was evangelizing the fiercely independent yeomen farmers and their dependents, and the diminishing number of "free miners" who still survived on the bleak wastelands of Bodmin Moor, men who resented any outside interference or control, whether it came from "foreign" capitalist or conference-appointed Methodist preacher.

O'Bryan had a passion for the salvation of souls, yet for the time he felt himself unequal to the task of working alone; it is more than likely that a proudly-remembered boyhood meeting with John Wesley, when the founder of Methodism had pronounced a blessing on him, made him regret his exclusion from the fold. He was persuaded by the minister, A. J. Odgers, to a reconciliation with the Wesleyans, and he made over to them the new societies and meeting houses he had founded.[48] Yet it still proved impossible to curb him; he was too independent to accept quietly the fettering rules that Wesley and his successors had devised to organize their Connexion. He continued and extended his individual missions to north-east Cornwall and visited the western part of the county in 1815; when he returned to his new home at St. Blazey it was to find that John Woodrow, superintendant of the St. Austell circuit had withheld his ticket of membership of the St. Blazey society. Thenceforward O'Bryan refused to have anything further to do with "official" Methodism, and forthwith went on another preaching tour in north Cornwall and in north-western Devon, a district in which Methodism had previously made very little progress. Around him gathered converts and Methodist mal-contents. The group left leaderless at Redruth through the death of Dr. William Boase, in 1813, formed the nucleus of a western "Bryanite circuit". The appearance of women preachers among his active adherents drew many. He and those who joined him

[48]S. L. Thorne: *William O'Bryan* pp. 90ff.

were preaching a religion based solely on the word of the Scriptures; they were appealing to all men and women by the outspoken message that each and all of them had a soul to be saved—or lost. True, O'Bryan wanted to drive men to Heaven along his own road, but now it was salvation without tarrying for any. If the old Methodists chose to waste their energies about temporary mundane organization and stray from the direct way the common man was under no compulsion or necessity to jeopardise his own eternal welfare by waiting for them. O'Bryan's faith was the spiritual counterpart of the economic forces that, impatient of any and every restraint, blindly believing in infinite and unlimited progress, were driving forward. Older Methodism had allied itself with restraining and reactionary forces in political and economic life, although its rebels and secessionists had now forced it to adopt a more radical religious policy; it had already been forced to make an aggressive defence of revivalism; the next step was to drop all pretence that it had any association with the Anglican Church which had, by this time, become wholly identified not with conservatism but with the blindest reactionary forces opposed to all progress.

During the second decade of the nineteenth century the Anglican Church reached the lowest ebb of its spiritual life. The austere Evangelical Movement had only checked its decline for a brief period; a progressive age wanted a religion of hope and, whatever it may have offered in earlier times, Calvinistic theology in the early years of the nineteenth century provided only despair; Malthusianism was all that it offered to the age of the Industrial Revolution. The majority of the clergymen of the day, however, had been little influenced by the Calvinistic Evangelicals. Worldliness was supreme. The evils of pluralism and non-residence were at their worst. In Cornwall at least a third of the parishes were held by clergy who were absentees or who had more than one living. The Rev. Richard Milles, son of the famous theological writer Jeremiah Milles, held four Cornish parishes, Mylor, Mabe, Kenwyn, and Kea, a Prebendal Stall in Exeter Cathedral, and the Sussex Rectory of Tarring, all of which he acquired between 1778 and 1781 and all of which he held till he died in 1823. More notorious still was the case of Fitzroy Stanhope who, incapacitated for further military service by the loss of a leg at Waterloo, was ordained with the most unseemly haste and, without the least enquiry into his fitness for a clerical career, given the Deanery of Buryan which he had probably never heard of before and certainly never was curious enough to visit after.[49] The worst case of all, however, was that of Thomas Wills, who held the living of Wendron for fifty-three years—from 1784 to 1837; the tradition that he never entered his church during his long incumbency was but slightly exaggerated; he was known to have had two illegitimate children at least; his main interests, outside the bottle and lechery, were hunting and farming, and the attitude of his parishioners towards him is revealed by the tale that he distributed the flesh of a dead cow, which he dared not give to his pack of hounds for fear of infection, to the poor of his parish.[50] Other prominent farming parsons were Robert Walker of St. Winnow and Jeremiah Trist of Veryan, although their lives were eminently respectable and they were not guilty of the scandalous neglect of their parishioners with which Wills was charged. Another of the "eccentric" parsons of the day was Richard Hennan of St. Austell, who also held the livings of St. Blazey and St. Michael Penkivel; he was held in some esteem by his parishioners not for his prowess in the pulpit but for his ability and fairness in refereeing wrestling matches held in the churchyard after services.[51]

Some indication of the state of the Established Church is given by the returns made by some of the Cornish clergy to questionnaires sent out by George Pelham, bishop of Exeter, in 1812, and by his successor, William Carey, in 1821. Out of thirty-seven parishes in 1812, there were resident incumbents in only twenty-two;[52] a dozen pluralist clerics were holding two or more livings, the greatest, with the exception of Richard Milles, being Cornelius Cardew, former master of Truro Grammar School and once mayor of that borough, who held the livings of St. Erme, Lelant, St. Ives, and

---

[49]C. Henderson: *Essays in Cornish History*, pp. 93-94. Stanhope held the Deanery for forty-seven years, receiving from it an income of over a thousand pounds a year, and paying three curates about a hundred pounds each yearly to look after the three parishes of Buryan, Sennen, and St. Levan into which it was divided after Stanhope's death.

[50]Canon. G. Doble: *Sithney and Wendron* pp. 45-47. Wendron was the parent church of the populous borough of Helston.

[51]Canon Joseph Hammond: *A Cornish Parish*, pp 238-9. Hennan was vicar of St. Austell for forty years, from 1775 to 1815. Robert Walker was vicar of St. Winnow from 1781 to his death in 1834, and Jeremiah Trist vicar of Veryan from 1782 until 1829. Trist had succeeded his father as vicar and was in turn succeeded by his son, the Trist "dynasty" holding the living for four years less than a century.

[52]Lanivet is included as a parish with a resident rector, although Nicholas Phillips informed his bishop—"I do not reside on account of my ill state of health, but am frequently at my Parsonage House at least three days in the week, and keep servants to inhabit it. I perform my own duty twice on Sunday . . ." Abstracts and Quotations from these returns are derived from the *Henderson MSS.*, in the Royal Institution of Cornwall.

Towednack. William Wheeler, rector of Ladock since 1796, preferred to live at the fashionable watering place of Leamington where he acted as curate for his aged father, paying a curate £60 a year to look after his Cornish benefice, £6 a year more than the vicar of Colan was paying a curate at his other living at St. Neots in Huntingdonshire. The non-resident vicar of Fowey also held the living of Perranzabuloe. Nicholas Kendell informed the bishop that he resided in his benefice at Lanlivery although not in the parsonage house, but he had a resident curate in the parish and another in his other living at St. Newlyn East, to both of whom he paid a salary of £40 a year. Kendell, however, omitted to inform Bishop Pelham that he himself acted as curate at Luxulyan for the Rev. John Lewis who preferred to live in Crowan and act as curate for "Mr. Robinson (who) resides chiefly at the watering Place by advice of his Physicians."[53] An even more fantastic situation was revealed by the Methodist-baiter, Richard Polwhele; he was employing a curate to live in Manaccan to serve that and the adjoining parish of St. Anthony in Meneage, whilst Polwhele himself resided at the Vicarage of Kenwyn, near Truro, to act as curate for Richard Milles in both Kenwyn and Kea since:-

"The schools at Truro necessary for so numerous a family as mine brought me to this neighborhood from Manaccan Vicarage where Mr. Edward Tippet is Curate. I hold rent free a highly taxed Glebe and Garden at Kenwyn, not seven acres, for serving Kenwyn and Kea. This is all my remuneration for service at two churches with two sermons . . . The Vicarage House at Kenwyn is an excellent house in very good repair; not so the Church, in the nave of which all the pillars incline considerably to the South; had they not been cramped with iron they would probably have fallen years (ago) together with the whole incumbent roof . . ."

The returns for the populous mining parishes of Illogan and Camborne were made by two curates; Keigwin, curate of Illogan, stated that he was being paid £60 a year for that parish and a further £40 a year for serving the chapel Lord de Dunstanville had erected at his seat at Tehidy; Nichols, curate of Camborne, told the bishop that his Rector, a member of the Basset family, was "not in sana mente" and that he was receiving a salary of £90 a year for his services.

The clergymen of Cornwall were performing their duties or ensuring that others performed them without any very excessive

---

[53]Robinson also held the rectory of Withiel.

zeal. The curates were, on the whole, too poorly paid to assume a prominent position in the society of the parishes they served.[54] In a few places the Church established Sunday Schools, notably in the towns of St. Austell and Penryn; in the former some 150 children were regular attendants in 1812. There were a number of smaller schools conducted by a few individuals; in St. Clements the daughters of the vicar, Francis Jenkins, ran such a school, whilst in Illogan the womenfolk of Lord de Dunstanville's family devoted a hour or so every Sunday to a similar school, although the curate, Keigwin, complained that there were two other schools:-

"with Methodistical Teachers, and both in a way endowed by Lord de Dunstanville, though I believe he is ignorant of their being Methodists."

Even more unsatisfactory was the revelation made by the vicar of Gorran to Bishop Carey in 1821:-

"There are schools for teaching the children to read kept by women. There was a school on Dr. Bell's plan for about six years, but it has been discontinued since Christmas, the subscriptions having failed."

In Crowan, however, largely through the support of Sir John St. Aubyn, education was in a much healthier state.

The attendance of the people at Anglican services was not very great. At St. Ewe the rector, John Cragoe, inducted in 1785, complained twenty-seven years later that the most prominent parishioners, who, presumably should have set a good example to the lower orders were "farmers who attend in their farms more than their Church." The greatest indication of the decline of the Anglican Church at this time, however, is revealed by the reports given in 1812 and 1821 of the numbers who participated in the celebrations of Holy Communion, a Sacrament that was in the greater number of parishes only taken four or five times in the course of the year.[55] Anthony Williams, the aged non-resident vicar of St. Keverne said in 1812 that there had been a hundred

---

[54]The salaries of curates varied. In 1812 W. Willcock served Ruan Minor for £35 a year with the tithes of pig, goose, and honey, besides fees. Richard Hennam paid his St. Austell curate, William Andrew (who also served St. Blazey for him) £73 a year. Anthony Williams paid his curate at St. Keverne an annual salary of £50, allocated to him the tithes of pig, goose, and honey, besides the vicarage to live in, which he reckoned to make up a salary of £100 a year. In this period the average salary of a curate could be reckoned as about £80 annually; thirty years before it had been about £50 at most; both sums were about the same as those earned by mine captains, and about double that of the working miners.

[55]See Appendix p.261.47 below.

celebrants at the last Easter Eucharist out of a population of 2,242, but the analysis of the returns which gave the general average number of celebrants at all Eucharist services indicate that only about one person in fifty participated. Two of the parishes that made returns in both years, St. Anthony in Meneage and Creed, showed a decline of half in the short intervening period. At Crowan, in 1821, the absentee rector, Robinson, complained:-

"Until lately the Communion Table has been nearly deserted. There is not a single gentleman resident in this large parish to encourage the Parishioners by his example and exhibition to attend this Ordinance. The officiating Minister being only a Deacon, many of them feel a dis-inclination, which it is very difficult to remove to receive the elements from a Stranger's hands . . ."[56]

Recently, however, there had been some improvement at Crowan, forty-seven having attended the last celebration and donating collections amounting to 10/6d. as against 1/10½d. a short time before when only seven had been present.[57]

If the Eucharist did not attract the common people the normal church service certainly failed to do so to an even greater extent. Where a clergyman held a single living and resided in his befefice there were usually two services every Sunday, but when a man held more than one living, and was, to a certain extent, dependant on curates, services were rather irregular. St. Ives, with a population of over three thousand, was left, through the pluralism of Cornelius Cardew, with one afternoon service on two Sundays out of three, held by the Lelant curate who was expected to hold services at

---

[56]It is more than doubtful if the example of the gentry encouraged the common people to participate in the Communion services. In the parish of Illogan where Lord de Dunstanville, when in residence at Tehidy, made a point of setting an example to the people (Joseph Farington: *Diary*, Vol. VI. p. 141) there were at most eighty communicants out of a total population that exceeded four thousand in 1812 and was more than five thousand in 1821. At Lanlivery the example of the Kendells was followed by about one in every thirty of their parishioners. It seems rather to have been the case that where the gentry partook of the Sacrament the majority of the common people felt that they were better advised to hold aloof; elsewhere they did not bother as at St. Denis where, in 1821, the vicar reported "Communicants 2 men, 5 or 6 women . . . The inhabitants are poor, and chiefly tenants at rack rents."

[57]This collection, averaging less than 3d. per person, may be compared with the Methodist collections in Cornwall in 1821; with 12,792 Society members the total was only £248—14—8d., or less than 5d. per member. These were the collections made for general Methodist funds, and others may have been taken, although not yet regularly and invariably at other services. (Minutes of Conference, Vol. V. pp. 180-187, 226). The 10/6d. Crowan collection was perhaps the Easter Offering.

Towednack as well; normally, however, a curate was maintained
by the corporation of St. Ives, although it was not always easy to
find one when a vacancy occurred. Hugh Peters, resident rector
of Camborne, suggested in 1821 that there should be a "general
institution of an Evening Service in the week especially as I believe
all denominations of Dissenters have one at least." Even had this
suggestion been widely carried into effect it is doubtful if it would
have drawn back Methodists to the Established Church. It was the
"Preaching" that, above all, drew the common folk to the
Methodist meeting houses and chapels, but the sermons of the
Anglican clergy for the most part seem to have been short, insipid,
and uninspired; the best of them were far too erudite to be
comprehensible to working people whose education had been of
the very slightest;[58] the majority of them were unoriginal,[59] more
or less didactic, and rarely took more than ten minutes to deliver.
The prevalent rationalist doctrine of men trained at the Universities
of Oxford and Cambridge called for an educated audience.
Although it is true that the more spectacular Methodist preachers
only offered the terrors of hell instead of erudite dogma, it should
be borne in mind then the generality of people, in greater or less
degree, then and always, have a psychological craving for the
horrific and terrible; the more lurid the picture a preacher could
depict of the torments of eternal damnation the greater his audience
in times when people had no other way to satisfy the urge for the
harrowing of their emotions; they desired neither reason nor reality
but to escape from a surfeit of both in their normal everyday lives;
until the Anglican Church again directed its appeal to the
psychological emotions and desires common to all men it was
bound to decline, but the older Methodists also had to learn the
same lesson.

The most prominent Anglican clergymen in Cornwall in the first

[58]The sermons of Thomas Grylls, for many years Vicar of Cardinham, may be quoted
as an example of the best Anglican sermonizing of the day. Although they represent the best
of "Broad Churchmanship" they could scarcely be more unreadable to-day had they been
written in Hittite.

[59]One of the absentee Deans of Buryan once took it into his mind to pay a visit to his
western living. The astonishment of the parishioners was great; one, however, ventured to
compliment him on preaching a very fine sermon. The Dean looked at him and candidly
remarked—"So it ought to be. I paid three guineas for it." (Canon J. Hammond: *A Cornish
Parish* p. 203 n. 2) Had the Dean preached more often he might have found that sermons
could be obtained at about a penny a dozen; he deserves credit for getting a hack to write
an original sermon for this occasion.

quarter of the nineteenth century were the pluralists Richard Polwhele and Cornelius Cardew. Polwhele, scion of a long-established Cornish family of country gentry, in more recent times would, in all likelihood, have remained in Oxford after graduating and devoted himself to scholarship and learning. He had a flair for light poetry of an ephemeral nature, and he also published voluminous histories of Devonshire and of Cornwall. The greatest defect of these historical works was an unbridled tendency to verbosity along with lack of judgment in the selection of detail, the faults that were revealed even more glaringly in his notorious *Anecdotes of Methodism*. Conciseness, to him, was a deadly sin; when, at last, after having had it in mind for over thirty years, he published a new edition of Bishop Lavington's *Enthusiasm of Methodists and Papists Compared*, he saw fit to write a preface nearly as long as the original work and, that not being enough, at the end he added an appendix of nearly another hundred pages, the greater part of all had no direct bearing on the original subject at all.[60] In addition to these works Polwhele published many volumes of sermons and poems, besides personal memoirs and reminiscences; had his tongue been as garrulous as his pen his congregations would have had more than enough of sermonizing. Essentially the cultured product of the erudite rationalism of the eighteenth century and of its decorous conventionalism, Polwhele lived on to 1838. He believed in the eighteenth century Established Church with a zeal hardly distinguishable from the fanaticism he attacked when manifested by other sects, and finally attacked Rome and Catholic Emancipation in the closing days of 1828. Pluralism was forced on him by the necessity of maintaining an extremely large family, but it stands to his credit that in his later years he contented himself with a single living, resigning the cures of St. Anthony in Meneage and of Manaccan, along with the curacies of Kenwyn and Kea, when he was presented to the living of St. Newlyn East in 1821.

Polwhele, too, can be commended for drawing the attention of his Bishop to the dangerous condition of the structure of Kenwyn Church in 1812; it is even likely that he was responsible for cramping the pillars with iron to stave off disaster. His contemporary, Cornelius Cardew, at St. Erme went further, and

---

[60]Polwhele's Preface covered 312 pages; Lavington's text 398 pages; Polwhele's appendix 98 pages; it was published in 1833 in consequence of the Methodist revival of that year, although four years earlier Polwhele and some of the Methodists had been allies against Catholic Emancipation. (*West Briton*: 2-1-1829)

having told Bishop Pelham that "the Church (is) in as good repair as it has been for the last forty years", proceeded, a few years later, on a drastic restoration that, in fact, amounted to pulling down the ancient church and rebuilding it at a cost of £1,400. In this "restoration" Cardew paid but little heed to the relics of the past, and it is certain that he quarrelled bitterly with one of his leading parishioners, Edward Collins, who objected to the removal of a memorial to the memory of his grandfather.[61] "Restoration", however, was preferable to the inactivity and neglect that caused the dilapidated condition of the chapel in the borough of Grampound, described as ruinous in 1821, but it is likely that the former Whig master of Truro Grammar School had less respect for the past than the Tory antiquarian historian Polwhele. A little later Cardew clashed with his parishioners in a prolonged and acrimonious dispute over tithes, a dispute doubtless aggravated by the extremely business-like qualities of a clergyman who, throughout a long life, kept yearly balance-sheets of his receipts and expenditures, and who died worth £20,000.[62] Cardew's career may be regarded as the epitome of the materialistic clergy

---

[61] Sir Alexander Cardew: *Cornelius Cardew*, pp. 71-73. The church at St. Erme was probably one of the oldest in Cornwall. Whilst the majority of the stories of churches having been founded by Celtic missionary saints can be given little credence, the tale that St. Piran established the original church of St. Erme on the site of a pagan temple deserves some attention in view of the original round graveyard. It is to be feared that Cardew destroyed more than the memorials of a few immediately preceeding generations. He was not the only clerical culprit in such matters. A contemporary curate ordered the abolition of wall paintings in St. Neot Church, whilst an earlier incumbent of the same parish sold the head of Christ on the Cross depicted in one of the late medieval stained glass windows; a later Vicar replaced it with the head of St. John the Baptist taken from another window. West Briton: April 1, 1825.

(a) Some other Cornish parish churches were being "restored" in this period. Polwhele in his return to Bishop Pelham, with a hint of slighting contempt, wrote "There is no Vicarage house at Kea—the Church there is a newly built Fabrick." A little later the church at St. Columb Major was enlarged by the addition of galleries. It was, perhaps, little wonder that the church founded by the medieval Knights Templars in the isolated and nearly deserted village of Temple fell into utter ruin in this period, but in the populous mining parish of Perranzabuloe the parishioners contributed a great amount of money and labour to build a new church in 1804, the old church being at one end of a long, narrow parish, remote from the main mining district, and well-nigh entirely buried by drift sand. (*Henderson MSS.* Vol X pp 355 ff.) A later age disinterred this older church, perhaps the oldest in Cornwall, encasing the walls in concrete for preservation, but there is no trace of the surrounding graveyard to-day. The Established Church made no attempt yet to build new churches in the mining districts where large villages had grown up in the past two or three generations. It was not until the 1840s that new churches were built at Chacewater and St. Day to remedy the inconvenient distance of the parent churches at Kenwyn and Gwennap. (*West Briton:* January 26, 1844.)

[62] Sir A. Cardew: *Cornelius Cardew*, p. 90.

of his age;· yet he does not seem to have shirked duties and responsibilities. Zealous he was not, but—save where money-matters were concerned—he was no bigotted fanatic, unlike Richard Polwhele against whom such a charge could have been levied by Methodists and by Catholics alike.

Polite learned culture and materialism were not the qualities to make religion a living force. It was not in the least surprising that the Anglican Church in Cornwall seemed almost moribund at this time; not until the work of the Oxford Tractarians began to influence some of the Cornish clergy was there any sign of more positive life than passive antagonism to the more rabid Methodist sectaries. Goaded on by secessionist rebels like William O'Bryan and the Primitive Methodists, the Wesleyans carried on their work with less heed to decorous conventional restraint than in the early days after the death of John Wesley. Like Richard Polwhele they took a firm stand against the Catholic claims in 1829.[63] The fervid antagonism of Methodism to the Church of Rome grew more pronounced and aggressive with passing years, and was accentuated when the increasing Anglican stress on the catholicity of the Established Church seemed to be leading into extremely strange spiritual havens. By 1830 there were at least four times as many class members of Methodist societies as there were communcants of the Church of England in the western county, and it seemed inevitable that successive revivals would increase the disproportion to an even greater extent.

Changes were taking place in Methodism itself, the most significant being the tendency to extreme puritanism. As early as 1823 the followers of O'Bryan made a determined but unsuccessful attempt to stop hurling at Germoe Feast,[64] and similar disturbances took place at St. Columb Major four years later in consequence of the growth of "Bryanite" puritanism in that parish long famous for wrestling and hurling matches than for excessive religious zeal.[65] Attempts of this kind to put an end to long-popular diversions were likely to check the progress of the persons and organizations making them; there were then, as always, many who believed that joy was not confined to another life, and many others that would not subscribe to the belief that worldly pleasure and deadly sin were

[63] *West Briton*: January 9 and 16, 1829.
[64] *West Briton*: May 9, 1823.
[65] *West Briton*: October 5, 12, and 19, 1827.

synonymous. The fanatic spirits, however, would not be dissuaded by any popular feeling, and by 1833 they were denouncing the Launceston Horse Races at St. Stephens Downs as "unreasonable, frivolous, cruel, impolitic, immoral, and unchristian."[66] A more rigid sabbatarianism was not confined to the Methodists,[67] but their sectaries early became associated with the temperance movement that, like the camp meetings of the Primitive Methodists, was of American origin.[68]

By this time the internal divisions and schisms of the Methodists had become acute. As their adherents increased in number in Cornwall and far beyond the Tamar, problems of organization troubled the Bible Christians; these difficulties culminated in 1829 when a head-on collision took place between the imperious individualism of William O'Bryan and "his" Conference; in consequence O'Bryan seceded from the sect he himself had founded. A handful of his adherents followed him; the majority remained behind and organized a Church in which lay members were given a greater role than in the orthodox Wesleyan Connexion and greater even than O'Bryan, through his exalted idea of the preacher's calling, had been ready to afford them. There was only a temporary check to the progress of the Bible Christian movement. The very qualities of democratic equality and independence that O'Bryan had emphasised in the beginning together with the fervour of the mission to save souls ensured its survival. The Bible Christian schism of 1829 was a conflict between the religious dictatorship of a single popular evangelical preacher and the very spirit of revolt against "priestly rule" to which that leader had himself appealed in his conflict with the ministers appointed by the Wesleyan Conference. O'Bryan had roused a spirit of radical egalitarian democracy in the realm of religion that had proved mightier than he himself.

Any hopes the older Methodists may have entertained that the breach between O'Bryan and the greater number of his adherents

[66] *West Briton*: August 30, 1833.

[67] *West Briton*: August 6, 1820 and May 17, 1833.

[68] *West Briton*: March 1, 1833. The first Primitive Methodist missions in Cornwall were held in 1827, about the time of the first appearance of the temperance movement in Britain; they gained their greatest Cornish triumphs in St. Austell, and it is significant that the sect had originated in the Potteries, one of its greatest early leaders being William Clowes, nephew of Josiah Wedgwood. The Primitive Methodists also made considerable progress in the traditionally radical Redruth district. (John Petty: *History of the Primitive Methodist* Connexion, pp. 196-9. J. Davison: *Life of Clowes* pp. 171ff.

would lead to a general reunion were soon dashed to the ground. Wesleyanism before long was distracted and torn by the clash of the imperious Jabez Bunting and Dr. Samuel Warren. Unlike the earlier squabbles of rival Methodist leading personalities in Conference forty years before this feud had speedy repercussions in Cornwall. Before the Conference of 1835 expelled Warren there were local secessions in Truro, Chacewater, Camelford and elsewhere. The quarrel in Conference among the preachers on account of the nomination of Bunting to the proposed presidency of a theological college was the occasion rather than the cause for a new revolt of discontented lay elements in the Methodist societies. The earliest Cornish secession came in the spring of 1834 when a Truro local preacher, James Sawle, and some of his friends broke away, quickly built a chapel of their own, and then threw in their lot with the Kilhamite New Connexion that had seceded forty years before.[69] By December, 1834, the demand that Conference hold all its sessions publicly and that in it voting should be by ballot, led to the expulsion of some local leaders by the Methodist Superintendant at Truro; the immediate consequence was a revolt at Chacewater against the "priests".[70] This spirit of discontent was, in part, the natural aftermath of the emotional excitement aroused during the "Great Revival" of 1833. In Truro the actual number of seceders was small, the numbers in society throughout the circuit only falling from 1,426 in 1833 to 1,377 in 1835, whilst during the next few years such a rapid recovery was made that, in 1842, it was found necessary to carve out the separate Perranwell Circuit.[71]

In Camelford Circuit, however, the Warrenite controversy almost annihilated "Confence Methodism", the numbers of members in society falling from 696 in 1834 to 59 in the next year, whilst even ten years later there were only 232 society members in that circuit.[72] The revolt broke out at the Quarterly Meeting held on December 29, 1834. Barker, the Superintendant, refused to put forward certain motions that had been presented to him; the layman William Grose took the chair, and another layman, Thomas Pope Roseveare, proposed motions that were passed with the only opposition coming from Barker and two others. These

[69] *West Briton*: March 7, April 4, and June 13, 1834.
[70] *West Briton*: December 12, 1834.
[71] *Minutes of Conference*: Vol. VII, pp. 271, 314, Vol. IX, pp. 171, 354.
[72] *Minutes of Conference*: Vol. VII pp. 386, 514; Vol. X, pp. 51, 204.

resolutions demanded that Conference should pass no new rules until they had been considered by all the local Methodist Socieites, that full scope be given in regular meetings for the discussion of all questions and issues on which the people wished to make their sentiments known to Conference, and that every circuit should send a lay delegate to the next Conference to join with the preachers in discussing all the rules of the Connexion and in codifying the rules that were found acceptable. The fate of earlier resolutions was remembered and, to make it more likely that the preachers would consider these, the meeting proceeded to a decision not to make any further contribution to the Conference funds for the time being; the cry of "No taxation without Representation" was being applied to the counsels of the Wesleyan Connexion.[73] Barker then aggravated the crisis by expelling Roseveare through the old method of withholding his ticket of membership to the Camelford Society.[74] At once the outcry of "Popish Tryanny" was raised; the rebels struck back by withholding Barker's allowance, and closed nearly all the chapels in the circuit to him.[75] Barker's fellow minister, John Averill, threw in his lot with the rebels and was suspended by the ministers of the District in May, 1835.[76] The outcome was the union of the Camelford Anti-Conference Party with the Wesleyan Reform Association. Only gradually did the older Methodists recover some of the chapels that were closed against Barker, but the schism in the Circuit was enduring.

The Camelford "Revolution" was the uprising of the discontented lay elements in Methodism; they believed that the Connexion had been founded for the people and not merely to set up ministers over them. The followers of Roseveare made much of the fact that, like William O'Bryan, he had been publicly expelled in a chapel that he had built himself. The lay supporters of Methodism felt that as they provided the funds of the Connexion they should dictate its policy, and felt that the business of organization was their concern whilst the preachers should restrict their activities to matters spiritual. A wealthy and prominent

[73] *West Briton*: January 2, 1835.

[74] At a full meeting of the local preachers of the Camelford Circuit on March 2, 1835 "it was declared that the conduct of our superintendant in excluding Mr. Roseveare was wholly illegal, and that the expulsion is to be regarded as null and void, being an act of arbitrary power, a violation of the rules of the Connexion, and an outrage on the rights of the members of the Methodist Societies". (*West Briton*: March 6, 1835.)

[75] *West Briton*: March 27 and April 10, 1835.

[76] *West Briton*: April 10, May 1 and 15, 1835.

layman, like Thomas Pope Roseveare, was not content with the subordinate and passive role that the Conference men allotted to him.

Another prominent layman led a similar revolt in the village of Polperro against:-

"the laws made by the Wesleyan Methodist Conference in 1835, and the consequent assumption of Arbitrary power by the Preachers, those in the Liskeard Circuit exerting this power with the utmost confidence and assurance."[77]

The surgeon, local preacher, and scientific scholar Dr. Jonathan Couch was too prominent a man in the little fishing community to submit to the behests of a minister who, in all probability, might not appear in Polperro more than once every month or two, and who was hardly likely to be a man of anything like his own mental calibre. Over thirty of the local Methodists followed his lead into secession. A new chapel was built with funds raised on a joint-stock basis, shareholders being given votes in proportion to their holdings,[78] and was opened on September 25, 1838, when the service was conducted by William O'Bryan, home for the time being from the United States. A few days earlier the Polperro Secessionists had met and agreed:-

"That a Committee of five Members be appointed to form a Court, before which all Complaints and Accusations involving Charges of faults against Members of Societies and Sins against the Law of Almighty God, shall be brought by any person thinking it his or her duty to do so.
"That the Names of such five members shall be severally proposed in the Public Meeting of the Society, and the appointment shall be determined by a Majority of the votes of the Members of Society then present, such appointment to continue for the space of one year."[79]

This may have the appearance of a religious and moral inquisition; it was such but it was one democratically elected by all members of the Society; the powers of religious jurisdiction and of expelling defaulters was taken away from the ministers, and entrusted to persons elected by the members of the Society; the

---

[77] *Records of the Polperro Wesleyan Methodist Association Chapel, now the Central Methodist Church,* MSS. (henceforth cited as *Polperro W.M.A.C. Records.*)

[78] *Polperro W.M.A.C. Records.* A similar device for raising funds to build a chapel was adopted by the Wesleyan Methodist Association at Liskeard, the chapel being opened in May, 1838. (L. Maker: *Cob and Moorstone* p. 77)

[79] *Polperro W.M.A.C. Records:* September 16, 1838.

minister was no longer able to expel a member by the over-simple expedient of withholding a ticket of membership, and accused were allowed a full opportunity to justify and defend themselves.

The final blow to Cornish Wesleyanism came in the autumn of 1841 in the birthplace of Methodism in the western county—St. Ives. A Temperance Society formed in that town in 1835 had met with little success, but a more fanatical Total Abstinence Group, starting two years later, was far more successful, and by 1840 was claiming to have "converted" nearly three-fifths of the population to teetotalism. The clash between the teetotallers and the ministers started from a quasi-theological dispute on the point whether or not the ordinance of the Sacrament should be symbolized in fermented wine; the ministers, moreover, were reluctant to allow the use of the chapels for the advocacy of total abstinence. The Conference of 1841 made a resolution that unfermented wine was not to be used in the administration of the Sacrament, and proceeded to pass regulations to the effect that no chapel was to be used for total abstinence meetings, and that no preacher was to go into another circuit to advocate total abstinence without first obtaining the consent of the Methodist Superintendant of the circuit he proposed to visit. The new Superintendant at St. Ives, Jonathan Turner, had hardly reached his new station before it was rumoured that he intended closing all the chapels in the circuit against the teetotallers, but, when the secretary of the teetotal society, Docton, interviewed him he professed that he was willing to propose the building of a temperance hall and, in the meantime, to allow monthly teetotal meetings in the Methodist chapel in St. Ives provided that he was allowed to choose the speakers. Docton, however, made a rather tactless attack on the brewing connections of Jabez Bunting. Turner, for his part, insisted that, at teetotal meetings, nothing was to be said in the chapel pulpit against those ministers who were not total abstainers nor would he permit moderate drinkers to be accused of error. Rumour then intervened with the report that the other St. Ives minister had had a barrel of beer brought into his house. Turner then withheld Docton's ticket of Methodist membership; the teetotallers met, and on September 24, 1841—a mere five days after the crisis had been precipitated by the first refusal of Turner to allow the chapel to be used by the teetotallers on a certain date—the total abstainers resolved on secession from the Wesleyan Methodist Connexion. In a last minute effort to avert schism, Turner proposed that a general meeting of the whole society be called; this was contemptuously rejected by Docton and his followers who, not choosing to mince their words, said they wished to hear no more of the "twaddle of Mr. Turner." In all some four hundred seceded from the parent sect at St. Ives, including three of the oldest stewards and trustees, fourteen local preachers, and twenty-four class leaders. In a few months a teetotal chapel was built in St. Ives, whilst elsewhere in the western county the movement had made great progress, and teetotal meetings were being held regularly in many chapels.[80] The older secessionists, Bible Christians and Primitive Methodists showed every disposition to adopt teetotal principles. The reduction of drunkenness was desirable, but the price paid was the triumph of a harsh, uncharitable, and bigotted intolerance, whilst sectarian quarrels grew more bitter. The triumph of the movement in Cornwall was symbolized by the meeting of three thousand total abstainers in a camp meeting held on July 4, 1843, in no very clement weather on the exposed summit of Roughtor; for a few years this Roughtor festival was kept up annually.[81]

This development of the total abstinence movement marks the end of the lax and easy-going toleration of an earlier time. It was marked by a fanaticism and by a readiness to interfere with the liberties of persons who held different opinions that amounted to a denial of individual liberty. Whilst there is no reason to deny that drunkenness had been only too prevalent among the Cornish people yet the advocates of teetotallism exaggerated its extent, and

[80] A full account of these events was given at the time in the anonymous pamplet *A Vindication of the Case of the Teetotal Wesleyan Methodists of St. Ives; with an incidental exposure of the Domination of the Wesleyan Priesthood*, published at Penzance in 1842. John Boaden described the movement, more than sixty years later, as beginning in the Cury district, in the Helston Circuit, in 1839:—"The first (teetotal) meeting at the Garras (Chapel) was held on April 9th . . . There had been a great revival at the Garras chapel just before; the hearts of the people were like molten wax and at the close of this epoch making meeting over 100 signed the pledge including all the officers of the society and most of its members. Thus was laid the foundations of that sobriety here which had distinguished the parish ever since. It was not long before the nine beer and cider shops in the parish were closed, not by any authorities but for want of custom. The Church has not yet put forth anything like its full power in abstaining from drink and faithfully proclaiming the fearful responsibility of those who stand on the other side . . . Christmas Day 1840 Rev. Mr. Budden preached there at Caclack in the morning, the Chapel was almost full. The temperance feeling was very warm. I recollect Alex. Wicks going out of a prayer meeting when my father engaged in prayer because at that time he was not a teetotaler. There soon began to be agitation on this question in consequence of some of the preachers not being abstainers. I signed the pledge in the fall of 1841 . . . Teetotal prayer meetings were held alternatively in the various chapels."(*MSS. Autobiography*)

[81] *West Briton*: July 7, 1843, and June 27, 1845.

certainly maximized the connection of inebriety and crime.[82] It is certain that those that signed the pledge saved more of their wages, may have worked better, and indirectly benefitted their employers besides, perhaps, reducing the burden of pauperism on parochial rates. It might be questioned, however, if the negation of toleration was not too high a price to be paid for the economic and social gains that were made, whilst, even granting that the majority of the advocates of total abstinence were genuine and sincere the movement, from its very nature, was peculiarly exposed to the insidious intrusion of cant and of hypocrisy.

Toleration, however, was in retreat, had been retreating ever since the Methodists had avowed that reason was not the sum total of their faith. The movement for Catholic Emancipation and the activities of the Oxford Tractarians raised the "Popish" bogy again, whilst, in the west, the Anglican Church that, for nearly three generations had made little attempt to meet the criticisms of Methodists within and without its communion was suddenly re-awakened by the dynamic although, perhaps, rather erratic personality of Henry Phillpotts, who had been appointed to the Bishopric of Exeter in 1831. Controversies about tithes and church rates arising from economic distress and from the very natural reluctance of religious dissenters to support an "alien" church in the 1830s were to be followed by even more bitter controversies on religious and doctrinal points; a compromise settlement could ofttimes be reached when all that was in dispute was a sum of money; when men failed to agree over religious principles no compromise could be reached for the dispute was not over matters finite.

Early in 1843 the Methodists of Western Cornwall opposed the Factory Bill introduced by the government of Sir Robert Peel on the grounds that it infringed "the civil and religious privileges" of the British people; the outcry, which played into the hands of the laissez faire exploiters of child labour, was directed against the educational provisions of the bill; these provided for the prosecution of parents who would not allow their children to attend schools that were placed under the trusteeship of local Anglican incumbents and churchwardens along with four other men who were not

---

[82]Claims of Methodists and teetotallers to have reduced crime cannot be proved. The records of eighteenth century assizes reveal no more crime than those of the later nineteenth, although, against this, it may be argued that in earlier times fewer criminals were caught.

elected by the whole parish but appointed by the justices of the peace.[83] An even greater storm arose over the conduct of certain "Pusseyite" clergy. William Marshall, vicar of Falmouth, thought it best to leave his parish in the hands of a curate.[84] Walter Blount, curate of Helston, after provoking bitter quarrels was hounded from the county.[85] Samuel Edmund Walker of St. Columb Major was, however, more of a fighting character; he engaged on a drastic "restoration" of the parish church thereby alienating those whom he had not already quarrelled with by his refusal to permit the National School Room to be used by the St. Columb Mutual Improvement Society for its meetings; in a few months the attendance at the Church Sunday School dropped from 450 to 70; parents were not allowing their children to be lured into the snares of "Rome".[86] Bishop Phillpotts provoked a storm when, in December, 1844, he ordered all the clergy in his diocese to wear the surplice; the outcry in the west was so formidable that he withdrew the order within a month.[87] There was another outburst of fanaticism against the Maynooth grant, more violent perhaps in the Cornish strongholds of Methodism than elsewhere in England. By 1850 religious and theological disputes were more bitter than at any time since 1688, the most significant feature being that the disputants were now drawn from every section of the community —the outcome of John Wesley's reassertion of individual

[83] *West Briton*: April 28, 1843,

[84] *West Briton*: September 22, 1843; October 23, 1846; and January 21, 1848.

[85] *West Briton*: March 14 and 28, 1845; April 8, 1845; and June 4, 1845. The churchwarden, Frederick Hill, was cited before the Consistory Court of Exeter for removing the church plate to prevent Blount holding Communion services.

[86] *West Briton*: December 27, 1844. S. K. Walker was not related to Robert Walker of St. Winnow, mentioned above, but came of a wealthy "foreign" manufacturing family; he bought the living of St. Columb Major in 1841 and held it to his death in 1869. A correspondent of the *West Briton* (September 6, 1844) described Walker's restorations as "the most daring and sacrilegious outrage on his church. Not content with bringing all the pews, as he would wish to bring the consciences of his congregation, to the same level, he has also pulled down two very spacious galleries which were not very long ago erected at a very great expense to the parish, and sold the materials by auction to the public; so that what was the door of Mr. A's pew, is now the door of Mr. P's pig sty. The flooring of the gallery is now being laid down in Mr. B's tap-room, and some part, indeed, has already been applied to a more degraded purpose, whilst the handsome columns that formerly supported it are propping up the back-wall of Molly Gummow's Mumpers' Inn. Some people are foolish enough to say that the Rector has driven away his congregation, and, therefore, has no need of a gallery. Slander! I know he has not driven them all away, for there are the two Miss P's, and the three Miss D's and the four Miss C's who follow in his train seven times a week and twice on Sunday, melodiously chanting the service in unison with this zealous tractarian."

[87] *West Briton*: December 13 and 27, 1844.

justification by faith and of William O'Bryan's insistent message that all had a soul to be saved.

With Methodism split between Wesleyans, New Connexion, Primitive Methodists, Bible Christians, Wesleyan Methodist Association, Teetotal Wesleyans, and one or two other sects, with the Anglican Church torn between the Tractarians and their opponents, and with a few Quakers, Baptists, and Congregationalists all to be found in Cornwall, religious controversy was inevitable. Nevertheless the long tradition of toleration, that had developed since 1688, was stronger than all the sectaries, although the most potent bond of union was the general and well-founded belief that Rome was the enemy of toleration and of religious individualism. The various Methodist bodies would reunite to conduct mass revival services; one chapel would generally suspend its services when its neighbour was holding anniversary services. Many of the staunchest Methodists still brought their children to the parish church to be baptised. Only in the more populous towns and mining parishes were sectarian burial grounds established. Toleration survived even the most rabid fanaticism of the extreme Teetotal Methodist sectaries and the dispute between Bishop Phillpotts and the Rev. C. C. Gorham of St. Just in Penwith over baptismal regeneration.

There also survived relics from an older time. The Bible Christian miller, farmer, and mining adventurer, Thomas Tregaskis, builder of the "cathedral" of his Connexion at Hick's Mill failed utterly in his efforts to suppress the pre- Christian festival of the Padstow Hobby Horse that from a pagan spring fertility rite had become a harmless popular fete.[88] Whatever they thought of the killjoy "Bryanites" and the Tractarianism of Samuel Edmund Walker and his vandalous "restoration" of their ancient church, the people of St. Columb Major still flocked to wrestling and to hurling matches. May Day revels were still retained; only a later generation saw the

[88]'It appears that for ages past, the inhabitants of Padstow have been in the habit, every May Day, of dressing up a man in grotesque and hideous form, and calling the figure A Hobby Horse. This Hobby Horse, it seems, is paraded through the streets, followed by multitudes of men, women, and children; and much indecency and other kinds of immorality are said to be the result. About eleven months ago . . . Mr. Tregaskis, in the hope of abolishing a custom which he thought was 'more honoured in the breach than the observance', offered to give a fat bullock to be distributed among the poor inhabitants on May Day, and to repeat the gift annually for seven years, if the patrons of the Hobby would give up their 'vain practice'; and on the 10th. ult. he had hand bills published repeating his offer. This offer was, however, ridiculed in a hand bill signed 'the Hobby Horse Fraternity', and great

passing of the yearly struggles of Pelynt and Duloe parishioners for
the possession of the prized maypole; Helston Floral Dance never
passed away, whilst the low flat granite boulder at the meeting
point of the four parishes of Morvah, Zennor, Gulval and Madron
may have the unenviable distinction of being one of the last
cock-fighting rings in England, but it was something at least that
this blood sport had been driven to the centre of a desolate moor
almost literally a mile from anywhere.

Sports condemned by many or even by nearly all the people as
brutal were not the only dark survivals of an earlier primitivism.
Belief in the evil-eye, in the malevolent powers of darkness, and in
the prowess of "white witches" was still prevalent at the beginning
of the Victorian Age, and lingered on for many years to come. As
late as 1836 a Scillonian farmer attributed the loss of several of
his farm stock to malign witchcraft, and, on the advice of one of his
neighbours, burnt a calf alive to break the spell.[89] At Tywardreath,
in 1841, a woman accused of witchcraft attacked her accuser, and
in the subsequent action for assault, that was brought against the
reputed witch, a witness told the magistrates that the defendant
had confessed to him that she had acquired by sinister powers:-

"attending the sacrament, and repeating the Lord's Prayer thrice
backwards, partaking of the wine, but securing the bread and giving it to

88 (cont.) excitement prevailed in the town—the cry being 'who is for the beef, and who is
for Hobby?' Still, Mr. Tregaskis persisted in his offer, and announced that on the 28th all
the bullock would be forthcoming, and a lecture given on the subject which had induced
him to present it; but on the animal making his appearance, the whole town was in an
uproar, the 'H. H. Fraternity' singing their doggerel 'May Songs' and preventing those who
wished to address the people from being heard. When the meeting had been closed, and
the bullock publicly rejected, Mr. and Mrs. Tregaskis were followed out of the town for a
quarter of a mile by hundreds of people shouting for the Hobby Horse as vociferously as
the craftsmen of a certain town once shouted for Diana of the Ephesians. To this comedy
succeeded tragedy, two of Mr. Tregaskis's friends being severely wounded by stones thrown
by the mob; and thus the affair ended, the enlightened 'H. H. Fraternity' being left in
possession of the field." (*West Briton*: May 9, 1845). Some account of the career of Tregaskis
is given by Lawrence Maker: *Cob and Moorstone*, pp. 44-49.
    89 *West Briton*: April 15, 1836. John Boaden, writing at the beginning of the twentieth
century remembered well—"that Mr. Jos. Dale (not long) since dead was driving a sow,
belonging to his father who farmed Gilly to Bonython when near Grygler Green she fell,
(and) died; they had also lost some cattle previously. Mr. Dale in returning by way of Bayoner
was advised by Mr. Josiah Thomas, a Baptist local preacher, to go back, take out the sow's
heart, stick it over with thorn prickles, then roast it in a fire: while this was proceeding a
blue cock would emerge from some hedge or thicket and while the blue cock was in sight
the person who had ill-wished Mr. Dale would be out of his mind. But though it was carried
out to the letter no blue cock appeared. I was an eye-witness. This happened in the early
'forties." (*MSS. Autobiography*)

a toad, which, according to the prediction of her instructors, she found on her way home, and took (the toad) with her and retained (it) as the magic power of her spell."[90]

At the Spring Assizes of 1843, Frederick Peter Statton of St. Dominic, a young man of twenty-three years, was charged with witchcraft and false pretences, since he had beguiled a credulous farmer into giving him three shillings for finding a lost heifer by "white magic"; the Judge took a serious view of the case as wilful deceit, but a facetious counsel poured ridicule on the charge, and, after a great deal of time had been wasted, a legal technicality led to the case being thrown out.[91] Many believed that a child could be cured of whooping cough by passing it under the belly of a living donkey, but it is likely that no-one tried the charm with a mule lest that uncertain-tempered beast effected the cure by kicking the infant's brains out.[92]

Strange remedies were believed to be efficacious in the treatment of disease. It was reported in 1844 that sufferers from a certain unnamed and politely unnameable complaint in Philliack who:-

"for want of moral courage, would not submit to the directions of their medical advisers, very readily caught hold of and applied every nostrum that the gossips made known. Experience proving that the boasted remedies were of no avail . . . to believe that they were ill-wished was the work of a moment, but to discover a person who could break the spell was not so easily accomplished. Every thought and action was centered in attaining this darling object. Finally, their wish was consummated, and a scatterer of witch spells stalked forth from Helston, to whom they disclosed every incident of their lives, fraught with uncertainty as tending to good or evil. The day was chosen, the dreaded hour of midnight fixed, and the abode of the silent dead of all that once was living was named as the place of assignation. The hour drew near, but their purpose became known from the impulse of their ecstasies, and their stealthy actions were closely watched. The asked-for fee was immediately given, and after silence was enjoined, the church-yard wall was scaled. Then the spell-breaker commenced the mysteries of his art, by making mysterious sounds and performing mysterious motions, as he walked over the dead hotly pursued by his frightened dupes. Having walked many times around the church, the doors and windows opened and shut at his bidding. Then he commanded them to remain open, and as they were passed in succession, he brought the persons who had ill-wished them to their face. Thus the

[90] *West Briton*: December 3, 1841.
[91] *West Briton*: March 31, 1843.
[92] *West Briton*: January 26, 1844.

spell was broken and dissolved, and a faith given that their cure would
be speedily effected. Some days have since elapsed, and either their faith
has failed, or the witch-spell is not broken for their disease still maintains
its hold, the effect of a visible cause."[93]

This account was doubtless exaggerated, but it must have had
some basis in fact; that such superstition and such practices survived
make it less surprising that Richard Polwhele saw fit to republish
to the world bishop Lavington's invidious comparison between
revivalist meetings and witches' sabbaths.[94] Compared with this
Phillack episode the thronging of public executions by persons eager
to secure a piece of the hangman's rope, believed to be a specific
for all the ills to which mortality was subject,[95] was trivial. Paganism
may have been dead; it certainly had not been decently interred.

Many of Wesley's followers believed as firmly as he himself did
in ghosts.[96] To Methodists and to the majority of the people of the
early nineteenth century the reality of the existence of malign
supernatural powers and forces was beyond all doubt. The famed
local preacher Billy Bray was the product of this credulous age,
but he possessed an unshakeable faith that the temptations of the
Devil—a personality that was as real and as near to him as his own
shadow—could be thwarted and overcome by accepting the word
and by following in the way of God.[97] To his crowded congregations this strangely eccentric Cornish miner brought a message
that they could withstand and triumph over the Devil and the
powers of darkness by positive faith, a faith that was absolutely
personal and individual; on them and in them alone were the forces
that would ensure their own eternal salvation—man and not God
was responsible for man's fallen state. Billy Bray's assurance of his
own salvation, his eccentricities in the pulpit, his shouting, exaggerated gestures, and "dancing" offended the sedate, but no-one

[93] *West Briton*: September 6, 1844.
[94] Bishop Lavington: *Enthusiasm of Methodists and Papists Compared*, (ed. R. Polwhele.) p. 326.
[95] *West Briton*: August 15 and October 10, 1845. (*vide* Thomas Hardy's story "The Withered Arm" (*Wessex Tales*).
[96] Thus William Clowes, co-founder with Hugh Bourne of the Primitive Methodist Connexion, thought he saw a ghost at the house where he lodged in St. Day in the autumn of 1833; although he believed it was the apparition of a "horrid blasphemer", the ghost was apparently seated at a table, quietly writing. (John Davison: *Life of the Venerable William Clowes*, p. 206.)
[97] F. W. Bourne's *Billy Bray, the King's Son* is the only biography of this remarkable personality; it has some of the faults of Methodist "hagiography", but, on the whole, presents a good picture of Billy Bray.

could doubt the reality of his faith or his sincerity. His faith, moreover was not originally born of emotions stirred to fearful heights of agitation in a revival meeting, though he delighted in such meetings, but from the studious reading of John Bunyan's *Visions of Heaven and Hell.*[98] Like most converts Bray made the most of the condition of his unregenerate days in his sermons; there is little doubt that he had been a drunkard and this, in part, accounts for his alliance with the more extreme teetotallers later; yet his Methodist family antecedents should not be forgotten even although he himself, sublime individualist that he was, only remembered his own youthful follies in his preaching, drawing from them warnings and lurid examples for the youths in his congregations. His great success was due to the fact that he spoke to the labouring people of Cornwall in their own language and lived as they did; from boyhood to age he laboured in mines in many parts of the county on week-days, and on Sundays walked long miles from one chapel to another to hold services as a local preacher.

Anecdotes of the eccentricities of Billy Bray have obscured his real significance.[99] He was the most famous local preacher of his time, and even of all time, in Cornwall, but he was one of many men of but little learning who felt themselves called to testify their faith to their fellow-men. His and their great message was the redemption and salvation of the individual soul; Billy Bray never claimed to do more than to guide men to salvation; indefatigable in his efforts to do so, his own religious experience and active temperament meant that he never uttered an opinion that all was done and that all would be well if a preacher convinced a man of the evil of his past ways, and that in itself conversion was not salvation. In the opinion of Billy Bray, expressed as vividly in his life as in his colourful preaching, man himself was left free to walk in the strait and narrow path from conversion to the end of his earthly days; chapel-services and revivalist missions were only signposts along that path; the individual was free to travel along the way if he would; he should allow nothing to distract him from it; looking neither to left nor to right nor to what lay behind he must steadily push on to the destination of final triumphant

[98]F. W. Bourne: *Billy Bray, the King's Son,* (1937 edition) pp. 16-17.
[99]Some of these anecdotes are related by S. L. Thorne in *Samuel Thorne, Printer,* (1875 edition) p. 166-170.

redemption beyond the grave. It was an individualist and dynamic faith. The way Billy Bray chose to go himself may have been too strait and too narrow, yet if he mourned the weaknesses and failings of others he rarely despaired of them; they could, if they would, achieve salvation, and he was ever ready to extend a helping hand to them. He had no use for an ecclesiastical organization that pronounced a formal absolution for all sins, whilst many of its preachers, by precept or example, made but little attempt that the absolved would strive to sin no more. On the other hand Billy Bray had no use for Calvinistic predestinarian doctrines, and even less for passive quietism.

Billy Bray's individualism almost amounted to religious anarchism. If he thought a chapel was necessary in any place he would forthwith set about building one, labouring with his own hands, inspiring some men to labour with him, and inducing others by the example of his own religious faith to contribute materials and money for the work.[100] Indeed, the conception of faith held by other men almost makes it a term too meekly passive to describe the fierce positiveness of Billy Bray. Nevertheless this forthright individualism and intentness on the way ahead was but typical of the age with its belief in illimitable progress that had been nurtured by past achievement. It is unlikely that such a man as Billy Bray could have lived in Cornwall at any other time; it may not have been a pure coincidence that his self-conversion took place round about the year 1823—the year when a wave of speculative enterprise promoted a great expansion of Cornish mining enterprise; when the depression of 1865 brought disaster to so many Cornish mines his work was nearly done, and he died in May, 1868, before the generality of Cornish miners realized that this was a depression from which the greater number of Cornish copper mines would not recover.

If Billy Bray looked into the future further than human eye could see the exact contrary was true of the most famous Cornish Anglican clergyman of the same time. Robert Stephen Hawker was all that Billy Bray was not.[101] Bray stressed the individual, Hawker

[100]F. W. Bourne: *Billy Bray, the King's Son*, pp. 49-64.
[101]The "official" biography of Hawker by his son-in-law, C. E. Byles (*Life and Letters of R. S. Hawker*) is much longer and considerably more reliable than the more famous biography written by S. R. Baring-Gould (*The Vicar of Morwenstow*), which was written and published within a few months of Hawker's death by a man who succumbed to the temptation of the novelist to sacrifice accuracy to sensationalism.

the social communion; Bray ignored all that lay behind, Hawker escaped further and further into the past as he grew old; Bray travelled and preached through all the populous mining districts of Cornwall, Hawker confined his ministry to the thinly populated agricultural parish of Morwenstow.[102] Both men have suffered in reputation through the exaggeration of their superficial foibles and eccentricities by those who wrote accounts of their lives, yet the ill-educated miner and the graduate of Oxford together represent all that was best in the religious life of Cornwall in the second and third quarters of the nineteenth century.

Born in December, 1803, Hawker became curate of North Tamerton in 1829, and in December, 1834, Bishop Phillpotts offered him the living of Morwenstow where he remained for practically the rest of his life; the curacy of the adjoining Devon parish of Welcombe was given to him in 1850. The Bishop had, at the time, been rather dubious whether Hawker would accept such an isolated and out-of-the-world parish as Morwenstow, and it is certain that his learning and social gifts would have won him greater preferment had he chosen to wait for a more populous parish.[103] He had already made something of a name for himself as a poet, though his authorship of the famous Trelawney Ballad—the "national anthem" of Cornwall—was not widely known at that time. In the course of a relatively long life, however, he wrote comparatively little, devoting practically all his attention to the care of his parish and to farming his glebe. Hawker's conception of the duties of a clergyman embraced a wider field than that of most of his contemporaries, and clerical cares in Morwenstow were particularly heavy for, through a long succession of absentee vicars, the parish had fallen into the hands of O'Bryan's followers and of other Methodists, whose theological doctrines were anathema to Hawker. He won many of the people of his parish back to the Anglican Church by sheer force of personality for, if

---

[102]Hawker wrote in July, 1867—"Every Minister has a Flock of his own whom he is bound to teach . . . and for what he does to them as teacher he will be requited by God. But no man is sent to address another man's people. No reward is promised to a man for any duty not laid upon him, nor have we any right to elect and choose what duties we will fulfil." (C.E. Byles: *Life and Letters of R. S. Hawker*, pp. 485-6). The addition of the curacy of Welcombe in 1850 to Hawker's charge can, with justice and reason, be called the amalgamation of two poor livings; together they could be looked after by a single incumbent, whilst the addition to his income enabled Hawker to perform his clerical duties more adequately.
[103]C. E. Byles: *Life and Letters of R. S. Hawker*, pp. 39- 40.

occasion arose, he could be every whit as blunt and forthright as the most extreme "Methody". Although he was over-scrupulous in the use of vestments for church ceremonies,[104] yet his everyday garb of high sea-boots and coarse-woollen fisherman's jersey convinced his parishioners that he was one of them. He was reckless in charity at the expense of his own well-being, and to the extent of being rarely more than on the verge of solvency. Above all he gained followers, esteem, and affection by his efforts, sometimes attended with grave personal danger, to recover the bodies of seafarers who had perished off the cruel coast of his parish for the purpose of giving them Christian burial.

The people of Morwenstow lived mainly by farming, and Hawker was one of the first to institute the festival of harvest thanksgiving.[105] At other times of the year he would decorate his parish church with plants and flowers, a departure from the austerity of Methodism and of rationalism alike, and an action that brought colour into the life of people whose everyday life was drab and dull, and he associated that colour with religion. His personal interests in myth and legend drew him further and further into the past in a parish too remote to have been yet touched by nineteenth century progress. He was, however, no mere scholarly recluse; life to him was active and not passive, to be lived to the full and not borne as a burden. Cut away from what was generally termed "society", he became all the more keenly aware of the human sentiment of community and of a more transcendental communion. Uncompromising himself in his opposition to "dissent", he was alienated by the attempt of the Anglican Church to achieve a compromise with the materialism of the first half of the nineteenth century,[106] whilst the later effort of bishops like Frederick Temple to effect a compromise between religion and the science of Charles Darwin and Thomas Huxley helped to bring about his death-bed conversion to Rome. Yet it was his own consciousness of a church community transcending the present by extending not into the future but into the past that was the underlying reason for his final renunciation of the Anglican Church. His poetry dealing with the myths of the ancient saints and with the Arthurian legend of the

[104]C. E. Byles: *Life and Letters of R. S. Hawker*, pp. 134, 137.

[105]This was in 1843 (C. E. Byles: *Life and Letters of R. S. Hawker*, p. 171.

[106]Hawker even tended to regard material prosperity as a snare of the devil. (C. E. Byles: *Life and Letters of R. S. Hawker*, pp. 441-2—letter of Hawker to J. G. Gordon, November 7, 1863.)

Holy Grail might have warned many that he would eventually take the same path that Newman and Wiseman had taken. Ever since the Gorham Case and the crushing defeat it brought to Bishop Phillpotts Hawker had been outspokenly critical of the negative nature of contemporary Protestantism;[107] in the end doubts whether Archbishop Tait had ever really been properly baptised, which made it debateable whether or not the historic continuity of the Anglican Church had been broken, helped to lead to Hawker's final decision to die in the Roman Communion. His death-bed conversion came as a shock to many and provoked considerable controversy; but the man who recanted life-long Anglicanism was no longer the parish clergyman of Morwenstow but the mystic religious poet, and, with the sands of life fast draining away, he made his peace not with the Church of Pius IX but with the older Church of the Celtic Saints.

Hawker may have been an escapist from his own age, but the past in rural Morwenstow was more present than the dark satanic mines and mills of the Industrial Revolution. Life there went on in its old rhythm of seed-time and harvest, the tranquil monotony only broken now and again by fearful tempest and dreadful wreck on the inhospitable coast of Morwenstow. Man, in that district, was the subject of the forces, friendly and inimical, of nature and of nature's God. The older agrarian community, going back to time immemorial, was still in existence. Parson Hawker was the product of that environment just as Billy Bray was the product of the expansion of Cornish mining occasioned by the triumph of individualist "economic" man. Even in the last hours of the two men the contrasting environments and what man's own spirit had made of those environments were manifested—Hawker accepting the same sacraments that St. Morwenna more than a thousand years before had received and joining the communion of all that was past, Billy Bray still the individualist in sight of his God and Redeemer with unquestioning triumphant faith in the future uttering the cry of "glory" for the last time.[108] Both men had lived by and for a faith that was real and transcending all other realities for them; they had lived lives of abundant service that benefitted

[107]"Neither am I going to proclaim myself a Protestant whose Creed is Nay Nay—nor an advocate for That universal No called the Reformation, the pretext for Royal lust and noble robbery." Hawker to his brother Charles Hawker, November 27, 1850. (C. E. Byles: *Life and Letters of R. S. Hawker*, p. 213)
[108]C. W. Bourne: *Billy Bray, the King's Son*, p. 121.

their fellow men. Both realized the existence of much that was evil and both fought against it in their own way. Yet in their time and, perhaps, at all times in the world in which they lived there was and is no reconciliation possible between the Churchman who wrote:-

"The truth is our Bishops and other Chief Captains have for long years done their best to annul and annihilate authority. The Bible cannot be enforced without the Church, and when the Mother is repudiated who is to prove the Birth and Parentage of the Children?"[109]

and the religious anarchism of the labouring miner who, when a youth, after having passed some critical remarks on his unorthodox methods of preaching, met his blunt question if he loved God with the prim answer that he belonged to the Wesleyan Connexion blazed forth:-

"Thee a Wesleyan! Thou art only a Wesley's bastard!"[110]

The communion of a church transcending time was all in all to Robert Stephen Hawker; to Billy Bray nothing mattered but the timeless individual soul. Together the spiritual community and the individual soul make up the entity of human religion, but throughout history they have been in greater or less degree antagonistic, and in an age of progressive and successful economic individualism it is not at all surprising that, instead of reconciliation, there was a wider divergence and a more bitter antagonism than before.

[109]C. E. Byles: *Life and Letters of R. S. Hawker*, p. 514. (letter of Hawker to J. G. Godwin, written in 1863)
[110]S. L. Thorne: *Samuel Thorne, Printer*, p. 170.

Appendix.

The Number of Communicants in the Anglican Church in Thirty-Four Cornish Parishes in 1812 or 1821.

Parish	Year	No. of Communicants	Population 1811	1821
St. Anthony in Meneage	1812	40	222	330
do.	1821	20		
St. Austell	1821	40	3,680	6,175
Breage	do.	30	2,888	3,668
Camborne	do.	25	4,714	6,219
St. Clements	do.	50	1,692	2,306
Colan	1812	10	221	259
St. Columb Major.	1821	80 to 100	2,070	2,493
St. Columb Minor.	1812	30 to 40	1,126	1,297
Constantine	1821	30	1,327	1,671
Crantock	do.	12	358	389
Creed	1812	28	226	279
	1821	11		
Crowan	1812	25	3,021	3,973
	1821	7 to 47		
Cuby	do.	30 to 40	152	140
Cubert	1812	20 to 30	289	322
St. Dennis	1821	7 to 8	478	592
St. Enoder	do.	20 to 30	881	833
St. Erme	1812	12	431	561
	1821	14		
St. Erth	do.	10	1,317	1,609
Feock	do.	12	968	1,093
Grade	do.	15	306	355
Gluvias	do.	60 to 100	3,427	3,678
Illogan	1812	50 to 80	4,078	5,170
St. Ives	do.	40	3,281	3,526
St. Just in Roseland	do.	50	1,639	1,648
Kenwyn	do.	10	5,000	6,221
Kea	do.	10	2,766	3,142
Ladock	do.	15 to 20	651	806

Lamorran	do.	10	94	93
Landewednack	do.	14	303	387
Lanivet	do.	12	687	803
Lanlivery	do.	35	965	1,318
Lelant	do.	12	1,180	1,271
Luxulyan	do.	40	1,047	1,276
Towednack	do.	10	532	582

The population of the whole of Cornwall was 220,525 in 1811 and 261,045 in 1821 (The above based on *Henderson MSS.*)

N.B. The Feock return of the Rev. John Symons read "7–8 communicants besides my own family."

CHAPTER VII

MEN AND THE SEA

CHAPTER VII

MEN AND THE SEA

IT MIGHT be rightly said that the sea has played a greater part in the life of the Cornish people than the land whereon they dwelt. The sea was the main "highway" between Cornwall and England until Brunel's Saltash Bridge, the last link in the railroad line from Penzance to Paddington, was completed in 1859. From the very beginning the traffic between Cornish copper mines and the smelters and colliers of South Wales was conducted by sea, whilst nearly every block of tin raised in Cornwall, until the Stannary organization had been reduced to a local law court in 1836, had been sent out of the county by sea. Tales of Phoenicians coming in galleys from distant Mediterranean lands and of Celtic missionary saints arriving in coracles strangely metamorphosed by an age of faith into millstones, despite the scorn of later scepticism, indicate that the sea was ever present in Cornish consciousness and that it played a role of supreme importance in the daily life of Cornish folk.

All told there are some three hundred miles of coast from the wide Tamar estuary round the Lizard and Land's End and back to Devon again, a coast of towering cliffs, sheltered havens, sandy beaches, tidal estuaries, sand bars and rocky reefs. There are sheltered harbours, like those of Fowey and Falmouth and Padstow—ere the Doom Bar began to creep across the entrance of the Camel Estuary—that attracted men to venture on to the vaster ocean; there are inlets and coves like those of Looe, Polperro, Newlyn, and St. Ives where shoals of pilchards swarmed in, providing a harvest nearly as reliable as that of the land; in one or two places, as at Par and Portreath, man has made ports to serve the demands of a busy hinterland. The history of the men who lived in those harbours, havens, and coves was one of fishing and trading, of fighting and smuggling. Picturesque scenery and the influx of tourist traffic in latter days have subtracted nothing from the legends of the past, too many of which had little foundation in fact but none of which exaggerated the debt of Cornish people to the sea. It provided their link to the outside world, perhaps not with half-mythical Phoenicia and Tyre but certainly with pre-Roman Spain, with early Bronze Age Ireland, with early Christian Brittany, and with the wider world revealed by the geographical renaissance of the late fifteenth century. Cornishmen sailed with Hawkins and Drake, nor is it beyond the bounds of possibility that some trading pilchards to Spain slipped away in Seville and Cadiz to join the galleons of the Spanish treasure fleets. Later, when growing nationalist sentiment and the increasing expenses of government imposed revenue duties which cut athwart the older commercial unity of the western European coast, stretching from Donegal to Gibraltar, the era of "free trade" began. The activities of the smugglers have been so obscured by the hazy meanderings of romantic writers that it is too often forgotten that smuggling was almost a regular occupation enabling many to earn, if not their daily bread, at least something to spread on that bread.

Smuggling, however, was not confined to Cornwall; the pilchard fishery was, although a few pilchards were secured off the South Devon coast in most years. The migration of pilchards in shoals from somewhere to the south-west of Scilly to arrive on the southern Cornish coast about mid-July and on the northern coast later in the autumn first attracted scientific speculation and investigation in the middle of the nineteenth century; previously it had been regarded like manna in the Biblical story, as the bounty of God, sometimes forthcoming, now and again withheld. Over long periods of years there occurred some considerable changes in the times the pilchards appeared off the Cornish coasts; in some years they failed to appear at all. Nevertheless, before the seventeenth century their visitations were regular enough to promote a considerable industry in catching and curing the fish for Mediterranean markets. Usually the fish came close enough inshore to be taken by seine nets, whose introduction Dr. Jonathan Couch, the great ichthyologist, attributed to the Phoenicians;[1] evidence to support this theory was not forthcoming, but the industry was of quite respectable antiquity, and the traditional Cornish toast "Fish, Tin, and Copper" may well represent the order in which these commodities came to play a dominant role in the economy of the county. The pilchard

[1]*Parliamentary Papers*, 1878-79, Vol. XVII, p. 259.

fishery may have developed on a large scale in the fourteenth century to complement the dwindling supplies of Baltic herring to the Mediterranean markets; while the contact of Cornwall with the Mediterranean is a matter of fruitful and, indeed, of endless archaeological surmise and speculation, there is no reason to seek beyond the Lenten fasts of Catholic peoples for the origins of the Cornish pilchard trade.

In seining a large net was used to enclose a shoal of fish, larger and larger nets being employed as time went by to ensure the capture of the whole shoal. The net was taken out in one rowing boat and "shot" around the shoal; at a very early time a second boat or *vollier* was used to work a second or *stop-net*; later a third boat or *lurcher* was employed from which the master seiner directed the operations of the other two boats; the lurcher, being unencumbered with nets, was also used to divert the direction of the fish and to frighten them into the closing circle of net, and for this purpose was manned by one or two of the best rowing-men. Once the circle of net was closed, it was hauled by the boats into shoal water, and the process of removing the fish by smaller *tuck-nets* began. Finally the fish were landed from these smaller nets, and carried in baskets called *gurries* or *mauns* to the curing cellars or *palaces*. Seining was only practicable close inshore, and before the seventeenth century drift nets that could be worked in deeper waters and far off-shore were in general use. Almost at once a bitter feud developed between seiners and drift-fishermen, the former complaining, particularly in bad seasons when the fish did not come close inshore, that the drifters broke or diverted the shoals; it was an argument which was still going on within living memory.

Apart from the feud of drifters and seiners, the significant development in the pilchard fishery during the seventeenth century was a tendency towards large-scale capitalistic organization. It was a seasonal industry since shoals appeared off the coasts and could be taken by seine nets for only a few weeks during the year; in most places, during a normal season, the greater part of the catch was taken in a few days, nor was it unknown for the entire catch to be made in a single day. Fish-curing afforded from six to twelve, though rarely more than eight, weeks of continuous employment to those engaged in it. Quite apart from any consideration of the best methods of maintaining a distant foreign market, the increasing size of nets, the development of the system of using three boats instead of one, and the maintenance of curing cellars all called for capitalistic organization, although the older system of share-fishing long survived, especially on the driftboats. The three-boat seining system meant a division of labour which made it harder to arrive at a just division of the catch among the actual fishermen without reckoning the complexities of apportioning the fish between boat-owners, net-owners, and fishermen, whilst some shares had also to be allocated to the casual labourers who helped to drag the heavy nets into shoal waters and to the *huers* who were stationed on the cliffs to watch for and give warning of approaching shoals.

Share-fishing was adequate for men who sold their catch locally to persons who could preserve it by various ways for their own personal future consumption. In late Tudor times pilchards had been preserved by smoking, pickling, or salting,[1] but by the eighteenth century only the third method of curing in "bulk" by salting was generally employed. By this method alternate layers of fish and salt were laid down and *bulked* up to heights between five or six feet in the specially-constructed cellars or *palaces*, which had elaborate drains to save the precious oil exuding from the fish. Cellars could be leased and shared by the working fishermen, whose families could lay out and salt the fish, but a capitalist system was more convenient especially since the cured fish had to be packed in casks and then sent to distant markets in far larger vessels than the open rowing-boats employed in seining.

In short, the cost of large nets which could only be employed on a very few days in any one season, the system of large-scale curing with a large amount of salt which was generally obtained from France, and dependence on a distant foreign market meant the inevitable development of capitalistic organization in the seine pilchard industry. For a long time, however, features of the older share-system survived. Thus at St. Ives, in 1838, a tenth of the catch was divided among the members of the crew of some seining outfits over and above monthly wages of 45s. to men and 37s. 6d. to "boys"; the huers were each paid £3 a month; the *blowsers* employed to haul in nets and to carry fish to the cellars were given an eighth of the catch or a compostition of 2s. 10d. per hogshead,

[1]Carew, pp. 102-103.

each hogshead containing from 2,500 to 3,000 pilchards; in
other outfits half the total catch was shared between all the
men engaged in catching and landing the fish but they were
given no wages. In Mount's Bay the huers were paid 18s. a
month and given a seventeenth part of the fish, whilst fishermen
were either given some fish along with a weekly wage of 9s. or
paid 10s. a week.[1] At Mevagissey, where no huers were employed after the beginning of the seventeeth century,[2] the men
were given a third of the fresh fish and a quarter of the salted
fish sold besides a weekly wage of 8s.[3] Such variations from
place to place in a single year, apart from changes on the same
stations over periods of years, make generalizations impossible,
but it is obvious that ownership of boats, nets, and cellars had
become distinct from labour employed in the fishery, whilst
dependence on Mediterranean markets had long before ensured the control of the industry to merchants trading to those
markets. Out of thirty seines divided into a variety of shares at
Newlyn and Mousehole in 1833, only ten actual fishermen
owned shares,[4] and the seine fishery had come to be known as
the "rich man's fishery", the complete seining outfit in 1835
representing a capital of nearly £1,000 whilst the average
drift-boat with nets was worth about £250.[5]

[1]Dr. J. Couch: "A Treatise on the Pilchard", *R.C.P.S.*, 1835, p. 99; J. S.
Courtney: "Fishery Statistics", *R.C.P.S.* 1838, p. 125.
    [2]J. Couch: *R.C.P.S.*, 1835, p. 37. With improved and more general intercom-
munications between the various fishing ports, itself partly the result of increasing
capitalist enterprise, with seine owners owning concerns or shares in concerns in
several places, there was no need to maintain permanent look-outs save at the
points where the shoals first appeared, at Mount Misery off Penzance for the
summer fishery of the South coast and at St. Ives for the autumn shoals that came
to the North coast; the experience of years indicated roughly how long shoals
would take to move further eastward to other places along those coasts.
    [3]J. S. Courtney: *R.C.P.S.*, 1838, p. 125.
    [4]*W.B.*: December 13, 1833. Shares in seines like shares in cost-book mines were
usually in eighths or sixteenths or by sub-divisions of those fractions. Thus, at
East Looe in July, 1819, the effects of a bankrupt advertised for sale (*W.B.*: July 2,
1819) included 11/32 of the Unity Seine, 7/16 of the Friends' Adventure Seine,
2/16 of the Poor Man's Adventure Seine, 7/16 of the Pilchard Seine, and 1/16 of
the Penwarne Seine. Four years later there were nine seines in all at Looe (Bond:
History of Looe, p. 74), but this particular bankrupt also had owned shares in other
seines at Polperro, Polkerris, Mevagissey, and Portwrinkle. He had also held a
¼ share in the 90 ton sloop *Industry* and 39/64ths of the 130 ton brig *Speculation*,
vessels which might have been employed in Mediterranean voyages, besides shares
in 60 and 70 ton "barges" and full ownership of a twelve ton "river barge or
lighter". This man had probably been engaged in general coastal trade, with Looe
as his centre; his trade in the immediate neighbourhood, besides that in fish, must
have consisted mainly in "exporting" grain and in "importing" lime and sand
from and to the immediate agricultural hinterland.
    [5]J. Couch: *R.C.P.S.*, 1835, p. 82.

The rivalry of drifters and seiners became acute in the early seventeenth century. Professing its concern to maintain public honour, wealth, and safety and deploring the "divers pernicious disorders and abuses of the times crept in", one of the first actions of the Long Parliament of the Restoration was to legislate against the "growing evils caused by Driving nets", and prohibit the use of drift, trammel and stream nets within one and a half leagues of the coasts of Devon and Cornwall from June 1st to November 30th every year.[1] The main charge against the drifters was that they diverted and broke up the shoals, preventing their coming close enough inshore to be taken by seine nets. The Act then went on to make provisions against persons found loitering near boats, nets, and cellars, to provide penalties against the purloining of fish, and to ban the "making" of "pilchards and Fumenthoes"[2] except by owners, partners and adventurers in "the Craft of Fishery" or by the persons to whom they had openly sold their fish. It is likely that this legislation had been prompted by a succession of poor seasons, during which the pilchard shoals had not touched inshore waters, and that consequent poverty and distress had forced the poor to steal fish to assuage the pangs of famine. There was no hint at this time that the drifters were accused of destroying small fish, and little to suggest that their activities had aught to do with the passing of the Act of 1715 providing against the importation of foreign-caught fish, laying down the sizes at which turbot, sole, plaice, brill, whiting, mullet and certain other fish were merchantable, and banning the use of small-mesh nets except in the herring, pilchard, and sprat fisheries.[3]

Before this first indication of a decline in certain branches of the British fisheries, ascribed, rightly or wrongly, to the destruction of small fry by narrow-meshed nets, Parliament had passed other legislation affecting the pilchard fishery and the people engaged in it. To "Dutch William" and his advisers was due the introduction into England of salt duties which long had been a sore grievance of the poorer classes on the Continent. These duties, first introduced for a period of three years in 1694, were made perpetual in 1697. At the time

---

[1] 13 & 14 Car. II, cap. 28.
[2] From the Spanish *fumadoe*, a smoked pilchard, corrupted to "fair maid" in Cornish dialect. It came to be applied to any kind of smoked pilchard.
[3] 1 Geo. I, Sess. 2, cap. 18.

they were relatively small; provisions to compensate the fish-curing and salted provisions trades, besides drawbacks on re-exported salt, created a complex system of salt laws which, naturally, led to widespread evasions and abuses. To the original excise duty of three-halfpence per gallon on English salt and a three-penny duty on imported salt was added a proviso for a bounty of 12s. on every fifty-gallon cask or hogs-head of pilchards or scads exported.[1] This was, perhaps, an excessive bounty, and led to flagrant abuses; curers packed off fish that had not been salted enough to preserve them; merchants shipped off casks, secretly brought them ashore again, took off the marked cask-heads, and claimed a second bounty on a re-headed cask. In 1702 a lengthy Act for the prevention of frauds in the duties on salt laid down that no person should cure and pack pilchards for sale:

"unless he or they be owner or owners or Part Owners of some Seyn or Seyns or of Drift net or Drift nets, or have the consent of such owners in writing, and that on each Cask or hogshead of Pilchards the word Seyn or Drift . . . shall be burnt with an Iron on some visible part thereof together with the name . . . of the Owner or Owners of the Same, as also the number of Pilchards contained in each Cask . . ."

on a penalty of twice the value of the fish in the defaulting hogshead.[2] This was ineffective, and early in 1718 further laws were passed to restore "the credit of the British fishery in foreign parts and for better securing the Duties on Salt", the export bounty on pilchards being reduced to 7s. per hogshead.[3] Although the salt duties were suspended in 1730, the bounty on exported pilchards was retained, perhaps on account of the influence of Cornish members in Walpole's Parliament; it was found necessary, however, to reimpose the salt duties in March, 1732, for three years, and twenty-one years later their permanent reimposition was deemed necessary.[4]

Little is known of the fortunes of the fisheries in the early eighteenth century. The illicit practices of the exporting merchants, the bounties on foreign sales, the abolition of the salt duties in the reign of George II, all may have had some association with the fluctuating fortunes of the fisheries, but the

[1] 5 & 6 Wm. & Mary, cap. 7. cl. 10.
[2] 1 Anne, Sess. 1, cap. 21, clause 31.: Carew, p. 104 note *c*.
[3] 5 Geo. 1, cap. 20, clauses 3 and 8.
[4] 5 Geo. 11, cap. 6, clause 1; 26 Geo. 11, cap. 3, clause 1.

last was certainly associated with a variety of greater and far more general interests than the local pilchard trade of Cornwall. The pilchard seining industry had known variable fortunes in Elizabethan times,[1] and in the seventeenth century the migratory habits of the pilchard had changed. In the late sixteenth century the main shoals arrived off the Cornish coasts in the late summer and early autumn, but in George I's time the greatest seining season was in December although a few pilchards were taken in Mount's Bay in some summers.[2] This change may have been due to changing biological phenomena either in the fish themselves or in the organic matter on which they fed, possibly affected in some degree by minor cyclical or long term climatic changes; all that is important in Cornish economic history is that there was no complete cessation of the visits of the pilchards to the Cornish coasts like that which occurred off the south-west coasts of Ireland about 1740;[3] the main difference between early and late fish was that the latter were not nearly so rich in oil.

Perhaps through the Act of 1662, the seiners practically monopolised the pilchard fishery until the middle of the eighteenth century. In 1750, however, when Parliament was considering the state of the British fisheries in general and in especial the threat of Dutch interlopers to the East Anglican herring fishery, the Cornish seining interests were alarmed by a report that:

"the towns of East and West Looe, Liskeard and Bodmin,[4] supported by men of considerable property and interest in Plymouth, have proposed a petition to Parliament for carrying on the Cornish fishery by drift nets, and for taking away the use of Seines, which at present is the universal practice of our fishery all along the coast from St. Ives to the Looes."[5]

The petition, however, was not presented to Parliament, and the only measure passed affecting the fisheries in this session was the "Act for the encouragement of the British White

---

[1] Carew, pp. 104-105.

[2] Carew, pp. 100 and 103 footnote (by Tonkin, written *circa* 1720).

[3] Howard Fox: "The Pilchard Fishery", *R.C.P.S.*, 1878, pp. 83-85. This abandonment of the Bantry Bay region by the pilchards seems to have coincided with their appearance in greater shoals off St. Ives and the north Cornish coasts where previously they had been rather rare.

[4] These places were all Parliamentary boroughs, the two Looes having each two seats.

[5] Walter Borlase MSS: Letter of Walter Borlase to John Harris, January 18, 1749/50.

Herring Fishery."[1] It seems that the seiners had been unduly alarmed by a group of men lobbying the numerous Cornish members at Westminster to support the Act which, for a period of twenty-one years, conferred very considerable privileges on the "Society of the Free British Fishery." Prominent among the men defending the seine fishery as more efficient, more gainful, employing more men, and benefitting the revenues of the realm was the Rev. Walter Borlase, Vicar of Madron and Kenwyn, adventurer and bound-proprietor of several tin mines in West Penwith, and Vice-Warden of the Stannaries, besides a share-holder in one of two seining outfits himself, who wrote, when rumour was most active, that the Looe men supporting the drifters were "mean and beggarly", who possessed none but a small and insignificant whiting fishery of their own, and that:

"Never was a project formed by men more mischievous to the country, or more absurd or unreasonable in itself than this, to destroy seyne fishing in favour of the driving. Besides the calamitous consequences that would ensue to private families and to the sinking in consequence the value of Gents' estates in this county, merchants and adventurers have been at great expenses in fitting up Seanes, which would all be lost and such great expense it must be to the poorer sort to furnish themselves with drift nets, that after losing their present craft, by it being rendered useless, they would not be able to repair the loss (so they say themselves) in fourteen years. The allegations of our opponents that Seane fishing destroys the spawn and that drift fishing makes a large nursery of seamen are plausible and have only this defect, that they are both absolutely false, which, if they give occasion, will be demonstrated."[2]

It is likely that the agitation of Borlase and other seiners was caused by some move to repeal the 1662 Act against drift-fishing off the south-western coasts during the summer and autumn months; there may have been some scheme mooted for establishing an organization that would monopolize the entire fishing industry of the British coasts; but, in the end, the seiners were unaffected by legislation detrimental to their interests in the reign of George II, or, indeed, in that of his grandson.

The earliest statistics of the pilchard fishery were those ob-

[1] 23 Geo. 11, cap. 24.
[2] Walter Borlase MSS: Walter Borlase to John Harris, January 18, 1749/50.

tained by Dr. William Borlase from the merchant George Blewett in January, 1758.[1] In the ten years 1747 to 1756, mainly years of peace, the average annual export of Cornish pilchards was 29,795 hogsheads. Blewett ranked Falmouth as the main exporting centre, sending out about half the total; four-fifths of the remainder went from the Mount's Bay harbours of Penzance, Newlyn, and Mousehole; Fowey was responsible for six and St. Ives for but four of the remaining ten per cent. Blewett's figures may have been incomplete, yet the scanty records of St. Ives at this time,[2] and the fact that seining was only introduced at Looe in 1778[3] and at Polperro four or five years later,[4] indicate that in the middle of the eighteenth century Mevagissey and its neighbouring coves were the main centres of the pilchard fishery. There was little fishing in Falmouth itself, and its domination of the export trade was due to its many general trading contacts with the Mediterranean lands. Blewett estimated the annual value of the exported fish, including the bounty, at rather less than £50,000. The amount of salt used in preparing the pilchards for export was about 2,250 tons a year; assuming that at least a fifth of the fish caught were sold for local consumption, about 350 tons of salt must have been used in Cornwall every year in preparing this single staple food; this amount must have progressively increased as the population grew, so that when, at the end of the century, the salt duties were raised to contribute more to the war budgets of the Younger Pitt and his successors at the Treasury, the poorer classes felt it hardly, complained bitterly, and resorted to wholesale smuggling of that necessity of life.

To the third quarter of the eighteenth century can be ascribed the rise of St. Ives to a predominating place in the pilchard fishery, though there were still years when hardly any fish appeared on the north coast, whilst now and again huge shoals were secured on the south Cornish coasts.[5] During its

---

[1] William Borlase MSS.

[2] Couch records that in 1756 a great shoal or shoals were taken on November 5th, and that in 1764 no less than 11,600 hogsheads were taken by the St. Ives fishermen (*R.C.P.S.*, 1835, pp. 100-101).

[3] Bond: *History of Looe*, p. 74.

[4] J. Couch: *History of Polperro*, p. 109.

[5] Thus in 1796, when perhaps the largest catches ever in a single season were made, 28,000 of the 65,000 hogsheads secured were caught in the Fowey region. (H. Fox: *R.C.P.S.*, 1878, pp. 94-95).

long domination of the fishery Mevagissey had adopted a customary regulation of the actual fishing by which the very limited area in which seining was possible was divided into *stations* or *stems*; since there came to be more seining concerns than there were stems, it became the rule for each seine to take a stem for a single day, giving it up at the end of the day and then taking another stem two, three, or four days later, and so on throughout the season.[1] This system eliminated the confusion and loss of shoals which would have occurred if, on the arrival of the shoal, each and every seining outfit had put to sea and started shooting its nets hither and yon, getting hopelessly entangled and losing part if not the whole of the shoal in the general pandemonium. At St. Ives, too, the seining area was limited, and, with a rapid increase in the number of seines there, a similar system of stems was adopted for which, to ensure its enforcement, Parliamentary sanction was obtained in 1776.[2]

With the outbreak of war occasioned by the American Revolution difficult days dawned for the pilchard fishery. The St. Ives Act of 1776 and one secured a year earlier for "completing and maintaining the Pier at the Town of Mevagissey"[3] indicate the expansion of the industry in immediately preceding years; the fact that these Acts were passed by the third and not the second Parliament of George III suggests that expansion had little to do with the financial boom which burst with such disastrous results to the mining industries in 1772, although the multiplicity of seining concerns in St. Ives may have been partly due to over-rash speculation. The price of pilchards exported to the Mediterranean averaged rather above £2 per hogshead from 1771 to 1778, thirty per cent above the level of the years analysed by George Blewett. The total quantity exported may have dropped a little,[4] and there

---

[1] The term "stem" was also applied to day labour in Cornish mines.
[2] 16 Geo. III, cap. 36.
[3] 15 Geo. III, cap. 62.
[4] Messrs. Fox of Falmouth, who were probably handling a third of the pilchard exports in these years (in 1796 they exported 23,216 of the Cornish record catch of 65,000 hogsheads), exported 58,813 hogsheads in the eight years 1771-78, receiving £130,290, or an average price of £2 4s. 3d. If they exported a quarter of all the pilchards sent out from Cornwall, the average export of these years would have been 29,400 hogsheads, or only slightly less than Blewett's estimate for the years 1747-56; it is hardly likely that they exported more than forty per cent of the total, but if they did the annual export from Cornwall would have been but 18,375 hogsheads, although the total price would still have averaged over £40,000 per annum. (H. Fox: *R.C.P.S.*, 1878, pp. 94-95).

is some indication of a declining foreign demand for, in May, 1779, an Act was passed to remove the duty on all salt used in curing pilchards, substituting a duty of 5s. 2½d. per fifty gallon hogshead. The avowed purpose of this Act, which was passed through all its stages in both Houses and received the Royal Assent in three weeks from May 10th to May 31st, was to encourage the home consumption of pilchards since there was more than enough fish to supply the foreign market. It is possible that this Act was promoted by the already tottering government of Lord North to conciliate a powerful Cornish political interest; the bill was drafted by the two county members, Sir William Lemon and Edward Eliot, by the Fowey and Bodmin representatives, Philip Rashleigh and Sir James Laroche, by Earl Nugent, a scion of the banking family of Craggs who were partners of the Eliots, and by one of the Grenvilles who, although sitting for Buckinghamshire, was a member of the famous West Country family.[1]

The year 1779 was one of the worst known in the fishery. Spain entered the war. Mediterranean markets were sealed off by the prolonged siege of Gibraltar. Worst of all a combined Franco-Spanish fleet was cruising in the western Channel, even achoring for some days in Plymouth Sound. Little drift fishing could be carried on under such circumstances, but it is also possible that few pilchards came to the Cornish coasts that year. More bad years followed, and at one time the people of Fowey were reduced to living on limpets.[2] In 1782 the price of pilchards had dropped to £1 per hogshead including the 7s. bounty; the average price in the years 1780-83 was only £1 6s. 4d. With peace the price recovered to £2 8s. 6d. in 1784, but that year Cornwall had less than 6,000 hogsheads to export.[3] During the war the situation had been aggravated by the cessation of much trade with France, from which country normally much salt had been obtained. Illegitimate "free trade", however, did not cease; war conditions fostered it, whilst the depression in the fishery drove the fishing folk to resort to it, to make a livelihood, on perhaps a greater scale than ever known before.

[1] 19 Geo. III, cap. 52: *J.H.C.*, Vol. 37, pp. 387, 390, 394, 396, 407.
[2] Maton, Vol. 1, p. 143.
[3] Messrs Fox exported 1,481 hogsheads in that year. (H. Fox: *R.C.P.S.*, 1878, pp. 94-95).

It was not particularly patriotic on their part but the
ordinary Cornish fishermen had little interest in the war into
which Lord North's Ministry had blundered; if they had any
strong political views they were likely to be more favourable
to the "free traders" on the other side of the Atlantic than to a
government which, if it suppressed the Colonial smugglers,
would in all likelihood next turn its attention against evaders
of the revenues nearer home. The bounties on pilchards only
benefitted the small group of exporting merchants and large-
scale fish-curers, not the common people; the latter's only way
of getting cheap salt to cure a small quantity of fish for their
own families and friends was by smuggling it into the country.
It required a bushel of salt to cure a thousand pilchards which
would hardly supply a moderately large family throughout a
winter, but the duty of 3s. 4d. on that quantity of English and
6s. 8d. on foreign salt, over and above the relatively low initial
cost, often represented half the wages they made in a poor
fishing season.[1] Spasmodic efforts, the result of the same bad
seasons, by the rich seining interests to enforce the 1662 statute
against the "poor" drift fishermen, and the exactions of fish
tithes by the clergy did not make them any more friendly to
the established order in state and church. Nor did the activities
of the press-gang stimulate patriotic sentiment, and it is not
entirely astonishing that, on one occasion during the
American War, the Carters of Prussia Cove turned a coastal
defence battery against the excisemen.[2]

Sheer economic necessity drove the Cornish seafarers to
smuggling. Their activities were connived at by local gentry,
by justices of the peace, and even by members of parliament.
Defrauding the revenues of the realm was not generally regarded then, or even more recently, as a crime; the only fault
was to be caught. Philip Hawkins a member for Grampound,
was slightly conscience-stricken on his death-bed, and left
George II a legacy of £600 to compensate the Crown for some
part of the revenue it had lost through the activities of Hawkins'

[1]Salt was also extensively used in curing pigs by cottagers, a ten-score (200 lb.)
pig requiring up to 20 lbs. of salt in curing. Dairymen and farmers also used salt
rather lavishly in butter-making.
[2]A. L. Cross: *Royal Forests, Sheriffs and Smuggling*, p. 309. *Vide* also J. B. Cornish's
preface to his edition of *An Autobiography of a Cornish Smuggler* (Henry Carter),
and Sir A. T. Quiller Couch: "King o' Prussia", *The White Wolf and Other Fireside
Tales*, 1928 Duchy Edition, pp. 91 ff.

tenants.[1] This sum was but an infinitesimal fraction of the
amount of customs duties lost by the revenue through the
Cornish "free-traders". In all probability it would be an underestimate to assert that throughout the eighteenth century, it
averaged yearly thrice the value of Cornish pilchards exported,
but, naturally enough, the smugglers themselves did not keep
records of their transactions, whilst estimates drawn up by
customs men would be generally based upon the unsuccessful
"runs" they had frustrated rather than the successful ones.
Officials, too, to justify their own employment, would tend to
underestimate the amount of smuggling that occurred. Moreover, the corruption of the customs and excisemen was notorious; many of them at Fowey, St. Mawes, Penryn, St. Ives, and
Bossiney regarded their posts as sinecures given them for their
good-will in parliamentary elections in those boroughs; when
excisemen were disenfranchised in 1783 Bossiney was left with
two members representing a solitary elector. Many customs
officials connived at the activities of smugglers; if, through inefficiency or graver offences, they were threatened with removal, they could usually find some influential borough patron
or member of parliament to protect them. Occasionally over-
zealous officials received hints from their superiors that painstakingly accurate accounts of trading transactions in the ports
where they were stationed were not required.[2]

Nevertheless, when a policy of economic retrenchment was
forced on the Government at the end of the Seven Years War,
the losses of revenue through smugglers were not ignored. The
glaring discrepancies between the amounts of wines and
brandy legally entered into Cornwall and the consumption of
those liquors in that county led the Treasury, in October, 1766,
to order the writing of a letter to the Customs Board, requesting

[1] J. B. Cornish: *An Autobiography of a Cornish Smuggler*, p. ix. The general attitude
of the local gentry seems to have been that the Government had only itself to
blame for its own inefficiency and for that of its agents. Writing as far back as
April, 1749, the cleric and magistrate Walter Borlase wrote:—"The smuggling
business was pretty much restrained in this bay (Mount's Bay) during the war,
but now it is over, is revived with as much application as ever. They embark in
fleets at noonday from Newlyn, from which parish only more than 1000 (£) has
been drained for that pernicious traffic since the ports have been open. I wonder
we have no Smack ordered to the Coast, nor any preventative means thought of
more effectual than stationed officers." (Walter Borlase MSS: Walter Borlase to
John Harris, April 5, 1749).
[2] A. L. Cross: *Royal Forests, Sheriffs and Smuggling*, pp. 265-266. (Report of Lisle
dated August 8, 1782).

them to give the matter urgent attention and to suggest the best remedies they could:

"to meet and correct this grievance, whether it be any change, to be made, in numbers, stations, and regulations of the cutters, or by visitation and inspection of the several ports, or by any other measures, which you may think it expedient, or which in your opinion are found to be wanting in the administration or collection of the revenue of customs. And their lordships . . . assure you that they shall be willing and zealous, on their parts, to promote, and to give vigour and execution to any such effectual plan."[1]

It seems, however, that this had no effect. In the 1770s it was estimated that the total amount of brandy yearly smuggled into Cornwall was 469,000 gallons, a loss of at least £100,000 to the revenue, whilst £50,000 more was lost by some 350,000 pounds of tea evading duty. Although only twenty-nine vessels, of between 30 and 100 tons burden, were known to be engaged in smuggling, most of these ships, unlike the "free-traders" of south-east England, were armed; possibly some three hundred seamen were engaged in the "trade," whilst a much larger number of landsmen assisted in landing and disposing of the run cargoes.[2]   At this time, however, smuggling was being carried on even more extensively in Kent and Sussex, with the vast London market in the hinterland, and also in Dorset and in Devonshire. The Cornish responsibility for £150,000 out of a total loss of revenue estimated at £3,000,000 was comparatively small, but it yet amounted to a twentieth of the whole smuggling carried on in the Kingdom, to a fifth of the amount of "free trade" in the Home Counties,[3] and the brandy run into Cornwall alone represented a yearly loss of revenue equivalent to the estimated yield of the notorious Stamp Duties from all the American Colonies.

The costs of the American War of Independence led to further attempts to tighten the Customs' administration. As a result of the report of Surveyor-General Lisle, made in August, 1782, excisemen were disenfranchised a year later. In 1784 fast-sailing long ships, whose length was more than three and a

---

[1]Elizabeth E. Hoon: *The Organisation of the British Customs System, 1696-1786,* p. 49 *n.* 5.

[2]A. L. Cross: *Royal Forests, Sheriffs and Smuggling,* p. 241.   The number of vessels was actually considerable; an official return of December 31, 1869, stated that there were then only 88 boats of over 15 tons burden registered in Cornish ports.

[3]A. L. Cross: *Royal Forests, Sheriffs and Smuggling,* p. 241.

half times their breadth were banned by statute, although licences could be obtained to construct and use them.[1] Parliament then investigated an aspect of "free trade" which has been ignored by the romantic chroniclers of smuggling— the evasions of duties and prohibitions on the export of certain commodities. The powerful woollen interests, unable to prevent the manufacture of cotton fabrics in England, lobbied Parliament in 1783, and again in 1786, to investigate the illegal exports of raw wool and live sheep from England to France, which, they believed, would enable the hated rival nation to rob Britain of Continental textile markets. The illegal exportation of wool from Cornwall to the Channel Isles had long been considerable; Cornish sheep had been vastly improved from the stock whose rough fleeces had been contemptuously described as "Cornish hair" and slightingly omitted from the types of wool whose export had been banned in late medieval times. In 1757 Richard Williams claimed that his woollen "manufactory" near Penryn was doing a great national service by providing employment for some six hundred hands and also by reducing smuggling; he had introduced a variety of looms to make different cloths not only to meet changing market demands but also to use the many different types of wool raised in Cornwall:

"which in this variety can all be worked in to advantage of the industrious poor and not sent as hitherto into other countries to be spun, and indeed I might add not be sent to France as usual where, to our very great loss and the inconceivable advantage of our treacherous neighbours, I may justly assert three fourths of the very short fine wools of the South and North coasts of this county were always transported in exchange for teas and brandy, and this owing to the want of a suitable market at home . . ."[2]

In the 1780s, however, much wool was still being smuggled out of Cornwall; in 1786 the customs seized in all 9,981 pounds weight of such illicit cargoes, but of that small quantity 1,889 pounds had sailed from Truro and other places on the Fal estuary, and a further 120 pounds from Penzance.[3] The inordinate amount of wool imported into St. Malo in the four

[1]24 Geo. III. Sess. 2, cap. 47, clause 4.
[2]William Borlase MSS: R. Williams to William Borlase, August 27, 1757.
[3]*Parliamentary Reports*, Vol. XI, p. 310. (Report from the Committee appointed to consider the several laws for preventing the Exportation of Live Sheep and Lambs, Wool, Wool Fells, Martlings, etc., 1788).

years following the end of the American Revolutionary War was alleged to have come from Guernsey or Jersey, but much of this must have been first brought to the Channel Isles by the smugglers of south-west England; in May, 1783, a seventy-ton vessel "from Cornwall" brought 37,800 pounds of wool into St. Malo, and in 1786 two Falmouth twenty-two ton ships brought in over 22,000 pounds more.[1] Much tin, which had never paid coinage duties, may also have gone out from Cornwall as "ballast"—a convenient term in the smuggling business then as at a later time. All that the Government could do was to increase the number of revenue cutters, improve their armament, and try to appoint more honest and efficient officials. With that the matter rested and Parliament turned its attention to the state of the Cornish pilchard fishery.

In a report from a Committee of Enquiry, presented to the Commons by Sir William Lemon in April, 1785, it was revealed that the average annual export of Cornish pilchards for the past four years had only been 12,500 hogsheads; this was ascribed partly to the normal fluctuations of the fishery, but mainly to the closing of the Mediterranean markets during the recent war. Little attention was paid to the fact that, during the war, some pilchards had been exported to the Azores, to the West Indies, and to Ostend, and even less to the revelation that tin was being exported as ballast on some ships taking fish from Cornwall to the Mediterranean. The merchants alleged that the war had drawn many seamen into the Navy, leaving craft and nets formerly used in the fishery to lie idle and rot. The number of seines at Mevagissey had fallen from 55 to 40, at St. Mawes from 16 to 10, and in Mount's Bay from 36 to 26, but no reference was made to the new seining ventures at Looe, Polperro, and Bigbury Bay. It was the merchant class, rather than fishermen, who resented the withdrawal of the drawback of the one per cent duty on cargoes sent to the Mediterranean; they alleged that this drawback had encouraged them to take out a losing cargo of fish since it and the profits of the return voyage more than made up the loss; merchants, too, naturally stressed that they brought cargoes of currants and other goods from Venice that otherwise would have come to Britain on Venetian ships. It was rather vaguely estimated that the fishery employed about 5,500 seamen and from four to five thousand

[1]*Parliamentary Reports*, Vol. XI, pp. 311-312.

persons in curing fish and other activities ashore, not, however, distinguishing casual and permanent employment. The capital invested in the fishery was reckoned at £207,750; there were from 110 to 140 seining concerns and some 180 drift-vessels, but the Committee did not make it clear if all these were in use or not. The actual losses of the industry during the past four years were stated by Fox, the Falmouth merchant, to have reached £91,215.[1]

This report led Parliament to increase the bounty on exported pilchards from seven to nine shillings per hogshead for the year from Midsummer 1785 to Midsummer 1786; Lemon and Fox, however, had asked for a twelve-shilling bounty, and had suggested that export bounties were less liable to fraud than direct subsidies to seining concerns which, of course, would have benefitted more fishermen than merchants. The only concession to the drift-fishermen was a relaxation of the strict licensing system of long boats, enacted the previous year to check smuggling. The merchants probably disliked the re-enactment of the clause in the 1732 Act against the relanding and "re-exportation" of pilchards; the reiteration of this provision suggests that this practice to get double or even treble bounties still went on.[2]

The season of 1785, however, also proved poor; although the price rose to £3 per hogshead, the Foxes of Falmouth only secured £7,029 since they collected but 2,343 hogsheads for export. Throughout these years the St. Ives fishery was far from flourishing, and it seems that the depression was due to natural and not commercial causes, and that, year after year, only small shoals reached the Cornish coasts. Indeed, there is evidence that the migratory habits of the pilchard had again changed. In Tonkin's time and in all probability in that of George Blewett as well, the main shoals had been arriving in the late autumn and early winter; between 1776 and 1785 they had again started appearing in the summer and vanishing from the Cornish coasts by mid-October;[3] the "summer" fishery from July to October had always been greater on the south than

[1]*Parliamentary Reports*, Vol. X, pp. 3-6. (Report from the Committee appointed to inquire into the State of the Pilchard Fisheries).

[2]25 Geo. III. cap. 58.

[3]J. Couch: *R.C.P.S.*, 1835, p. 84. Anon: *Pilchard Fishery Cornwall*, p. 3. This last pamphlet, published by W. Phillips of Lombard Street, London, speaks of the winter fishery being usual "thirty or forty years ago"; it is undated, but references to the Peace of Amiens, to the later loss of Continental markets through Napoleon's Continental System, and to non-importation and non-intercourse acts suggest that it was written before the outbreak of war with the United States in June, 1812.

on the north coast, and throughout the 1780s very few pilchards were taken at St. Ives. Early in 1786 the petitions of the "principal Persons concerned in the Pilchard Fishery" were referred to a second Parliamentary Committee, with Lemon as chairman, which recommended that the additional two shillings bounty be extended for at least seven years. Parliament agreed to extend it for five years from June 24, 1786, but laid down that it was not to be paid on more than 20,000 hogsheads in any one year; if, in any season, more than that quantity was exported, the sum of £40,000 was to be divided proportionately among the exporting merchants.[1]   In 1791 the additional bounty, reduced to 1s. 6d. per fifty gallon hogshead, was extended for seven years, and this was again renewed in 1798, 1805, and 1812 for similar periods. These additional bounties, unlike the original seven shillings bounty, were direct subsidies to the exporting merchants, and did not represent compensation for the duties on salt.

The season of 1790 was one of the best ever known, over 52,000 hogsheads of pilchards being secured. Throughout the period of the French Revolutionary and Napoleonic Wars the pilchards were plentiful in most seasons, but from 1798 to 1801 and again from 1807 to 1810 the foreign markets were closed. Abundance of fish and the difficulty of finding markets kept down the prices made by the merchants; the highest price obtained by the Foxes in the first war was 54s. for a part of the fish they exported in 1795, and the glut of fish the next season sent down the price to 26s.[2] These prices included the bounty, but the fish-curers if not the merchants gained substantial additional prices through the increased war-time naval demands for pilchard oil; in some years it even paid to bulk the fish without salt merely to obtain the oil which realized about £1 for ten gallons—a quantity that could be obtained from about two hogsheads of pilchards—and then selling off the fish for manure, as at St. Ives in 1801, at about tenpence a cartload.[3] Whatever the fortunes of merchants and fish-curers in the war years, there was plenty of fish for the poor to eat and to cure for their own use if they could get the salt to preserve them. On the return of peace prices immediately soared

[1]*Parliamentary Papers*, Vol. X, pp. 7-8. 26 Geo. III, cap. 45.
[2]H. Fox: *R.C.P.S.*, 1878, pp. 94-95. In 1793 a low price of 18s. 6d. was recorded, but some pilchards realized 40s. that year.
[3]H. Fox: *R.C.P.S.*, 1878, p. 95. Anon: *Pilchard Fishery Cornwall*, p. 8.

—to 67s. 9d. in 1802, to 55s. in 1814, whilst in 1815 they
reached the record high level of 110s. in a year of scarcity.[1]

The costs of war led Pitt to increase the duty on English
salt from 5s. to 10s. per bushel and on foreign from 10s. to
13s. 4d. in 1798, with a reduced duty of 6s. 6d. on Scottish salt.
This was a blow to the poorer classes, and in 1805 these duties
were to be increased by a further fifty per cent. Much of the
salt used in the Cornish pilchard industry was foreign, the
curers believing English salt to be inferior in quality. It may
be questioned, however, if all the salt used paid duty. It was
perhaps significant that in 1796, when the disintegration of the
First Coalition had left Britain alone fighting Revolutionary
France, the St. Ives seiners, with a phenomenal catch in their
nets, pulled them into shoal water and, without let or hindrance, sent a boat to France for salt to cure the fish which were
left in the nets till the salt arrived.[2] War, it is true, until 1807,
did not mean an entire suspension of trade between belligerents,
but this very strange and open transaction suggests that secretly
much salt was being smuggled into Cornwall. Curers could
afford foreign salt since they were granted a drawback of duty
on a specific quantity, although they complained that the 280
pounds weight per hogshead of pilchards granted by the Act
of 1798 was inadequate even if allowance was made for the
considerable amount that could be used twice over.[3] In 1802,
however, the curers were allowed 336 pounds to the hogshead,
but were forbidden to use salt more than twice.[4] These concessions, nevertheless, entailed the observance of endless legal
formalities which, at times, were needlessly complicated and
aggravated by the incompetence and even malice of customs
and excise officials. Penalties against the illegal use of duty-free
salt were heavy, but many of the women employed curing
pilchards secreted small packages of it about their persons when
they left work in order to cure fish and pork in their homes for
their own use.[5]

[1]H. Fox: *R.C.P.S.*, 1878, p. 95. J. Couch: *R.C.P.S.*, 1835, p. 79.
[2]J. S. Courtney: "Pilchard Statistics", *R.C.P.S.*, 1838, p. 119.
[3]38 Geo. III, cap. 89, clause 104. Bond: *History of Looe*, pp. 81 ff.
[4]42 Geo. III, cap. 93, clauses 20 and 21.
[5]*Parliamentary Papers*, Vol. XVIII (1866)—Report on the Sea Fisheries of the
United Kingdom—p. 496 (Evidence of Joseph Elvins to T. H. Huxley and
J. S. Lefevre at an inquiry at Mevagissey on March 29, 1864—"we had little
cellars . . . and we had a difficulty in getting salt. We used to tie the salt bags
round the women's legs and smuggle it in").

When Napoleon cut off the Mediterranean markets an effort was made to find an alternative market, but with indifferent success, in the West Indies; by the time the negro slaves had acquired a taste for pilchards in preference to North American cod and herring the Mediterranean markets were open again, and, moreover, a series of bad seasons followed. Hardly any fish were taken at St. Ives in 1815 and 1816, and none whatever in the following four years,[1] although the south coast ports sent 24,000 hogsheads to Italy in 1817. After 1815, however, an export of over 30,000 hogsheads only occurred seven times in the sixty-year period ending in 1875. The Italian markets could normally take all and more than all the pilchards Cornwall exported; there was no need to incur the cost of the extra salt needed to cure fish for the long voyage to the tropical West Indian Islands. The traditional conservatism of a long-established industry should not be forgotten. The fish-curers and traders of Cornwall had grown accustomed over decades and centuries to supplying Italians with pilchards packed in fifty or fifty-two gallon hogsheads; they did not welcome the idea of changing their methods to supply a Caribbean market with fish packed in thirty-two gallon casks, even though at one time the Government had offered additional bounties on fish sent to the West Indies. Last but not least was a fear that the trade, revolutionized by this development of a new market, would fall into the hands of "foreign" Plymouth merchants, whilst the Quaker Foxes of Falmouth disliked trading with the slave-owning planters of the British West Indies, and to this humanitarian prejudice was added the common knowledge that those planters had long been notorious for the tardy settlement of their debts.[2]

Local demand helped to keep the fishing industry going through the long years of war. It is impossible to reckon the quantity of fish consumed in Cornwall; vague estimates that between a fifth and a third of the total catch was normally consumed either fresh or salted by the local population indicate that the pilchard was a staple food in the county, and it is possible that in normal years no less than fifteen million pilchards, or between five and six thousand hogsheads of pil-

[1] J. Couch: *R.C.P.S.*, 1835, pp. 100-101.
[2] Anon: *Pilchard Fishery Cornwall*, pp. 12-15. William Burt: *Review of the Commerce of Plymouth*, (1816), pp. 88-89, 165-167, 169.

chards, worth about £7,500 at the fairly common price of a shilling a hundred, were eaten by the Cornish people besides other fish.[1] Apart from this local demand the chance of running a cargo through the French continental blockade, especially when it became known that the Italian price was 180s. per hogshead in 1811, was not one to be spurned by a community that paid little heed to its own customs laws.[2] In the last resort the fish could always be used as manure, and West Cornwall farmers in 1812 and 1813 were taking shares in seines, paying wages to men working them, and carting the catches directly from the beaches of St. Ives and Mount's Bay to their fields. The fearful poverty and hunger of many labouring people in these years might make this seem a frightful and criminal waste of food, but starving times invariably occurred not in the autumn months when the pilchards came but in the spring and early summer, when grain stocks were exhausted as well as such store of pilchards as the poor had been able to afford the salt to preserve. Fish manure was the best fertilizer then known to Cornish farmers, and by using it they were preparing for better grain and potato crops; for their part, the fisherfolk were quite ready to work for the farmers who were willing to pay them wages or to buy the fish from them at 12s. 6d. or 15s. the hogshead.[3]

The long wars and the series of poor fishing seasons which followed, caused considerable distress in the Cornish fishing ports. In the war years near starvation had reigned in a land of plenty; there had been plenty of fish, but with foreign markets closed the fisherfolk engaged in curing pilchards had not earned enough wages to buy the salt needed to preserve a family supply of about a thousand pilchards.[4] The fifteen shilling duty on salt had raised its price to 24s. a bushel or nearly 6d. a pound; the normal cottage family used about two pounds of salt a week, but the great difficulty arose from the fact that it was not a regular item in family budgets; there would be a demand for a half-bushel or bushel by the ordinary household when the pilchard shoals were secured; there would be another and even greater quantity required when the cottager killed his pig; oftentimes he could not afford the salt,

[1] J. S. Courtney, *R.C.P.S.*, 1836, p. 125. *W.B.*: September 6, 1811.
[2] *W.B.*: August 24, 1812.
[3] *W.B.*: August 24, 1812 and September 3, 1813.
[4] See p. 281 note 5 above.

and local markets were glutted with pork that might finally be sold off at a mere three-halfpence a pound.[1] The merchants and fish-curers dealing with fish for exportation, however, were exempt. Thus, whereas in 1786 the Cornish fishing interest had successfully pressed Parliament to relieve them, in February, 1822, only Sir William Lemon and but four other members of the total Cornish parliamentary contingent of forty-four were in the minority who demanded a reduction in the duties on salt.[2] This motion, however, was only defeated by 169 votes to 165, and the Government reduced the duties on salt from 15s. to 2s. a bushel a little later; the seining interests then sent a deputation to Vansittart, the Chancellor of the Exchequer, to ask for the abolition of this duty, but were content to receive a promise of a drawback on salt used in curing fish for export. Three years later the salt duty was finally abolished.

The war-time demand for pilchard oil had stimulated the early summer fishery which was carried on by the drifters in deep waters rather than by seiners. Drift-fishing, too, tended to supply fish for a longer season, whilst its equipment could also be used in mackerel and herring fisheries. In the war years the Government had tended to favour the drifters, who were seamen, not "landlubbers" who could only pull an oar two or three days in the year in shallow inshore waters to catch a shoal of pilchards. With peace and a series of bad seasons the old complaints of seiners that drift-men broke up and frightened away the shoals were renewed. A seiners' meeting at Falmouth in February, 1819, determined to consult the Attorney-General about the enforcement of the 1662 Act to keep the drifters and the new trawlers, which were coming down from Brixham and Plymouth in increasing numbers, outside the one and a half league line.[3] In the next few years a few drifters were prosecuted for breach of this Act,[4] but to all intents and purposes it was obsolete. The St. Ives drifters started participating in the Irish herring fishery in 1816; the Mount's Bay men followed suit a few years later, and by 1838 Newlyn alone had a hundred boats engaged in the Irish Sea fishery.[5]

[1]*Parliamentary Papers,* Vol. XIV (1817), p. 400.
[2]Hansard: *Parliamentary Debates* (Second Series) Vol. VI, 860 ff.
[3]*W.B.:* February 12, 1819.
[4]*W.B.:* April 11, 1823; September 15, 1826 (case at Looe); and September 5, 1828 (case at St. Agnes).
[5]J. S. Courtney: *R.C.P.S.,* 1838, p. 132.

Smuggling, the other resource of Cornish seafarers in hard times, also received a great impetus from the wars. At no time was that calling regarded with less official disfavour than when Napoleon tried to exclude British goods from Europe. Unfortunately the Cornish held very individualist notions of the best return cargoes to bring back with them; they seemed to think it necessary to avoid officials in authority on both sides of the Channel; nor did they see the need of giving up "free trade" when Napoleon had been exiled to St. Helena. The first quarter of the nineteenth century, perhaps, saw the zenith of Cornish smuggling; there were incidents as sensational as that when the Carters of Prussia Cove had turned a coastal battery against the excisemen. Jacob Denny, indicted at the Old Bailey in February, 1813, for landing a contraband cargo in Cornwall, after exchanging shots with naval cruisers in the Channel, was convicted, but was recommended to mercy by the jury on the ground that he was the first to be convicted by a new law, although that law had been on the statute book for five years; possibly more than one juryman felt some regard for a man who had defied the navy which had proudly patrolled the Channel since Trafalgar.[1] A sensation was caused in Cornwall a few months later when the Coroner's jury at the inquest on Thomas James returned a verdict of "Wilful Murder against Persons Unknown." James, a "respectable eating-house and lime-kiln proprietor" of Flushing, had been shot just after nine o'clock on the night of December 7, 1814, going home with his son from St. Mawes in an open boat. The hour was suspiciously late and James had not heeded the command of four Customs men in another boat to lay-to. Since the names of three of the four Customs men were known it is not unlikely that the jury returned the open verdict with some idea of thereby securing the committal of the entire Customs establishment at Falmouth; two of the four were immediately committed to Bodmin jail to await trial at the next Assizes; a third man, called Paynter, who had actually fired the shot, escaped on the first horse he could find, thereby running the risk of being charged as a horse-thief as well. Until March, 1815, the two men were held in prison, doubtless to the benefit of Falmouth "free traders"; the Assizes jury found them not guilty, but also found a true bill against Paynter, who then

1 *W.B.*: February 26, 1813.

gave himself up, and was sentenced in July to a year's imprisonment and a fine of a shilling for manslaughter. Paynter had been culpably if not criminally rash in firing the shot; at no stage in the trials was it suggested that it was merely a warning shot; there was no evidence that James had made threatening moves; nor was there any hint that he and his son had acted as decoys to lure the preventive men away from less innocent craft then their own. Paynter had not improved his case by flight, but it was likely that he was afraid of facing a Cornish jury on a capital charge—too many Cornish juries in the past had acquitted smugglers to make it seem feasible that they would be unbiassed in a charge brought against an exciseman.[1]

At this time the Falmouth Customs officials had gained notoriety by over-officious zeal and efficiency, but the same could not be said of the preventive men at Fowey. In February, 1815, the latter seized a contraband cargo from a French ship, and then proceeded to open the casks they brought from her in the roadway by the Customs House; everyone joined in to have a taste, and a free fight ensued over the division of the spoils; the local magistrates thought discretion the better part of valour, and did not intervene to uphold the laws of the land.[2] In later years the personnel of the Customs at Fowey improved, but the same cannot be said of its magistracy, for in July, 1824, £300 worth of contraband brandy was seized in the house of the Mayor, Bennet, who had only allowed the preventive men to enter his house when the chief collector of the port had arrived on the scene, he had refused entry to the subordinate officers and spent the period of grace gained thereby to throw a vast quantity of spirits into the river.[3] Smuggling went on at Fowey many years after this incident; a violent affray between a gang of "armed" smugglers, estimated and perhaps over-estimated at "a hundred strong and more", with the preventive men early in 1835 had a sequel at the Assizes the following August; five men were charged with having feloniously assembled to defraud the revenue; the Cornish jury, finding that the sticks with which they had been armed were not offensive weapons, acquitted them.[4]

[1] *W.B.*: December 9 and 16, 1814; March 31, July 7 and 28, 1815.
[2] *W.B.*: February 3, 1815.
[3] *W.B.*: July 30, 1824.
[4] *W.B.*: April 3 and August 7, 1835.

Violent clashes between smugglers and excisemen were not rare. In the second decade of the nineteenth century smuggling grew so flagrant that, early in 1816, the revenue cutters were transferred to the Navy which meant that the Admiralty had been called in to suppress the "free traders"; a little later Inniskilling Dragoons were stationed at Truro to assist in the suppression of smuggling.[1] In the long run these measures were effective. The extent of the activities of the rival parties—preventive men and smugglers—can be gauged from the Spring Sessions held at Torpoint in 1816 when between seventy and eighty persons were fined for infractions of the revenue laws a few days after over a hundred people had been found guilty of similar offences at Devonport.[2] Gradually the "trade" declined—or the smugglers became more adept in avoiding apprehension. There were still quite frequent affrays between "shore-gangs" and excisemen, but the hapless James seems to have been one of the last fatal casualties. Most amazing of the later incidents was that at Millhook Haven, near Boscastle, on November 11, 1820, when some excisemen headed by Sampson Woodcock seized:

"from four to five hundred tubs of foreign run Spirits and hauled their boat on the beach and remained to guard their seizure; that soon after a smuggling cutter came in sight and afterwards two armed boats were sent from her, the crews of which, together with the crew of the cutter, commenced firing upon the beach, which the preventative men returned until their ammunition was expended; that the Smugglers then came on shore and attacked the said Sampson Woodcock and his men, and by superiority of numbers overpowered them and compelled them to retreat, and after having driven them from their Seizure, the said Smugglers carried off the six-oared galley belong to the preventive station (at Boscastle) and her materials, together with the tubs which the Officers had seized, and went off to sea."[3]

Woodcock and his men had probably beaten a more hasty retreat than the stilted language of this official proclamation suggests, but the fact that no one seems to have been seriously hurt or killed leads to a suspicion of collusion between smugglers and officials.

Gradually the epic days of smuggling drew to a close.

[1] *W.B.*: March 8 and 22, 1816.
[2] *W.B.*: April, 5, 1816.
[3] Proclamation of Reward of £200 offered by the Board of Customs, London, December 7, 1820. (*W.B.*, advert., January 12, 1821).

Excisemen became more efficient; Cornish gentry and magistrates became a little more conscientious of their duties as citizens to contribute to the revenues and to uphold the laws of the realm; the poorer classes had their great grievance redressed by the abolition of the salt duties in 1825. Religion, and especially the growing temperance movement, which spread rapidly in the fishing villages in the 1830s, contributed to the decline of the trade. Falmouth had its last fling at the hated Customs men in March, 1832, when its constables arrested two Plymouth officials as suspected "resurrection men".[1] The "trade" fell into disrepute through the activities of hawkers who sold as the best "smuggled French brandy" spirits adulterated with oil of vitriol up and down the county.[2] The infliction of heavy terms of imprisonment and fines on smugglers helped to suppress illegal practices after 1835. Matters had become very quiet and respectable indeed by the middle of the nineteenth century, when the burning of the mere effigy of an overactive, over-efficient, and unpopular exciseman at St. Mawes could be described as "disgraceful proceedings" and as "uproar and riot".[3]

The effort to suppress smuggling after 1815 may have made the authorities more sympathetic to the clamour of the seiners against the deep-sea drifters and their disregard of the Act of 1662; one breach of the law provoked others, and the drifters were too well acquainted with the routes across the Channel. The cause of the almost complete failure of the St. Ives fishery for six successive seasons after 1815 will probably never be known; it seems most probable that it was due to a succession of poor spawning seasons, or to a dearth of the food the pilchards fed on, or even to epidemic disease in the fish,[4] that is to biological phenomena of which the time had little knowledge. As always the seiners were ready to blame the drifters for breaking up the shoals and frightening them away from the coasts. Others, however, advanced more fantastic reasons for the non-arrival of the pilchards, to sinfulness and sabbath breaking on the part of the fisherfolk, and to the depredations of

[1] *W.B.*: March 2, 1832.
[2] *W.B.*: February 25, 1842 and August 4, 1845.
[3] *W.B.*: July 20, 1849.
[4] J. Couch recorded that in 1834, a relatively good season in Mount's Bay and St. Ives, the early fish caught at Polperro had been small and spotted, which he thought indicated disease (*R.C.P.S.*, 1835, p. 90).

strange aquatic monsters.[1] Whatever the cause, the pilchards practically deserted St. Ives during the first years of peace, whilst the four seasons from 1818 to 1821 were extremely bad on the South Coast as well, the total average annual export of Cornish pilchards in those four years being but 1,850 hogsheads, a quantity which, in some past seasons, had been taken by a single seine in a day's working. High prices, ranging from 60s. to 90s. did not compensate for the dearth of fish.[2]

The majority of seiners, however, blamed the drifters and the increasing numbers of South Devon trawlers for the succession of bad seasons, and called a meeting at Truro on February 12, 1819, of "all concerned in the Pilchard Fishery", with Joseph Banfield, banker, merchant, and deputy-recorder of Falmouth in the chair.[3] In consequence of this meeting, Parliament extended the additional 1s 6d. bounty for a further seven years to June, 1826,[4] and the Attorney-General was consulted about enforcing the Act of 1662 banning drift-fishing within one and a half leagues of the coasts during the pilchard season. There was some talk that Spanish and French competitors had appeared in the Italian markets where they were either underselling the Cornish merchants or else defrauding the Italian consumers by falsified Cornish markings on the casks they sold. The drifters, in reply, stressed that they were deep-sea fishermen, occupied in that calling the whole year, providing fresh fish at all seasons, and training men in seamanship, whilst some of them asserted once more that drifting was the "poor man's fishery" and attacked the "rich" seine owners.[5]

The pressure of the seining interests on Parliament and their influence in some of the Cornish Parliamentary boroughs had, in the past, helped to secure the continuation of the bounties on exported pilchards, bounties that had become subsidies pure and simple since, in 1798, the seiners had been granted duty-free salt to cure fish for export although the original bounties had been granted as compensation for the salt taxes. This may explain the indifference of the seiners to the agitation for the abolition of the salt duties. When, however, Vansittart

[1]*W.B.*: October 20, 1815.
[2]William Roberts: "Quantity and Prices of Pilchards Exported, 1815-1871", *J.R.I.C.*, Vol. IV, p. 159. See Appendix V below, p. 334.
[3]*W.B.*: February 12, 1819.
[4]59 Geo. III, cap. 77.
[5]*W.B.*: February 26, 1819 (letters of Thomas Jago and "Old Fisherman"), March 5 and 26, 1819.

K

reduced the duties to 2s. a bushel on English salt and to 2s. 3d. on foreign, in 1822, and omitted to make any provision to continue the exemption on salt used in curing fish for export, there was an immediate outcry by the "fishermen" of Cornwall, headed by the merchant families of Fox, Banfield, Lake, and Blake of Falmouth and the Carnes of Penzance. They met at Truro to pass a resolution that Vansittart's new reduced duties would:

"utterly annihilate the Pilchard Fishery on the Coasts of Cornwall and Devon, by which means property to a considerable amount invested in Craft, Seans, and Cellars, will in a great measure be destroyed, and the numerous class of persons employed in the catching and curing of Pilchards, in the building and repairing of Boats and other Craft, in the manufacturing of Netting and Cordage for the Seans, in the making of Casks . . . will be deprived of employment and be under the necessity of applying for relief to their already overburdened parishes."[1]

It seemed to be a strong argument, yet it might have been asked whether a seasonal occupation dependent on a foreign market was one deserving government assistance. No disinterested person could have held that the seine fishery should have been regarded as more than a supplementary industry, giving additional employment to men and women who for the greater part of the year lived by other callings. A drifter, engaged in mackerel, herring, crab, and lobster fishing besides that for pilchards, could find work for the greater part of the year, supply local markets with his catches, and thus benefit the persons he supplied with cheap fresh fish at all seasons. If a man relied on seining alone for work he would have been a charge on the rates for the greater part of the year and for the whole year when the season failed.

The relationships of capital and labour in the seining industry were complicated. Ownership of the means of production—boats, nets, cellars, and so forth—had become divorced from labour in the seining ports of Mevagissey, Mount's Bay, and St. Ives at a very early period, but the tradition of sharefishing lingered. A relatively large capital was required to prepare and market the fish. Above all, it had become less of an industry than a speculation. One or two good seasons led too many men to speculate either singly or, more often, in

[1] *W.B.*: June 7, 1822.

groups, in buying boats, nets, and cellars to participate in the next season when, perhaps, the pilchards failed to appear. The custom that developed at Mevagissey and St. Ives of dividing the bays into *stems* represents an attempt to control but not to check this over-speculation; if there was only room at St. Ives for twenty seines to be worked at once, twenty seines were enough; a generous margin to allow for all accidental contingencies would perhaps double that number, but the number of seines in St. Ives was 146 in 1838, and by 1864 had reached 247.[1] In 1828 about 16,000 hogsheads of pilchards were caught at St. Ives,[2] but shared among 120 seines this represented only 133 hogsheads per seine; the highest price of the year was 45s. 6d., but since a great quantity remained unsold in Naples for some time,[3] the average value of the catch per seine cannot have exceeded £275; with costs of wages, salt, curing, and shipping abroad, few seines could have shown a clear profit of £100 on a capital investment of at least £1,000. Moreover, such catches were abnormal, occurring at most but once in every seven years, whilst there was almost a complete failure of the fishery in one season out of five.[4] It is doubtful if, on an average, all the St. Ives seining concerns averaged a profit of five per cent a year. The nets, which were a considerable item of capital expenditure, rarely lasted more than ten or twelve years. Some did make considerable gains for it is doubtful if more than two-thirds of the St. Ives seining outfits were ever in a fit state to be used in any one season, which meant that the catch was divided among fewer adventurers.

Apart from the little fishing coves where one or two seines were maintained, however, there is little doubt that the seine-fishery had been over-capitalized by 1820; the rash speculators had no reason and less justice to demand government subsidies to alleviate the losses they had incurred through their own folly. As for the labour the industry employed, that, too, was exaggerated. In 1827 it was estimated that the Cornish fisheries employed about 10,500 persons;[5] only the 1,600 driftmen can be regarded as permanently employed; 2,674 men

[1] J. S. Courtney: *R.C.P.S.*, 1838, p. 122. *Parliamentary Papers*, Vol. XVIII (1866) p. 546.
[2] *W.B.*: March 13, 1829.
[3] *W.B.*: March 13, 1829.
[4] This estimate is based on the records of the St. Ives fishery from 1840 to 1877. (H. Fox: *R.C.P.S.*, 1878, pp. 96-98).
[5] *W.B.*: March 7, 1827.

were said to be "employed at sea on seines", but with the local length of a seining season varying from two or three days to ten weeks, it cannot be reckoned that two thousand men were thus employed for more than six weeks in the year. On shore, 6,500 more persons were employed in curing pilchards and other work connected with the fishery, but they could hardly have been thus employed for more than three months in the year. At best the seining industry provided seasonal employment to many casual labourers, but more than a quarter of its labour force were housewives and other women engaging in it just to supplement family budgets. The rest were labourers who at other times were engaged on the farms and mines, especially the latter since the tribute and tutwork systems enabled them to change their occupations for two or three months.[1] The less arduous tasks of repairing nets and curing the fish in bulk must have employed many people who, physically incapable of heavier tasks, would otherwise have been, and at other seasons were, subsisting on parochial relief. But there is no reason to believe that seining provided more employment than this, whatever the merchants saw fit to publish abroad when trying to secure special privileges from the Government.

Nevertheless, in their campaign against the salt duties, in June, 1822, the seining interests went on to declare that:

"for several years past the Pilchard Fishery of this Kingdom has experienced great rivalship in the Italian markets from the Fisheries of France and Spain; and in consequence of the low prices at which the produce of these Fisheries has been sold, it is with the greatest difficulty, and by the application of the most rigid economy in every respect, that the British Fishery has been able to compete with them; but this competition will be rendered absolutely impossible, if, by a Duty on Salt, or by any other means, the charges of curing Pilchards are increased."

They also stressed the shipping employed in carrying fish to the Mediterranean markets, the value of the fishery as a school of seamanship, and the hardship entailed by taxing salt already

[1] The later St. Ives fishery may have benefitted the miners who, before the use of mechanically worked pumps became general, were driven by flooding from the lower mine levels in the wet autumns. On the South Coast, however, the pilchard season coincided with harvest time, and few farm-hands could have been spared to help the seiners, although some may have been released by the practice of putting the sheaves of corn into arrish-mows which could stand the ravages of weather undamaged till November or even December.

stored by the curers who had been hard hit by the succession
of bad seasons. Vansittart, however, was not moved by their
pleas and refused to abolish a tax he had just cut by eighty-
five per cent; he promised a drawback on the salt used to
cure fish that were actually exported, but he insisted that the
curers first pay the salt duty, whilst they could only secure
the drawback he promised by complying with rather intricate
formalities.

Popular pressure and a formidable opposition minority in
Parliament had forced Vansittart to reduce the salt duties
drastically; he knew that there was considerable opposition to
the small duty retained, and the duty was to vanish three
years later. If the condition of the poorer classes was slowly
improving after the post-war depression, the demand of richer
classes for reduced taxes grew as the years passed. The small salt
tax that was retained was hardly worth the costs and trouble of
collection, without considering its unpopularity. Expenditure,
however, could be reduced—notably by the reduction and
abolition of bounties. In 1824 Parliament determined to abolish
the bounties on exported pilchards by gradual reduction, to 7s.
until July, 1826, to 6s. for the next year, and then further
yearly 2s. reductions to terminate the bounty on July 5, 1829.
The seining interests—or rather the exporting merchants—
petitioned Parliament in July, 1827, and again in March, 1828,
against this but in vain. Their failure is not surprising; even if
some Cornish members supported them, their great champion,
Sir William Lemon, had died in 1825; the bounties had originally been granted as compensation for the salt duties which
had been abolished in 1825; if they argued that the small
catches in recent seasons[1] meant that the actual bounties paid
would be a trivial item in the national budget, they met the
rejoinder that their trade was not merely insignificant, but
dying, and that but a very small group of merchants were asking
for the reprieve of the bounties.

The series of bad seasons embittered the feud of drifters and
seiners; in those seasons the drift-men often secured better

[1]Over the twelve years 1818-1829, the average yearly export of Cornish pilchards had been 8,626 hogsheads; if the two good seasons of 1823 and 1828 are
excluded, with their respective exports of 24,109 and 26,018 hogsheads, the yearly
average was but 5,339, which, far from employing a vast amount of merchant
shipping, could be taken to Italy by a dozen of the vessels then normally employed
in that trade, the round voyage taking, at most, three months.

catches than their rivals, and consequently there was a steady
increase in the number of drifting concerns, which went on
although in the 1830s and 1840s the seiners enjoyed several
good seasons. The drifters were improving their methods,
adopting deep-sunk nets after experience in the Irish Sea
herring fishery,[1] but few of them heeded suggestions, made by
Dr. Jonathan Couch and others,[2] that they use luring lights
to attract fish to the nets. The increase of drift-fishing, for
mackerel, herring, and other fish besides pilchards, in Mount's
Bay, contributed to the next startling conflict in the Cornish
fishing industry—the outbreak of tithe-warfare in Mousehole
in December, 1830. Although sensational, this conflict is
closely related to the struggle that farmers had been inter-
mittently fighting against tithe since the beginning of the post-
war slump.[3] The Mousehole troubles came after two bad
seasons; hardly any pilchards had been taken in Cornwall in
1829, whilst in 1830 a fairly productive season had coincided
with the lowest prices since the war.[4]

Tithe of fish fell into the category of things that went back to
"time immemorial", and the general temper of the age had
become more than impatient of the dead hand of the past.
Cornish farmers and fishermen probably knew nothing of the
writings of Bentham and the other utilitarian anti-tradition-
alists, but the theorists were expressing the feelings and sentiments of the age rather than leading public opinion. There had
been some trouble over tithes of fish in the past, but the matter
had become increasingly complicated with the development
of the industry into diverse interests. It had been reasonably
easy for the tithe-owners to arrive at a composition with the
actual owners of seining outfits, especially when some of them

[1] *W.B.*: August 9, 1822.
[2] Couch stressed the success of this method in the Chesapeake Bay fishery
(*R.C.P.S.*, 1835, p. 71); it was also advocated by Lawrence Samuel Boyne of St.
Mawes at the end of the poor season of 1829. (*W.B.*: November 6, 1829).
[3] See above pp. 242 ff.
[4] W. Roberts: *J.R.I.C.*, Vol. IV, p. 159. In 1830, 22,000 hogsheads were
exported; the bounties had ended, and the prices realized were from 32s. to 35s.
per hogshead; the cost of curing was about £1 per hogshead. Low prices continued for the next seven years, and cannot be ascribed to the troubled political
situation in Italy in 1830 and 1831. There was some French and Spanish competition, but there were also Italian complaints that the quality of the pilchards
supplied by the Cornish merchants had been bad (*W.B.*: July 27, 1827). The
Neapolitan markets, moreover, were closed as a quarantine measure in 1831
on account of the outbreak of cholera in England in the late autumn of that year
(*W.B.*: December 16, 1831).

were part-owners in seines themselves,[1] and when even more of
them were related to owners of seines; it was more difficult to
arrive at any satisfactory arrangement with share-fishermen
in the seine fishery, and still more difficult to make terms with
the drift-men. The latter not only had a complex system of
allocating the catch in shares of an eighth to the boat, three-
eighths to the nets, and the rest to the men, but also frequently
landed their catches not in their own parishes but elsewhere,
sometimes to market the fish more conveniently, at others
simply through stress of weather.[2] The worst feature of all was
the commercialization of tithe, a tendency that had begun in
the Stuart period. Whatever the original purpose of tithe in
England, whether it had been designed to support charity as
well as to maintain religious faith, it is certain that by 1800
tithes were regarded as speculative investments; they had
become entirely divorced from things spiritual and religious,
and the relics of their connection with the Established Church
only served further to discredit that Church. Lay impropriators and absentee pluralist beneficed rectors had transformed tithes into a property right, and in the case of the tithes
on fish such exactions could not be regarded as having any
association with real property, but merely a right claimed by a
few favoured individuals to tax the labours of poor fisherfolk.
The growing commercial materialism of the age, too, meant,
especially in times of economic stress and of financial fluctuations, that tithe-owners would be all the more insistent on the
exaction of the last penny they could claim.

[1]*E.g.* Walter Borlase. (Walter Borlase MSS: letters of Walter to Peggy Borlase
of November 21, 1748 and March 27, 1749).
[2]A seiner resident in one parish often operated from another. One of Walter
Borlase's parishioners at Madron, Langford, became the partner of a Buryan man
in a seine about 1742, and in consequence both Borlase and Dr. A. A. Sykes, the
Dean of Buryan claimed tithes from him. (Penlee MSS: Letters of A. A. Sykes to
Walter Borlase, January 31, 1743/44; March 1, 1743/44; and May 8, 1744). Sykes
finally told Borlase: "As to what Right you may have at Madron, or what Custom,
I am not a judge nor am I concerned in it. My own right is what I am concerned
for: and as the custom is to have the tithe of Fish, landed, cured, etc., in the
Deanery, especially where the tackle is kept, the houses all repaired there, and all
fitted for that use, and everything done in my district, I can hitherto see no reason
to give up a Right which my Predecessors have all long enjoyed. That Mr. Langford by hiring the Cove, Sheds, etc., is *quoad haec* an inhabitant of the Deanery."
It might be added that at no point are the coasts of the parish of Madron and those
of the former Deanery of Buryan contiguous. The very nature of the coast makes
it unlikely that Langford was operating a seine from Lamorna Cove, adjoining
Paul parish, the nearest point to Madron; he was probably seining at Sennen
Cove, north of Land's End, the only other "Cove" on the coast of the Deanery
which was made up of the present parishes of Buryan, St. Levan, and Sennen.

The drift-fishermen of Newlyn and Mousehole had never entirely acquiesced in the exactions of tithe by the rectors of Paul parish. In 1680 they had argued in the courts against William Gwavas that fish caught in drift-nets were not tithe-able, since such fish were caught by being hung by the head in the meshes of the nets and, therefore, came in the same class as fish *meased* in the sleeves of seine-nets which, by immemorial custom were exempted from tithe. Gwavas, alleging that the fishermen had resorted to drifting for the deliberate purpose of defrauding him of his tithes, finally won his case in the Court of Exchequer. The fishermen then paid tithes until 1722, when several of them again refused to pay tithes on fish caught in drift-nets; this time the issue was complicated by the fact that the drifters were landing many of their fish not at home but at St. Ives, Fowey, and elsewhere; they argued that the tithe would take away the greater part if not all their profits, and that they held no land at all in Paul, where they had to pay rents to other individuals for mooring their boats. To secure a fair trial, Gwavas more than distrusting the impartiality of Cornish juries, the case was tried in London in December, 1728. Many aged witnesses were taken up from Cornwall to testify the nature of ancient customs, but the Court decided in favour of Gwavas. The fishermen then appealed to Parliament, alleging that holding the trial in London had been unfair to them since there were a host of witnesses they could not afford to bring a distance of some three hundred miles to give testimony in their favour; they also stated that a Middlesex jury was incompetent to judge the customs of Cornwall. But Gwavas again won the day.[1]

The new struggle began with the sale of the tithes of Paul late in 1829.[2] In November, 1830, there was some talk in Newlyn and Mousehole of petitioning Parliament to abolish the tithe on fish,[3] but in December the fisherfolk took matters into their own hands. An attorney who came for the tithe-owners to persuade the Mousehole men that it was right that tithe be paid, met with a stormy reception from men who, after a poor drifting season, were hard put to it to procure bread for their families; the attorney was glad to escape with a whole skin,

[1] Josiah Brown: *Cases in Parliament*, (1780), Vol. III, p. 479.
[2] *W.B.*: November 13, 1829.
[3] *W.B.*: November 19, 1830.

albeit with some disorder to his attire. On Christmas Eve a bailiff came to Mousehole to serve writs on the defaulters; mobbed by the women of the village, he rashly drew a pistol from his pocket which was quickly seized from him and thrown into the sea; not wishing to share the fate of his weapon, he escaped, battered and clothes torn by his assailants, only to have to run the gauntlet of the enraged women of Newlyn; beaten and bruised he at last reached his home, while at Mousehole men were posting placards with the legend "It is better to die than to starve. No tithe; we will die first. One and All."[1] The fishermen justly argued that the tithes had become exorbitant; the new tithe-owners were claiming £6 on every boat, double what it had been before, whilst, within memory, only 6s. had been charged; moreover, a further guinea was claimed from the boats engaged in the Irish herring fishery, whether they caught any fish or not. Some started denouncing tithe as the relic of "a free will offering made in the days of Catholic superstition."[2] Magistrates met and consulted; prosecutions were anticipated and led to some mob-scenes, but the tithe-owners were terrified and fish-tithes were nevermore collected in the parish of Paul.

Elsewhere fish-tithes survived; seiners usually compounded at a flat rate of £1 13s. 4d. per seining outfit, but at St. Ives this caused several disputes since the large number of seines there made it an inequitable charge on the fortunate and unfortunate alike, until, in 1837, the tithe-owners agreed to accept a flat rate of 6d. on every hogshead caught if the price was at or below 30s. and a graduated rise of 3d. for every 5s. above that price, no charge being made on the working fishermen or on the drifters. At Porthleven and Mullion a levy of £5 on drift-boats met no resistance. There was some litigation over tithe-claims; the Rector of St. Just in Roseland, after a lapse of several years, attempted to levy a tenth on the seiners in 1865, but agreed in the court to accept a guinea from every seine in the parish yearly as in former times.[3] In 1870, the Vicar of Mevagissey successfully brought an action against some seine-owners registered in that port for the share of 1/12 claimed

[1] *W.B.*: December 31, 1830.
[2] *W.B.*: January 7, 1831.
[3] H. Fox: *R.C.P.S.*, 1878, p. 91. At that time there were only 8 or 10 seines in St. Just in Roseland, which included St. Mawes.

in the portion of the fish allocated to the men whom they had paid in money, besides the £1 13s. 4d. charged on each seine, although most of the men so employed were St. Mawes and not Mevagissey men.[1] With the exception of Mullion and Porthleven, however, the tithes claimed after 1830 were tithes on seines, and the victory of the Newlyn and Mousehole men and women almost completely freed the drifters from liability to tithe.

Exemption from tithes, more or less full-time employment, and far more regular returns all tended to encourage the drift rather than the seine fishery, especially on the south coast of Cornwall. As the nineteenth century went on, improved transport by sea and land increased the markets for fresh fish whereas there had never been any English sale for salted pilchards outside Cornwall and Devon. True the old feud of seiners and drifters went on, but in most places they came to some agreement since the former could only operate by day and the latter by night.[2] At Mevagissey and St. Ives the smaller seiners were driven out by the the larger concerns, in St. Ives by an 1841 Act of Parliament[3] which, besides prohibiting all other modes of fishing within a thousand fathoms of the shore during the pilchard season, stipulated that no seine nets less than 160 fathoms in length and 8 in depth should be employed. In 1868 this ban on other modes of fishing close inshore was extended to the entire coast of Cornwall, save to the north-east of Trevose Head, but this resulted from the belief of both seiners and drifters that "foreign" trawlers were destroying fish spawn and small fry by coming too close inshore. At the same time the crab and lobster fishermen were also complaining that their pots and creels were being swept away by the beam trawls.

By the 1860s fears were being entertained of the exhaustion of the fisheries, not only of pilchards but of the larger fish, and even more of the crabs and lobsters that were taken to London by rail in great quantities. Whatever marine biologists were to discover on the subject in later years, contemporary fisherfolk believed that certain types of nets—particularly the small-meshed nets, the beam-trawl nets, and the ground-seine nets—

[1]H. Fox: *R.C.P.S.*, 1878, pp. 91-92.
[2]*Parliamentary Papers*, (1866), Vol. XVII, p. 465 and Vol. XVIII, p. 598.
[3]4 and 5 Vict. cap. 57. *Parliamentary Papers*, (1866), Vol. XVII, p. 630 and Vol. XVIII, pp. 503-504.

were wastefully destructive of fish spawn and small fry.[1]
Pilchard exports had certainly declined, but this may have
been offset by the demands of the increased Cornish population
at home, especially after the abolition of the salt duties in 1825.
The fluctuating nature of the seining industry led to its decline
in an age of free capitalist enterprise; by 1841 the St. Ives
seiners had agreed to set up rigid controls of the fishery, and
by 1864, although there were over 240 seining outfits at St.
Ives, five companies controlled and shared the fishery and only
employed 230 men at most as fishermen.[2] By 1877, even at
St. Ives, it was recognised that the drift fishery was more important than seining,[3] and the drifters had triumphed in
Mount's Bay and at Mevagissey long before. Seines were still
maintained in readiness to be used when shoals came close
inshore, but the drifters had triumphed, although now they in
their turn were being organized into capitalist companies,
some of which owned small fleets of fishing vessels. The "little
man", however, survived, but the largest profits were now
reaped by a new middleman interest, the great fishmongers of
London and other markets who, minimizing the loss of deteriorated fish by the use of ice, in the 1870s were clearing three-
and four-fold profits.[4]

The sparse early records of the Cornish fisheries do not make
it possible to form more than a rough general idea of the progress of drift-fishing and of the decline of seining. In 1785 there
had been 180 Cornish drift-boats, employing about 900 men,
whilst 110 to 140 seines employed from 1,870 to 2,380 hands;
about a third of the seines were at Mevagissey, a quarter in
Mount's Bay, and a sixth at St. Mawes and other south coast
fishing coves, the remaining quarter being at St. Ives. By
1835 out of about 200 Cornish seines 132 were at St. Ives,
although nearly half of these were unfit for use, whilst the
number of Cornish drift-boats had doubled and were now em-

[1]"Report of the Sea Fisheries of the United Kingdom", *Parliamentary Papers*,
(1866), Vol. XVII, pp. 571-721, and Vol. XVIII, pp. 466-556. "Destruction of
Spawn by Trawling and Ground Seining", *ibid*, (1878-79), Vol. XVII,
pp. 259-306. J. N. Hearder: "The Degeneration of our Sea Fisheries", *Transactions Devonshire Association*, Vol. IV (1870), pp. 213 ff. A defence of the trawlers
was made by E. W. H. Holdsworth in his *Sea Fisheries of Great Britain and Ireland*,
(1883) pp. 39-45, 121.
[2]*Parliamentary Papers*, (1866), Vol. XVIII, pp. 546, 552.
[3]*Parliamentary Papers*, (1878-79), Vol. XVIII, p. 301 (evidence of J. B. Rosewall).
[4]"The British Sea Fisheries": *Blackwood's Magazine*, Vol. CXVIII (1875),
p. 460. E. W. H. Holdsworth: *The Sea Fisheries of Great Britain and Ireland*, p. 10.

ploying 1,600 men. In 1870 there were 379 seines in Cornwall, 285 of them at St. Ives, 23 in Mount's Bay, 10 at Mevagissey, 9 each at Newquay and St. Mawes, and the remaining 43 distributed among fifteen other harbours and havens. The number of drift boats had risen to 635, of which 339 were in Mount's Bay (130 at Newlyn, 105 at Mousehole, and 104 at Porthleven), 186 at St. Ives, 61 at Mevagissey, and 22 at Looe, the remaining 37 belonging to seven other ports; of the 261 first-class boats Newlyn possessed 90, St. Ives 86, Mousehole 55, and Porthleven 30. Of the total capital invested in both fisheries, estimated at £236,500, over half was at St. Ives with a total investment of £118,750, whilst the Mount's Bay ports had £82,710 and Mevagissey but £14,460; in the drift fishery, however, the Mount's Bay ports accounted for over 47% of the capital of £139,690 and St. Ives rather less than 30%, whereas in the seining industry St. Ives was responsible for nearly 65% of the capital invested and the Mount's Bay ports for less than 6%. St. Ives, however, only employed 260 men in seining and 602 drift-fishermen, whereas the Mount's Bay seines employed 169 and its drift-boats 1,415 men; Mevagissey was employing 149 men in seining and 205 drift-fishermen out of a total of 3,972 employed in both fisheries, of whom 2,462 were working on drifters. Since 1827 the relative importance of the seining and drift fisheries in providing employment had been reversed; in 1827 the seines had employed 2,672 at sea and the drifters 1,599, in 1870 the seiners only employed 1,510 men and the drifters 2,462.[1] Taken together the figures show a diminution of the number of men employed "at sea", but over the whole half-century the number of men in full-time employment at sea in the fisheries had increased by fifty per cent, whereas that of hands employed in the short season seining industry had fallen forty per cent. Casual labour had declined; specialized labour following the same pursuit, day in, day out, throughout the year, had increased. Efficiency, skill, and greater economic security had been gained at the cost of freedom to change from one calling to another.

It was an arduous calling and a dangerous one that these fishermen "at sea" followed. Every fishing village has its

[1]*Parliamentary Reports* (1803), Vol. X, pp. 3-6. *W.B.*: March 7, 1828. J. Couch *R.C.P.S.*, 1835, p. 82. W. Jory Hancock, "The Cornish Fishery in 1870": *J.R.I.C.* (1871), p. iii.

records and tales of storms and disasters, from the half-legend of the night when all the men of Port Quin put to sea never to return. Occasionally storms destroyed vessels as they lay anchored in harbour, the tiny haven of Polperro alone losing nineteen boats in the storm of November 22 and 23, 1824.[1] In 1823, out of 556 vessels recorded at Lloyds as rounding Land's End, 50 were stranded or damaged or totally wrecked, and 48 others dismasted or suffered other superficial damage on the coasts from Portland round to the Bridgewater River;[2] at least half of them met disaster on the Cornish coasts. There was no need for the legendary wreckers to risk life and limb displaying luring lights on the cliffs. But these were vessels on Lloyd's Registers and did not include the host of small fishing boats wrecked or damaged by storms. The Cornish people did much to try to reduce the loss of vessels and of life; Henry Trengrouse spent the greater part of his days perfecting the rocket life-saving apparatus, whilst the Killigrews had set up the first Lizard lighthouse in early Stuart times. The construction of the first successful light on the Eddystone by Smeaton led to plans to set up warning lights at the equally dangerous rocks further west; the Longships Lighthouse, off Land's End, was completed by 1794.[3] About the same time a plan to erect a gigantic effigy of a wolf in copper on the notorious Wolf Rock between Land's End and Scilly, so designed that the surge of wind and wave would cause it to "emit a dreadful sound, corresponding to the howlings of a wolf" came to naught, nor was the offer of Curtis, who had started the Wherry Mine, to blow up the rock accepted.[4]

The toll of the sea in the eastern part of Mount's Bay, where no less than eleven ships worth £300,000 and over 250 lives were lost in the five years 1807-11, led to an Act of Parliament for building a harbour of refuge at Porthleven, which, however, took fifteen years to complete.[5] The wreck of the frigate *Anson* on the notorious wrecker's coast of Breage and Germoe

[1] *W.B.*: December 10, 1824.
[2] *Life of Thomas Telford* (1838), p. 621. Lloyds estimated that at this time 42½ vessels were totally wrecked every year on this route, and 62 others damaged. On the single stretch of coast between St. Gennys and Morwenstow there were 37 wrecks between 1756 and 1832. (C. E. Byles: *The Life and Letters of R. S. Hawker*, pp. 157-158).
[3] Maton, Vol. I, p. 217; Warner, pp. 158 ff.
[4] Drew, Vol. II, p. 416; Hunt, p. 79.
[5] Drew, Vol. II, pp. 602-609.

led to the Act, promoted by the Cornish member J. H. Tremayne, for the Christian burial of bodies cast up by the sea;
thereafter the burial registers of the Cornish coastal parishes
give some indication of the toll of human life exacted by the
sea. In Breage ten shipwreck victims were buried in December,
1828, and four more in November, 1833. whilst the record of
the burial of Lieutenant Henry Smith on April 27, 1841, shows
that Breage had atoned for its past notorious reputation for
wrecking, Smith and five others being drowned on March 22,
1841, going to the assistance of a vessel in distress.[1] Whilst the
more sensational wrecks were longest remembered, a truer
estimate of the ravages of the sea can be gained from a summary
of details of wrecks and drownings given by local papers in
years not associated with any startling disaster; thus in 1846
the *West Briton* recorded the wreck of twenty ships off the
Cornish coasts, besides finds of unidentified wreckage cast up
on the beaches; it specifically detailed the loss of fifty lives by
drowning quite apart from a few ships "lost with all on board";
storm-damaged ships were so common in Cornish ports in
winter that they were not even enumerated. In only two cases
this year was the plundering of wrecked vessels recorded,
and one of these led to the conviction of over twenty persons
at St. Eval for depredations on the Liverpool ship, *Samaritan*,
lost with ten of her crew of twelve on a voyage to Constanti-
nople off Bedruthan Steps in October.[2]

The sea brought wealth to some Cornishmen; it brought a
livelihood to many more; but to a few it brought loss, disaster,
and death. It was even more fickle and wayward than the
mines in its favours and depredations, an untrustworthy friend
and a deadly foe. Later, when the fisheries declined, it compensated that loss by attracting tourists and holiday-makers
in their hundreds and thousands; even in the later days of the
reign of George III there were some indications of this new
"industry". Perranporth was frequented by summer guests

[1]The Breage Burial Registers also record that on Midsummer Day, 1788, six
youths and young men of Breage were drowned with 15 others from neighbouring
parishes in a boat which capsized at Porthleven, and that in January, 1796, ten
Breage men lost their lives in another wreck, only three of the bodies being recovered.
[2]*W.B.*: October 30 and November 13, 1846. The other ship plundered by
"wreckers" was the Hull barque, *Mary Anne*, off Zennor; this ship was not a
"total wreck", and was towed into Hayle for repair. (*W.B.*: October 30 and
November 6, 1846).

and had at least one established boarding-house by 1820;[1] but the bathing machine set up at Looe in 1820, perhaps in the hope that members of the Royal Family would tire of Brighton and Weymouth and venture further west, found so little patronage that it was suffered to fall into ruin.[2] Some of the earlier visitors to Cornwall were not enamoured of the reek of the fishing villages now so generally regarded as picturesque and entrancingly quaint,[3] but the wild cliff-scenery round Portreath kept the artist Joseph Farington busy when he visited Lord de Dunstanville in 1810.[4] Before Victoria's accession Cornwall had gained a reputation as a health resort to which many, particularly consumptives, repaired in an endeavour to repair shattered constitutions. In July, 1844, some of Boscastle's residents were considering plans for an "omnibus" service to Plymouth, for "more" lodging houses and a bathing house, and for reviving the old market, whilst it was doubtless hoped that the example of the King of Saxony, who at that time visited Penzance, Land's End and Botallack Mine would attract others to West Penwith.[5]

The tourist industry, however, only really began with the coming of the railway; even after the opening of Saltash Bridge in 1859, the passenger to Cornwall had to change since portions of the track in Cornwall retained the broad gauge for years to come. Until 1870 the fisherfolk, merchants, and tradespeople were left to live in the coastal towns as well they might, now in affluence, now in poverty, now and again wondering fearfully whether there was any association between the stench of pilchard cellars and epidemic disease as when the dread cholera struck Newlyn in 1832 and Mevagissey in 1849. Most of them realized full well that they lived by the sea, on the sea, and from the sea, yet even in old, far-off days there were some who appreciated the colourful and romantic atmosphere, which had not yet been turned into a commercial asset. Thomas Bond, a burgess of East Looe, writing of his native town in 1823, waxed poetical describing the fishery:

"conceive to yourself", he wrote, "the effect of the splashing of tens of thousands of fish must produce; the sea appears full of glow-worms

[1] Drew, Vol. II, pp. 543-544.
[2] Bond: *History of Looe*, p. 30.
[3] Maton, Vol. I, p. 227.
[4] J. Farington: *Diary*, Vol VI, pp. 123 ff.
[5] *W.B.*: July 12, 1844.

of the most splendid lustre, the ropes hauling up from below appear like chains of fire, in short the scene is beyond description beautiful. A universal colour o'erspreads the sea; its waters are hushed, no noise is heard but from the fishermen and the fish, the land appearing with sombre hue, contrasted to the light of a summer evening sky, charmingly defines the visible horizon of the high hills around, and the spangled canopy of heaven, and shooting meteors of the atmosphere, contribute to produce the utmost tranquillity of the mind and purest and finest of pleasures."[1]

Bond, it is true, wrote in the age of Scott and the great Romantic revival, which loved wild, picturesque, and, perhaps, slightly sinister natural beauty. Yet nearly eighty years before, in the heyday of the Age of Reason, of Pope, of conventional formalism, we find that worldly cleric Walter Borlase writing to his daughter, commiserating the lot of those forced to spend all their days in London, that their friend, the fashionable and rich socialite Mrs. Harris of Keneggy, in her Cornish home:

"extends her view over the smooth glassy deep and kens afar off the ships wafted thro' the widening Channel into the Atlantic Ocean, the hills stretching out on both sides their barren heads to form a deep bay and commodious harbour. The waves below dash lazily against the pebbled shore, and spend their rage in pulsating murmurs. On the other hand stands the Mount, a stupendous pile, a most romantic piece of rock work, on the other a town most charmingly situated in the centre of the Bay, gently descending to a stately pier filled with trading vessels, and sea covered over with boats, the shores resound with huzzas from eager fishermen, answering their signals from their Hewers, who with their brushes from the adjacent hills point out the courses of the scaly tribes, till captiv'd in the fatal nets they struggle for their liberty in vain. How delightful are these scenes of nature. With what pleasure may we contemplate the great variety and workmanship of her production. What relief I should think to minds tired with artificial life, with pageantry, noise, compliments and show, with a perpetual circle of vanity and folly."[2]

With all his mining and other business activities, his numerous family cares, and his work as a magistrate, Walter Borlase may have been but an indifferent sermonizer; in his long clerical career, however, he must have preached many sermons; they are forgotten and lost, but it is unlikely that he ever chose for his text "And there shall be no more sea."

[1]Bond: *History of Looe*, pp. 83-84.
[2]Walter Borlase MSS: Walter to Peggy Borlase, August 1, 1747.

EPILOGUE

THE END OF THE COPPER KINGDOM

THE MINING industries quickly recovered from the depression which had accompanied the famine-time of 1847. The output of copper ore from Cornwall and the Tamar Valley reached its maximum in 1856 when 209,000 tons were raised—a quantity nearly fifty per cent greater than that of 1849, although the actual metallic content of these ores had increased by little more than ten per cent, from 12,052 to 13,274 tons; the level of the copper standard had risen from £93 to £140, but the produce of the ores sold had dropped from 8¼ to 6⅜.[1] Declining produce indicated the increasing poverty of the Cornish copper ores although, at the time, the copper interests boasted that improved methods of treating the ores made it possible to gain a profit from mineralized rocks which, a generation earlier, would have been cast aside as halvans or even as worthless mundic. Tin-mining, however, made but slow progress for, although the price of tin ore rose from £55 per ton in 1849 to £76 in 1857, the output of 10,719 tons reached in 1849 was not surpassed until 1862.[2] The value of the copper mined in Cornwall in the 1850s was about twice that of the tin, and it can be estimated that about three out of every four miners in Cornwall were employed by copper mines.[3]

The most sensational change was the pre-eminent position gained by Devon Great Consols.[4] It had made its first sales in 1844, but in 1850 it sold a ninth of the total quantity of ores sold at the Cornish ticketings, whilst, owing to superior

[1]Hunt, p. 892.
[2]*Ibid.* p. 889.
[3]Clay workers were not classed as miners in Cornwall, whilst it is unlikely that the lead mines at this time employed more than 500 persons, 200 at Cargoll in Newlyn East, 120 at Herodsfoot Mine, and the rest in smaller mines; at least a third of these were women and boys. (T. Spargo: *Mines of Cornwall and Devon,* 1865 ed., pp. 133, 139; Hunt, pp. 433 ff.). East Wheal Rose Mine had never recovered from the disaster of 1846 (see above p. 155 n. 5) just as Levant never rallied from the disaster in 1919 when forty men were killed through the breaking of the man engine.
[4]Devon Great Consols, in Tavistock parish, just over the Devon border, was invariably classed as a Cornish mine because it sold its ores at Cornish ticketings.

metallic produce, the proportion in value was fully an eighth. The Consolidated Mines of Gwennap ("Consols"), long pre-eminent, had fallen to fifth place, and now accounted for less than five per cent of the ticketing sales; Par Consols still ranked third, over 95 % of the value of ores now raised at Dolcoath came from tinstuff.[1] After 1850 Devon Great Consols easily held its premier position, although some of the "western" mines revived. In the peak year ending on June 30, 1856, however, Consolidated Mines only sold 2,768 tons of ores for £13,651 10s. 6d., Tincroft 4,438 tons for £18,300, whilst once mighty Tresavean sold little over 3,000 tons for about £10,000 its poor grade ores being worth £3 7s. per ton as against the general average of £6 2s. 6d.[2] Early in 1857 it was estimated that fifty-five mines in the West Country were paying dividends, but of the total dividends of over £300,000 a fifth fell to the lot of the Devon Great Consols shareholders;[3] about the same number of copper mines were either barely paying their way or being worked at a loss.[4] In the closing quarter of 1856, too, whilst Devon Great Consols maintained its lead, South Cara-don, another "eastern" mine, leapt into second place.[5] The prosperity of the new eastern mines became even more marked with a slight economic recession in 1857. In this year only three mines in Gwennap, once the centre of Cornish copper mining, paid dividends; Wheal Clifford paid £4,250,

[1]Cornish ticketing sales in the year ending June 30, 1851 amounted to £808,244 for 154,299 tons of ore. The leading mines were:

			£	s.	d.
Devon Great Consols	selling 18,171 tons for	101,017	13	6
Carn Brea Mines	„ 8,500 „	48,928	5	0
Par Consols	„ 7,227 „	44,495	3	0
United Mines	„ 8,414 „	37,714	0	6
Consolidated Mines	„ 6,777 „	34,099	16	6
Fowey Consols	„ 5,831 „	33,332	4	0
Wheal Basset	„ 5,184 „	32,016	17	6
Tincroft	„ 7,611 „	27,067	1	0
Wheal Seton	„ 5,816 „	25,659	18	6
Tywarnhayle	„ 6,123 „	23,204	10	0
North Pool	„ 6,677 „	23,178	5	6

Twenty-two other mines brought between a thousand and five thousand tons of ores to the ticketings, and forty-three other mines each sold less than a thousand tons. (*W.B.*: August 1, 1851.)
[2]The total sales amounted to 209,305 tons of ore for £1,283,639 8s. 6d. (*W.B.*: July 11, 1856).
[3]*W.B.*: January 9, 1857.
[4]In the year ending June 30, 1856, 9 mines sold over 5,000 tons of ores, 36 between 1,000 and, 5000 tons, and 57 less than 1,000 tons, besides a group classed as "sundry small mines". (*W.B.*: July 11, 1856).
[5]*W.B.*: January 2, 1857.

Wheal Damsel £1,536 and Grambler and St. Aubyn £1,458, making a total dividend of £7,244 in the parish but South Caradon in St. Cleer divided £14,336 between 256 shares. In the following year South Caradon dividends fell to £11,264, those of Grambler and St. Aubyn rose to £2,673, but the other two Gwennap mines paid nothing.[1]

Relatively high prices for copper were maintained until 1862 when the standard fell below £124.[2] Profits, however, fell more rapidly; by 1865 only eleven mines were paying dividends of over £5,000, and but twenty-seven in all paid any dividends to their shareholders.[3] Increased working costs and the growing poverty of the deeper lodes rather than any great fall in the price of copper accounted for these declining profits. The decline of the older copper mines was strikingly exemplified by Fowey Consols, whose shareholders were told by the management in February, 1859, that:

"many of our old pitches are fast wearing out; and, were it not for the recent improvements in the mine, our returns would be seriously diminished. Should our present bright prospects continue, and discoveries be made in the lodes lately added to our set, and of which there are strong grounds to hope for, it will be necessary to incur a considerable expense in new machinery before the adventurers can derive any pecuniary benefit from them; therefore, it would be encouraging false hopes to calculate on an early resumption of dividends; but we hope, and believe, that at no very distant period we may calculate on a good dividend paying mine."[4]

The days of Fowey Consols, despite this optimistic report on the possibilities of lateral extension, were numbered. In the thirty-five years from 1822 to 1857 it had raised 282,759 tons of ore which had realized £1,645,479; its yearly profits in that period averaged about £5,000. During the year ending June 30, 1859, in which this report had been presented it sold 5,286 tons for rather less than £35,900, an average price of £6 16s. per ton which compared very favourably with the previous long term average price of less than £5 10s. per ton. In the year ending June 30, 1862, production fell to 4,456 tons,

[1]*W.B.*: April 9, 1858 and January 14, 1859.
[2]Hunt: p. 892.
[3]Devon Great Consols paid £56,320, South Caradon £22,528, but the third dividend mine was the tin mine of Wheal Vor, paying £20,678. Three other mines paying over £5,000 were the tin mine of Dolcoath and the lead mines of West Chiverton and Herodsfoot. (*W.B.*: February 16, 1866).
[4]*W.B.*: February 25, 1859.

the average price to £5 18s., and total sales to £26,332 4s., whilst in its last working year, 1867-68, Fowey Consols sold 176 tons of ore for rather less than £770.[1]

Although it was a financial crisis which precipitated the collapse of Cornish copper mining in 1866, there had been many earlier warning signs. The old protected interests had foretold doom in the early thirties, but, as in the case of corn, a modicum of continuing prosperity coincided with the first decades of free trade. In the thirties Chili and Cuba together had produced only about three-eighths of the amount raised in Cornwall; in the next decade they exceeded it, whilst two other significant competitors had appeared—South Australia and Michigan. The smelting interests, which had been so persistent in demanding free trade, must have been disturbed by the steady decline in the quantities of foreign and colonial copper ores imported after 1845; semi-finished and fine overseas copper began to compete with British in both foreign and home markets. Chilian production of copper ore in the fifties was half as great again as that of Cornwall, and in the same decade Michigan and South Australia each raised about a quarter of the Cornish quantity. When, after 1856, the Cornish output began to fall away, there seemed to be unlimited prospects of expansion in Chili, South Australia, and Michigan, although Cuban production had declined. Fluctuations in the prices and standards of copper after 1855 suggested that world production had caught up with demand; it is possible that the American Civil War postponed the final Cornish collapse for a year or two, whilst there is no doubt whatever that the formidable competitor was Michigan, the State to which many Cornish miners had already migrated, where new extensive finds were being made almost every year. Michigan, too, challenged the British commercial smelting interests, which had been able to exercise considerable control over the South Australian mines and, to a less extent, over those of Chili and Cuba; albeit there was considerable British investment in American mining, the Michigan industry was firmly in the grasp of New England capitalists. By 1868 the Michigan output of copper had surpassed that of Cornwall, although the great

[1] J. A. Phillips and J. Darlington: *Records of Mining and Metallurgy.* p. 259. T. Spargo: *Mines of Cornwall and Devon* (1865 ed.) p. 129. *W.B.*: August 15, 1862 and July 23, 1868.

mines of Calumet and Hecla had only just been opened. Civil War and the depression of 1866 had only checked the development of American copper mining to a slight degree, but the copper mining industry of Cornwall had already declined to an extent which made it impossible to withstand financial panic.[1]

The tin mining industry enjoyed no more prosperity than that of copper. Early in 1859 the North Levant adventurers, having spent £13,000 in the past few years over and above the value of the tin they had raised and sold, were forced to ask the landowners for a remission of dues; Wendron Consols had been forced to replace horse whims with costly machinery; Ding Dong and Wheal Vor, too, had recently incurred heavy losses, but Dolcoath paid dividends amounting to £6,444 in 1857 and to £7,518 in 1858.[2] The economic recession that set in in 1857 accounts for tin prices falling from £136 in that year to below £120 in 1858; prices revived in 1860, but at the end of 1861 started falling again to a level below £90 in 1866.[3]

Yet, whatever the prices of copper and tin, there were mines like South Caradon and Dolcoath that were able to go on making profits, paying dividends, and attracting shareholders. The trade depression of 1857 had comparatively little effect on Cornish mining enterprise, and, with general economic recovery in 1860, speculation in Cornish mines reached a scale hitherto unknown. More and more of these speculators and investors, however, were "foreigners"; even in October, 1859, William Richards, who acted as purser for four mines, stated that out of 640 shareholders with whom he was concerned over four hundred were London capitalists.[4] An indication of the

---

[1]W. B. Gates: *Michigan Copper and Boston Dollars*, pp.9-10, 12-14, 39-45, 203. Brown and Turnbull, pp. 7, 8, 10. (1906 ed.). Hunt, pp. 892-3. The decennial production of fine copper (in tons) was as follows:

		1831-40	1841-50	1851-60	1861-70
Britain	.. ..	144,000	138,200	142,200	116,300
Chili	.. ..	65,000	88,100	214,500	447,400
Cuba	.. ..	9,580	56,400	47,500	25,600
United States	..	—	2,400	37,000	97,100
S. Australia	..	—	15,700	35,500	71,300
Total World	..	325,400	440,900	677,749	1,026,200

[2]*W.B.*: April 9, 1858, January 7 and 14, March 11 and 25, and June 3, 1859.
[3]These are prices for metallic tin; black tin or tin ore prices were about 5/9ths of this price. (Hunt: p. 889). For the international trade depression of 1857 *vide* J. H. Clapham, *Economic History of Modern Britain*, Vol. 11 pp. 368ff : L. Hacker: *The Triumph of American Capitalism*, pp. 329 ff. A. Nevins: *The Emergence of Lincoln* Vol. 1. pp. 176 ff.
[4]*W.B.*: October 14, 1859.

speculation that went on is given by the fluctuating prices of shares in the Caradon Mines. Since the discovery of the riches of this district and news of fortunes gained by the discoverers, anything with the name of Caradon could be sold on the stock markets; Caradons sprang up everywhere, some of them miles from the copper hill on the boundaries of St. Cleer and Linkinhorne. In November, 1859, shares in East Caradon were quoted at £8, those in West Caradon at £142 10s., whilst South Caradon shares were selling at £245. By the beginning of 1861 East Caradon shares had advanced to £11 15s., West Caradons to £156, whilst South Caradons could not be obtained below £300. In May, 1862, however, whilst East Caradons had soared to £42 10s. and South Caradons to £355, the halved shares (1/1024) of West Caradon had receded to £70. East Caradons reached a peak of £53 in October, 1862; two years later they were hardly realizing a third of that price. The shares of South Caradon, however, continued to rise, and at the end of 1864 stood at £540, making the selling price of the mine, which was divided into 512 shares, £276,480; before 1863 it had paid dividends of £385 on every share, the calls on the shares having been only 25s. each. West Caradon had paid out dividends totalling £110,000, or, approximately, £215 per original share, whilst East Caradon had returned profits of nearly £30,000 over and above an expenditure of rather less than £17,000.[1] It was little wonder, indeed, that speculators were attracted, and the more unwary trapped, into acquiring shares in such projects as Caradon Vale, New South Caradon, Caradon Hill, Caradon and Phoenix Consols, Wheal Caradon, and Great Caradon.

This renewed speculation in Cornish mines checked the rate of declining copper production for a time, but when financial depression set in with the panic of May, 1866, the output of Cornish copper ores slumped. In 1865 nearly 160,000 tons had been sold; two years later only 120,000 tons, and in 1870 but 80,000 tons; this last figure was halved again in the next decade, making a total decline of seventy-five per cent in fifteen years.[2]

[1]Webb and Geach: *History and Progress of Mining in the Caradon and Liskeard Districts,* pp. 13-16. 31-36. *W.B.*: Oct. 28 and Nov. 11, 1859; Jan. 18, 1861; May 30 and Oct. 10, 1862; Nov. 18 and Dec. 30, 1864. *Mining and Smelting Magazine,* Vol. II, (Dec. 1862), pp. 339-344.
[2]Hunt, p. 182.

Even before the slump the condition of Cornish working miners had not been good; they were not the people who were enjoying dividends. In the earlier recession of 1857 there had been signs of industrial unrest, and in July that year, the Rev. J. R. Prettyman Berkeley, Vicar of St. Cleer, had told a Committee that had been set up to investigate the rating of mineral royalties that, in his opinion, the miners were ill-paid and could not be expected to be "saving men".[1] The working of poorer grade ores had led to some decline in the gains of tributers. The first strike in Cornish mining history occurred in December, 1857, when the surface workers at Balleswidden stopped work when the adventurers tried to cut their wages. It should be stressed, however, that day-labourers employed on the surface and not the underground tributers and tut-workers came out on strike, but the latter ultimately suffered since the adventurers suspended the mine rather than maintain wages at the former level.[2] The closing of other mines at this time and later caused local unemployment. Tributers, with some savings, realizing the increasing poverty of the deeper mines, emigrated rather than remain in Cornwall to compete against each other in a glutted labour market. They had started a movement that was to spread all over the world. In the early fifties Cornish copper miners in Tennessee caused the Americans no little embarrassment by hoisting the Union Jack and singing the British National Anthem at Fourth of July celebrations.[3] Others had gone to the Californian gold diggings, whilst, by 1860, not only were "Cousin Jacks" working the copper deposits of the Lake Superior region, but the machines employed there were supplied by the Vivians who had moved their engineering works from Camborne to Pittsburgh.[4] Cornish miners had been exploiting copper and silver-lead in South Australia before the gold discoveries in New

---

[1] *W.B.*: July 17, 1857. Berkeley was one of the Tory Democrats. On the accession of Lord Derby's short-lived ministry early in 1852 he had been associated with the group that urged the revival of protectionism; the "liberals" had then resurrected the Anti-Corn Law League and raised the spectre of insurrection against the threat of the "little loaf"; Berkeley had thereupon gained notoriety by publicly declaring: "I have no hesitation in saying that no men would be more thankful to see the faces of a corps of yeomanry than those individuals who threaten us with insurrection; the land cannot be destroyed in an hour, but what pretty bonfires would their factories make." (*W.B.*: March 26, 1852).

[2] *W.B.*: Dec. 4 and 11, 1857; Jan. 22, 1858.

[3] F. L. Olmstead: *Our Slave States—A Journey into the Back Country*, p. 273.

[4] *W.B.*: Feb. 24, 1865.

South Wales and Victoria.[1] Many Cornish miners, too, had
migrated to the collieries of Northern England and Scotland.
Before the great depression of 1866 mining adventurers were
complaining that the cost of labour had been increased by
emigration.[2]

By this time the ill-health and short lives of the Cornish
mining population had attracted much attention. Richard
Quiller Couch, a doctor like his father Jonathan Couch, carefully investigated conditions among the miners of St. Just in
Penwith. He found that the average age of the underground
miners at Balleswidden in 1857 was twenty-nine years and
four months; of 303 men, 41 were under fifteen, the youngest
being a boy of eleven; there were 91 between fifteen and
twenty-five, and only 40 above forty-five years of age. At
Levant the average age of 206 men was twenty-eight years and
ten months, whilst at Ding Dong, in the adjoining parish of
Gulval, the average age of 206 male workers was but twenty-
six years and one month; Ding Dong employed 61 boys under
fifteen, two being eight year old children, whilst 52 others
had not reached twenty. Couch attributed more than half the
deaths among the mining population to chest complaints, and
estimated the average age of death of miners in the St. Just
district during the last twenty years (1837-56) to have been
forty-seven years. He was alarmed by the rate of infant mortality, and calculated that in the whole county of Cornwall 64.07
per cent of all males and 45.73 per cent of all females died
before reaching five years of age; he attributed this to the
debilitated condition of the parents, but did not stress the
underlying causes of poverty and malnutrition.[3]

Similar conclusions were reached by the Royal Commission
on Mines in 1864 as a result of investigations in St. Agnes. In
the three years 1859, 1860 and 1861 forty-two copper-miners
died in this parish. Only one was over eighty, and three over
seventy—in fact the report of the Commissioners suggests that
it was so strange for a copper-miner to reach seventy-seven
years of age that an inquest was held at which was returned
the verdict "Visitation of God". Only half of them reached
fifty, the average of the forty-two being forty-three years and

[1] *W.B.*: June 16, 1848. The name "Wheal" was given by the Cornish to some
South Australian mines.
[2] *W.B.*: Jan. 27, 1865.
[3] *W.B.*: Nov. 27, 1857.

five months. Eighteen of the deaths were ascribed to consumption, three to congestion of the lungs, two to accidents, and four to "natural decay". In the same three years forty-six tin-miners died in St. Agnes, four being over eighty and seven others over seventy, but thirteen never reached fifty. The average age of the "tinners" was fifty-four years and five months, eleven years more than that of the copper-miners, but twenty-one of them died of consumption and only one death was accidental. These figures were contrasted with the mortality of agricultural labourers in the same parish; out of twenty-four men thus employed and dying in these three years, three were over eighty and six more over seventy, but nine were under fifty. Two of the farm labourers, however, were killed in accidents, and a third death ascribed to blood-poisoning might be included in the same category; only two died of pulmonary diseases, bronchitis carrying off one, the other dying of consumption when sixty-seven years of age. The average age of death in these cases was a year more than that of the tin miners being fifty-five years and five months.[1]

There was no indication that Cornish mine surgeons and doctors suspected that the higher incidence of "pulmonary complaints" among miners was mainly due to the inhalation of metallic dust, although bad air in some of the mines was sometimes blamed.[2] Most doctors attributed the ill-health and short lives of the miners to the great differences in temperature between the hot bottom levels of mines and those at the surface; miners, at the end of their shifts, came "to grass" and, without donning adequate additional clothing, walked to their homes, sometimes five or more miles away, often through driving rains, chilly mists, or in the blast of bitter winds. One or two blamed the early ages at which miners started working, and Berkeley, the Vicar of St. Cleer, asserted that a miner starting work at the age of fifteen had but seventeen years expectancy of life whereas lads adopting other callings could, on the average, expect to live to forty-six.[3]

After the publication of the Report of the Commissioners

---

[1] *Report of the Commissioners on Mines of Great Britain,* (1864) Appendix B, pp. 370-372. The term "consumption" at this time included phthisis, silicosis, and possibly other pulmonary diseases, just as 'decline' might indicate anaemia and even cancer besides tuberculosis.

[2] *Report of the Commissioners on Mines of Great Britain,* (1864), Appendix B, p. 289.

[3] *W.B.:* May 19, 1865.

of Mines of 1864, it was rumoured that Lord Kinnaird would propose legislation providing close governmental inspections of metallic mines. Certain prominent Cornish "miners" at once raised an outcry that such laws would force two-thirds of the Cornish mines to close down,[1] and called meetings of protest at Camborne and at Liskeard. At the Camborne meeting it was asserted that Lord Kinnaird's well-meant philanthropic efforts were being abused by agitators in the mining district to stir up unrest against alleged oppression and injustice. At Liskeard the majority of the "representatives of landowners, mine agents, adventurers, and gentlemen interested in mining property" agreed that "legislative interference, should, if possible, be avoided in metalliferous mining, which, as an uncertain and hazardous pursuit, would be unable to survive any degree of discouragement".[2] Lacking support from Palmerston's government, Lord Kinnaird withdrew his Bill. The "miners" for their part had asserted that they had done all within their power to improve the working conditions and promote the welfare of the men employed underground, alleging that every practicable device to improve ventilation had been adopted, but regretting that it was not possible in many Cornish mines to instal man-engines, like the one Michael Loam had constructed at Tresavean a quarter of a century before. In the interests of economy, working miners had to go on wearing out hearts and lungs climbing and descending fathoms of ladders from and to their places of employment.[3]

The failure of Lord Kinnaird's Bill had two results in Cornwall. First was the rather amazing proposal by certain mining adventurers to call a Stannary Parliament; none had been convened for more than a century, but the men who suggested it expressed their belief that it was better than legislative

---

[1] *W.B.*: May 12, 1865.

[2] *W.B.*: May 19, 1865.

[3] At the Liskeard meeting it was alleged that it would take ten years to sink a man-engine shaft at South Caradon. At that time South Caradon was employing about 650 hands, and probably between 250 and 300 of them worked underground; the depth of the mine was over 200 fathoms; it may have been a hard "country" of granite and elvan through which to sink a shaft, but the mine had paid dividends of some £200,000, and the expense might seem well justified not merely to benefit the workpeople but to increase the efficiency of the miners by eliminating a cause of fatigue and of frequent accidents. (*W.B.*: May 19, 1865. Webb and Geach: *History . . . of Mining in the Caradon and Liskeard Districts*, pp. 31-34).

interference by Parliament in the conduct of mining; at least it meant that "irregularities in mining operations" might be remedied by the adventurers themselves rather than by:

"Board of Trade interferences, and inspections and reports by official scientific men who know nothing of the necessities and difficulties that are involved in the practical working of mines."[1]

The second, and more serious consequence was the embitterment of the relationships between the adventurers and the working miners. Some of the latter had voiced support of Lord Kinnaird's Bill in no uncertain terms, and they had the backing of the firebrand Tory Vicar, Berkeley, who, not content with stating that ameliorative laws were necessary, had made a forthright declaration that:

"looking at the nature of the employment and the risk connected with it, there is no class of men in England so badly paid as the miners."[2]

Falling copper prices towards the end of 1865 aggravated the situation. The adventurers were trying to reduce costs, particularly those of labour although they were low already. Knowledge of the aims and activities of trade unions elsewhere in England had reached Cornwall, and, in that county, experience as class-leaders and stewards in Methodist societies had developed among the labourers themselves the qualities necessary for organizing and leading a working class movement. By February, 1866, the Miners' Mutual Benefit Association had been formed in the eastern mining districts. This was organized primarily and ostensibly as a friendly society. There was an entrance fee of 2s. 6d., and monthly subscription of 6d. from workers aged fifteen and over; the chief benefits were pensions of 7s. a week for "worn-out miners" and for those who had lost their sight in mining accidents, provided that they were fully paid-up members of at least five years' standing. Against such provisions mine-owners could not quibble, but the next article laid down that:

"In every mine where there are fifty men working there shall be a committee formed of nine men, to be chosen by a majority, to whom miners shall go when they deem the price offered by the mine agents for doing certain work insufficient, and this committee shall

[1] *W.B.*: June 2, 1865.
[2] *W.B.*: May 19, 1865.

see the place in dispute, and decide whether the price offered is sufficient or not, and if it is, the men must bear their own responsibility, but if not, the committee shall consult the agents and ask them to advance (their price), and in case of the agents refusing to do this at the expiration of a fortnight, such committee shall compound with the general secretary (of the Miners' Mutual Benefit Association), who shall call a delegate meeting to decide what steps shall be taken."[1]

This meant that the trade union committee in every large mine with more than four or five tribute pitches was to decide what was a fair tribute or tut-work contract. If mine agents rejected the final offer from the delegate meeting of the Association, the latter would then call a strike. Provisions were made for strike pay of 12s. a week with an additional allowance of a shilling a week for each dependent child, under twelve years' old, of striking miners. Furthermore, "blacklegs" taking tribute pitches hitherto worked by strikers were to be expelled forthwith and forfeit any claim they had on the Association.

On February 24, 1866, the adventurers of Drakewalls, Latchley Consols, and other Gunnislake mines, refused to employ any members of the Association on tribute contracts. The Drakewalls men at once came out on strike, but probably did their cause no good by seizing a blackleg and riding him on a rail through Gunnislake village. Two days later the East Caradon and Marke Valley men went on strike. The same day, the managers of forty-three mines in the Caradon and Tamar districts, along with those of Par and Fowey Consols, met and agreed not to employ any member of the Association. In consequence, some managers were threatened with physical violence, and the miners forced the engine-men to join them even at the danger of flooding the mines. Troops were then brought to Tavistock, whereupon divisions and dissensions appeared among the miners, some being willing to restrict the Association to the role of a mere benefit club, others demanding a minimum monthly wage of £4. At Devon Great Consols, then normally employing 1,300 persons, but four tribute

---

[1]*W.B.*: March 2, 1866. The greater number of the working mines in this district employed more than fifty men at this time. On the Cornish side of the Tamar the mines employing most hands were Phoenix (320 men, 60 females, and 80 boys), West Caradon, Gunnislake Clitters, East Caradon, Hingston Down Consols, and Craddock Moor, in that order. (T. Spargo: *Mines of Cornwall and Devon*, pp. 140 ff).

pitches were taken up on the setting day on March 2—not enough to keep fifty hands at work above and below ground. All the employees at South Caradon were locked out since they had, one and all, joined the Association; with similar lock-outs occurring at Phoenix and Gonamena, more than two thousand labourers were involved in the Eastern Mining District. "Western" miners, however, were brought in to work Devon Great Consols, and by the end of March the Association had collapsed.[1]

Apart from the initial clash of the men and the mines adventurers at Drakewalls it had been a lock-out, not a strike. The "masters" had won the day; they had been able to find "blackleg" labour in the west where the decreasing production of local mines had already caused some unemployment and where, too, the general level of wages was lower than in the Eastern District. The violence of some of their leaders brought no little discredit to the men.[2] The times, moreover, were not propitious for miners to embark on a struggle for higher wages, or even for the maintenance of those already being paid, since the general fall in copper prices[3] made adventurers reluctant if not unable to incur increased labour costs. If the men held out there was a real danger that the only result would be the complete suspension of some mines and consequent unemployment.[4]

One by one mines were closing down. Crenver and Wheal Abraham in Crowan were "knocked" in August, 1865.[5] Buller and Basset United in Wendron, North Hallenbeagle in St. Agnes, and many other mines which had been losing concerns for years soon suffered the same fate.[6] In April, 1866, no less than four mines in the single parish of Perranzabuloe

---

[1] *W.B.*: March 9, 16, 23, and 30, 1866.

[2] Eight men were tried for the riding of the blackleg on a rail through Gunnislake and were each sentenced to eight months hard labour. The threats of certain violent agitators against mine agents should, however, be contrasted with the orderly mass meeting of miners at Caradon where proceedings opened, like a Methodist meeting, with hymn-singing and prayer. (*W.B.*: March 9, 1866).

[3] During the nine years, 1853-61, the copper standard had been over £130; it had fallen to £119 5s. in 1863, recovered to £127 19s. in 1864, fell to £122 12s. in 1865, and then slumped to £109 7s. in 1866. (Hunt: p. 892).

[4] Some mines had already closed down in the Eastern District, notably Wheal Pollard, West Drakewalls, Caradon Vale, and West Phoenix. (T. Spargo: *Mines of Cornwall and Devon*, pp. 140, 141 and 146).

[5] *W.B.*: August 4 and 18, 1865. The Company that suspended operations had only acquired the mines the previous year. (T. Spargo: *Mines of Cornwall and Devon*, p. 56).

[6] *W.B.*: April 6, 1866.

were being sold up,[1] whilst other mines were struggling to survive. Costly litigation, lasting more than twenty years, about its underground boundaries with West Basset, sent the price of South Francis shares down from £360 to £18.[2] The optimistic speculators of a few years before were abandoning their shares and loudly blackening the besmirched name of Cornish mine investment. Nor were matters helped when the Central Criminal Court in London sentenced the former Redruth surgeon John Permewan to seven years penal servitude for his part in forging Wheal Seton shares.[3] Still there were a few optimists for, in April, 1866, a group of "adventurers", with their offices in Manchester, started the Ellen United Copper and Zinc Mining Company Limited to work a mining property they had acquired in St. Agnes; two of the directors lived in Manchester; the other five at Macclesfield, Bolton, Doncaster, Stockport and Titchfield. The Company went to the expense of laying the foundation stone of its engine-house with a silver trowel, but its hopes of profits were soon dashed.[4]

The financial panic caused by the failure of Overend, Gurney, and Company in London transformed a Cornish mining recession into a catastrophe. Every type of mine, unable to face falling mineral prices, foreign competition, and the emigration of so many of the better and more enterprising workmen, was closing down. By the end of May, 1866, the casualties included the tin mines of Carnyorth and Wheal Hearle in St. Just, Treloweth copper mine in St. Erth, and the lead mines of Botalet in Lanreath and Wheal Ludcott in St. Ive.[5] Pendeen Consols in St. Just and Drakewalls[6] abandoned their less productive levels. The cessation of dividends from Cargoll lead mine in Newlyn East, and from East Rosewarne copper mine in Gwinear meant little, for neither had been regularly or prominently in lists of dividend-paying mines, but the revelation that the Carn Brea Copper Mines in Illogan, after paying dividends for thirty years, had incurred a loss of nearly £6,000 came as a shock to others besides shareholders.[7]

[1]Wheal Hope, Mineral Bottom, Wentworth Consols, and Wheal Albert, the last a lead mine. (*W.B.*: April 27, 1866).
[2]*W.B.*: December 15, 1865, and January 12, 1866.
[3]*W.B.*: December 15, 1865, and March 2, 1866.
[4]*W.B.*: April 27, 1866.
[5]*W.B.*: May 18 and 25, 1866.
[6]*W.B.*: May 25 and June 1, 1866.
[7]*W.B.*: June 1 and 15, 1866.

Fears of unemployment in St. Just intensified with the publication of Balleswidden accounts showing a debt of £6,000 and
an annual loss of £4,000.[1] Early in June South Wheal Tolgus
in Redruth was on the verge of closing, and Wendron Consols
had gone under.[2]   Great Wheal Busy, in Kenwyn, after a ten-
year trial by the present group of adventurers, was in a perilous
condition, and it was feared that its suspension would entail
unemployment and destitution to two thousand miners and
their dependents.[3] Other mines were resorting to the most
desperate economies, Levant, for example, using sea water in
the boilers of its pumping engines despite the fears of the
engine-men that this might cause explosions.[4] There was no
change for the better, however, and Great Wheal Busy was
stopped in mid-August, and a few weeks later South Tolgus
ceased working.[5]   Before the end of the year, the most disastrous within memory, other mines had closed down or were
working only their best and more accessible levels. There was
as yet, however, comparatively little unemployment, since
nearly 1,500 miners had already gone off to the collieries of
Ayrshire and Lanark from Cornwall;[6] others had gone still
further afield—to America and to Australia, one estimate
being that in the year no less than five thousand Cornish
miners had emigrated.[7]

In 1867 conditions, instead of improving, grew worse.
Copper mining in western Cornwall was becoming an industry
of the past. The New Year came in with the news that Wheal
Reeth, having lost £30,000, had closed down and thrown four
hundred hands out of work, and that Hallamannin and Croft
Gothal having cost their hopeful adventurers £80,000, had
ceased to exist in St. Hilary.[8] During the last working year,
ending on June 30, 1866, the number of mines producing over
a thousand tons of ore had dropped to thirty, whilst a sixth of
the ores sold at the Cornish ticketings had been raised by
Devon Great Consols.[9] Many families in St. Agnes were living

---

[1] *W.B.*: June 8, 1866.
[2] *W.B.*: June 8 and 15, 1866.
[3] *W.B.*: June 8, 1866: T. Spargo: *Mines of Cornwall and Devon*, p. 95.
[4] *W.B.*: June 15, 1866.
[5] *W.B.* August 17 and 31, and September 28, 1866.
[6] *W.B.*: October 26, November 16 and 30, and December 28, 1866.
[7] *W.B.*: January 4, 1867.
[8] *W.B.*: January 4, 1867.
[9] *W.B.*: July 27, 1866.

on remittances sent home by emigrants to California.[1] A bitterly cold and stormy winter made matters worse; snow followed by heavy rains flooded out North Downs, Wheal Rose, Hallenbeagle and Great South Tolgus, which normally employed seven hundred persons, for nearly two months.[2] The less unfortunate tin mines suffered through the emigration of those more enterprising miners who decided to get out of Cornwall while they still had some savings wherewith to start a new life elsewhere. When spring came it was alleged that half the miners in Cornwall were literally starving, and that many families were trying to live on half a crown a week.[3] Late in April the closing of the St. Day United Mines increased misery in Gwennap; not only were four hundred immediate employees of the concern thrown out of work, but Clifford mine had to abandon its lower levels which were flooded out by the stoppage of the St. Day pumping engines.[4]

On July 19, 1867, a sub-committee appointed by the Justices in Quarter Sessions to enquire into the distress prevalent among the labouring classes in West Cornwall met in the counting-house of Wheal Reeth in Lelant—a building no longer required for mine administration was being used as the venue for the inquest on western copper mining. Joseph Giles, the Relieving Officer of the St. Ives district,[5] reported that during the last two years the wages of working miners had fallen from sixty-five to forty-five shillings a month; that men were destitute of the necessities of life and many of them deeply in debt; that the numbers applying for Union Workhouse relief had risen from 72 to 131; that many heads of families had left the district leaving their dependents destitute; and that, although at that season of the year, children were able to work in the fields they were earning barely enough to keep themselves let alone help their families as they had been able to do in time past. In one parish, Ludgvan, 64 heads of families had left since 1865, but nearly 50 of them had left their families behind. Some miners, rather than remain idle, were taking up old tribute pitches, but the cost of working such pitches was

---

[1] *W.B.*: February 1, 1867.
[2] *W.B.*: February 8 and April 5, 1867.
[3] *W.B.*: April 19, 1867.
[4] *W.B.*: May 3, 1867.
[5] This district included the parishes of St. Ives, Lelant, Zennor, Towednack, St. Erth, Ludgvan, Marazion, St. Hilary, and Perranuthno.

often more than the value of the ores gained from them. Elsewhere miners worked overtime in a desperate effort to maintain their personal wage levels. In Lelant parish five mines had stopped in two years, throwing 360 men and several women and children out of work; some found employment elsewhere, but whereas 881 men had been working in the parish in June, 1865, two years later the number had fallen to 671, whilst the number of people left in Lelant, including dependents, without the means of subsistence was nearly a thousand.[1] The labouring classes had run into debt with shopkeepers who now, themselves, could obtain no further credit from the wholesale merchants who supplied their stocks. From Marazion thirty miners had emigrated. In St. Hilary two able-bodied miners, receiving wages of only twenty-five shillings a month to maintain families of six and seven, had been forced to apply for Union relief. At a similar meeting at Marazion, the Rev. T. Pascoe condemned a system whereby miners might work eight or nine weeks before they were paid any wages, and even then be only paid for a single month's work; such a system drove them to get the necessities of life on credit, to run into debt, and often to become not only improvident but even dishonest; he suggested that they should be paid fortnightly, apparently without realizing that this would, almost of necessity, mean the revolutionary abandonment of the tribute system of working, and, probably the ticketing system of selling ores as well.[2]

Emigration only solved or ameliorated individual problems; in many places it only aggravated the social distress. From St. Austell, Helston, and Penzance Union Districts about six hundred men had emigrated in two years, each leaving behind, on the average, a wife and three children to whom he sent meagre and irregular remittances.[3] The departure of these men, in a quest for higher wages and better living conditions, further reduced the productivity of the mines where, hitherto, they had worked, and immediately threw ancillary workers, who were generally less able-bodied, out of work. Relief expenses in the Penzance and Helston Unions doubled between

[1]The population of Lelant fell from 2,319 in 1861 to 2,178 in 1871, and to 1,720 in 1881.
[2]*W.B.*: July 26, 1867. (Reports of enquiries at Lelant and Marazion held on July 19th). The delay of wages and disputes over the length of the month led to a strike at South Condurrow mine, Camborne, in March, 1874.
[3]*W.B.*: August 16, 1867.

June, 1865, and June, 1867, whilst those in the St. Austell and Redruth Unions increased by fifty per cent. There was also considerable distress in the Calstock district, although at Liskeard the main grievance was the high price of provisions rather than unemployment.[1] Real wages throughout the county had been reduced by full fifty per cent, mainly through the increased prices of provisions since the actual fall in average money wages had only been about a sixth.[2] A County Distress Fund was started in August to aid the reunion of families whose heads had migrated, to pay the expenses of men willing to go elsewhere in search of work, and to supply poor families with clothing, bedding, and sick relief.[3] In less than five months nearly £3,000 had been raised, but this was inadequate to "tide over the pressure of misery", for by that time there were a thousand persons in Chacewater, 1,413 in St. Just, and 240 in St. Agnes, trying to live on eighteenpence each a week.[4] Some fared a little better, but scenes of appalling poverty and misery were only too common. A group of philanthropists visiting distressed families and distributing relief found in Redruth:

"In one house . . . a poor sick woman in bed, her daughter, a married woman, and five children . . . neither of whom had tasted a morsel of food for the day. Every scrap had been baked into two 'pasties' for the husband and brother to carry to work with them. The two latter, who had lately gone to work in a new mine, after being out of employment for some time, had gone underground without breakfast. All had supped the evening before on a little soup without bread."[5]

The number thrown out of work in the mining districts of Cornwall and West Devon in eighteen months ending in December, 1867, was estimated at nearly 11,400. About two-thirds of them left the western counties, leaving nearly 20,000 dependents behind them.[6] The mining adventurers, for their part, sought to continue working by dint of intensified economies. Grumblings about monopolist and extortionate smelters of both copper and tin were a feature of these distressed times

[1] *W.B.*: August 16, 1867.
[2] *W.B.*: August 30, 1867.
[3] *W.B.*: August 16, 1867.
[4] *W.B.*: January 2, 1868.
[5] *W.B.*: January 25, 1868.
[6] *W.B.*: December 27, 1867.

as they had so often been in the past. There was also an attempt to break the "monopoly" of coal which had been established by a small ring of "importing" Cornish merchants.[1] The main mechanical improvements were those effected in boring and drilling machines, and in the processes of preparing the ores for sale.[2] Yet it was but a desperate bid to stave off the ruin of Cornish copper mining. Minerals once taken from their parent lodes and veins were irreplaceable. Many of the Cornish mines had been exhausted by years of exploitation; Dolcoath, Tresavean, and the Consolidated Mines had all been worked down to a depth of 350 fathoms, and Cook's Kitchen nearly to that depth, whilst many others were over 200 fathoms.[3] Richer ores had been removed; what were left were worked as long and, in many cases, even longer than they were profitable. The richer and more extensive deposits of Chili, South Australia, Michigan and later, of Montana, made it impossible for the longer worked Cornish mines to survive in the fiercely competitive world markets.

In 1870 there were still vast deposits of deep tin left in Cornwall, but, save in the eastern districts, the remaining copper reserves were comparatively small and generally poor in quality. By 1874 the Cornish output of copper ore had fallen below 50,000 tons, and, though there followed a slight and temporary revival, by 1880 hardly 40,000 tons were raised. The contrast between the statistics of Cornish mines for the year ending on June 30, 1876, and that of the peak year twenty years before is amazing. Output had fallen by three-quarters. Instead of nine mines selling more than five thousand tons of copper ore there were but two—Devon Great Consols which sold 8,500 tons for £35,000 and South Caradon which secured £42,500 for about 6,000 tons of richer ores. There were still twenty-nine mines making sales of over £1,000 and forty-nine making smaller sales, but the number of mines selling between a thousand and five thousand tons of ores was only thirteen as against thirty-six in 1856, whilst once-mighty Poldice sold but

[1]*W.B.*: January 2, 1868.
[2]The Darlington-Jordon rock drill was patented in 1865, and Doering's boring machine was first used in Cornwall at Tincroft in 1867. Stamping machinery had been greatly improved since Arthur Woolf had installed steam-driven stamps at Wheal Vor in 1812. Another new device was the improved continuous 'jigger' invented by John Hunt in 1866 for separating ore-stuff in suspension in water. (Hunt: pp. 324, 566-7, 695-6, 726).
[3]Hunt: p. 310.

ten tons of truly miserable ores for a mere £10[1] Ten years
later Devon Great Consols once more made the greatest sales,
but its sales for the year ending June 30, 1886, were only
£9,875, its 8,617 tons of low grade ores only averaging £1 3s.
per ton; the second place had been taken by the St. Erth mine of
Mellanear, selling 5,303 tons at £1 17s. per ton £9,841; the
third place was taken by Wheal Crebor in Tavistock which
sold 3,104 tons for £6,494; Glasgow Caradon, South Caradon,
and Gunnislake Mine each sold over a thousand tons of better
quality ores fetching an average price of £3 16s. 6d. per ton.
Out of 39 mines selling copper ores in this year, 1885-6, 20 sold
less than a hundred tons each, most of them having only raised
the ores as the "by-product" of tin mining.[2]

Tin mining had ousted copper from its pre-eminency very
early during the rapid decline of the latter industry from its
peak level of 1856 in Cornwall. The total value of the copper
ores sold in Cornwall in that year had been nearly £1,300,000,
whereas that of tin had been only £663,850, or little more than
half that of the copper. By 1861 the copper sales had fallen to
little over £1,000,000 and those of tin had risen to £722,000
whilst in 1862 the figures were £1,045,000 and £883,382
respectively. The change came in 1863 when tin sales leapt to
£1,170,000 and those of copper ores fell to £841,346.[3] In the
following years the disparity rapidly increased, owing mainly,
however, to the declining sales of copper, since the output of
tin did not rise much above the 1863 figure of 15,157 tons.
Even if tin, after more than a century, had regained its place as
the Cornish mineral, the tin mines did not afford employment
to men thrown out of work by the closing down of copper mines.

To what extent the Cornish miners resorted to clay-working
when the mines failed is problematical. Although the majority
of the miners looked down on clay-working as an inferior
occupation, it seems likely that many in the St. Austell area
were glad enough to turn to it rather than emigrate when the
copper mines of that district closed down. In 1857 it was
estimated that about 1,700 men were employed in the clay
works of St. Austell and the neighbouring parishes.[4] This
labour force raised about 68,000 tons of china clay and china

[1]*W.B.*: July 11, 1856 and July 23, 1876.
[2]*W.B.*: November 4, 1886.
[3]*W.B.* July 11, 1856 and July 19, 1861. Hunt: pp. 889, 892 and 895.
[4]*W.B.*: July 24, 1857.

stone, or, approximately forty tons per man.[1] In the period immediately following it is unlikely that the output per man was increased to any considerable extent; any application of improved machinery and mechanical methods was offset by the increasing depth of the open-cast workings, by the greater amount of labour required to dispose of waste, and by the problem of draining many of the "pits". The output of china clay increased rapidly in the next few years, but the rise to 118,000 tons by 1864 occurred before the situation of the copper mining industry had become alarming, although it may have aggravated the woes of some mining adventurers by giving work to nearly 1,250 more men. By 1867 clay production had reached 160,000 tons, and the industry was probably employing some four thousand men, but in the next two years, instead of providing work for unemployed miners, the clay industry must have turned away at least eight hundred of its own hands, since output receded to 131,000 tons. The 1867 level was regained in 1871, and the 1874 output of 193,000 must have meant a labour force of at least 4,800 men.[2] It may, therefore, be assumed that from 2,500 to 3,000 men formerly employed in copper mining found temporary or permanent work in the china clay industry, but that was only about a quarter of the men that lost their livelihood through the catastrophic collapse of the copper mining industry of Cornwall.

The majority of the others emigrated. As early as 1870 there were no less than 85 Cornishmen at the Tocapilla mine in Brazil, and earning five guineas a month above the cost of living, or a total wage thrice that which they had been able to secure even in "good times" in Cornwall.[3] A few years later there were more Cornishmen working at Calumet and Hecla mines in Michigan than there were at any other copper mine in the world, whilst even back in 1869 Camborne men in California and Nevada were sending home to their families and relatives between £15,000 and £18,000 in the year—a sum equal to the combined monthly wage bill of a score of

---

[1] *J.R.I.C.*, Vol. V., p. 257.

[2] *J.R.I.C.* Vol. V. p. 257. Rather lower figures for the output of china clay were given by David Cock (*Treatise on China Clay*, p. 123), but this was through the omission of "china stone". Allowing the lower annual man-output of 35 tons per annum, the labour force of 1874 would have been 5,514 or about 3,800 more than in 1857.

[3] *W.B.*: January 26, 1871.

mines in the Camborne district at that time.[1]   Many tin mines
were adversely affected by the emigration of skilled miners,
whilst knowledge of fortunes made abroad by relatives and
friends meant that, at the slightest sign of recession in tin
mining, the miner with some savings put by, or one who had
recently had a "lucky strike" from a tribute pitch, would take
his departure. The history of Cornish mining and of the Cornish
miner went on, but the scene had changed. Calumet and Hecla
and Anaconda had taken the place of Hallamannin, Wheal
Busy, Par Consols and Poldice. Before long there were to be as
many Cornish miners in Johannesburg and Butte City as there
were in Redruth and St. Just. Mining was bred into the blood,
into the bones, even into the very souls of the men of Cornwall.
If they could not live by that calling in their homeland there
were other places. They could not live without the mines, and
many of them felt that without mining they were not living.
So, with reason, it came to be said that wherever there was a
pit in the world a Cornishman would be found at the bottom
of it—digging away for copper or tin, for silver or lead, for
gold or diamonds. Cornish mining went on while in Cornwall
gorse and heather were creeping over the unsightly heaps of
"attles" and "deads" which the old miners had rejected and
cast aside, while engine houses were crumbling down into
ruins until all that remained were a few gaunt stacks, defying
storm and time itself, memorials of a bygone industry, memorials of a past age dead and gone like that in which menhirs
and cromlechs were erected.

[1] *W.B.*: August 12, 1869.

APPENDIX I

CORNISH STATISTICAL MATERIAL

The cliche that statistics can be employed to support every and any false statement is exaggerated, but has in it a grain of truth. Early statistics are particularly suspect, and certain additional considerations must be kept in mind in considering the industries of Cornwall.

In the case of tin G. R. Lewis made a complete estimate of yearly production after 1673 (*The Stannaries*: App. J, pp. 255-6). These were, however, only the amounts of tin actually coined, with the year ending at Michaelmas, and can only be regarded as a rough guide to production in view of the time-lag between the actual mining of the tin and its coining; Sometimes, too, tin-stuff and smelted tin were smuggled out of the country without coining. Averages over a group of years derived from these figures, however, will give an indication of the expansion or contraction of the mining industry, whilst abnormally high or low coinages reflect boom speculation or recession in marketing tin which would affect actual mining activity after a fairly short time.

The output and prices of copper ores in the period 1726-75 given by Dr. W. Pryce (*Mineralogia Cornubiensis* p. xv) may have been derived from ticketing records; they do not include private sales of copper-ores, although smaller mines may have sold their ores to the larger ones who sold them along with their own product. The later copper statistics of Robert Hunt (*British Mining*, pp. 891-2) seem reasonably accurate, but they were apparently derived from smelting rather than from mining sources. In the case of copper a complication arises from the mining year beginning sometimes on July 1st and not on January 1st.

Prices for copper are obscured by the distinction between the actual selling price of copper ores and the smelters' 'standard' which, too, was not the same as the market price of 'fine' copper. Tin prices are confused by the distinction between 'black' tin, or unsmelted tin ore, and refined 'white' tin, or unsmelted tin ore, and refined 'white' tin, over and above the distinction between 'mine' and the more valuable alluvial or 'grain' tin. The old Cornish tin measure of the thousand-weight, of 1,200 pounds, however, had fallen into disuse by the eighteenth century, although both tin and copper miners still allowed extra weight for 'breakages'.

Agricultural statistics are confused by the survival of the Cornish bushel of 24 gallons, and by the impossiblity of distinguishing Cornish from statute acres.

APPENDIX II

The Construction and Lease of a
Tin Stamping Mill in 1728

Memorandum Nbr. ye 9th 1728. It is this agreed by William Busvargus of Busvargus in ye parish of St. Just Gent, & Nicholas Tresise, Tynner of ye aforesd Parish as follows—

The sd Nicholas Tresise for ye consideration here-after mention'd do oblige himself to build a good Stamping Mill on ye sd W.B.'s tennement of Tregasaseall in ye place allready agreed on; & to make a good and convenient House with good Thatch, & good English Oack in ye Exle Tree & Ring & Inner frames of at least four Inches Thick, wth Three working frames & catches wth places for too leaving frames & all other conveniencies (stampheads only excepted) for to make ye sd Mill compleate as belong to any other convenient stamping mill, according to ye true intent & meaning of this Article, for ye sum of £27-12-6 to be pd as follows, £5 on beginning, £5 when any honest man can judge there is £10 of work done about erecting ye sd Mill, £5 when ye House is cover'd & conveniency made for Taking ye wheele, £5 when ye Wheel is in her place, & ye remaining sum of £7-12-6 when ye sd stamping Mill to a Publick sale for three lives within six months after it is finish'd, & wtever sum ye sd Mill will bring at such a sale above £55-5s to pay ye one half of such overplus if any to ye sd Nicholas Tresise, in witness hereto ye parties here mutually sett their hands ye day above mentioned.

(On Obverse) Memorandum before ye signing ye within Articles, ye within named Nicholas Tresise do promise to bring home ye water & make a good & sufficient watercourse, & likewise to bring Hallgolower water brought to sd stamps, & to leave at least 26 feet of Levell from ye Pullrose of this Stampe, wth conveniency for carrying ye sd water, if it shall hereafter be thought proper to build any more stamping Mills betwixt this stamps & Bosvargow Mill-Poole wch sd Mill Poole is to ye Hill of James Nankervis's Stamping Mill, and yn signed by

W. B.

N. TRESISE,

witnessed by Richard Polkinhorne,
James Millet,
Stephen Usticke,
James Toms.

(From *Toup MSS.*, Bodleian Library).

APPENDIX III

Statistics of Cornish Production of Copper Ore, Value, and Relationship with Smelters' Prices of Fine Copper, 1801-1829

	Copper Ore raised in Cornwall (Tons)	Fine Copper produced from Cornish Ores (Tons)	Value	Cost of Ore per Ton			Tons of Copper produced per 100 tons of Ore (*i.e.* Produce)	Cost of Fine Copper per Ton			Smelters' Standard Price		
			£	£	s.	d.		£	s.	d.	£	s.	d.
1801	56,611	5,267	476,313	8	8	6	9¼	90	16	3	117	5	0
1802	53,937	5,228	445,094	8	5	0	9⅝	85	14	3	110	8	0
1803	60,566	5,616	533,910	8	16	6	9¼	95	8	1	122	0	0
1804	64,637	5,374	570,840	8	16	6	9⅜	94	2	8	136	5	0
1805	78,452	6,234	862,410	10	9	10	7⅞	139	13	0	169	16	0
1806	79,269	6,863	730,845	9	4	4½	8⅝	106	19	1½	138	5	0
1807	71,694	6,716	609,002	8	9	10½	9⅜	90	13	4	120	0	0
1808	67,867	6,795	495,503	7	6	0	10	73	0	0	100	17	0
1809	76,245	6,821	770,028	10	2	0	8⅞	113	16	0	143	12	0
1810	66,048	5,682	569,981	8	12	6	8½	101	9	4	132	5	0
1811	66,499	5,948	563,742	8	9	6	9⅛	92	17	6	120	10	0
1812	75,510	7,248	608,065	8	1	0	9⅜	85	17	4	111	0	0
1813	86,713	8,166	685,572	7	18	0	9¼	85	8	1	115	7	0
1814	87,482	7,936	766,825	8	15	6	8½	103	4	8	130	12	0
1815	79,984	6,607	582,108	7	11	0	8¼	91	10	4	117	16	6
1816	83,058	7,045	541,737	6	10	6	8⅝	75	12	7	98	13	0
1817	75,816	6,608	422,426	5	11	6	8½	66	15	4	108	10	0
1818	80,525	6,714	587,977	7	6	0	7⅞	92	14	0	134	15	0
1819	93,234	7,214	728,032	7	16	0	7⅝	102	6	0	127	10	0
1820	92,672	7,464	620,347	6	14	0	8⅛	82	13	1	113	15	0
1821	98,803	8,163	628,832	6	7	0	8⅝	73	18	1	103	0	0
1822	106,724	9,331	676,285	6	6	6	8¾	72	5	9	104	0	0
1823	97,470	8,070	618,933	6	7	0	8¼	76	19	6	109	18	0
1824	102,200	8,022	603,878	5	18	0	7⅞	74	18	5	110	0	0
1825	110,000	8,417	743,253	6	15	0	7⅝	88	10	6	114	0	0
1826	118,768	9,140	798,790	6	14	6	7⅜	91	3	9	123	3	0
1827	128,459	10,450	755,358	5	17	6	8⅛	72	6	2	106	1	0
1828	130,866	9,961	759,175	5	16	0	7⅝	76	1	4	112	7	0
1829	125,902	9,763	725,834	5	15	6	7¾	74	10	3	109	14	0

(Based on *R.C.P.S.*, 1838, pp. 137-8 and Robert Hunt, *British Mining*, p. 892)

APPENDIX IV

The Copper Speculation Mines of 1823-26 in Cornwall

Mine	Working	Tons of Ores Raised	Value of Ores Sold £
Wheal Barton	1823-26	163	2,003
East Wheal Basset	1825-27	505	5,318
South Wheal Basset	1825-56*	94,649	614,243
Bottle Hill	1823-35	1,771	?
Wheal Busy	1823-56*	33,486	126,230
Cabilla	1823-24	26	196
Cardrew	1826-38	17,143	83,618
Wheal Caroline	1826-31	9,823	44,897
Wheal Cecilia	1823	6	?
Chacewater Mine	1823	198	?
Wheal Chance Consols ..	1826-27	3,998	25,111
Cliff Downs	1823-41	316	1,483
Wheal Clowance	1823-24	342	?
East Wheal Cock	1823-24	495	3,165
Friendly Mines	1823-25	100	1,183
South Wheal Friendship ..	1824	7	?
George the Fourth	1823-24	102	456
Wheal Gerry	1824-25	187	671
Gewans	1825	31	111
Wheal Good Luck	1826	37	?
Wheal Hope	1824-32	5,584	41,981
Wheal Kayle	1826-46	575	3,714
Wheal Lamb	1823	114	394
Wheal Lambo	1823-25	350	2,289
Little Duke	1824	40	?
Wheal Lopes	1825	26	?
Wheal Maudlin	1823-24	84	360
Prince Royal	1825-26	206	1,576
West Wheal Prudence ..	1825-26	55	349
Wheal Raven	1825-28	1,447	9,546
Wheal Robert	1825-26	106	?
Wheal Rodney	1824-48	6,844	32,276
Rosplethan	1823	10	?
Wheal Sisters..	1825-48	3,006	16,257
Wheal Speed	1825-43	4,096	23,606
Great Towan Consols ..	1825	20	103
Wheal Treasury	1826-44	6,787	32,606
Wheal Trenwith	1825-56	13,080	115,116
Treskow	1824	6	55

Trevea	..	1823	10	92
Wheal Unity Wood ..	..	1823-42	32,756	192,652
United Hills	..	1826-47	54,473	266,075
Wheal Uny	..	1826-56*	755	3,472
Wheal Valley	..	1825-28	498	2,312
Virtuous Lady	..	1825-33	3,843	?

* Still working after 1856

(Based on J. A. Phillips and J. Darlington—*Records of Mining and Metallurgy.* 1857, pp. 256-265).

APPENDIX V

Annual records of the pilchard fishery for the period 1815-1871 were given by William Roberts in the *Journal of the Royal Institution of Cornwall*, Vol. IV, p. 159; further records were given by Howard Fox in the *Reports and Transactions of the Royal Cornwall Polytechnic Society*, 1878, pp. 105-119. These records show a few minor divergencies, but the general progress, or decline, of the export trade is better shown by decennial averages which tend to eliminate seasonal fluctuations.

Period	Average Yearly Export	Highest Export	Lowest Export	Price Low	High
1820-29	9,892 hhds.	26,018 (1828)	700 (1829)	34s. (1826)	84s. (1820, 1823)
1830-39	19,430½ ,,	31,930 (1832)	7,580 (1838)	26s. (1832)	62s. (1838)
1840-49	21,6285 ,,	41,623 (1847)	7,593 (1848)	30s. (1846, 1847)	78s. (1840)
1850-59	15,766 ,,	26,743 (1851)	3,145 (1859)	30s. (1852)	75s. (1855)
1860-69	15,650½ ,,	26,057½ (1863)	3,920½ (1860)	41s. (1863)	80s. (1860)
1870-77	17,216¾ ,,	45,683 (1871)	6,048 (1870)	25s. (1871, 1873)	100s. (1876)

The total export for 58 years amounted to 960,051½ hogsheads, or an average of 16,553 hogsheads per annum.

The number of years with catches of :

Under 5,000 hogsheads were		5
5,000 to 10,000 ,,	,,	15
10,000 to 15,000 ,,	,,	7
15,000 to 20,000 ,,	,,	11
20,000 to 25,000 ,,	,,	7
25,000 to 30,000 ,,	,,	7
Over 30,000 ,,	,,	6

Prices of over 50s. per hogshead were obtained in 28 years; for 21 years prices ranged from 30s. to 50s.; in no year was the average below 30s.; although in six years some fish were sold at or below that price; in nine years there were wide variations in price, *e.g.*, in 1820 the range was between 55s. and 84s., whilst in 1871 the first catches fetched 68s. and those at the end of the season but 25s. There is no absolute correspondence between scarcity of pilchards and high prices, but generally the twenty years with exports of more than 20,000 hogsheads correspond to the twenty-one with prices below 50s., and the twenty-seven with an export of less than 15,000 to the twenty-eight with prices above 50s.

BIBLIOGRAPHY

MANUSCRIPTS

BRITISH MUSEUM
Additional MSS., 21553, 28554, 29281.

PUBLIC RECORD OFFICE
Assize Records
Chatham Papers

BODLEIAN LIBRARY, OXFORD
Jonathan Toup MSS. Toup, one of the most renowned classical scholars of his age, left his papers on classical subjects to Oxford University. A number of his notes were jotted down on any scrap of paper that came to hand, which included leases of property, certificates that Quakers had been properly buried in woollen shrouds, private letters and even the butcher's bill.

CORNISH COLLECTIONS

i. John Boaden MSS. These include a number of leases of landed properties, chiefly in Mawgan in Meneage and neighbouring parishes, the earliest belonging to the year 1628 and the latest 1860, besides Boaden's MSS Autobiography, written in 1902-3. They were in the possession of the late H. E. Boaden, Esq., Falmouth.

ii. Walter Borlase MSS. Letter-books, February 12, 1746/47 to June 2, 1752; tin bounds book, April, 1751. In the possession of C. W. B. Parker, Esq., Penzance.

iii. Borlase MSS. Letter-books of William Borlase, December 12, 1722 to May 13, 1772. In the Morrab Library, Penzance.

iv. Church Warden's Accounts. St. Cleer, St. Erme, Illogan, Lanteglos-by-Camelford and Ludgvan.

v. Coinage Resolution Book. Minutes of the Meetings of the Associated Tinners at Truro, Penzance, and Redruth, February 29, 1780 to July 31, 1818. In the Museum of the Royal Geological Society of Cornwall, Penzance.

vi. J. R. Cunnack MSS. Notes on a number of mines, chiefly in the Helston district written in 1883. In the possession of E. M. Cunnack, Esq., Four Winds, Helston.

vii. C. G. Henderson MSS. Royal Institution of Cornwall, Truro.
viii. Hoblyn MSS. Estate documents now in the possession of G. White, Esq., Newquay.

ix. Parish Burial Registers. St. Cleer, St. Erme, St. Just-in-Penwith, St. Just-in-Roseland.

x. Penlee MSS. Estate Papers of various small estates in Buryan. Gulval Parish Investigations under the Laws of Settlement. Correspondence of the Rev. A. A. Sykes, Dean of Buryan and Walter Borlase.

xi. Tehidy MSS. Estate Accounts of Tehidy 1730-1840, including Account Books of Dolcoath and Cook's Kitchen Mines. At present in the possession of F. L. Harris, Esq., Redruth and T. R. Harris, Esq., Camborne.

xii. Wilson MSS. Correspondence of Boulton and Watt with their Cornish agent Thomas Wilson from June 5, 1780 to November 25, 1803 now in the possession of the Royal Cornwall Polytechnic Society at Falmouth.

PRINTED RECORDS, PARLIAMENTARY REPORTS, LEGAL DOCUMENTS

Brown, Josiah, *Cases In Parliament*, 1780.

Concanen, G., *A Report of the trial at bar, Rowe v. Brenton . . . as to the right to minerals in the assessional lands of the Duchy of Cornwall*, 1830.

Calendars of Home Office Papers.
Calendars of State Papers, Domestic.
Calendars of Treasury Books and Papers.

Cross, A. L., *Eighteenth Century Documents relating to the Royal Forests, the Sheriffs, and Smuggling*, 1928.

Davies, J. H., *The Letters of Lewis Richard, William and John Morris 1728-1765.* (Aberystwyth) 1907.

Hansard, *Parliamentary Debates.*

Harrison, Sir George, *Substance of a Report on the Laws and Jurisdiction of the Stannaries in Cornwall*, 1835.

Journals of the House of Commons:

Reports from Committees of the House of Commons—

Report from the Committee appointed to Enquire into the State of the Pilchard Fisheries, 1785.

Report from the Committee appointed to Enquire into the Matter of the Petition of the Principal Persons concerned in the Pilchard Fisheries on Behalf of Themselves and Other Adventurers therein, 1786.

Report from the Committee on Illicit Export of Wool, Live Sheep, Worsted and Yarn, 1786.

Report from the Committee appointed to Consider the Several Laws for Preventing the Exportation of Live Sheep and Lambs, Wool, Wool Felts, and Martlings, etc., 1788.

Report from the Committee appointed to Enquire into the State of the Copper Mines and Copper Trade, 1799.

Report on the Salt Duties, 1816.

Report of the Sea Fisheries of the United Kingdom, 1866.

Report on the Cod and Lobster Fisheries, 1877.

Report on the Destruction of Spawn by Trawling and Ground Seining, 1878-79.

Report of the Commissioners of Mines of Great Britain, 1864.

Report of the General Board of Health on the Epidemic Cholera, 1850.

U.S. Geological Survey, Annual Reports.

PERIODICALS AND NEWSPAPERS

Annals of Agriculture.
Annual Register.
Economic History Review.
Economic Journal.
Gentleman's Magazine.
Journal of the Bath and West of England Society.
Journal of the Royal Agricultural Society of England.
Mining and Smelting Magazine.
Penzance Gazette and West Cornwall Advertiser.
Philosophical Transactions.
Reports of the Penzance Natural History and Antiquarian Society.
Reports of the Royal Cornwall Polytechnic Society.
Reports and Journals of the Royal Institution of Cornwall.
Royal Cornwall Gazette.
Statistical Society Journal.
Transactions of the Devonshire Association for the Advancement of Science, Literature and Art.
Transactions of the Newcomen Society.
Transactions of the Royal Geological Society of Cornwall.
West Briton.
Western Antiquary.

BOOKS, PAMPHLETS AND ARTICLES

Abbott, G. *An Essay on the Mines of England.* 1833.

Agricola. *De Re Metallica* (edited H. C. and L. H. Hoover), 1912.

Allen, G. C. 'An Eighteenth Century Combination in the Copper Mining Industry'—*Economic Journal*, 1923.

Allen, J. *History of Liskeard.* (Liskeard) 1856.

Anonymous *Aggravii Venetiani, or the Venetian and other Grievances together with a Proposal for raising the Price of Tin.* 1697.

Anonymous   *A Statement of the Proceedings of the Convocation, or
                          Parliament, for the Stannaries of the County of
                          Cornwall. 1751.*

do.   *An Address to the Gentlemen of the County of Cornwall
                          on the Present State of Mining in that County: with
                          some observations on the Tin and Copper Trade.* 1772.

do.   *Pilchard Fishery, Cornwall,* c. 1811 (see above, p. 279,
                          note 3).

do.   *Life of Thomas Telford.* 1838.

Ashton, T. S. &   *The Coal Industry in the Eighteenth Century.* (Man-
Sykes, J.   chester) 1929.

Barr, A.   *James Watt and the Application of Steam to the
                          Mechanical Arts.* (Glasgow) 1889.

Batten, J.   *The Stannaries Act.* 1869.

Bellamy, J. C.   *Housekeeper's Guide to the Fish Market.* 1862.

Boase, G. C.   *Collectanea Cornubiensis.* 1890.

Boase, G. C. &   *Bibliotheca Cornubiensis.* 1874-1882 (3 Vols.).
W. P. Courtney.

Bolitho, T. S.   'On the Pilchard'—*Reports of the Penzance Natural
                          History and Antiquarian Society.* 1850.

Bond, T.   *Topographical and Historical Sketches of the Boroughs
                          of East and West Looe in the County of Cornwall.*
                          1823.

Borlase, W.   *Observations on the Ancient and Present State of the
                          Isles of Scilly and their Importance to the Trade of
                          Great Britain.* (Oxford) 1756.

do.   *The Natural History of Cornwall.* (Oxford) 1758.

Borlase, W, C,   *Historical Sketch of the Tin Trade in Cornwall.* 1874.

do.   *Borlase of Borlase.* 1888.

Boys, J.   *General View of the Agriculture of Kent.* 1796.

Brown, N. &   *A Century of Copper.* 1900.
Turnbull, C. C.

Calamy, E,   *The Nonconformists' Memorial.* Edited by Samuel
                          Palmer, 1802 (3 Vols.).

Cardew, Sir A.   *Cornelius Cardew.* (Truro) 1926.

Carew, R.   *Survey of Cornwall.* (Edited by Lord de Dunstan-
                          ville) 1811.

Carne, J.   'The Tin Mines of Cornwall'—*Journal Statistical
                          Society.* Vol II, 1839.

Coate, M.   *Cornwall in the Great Civil War.* (Oxford) 1933.

Cock, D.   *A Treatise on China Clay.* 1880.

Collins, J. H.   *Observations on the West of England Mining Region.*
                          1912.

*Communications to the Board of Agriculture on Subjects relative to the Husbandry
and Internal Improvement of the Country.* 1804-1808 (6 Vols.).

Cornish, J. B. (ed.) — *The Autobiography of a Cornish Smuggler, Captain Harry Carter of Prussia Cove*, 1749-1809. 1894.

Couch, J. — *History of Polperro.* 1872

do. — 'Treatise on the Pilchard'—*Royal Cornwall Polytechnic Society Reports.* 1835.

do. — 'Observations on the Pilchard Fishery'—*Royal Cornwall Polytechnic Society Reports.* 1840.

do. — 'A Natural History of the Mackerel'—*Royal Cornwall Polytechnic Society Reports.* 1844.

Couch, R. Q. — 'The Mackeral'—*Reports of the Penzance Natural History and Antiquarian Society.* 1848.

Courtney, J. S. — 'Fishery Statistics'—*Royal Cornwall Polytechnic Society Reports.* 1838.

Courtney, W. P. — *History of Parliamentary Representation in Cornwall.* 1889.

Darling, J. & Phillips, J. A. — *Records of Mining and Metallurgy.* 1857.

Defoe, D. — *A Tour Thro' the Whole Island of Great Britain.* (Edited G. D. H. Cole) 1927 (2 Vols.).

Delany, M. — *Autobiography and Correspondence of Mary Grenville, Mrs. Delany.* (Edited Lady Llanover) 1861-62 (6 Vols.).

Dew, R. — *The History of the Parish and Church of Kilkhampton.* 1926.

Dickinson, H. W. — *Matthew Boulton.* (Cambridge) 1936.

Dickinson, H. W. & Jenkins Rhys. — *James Watt and the Steam Engine.* (Oxford) 1927.

Dickinson, H. W. & Titley A. — *Richard Trevithick—the Engineer and the Man.* (Cambridge) 1934.

Dictionary of National Biography.

Doble, G. H. — *Sithney and Wendron.* (n.d.).

Dodd, A. H. — *The Industrial Revolution in North Wales.* (Cardiff) 1933.

Drew, S. — *History of Cornwall.* (Helston) 1824 (2 Vols.).

Edmonds, R. — *The Land's End District.* 1862.

English, H. — *A General Guide to the Companies formed for Working Foreign Mines.* 1825.

English, H. — *A Compendium of Useful Information relating to the Companies formed for working British Mines.* 1826.

Farington, J. — *Diary.* (Edited J. Greig) 1922-28 (8 Vols.).

Fay, C. R. — *The Corn Laws and Social England.* (Cambridge) 1932.

Fiennes, C. — *Through England on a Side Saddle.* (Edited Hon. E. Griffiths) 1888.

Flower, P. W. — *A History of the Trade in Tin.* 1880.

Fox, H.   'The Pilchard Fishery'—*Royal Cornwall Polytechnic Society Reports.* 1878.

Francis, W.   *Gwennap—a Descriptive Poem.* 1845.

Fraser, R.   *General View of the County of Cornwall.* 1794.

Galphin, W. F.   *The Grain Supply of England during the Napoleonic Period.* (New York) 1925.

Gay, S. E.   *Old Falmouth.* 1903.

Geach, E. & Webb   *History and Progress of Mining in the Liskeard and Caradon Districts.* 1862.

Gee, T.   *The Trade and Navigation of Britain Considered.* 1729.

Gilbert, D.   *Parochial History of Cornwall.* 1838 (4 Vols.).

Gott, Bishop T.   *The Ideals of a Parish.* 1897.

Grant Francis G.   *The Smelting of Copper in the Swansea District of South Wales from the Time of Elizabeth to the Present Day.* 1881.

Hals, W.   *Parochial History of Cornwall.* 1750.

Hamilton, H.   *The English Brass and Copper Industries to 1800.* 1926.

Hammond, T.   *A Cornish Parish—an Account of St. Austell.* 1897.

Hawker, R. S.   *Cornish Ballads.* 1869.

do.   *Footprints of Former Men in Far Cornwall.* 1870.

Head, Sir F. B.   *Report Relating to the Failure of the Rio Plate Mining Association.* 1827.

Hearder, J. N.   'The Degeneration of our Sea Fisheries'—*Transactions Devonshire Association.* Vol. IV, 1870.

Henderson, C. G.   *Essays in Cornish History.* (Oxford) 1935.

Henwood, W. T.   'The Cornish Fishery in 1870'—*Journal Royal Institution of Cornwall.* 1871.

Holdsworth, R. W. H.   *The Sea Fisheries of Great Britain and Ireland.* 1883.

Hoon, E. E.   *The Organisation of the British Customs System, 1696-1786.* (New York) 1938.

Humphreys, R. A.   *British Consular Reports on the Trade and Politics of Latin America, 1824-1826.* 1940.

Hunt, R.   *British Mining.* 1884.

James, C. C.   *A History of Gwennap.* 1949.

Jars, G.   *Voyages Metallurgiques.* (Lyons) 1774-81 (5 Vols.).

Jenkin, A. K. H.   *The Cornish Miner.* 1927.

do.   'Boulton and Watt in Cornwall'—*Royal Cornwall Polytechnic Society Reports.* 1927.

Jenkins, Rhys.   'Savery, Newcomen, and the Early History of the Steam Engine'—*T.N.S.* Vols. III & IV, 1923-24.

do.   'Jonathan Hornblower and the Compound Engine'—*T.N.S.* Vol. XI, 1931.

Jenkins, Rhys.	'A Cornish Engineer. Arthur Woolf, 1766-1837'— *T.N.S.* Vol. XIII, 1933.
do.	'The Reverberatory Furnace with Coal Fuel'— *T.N.S.* Vol. XIV, 1934.
do.	'Hammer Mill in Cornwall'—*T.N.S.* Vol. XVIII, 1938.
Jewitt, L.	*The Wedgwoods.* 1865.
Jones, W. R.	*The Tinfields of the World.* 1925.
Karkeek, W. F.	'On the Farming of Cornwall'—*J.R.A.S.* Vol. VI, 1845-46.
do.	'Richard Davey, M.P.'s Farm at Polsew in Philleigh'—*J.B.W.* Vol. VIII, 1858.
Lake, W. (publisher)	*Parochial History of Cornwall.* (4 Vols.) 1872.
Lardner, D.	*Cabinet Cyclopedia; Manufactures of Metal.* 1834.
Lawrance, W. T.	*Parliamentary Representation of Cornwall,* (Truro) 1924.
Lean, T.	*Historical Statement of the Improvements Made in the Duty Performed by the Steam Engines in Cornwall.* 1839.
Lecky, W. E. H.	*History of England in the Eighteenth Century.* 1878-90 (7 Vols.).
Lemon, Sir C.	'The Copper Mines of Cornwall'—*Statistical Society Journal.* Vol I, 1838.
do.	'Notes on the Agricultural Produce of Cornwall'— *Statistical Society Journal.* Vol. IV, 1841.
Lewis, G. R.	*The Stannaries.* (Harvard) 1908.
Lockyer, C.	*Account of the Trade in India.* 1711.
Lord, J.	*Capital and Steam Power, 1750-1800.* 1923.
Lorre, L. F.	'The First Steam Engine in America'—*T.N.S.* Vol. X, 1930.
Lovett, W.	*Life and Struggles of William Lovett.* 1876.
MacDermott, E. T.	*History of the Great Western Railway.* 1927 (2 Vols.).
Macgregor, J.	*Commercial Statistics.* 1844-1850 (5 Vols.).
Maclean, J.	*Parochial and Family History of the Deanery of Trigg Manor in the County of Cornwall.* 1876 (3 Vols.).
Mantoux, P.	*The Industrial Revolution in the Eighteenth Century.* 1927 (Revised Edition).
Marshall, C. F. D.	*A History of the Southern Railway.* 1936.
Marshall, T. H.	*James Watt.* 1925.
Marshall, W.	*The Rural Economy of the West of England.* 1796.
do.	*Review and Complete Abstracts of the Reports to the Board of Agriculture for the Southern and Peninsular Departments of England.* 1817.

Mason, W. W.	'Trevithick's First Rail Locomotive'—*T.N.S.* Vol. XII, 1932.
Maton, W. G.	*Observation of the Western Counties of England 1794-1796.* 1797 (2 Vols.).
Matthews, J. H.	*A History of the Parishes of St. Ives, Lelant, Towednack and Zennor.* 1892.
Milburn, W.	*Oriental Commerce.* 1813.
Morshead, Wm.	'The Relative Advantages of Steam, Water, and Animal Power'—*J.B.W.* Vol. IV, 1856.
do.	'Practical Hints as to the Selection and Management of Agricultural Steam Engines'—*J.B.W.* Vol. IX, 1861.
Muirhead, J. P.	*The Origins and Progress of the Mechanical Invention of James Watt.* (Glasgow) 1854 (3 Vols.).
Olmstead, F. L.	*Our Slave States: a Journey into the Back Country in 1853-54.* (New York) 1860.
Pearce, W.	*General View of the Agriculture of Berkshire.* 1794.
Peters, T. C.	*Glasney Collegiate Church.* 1903.
Polwhele, R.	*The History of Cornwall.* 1816 (7 Vols.).
do.	*Traditions and Recollections domestic, clerical and literary.* 1826.
do.	*Biographical Sketches in Cornwall.* 1831.
do.	*Reminiscences in Prose and Verse, consisting of Epistolary Correspondence of many distinguished Characters.* 1836.
Pounds, N. J. G.	'The Discovery of China Clay'—*Economic History Review.* 2nd Series, Vol. I, 1948.
do.	'Population Movements in Cornwall and the Rise of Mining in the Eighteenth Century'—*Geography.* XXVIII, 1943.
Pryce, W.	*Mineralogia Cornubiensis.* 1778.
Rashleigh, W. W.	'Ancient Cornish Fishery'—*Western Antiquary.* Vol. III, 1883-84.
Redding, C.	*Illustrated Itinerary of the County of Cornwall.* 1842.
Rickard, T. A.	*History of American Mining.* (New York) 1932.
Roll, E.	*An Early Experiment in Industrial Organisation—the Firm of Boulton and Watt, 1775-1805.* 1930.
Rowse, A. L.	*Tudor Cornwall.* 1941.
Russell, P. & Price, O.	*England Displayed.* 1769 (2 Vols).
Savery, T.	*The Miner's Friend, or, an Engine to raise Water by Fire described, and the Manner of Fixing it in the Mines.* 1707.
Scott, W. R.	*The Constitution and Finance of English Scottish, and Irish Joint Stock Companies to 1720.* (Cambridge) 1910-1912 (3 Vols.).

Smiles, S.	*Lives of Boulton and Watt.* 1865.
Spargo, T.	*Mines of Cornwall and Devon.* 1865.
Stoker, H. M.	'Essay on the China-stone and China Clays of Cornwall'—*Edinburgh New Philosophical Journal.* Vol. IV, 1854.
Stuart, R.	*A Descriptive History of the Steam Engine.* 1824.
Taylor, J.	*Records of Mining.* 1829.
do.	*Reply to Observations on the Statement of the Committee of the Consolidated Mine Adventures.* 1838.
Thomas, J.	'Changes in the Agriculture of Cornwall since 1800'—*Statistical Society Journal.* 1869.
Titley, A.	'The Account Books of Richard Trevithick, Senior'—*T.N.S.* Vol. XI, 1931.
Toy, H. S.	*History of Helston.* 1936.
Tredgold, T.	*On the Steam Engine.* 1838.
Trevithick, F.	*Life of Richard Trevithick.* 1872 (2 Vols.).
Unwin, G.	*Letters, Remarks, etc., with a View to open an Extensive Trade in the Article of Tin from the County of Cornwall to India, Persia and China.* 1790.

Victoria County History of Cornwall. 1906.

Victoria County History of Shropshire. 1908.

Voelcher, A.	'The Use of Lime, Marl, and Shell Sand in Agriculture'—*J.B.W.* Vol. VI. 1858.
Wailes, R.	'Tide Mills in England and Wales'—*T.N.S.* Vol. XIX., 1938.
Ward, H. G.	*Mexico in 1827.* 1828 (2 Vols.).
Warner, R.	*A Tour through Cornwall in the Autumn of 1808.* 1809.
Watson, T. Y.	*A Compendium of British Mining, with Statistical Notices of the Principal Mines in Cornwall.* 1843.
Welch, C.	*History of the Worshipful Company of Pewterers of the City of London.* 1902 (2 Vols.).
Whitley, N.	'On some Peculiarities of the Climate of the South-West of England'—*J.B.W.* Vol. III. 1855.
do.	'The Physical Geography of the South Western Counties'—*J.B.W.* Vol. IV, 1856.
do.	'Development of the Agricultural Resources of Cornwall'—*J.B.W..* Vol. IX, 1861.
Williams, J. B.	*Guide to the Printed Materials for English Social and Economic History.* (New York) 1926 (2 Vols.).
Worgan, G. B.	*A General View of the Agriculture of Cornwall.* 1808.
Worth, R. N.	'William Cookworthy and the Plymouth China Factory'—*Transactions of the Devonshire Association.* Vol. VIII, 1876.
Yarranton, A.	*England's Improvement in Sea and Land.* 1677-81 (2 Parts).
Young, A.	*A Six Weeks' Tour through the Southern Counties of England and Wales.* 1768.

SUPPLEMENTARY BIBLIOGRAPHY: CHAPTER II(i)
AND CHAPTER VI(i)

CORNISH COLLECTIONS

Polperro Wesleyan Methodist Association Chapel Records.
Richard Treffry MSS. Diary, January 7, 1802-November 7, 1809; at
present in the possession of Dr. F. L. Harris, Redruth.

PERIODICALS

Arminian Magazine.
Evangelical Magazine.
Methodist Magazine.

BOOKS, PAMPHLETS AND ARTICLES

Baring Gould, S. R.	*The Vicar of Morwenstow*, 1876.
Bourne, F. W.	*Billy Bray, the King's Son*, 1872.
Byles, C. E.	*Life and Letters of Robert Stephen Hawker*, 1905.
Christophers, S. W.	*The Poets of Methodism*, 1875.
Davison, J.	*Life of the Venerable William Clowes*, 1854.
Drew, J. H.	*The Life, Character and Literary Labours of Samuel Drew*, 1834.
Drew, J. H.	*Samuel Drew—the self-taught Cornishman*. 1861.
Drew, S.	*Observations (in behalf of the Methodists) on a Pamphlet . . . by the Rev. R. Polwhele . . . entitled Anecdotes of Methodism*, Falmouth, 1800.
Gott, Bishop. T.	*The Ideals of a Parish*, 1897.

Huntingdon—Life and Times of the Countess of, 1839-40 (2 Vols.)

Jackson, T.	*Life of Charles Wesley*, 1841 (2 Vols.)
Jackson, T.	*Methodist Biography*, 1837-8 (3 Vols.)
James, W.	*The Varieties of Religious Experience*, 1902.

Kilham—Life of the Rev. Alexander, Nottingham, 1799.

Lach-Szyrma, W. S.	*A Church History of Cornwall*, 1887.
Le Grice, C. V.	*Proofs of the Spirit, or Considerations on Revivalism*, 1814.
Maker, L.	*Cob and Moorstone*, 1935.

Methodist Minutes of Conference, 1744-

Niebuhr, R.	*Contribution of Religion to Social Work*, 1932.

Petty, J.   *History of the Primitive Methodist Connexion, from its Origins to the Conference of 1859. 1860.*

Polwhele, R.   *Anecdotes of Methodism, to which is added a Sermon (on 2 Cor. 1-12) on the Conduct that becomes a Clergyman. 1800.*

Polwhele, R.   *Bishop Lavington's 'Enthusiasm of Methodists and Papists Compared', 1833*

Redfern, W.   *Modern Developments in Methodism, 1906.*

Riles, J.   *Account of the Revival, Truro, 1814.*

Ryle, J.   *The Church Leaders of the Last Century, 1869.*

St. Ives—A Vindication of the Teetotal Wesleyan Methodists of—with an Incidential Exposure of the domination of the Wesleyan Priesthood, 1842.

Smith, G.   *History of Wesleyan Methodism 1859-65. (3 Vols).*

Thorne, S. L.   *William O'Bryan—Founder of the Bible Christians, 1878.*

Thorne, S. L.   *Samuel Thorne, Printer, 1875.*

Treffry, Rev. R. Snr. *Letter to the Rev. C. Val Le Grice occasioned by his Sermon entitled Proofs of the Spirit or Considerations on Revivalism, Penzance, 1814.*

Treffry, Rev. R. Snr. *Select Remains of the Rev. Francis Truscott, 1833.*

Treffry, Rev. R. Snr. *Memoirs of the Rev. R. Treffry, Junior, 1838.*

Treffry, Rev. R. Snr. *Memoirs of Mr. Richard Trewavas, Senior, of Mousehold, Cornwall, 1839.*

Treffry, Rev. R. Jnr. *Memoirs of Mr. John Edwards Tresize, 1837.*

Troeltsch, E.   *The Social Teaching of the Christian Churches, 1931 (2 Vols).*

Tyerman, L.   *Life and Times of John Wesley, 1890. (3 Vols).*

Warner, W. J.   *The Wesleyan Movement in the Industrial Revolution, 1930.*

Wesley, J.   *Journal* (ed. N. Curnock), 1909-16 (89B] VOLS.)

Wesley, J.   *Letters* (ed. J. Telford, 1931 (8 Vols.)

Wills, — Memoirs of the Life of the Rev. Thomas, 1804.

INDEX

ACLAND, Sir Thomas Dyke (1787-1871), 248.

Acre, Cornish, 230 *n. 3.*

Adit-driving, 51, 54, 55. See also Levels.

Adit, the Great, 54, 55 *n. 1*, 219 *n. 1.*

Adventurers, Cornish Mines, 68. See also Basset, Sir Francis; Consolidated Mines; Cost Book System; Daniell, Ralph Allen; North Downs; Speculation in Mining; Tincroft, etc.

— 'Foreign' in Cornish Mines, 47-9, 55, 65-6, 68, 95, 188.

— General Meetings of those in Tin, 43, 44, 195, 201, 202.

Africa, tin trade with, 58, 61.

Agrarian Society, changes in during early eighteenth century, 2, 39.

Agriculture, 208-61; child labour in, 260; depression of, 239, 249-52, 259; mechanization of, 233, 239-40, 254-5; open field, 212-3; run rig, 212-5.

Agricultural College, proposed in Cornwall, 255.

Agricultural Distress (in 1822), 239.

Agricultural Societies, of Kerrier, 236 *n. 1*; of Probus, 252, 253; of Wadebridge, 248, 250, 252; of West Penwith, 256.

Ale and Cakes (mine), 115 *n. 1.*

Allen, John (mine adventurer), 148.

Allotments, 239. See also Smallholdings.

Alternun, 209.

America, North, 40 *n. 3*, 58, 61, 308-9.

America, Spanish, 3 *n.1*, 115, 120 *n. 2*, 126, 128-30, 133, 135, 138-41, 144-5, 216.

Anaconda, 326.

Angarrack, 117 *n. 2*, 148.

Anglesey, 61, 68, 71-2, 76, 80-3, 85, 87, 90-1, 112, 117, 119, 141; Cornish agreement with to restrict copper production, 82-3; Cornish miners in, 91 *n. 1.*

Anglo-Chilean Mining Association, 145

Anti-Corn Law League, 247-51, 311 *n. 1.*

Apprentices to Husbandry, 239.

Arable Farming, 221, 223-4, 228, 230-33, 236-7, 258; increase of to meet needs of mining population, 116.

Archer, Edward (landowner), 251, 256-7, 260.

Arkwright, Richard (inventor), 94, 95, 96, 97, 98, 103.

Arrish Mow, 229, 230, 258, 292 *n. 1.*

Arsenic, 48.

Assizes, 37, 104-5, 143, 219, 285-6.

Associations, Armed against threatened French Invasion in 1793, 104.

Atmospheric Engine, 7, 101. See also Newcomen Watt.

Attorneys, Associated of Cornwall, 183.

Austen, Joseph Thomas (mine adventurer), 117 *n. 3*, 126 *n. 6*, 136, 143-4, 158, 195, 203.

BALDHU, 102, 192.

Bal Maidens, 28.

Baltic, trade in tin to, 57 *n. 1.*

Balleswidden, 311, 312.

Balwath, 53 *n. 2.*

Banca, 165, 185, 189, 199, 202, 204, 206. See also Tin: East Indian.

Banfield, Joseph (merchant and banker), 289, 290.

Banking, 11, 59.

Barley, 223, 224, 230-1.

Basset family of Tehidy, 30, 63 *n. 2*, 217, 225, 245, 260.

Basset, Francis (d. 1769), 50, 52, 55 *n. 1*, 226.

Basset, Sir Francis (1757-1835), 68, 89, 95, 102 *n. 1*, 120, 136, 179, 233, 303; and Cornish Metal Company, 83-8; farming of 223 *n. 2*, 234; promotes Portreath tramroad, 117; reclaims waste lands, 90, 225; supports Tinners' Association, 166; suppresses riot in mining district, 104-5.

Basset, John (landowner), 203.

Basset, Lady Frances, 155.

Bath and West Agricultural Show, 240, 259.

Bath, Michael (smelter), 181.

Batten, John (merchant), 170.

Bawden, Joseph (miner), 186.

Beaglehole, Captain (miner), 187.

Bedruthan Steps, 302.

Belwathland, 213, 214 *n. 1.*

Bennelleck, Francis (attorney), 59.

Bennet (Mayor of Fowey), 286.

Berkeley, Rev. J. B. Prettyman, 311, 312, 315.

Bible Christian Movement, 247.

Bickford, William (inventor), 9.

Bickford, William (landowner), 214.

Birmingham, 48, 68, 84; market for copper in, 72; agents of Tinners' Association in, 168. See also Boulton, Soho, Watt.

Bissoe, 10.

Black, Dr. Joseph, 73, 74, 78, 79 *n. 1*.

Blackstone, Sir William, 59, 192.

Blake family (merchants of Falmouth), 290.

Blewett (farmer of Perranzabuloe), 219-20.

Blewett, George (merchant) 271, 272, 279.

Blewitt, James (merchant), 59.

Blisland, 218.

Boaden, John (farmer), 242.

Boase, John (farmer), 241.

Boconnoc, 234, 251.

Boddy, John (farmer), 216.

Bodmin, 102 *n. 1*, 148, 193, 194, 209, 246, 248, 250, 269, 273; anti-tithe meeting at, 243; assizes, 12 *n. 3*, 104, 143, 285; coinage town, 13 *n. 1*; prison, 104, 143, 161, 285.

Bodmin Moors, 209, 227.

Bodmin and Wadebridge Railway, 148.

Boiler, tubular, 124.

Bolingey, 219.

Bolitho family, 60, 170, 201.

Bolitho, Thomas (smelter), 203.

Bond, Thomas (landowner and writer), 230, 303-4.

Booth, Rev. (of Gwennap), 181.

Borlase family, 217.

Borlase, John (squire of Pendeen), 11, 30, 31, 32.

Borlase, John (Steward of the Stannaries), 193.

Borlase, Rev. Walter, 30, 36 *n. 2*, 295 *n. 1*, 295 *n. 2*, 304; mine adventurer, 270; religious views of, 31; seine-owner, 270; tin bounds owned by, 17; Vice-warden of the Stannaries, 196, 270.

Borlase, Rev. Dr. William, 8 *n. 1*, 30, 51, 218, 219, 221, 222, 228, 231, 232, 236 *n. 1*, 271.

Borough Representation in Parliament, 245.

Boscastle, 287, 303.

Boscaswell, 17.

Boscawen family, 6 *n. 2*, 38, 45, 68, 85, 227, 245. See also Falmouth, Edward Boscawen, Earl of; George Evelyn Boscawen, Viscount; and Hugh Boscawen, Viscount.

Bossiney, 275.

Botalet (mine), 318.

Botallack, 17, 176, 303.

Boulton and Watt, firm of, 74, 111, 114, 172 *n. 6*, 188; became shareholders in Cornish mines, 82; and Jonathan Hornblower, 93, 96-7, 98, 107; monopoly of steam engines in Cornwall, 95; breach with Edward Bull, 96; attempt to buy Hornblower patent, 98; lose monopoly of engines in Cornwall, 101; premiums paid to them or due them from Cornish mines, 79-81, 94, 97, 102-3, 111-2; business associates in Cornwall, 102; relations with the younger Richard Trevithick 102, 108-10; secure injunction against Bull, 102, 106; clash with R. A. Daniell, 103, 108; riots instigated against in Cornwall, 105-6; become engine manufacturers, 107; win legal action against Hornblower 108; evaluation of their services to Cornish mining, 112-3.

Boulton, Matthew, 68, 72, 80, 81, 87, 91, 93, 94, 96, 97, 98, 111, 115: meeting and partnership with Watt, 73; secures extension of Watt's patent by Act of Parliament, 74; early dealings in Cornwall, 75, 77-8; and the Cornish Metal Company, 82-6, 101; relations with Sir Francis Basset, 84-6; suggests migration to relieve Cornish mining distress, 88; lacks real knowledge of mining conditions, 89; character of, 95; quarrel with John Wilkinson, 107. See also Boulton and Watt: Soho: Watt.

Bounds, Tin, 17, 47.

Bounties on exported Pilchards, 268, 271, 274, 279-80, 289, 293.

Bowden, Collan (mine adventurer), 166.

Brass Wire Company, 21 *n. 1*.

Bratt (engineer), 186-7.

Brazil, 325.

Breage, 10, 48, 52, 186, 239, 301, 302; wreckers of, 35-6.

Bristol, 95, 149; agents of Tinners' Association in, 166, 167, 168; copper merchants and smelters of, 11, 19, 20, 22, 41, 68, 77; prices of tin in, 166, 167, 168, 169, 178.

Britannia Metal, 165.

British Mining or Royal Stannary Association, 134, 138.

British United Mine Company, 134.

Brixham, 284.

Brown, Willy, 209, 210.

Brunel, Isambard Kingdom, 149, 262.

Buddle Boys, 28.

Bude, 221.

Bull, Edward (engineer), 100, 102, 103, 107, 109, 110, 111; employed by Boulton and Watt, 96; quarrels with Boulton and Watt and erects engine infringing Watt's patent at Wheal Virgin, 96; erects engine at Dolcoath, 97; Boulton and Watt secure injunction against him, 97; employed at Poldice and riots follow a second injunction, 106.

Buller family, 38.

Buller, Judge (1746-1800), 232.

Buller and Basset United Mine, 317.

Burning Beat, 228-9.

Buryan, 244, 295 *n. 2*.

Butte City, 326.

CALIFORNIA, 41 *n. 1*, 311, 320, 325.

Callington, 38, 157, 247, 248, 250; miners invade and fix maximum prices at weekly market in 1847, 159-60, 161.

Calstock, 10, 48, 322.

Calumet, 309, 325, 326.

Camborne, 31, 52, 59, 63, 66, 83, 110, 117, 123, 134, 139, 140, 146, 151, 181, 183, 225, 326; anti-Chartist league in, 147; miners of in Anglesey 90-1, in California, 325, in Caradon, 147, and in Nevada, 325; Trevithick's locomotive trial at, 115-6; Vivians of move their engineering works to Pittsburgh, 311; meeting protesting against proposed governmental inspection of mines, 314.

Camel River, 221, 262.

Camelford, 148, 194, 246; disturbance at Anti-Corn Law meeting at, 248.

Camelford, Thomas Pitt, Lord (1737-93), 234.

Canals: Liskeard and Looe, 148, 228; projected, 221.

Capital: antagonism of and labour in mining, 143, 162-3, 311, 316-7; increasing demand for with the development of deep mining, 40; in the pilchard fishery, 264-6, 279, 290-1. See also Cost Book System: Speculation in Mining, etc.

Captains, mining, 25.

Caradon, 71 *n. 1*, 147, 149-51, 159, 310, 316. See also East Caradon: South Caradon.

Caradon Hill, 310.

Caradon Railway, 148.

Caradon Vale, 310, 317 *n. 4*.

Caradon and Phoenix Consols, 310.

Cardrew, 139.

Carew family, 38.

Carew, Richard, 210, 212, 215, 216, 221, 228, 240.

Cargoll, 305 *n. 3*, 318.

Carhayes, 217.

Carloose, 53, 84.

Carlyon, Dr., 155.

Carn Brea, 66, 318.

Carn Entral, enclosure of 225, 226.

Carne, Joseph (smelter and merchant), 203, 290.

Carne, William (mine agent), 137.

Carnmenallis, 147, 149, 209, 217.

Carnon Stream Work, 176, 188, 219 *n. 1*

Carnyorth, 318.

Carpenters, Mine, 25.

Cartels, See Cornish Metal Company: Tinners' Association.

Carter brothers (smugglers), 274, 285.

Carvinnick, 214.

Castle Horneck, 217, 241.

Cathedral Mine, 136.

Cattle, 234-5, 238, 259; diseases of, 227; depasturing of on moorlands, 227; dairy, 235-6; draught, 240, 253, 254; feeding with potatoes, 232; stall or winter feeding of, 223, 232, 253, 255, 257.

Cerro de Pasco (Peru), 130.

Chacewater, 21, 39, 63 *n. 1*, 74 *n. 5*, 83; Boulton and Watt's engines at, 78-80; poverty of miners of in the depression of 1867, 322.

Chartism, 156-7, 248, 250.

Cheesewring, 148.

Chilean Mining Association, 145.

Chilean-Peruvian Mining Association, 145.

Chili, 130, 145, 308, 323.

Chiverton, 83.

Cholera, 154, 294 *n. 4*, 303.

Church of England: and agrarian society, 2. See also Borlase, Rev. Walter: Methodists, etc.

Church Rates, 156, 248. See also Tithes.

Chyandour, 10, 11, 60.

Clark, Sir Talbot (smelter), 19.

Class War: fears of in 1793, 104, 158.

Clay, China, 48-9, 90, 117 *n. 3*; employment provided by, 324-5.

Clergy, Cornish Parish, 1, 30-1. See also Borlase, Rev. Walter.

Clifford Mine, 320.

Climate of Cornwall, 208-10, 232-3.

Clive family, 38.

Clowance, 30, 37.

Clymo brothers (miners), 148.

Coal: abolition of duties on, 142; cost of, 7, 64, 71; drawbacks of duties on, 9, 41-2; duties on, 7, 9, 41-2, 142; measures of, 99; use in farmhouses, 224; use in smelting minerals, 9; use in smelting tin, 16.

Coal Merchants: 'ring' of, 323.

Coalbrookdale, 74 *n. 3*, 109, 110.

Cobalt, 48.

Coinage, of Tin, 45, 59; accounts and statistics of, 3 *n. 2*, 3-4; Dues, 194, 196-7, 199, 202, abolished, 203; Duties, 16, 64 *n. 2*, denounced as obsolete and abolition demanded, 199-202, abolished, 203; towns, 13 *n. 1*, 197. See also Cornwall, Duchy of: Stannaries.

Colan, 215 *n. 2*.

Cole family, 6 *n. 2*.

Collins family, 6 *n. 2*.

Collins, George (Supervisor of Tin Smelting Houses), 10.

Columbian Mining Association, 145.

Complete Suffrage Movement, 157.

Compound Engine, 93, 112.

Concanen, George ('foreign' mine adventurer), 195.

Condenser, Separate, 53 *n. 3*, 54, 73, 74, 76, 80, 94, 96, 112. See also Watt, James.

Consolidated Mines ('Consols'), 6 *n. 2*, 112, 121 *n. 5*, 123, 131, 135, 136, 150, 195, 217, 323; Boulton and Watt shareholders in, 82 *n. 1*; employ Edward Bull, 96; number of Watt's engines at, 80; refuse further payments of premiums to Boulton and Watt, 103; sales of copper ores in 1792, 92, and in 1856, 306; Woolf's engine at, 126.

'Consols' Mine, 137.

Constables, Parish, 105.

Cook's Kitchen, 83; female labour at, 8 *n. 1*; sales of copper by, 146 *n. 2*; tin of, 177; types of labour employed at in 1786, 28; use of water power in, 56.

Cookworthy, William, 48, 51.

Copper: Cornish domination of world supplies, 128; duties on foreign from 1814 to 1819, 122; free trade in, 140-2, 144-5; increasing foreign production, 128, 140, 141, 145; smelters of favour free trade whereas mining interest demand protection, 140-2, 144-5; smelting attempts and projects of in Cornwall, 19-20, 63-5; statistics of production, 309 *n. 1*. 331.

Copper Bank Smelting Works, 121.

Copper Hill Mine, 134.

Copper Markets: See Bristol: Birmingham: Boulton: Cornish Metal Company: South Wales: Wilkinson: Williams, Thomas.

Copper Merchants, 2, 11, 19, 20, 22, 68, 121, 145, 198.

Copper Miners: numbers of in 1720-30, 18. See also Miners.

Copper Mines: profits of different, 122; prosperity after 1815, 127;

signs of exhaustion in particular, 146; declining profits of in 1860, 307; closing down of in 1788, 88, 90, and in 1866, 317-20. See also Mines.

Copper Mining, 2, 17-9, 40, 175, 305; depressions in, 56, 68, 88, 90, 317-24; effects of Napoleonic War on, 119-21; prosperity of after 1815, 127. See also Mines.

Copper Ores, 2, 41, 56, 118-22, 305; attempted restriction of production by the Cornish Metal Company, 91; exports of, 40, 121-2; foreign, 83, 110, 122, 130, 140-1, 308-9; increasing costs of production with deeper mines, 91; metal produce of Cornish, 69-70, 118-9, 305; output of in Cornwall, 41, 56, 69, 76 *n. 2*, 118-9, 135, 176, 306, 310, 323, 324, 331; prices of, 56, 118, 122, 315, 317; profits from, 81, 92, 317; reservation of Cornish stocks of for the East India Company, 119-21; value of to Cornwall, 19, 41, 305, 324, 331. See also Mines.

Copper Smelting Companies, 19-20, 21, 21 *n. 1*, 21 *n. 4*, 21 *n. 6*, 41, 63-5, 84, 87, 94, 121, 141, 144-5. See also English Copper Company: Entral: Hafod Copper Works: Lockwood, Morris, and Company: Morfa Copper Works.

Copper Standard, 68 *n. 3*; fluctuations in, 118, 127-8, 305, 307, 317 *n. 3*

Copper Warehousing Bill, 140, 197.

Copper Workers, ill-health of, 64 *n. 1*.

Corn, 236-7, 258; Laws, 142, 207, 229, 230, 237, 238, 247-50, 252, 255, 257; prices, 249, 255; scarcity of, 33, 89, 104-5, 142, 158-63, 181-4, 211, 223, 231. See also Anti-Corn Law league: Arable Farming: Barley: Oats: Wheat.

Cornish Equitable Mining Association, 138.

Cornish Language, 37-8.

Cornishman, locomotive, 149.

Cornish Metal Company, 21 *n. 6*, 81-8, 91, 94-7, 101, 112.

Cornish people, 30, 32; Watt's opinion of, 78, 80.

Cornish Tin Company, 59-60, 161.

Cornish Wain, 229.

Cornish, William (mine adventurer), 166.

Cornwall Central Railroad, 221.

Cornwall, Duchy of, 3 *n. 2*, 12, 13, 26, 44, 147, 193, 194, 195, 196, 203; mineral rights of, 188-91. See also Coinage of Tin, Duties: Stannaries.

Cornwall, Duke of, 58, 189.

Cornwall Great United Company, 147.
Cornwall United Hills Copper Mines, 134.
Cost Book System, 22, 23-5, 47, 62, 65, 86, 133.
Coster, John (inventor), 8, 21.
Coster, Richard (smelter), 20.
Cottagers, reclamation of waste-lands by, 225-6.
Couch, Dr. Jonathan, 263, 294, 312.
Couch, Dr. Richard, 312.
County Adit, 54, 55 *n. 1*, 219 *n. 1*.
County Relief Committee of 1867, 322.
Cows, renting of, 235-6.
Coxe, Dr. Daniel, 209, 218, 219.
Crantock, 22.
Creese, Henry (lessee of Duchy mineral duties), 190-1.
Crenver, 132; closed down in 1866, 317.
Crinnis, 119, 122-3, 147, 186; early profits of, 132-3; Duchy claims of mineral rights and ensuing lawsuit, 189-90.
Croft Gothal, 319.
Croft-land, cultivation of, 211, 224.
Crofty Mines, 148.
Crops, Rotation of, 222.
Crowan, 37, 66, 181, 239, 317.
Cuba, 130, 141, 308.
Cubert, 220.
Cunnock, R. J., 186.
Customs Officials, 275, 281; of Falmouth, 285-6; of Fowey, 286.

DAIRY FARMING, 235-6.
Daniell family, 96.
Daniell, Ralph Allan (Merchant and mine adventurer), 86 *n. 1*, 166; induces adventurers of Consolidated Mines to refuse further premiums to Boulton and Watt, 103; ally of Jonathan Hornblower against Boulton and Watt, 108; adventurer in Great Towan Mine, 131; acting chairman of Tinners' Association, 172 *n. 6*.
Daniell, Thomas (merchant and mine adventurer), 59, 166.
Darlington-Jordan Rock Drill, 323 *n.2*.
Daubuz family, 60, 201.
Daubuz, L. C. (smelter), 199, 202.
Davey family, 24 *n. 1*, 102, 163, 164 *n. 1*, 240 *n. 1*, 255.
Davey, Richard (mine adventurer and farmer), 259.
Davey, Stephen (mine adventurer and farmer), 195.
De Dunstanville, Francis Basset, Lord; see Basset, Sir Francis.
Deep Mines, cost of working, 62.
Defoe, Daniel, 18 *n. 1*, 34 *n. 1*, 35.

Deforestation of Cornwall, 9, 10, 224.
Delabole, 148, 159.
Denny, Jacob (smuggler), 285.
Denshiring, 228-9.
Depression, economic, 42, 43, 47, 68; in farming, 236; in mining, 56-7, 62, 68, 88, 90, 317-24.
Devon, 3 *n. 3*, 10, 134, 160.
Devon Great Consols, 319, 323, 324; early sensational profits of, 150, 307 *n. 3*; premier position among copper mines after 1850, 305-6; strike at, 316-7.
Devonshire, Thomas (copper assayer), 59.
Devonshire and Cornwall Mining Association, 132-3, 134, 137.
Ding Dong, 11, 17, 39, 40, 60, 188, 309; Edward Bull starts erecting engine at but is stopped by injunction from Boulton and Watt, 97; Boulton and Watt attempt to recover premiums from, 102; the younger Trevithick completes Bull's engine, 106, 109, 110; ages of underground workers at in 1857, 312.
Discontent of Labouring Classes, 43, 104, 158. See also Corn, scarcity of: Riots.
Divining Rod, 51.
Division of Labour in Mining, 40. See also Labourers: Tributers: Tutworkers.
Doctor's Pence, 153, 155.
Doering's Boring Machine, 323 *n. 2*.
Dolcoath, 4, 59, 74 *n. 3*, 91, 123, 135, 136, 139, 307 *n. 3*; Sir Francis Basset's interest in, 83, 84, 87; Boulton describes as a poor mine in 1788, 86; Bull erects engine at infringing Watt's patent, 97; depth of, 323; dividends from, 309; exhaustion of copper and discovery of lower tin zone in, 89; female labour employed at, 8 *n. 1*; mechanical improvements of the elder Richard Trevithick at, 53, 54; output of copper from 1815 to 1854, 150; poverty of copper ores in lower levels of, 146; suspension of from 1790 to 1798, 88-9; tramroad constructed from to Portreath, 117; wage bill of in 1786, 28; Watt engine at, 84.
Domestic Industries, 90.
Donnithorne, Nicholas (mine adventurer), 11, 170, 172.
Doom Bar, 262.
Drakewalls, 40, 318; strike at, 316, 317.
Drifters and Seiners, feud of, 264, 266, 267, 269-70, 274, 284, 288, 289, 293-4 298, 299. See also Fisheries, drift.

Drills: Rock, 55 *n. 1*, 323; Seed, 221, 241-2, 252, 256.
Dulany, Mrs. (Mary Granville), 29-30.
Dumfee, John Lucius (Vice-Warden of the Stannaries), 196.
Dutch Tin Trade, 61. See also Tin, East Indian.
Duty of Steam Engines, 99. See also Engines, trials of: Lean, Joel.

EAST CARADON: speculation in shares of, 310; strike at, 316.
East Crinnis, 135.
East India Company, 55, 62, 119-21, 171-5, 177-9, 184-5, 197.
East Rosewarne, 318.
East Wheal Rose, mining disaster at, 155 *n. 5*, 305 *n. 3*.
Ecclesiastical Organisation, 67.
Eddystone Lighthouse, 301.
Edgcumbe family, 46.
Edwards, William (mine adventurer), 166.
Egloskerry, 244.
Eliot family, 1, 45, 234, 245, 273.
Eliot, Edward, Lord (1727-1804), (banker), 59, 273.
Elizabethan Poor Law, 67, 89.
Ellen United Copper and Zinc Mining Company, 318.
Elliott, William (receiver-General for Cornwall), 38.
Emigrants, problems of relieving forsaken families of, 320.
Emigration, 320-1, 324; Boulton suggests to relieve mining unemployment, 89; of farm labourers from North Cornwall to Canada, 238 *n. 1*, 239; of farmers to New Zealand and South Australia, 252; of miners to Australia, 311-2, 319, to Brazil, 325, to northern collieries, 312, 319, and to the United States, 311-2, 319, 325-6.
Enclosure of Land, 211, 212, 224, 225.
Engines, Steam: atmospheric, 7, 101 (see also Newcomen: Watt); compound, 93, 112, 187; Cornish in Holland and South America, 127; deterioration in performances of after the withdrawal of Boulton and Watt from Cornwall, 114; efficiency o`in Cornish mines, 72 *n. 1*, 99, 114, 123, 124-6, 135, 187; first in Cornwall at Balwath, 53 *n. 2*; forty erected in Cornwall between 1740 and 1775, 51; trials of, 98, 114, 123, 124-6, 135. See also Bratt: Grose: Hornblower: Newcomen: Nancarrow: Sims: Trevithick: Watt, etc.
Engineers, Mining in Cornwall, 25, 41, 51-6, 68, 71, 72, 74, 75, 175. See also

Hornblower: Trevithick: Watt: Woolf, etc.
English Copper Company, 21, 83.
Entral, 52, 63, 64, 65.
Enys (landowner), 219, 220.
Epsley, Thomas; introduces gunpowder into Cornwall, 9.
Estates; small size of Cornish landed, 217.
Excisemen, 275, 276, 281, 287.
Explosives, 4, 9.
Export, Bounties on Pilchards, 268, 271, 274, 279, 280, 289, 293; Duties on Copper and Tin, 84.

Facey v. Harden, 244.
Fal Estuary, 117, 277.
Falmouth, 38, 149, 158, 183, 196, 262, 282, 289, 290; corn riots at, 33; Customs men of, 285-6, 288; export trade of, 271, 279; seiners' meeting at, 284; smuggling of wool from, 278.
Falmouth, Edward Boscawen, Earl of (1787-1841), 141, 191, 195, 200, 202.
Falmouth, George Evelyn Boscawen, Viscount (1758-1808), 83, 84, 87, 173 *n. 1*.
Falmouth, Hugh Boscawen, Viscount (1680-1734), 6 *n. 2*, 20.
Fal River, 148, 221; silting of, 10, 218.
Farington, Joseph (artist), 104, 303.
Farmers, 260-61; conservatism of, 255-6; influence of mining on, 254-5; living conditions of in the 1840s, 242.
Farming, Mixed, 258.
Farm Labourers, 313; scarcity of, 233, 258, emigration of, 254.
Farms, small size of Cornish, 239.
Faull, Charles (miner), 162.
Feasts, Village, 33.
Female Labour: in mining, 7-8, 25, 28, 70; in farming, 260; in pilchard curing, 292.
Fences, 253.
Fenton Copper Company, 63 *n. 1*.
Fiennes, Celia, 6 *n. 1*, 11, 18 *n. 1*, 29, 223 *n. 2*.
Financial Crisis of 1866, 308.
'Fire Engines', 41, 70, 71.
Fish Cellars or Palaces, 264, 265.
Fish Curing, 264, 265.
Fisheries: 263-6, 269, 273-4, 278-9, 284, 288-92, 294, 297-8; crab, 290, 298; drift, 264, 273, 274, 279, 284, 290, 298; herring, 269, 284, 290, 294, 297; inshore, 264; labour employed in pilchard, 265-6, 278-9, 283, 291-2; lobster, 290, 298; mackerel, 284, 290, 294; pilchard, 221, 263-5, 269, 270-1, 273, 288-92, 293 *n. 1*, 299-300; profits of, 291; share system in boats

and nets, 265-6; statistics of pilchard, 270-1, 291-2, 293 *n. 1*, 299-300, 334-5; trawl, 284, 289, 298; value of as a nursery of seamen, 270, 278, 284, 292. See also Bounties on exported Pilchards: Drifters and Seiners, feuds of: Huers: Mediterranean: Pilchards: Salt Duties: Seine fishery: Tithes: West Indies.

Flails, 230, 233, 239, 240 *n. 1*.

Flour, American arrives in Falmouth in 1812, 183.

Flushing, 285.

Food: prices of in 1843-47, 163; scarcity of occasions discontent and riots, 33, 89, 104-5, 142, 158-63, 180-84, 211, 223, 231.

'Foreign' Mine Adventurers, 47, 48-9, 55, 65-6, 68, 95, 188, 309; Cornish distrust of, 45, 48-9, 68, 95, 180; improvements suggested by 8, 55.

Foreign Miners in Cornwall, 5.

Foreign Tin Markets, 57, 59, 61. See also Tin, export of: Unwin, George.

Fortesque (landowner), 251.

Fowey, 29, 262, 296; inefficiency of Customs Officials at, 275, 286; distress at during American Revolutionary War, 273; mayor of an active smuggler, 286; pilchard fishery of, 271; smugglers of, 286.

Fowey Consols, 139, 147; owned by Joseph Thomas Austen, 126 *n. 1*; profits of before and decline after 1860, 307-8; refuse to employ men belonging to the Miners' Mutual Benefit Association, 316; steam engine of William West at, 126-7; strike at, 143.

Fowey River, 221.

Fox, Alfred (merchant), 145.

Fox family (of Falmouth), 102, 170 279, 280, 282, 290.

Fox, George (merchant), 181.

Fox, George C. (merchant), 145.

Fox, George C. and Son (merchants), 170.

Fox, Phillips, and Fox (merchants), 170.

Fraser, Robert (agricultural writer), 223 *n. 1*, 228, 232, 233.

Frederick, Prince of Wales, 43, 46.

Freeman and Company (copper smelters), 83.

'Free' Miners, 26, 41, 90.

Friendly Mines, 139.

Friendly Societies, 153, 315-7. See also Doctors' Pence.

Frosse, Ulrich (miner), 5.

Frost, damage done by in Cornwall, 209, 232-3.

Furnace, Reverberatory, 9, 11.

Furze, importance of for fuel, 224, 226.

Fuse, Safety, 9.

GATES, farm and field, 253.

Geake, Anthony (farmer), 243-4.

Gentry, Cornish, 29-30. See also Landowners.

George the Fourth Mine, 139.

Geology of Cornwall, 209-10.

German Miners in Cornwall, 5.

Germoe, 301; wreckers of, 35-6.

Giddy, Davies alias Gilbert (landowner and Member of Parliament): and Associated Tinners, 179; part in revival and reform of the Stannary Jurisdiction, 193, 194; and abolition of Tin Coinage Duties, 203.

Gilbert family (landowners), 251, 259.

Giles, Joseph (Relieving Officer), 320-1.

Glasgow Caradon, 324.

Glasgow University, 73, 126.

Glasney College, 213.

Gluvias, 213, 214 *n. 1*.

Glynn, Thomas (miner), 170.

Gnoll Copper Works, 83.

Godolphin family, 30, 38, 45.

Godolphin, Sidney Earl of (1645-1712), 9, 14, 15, 20.

Godolphin Tin Smelting House, 10, 11.

Goldsithney, 186.

Gonamena, 317.

Goon-lez Mine: Artificial Ventilation introduced at, 53 *n. 1*.

Goonzion Downs, 151.

Grain: exportation of from Cornwall forbidden in 1748, 43; scarcity of in Cornwall, 68, 181-2 (see also Food); yields of per acre in Cornwall, 230-1.

Grambler and St. Aubyn Mine, 307.

Grampound, 148, 157, 218, 221, 259. 274.

Granville, John, Lord (Lord Warden of the Stannaries), 14.

Great Caradon, 310.

Great South Tolgus, 320.

Great Towan Consols, 139.

Great Wheal Busy, 319.

Great Wheal Fortune, 132.

Great Work Mine, 52.

Gregor family, 6 *n. 2*.

Gregor, Francis (Member of Parliament), 173, 175.

Grenfell family, 121, 141.

Grenfell, Pasco (smelter), 121, 145, 198.

Grenville family, 273.

Grose, Samuel (engineer), 126.

Grylls, Thomas (lawyer), 181.

Grylls, Rev. William, 239.

Gulval, 10, 17, 39, 236 *n. 1*, 312.

Gundry family, 186, 187, 188.

Gundry, Captain John, reopens Wheal Vor, 186, 187.
Gundry, Thomas (mine adventurer), 108.
Gunnislake, 140; violence of striking miners at, 316.
Gunnislake Mine, 71 *n. 1*, 324.
Gunpowder, 9.
Gunwalloe, 36.
Gwatkin, R. L. (landowner), 235.
Gwavas, William (tithe-owner), 296.
Gweek, 59.
Gwennap, 59, 66, 83, 181; mines of, 18 *n. 1*, 139, 146, 150, 177, 217, 219 *n. 1*, 306-7, 320; poor rates spent on relief of mining distress in 1812, 183-4; population of in 1811, 184 *n. 1*; tin smelting house at, 10; unemployment in the parish of in 1867, 320; Williams family of, 60.
Gwennap Pit, 157.
Gwennap Tin and Copper Mining Company, 136.
Gwinear, 52, 66, 132, 148.
Gwithian, 123, 219.

HAFOD Copper Works, 121.
Half Crease system of Pastoral Farming 236.
Hall, Frederick (merchant), 192.
Hallamannin, 83, 97, 102, 319, 326.
Hallenbeagle, 320.
Hand Pumps, used in mines, 70.
Harris, John (London Agent of Tinners' Association), 170.
Harvesting, methods of, 252-3.
Harvest Journeys, survival of in conditions of land leases, 215.
Harvey family, 127.
Hawker, Rev. Robert Stephen, 1, 301 *n. 2*.
Hawkins family, 6 *n. 2*, 217, 245.
Hawkins, Sir Christopher; mining property of, 83, 95; farming of at Trewithian, 233, 254.
Hayle, 10, 29, 71, 117 *n. 2*; copper works at, 63, 64, engineering works at, 127, 149; Railway Company, 148; becomes a Tin Coinage town in 1833, 197.
Heam and Treave Company, 170.
Hecla, 309, 325, 326.
Hedges, 253.
Helston, 45-6, 59, 60, 102 *n. 1*, 157, 177, 181, 260, 321; Coinage and Stannary town, 13, 44; floral dance, 33; food riot in, 160; meetings of Tinners' Association in, 166, 167, 170, Stannary Parliament at, 14 *n. 1*.
Hendy (farmer), 239.
Hensbarrow, 209.

Heriots, 215, 216.
Herland, engine of in 1757, 52, 54; reworking of, 132; Watt's engines at, 100, 101.
Herodsfoot, 305 *n. 3*.
Hertford, Francis Seymour, Marquis of (Lord Warden of the Stannaries), 194.
Hewas Mine, 101.
Hodge, Edward (farmer), 214, 215.
Hornblower family, 7, 38, 72, 81, 103, 107.
Hornblower, Jabez (engineer), 108.
Hornblower, Jethro (engineer), 96 *n. 3*, 98, 108.
Hornblower, Jonathan the elder (engineer), 42, 51, 53, 55, 78.
Hornblower, Jonathan the younger (engineer); asserts that Edward Bull's Wheal Virgin engine does not infringe Watt's patent, 96; attempts of Boulton and Watt to buy his patent, 98, to disparage his ability, 93, 94, and to prevent the extension of his patent by Act of Parliament, 99; competitive engine trials suggested by Boulton and Watt, 98; compound engine of, 93, 94, 95, 97, 112, 124; Cornish mines adventurers support him against Boulton and Watt, 101-2, 107; criticism of Watt's engines, 78, 81, 92, 97; engines of at Tincroft, Tresavean, and Wheal Unity, 99, 100; financial ruin of, 109, 114; infringes Watt's patent, 84, 94, 99; litigation with Boulton and Watt, 73 *n. 1*, 97, 102, 103, 107, 108, 111; partnerships with John Winwood at Radstock, 95, 97, and D. A. Maberley, 108; patent of, 93, 98, 99; a practical engineer rather than a radical innovator and inventor, 110; reluctance of some Cornish mines adventurers to employ his early machines, 94.
Hornblower, Josiah (engineer), 42.
Horse Drill, 241.
Horses, 240-1, 254, 258.
Hosken, John (miner), 105.
Hospitals, 154.
Huers, 265, 266.
Hurling, 32.
Husbandry, apprentices to, 239.
Hussey Reaper, 252-3.

ILLOGAN, 66, 177, 181, 226, 318.
Infant Mortality, 151-2, 312.
Insurance of sea-borne cargoes in wartime, 57, 189.
Irish Sea Fishery, 284, 294, 297.
JACOBITISM in Cornwall, 33.

James, James (mine adventurer), 166.
James, John (mine adventurer), 166.
James, Thomas, killed in clash with Excisemen at Falmouth, 285, 287.
Java, exports of tin from, 206.
'Jigger', continuous, 323 *n. 2*.
Joint Stock System, 133. See also Cost Book System.
Johannesburg, 326.
Johannes, Rector of Lezant, 243.
Johns, Edward (landowner), 213-4.
Johns, William (miner), 50.
Jordan, William (writer), 38.

KARKEEK, W. F. (veterinary surgeon), 210 *n. 2*, 230, 236 *n. 1*, 240 *n. 4*.
Kea, 10, 181, 192, 220, 235, 243.
Keigwin, John (writer), 38.
Kelynack Smelting House, 10.
Kendall (farmer of Probus), 259.
Kendall, Nicholas (landowner and Member of Parliament), 161, 251, Kenwyn, 10, 39, 66, 132, 181, 217, 220, 270, 319.
Kerrier Agricultural Association, 236 *n. 1*.
Kestell, Richard (miner), 162.
Kevill, Thomas (estate agent), 84.
Killigrew family, 301.
Kinnaird, George William Fox, Lord, (1807-78) 314, 315.
Kittow brothers (miners), 148.

LABOUR: casual in mining, 19, 70; cost of in mining, 70; division of, 40 female in mining, 7-8, 25, 28, 70; farm, 238, 239, 252, 254, 258; fisheries, 265-6, 279, 290, 291-2, 300; juvenile in agriculture, 260, and in mines, 25-6, 28, 70; conflict of with capital in mining, 143, 162-3; mortality of mining and farm labourers in St. Agnes compared in 1864, 312-3.
Labouring Classes: 2, 43; conditions of mining, 26, 28-9, 66, 311; types of mining, 40, 311.
Ladock, 220.
Laissez Faire, 58, 160, 165.
Lake family (merchants of Falmouth), 290.
Lake Superior, 129, 311.
Lamorna Cove, 295 *n. 2*.
Landewednack, 38.
Landlords of Mineral Rights, 50-1, 84. See also Cornwall, Duchy of.
Landowners, 2, 245, 251, 256-7, 260.
Land Reclamation, 90, 211, 212, 224, 225, 228, 233; estimate of amount of between 1700 and 1860, 225; to provide employment, 164.

Lanescot, 135 *n. 3*, 136, 147; strike at 143-4.
Lanreath, 318.
Lanteglos-by-Camelford, 183, 231.
Lanyon, Dr. Richard, 155 *n. 5*, 157.
Larkholes Mine, 201.
Latchley Consols, 316.
Launceston, 148, 157, 247, 248, 252; Assizes, 12 *n. 3*, 37; food riot at, 160.
Law Cases: *Creese v. Barrett*, 191; *Facey v. Harden*, 244; *Paynter and others v. Permewan*, 211 *n. 2*, 244; *Rex v. Rowe and Brenton*, 190; *Rowe v. Brenton*, 189. See also Arkwright: Assizes: Bull: Hornblower, etc.
Lawyers, as a caste, 2, 6, 183.
Lead mines, 88, 305 *n. 3*, See also Cargoll: East Wheal Rose, Herodsfoot.
Lean, Joel (engineer), 72 *n. 1*, 114, 123, 135.
Leases: conditions of farm, 237; three life system of, 215-7, 225, 227.
Leather, use of in mining, 8.
Lelant, 320, 321.
Lemon family, 60, 217.
Lemon, Sir Charles, 195, 200, 203, 205
Lemon, William (mine adventurer), 8 *n. 3*, 54.
Lemon, Sir William (landowner and Member of Parliament); shareholder in Wheal Unity, 101; and Tinners' Association, 175, 179; drafts Act removing duties on salt used in curing pilchards for export, 273; Chairman of Parliamentary Committees into the Fisheries which recommended increased export bounties on pilchards, 278, 279, 280; supports demand for reduction of salt duties, 284; champion of the Cornish seining interests, 293.
Levant Mine, 139, 305 *n. 3*, 319.
Levant Trade in Tin, 57 *n. 1*.
Levels, underground in mines, 40, 50, 51, 54, 55.
Lewannick, 251, 256-7.
Ley Farming, 222.
Lezant, 243.
Lifts in Mines, 155. See also Man Engines.
Lighthouses, 301.
Lime, deficiency of in Cornish soils, 210, 221, 241.
Linkinhorne, 10, 188, 196, 246, 310.
Liskeard, 60, 229, 248, 269; Coinage town, 10, 13, 44, 45; and Looe Canal, 148, 228; May market prices at from 1843 to 1847, 163; meeting at protesting against proposed governmental regulation of mines, 314.
Liverpool, 166.

Live-stock, Winter feeding of, 223, 253, 255, 257.
Lizard, 34 *n. 1*, 262, 301.
Loam, Michael (engineer), 155, 314.
Lockwood, Morris, and Company, 21 *n. 4*, 83.
Locomotives, 115-6, 149.
Lodes, tracing of mineral, 50.
London: Capitalist interests of, 44, 45; prices of tin in, 166, 167, 168, 169, 178; agents of Tinners' Association in, 166, 167, 168. See also Pewterers.
Longships Lighthouse, 301.
Looe, 29, 252, 262, 269; number of drift fishing-boats at in 1870, 300; seines at, 266 *n. 4*, 271, 278; and Liskeard Canal, 148, 228.
Looe, East, 266 *n. 4*, 269. 303.
Looe, West, 269.
Lord Warden of the Stannaries, 13, 194.
Lostwithiel, 49 *n. 2*, 60, 161; Coinage town, 10, 13, 44; meeting of Stannary Parliament of 1750 at, 14 *n. 1*.
Lostwithiel Mine, 102.
Lovett, William, 156.
Lubbock Banking House, 59.
Ludgey, Richard (landowner), 213.
Ludgvan, 180, 217, 320.
Lugger, Nathaniel (Supervisor of Tin Smelting Houses), 10.
Luxulyan, 158, 247.
Lyndhurst, John Singleton Copley, Lord, 191.

Maberley, D. A., partner of Jonathan Hornblower the younger, 108.
McCormick, General William, 101, 102 *n. 1*.
Machine parts, 112.
Machines, Threshing, 124, 233, 257.
Madron, 17, 217, 256, 270, 295 *n. 2*.
Malaya: difficulties of early tin mining in, 206.
Manaccan, 181 *n. 2*, 215.
Man Engines, 154, 305 *n. 3*, 314.
Manures, 210, 218, 221, 232; 'artificial' 255, 256.
Marazion, 29, 228, 321.
Markets, local weekly, 162-3.
Marke Valley, 147, 150; strike at, 316.
Marshall, William (agricultural writer) 228.
Mawgan in Pyder, 230.
Maypole Dances, 33.
Mechanization: of farming, 124, 233, 238, 252-4, 258; of mining, 70, 134-5. See also Engines, etc.
Mechi, John Joseph (farmer), 256, 257.
Mediterranean: pilchard trade to, 166, 221, 263, 264, 266, 271, 272-3, 278-80, 282-3, 289, 292, 334-5; tin trade, 57 *n. 1*.

Mellanear, 324.
Meneage, 231, 252.
Menheniot, 223 *n. 1*.
Merther, 220.
Messer, John (mine adventurer), 166.
Methodists and Methodism, 31, 32, 110, 157, 247, 315, 317 *n. 2*.
Mevagissey: cholera outbreak at, 303; drift fishery, 299, 300; fish tithes at, 297-8; payment of fishermen at, 266; regulation of seining stations at, 272, 291; salt smuggling at, 281 *n. 5*; seine fishery of, 271 278, 298, 299, 300.
Mexico, 127, 130.
Michigan, 130, 308, 323, 325.
Middlecoate, Nicholas (Supervisor of Tin Smelting Houses), 194.
Midland Manufacturers, 87. See also Birmingham: Boulton: Wilkinson.
Millhook Haven, smuggling affray at, 287.
Mine Doctors, 154. See also Couch, Dr. Richard: Lanyon, Dr. Richard: Pryce, Dr. William.
Mineral and Battery Works, 44.
Mineral Bottom Mine, 318 *n. 1*.
Mineral Dues and Rights of Landowners, 50-1, 69; of the Duchy of Cornwall, 188-91. See also Basset, Sir Francis: Hawkins, Sir Christopher, etc.
Miners: 26-8, 152-6, 311-5, 320-1; inability of to combine in 1812, 185-6; living conditions of, 152, 154-6, 322; mortality of, 153, 155, 312-3; numbers of, in 1720-30, 18, in 1787, 85; unemployment among in 1867, 320-1; wages of, 152-3, 321; working conditions of, 204, 313, 315. See also Copper: Engineers: Labour: Tin: Trades Unions, etc.
Miners' Mutual Benefit Association, 315-7.
Mines: Ale and Cakes, 115 *n. 1*; Anaconda (Montana), 326; Baldhu, 102, 192; Balleswidden, 311, 312; Balwath, 53 *n. 2*; Boscaswell, 17; Botalet (Lanreath), 318; Botallack, 17, 176, 303; Buller and Basset United, 317; Calumet (Michigan), 309, 325, 326; Caradon and Phoenix Consols, 310; Caradon Hill, 310; Caradon Vale, 310, 317 *n. 4*; Cardrew, 139; Cargoll, 305 *n. 3*, 318; Carn Brea, 318; Carnon Stream Works, 176, 188, 219 *n. 1*; Carnyorth, 318; Cathedral Mine, 136; Cerro de Pasco (Peru), 130; Clifford, 320; Consolidated Mines, 6 *n. 2*, 80, 82 *n. 1*, 92, 96, 103, 112,

121 *n. 1*, 123, 126, 131, 135, 136, 150, 195, 217, 306, 323; 'Consols' Mine, 137; Cook's Kitchen, 8 *n. 1*, 28, 56, 83, 146 *n. 2*, 177; Copper Hill, 134; Crenver, 132, 317; Crinnis, 119, 122, 133, 147, 186. 189, 190; Croft Gothal, 319; Crofty, 148; Devon Great Consols, 150, 305-6, 307 *n. 3*, 316-7, 319, 323, 324; Ding Dong, 11, 17, 39, 40, 60, 97, 102, 106, 109, 110, 188, 309, 312; Dolcoath, 4, 8 *n. 1*, 28, 53, 54, 59, 74 *n. 3*, 83, 84, 86, 87, 88, 89, 91, 97, 117, 123, 135, 136, 146, 150, 307 *n. 3*, 309, 323; Drakewalls, 40, 316, 317, 318,; East Caradon, 310, 316; East Crinnis, 135; East Rosewarne, 318; East Wheal Rose, 155 *n. 5*, 305 *n. 3*; Fowey Consols, 126, 127, 139, 143, 147, 307-8, 316; Friendly Mines, 139; George the Fourth, 139; Glasgow Caradon, 324; Gonamena, 317; Goon-lez, 53 *n. 1*; Goonzion Downs, 151; Grambler and St. Aubyn, 307; Great Caradon, 310; Great South Tolgus, 320; Great Towan Consols, 139; Great Wheal Busy, 319; Great Wheal Fortune, 132; Great Work, 52; Hallamannin, 83, 97, 102, 319, 326; Hallenbeagle, 320; Hecla (Michigan), 309, 325, 326; Herland, 52, 54, 100, 101, 132; Herodsfoot, 305 *n. 3*; Hewas, 101; Lanescot, 135, 136, 143-4, 147; Larkholes, 201; Latchley Consols, 316; Levant, 139, 305 *n. 3*, 319; Lostwithiel, 102; Marke Valley, 147, 150, 316; Mineral Bottom, 318 *n. 1*; New South Caradon, 310; North Downs, 8, 18 *n. 1*, 63 *n. 1*, 75 *n. 1*, 80, 82 *n. 1*, 85, 87, 92, 146, 320; North Hallenbeagle, 317; North Levant, 309; Oatfield, 132; Par Consols, 158, 306, 316, 321; Parys Mountain (Anglesey), 71-2, 91, 119; Pednandrea, 18 *n. 1*, 132, 176; Pembroke, 131; Pendeen Consols, 318; Penstruthel, 135, 139; Phoenix 147, 316 *n. 1*, 317; Polberro, 11, 44, 60; Poldice, 18 *n. 1*, 54, 55, 60, 80, 100, 103, 106, 155 *n. 3*, 323-4, 326; Poldory, 74 *n. 3*, 75 *n. 1*; Polgooth, 8 *n. 3*, 11, 42, 44, 60, 126 *n. 1*, 132, 176, 188; Pool Adit, 18 *n. 1*; Porth Stream Workings, 176; Real del Monte (Mexico), 121 *n. 1*, 127, 130; Rosewarne, 44 *n. 3*; Roskear, 18 *n. 1*, 21 *n. 7*, 148, 155; St. Day United, 320; South Caradon, 147, 148, 149, 150, 306, 307, 309, 310, 317, 323, 324; South Francis, 318; South Wheal Basset, 139; South Wheal

Tolgus, 319; Tincroft, 59, 84, 92, 98, 99, 100, 101, 112, 306, 323 *n. 2*; Ting Tang, 77-8, 92; Tin Hatches, 151; Tocapilla (Brazil), 325; Towan, 131; Treloweth, 318; Trengale, 151; Tresavean, 100, 102, 123, 148, 151, 155, 306, 314, 323; Trevenen, 178; Trewellard, 39; United Hills, 139; United Mines, 80, 112; Wendron Consols, 309, 319; Wentworth Consols, 318 *n. 1*; West Basset, 318; West Caradon, 147, 150, 310; West Chiverton, 307 *n. 3*; West Drakewalls, 317 *n. 4*; West Phoenix, 317 *n. 4*; West Wheal Prudence, 139; Wheal Abraham, 126 *n. 2*, 132, 317; Wheal Albert, 318 *n. 1*; Wheal Alfred, 132; Wheal Bank, 151; Wheal Barnard, 132; Wheal Basset, 306 *n. 1*; Wheal Busy, 42, 78, 132, 139, 326; Wheal Butson, 79, 99, 100; Wheal Caradon, 310; Wheal Chance, 126 *n. 1*; Wheal Charles, 134, 138; Wheal Clifford, 155 *n. 3*, 306; Wheal Cock, 176; Wheal Crebor, 324; Wheal Damsel, 307; Wheal Dream, 132; Wheal Fortune (Gwennap), 126; Wheal Fortune (Ludgvan), 18 *n. 1*; Wheal Hearle, 318; Wheal Hope, 318 *n. 1*; Wheal Kitty, 21 *n. 7*; Wheal Ludcott, 318; Wheal Maid, 80; Wheal Malkin, 134, 138; Wheal Margaret, 102; Wheal Mary, 147; Wheal Pollard, 317 *n. 4*; Wheal Pool, 102; Wheal Prosper, 123; Wheal Ram, 50; Wheal Raven, 139; Wheal Reeth, 100, 319, 320; Wheal Rose, 42, 320; Wheal Seton, 306 *n. 1*, 318; Wheal Sparnon, 132; Wheal Tregothnan, 102; Wheal Trenwith, 139; Wheal Triumph, 151; Wheal Unity (Gwennap), 8 *n. 1*, 92, 100, 101, 112, 177; Wheal Unity Wood, 139; Wheal Virgin, 74 *n. 3*, 96; Wheal Vor, 11, 14, 40, 126-32, 186-8, 201, 307 *n. 3*, 309; Wherry Mine, 176, 188, 301.

Amalgamation of: 65; deep, 2, 3, 4, 40, 41, 62, 70; difficulties of reworking abandoned, 89; duration of 1823 speculative, 139, 332-3; exhaustion of, 307-8 323; numbers of selling copper ores in 1775, 65; proposed inspection of, 314-5; rating of, 310; 'submarine', 176; surface, 2, 40 (see also Stream Tin and Tinners).

Mines Royal Acts, 12, 17.
Mines Royal Company, 12, 44, 47, 83.
Mining Accidents and Injuries, 153-4, 305 *n. 3*.

Mining Associations and Companies: Anglo-Chilean, 145; British Mining or Royal Stannary, 134, 138; British United Mines, 134; Chilean, 145; Chilean-Peruvian, 145; Cornish Equitable, 138; Cornwall Great United, 147; Cornwall United Hills Copper Mines, 134; Devonshire and Cornwall, 132-3, 134, 137; Ellen United Copper and Zinc, 318; Gwennap Tin and Copper, 136; Redruth Consolidated, 151; St. Cleer and St. Neot Consolidated, 151; West Cornwall Mines Investment, 151.

Mining Frauds, 135-6, 138, 318.

Mining Interest: lack of unity in Cornish, 72-3.

Mining Laws, 2. See also Stannaries: Cornwall, Duchy of.

Mining Speculation, 19, 44, 57, 61, 69, 76-7, 130-9, 150-1, 189, 309-10. See also Cost Book System: Scrip System.

Mining, Slumps in, 56-60, 68, 166, 168, 201, 317-23.

Mitchell (borough of), 38, 102 n. 1, 213.

Mitchell, Robert (mine adventurer), 181.

Mitchell, Tobias (surgeon), 154.

Mixed Farming, 258.

Molesworth family, 217, 245, 260.

Molesworth, Sir John (1729-75), 59.

Molesworth, Sir William (1810-55), 247, 248, 250.

Monopoly and Patent Rights, 77, 93, 95, 111-3. See also Watt's Patent.

Monopoly: of coal, 323; of tin, proposed in 1750, 44-5. See also Cornish Metal Company: Tin, farm of: Tinners' Association.

Montana, 323.

Moorland Pastures, 227, See also Croftland.

Moorswater, 148.

Morfa Copper Works, 121.

Morshead, William (engineer), 240 n. 3

Mortality: in mining parishes, 151-2, 312-3; infant, 151-2.

Morton, Rev. Charles, 218-9.

Morvah, 209.

Morval: 'Swing' Riots threatened at, 142, 246.

Mount's Bay, 271, 304; drift fishery of, 299, 300; early potato industry of, 232; fishermen of and the Irish Sea herring fishery, 284; mode of payment of fishermen of, 266; seine fishery, 278, 300; summer pilchard fishery, 269; wrecks in, 301-2.

Mousehole, 271; drift fishery of, 300; shares in seines at, 266; tithe disputes at, 294, 296-7, 298.

Moyle, John (mine adventurer), 181.

Moyle, Dr. Richard, 228.

Mules, 240-1.

Mullion, 297, 298.

Murdoch, William (engineer), 81, 91, 96, 103, 111, 115 n. 1.

Mylor, 214 n. 1.

NANCARROW, John (engineer), 42, 52, 54, 72.

Nancekuke, 52, 225, 226.

Nankivell, Benjamin (mine adventurer) 166, 170, 171, 172 n. 6.

Nankivell, Rev. (of Stithians), 181.

Nevada, 325.

Newcomen, Thomas (engineer), 4, 7, 38, 51, 53 n. 2, 54, 93; engines of in Cornwall, 42, 49, 52, 53, 71, 72; patent of extended by Act of Parliament, 74 n. 2; Watt's experiments with model of engine at Glasgow University, 73.

Newlyn, 156, 262, 271; cholera epidemic at, 303; drift fishery of, 300; fishermen of engaged in Irish Sea herring fishery, 284; shares in seines at, 266; tithe troubles at, 296-7, 298.

Newlyn East, 220, 318; mine disaster at East Wheal Rose in parish of, 155 n. 5, 305 n. 3.

Newquay, 209, 221, 300.

New South Caradon, 310.

New South Wales, 311-2.

Nicholas, Wearne (landowner), 215, 216.

North Downs, 18 n. 1, 320; amount of ropes and leather used in mining at, 8; attempt to smelt copper at, 63 n. 1; Boulton and Watt's transport difficulties in sending engine parts to, 75 n. 1; Boulton and Watt shareholders in, 82 n. 1; suspension of in 1787, 85; threats of unemployed miners force adventurers to re-start, 87; although selling more copper ores than any other Cornish mine incurs heavy losses in the period 1792-7, 92; Watt's engines at, 80; increasing poverty of copper ores of in 1828, 146.

North Hallenbeagle, 317.

North Levant, 309.

Nullum Tempus Act, 191, 202.

OATFIELD (mine), 132.

Oats, 230, 231.

O'Bryan, William, 247.

Olver, Thomas (farmer), 250, 251, 255, 256, 257, 260, 261.

Olver, William (farmer), 230.
Open field system of agriculture, 212-3.
Organization, large scale economic, 40-1.
Overend, Gurney, and Company, 318.
Oxen, use of in agriculture, 240, 253, 254.
Oxnam family, 60, 170.
Oxnam, Richard (smelter), 177.

PACK-HORSE transportation, 229, 233-4. See also Mules.
Padstow, 181 *n. 2*, 233 262; corn riots at, 142; corn stealing at, 105; emigration from to Canada, 239; railway projects, 148, 221.
Par, 29, 119, 262.
Par Consols, 306, 326; corn riots averted at through J. T. Treffry's benevolence, 158; adventurers refuse to employ men belonging to the Miners' Mutual Benefit Association, 316.
Parliament: influence of Cornish Members of during Walpole's administration, 41; Cornish borough seats in increasingly held by 'foreigners', 245; inquiry into the tin trade in 1772, 165; petition to asking for the abolition of the export duty on tin in 1772, 61; and the pilchard fisheries, 278, 279, 280; debate on mining speculation, 114; Acts of against Drift Fishery, 267, for encouraging the British White Herring Fishery, 269-70, extending Watt's patent, 74. See also Bounties on exported Pilchards: Salt Duties.
Parliamentary Representation, 38, 245; reform of demanded by Cornish farming interests, 244-6.
Parliamentary Sovereignty, 58-9.
Parliament, Stannary. See Stannary Parliament.
Parys Mountain, 71-2, 91, 119, 121, 123, 146, 147. See also Anglesey: Williams, Thomas.
Pascoe, Rev. T., 321.
Pastoral Husbandry, 223, 227, 228, 234-5, 236, 237, 238, 258, 259.
Pastures, use of moorlands for summer, 227.
Patent Rights, 68, 81-2, 84, 91, 93, 96, 111-3, 114; lawsuits over, 94-5, 97, 98, 102-3, 106-12; monopolistic tendency of, 77, 93. See also Bul., Edward: Hornblower, Jonathan the younger, etc.
Paul (parish), 37, 296, 297.
Paul, William (mine adventurer), 59.
Paynter (exciseman), 285-6.

Paynter, John (landowner), 149, 158.
Paynter and others v. Permewan, 211 *n. 2*, 244.
Pednandrea, 18 *n. 1*, 132, 176.
Peel, Sir Robert: Cornish criticism of policy of, 205, 207.
Pelynt, 234.
Pembroke Mine, 131.
Pencarrow, 247.
Pendarves family, 30.
Pendarves, Alexander (landowner), 29, 213, 214.
Pendarves, E. W. Wynn (Member of Parliament): and cholera outbreak, 154; supports revival of Stannary Jurisdiction, 193; supports protective duties against foreign tin, 200, 203; favours the abolition of the Duchy Coinage duties, 201.
Pendarves, Mary (Mrs. Dulany), 29-30.
Pendarves, Sir William, 20, 29, 30, 32.
Pendeen, 39.
Pendeen Consols, 318.
Pendennis, Castle, 182.
Pengigan Moor, 226.
Penheske (farm), 212.
Penrhyn Foreign, Manor of, 214.
Penryn, 59, 196, 247, 275; open field system near, 213; projected porcelain works, 48; tin smelting houses, 10, 15 *n. 2*; wool factory near 277.
Penstruthnel, 135, 139.
Pentewan, 117, 158; railway, 117, 148.
Pentreath, Dolly, 37.
Penwith, West, 31, 44, 321; Agricultural Society of, 256.
Penzance, 10, 29, 59, 60, 158, 170, 177, 197, 199, 241, 271, 290, 303, 321; becomes a tin coinage town, 13; coinage meetings of Tinners' Association at, 173, 175, 178, 184; fishery, 266 *n. 2*, (see also Mount's Bay); food riot at, 160; market prices, 163; railway to, 149, 262; smuggling of wool from, 277.
Permewan, John (surgeon), 318.
Perranarworthal, 127, 234.
Perranporth, 148, 219, 221, 302-3.
Perranzabuloe, 181, 219, 220, 230, 317-8.
Peters, John Penhallow (farmer), 237, 238, 256, 259, 261.
Pewter, 64 *n. 2*.
Pewterers, London, 14-5, 47, 60, 64, 165; wish to restrict exports of tin, 14.
Phillack, 213 *n. 2*.
Philleigh, 237.
Phoenix, 147, 316 *n. 1*; lock out at, 317.
Phthisis, 153.
Pigs, 235, 258, 274 *n. 1*,

Pilchard Oil, 279, 284.

Pilchards: consumption of in Cornwall, 271, 273, 274, 282-3, 298, 299; Mediterranean Markets of, 166, 221, 263, 264, 266, 271, 272-3, 278-80, 282-3, 289, 292; migration of, 262, 263, 266 *n. 3*, 269, 271, 279-80; used as fertilizer, 210, 221, 280, 283. See also Fisheries.

Pillas, 223-4.

Pitt, Thomas (Lord Warden of the Stannaries), 43, 46.

Pittsburgh, 311.

Ploughs, 234, 241, 254.

Plunger-pole Engine, 109, 115, 123, 126. See also Trevithick, Richard the younger.

Pluralism, clerical, 30.

Plymouth, 48, 148, 149, 269, 273, 282, 284, 303.

Poland, 57.

Polberro, 11, 44, 60.

Poldice, 18 *n. 1*, 60, 326; Edward Bull and, 106; decline of, 103, 323-4; Great Adit to constructed by John Williams, 54-5; riots at, 106; Watt's engines at, 80, 100-1, 103, 106.

Poldory, 74 *n. 3*, 75 *n. 1*.

Polgooth, 60; mine materials used in, 8 *n. 3*; Newcomen engine at, 42; Sims' engine at, 126 *n. 1*; suspension of in 1807, 176, and re-working of in 1823, 132, 188; tin production of, 44; tin smelting house at, 11.

Pollard, John (copper smelter), 20.

Polperro, 262; pilchard seines at, 266 *n. 4*, 271, 278; storm at, 301.

Polruddan 19.

Polwhele, Rev. Richard, 181 *n. 2*, 223.

Pont's Mill, 117 *n. 2*.

Pool, 18 *n. 1*, 161.

Poor, distribution of food and clothing to, 157.

Poor Laws, 67, 89, 90, 155-6, 163, 246-7, 320-2.

Poor Rates and Relief, 66, 156-6, 238, 244, 246, 320-2.

Population, increase of, 38-9, 66 *n. 1*, 116, 151, 211.

Porkellis, 53 *n. 2*.

Porthleven, 35; drift fishery, 300; fish tithes at, 297, 298; harbour of refuge constructed at, 301.

Porth Stream Works, 176.

Porth Towan Tin Smelting House, 179, 180, 185.

Port Quin, 301.

Portreath, 226, 303; construction of harbour at, 63 *n. 2*, 262; tramroad, 116-7.

Port Towan, 226; smelting house at, 179, 180, 185.

Potatoes, 222, 231-3; use of for cattle food, 232.

Poverty of Working Miners, 152-3, 155, 320, 322.

Practical Miners' Society, 154.

Praed, Humphrey Mackworth (banker) 59.

Premiums, due to Boulton and Watt from Cornish Mines, 79-81, 97, 102, 111-2.

Privateers, damage done by to Cornish interests in wartime, 42, 49-50, 174.

Probus, 217, 220, 259; agricultural Society, 252, 253.

Prussia Cove, 35.

Pryce, Dr. William, 5, 51.

Pumping Machinery: need of better and cheaper in 1740, 41; Trevithick's improvements of, 115. See also Engines, etc.

Pumps, hand, 5.

Pumps, steam, 4, 70. See also Engines, etc.

Puritanism, 1, 2.

QUARTER Sessions, 181, 320.

Quick, Dagges, and Company, 59.

Quit Rents, 215. See also Three Life System of Leases.

RACK Leases, 215, 217.

Radstock, 95, 97, 102.

Rag and Chain Pump, 5.

Railways: Bodmin and Wadebridge, 148; Pentewan, 117, 148; Portreath, 116-7; projected, 148-9, 221; West Cornwall, 149.

Rashleigh family, 38.

Rashleigh, Philip (Member of Parliament and landowner), 158, 273.

Rashleigh, William (Member of Parliament), 248.

Raspe, Erich, 96 *n. 2*.

Rates, Poor, 66, 238, 244.

Rawlins, Thomas (merchant), 181 *n. 2*.

Rawlins, William (smelter), 15.

Real del Monte, 121 *n. 1*, 127, 130.

Reaping Machines, 252-3.

Reclamation of Wasteland, 90, 211, 212, 224, 225-6, 228, 233, 244.

Redruth, 18 *n. 1*, 39, 66, 88, 115, 123, 132, 139, 140, 146, 149, 176, 225, 318, 319, 326; Corn riots at, 105, 161, 182-3; distress of labouring classes at, 180-1, 322; meeting to consider relief of distress of labouring classes, 180-1; population of in 1811, 184 *n. 1*; Practical Miners' Society formed at, 154; railway at,

148; Tinners' Association meetings at, 119, 120, 171, 172, 179, 180; tin smelting house at, 10; tramroad to Portreath from, 116; vitriol manufacture at, 48; wages of miners at, 143 *n. 3*; Watt at, 79 *n. 1*; meeting of mining interest to protest against reduction of import duties on foreign copper ores, 205.
Redruth Consolidated Mining Company, 151
Reed family, 102.
Reed, Thomas (mine adventurer), 166.
Religious Faith, of early eighteenth century, 31-2.
Religious Nonconformity, 247.
Religious Revivals, 156.
Rents, 215, 217, 251, 257.
Reskajeage Downs, 225, 227.
Reskymer Smelting House, 10.
Restronguet Creek, 177.
Reverberatory Furnace, 9, 11.
Rex v. Rowe and Brenton, 190.
Revolution: of 1688, 1; French, disturbing effects of in Cornish mining districts, 104-5.
Reynolds, William (mine adventurer), 181.
Richards, Captain (miner), 126.
Richards, Philip (banker and mine adventurer), 59.
Richards, Thomas (engineer), 187.
Richards, Thomas (wrecker), 36.
Richards, William (mine purser), 309.
Riots, 33, 68, 89, 103-6, 142-3, 246-7.
Roads, 29, 116, 213.
Robartes family, 1.
Robartes, T. J. Agar (Member of Parliament and landowner), 250-1.
Robinson, John, 74, 78.
Roche, 158.
Rock Drills and Drilling, 55 *n. 1*, 323.
Rodd, Francis Hearle (landowner), 237, 255.
Roebuck, Dr. 73, 74, 77.
Rogers, Henry, 37.
Rogers, Rev. Hugh, 157, 180, 181, 182
Root Crops, 218, 222, 223, 231.
Rope, amount used in mines, 8.
Roscrow, 29, 213.
Roseland, 104.
Rosewarne Mine, 44 *n. 3*.
Rosewarne, Henry (mine adventurer), 59, 166, 196.
Roskear, 18 *n. 1*, 21 *n. 7*, 148, 155.
Rotation of crops, 222, 237, 257.
Rouby, Dr. 48.
Roughtor, 209.
Rowe, Josiah (mine adventurer), 189.
Rowe v. Brenton, 189.

Royal Commission on Mines of 1864, Report of, 312-4.
Ruan Lanihorne, 104.
Rule, John (mine captain), 130.
Rundle, John (landowner), 246, 247-8.
Run Rig system of Agriculture, 212-5.
Russia, 57.

St. Agnes, 44, 53 *n. 1*, 131, 196, 211 *n. 2*, 247, 317, 318; distress of mining population of in 1867, 319-20, 322; Duchy mineral claims in, 189; mortality of working men in, 312-3; parochial relief in 1811-12, 183; population of in 1811, 184 *n. 1*; remittances sent home by emigrants to California, 319-20; smelting of copper in, 20, of tin in, 10, 11; Trevithick's engine in, 110.
St. Allen, 10, 220, 227, 230.
St. Aubyn family, 30, 38, 227.
St. Aubyn, Sir John (1696-1744), 30, 37.
St. Aubyn, Sir John (1758-1839), 239.
St. Austell, 6, 10, 51, 71 *n. 1*, 101, 139, 140, 147, 158, 159, 321, 322; china clay of, 48, 186, 324-5; becomes a coinage town, 197; copper smelting attempt near, 19; food riots at, 161-2; market prices, 163; and Pentewan Railway, 117; population in 1801, 186.
St. Blazey, 10, 29, 117 *n. 2*, 131, 143.
St. Cleer, 140, 147, 201, 307, 310, 311, 313; mortality at, 151-2.
St. Cleer and St. Neot Consolidated Mining Association, 151.
St. Clement, 220.
St. Columb Major, 215 *n. 2*.
St. Day United Mines, 320.
St. Enoder, 18 *n. 1*, 220, 230.
St. Erme, 220.
St. Erth, 215 *n. 2*, 324.
St. Eval, 302.
St. Ewe, 10, 11,
St. Germans, 223 *n. 1*, 234, 254.
St. Germans, Edward Granville Eliot, Earl of (1798-1877), 247.
St. Hilary, 319, 321.
St. Ive, 318.
St. Ives, 11, 64, 262, 269, 275, 296, 320; attempt to smelt copper at, 20; disturbances on account of the Union Workhouse system, 247; drift fishery, 284, 300; Methodism in, 157; pilchard fishery of, 271, 272, 280, 283, 288, 289, 292 *n. 1*; seining at, 272, 281, 291, 298, 299, 300; tithe disputes at, 297; wages of fishermen at, 265.
St. Juliot, 228.

St. Just in Penwith, 11, 39, 60, 139, 201, 318, 319, 326; distress in 1867, 322; disturbances caused by the new Union Workhouse system, 247; ill-health and mortality of mining population of, 152, 312; population in 1801, 186; submarine mines of, 176.

St. Just in Roseland, 297.

St. Just Pool, 221.

St. Keverne, 215, 216.

St. Leven, 215 *n. 2*, 295 *n. 2*.

St. Mawes, 218, 275, 285, 294 *n. 2*, 298; seine fishery of, 278, 299, 300.

St. Michael's Mount, 35.

St. Mewan, 132, 176, 212.

St. Neot, 10, 246.

St. Stephens in Brannel, 10, 221, 252; china clay works of, 90, 117 *n. 3*, 148.

St. Winnow 181 *n. 2*, 235, 237; 'Swing' disturbances at, 142, 246.

Salt, 265, 267-8, 271, 274, 280, 281, 283-4; foreign, use of in Cornwall, 265, 273, 281; smuggling of, 271, 274, 281.

Salt Duties, 267-8, 271, 273, 274, 283-4, 289-90, 292-3, 299; burden of, 271; exemptions of for pilchard curing industry, 273, 290.

Saltash, 238, 262, 303.

Saltpetre, 55.

Sampson, Benjamin (mine adventurer) 181.

Sampson, William (rioter), 105.

Sand, used as fertilizer, 210, 218.

Sandys, Carne, and Vivian Company (engineers), 149.

Savery, Thomas (inventor), 4, 7, 38, 51, 53 *n. 2*.

Scilly Isles, 34 *n. 1*, 35, 209, 263.

Scobell family, 19.

Scobell, John (farmer), 238, 241, 256.

Scott, David (Director of the East India Company), 172.

Scrip System of Mining Investment, 150, 151.

Scythes, 252.

Sea: Communications, 28, 42, 49-50, 57, 174, 262, 263; Dangers of the, 28, 42, 49-50, 174, 300-1.

Seamen: impressment of, 274, 278; value of fisheries as a nursery of, 270, 278, 284, 292.

Sea Weed, use of as fertilizer, 210, 221, 232.

Seed Drills, 221, 222, 241-2, 252, 256.

Seine Fishery: 263, 267, 269-70, 272, 274, 284, 288-91, 298, 299; Capital invested in, 264-6, 279, 290-91; nets used in, 263-4; stations or stems at Mevagissey and St. Ives, 272, 291.

Seiners and Drifters, feuds of, 264, 266, 267, 269-70, 274, 284, 288, 289, 293-4, 298, 299.

Sennen 236 *n. 1*, 295 *n. 2*.

Settlement, Laws of, 90.

Separate Condenser, 53 *n. 3*, 54, 73, 74, 76, 80, 94, 96, 112.

Shaft Sinking, 40.

Sheep, 223, 227, 228, 234, 237, 258, 259.

Shovell, Admiral Sir Cloudesley, 34 *n. 1*, 35.

Shipwrecks, 34 *n. 1*, 35, 301-2.

Siliocosis, 26 *n. 1*, 153.

Sims, James (engineer), 126.

Skewis (tenement), 37.

Skimmington Ride, 33.

Skues, William (secretary of the Tinners' Association), 170.

Sledges or Sliding Butts, 229, 233.

Small, Dr. William, 75, 78.

Smallholdings, 225, 239.

Smeaton, John (engineer), 72, 73.

Smelters: Copper, 20, 22, 41, 62-3, 71, 72, 82, 83, 85, 87, 94, 121, 145, 322; Cornish distrust of 'foreign', 19, 20, 21, 82; Cornish Copper, 19-20, 63-5, 71, 121; Tin, 10-1, 15-6, 44, 47, 64 *n. 2*, 169-70, 199-204, 322; Welsh, 20, 22, 41, 83, 85, 87, 94; Ring of Copper, 62-3, 72; Copper favour free importation of foreign ores, 145.

Smelting Houses, Tin, 8 *n. 3*, 10-1, 15, 194.

Smelting, Improvements in, 59.

Smith, Adam, 58.

Smith, Edward (lessee of Duchy rights), 189.

Smith, Lieut. Henry, 302.

Smuggling, 57 *n. 1*, 105, 172, 177, 263, 271, 273-8, 279, 285-8; attitude of local gentry to, 36 *n. 2*, 274-5, 286, 288; connivance of Customs Officials in, 275; efforts to check, 276-7, 279, 287; estimate of amounts of revenue lost through, 275, 276; of tin out of Cornwall, 57 *n. 1*, 177; of wool out of Cornwall, 277-8.

Sod Burning, 228-9.

Soho Foundry, 68, 73-4, 77, 93, 106, 107, 112. See also Boulton and Watt.

Soils of Cornwall, 210, 221, 241.

South Australia, 130, 308, 311, 323.

South Caradon: discovery of copper at, 147, 148; dividends paid by, 306, 307, 309; value of sales of copper ores by, 149-50, 323, 324; value of shares of, 310; lock out at, 317.

South Francis, 318.

South Petherwin, 246.

South Wales, 18, 19, 48, 64, 65, 68, 90, 116, 121.

South Wheal Basset, 139.

South Wheal Tolgus, 319.

Speculation in Mining: 19, 57, 61, 69, 76-7, 130-9, 189, 309-10; 'wild cat', 61, 130-9, 189, 309-10. See also Cost Book System: Scrip System; Wilks, John.

Speenhamland System, 163, 246. See also Poor Rates and Relief.

Spry family, 6 *n. 2.*

Spurr, Richard (Chartist), 156.

Stackhouse, Edward (landowner), 181, 181 *n. 2*, 182.

Staffordshire Potteries, 48.

Stall and Winter Feeding of Cattle, 253, 255, 257.

Stamping Mills, Tin, 25-6, 47, 70.

Stanley (mine promoter), 131.

Stannaries, 12-3, 14, 20, 43-7, 58, 195-6, 203, 262; Courts of, 13, 192-5; laws and jurisdiction of, 12 *n. 3*, 13, 20, 45-7, 192-6; privileges of, 192-3; reforms of, 196, 203.

Stannary Local Militia Royal Artillery, 182.

Stannary Parliament: 13; of 1703, 14; of 1710, 14; of 1750, 43-7; proposed convocation of in 1835, 195, in 1865, 314-5.

Steam Power: 4, 6-7, 91, 115, 123-4, 165, 175; use of in agriculture, 124, 234, 240, 255. See also Engines: Hornblower: Trevithick: Watt, etc.

Steam Ploughs, 255.

Steam Threshing Machines, 124, 240 *n. 1.*

Stephens, Edward (farmer), 250.

Stephens, Edward (magistrate), 158, 159, 162.

Stitches of Land, 212, 213.

Stratton, 238, 248; riots against the new Union Workhouse system at, 246.

Stream Tin and Tinners, 2, 40, 47, 176, 188, 208, 219 *n. 1.*

Strikes: of farm workers, 252; of miners, 143-4, 311, 316-7.

Swansea, 20, 121.

Swayne, Sampson (engineer), 52, 54, 63, 93.

Swing Riots, 142, 246.

TAMAR River, 221, 238, 262.

Taylor, Robert (mine adventurer), 202, 203.

Teague, Thomas (mine adventurer), 137, 203.

Teague, William (mine agent), 181.

Tehidy, 241.

Tellum, William (rioter), 162.

Temperance Movement, 156, 288.

Temple, 149.

Tennessee, 311.

Thomas, John (mine adventurer and Vice-Warden of the Stannaries), 181 *n. 2*, 196.

Three Life Systen of Leases, 215-7, 225, 227.

Threshing, 229-30; machines, 124, 233, 239-40, 257.

Ticketing System of Selling Copper Ores, 21-2, 62-3, 71, 321.

Timber Duties, Drawback of for Mines, 177.

Tin: Alluvial or Stream, 2, 40; adulteration of, 47; bounds, 16-7; demand exceeds supply of in closing years of the eighteenth century, 174; East Indian, 15, 60-1, 165, 166, 171, 172, 185, 189, 197-8, 199, 202, 204, 206; export of 14, 40, 57 *n. 1*, 58, 61, 165-6, 171-9, 184-5, 197, 207 *n. 1*; export duty, 61, 177; farm of, 15; foreign, 196-8, 204-6, duties on reduced and abolished, 140, 204-5; 'Miners' of antagonistic to smelters of, 178, 198, 202-3, 204; mining of, 4, 165, 305, 309, 323, adversely affected by expansion of copper mining, 176; mining interest, meetings of, 43, 59, 191, 202, 205; output of Cornish, 2-3, 14, 19, 57-8, 171 *n. 1*, 174, 188, 324; pre-emption of, 13-4; prices, 42, 43, 45, 57, 166-7, 171, 174, 179, 188-9, 198-200, 204, 206, 305, 309; proposed China trade, 171-2 (see also Unwin, George); slumps in mining of, 56, 57, 165, 180; smelting and smelters, 10, 11, 15-6, 64 *n, 2*, 169-70, 199-204, 322; smuggling of, 57 *n. 1*, 177, 278; stamping mills, 25-6, 47, 70; stocking of Cornish for the East India Company, 177-80, 184-5; used in making dyestuffs, 48; Warehousing Bill exempting foreign ores for re-export from import duties, 140, 197; working miners of in 'hungry forties', 204.

Tincroft, 59, 84, 306; Doering's boring machine at, 323 *n. 2*; Hornblower's engines at, 98, 99, 100, 112; profits of a threat to reputation of Boulton and Watt whose engines associated with losing mines, 92; shares of held almost exclusively by Cornish adventurers, 101.

Ting Tang, 77-8, 92.

Tin Hatches, 151.

Tinners' Association of 1780, 167-8, 169, 172-9, 184-5, 202; dealings with

East India Company, 172-5, 177-9, 184-5; proposed direct trade to the Orient independently of E.I.C.'s vessels, 173, 179; unity of, 167, 169.
Tin Plate Industry, 28, 48, 49, 174, 185, 198, 201, 205; clash with tin smelting interest, 199-200.
Tippetts, Peter (mine adventurer), 102.
Tithes, 216, 242-4, 246, 295; exemption of reclaimed lands from, 211 n. 2, 244; of fish, 274, 294-8.
Tocapilla Mine (Brazil), 325.
Tonkin, Anthony (farmer), 215, 216.
Tonkin, Thomas (historian), 29, 229, 240 n. 4, 279.
Torpoint, 287.
Tourist Traffic, 262, 302-3.
Towan Mines, 131.
Towans, right of taking sand from for fertilizer, 219-21.
Trade Unionism, 315-7.
Tram Roads, 116, 117.
Transportation: costs and difficulties of, 55 n. 2, 64, 75, 116, 147, 237, 240-1; dangers and losses in sea in wartime, 42, 49-50, 57, 174; on farms, 229, 233.
Trawl Fishery, 284, 289, 298.
Trebartha, 237, 255.
Treffry, Joseph Thomas, See Austen, Joseph Thomas.
Tregonning (farmer), 220.
Tregony, 148, 194, 221.
Trelawney, Bishop Jonathan, 1, 38.
Trelawney, Sir Harry, 234.
Treloweth Mine, 318.
Tremayne, John Hearle (Member of Parliament), 143, 179, 302.
Trengale, 151.
Trengrouse, Henry (inventor), 301.
Tresavean, 102, 123; depth of, 323; decline of, 151, 306; Hornblower's engine at, 100; man engine at, 155, 314; railway to from Hayle, 148.
Tresillian, 219.
Trestrail, Thomas, 181.
Treswithian Downs, 50, 225.
Trethewey (farmer), 259.
Trevanion, Charles (landowner), 218.
Trevanion family, 217.
Trevanion, Rev., 60.
Trevanson Marshes, 228.
Trevenan, 178.
Trevithick family, 7.
Trevithick, Richard the elder : 42, 55, 84, 88; improvements in a Newcomen engine at Dolcoath, 52-4.
Trevithick, Richard the younger: 4, 102, 107, 112, 175; 193 n 4, 240, 254; completes engines when Bull is stopped by Boulton and Watt's injunction, 97; completes Bull's engine at Ding Dong, 106; offers services to Boulton and Watt, 108; visits Soho and injunction served on him there, 109; asks terms from Boulton and Watt, 110; radical inventiveness of, 110; character of, 115, 125-6; constructs locomotive, 115-6; fails to attempt to solve problem of constructing a suitable permanent way for locomotives, 116; goes to South Wales, Tyneside, and London, 116; returns to Cornwall and erects a high pressure plunger-pole pumping engine at Wheal Prosper, 123; designs a steam threshing machine, 124, 233; claims that all agricultural work could be performed by steam power, 124; in South America, 126, 130.
Trewellard, 39.
Trewithian, 217, 219, 233, 254.
Tributers, 26-7, 311.
Tribute System, 68, 70, 321.
Tribute Work, 64, 316.
Trist, Rev. Jeremiah, 104.
Trist, Rev. John, 181 n. 2.
Troutbeck, Rev. John, 35.
Truck System, 153.
Truro, 18 n. 1, 59, 60, 71, 88, 96, 101, 102 n. 1, 157, 158, 173, 177, 196, 220, 238, 246, 277, 287, Bath and West Agricultural Show at, 240, 259; Chartists in, 248; church rate troubles, 156, 248; coinage and stannary town, 13, 44, 45, 197; miners' demonstrations at, 33, 85, 87; Mining Interest meeting at in 1830, 141, and in 1833, 199; new Stannary Court at, 196; Quarter Sessions and prevalence of distress in 1812, 181-2; railway plans, 148, 149, 221; Stannary Parliament of 1710, 14 n. 1, 33; tin mining adventurers' meetings, 43, 44, 195, 201, 202; Tinners' Association meetings at, 166, 167-8, 170, 175, 178; Watt at, 78 n. 3.
Truscott, L. B. (millwright), 252.
Turf Fuel, 226.
Turkey, 57
Turnip Cultivation, 218, 222, 223, 231 256.
Tut-work, 64, 316.
Tut-workers, 26-8, 311.
Tywarnhayle, 163, 164 n. 1, 240 n. 1.

UNEMPLOYMENT: among miners, 68, 70, 75, 319-22; leads to demonstrations at Truro, 85, and North Downs, 87.

United Hills, 139.
United Mines, 80, 112.
Unwin, George, 171, 172, 173, 174, 175, 177.
Upcott, William (supervisor of smelting houses), 10.

VENTILATION of Mines, 53 *n. 1*.
Vercoe (farmer), 252.
Veryan, 104, 181 *n. 2*.
Vice-Warden of the Stannaries, 17, 166, 172 *n. 6*, 178, 192, 193, 196, 270.
Victoria (Australia), 41 *n. 1*, 312.
Vincent, Dr. Philip, 157.
Vitriol, 48.
Vivian, Andrew (engineer), 109, 181.
Vivian family (engineers), 311.
Vivian, James (Sheriff of Cornwall), 59.
Vivian, John (mine adventurer), 84, 95, 181 *n. 2*; deputy governor of Cornish Metal Company, 82, 86 *n. 1*; connections with copper smelters, 82-3; dispute with Sir Francis Basset about compensation to closed-down mines in attempt to restrict copper production, 88; Sheriff of Cornwall, 182; and distress of 1812, 182; Vice-Warden of the Stannaries, 192, 196.
Vivian, John (miner), 50.
Vivian, John (mine manger), 84 *n. 1*.
Vivian, John Henry (copper smelter), 121.
Vivian, Richard Hussey (copper smelter), 121.
Vivian, Simon (engineer), 105.
Vyvyan family, 227, 260.
Vyvyan, Sir Richard Rawlinson (Member of Parliament), 158, 205, 245; advocates revival of Stannary jurisdiction, 193, 194; and removal of sand from Perranzabuloe towans, 219, 220.

WADEBRIDGE, 228; Agricultural Society, 248, 250, 252; food riots at, 142, 158-9.
Wages: of agricultural labourers, 142, 238, 252; of fishermen, 265-6, 283; of miners, 143 *n. 3*, 320; real, 160, 322.
Wain, Cornish, 229, 233.
Wales, South. See South Wales.
Walker, Rev. Robert, 181 *n. 2*, 235, 237, 246.
Wallis, John (Vice-Warden of the Stannaries), 193, 196.
War: effect of on Cornish trade and industry, 56-7; of that of the Austrian Succession, 41-2; of that of the American Revolution, 165-6, 168, 272-4, 278; of the French Revolu-

tionary and Napoleonic, 119-20, 174, 184, 280, 281, 282, 283.
Warehousing of Copper and Tin Bill, 140, 197.
Wasteland Reclamation, 90, 211, 212, 224, 228, 233; by cottagers, 225-6.
Water Power, 6, 93; in farming, 240, 254-5; in mining underground, 56.
Water Rights, 6, 47.
Watt, James: 4, 124, 125, 126, 132; first approached by Cornish mining adventurers, 73; work at Glasgow University, 73; repairs and improves model of a Newcomen engine, 73; partnership with Roebuck, 73-4, 77; meets Boulton, 73; partnership with Boulton, 74, 77 (see also Boulton and Watt); Act of Parliament secured to extend period of his patent rights, 74, 77; precise engineering technique of, 75, 112; Dr. Small draws attention to potential Cornish engine market, 75; his separate condenser enables Cornish copper mining to survive Anglesey competition, 76, 80-1; engine order from Ting Tang, 77-8; goes to Cornwall, 78; quarrels with Cornish engineers, 78; poor opinion of Cornwall and the Cornish, 78; engines of at Chacewater and elsewhere in Cornwall, 79; adopts premium system of payment for engines, 79-80; numbers of his engines in Cornwall, 80; his Dolcoath engine, 84, 88; his North Downs engine, 92; Hornblower's challenge to his patent, 92-3; disparages Hornblower's engine, 93, 97; his lack of success with double-cylinder engines, 93; alienates Cornish mining interest, 95; attempts engine trials to prove his engines superior to Hornblower's, 99-100; deterioration of his engines in Cornwall, 100-1; contrast with Trevithick, 110; services and disservices to mining progress, 111, 113: Separate Condenser of: 53 *n. 3*, 54, 73, 74, 76, 80, 94, 96, 112: patent of, 54, 68, 73, 74, 77, 93, 96, 97, 103 (see also Bull, Edward: Hornblowe, Jonathanr the younger: Trevithick, Richard, the younger). Engines of in copper rather than tin mines in Cornwall, 188. See also Boulton, Matthew: Boulton and Watt: Soho.
Wayne and Company, 21.
Welsh Copper Smelters, 41, 85, 87, 94.
Wendron, 10, 11, 317.
Wendron Consols, 309, 319.
Wentworth Consols, 318 *n. 1*,

Wesley brothers, 67.
Wesley, John, 29, 32, 52, 156.
West Basset, 318.
West Caradon, 147, 150; fluctuations in shares of, 310.
West Chiverton Mine, 307 *n. 3.*
West Cornwall Mines Investment Association, 151.
West Cornwall Railway. 149.
West Drakewalls, 317 *n. 4.*
West Indies, 124; attempt to find pilchard market in, 278, 282.
Weston, John (mine adventurer), 52.
West Penwith, 160, 161, 209, 217, 235, 238, 270, 303; Agricultural Society of, 256.
West Phoenix, 317 *n. 4.*
West Wheal Prudence, 139.
West, William (engineer), 126, 127.
Wheal Abraham, 126 *n. 2*, 132, 317.
Wheal Albert, 318 *n. 1.*
Wheal Alfred, 132.
Wheal Bank, 151.
Wheal Barnard, 132.
Wheal Basset, 306 *n. 1.*
Wheal Busy, 132, 139, 326; Newcomen engine at, 42; Watt engine at, 78.
Wheal Butson: Watt's engine at, 79, 99, 100.
Wheal Caradon, 310.
Wheal Chance, 126 *n. 1,*
Wheal Charles, 134, 138.
Wheal Clifford, 155 *n. 3*, 306.
Wheal Cock, 176.
Wheal Crebor (Tavistock), 324.
Wheal Damsel, 307.
Wheal Dream, 132.
Wheal Fortune (Gwennap), 126.
Wheal Fortune (Ludgvan), 18 *n. 1.*
Wheal Hearle, 318.
Wheal Hope, 318 *n. 1.*
Wheal Kitty, 21 *n. 7.*
Wheal Ludcott, 318.
Wheal Maid, 80.
Wheal Malkin, 134, 138.
Wheal Margaret, 102.
Wheal Mary (St. Neot), 147.
Wheal Pollard, 317 *n. 4.*
Wheal Pool, 102.
Wheal Prosper, 123.
Wheal Ram, 50.
Wheal Raven, 139.
Wheal Reeth, 100, 319, 320.
Wheal Rose, 42, 320.
Wheal Seton, 306 *n. 1*, 318.
Wheal Sparnon, 132.
Wheal Tregothnan, 102.
Wheal Trenwith, 139.
Wheal Triumph, 151.
Wheal Unity: employment of female labour at, 8 *n. 1*; Hornblower's engine at, 100, 101, 112; profits of, 92.
Wheal Unity Wood, 139.
Wheal Virgin, 74 *n. 3*, 96.
Wheal Vor, 14, 40, 132, 307 *n. 3*, 309; closing of in 1715, 11; re-opening by Captain John Gundry in 1814, 186-8; clash of adventurers of with tin smelters, 201; Richards' engine at, 126.
Wheat, 221, 223, 224, 230, 258.
Wheeled Vehicles in Farming, 229, 233.
Wherry Mine, 176, 188. 301.
Whim, 8.
Wilbraham, Roger (Member of Parliament), 101, 102 *n. 1.*
Wilkinson, John 107, 108, 109, 110.
Wilks, John, jnr. (professional company promoter), 132-4, 135, 136, 137, 138, 151.
Williams family of Scorrier, 24 *n. 1*, 60, 121, 123, 136, 201, 217, 234.
Williams, John (mine manager), 54, 55.
Williams, John, director of Chilean Mining Association, 145.
Williams, Michael, 181, 199, 202, 203.
Williams, Owen (of Anglesey), 121.
Williams, Richard, 277.
Williams, Thomas (of Anglesey), 68, 72, 85, 90, 119, 121; relations with Cornish Metal Company, 82, 83, 88; attempts to monopolize control of the copper industry, 87.
Wilson, Thomas, agent of Boulton and Watt in Cornwall, 98, 99, 102, 103, 107, 108, 172 *n. 6.*
Winter Feeding of Livestock, 223, 223 *n. 2*, 253, 255, 257.
Winwood, John, partner of Jonathan Hornblower the younger, 95, 96 *n. 3*, 98, 108.
Wolf Rock, 301.
Wood, smelting tin with, 9.
Woodcock, Sampson (exciseman), 287.
Wool, 210, 211, 223, 234, 237, 257; illegal exportation of from Cornwall, 277-8; poor quality of medieval Cornish, 211.
Woolf, Arthur (engineer); associated with the Hornblowers against Boulton and Watt, 108 *n. 3*; in London, 114, 123; returns to Cornwall, 123; tubular boiler patent of, 123; in charge of mines in Crowan, 125 erects engines at Wheal Abraham and Wheal Vor, 125; character of, 125; compound engine of, 126; his single-cylinder engine at Wheal Fortune, 126; Wheal Vor engine, 187.
Worcester, 48.

Worgan, G. B. (agriculturist), 223 *n. 1*, 233, 235, 240 *n. 4.*
Workhouses, Union, 155, 156, 320-2.
Worth, Thomas (farmer), 213-4.
Worth, Thomas (smelter), 20.
Wrecking, 34, 35, 36, 301, 302.
Wrecks, 34 *n. 1*, 35, 301-2.

Wrestling, 32-3.

YOUNG, Arthur, 223 *n. 1*, 225, 228.

ZELAH, 221.
Zennor, 209, 236 *n. 1*, 302 *n. 2.*

SUPPLEMENTARY INDEX: CHAPTERS II(i) and VI(i)

Anecdotes of Methodism, 261.4-261.6.
Anglican Church, 67.1-67.9, 261.1, 261.4, 261.20-261.28.
Anglican Clergy, 67.3-67.4: Sermons of, 261.25.
Anglican Communion Services in 1745 and 1779, 67.40, in 1812 and 1821, 261.47.
Anti-Jacobin press, 261.4.
Averill, John, Methodist Minister, 261.31.

Baptists, 67.9, 67.30, 67.31.
Barker, Rev., Methodist minister, 261.30-261.31.
Baring-Gould, Rev. S. R., 261.42 *n*101.
Basset, Rev., rector of Camborne, 261.22.
Beauchamp, Francis, magistrate, 67.13.
Bell, Dr. Andrew, 261.23.
Bennet, Rev. John, vicar of Tresmere, 67.12, 67.12*n*12, 67.15*n*23, 67.20, 67.25, 67.36.
Bible Christians, 67.15, 67.36, 67.37, 261.7, 261.29. See also O'Bryan, William; Bray, Billy.
Bishops of Exeter, see Carey; Cleggett; Lavington; Pelham, Phillpotts, Ross; Temple.
Blount, Rev. Walter, Helston curate, 261.36.
Boase, Dr. William, 261.2-261.3, 261.8, 261.9.
Bodmin, 261.34, 261.18; Circuit members, 1810-13, 261.13 n47
Borlase, Rev. Walter, 67.3; 67.8, 67.12, 67.13, 67.17 *n*25, 67.18 *n*26, 67.21 *n*32, 67.23, 67.23 *n*35.
Borlase, Dr. William, 67.3, 67.4, 67.5 *n*3, 67.6, 67.8, 67.17 *n*.25.
Bosanhoe, R., 261.10 *n*.21
Boscastle, 67.11 *n*11
Bourne, Hugh, Primitive Methodist, 261.7, 261.18 *n*46.
Bray, Billy, preacher, 261.13, 261.40-261.42, 261.45.
Bray, vicar of, 67.2.
Breage, 67.5, 67.9 *n*8, 67.22-67.24; 67.22 *n*33, 67.26.
Bristol, 67.16.
Bryan, Thomasine née Lawry, 261.16.
Bryan, William, senior, 261.17.
Bryan, William, founder of Bible Christians, see O'Bryan.
Budden, Rev., Teetotal Methodist minister, 261.34 *n*80.

Bullock, Rev. Jacob, 67.32 *n*52.
Bunting, Rev. Jabez, 261.30, 261.33.
Buryan, Deanery of 261.20, 261.25 *n*49. *See also St. Buryan.*

Camborne, 67.4, 67.9 *n*8, 67.32 *n*. 32, 67.35, 261.6, 261.22.
Camelford, 67.29 *n*46, 261.10 *n*21, 261.11 *n*27, 261.13 *n*31, 261.30-261.31.
Caneggy, 261.12.
Cardew Rev. Cornelius, schoolmaster and pluralist, 261.21, 261.22, 261.24.
Cardigan, Earl of, 67.12.
Cardinham, 261.19, 261.25 *n*58.
Carey, William, Bishop of Exeter, 261.21, 261.23.
Castle Horneck, 67.13.
Carvosa, Benedict, Methodist preacher, 261.3.
Carvosa, William, Methodist preacher, 261.3.
Catholic Emancipation, 261.26, 261.28, 261.35.
Celtic provincialism, 67.16; temperament, 67.36 (see also Hawker, Rev. R. S.).
Chacewater, 67.9, 67.30, 67.31, 261.27*n*61, 261.30.
Charles I, commemoration of execution, 67.7-67.8.
Charles II, 67.2.
Cheriton Fitzpane, 67.4.
Church, attendance, 67.9*n*9; fees and tithes, 67.5; restorations, 261.26-261.27, 261.27*n*61; at St. Columb, 261.36*n*86.
Clowes, William, founder of Primitive Methodists, 261.7, 261.15*n*46, 261.29*n*68, 261.40*n*95.
Cleggett, Bishop of Exeter, 67.12*n*12, 67.14.
Collections, 261.24, 261.24n57.
Collins, Edward, 261.27.
Colon, 261.22.
Cock fighting, 67.11, 67.31, 261.38.
Communion Services, 67.18, 67.32, 67.40, 261.23-261.24, 261.47-261.48.
Conference, Methodist, 67.28, 67.29, 67.36 (2), 67.39.
Congregationalism, 67.31, 67.34; church at Truro, 67.30; early relations with Methodists, 67.34-67.35.
Conon, Truro schoolmaster, 67.20.
Converts, lapsed Methodist, 67.20.
Cornish Language, 67.16.

Cory, Rev. John, 67.12n12.
Couch, Dr. Jonathan, 261.32.
Cragoe, Rev. John, 261.23.
Creed, parish, 261.24.
Crowan, 67.9n8, 67.12, 67.13, 261.22, 261.23, 261.24.
Curates, eighteenth century, 67.5-67.8.
Cury, 67.5, 261.34n80.

Daniell, Thomas, merchant and mine adventurer, 261.3
Darwin, Charles, 261.44.
Dawe, John Nanscawen, 261.9.
De Dunstanville, Francis Basset Lord, 261.22, 261.23, 261.24n56.
Docton, St. Ives teetotal Methodist, 261.33.
Dolcoath, 261.3.
Donnithorne, family, 67.25.
Draynes, 261.19.
Drew, Samuel, Methodist controversialist, 261.4-261.7.
Duloe, 261.38.

Edgcombe, Lord, 67.23.
Evans, James, Methodist minister, 261.18.
Excommunications, 67.7, 261.10n24.

Factory Act, Methodist opposition to, 261.35.
Falmouth, 67.17, 67.26n44, 67.31, 67.34, 261.13, 261.36; anti-Methodist riot at in 1745, 67.14.
Food riots, 67.33, 261.6.
Fowey, 261.17, 261.22.

Garras Chapel, 261.34n80.
George III, 67.37n63.
Georgia, 67.12.
Germoe, 67.5, 67.9n8, 67.22, 67.24, 261.28.
Gorham, Rev. C. C., 261.6, 261.37, 261.45.
Gorran, 261.23.
Grampound, 67.25.
Greenfield, Edward, Methodist preacher, 67.16n24, 67.19.
Gregor, magistrate, correspondent of Walter Borlase, 1749, 67.18n26, 67.23n35.
Gregor, Francis, M. P. for Cornwall, 1790, 67.37n63.
Grose, William, Methodist layman, 261.30.
Grylls, Rev. R. Garveys, pluralist, 67.5n58.
Gulval, 67.3, 67.4, 67.24, 261.38.
Gundry, Capt. 'Jack', 261.9, 261.10n20.
Gunwalloe, 67.5.
Gunwen, 67.37, 261.16, 261.18.
Gwennap, 67.9, 67.9n8, 67.9n9, 67.13, 67.19, 67.25, 261.27n61. Gwennap Pit, 67.9;
Gwinear, 67.9n8.
Gwithian, 67.9n8.

Hall, George, wrecker, 67.10n10.
Harris, magistrate, 67.23.
Harvest festivals, 261.44.
Harvey, Stephen, mine captain or engineer, 261.3.
Hawker, Rev. Robert Stephen, 261.42-261.44.
Hawkins, magistrate, 67.23.
Hawkins, Rev. G., curate of St. Just, 67.7, 67.8.
Hayle, 67.8.
Heath, Rev., Baptist minister, 67.30.
Helston, 67.8(2), 67.9n8, 261.34n80, 261.38.
Hennan, Rev. Richard, 261.21.
Hill, Frederick, churchwarden, 261.36n85.
Hills Chapel, 261.13n30.
Hoblyn, Rev. R., curate of St. Ives, 67.11, 67.13.
Hornblower, Jonathan the Elder, engineer, 67.30.
Huntingdon, Countess of, 67.31, 67.32, 67.34, 67.35.
Hurling, 67.10, 67.21.
Huxley, Thomas, 261.44.
Hymn singing, 67.16.

Illogan, 67.4, 67.9n8, 261.22, 261.23, 261.24n56.

Jaco, Peter, Methodist preacher, 67.36.
Jeffree, William, mine captain or engineer, 261.3.
Jenkins, Rev. Francis, vicar of St. Clements, 261.23.
Justification by faith, 67.2, 261.1.

Kea, 67.3, 261.20, 261.22, 261.26, 261.27n61.
Keigwin, Rev., curate of Illogan, 261.22, 261.23.
Kelk, Rev. Thomas, Methodist minister, 261.8, 261.11n27, 261.18n47.
Kendell, Rev. Nicholas, 261.22; Kendell family, 261.24n56.
Kenwyn, 67.3, 67.5n3, 67.8, 67.9, 67.9n8, 67.33, 261.20, 261.22, 261.26, 261.27n61
Kerrier, 67.23.
Kilham, Alexander, 261.3: Kilhamite New Connexion, 261.30.
Kilkhampton, 67.12.
Kingsand, 261.19.
Kingswood, 67.37.

Ladock, 261.22.
Laneast, 67.12n12.
Lanivet, 261.21n52.
Lanlivery, 261.22, 261.24n56.
Lanner, 67.9.
Launceston, 67.25, 67.29n46., 67.33, 261.29.

Lavington, George, Bishop of Exeter, 67.14-67.15, 67.18n26, 67.26, 67.28, 261.5, 261.14, 261.26, 261.40.
Leaver, Rev. William, vicar of Kilkhampton, 67.12n12.
Le Grice, Rev. C. V., 261.14-261.15.
Lelant, 261.21, 261.24.
Lessey, Rev. Theophilus, President of Methodist Conference, 67.36.
Lessey, Theophilus, senior, 261.3.
Lewannick, 261.9.
Lewis, Rev. John, 261.22.
Lincoln College, Oxford, 67.10.
Lindiven, Rev., vicar of Sithney, 261.9.
Lisburn, 67.37.
Locke, John, 261.7.
London, 67.16.
Ludgvan, 67.3, 67.4, 67.5n3, 67.6, 67.9n8, 67.25.
Luxulyan, 67.5n3, 67.36, 261.16, 261.17, 261.18, 261.22.

Mabe, 261.20.
Madron, 67.3, 67.5n3, 261.38.
Manaccan, 261.4, 261.5, 261.22, 261.26.
Mangles, Rev., vicar of Lewannick, 261.9.
Marazion, 67.8, 67.9n8.
Marhamchurch, 67.12n12.
Marshall, Rev., vicar of Breage and Germoe, 67.5, 67.5n3.
Marshall, Rev William, 261.36.
Martyn, Rev. Henry, 261.3.
Martyn, John, mine clerk, 261.3.
Mason, John, Methodist minister, 67.37.
Matthews, James, mine captain or engineer, 261.3.
Maxfield, Methodist preacher, 67.12, 67.13.
May Day revels, 261.37-261.38.
Maynooth grant, 261.36.
Meriton, Methodist preacher, 67.15n23.
Methodism: development in Cornwall, 67.8, 67.19, 67.24-67.25, 67.29, 67.38, 261.4, 261.7, 261.14; drift towards secession from Anglican Church, 67.26-67.28, 67.33; schism in, 67.19. See also Bible Christians, Kilham; O'Bryan, Primitive Methodism, Roseveare, Teetotal Methodists.
Methodist Conference, 261.2, 261.7, 261.8, 261.18, 261.29, 261.30, 261.32, 261.33.
Methodist membership, in Camelford in 1834-5, 261.30; in Truro in 1830, 261.30.
Methodist New Connexion, 67.9n9.
Methodist Organization, 261.1, 261.10; sermons, 261.25; societies and classes, 67.21.
Mevagissey, 67.25.
Miles, Rev. Richard, vicar of Kenwyn, 67.33.
Milles, Jeremiah, theologican, 261.20.
Milles, Rev. R., 261.20, 261.22.
Minerals, origin of, 67.2n1.
Mitchell, 67.26n43.
Mithian, 67.35.
Moravanism, 67.26.
Morgan, Mrs., alleged Wesley scandal, 67.26n43.
Morvah, 67.5n3, 67.32n52, 261.38.
Morwenna, Saint, 261.45.
Morwenstow, 261.43-261.45.
Mount's Bay, 67.22.
Mousehole, 261.3.
Murdock, William, 261.8.
Murlin, John, Methodist preacher, 67.36.
Mylor, 261.20.

Newlyn, 67.19.
Newquay, 261.18n47, 261.19.
Newman, Cardinal, 261.35.
Nichols, Rev., curate of Camborne, 261.22.
Nichols, Stephen, Methodist preacher, 67.36.
North Tamerton, 67.12n12.

O'Bryan, William, 67.36, 67.37, 261.7, 261.13, 261.16-261.20, 261.28, 261.29, 261.32, 261.43.
Odgers, Rev. A. J., Methodist minister, 261.19.
Oliver, Dr. William, 67.18n26, 67.21n32.
Oxford Holy Club, 67.10.

Padstow Hobby Horse, 261.37.
Paley, William, 261.15.
Passmore, Rev. John, curate of Cury and Gunwalloe, 67.5.
Paul, parish, 67.7.
Paul, Giles, local preacher, 261.9.
Pearse, William, wrecker, 67.24.
Pelham, Bishop George, 261.21, 261.27.
Pelynt, 261.38.
Pendarves, Rev. Henry, 67.3.
Pendeen, 67.3, 67.8.
Pengreep, 67.13.
Penneck, Rev. John, 67.4.
Penrose, Paul, mine captain, 261.3.
Penryn, 67.8, 67.23, 67.31, 261.3, 261.23.
Penzance, 67.8, 261.8, 261.11, 261.13, 261.14.
Perranarworthal, 67.9n8.
Perranwell, 261.30.
Perranzabuloe, 261.22, 261.27n61.
Penwith, 67.23.
Peters, Rev. Hugh, rector of Camborne, 261.25.
Phillack, 67.9n8, 261.39.
Phillpotts, Bishop Henry of Exeter, 261.6, 261.35, 261.36, 261.37.
Pius IX, 261.45.

Pluralism of clergy, 67.3, 67.5n3.
Plymouth, 67.30; Plymouth Dock, 261.11n27, 261.13n31.
Polgooth, 261.3.
Polkinhorne, excommunicated, 67.7.
Pollard, William, Baptist, 67.30.
Polperro, 261.32.
Polwhele, Rev. Richard, 67.15, 261.4, 261.5, 261.9, 261.14, 261.22, 261.26 261.26n30, 261.27, 261.28, 261.40.
Ponsanooth, 261.3.
Population, 1779 estimate, 67.9n8.
Pool, 67.12.
Port Isaac, 67.19, 67.25.
Praed, Rev. Herbert, 67.4.
Presbyterianism, 67.1.
Primitive Methodists, 67.15, 261.7, 261.14, 261.18n46, 261.29.
Prospidneck, 261.10n24.
Pryce, Dr. William, 67.2n1.
Puseyite clergy, 261.36.

Quaker, antecedants of William O'Bryan, 261.16.

Redruth, 67.9, 67.9n8, 67.12, 67.29, 67.35, 67.38, 261.1, 261.2, 261.3, 261.8, 261.10, 261.13, 261.18n47, 261.19, 261.29n68.
Reeves, Jonathan, 67.14n20.
Religious schisms, 67.28-67.29.
Restoration (1660), 67.2.
Revolution, French, 261.4.
Revivals, 261.4, 261.14-261.16; see also Drew, Samuel and Le Grice, C. V.
Rhodes, Benjamin, Methodist minister, 67.38.
Riles, John, Methodist minister, 261.15.
Robbins, Joseph, Methodist minister, 261.10n21.
Roberts, James, 67.20n31.
Robinson, Rev., rector of Crowan, 261.22, 261.24.
Rodda, Nicholas, mine captain or engineer, 261.3.
Rodda, Richard, Methodist preacher, 67.25, 67.36.
Rogers, Henry, 67.12.
Roman Catholicism, 67.1.
Roseveare, Thomas Pope, Methodist layman, 261.30-261.32.
Ross, Bishop of Exeter, 67.9n8, 67.32, 67.40.
Roughtor, teetotal camp meetings at, 261.34.
Ruan Minor, 261.23n54.

St. Agnes, 67.8, 67.9n8, 67.25, 67.29n47, 67.30, 67.31, 67.34, 67.35, 261.11.
St, Anthony in Meneage, 261.22, 261.24, 261.26.

St. Aubyn, Sir John (d. 1744), 67.5n3.
St. Aubyn, Sir John (d. 1839), 261.33.
St. Austell, 67.17, 67.25, 67.37(2), 261.10n21, 261.17, 261.19, 261.21, 261.23, 261.29n68.
St. Blazey, 261.19, 261.21, 261.23n54.
St. Buryan, 67.12, 67.17n25, 67.34, 261.20, 261.25n49.
St. Cleer, 261.13n30.
St. Clements, 261.23.
St. Columb Major, 67.34, 261.6n13, 261.27n61, 261.28, 261.36, 261.36n86, 261.37.
St. Day, 67.9, 67.31, 261.27n61.
St. Dennis, 261.24n56.
St. Dominic, 261.39.
St. Erme, 261.21, 261.26-261.27.
St. Erth, 67.9n8.
St. Ewe, 261.23.
St. Gennys, 67.12, 67.25.
St. Hilary, 67.9n8, 67.17n25.
St. Ives, 67.10, 67.11-67.12, 67.13, 67.32n52, 261.3, 261.21, 261.24, 261.25, 261.33.
St. Just in Penwith, 67.3, 67.4, 67.5n3, 67.6. Methodism in, 67.8, 67.10n10, 67.17, 67.24, 67.32n52; smuggling and wrecking in, 67.10n10.
St. Keverne, 261.23, 261.23n54.
St. Levan, 261.21n49.
St. Mary's Church, Truro, 67.29.
St. Michael's Mount, 67.23.
St. Michael Penkivel, 261.21.
St. Neot, 261.19.
St. Neots (Hunts), 261.22.
St. Newlyn East, 261.22, 261.26.
St. Stephen in Brannell, 67.36.
St. Stephen's Downs, 261.29.
St. Winnow, 261.21.
Sancreed, 67.4, 67.5n3, 67.25, 67.36.
Sawle, James, local preacher, 261.30.
Scobell, Rev. G. P., 67.4, 67.5n3.
Sems, James, mine captain or engineer, 261.3.
Sennen, 261.21n49.
Serle, Rev. Thomas, 67.12.
Shelmerdine, Methodist minister, 261.8, 261.11.
Simons, William, Excise officer, 67.12n12.
Sithney, 67.7, 67.9n8, 67.23, 261.6, 261.9.
Skewis, 67.12.
Slade, Charles, St. Ives methodist, 261.3.
Smith, Rev. William, 67.3.
Smuggling, 67.21-67.22.
Staffordshire, 261.7.
Stanhope, Fitzroy, Dean of Buryan, 261.20-261.21.
Statton, Frederick, 'white witch', 261.39.
Stephens, John, Mayor of St. Ives, 67.12.
Stithians, 67.9n8.
Sykes, Rev. A. A., 67.17n25.

Tait, Archbishop of Canterbury, 261.45.
Teetotal Methodists, 261.33-261.34; see Temperance Movement.
Tehidy, 261.22.
Temperance Movement, 261.17*n*45, 261.29, 261.33-261.24.
Temple, parish, 261.27*n*61.
Temple, Frederick, Bishop of Exeter, 261.44.
Thompson, Rev. George, 67.12, 67.12*n*12, 67.15*n*23, 67.20, 67.25, 67.26, 67.34.
Thorne, S. L., 261.18*n*47.
Tintagel, 261.10*n*24.
Tippet, Rev. Edward, 261.22.
Tithes, 67.17.
Torney, Rev. John, 67.12.
Towednack, 67.32*n*52, 261.28, 261.35.
Tractarianism, 67.28, 261.28, 261.35.
Transportation sentences, 67.11*n*11.
Treffry, Rev. Richard, methodist minister and President of Conference, 67.10*n*10, 67.36, 261.4, 261.6*n*13, 261.8*n*17, 261.11*n*27, 261.13-261.16.
Tregarthen, Rev., curate of St. Just in Penwith, 67.6-67.7, 67.8.
Tregaskis, Thomas, 261.37, 261.36*n*88.
Tregony, 261.4.
Trelawney, Sir Harry, 67.31-67.32, 67.34; Trelawney 'ballad', 261.43.
Trembath, John. 'lapsed' Methodist preacher, 67.20*n*30.
Trenant Chapel, 261.13*n*30.
Treneglos, 67.12*n*12.
Tresmere, 67.12, 67.15*n*23.
Trevadlock Cross, 261.9.
Trevithick, Richard senior, 261.3.
Trist family, 67.3: Rev. Jeremiah, 261.21; Rev. John, 67.3.
Truro, 67.9*n*8, 67.20, 67.25, 67.27, 67.29-67,30, 67.33, 261.13, 261.15, 261.22, 261.27, 261.30.
Truscott, Francis, Methodist preacher, 261.4.
Turner, Captain of St. Ives, 67.10, 67.11.
Turner, Rev. Jonathan, Methodist minister, 261.33, 261.34.
Tyneside, 67.16.
Tywardreath, 261.38-261.39.

Uniformity, Act of, 67.31.
Usticke, magistrate, 67.12, 67.13.

Valtan, John, Methodist preacher, 67.38.
Veryan, 67.3, 261.21.
Vivian, John, Mine captain or engineer, 261.3.
Vowler, Rev., curate of St. Agnes, 67.25, 67.26.
Vyvyan, Sir Francis, 67.14*n*19.

Walker, Rev. Robert, vicar of St. Winnow, 261.21.
Walker, Rev. Samuel, 67.20, 67.29, 67.32; differs from Wesley on predestination, 67.25-67.26; warns Wesley against separation from Anglican Church, 67.26-67.27.
Walker, Rev. Samuel Edmund, rector of St. Columb, 261.36, 261.36*n*86, 261.37.
Warbstone, 67.12.
Warleggan, 261.19.
Warner, Dr. Samuel, 261.30.
Westell, Thomas, Methodist preacher, 67.12.
Wedgwood, Josiah, 261.29*n*68.
Week St. Mary, 67.12.
Welcombe, 261.43*n*102.
Wendron, 67.9*n*,8, 67.10*n*10, 67.32*n*52.
Wesley, Charles, 67.11, 67.12, 67.15*n*23, 67.36; hymns of, 67.16.
Wesley, John, 67.9, 67.11, 67.13-67.14, 67.19, 67.21, 67.24-67.25, 67.29, 67.33, 261.1, 261.7, 261.13, 261.19; Anglicanism of, 67.9, 67.26-67.28; differences between Methodists and Anglicans, 67.25-67.28.
Wesleyan Reform Association, 261.31.
Wesleyan Reformers, 67.36.
West Looe, 67.31.
West Penwith, 67.32*n*52.
Wheal Vor, 67.23, 261.10*n*20.
Wheeler, Rev. William, rector of Ladock, 261.22.
Willcock, Rev. W., curate of Ruan Minor, 261.23*n*54.
Williams, Rev. Anthony, vicar of St. Keverne, 261.23, 261.23*n*54.
Williams, Richard, preacher, 261.2.
Wills, Rev. Thomas, congregationalist, 67.31, 67.34-67.35, 67.37.
Wills, Rev. Thomas, Anglican pluralist, 261.21.
Wiseman, Cardinal, 261.45.
Witchcraft, 67.11*n*11, 261.38-261.40.
Wolsey, Cardinal, 67.3.
Women preachers, 261.19.
Womersley, Joseph, Methodist preacher, 261.18.
Wrecking, 67.22-67.24.
Wrestling, 67.10, 67.22, 261.6*n*13, 261.21, 261.37.
Wrigley, Francis, Methodist preacher, 67.37.

Zennor, 67.3, 67.5*n*3, 67.32*n*52, 261.38.